ETHICAL ISSUES IN THE PROFESSIONS

PETER Y. WINDT
PETER C. APPLEBY
MARGARET P. BATTIN
LESLIE P. FRANCIS
BRUCE M. LANDESMAN

University of Utah

PRENTICE HALL, ENGLEWOOD CLIFFS, NEW JERSEY 07632

Library of Congress Cataloging-in-Publication Data

Ethical issues in the professions.

Bibliography.
1. Business ethics. 2. Professional ethics.
I. Windt, Peter Y.
HF5387.E813 1989   174'.4   88-19652
ISBN 0-13-290081-5

Editorial/production supervision and
   interior design: **Marjorie Borden Shustak**
Cover design: **20/20 Services, Inc.**
Manufacturing buyer: **Peter Havens**

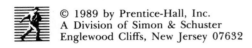 © 1989 by Prentice-Hall, Inc.
A Division of Simon & Schuster
Englewood Cliffs, New Jersey 07632

Printed in the United States of America

10 9 8 7 6 5 4 3 2 1

ISBN 0-13-290081-5

Prentice-Hall International (UK) Limited, *London*
Prentice-Hall of Australia Pty. Limited, *Sydney*
Prentice-Hall Canada Inc., *Toronto*
Prentice-Hall Hispanoamericana, S.A., *Mexico*
Prentice-Hall of India Private Limited, *New Delhi*
Prentice-Hall of Japan, Inc., *Tokyo*
Simon & Schuster Asia Pte. Ltd., *Singapore*
Editora Prentice-Hall do Brasil, Ltda., *Rio de Janeiro*

Contents

3   Personal, Professional, and Institutional Obligations

4   Access to Professional Services   *353*

5   Regulation of the Professions   *439*

Appendix I   *527*

Appendix II   Selected Codes of Professional Ethics   *535*

Preface

For a number of years, the philosophy curriculum at the University of Utah has included several courses in applied ethics. This book is the product of our efforts to provide a suitable text for one of these courses—one which we are persuaded is highly valuable, but for which existing texts have seemed, to us, to be not entirely appropriate. The course, titled simply *Professional Ethics*, is founded on three premises: (1) that there are families of important ethical issues which arise for many professions or occupations, rather than being peculiar to a single profession or cluster of occupations; (2) that the contemporary changes taking place in professional life make these issues both more important and more complex; and (3) that it is important for some understanding of such ethical issues to be achieved not only by those contemplating or pursuing professional careers, but by everyone who is affected by professional practice and conduct—that is to say, by all of us.

A course based on these premises should be designed as if it were to be offered as part of the liberal education curriculum, open to undergraduates from all academic areas, and presuming no special familiarity with philosophical literature and methods or with the fundamentals of any particular profession or occupation. It should also present the character and structure of the ethical issues in a way that underscores what is common to the ethical concerns of a wide range of professions and occupations, but that also represents the variety of different ways in which those common concerns can arise in the context of varying professional functions and aims. A text for such a course, then, should be accessible and relatively non-technical, should represent a wide range of professions and occupations, and should seek to put recurrent ethical themes in bold relief. Literature which concentrates on a single occupational area—for example, texts in medical ethics, or in business ethics—has too narrow a focus. Large anthologies are too fragmentary and tend to leave important recurrent themes obscured by an overabundance of diversity and detail. But single-author discursive texts tend to lose the flavor of the diversity and variation which it is so important to represent.

Our attempt to provide an improved text involves a combination of approaches. Each chapter focuses on a family of ethical issues which arise for a broad range of professions and occupations. A substantial introductory text characterizes that set of issues, introduces a basic conceptual apparatus, and provides a framework from which to approach and evaluate the literature about those issues. This text is followed by a carefully selected anthology of readings which presents both a diversity of viewpoint and a variety of occupational interests. Cases for discussion, and appendixes which provide an elementary introduction to ethical theory and a sampling of codes of professional ethics, complete our presentation. Our aim is to enhance the reader's access to the literature without sacrificing too much detail, on the one hand, or scope, on the other.

Virtually everything in this text is a product of group deliberation and critical interchange. Primary responsibility for the content and structure of each chapter was determined as follows: Chapter 1, Peter Windt; Chapter 2, Margaret Battin; Chapter 3, Peter Appleby; Chapter 4, Bruce Landesman; Chapter 5, Leslie Francis. We gratefully acknowledge the energetic and enthusiastic assistance of Katie Berger in locating and acquiring resources for our project. The thoughtful comments, both favorable and adverse, of our reviewers—Alan Goldman, University of Miami; Robert Corrington, Pennsylvania State University; Michael Phillips, Portland State University; and Tom Grassey, Naval Postgraduate School—helped greatly in bringing the book to its present form. Nathalie Jensrud, Cindy Allen, and Judy Schalow provided valuable help in typing and assembling the manuscript. And, finally, we wish to thank the University of Utah's Department of Philosophy and College of Law for their support.

P.Y.W.
P.C.A.
M.P.B.
L.P.F.
B.M.L.

ONE

Professions and Professional Ethics: The Theoretical Background

Contemporary attitudes toward professionals and their professions range over a broad and diverse spectrum. Professionals are widely regarded as experts and authorities who give us access to the benefits of knowledge and techniques that we have not mastered for ourselves. We routinely turn to them for guidance and help that we hope will make our lives rich, fruitful, and worth living. In more desperate circumstances, we hope that professional aid will protect life itself, minimize our losses, and help to make our losses bearable. Professional expertise seems indispensable to most of us, and we rely upon it, in both recognized and unrecognized ways, on a daily basis.

In addition, professional careers are widely sought after in our society. Professionals are seen as having desirable social status, good economic rewards, and work that is worthwhile. Many of us seek careers in recognized professions; and many more of us seek to have our own occupations upgraded, so that they may become recognized as professions and we may become recognized as professionals.

On the other hand, there is also widespread mistrust and criticism of professionals and professions. We often hear complaints that professionals abuse their power and that they refuse to acknowledge the rights of their clients or their obligations to society. Some portray professionals as arrogant, self-interested persons whose protection of their own favored status impedes genuine improvements in service or social progress. Others accuse professionals of tunnel vision, noting that their pursuit of the narrower, limited goals of their own professions interferes with meeting the more basic needs of the individual and the broader needs of the larger society. The conduct of professionals and the standards of their professions have recently been subjected to both scholarly and popular scrutiny. There have been numerous challenges to the status quo, often accompanied by pleas or demands for reform, and sometimes accompanied by legislative attempts to impose reform.

Such challenges and criticisms have not come entirely from outside the professions. Increasing numbers of professionals are themselves expressing doubts about the existing structure and standards of conduct in their professions. Journal space and conference time are being devoted to discussion of the objectives and standards of conduct of the professions. Committees are being formed to debate ethical issues and to formulate or revise codes of ethics and conduct. We are ambivalent about our professions: We acknowledge a need for them, reward professionals in a variety of ways, and seek to join their ranks; but we are often dissatisfied with the services they provide, and we sometimes suspect that professional conduct is improper, in ways that range from mere incivility on the one hand to deep immorality on the other.

This ambivalence is the product of a multitude of concerns, including interest in making professional services more efficient; interest in making various occupations more rewarding; concern for the most effective division of labor; concern for the most useful or most profitable way to organize an occupation; and interest in increasing the availability of professional services. But a persistent and fundamental theme in debates about the status of the professions is concern over whether the aims of the professions and the conduct of professionals are *ethically* acceptable. If they are not, what would count as ethically superior aims and conduct, and how should ethical improvement be achieved? What ethical principles should govern the relationships between professionals and their clients, their society, their colleagues, their employees, their employers or sheltering institutions, and the discipline or art they practice? This book is concerned with the debate about these ethical principles.

SPECIAL ETHICAL STATUS FOR PROFESSIONALS?

One complaint that is sometimes raised against professionals is that, when they are engaged in their professions, they do things that no ethical person would do; or else they refuse to do things that any ethical person would do. For example, many people are concerned when they find lawyers defending clients whom, it would seem, no decent person should be willing to defend. Many complain that physicians ignore the wishes of their patients, when an ethical person could not ignore those wishes. Some condemn public administrators for devising and carrying out policies that aim at the general public good but cause hardships for some people that, it seems, no decent person should be willing to impose.

In responding to such complaints, professionals often acknowledge that their actions are not those of an ethical *lay person* but claim that their actions are nevertheless ethically permissible, or even ethically required, for a professional. Such a response sometimes amounts to the familiar "I'm only doing my job" plea, of which we have rightly learned to be suspicious. But often the response seems to involve the view that the professional has a *special ethical* status, so that the rights, duties, or ethically significant interests of the professional are thought to differ in kind, or at least in degree of importance, from the rights, duties, and significant interests of the ordinary layperson or employee. In some cases, ethical requirements for the professional may seem more demanding than requirements for the layperson. In other cases, they may seem less demanding. And at times they may seem merely to be different.

This alleged special status of professionals is the primary concern of this chapter. Do professionals have such a special status, or are the ethical principles that apply to them the same as those that apply to any ordinary person? If professionals do have a special ethical status of some sort, then what is that status and why do they have it? Our answers to these questions will have considerable importance for our approach to the more specific ethical issues addressed in succeeding chapters.

Our task, then, is to explore the question of whether professionals have special ethical status, in the sense just explained. In order to understand this question more clearly, we need to consider two other issues: (1) Who are the professionals, and what distinguishes them from members of other occupations? (2) What is this "ethical status" we're interested in, and how does one acquire a particular ethical status? Exploring this second issue will also involve us in an examination of a few basic ideas in ethical theory.

WHO ARE THE PROFESSIONALS?

On any normal day, most of us encounter a multitude of claims about allegedly professional service. We are urged to patronize the dry-cleaner who will give our drapes professional cleaning, to visit the bank whose loan officers will deal with us in a professional manner, and to buy an automobile from the dealer with the professional sales staff. Professional advertisers construct commercials urging us to vote for the candidate who promises to fight professional criminals (although they may be careful to avoid saying that the candidate is a professional politician!). When we retire from our day's (professional?) activities, we are entertained by professional actors, artists, and athletes. Our children are encouraged by professional educators to study hard so that they can grow up to enter professions themselves. Is there really anything at all distinctive about being a professional? Whatever happened to ordinary *work*?

If we think carefully about such claims to professionalism, several underlying themes emerge. One function of the claim that someone does something professionally is to point out that the activity is done for a living, rather than for recreation, as a hobby, or as part of conducting one's personal life. In many contexts, a second function of the claim of professionalism is to imply competence or expertise, and efficiency. Professionals are the ones who know what they are doing and who do it well. Professional work, then, is good work, and the professional worker is skilled or expert. In still other contexts, the assurance that someone is professional is an assurance that she is reliable, trustworthy, fair, and sympathetic to our needs. Depending on the context, then, the claim that someone is professional, does professional work, or has a professional attitude can be interpreted to mean one or more of these things. Are there other important interpretations?

It seems clear that there are. Nearly anyone who considered the following list would identify some people (for example, lawyers and physicians) as professionals and others as nonprofessionals (for example, contestants and janitors) and be left with a group of those who are difficult to classify:

accountant	contestant	librarian	psychiatrist
actuary	dentist	model	soldier
architect	engineer	nurse	teacher
artist	farmer	photographer	thief
athlete	gambler	physician	undertaker
building contractor	janitor	plumber	veterinarian
carpenter	judge	police	zoologist
clergy	lawyer	politician	

How can we distinguish the *real* professions from other occupations? Scholars from many disciplines, as well as interested members of many occupations, have addressed the problem of definition, but no widely accepted account of the nature of a profession has been produced. It will be useful to explore briefly some of the difficulties involved in arriving at a definition.

The Problem of Definition

One approach to the problem of defining the nature of a profession is to choose a few occupations that we are sure must be counted as professions, study them to see what characteristics they share, and then propose a definition in terms of those characteristics. Other occupations may then be found to be professions if they are similar enough, in terms of the identified characteristics, to the selected models. Now, it is widely agreed that if any occupations at all are to be counted as professions, then law and medicine, especially as they existed in the mid-twentieth century, must be counted. Suppose we choose them as models.

Studies of the legal and medical professions vary considerably in detail, but there is substantial agreement about a number of general features that these two professions exhibit. These features include the following:

> *Expertise.* It is characteristic of law and medicine (as well as many other plausible candidates for the status of profession) that they involve mastery of a large and complex body of information and skills, which is based on a sophisticated theoretical foundation. Extensive education and training are required to learn this theoretical foundation and to acquire the knowledge and skills that are based on it.

> *Authority.* The expertise possessed by the physician or lawyer is frequently expressed in the form of authoritative advice or guidance—that is, advice that is to be followed by patients or clients without their understanding why it is good advice, and often in spite of their inclination not to follow it. Often, too, members of these profesions are called upon to guide the formation of public policy concerning their areas of expertise in the same authoritative way. (It is important to see that expertise and authority are two related but different qualities. It is possible to have either one without the other.)

> *Social importance.* The expertise and guidance provided by lawyers and physicians are important both to individuals who need their services and to society in general. Our health, lives, and liberty depend upon the quality of the services provided to us by these professionals.

Autonomy and self-regulation. Both these professions have been relatively independent of external controls. Standards of acceptable practice come from within the professions, and much of the responsibility for maintaining the quality of practice remains within the professions. These professions also control the structure and content of education and training, as well as the power to determine who will be allowed to enter the profession. In addition, individual lawyers and physicians have largely been free to choose the kind of service they will provide, both in selecting a specialty or kind of practice and in choosing which clients or patients they will serve.

Professional Commitments. By the time they begin to practice, members of these professions have undertaken a number of commitments that are supposed to provide ethical guidance for their conduct as professionals. These include a commitment to promote the interests and well-being of the patient or client; a commitment to protect and promote the well-being of the community; a commitment to promote excellence in the practice of their professional arts and skills; and a commitment to regard other members of their profession in a fraternal way. These commitments are presented in one or more codes of ethics, which have been drawn up and formally adopted by various professional organizations and their members.

Rewards. In comparison with other occupations, both law and medicine offer a number of substantial rewards, including good economic rewards, high social prestige and influence, and the satisfaction that comes from engaging in interesting and worthwhile work.

If we take seriously the idea that the features just listed define what it is for an occupation to be a profession, then we are in a position to look at other occupations to see whether they have the same or very similar features so that they, too, should be regarded as professions. And, indeed, we might even want to devise other categories of occupations. For example, we might designate some of them *semiprofessions,* for which required training and education may be less extensive, autonomy less complete, or other features less pronounced than in the professions proper. And, of course, we are familiar with the notion of the paraprofessional, one who learns to do specific, limited tasks that the professional also does, but on the basis of much less comprehensive training, greatly reduced autonomy (paraprofessionals typically must work under the direct supervision of professionals), and with substantially reduced rewards.

But such an approach has difficulties. First, there is an important distinction between features that are *essential* and those that are merely *accidental.* That is, we must ask whether all the features we have mentioned are what actually make an occupation into a profession, or whether some of them might be features that our two model professions just happen to have, but that could be altered or eliminated without endangering an occupation's claim to be a profession. Would law, for example, still be a profession if lawyers continued to do the work they do, but enjoyed much less prestige and vastly poorer compensation? Would medicine still be a profession if physicians lost much of their autonomy?

A second difficulty involves the confusion of *descriptive* and *normative* attempts to define a profession. A purely descriptive definition would outline features that are essential for an occupation to count as a profession, but would not attempt to tell us, beyond that, what professions *should* be like. On the other hand, a normative definition portrays the ideals that professions should strive to realize.. But in the debate over the proper definition of a profession, it may not be clear which sort of definition is intended. For example, when we are told that members of a profession have a commitment to protect and promote the interests of their clients, is this offered as a *descriptive* remark (the claim that such a commitment does in fact exist) or is it *normative* (the claim that members of the profession *should* have such a commitment)?

Finally, distinguishing essential and accidental features seems to depend to some extent upon one's reasons for seeking a definition in the first place. Historians, wondering how professions come into existence and how they contribute to the structure and development of societies, tend to emphasize somewhat different features than do economists, who want to understand the impact of professionalization on economic systems. Scholars from other disciplines, with other questions to ask, tend to sort out the essential from the accidental in other ways. And, not surprisingly, almost everyone tends to regard the features that his own occupation shares with the recognized professions as more significant than features that his occupation lacks.

PROFESSIONALIZATION AND DEPROFESSIONALIZATION

The seriousness of these difficulties can be appreciated if we consider their impact for those who are concerned to change the status of their occupations or to protect their occupations from such change. Let us first consider the process of *professionalization*—that is, the process of altering a nonprofessional occupation so that it becomes more like a profession, and perhaps eventually achieves the status of genuine profession. It is easy to see why such changes in status are attractive to those working in many occupations. Autonomy, authority, and social and economic rewards are powerful incentives to seek recognition as a professional. Workers in many occupations are persuaded that the increased autonomy and authority that they might win by becoming recognized as professionals would allow them to do their jobs more effectively, ultimately providing improved service to their clients or the public. But how is a claim to professional status to be supported?

Here it is clear that any confusion between accidental and essential characteristics of a profession could have serious consequences. For instance, librarians have been involved for years in the effort to achieve widespread recognition as professionals. They refer to their discipline as *library science*, the foundation upon which their special skills and abilities are based, and they have devised and revised several times a code of ethics that spells out their commitment to serving the interests of their patrons, the broader public, and the arts and sciences. They seek more autonomy and authority in their work. They anticipate, perhaps, greater economic rewards and social status in the future. But what of the social importance of their work? This is not to say that what librarians do is trivial, for it is not—especially to those of us who rely upon their efficient performance and knowledgeable advice on a regular basis. But if a profession *must* have the grinding, life-or-death sort of importance that we find in medicine or law, then many occupations will not qualify, no matter how they work at providing theoretical foundations for their expertise or dedicate themselves to service.

A similar issue arises for nursing. It is a contention of the majority of nurses that patient *care* is different in kind from medical treatment and that the knowledge and skills required for effective nursing care are different in kind from the knowledge and skills required for medical diagnosis and treatment. It can be argued, then, that nurses would be more effective in providing their services if they had a greater share of autonomy and authority than they have traditionally had, and that their direction and supervision by medical (rather than nursing) staff is a misplacement of authority. This has been one strong incentive (among others) for nurses to seek recognition as independent and equal professionals, rather than as "physicians' helpmeets." But what, then, of the "requirement" that a profession be founded on a sophisticated theoretical basis? Is there a theoretical foundation for a science of nursing that is different from, but as sophisticated as, the theoretical foundations of medical science? Many nurses who believe so are energetically pursuing the discovery and organization of that theoretical foundation, along with the development of appropriate programs in research, graduate study, and the academic structures that go with the development of such theoretical work. Other nurses are doubtful that such theoretical foundations are possible or needed. Their claim is that the particular skills and expertise involved in nursing are important enough to justify recognition as professionals (and with the autonomy, authority, and rewards accompanying that recognition) whether or not sophisticated independent theoretical foundations can be provided.

Part of the disagreement among nurses about how best to professionalize, then, is disagreement about whether sophisticated independent theoretical foundations are an essential or an accidental feature of a profession. But a second source of trouble is suggested by this discussion. Suppose that such a theoretical foundation is possible, and is actually provided, so that future nursing practice is just as scientifically founded as present medical practice. *How* will that affect the campaign for recognition as a professional? Some nurses discuss this issue as if they expect the theoretical foundation of their expertise to *produce* their authority and autonomy. Others make a point of claiming that it would *entitle* them to such authority and autonomy. But these two claims differ in an important way. The first is *descriptive*, stating how social processes actually work. It says that authority and autonomy are products of properly established expertise. But the second claim is *normative*, saying that those with properly established expertise *deserve* autonomy and authority and should have them. If there is confusion of these two claims, there is likely to be disappointment as well. For example, nurses may succeed in proving that they should be recognized as professionals but might nevertheless fail (in an unjust world) to get that recognition.

Similar problems arise concerning the process of deprofessionalization— that is, the alteration of an occupation so that it loses its status as a profession. Typically, this is an unintended process which professionals fear and try to avoid.[1] But uncertainty about what, precisely, makes their occupation a profession also leads to uncertainty about what is most to be feared in changes that the occupation might undergo. In medicine, for example, there has been a drastic change as the number of physicians in private practice has declined, and the number of physicians working as employees or shareholders in various kinds of healthcare corporations has increased. This has had the effect of reducing certain aspects of physician autonomy, since those not in private practice are less free to select patients or to decide on courses of therapy. It also has introduced a relationship with an employer/manager, which is relatively new for physicians. Some physicians see this as a threat to the very existence of their profession—that is, as a move toward deprofessionalization. Others regard these particular aspects of their autonomy as accidental and see the trend away from private practice as merely a change *within* the profession. Once again, uncertainty about the defining characteristics of a profession, as well as about the importance of having professional status, contributes to the difficulty of evaluating this new stage in the evolution of an occupation.

Moving Beyond Definition

How seriously does uncertainty about how to identify professionals affect the study of professional ethics? It might seem that if we cannot tell who the professionals are, then we have virtually no way to decide whose ethical problems we want to study, or whose resources and standards of conduct may be brought to bear on those problems. But things are not quite that grim. First, there are some occupations that we are sure are professions and some that we are sure are not. Even if we are unsure about how to construct a precise definition, it is not as if we have no idea at all what we are talking about. Second, we should recall that the way in which one decides who the professionals are is in part a function of one's *reason* for deciding. In our case, the question arose in the context of asking whether professionals have a special ethical status or not. Perhaps, then, we can simply ask whether there are any *occupations* whose practitioners have such special ethical status. If there are not, then members of all occupations, including professionals, must abide by the same principles and resolve their ethical problems in the same way as the rest of us do. If people in some occupations do have special ethical status, then we need to understand what the special status of each such occupation is, and why it has that status. We can speculate that the answers to these questions depend on the character of each occupation but do not depend on whether the occupation is a profession. If that is so, then we can go on to the ethical issues even if we are not sure how to draw a sharp distinction between professions and nonprofessions. If it is not so, then perhaps trying to get a clearer idea of what could give an occupation

---

[1] It may occasionally happen that members of an occupation deliberately seek to avoid recognition as professionals. For example, English journalists were confronted recently with the possibility of having to be licensed or certified as physicians and lawyers are. Perceiving that as a severe threat to their autonomy, some of them replied that they were not professionals, but only doing a job, and that this form of regulation would thus be inappropriate. See Geoffrey Robertson's *People Against the Press* (London: Quartet Books, 1983).

special ethical status will actually help us to understand better how to define the professions.

Let us then sidestep the interesting question about how to identify professions and professionals and turn our attention to questions about *ethical status*. What is ethical status, and how does one come to have it? And how could one come to have a *special* ethical status that is different from the ethical status of anyone else?

SOME BASIC IDEAS ABOUT ETHICS

Before we can come to grips with the idea of special (or, for that matter, ordinary) ethical status, we need to understand some basic ideas about ethics and the study of ethics. The study of ethics is the study of *good* and *bad* and the differences between them; of *right* and *wrong* (and also of what is merely *all right*) and their differences; of *duties* and of *rights* and their relationship; and of *virtues* and *vices* and related traits of character. But as soon as this much has been said, amendments are in order. Ethics is not concerned with *every* sort of good, bad, right, wrong, and so on. For example, what is legally all right may still be ethically wrong, or vice versa; the boundaries of legal behavior and ethical behavior are not identical, and the study of ethics is not the same as the study of law. Again, one may behave badly and be merely rude. Good manners sometimes have ethical value, but not always; the study of ethics is not the same as the study of etiquette. And, of course, in doing the wrong thing, we sometimes do what is merely stupid or impractical, and in doing the right thing we do what is clever or efficient. But what is practical may not be ethically correct, and the study of ethics is not the same as the study of prudence. It is important to remember that appraisals of human behavior from the points of view of ethics, law, etiquette, and prudence are all different from one another, even though they do overlap at some points. We must not confuse one of these enterprises with another.

What, then, does ethics study? A precise answer to this question would be quite complex, and there is disagreement about what that answer should contain. But as we explore some of the ideas that are basic to ethical thought, the nature of ethical values and principles, and their difference from other sorts of values and principles, will begin to come into focus.

The distinction between *descriptive* and *normative* questions has already been introduced; it is important to see that we can take two quite different approaches to the study of ethics, depending on which sort of question we ask. We might approach the study of ethics from the descriptive point of view, attempting to discover what people actually do value, what sorts of rules and principles they follow, and how they decide what their behavior and character should be. Alternatively, we might approach ethics from a normative point of view, trying to understand what people *should* value, what principles they *ought* to follow, and what their character and behavior really *should* be like. It is often fruitful to consider descriptive and normative questions together, but it is important not to mistake one for the other. What we actually do is not always what we should have done, nor is what we think we should do always what we really should do; and a purely descriptive account of our behavior and values will not be an account of the ideals and principles that should guide us. Although this book is seasoned with descriptive material, our primary concern is with normative issues—that is, with discovering how professionals ought to conduct themselves, rather than how they actually do conduct themselves.

Fundamental and Derived Values and Principles

Consider this hypothetical case: Suppose that one night, as I am preparing to retire, I find that the cat has knocked a drinking glass from the kitchen counter and that the kitchen floor is now littered with shards of broken glass. I'm tired, and I really don't want to start cleaning up broken glass at one o'clock in the morning, but I will, because I think *I ought to do so.*

And now suppose that I am asked *why* I think I ought to clean up the glass. Several answers could be given, but suppose mine is that if I don't clean up the glass, someone might come barefooted into the darkened kitchen during the night, step on the glass and be injured, and it would be wrong of me not to prevent such injury. But, now, why would it be wrong not to prevent such injury? My response is that injuries like that are painful, and I shouldn't do anything to cause needless pain. But, a determined questioner might go on, why is it wrong to cause needless pain? Response: Because pain is a bad thing, and we ought to prevent bad things. Now a very, very determined questioner might try two more queries: Why is pain a bad thing, and why should we prevent bad things? At this point I could only give a different kind of response. It should be obvious, I might say, that pain is bad, and equally obvious that we all should prevent bad things. This is so clear, so fundamental, that no further explanation can be given.

In this hypothetical case, we can distinguish among the following: (1) the *specific* ethical judgment about the particular situation (that I ought to clean up this broken glass, here, now); (2) general values and principles that are dependent upon other values and principles; (3) general values and principles that are independent of other values and principles. It is clear that even though I think I ought to clean up the glass, this is not an activity that I find valuable in itself. The ethical value I attach to the cleaning up in this case is based on my belief that cleaning up is a way to prevent injury; it is a means to an end. Similarly, the general value of preventing injury is explained in terms of the value of preventing pain and my beliefs about the connection between injury and pain. In each case, a value or rule is based upon some other value or rule, along with beliefs indicating that the former value can be promoted or protected by pursuing the latter one. Some things, then, have their value, or some rules are correct, because of the value, or ethical correctness, of something else. We can call such values and principles *derived,* because they get whatever ethical importance they have from elsewhere; their value or ethical correctness is derived from that other source. But not every value and principle can be derived. If the whole system of values is not to collapse in an infinite regress, we see that there must be some values and principles that are not derived but are *fundamental,* in the sense that they are not based on any other values or principles but have whatever ethical importance they have *in themselves.* In our present example, the negative value of pain and the principle that one ought to prevent bad things are offered as fundamental.

This little case also illustrates the process of *justification.* When we justify a specific ethical judgment, we explain how that judgment is derived from more basic values or principles. We may then go on to explain how those values or principles are derived from ones still more basic. In a complete justification, this process of explanation would go on until one or more fundamental values had been reached; in practice, however, justification often goes on only until some values or principles have been reached that seem acceptable to everyone involved in the discussion. It should be clear that only derivative values and principles can be justified in this way. Our fundamental values and principles must be established or determined in some other way. How that is to be done is a difficult question, much debated in the study of ethical theory, and to pursue that topic here would take us too far from our primary objectives. Instead, let us consider the variety of values and principles that people actually do take to be fundamental.

In both theory and practice, we find four general categories of fundamental values and principles. First, we tend to identify certain events, states of affairs, conditions, or situations as *good* or *bad.* For instance, many people regard pleasure, happiness, health, or life as fundamental goods; and pain, unhappiness, illness, or death as fundamental evils. Second, we tend to formulate rules or principles about various kinds of behavior, which we regard as *right* or *wrong.* For example, many people believe that there are fundamental principles requiring us to tell the truth and keep our promises (right things to do) and requiring us not to kill or steal (wrong things to do). Third, we often identify individuals whom we believe are entitled to be treated in certain ways and say that they have fundamental *rights,* such as a right to life, or to liberty, or to own property, and so on. And, finally, we identify certain states of character or traits of personality, which we regard as *virtues* or *vices.* Honesty, courage, and generosity are examples of virtues; and cruelty, selfishness, and untrustworthiness are examples of vices.

Now, most of us speak and act as if we were committed to values or principles in all four of these categories. But do we think that values or principles in all four categories are *fundamental?* Consider, for example, a case of lying to avoid personal embarrassment. Many people will condemn such behavior and insist (one of their ethical principles) that one should not lie. But if we ask *why* one should not lie, we will find an interesting divergence in answers. Some people will say that this is just an obvious, basic ethical principle and that there is no further explanation to be given. They regard the principle as a genuinely fundamental one. But others will respond by offering a justification. Some, for example, will say that lying causes mistrust and disharmony, and that these make social interaction less effective, so that in the end we are less able to promote goods or avoid evils for ourselves and others. Those who give such a justification of the rule against lying thus show that they regard it as derivative, and that their fundamental values (at least with respect to this area of ethics) are the goods and bads that lying may prevent or promote. Others may say that lying contributes to the development of a dishonest and untrustworthy character, and that the reason we should not lie is that doing so contributes to the development of vice and the suppression of virtue. For such people, too, the rule against lying is derivative, but the underlying fundamental values are virtues and vices rather than goods and evils.

Some people, then, may believe that fundamental values or principles are to be found in all four of the categories just outlined. Others may believe that some entire categories are derivative in character, so that every value in one category can be derived from (justified in terms of) values in other categories. Still others may believe that fundamental values are all of a single kind, and that values in all other categories are derivative. Finally, some members of this last group believe that there is only *one* fundamental value, in a single category, and that everything else can be traced back to that value if we only take the time and care to give a complete justification. We will call people who believe that fundamental values or principles exist in only one category *ethical monists,* and those who believe that there are fundamental values in more than one category will be called *ethical pluralists.*

We also can distinguish among various approaches to justification. A justification of some derivative value or principle that is based on consideration of the goods it will promote, or the evils it will prevent, can be said to be a *consequentialist* justification (it is based on considerations of the consequences of our behavior). A justification that is based on fundamental principles of right and wrong action or on appeals to individual rights (our second and third categories) is called a *deontological* justification (the Greek root *deon* refers to duty, or what is obligatory). Finally, there can be justifications based entirely on considerations of virtue and vice. Ethical pluralists, of course, may give justifications of all three sorts or even mix different kinds of fundamental values in a single justification. But ethical monists are restricted to a single kind of justification with which to explain the whole variety of ethical values and principles. It is worth examining some of the basic differences among monistic approaches to ethics.

Three Basic Kinds of Ethical Theory

Those ethical monists who believe that all fundamental values are in the category of goods and evils are committed to employing only consequential justifications where a complete justification is to be given. Accordingly, we can call such persons *consequentialists,* and any theories that they construct to explain normative ethics can be called *consequential* ethical theories. From a consequentialist viewpoint, ethical understanding begins with the identification of fundamental goods and evils. All the rest of ethics is to be understood in terms of tendencies to promote goods or prevent evils. When we have to choose a course of action, the choice that would result in the greatest balance of good over evil (or, when life is hard, the smallest balance of evil over good) is our duty, and the right thing to do. Other choices are wrong, and we ought not do them. Traits of character will be counted as virtues if they are traits that contribute to the production of goods or the suppression of evils, while traits of character with the reverse tendencies will be counted as vices.

The best-known and most thoroughly developed and criticized conse-quentialist ethical theories are those known as *utilitarian* theories. Utilitarians regard human happiness, pleasure, or satisfaction as the fundamental good; and human unhappiness, suffering, or dissatisfaction as the fundamental evil. Right and wrong action, then, as well as virtues and vices, are to be determined by estimating their impact on human happiness in the ways just indicated.

Consequentialist views are quantitative. If the crucial question is always whether one course of action will promote more good or less evil than another, then we must be able to measure and compare amounts of good or evil. Critics of consequentialism argue that it is impossible to measure goods and evils with the precision and foresight required. Consequentialists also are criticized because they seem to hold that ends definitely do justify means, and that a sufficiently good outcome could justify any kind of action at all.

Deontologists are those ethical monists who think that all complete jus-tifications must be based on fundamental principles of right and wrong action, or on appeals to individual rights. There are important differences between these two emphases, but in either case, the primary concern is with the correctness or incorrectness of our actions. Certain behavior is simply wrong, and other behavior is simply required, regardless of the goods or evils that result. Some deontologists have tried to describe a single fundamental prin-ciple, from which other rules might be derived; others have worked with a system of fundamental rules. Concern with goods and evils is limited and often secondary. Good will and good character, for example, might be regarded as ethically important because they contribute to right action, but many other goods and evils are held to be of little or no ethical significance. A deontologist might claim, for instance, that it is ethically wrong to inten-tionally cause suffering, and admit that suffering is an evil, but deny that suffering is an *ethical* evil itself. The act, then, is not wrong because of its result, but because of its own character. The difficulty of establishing fun-damental values seems somehow more pressing for deontologists than for consequentialists, and those who adopt more than one fundamental principle have difficulty with conflicts among them. Critics accuse deontologists of being rigid and uncaring, since the deontologist will not consider harms or goods that might result from our actions to be more important than the principles of action. For the deontologist, ends *cannot* justify means.

Finally, those who believe that complete justifications must always end in appeals to virtue or vice are often said to subscribe to *virtue ethics.* Such an ethical view has a peculiar inward-looking character. For each person, the fundamental goal is the cultivation of the virtuous traits of character and the suppression of vicious traits of character. Ethical success results in a harmoniously balanced, virtuous personality. Ethical failure results in tension and self-conflict. Our actions and interactions with others, then, are evaluated on the basis of two considerations: (1) Is the action a contribution to developing virtue? (2) Is the action an expression of virtue already developed? Paradox-ically, the fundamental reason to be considerate toward others is not the impact on them, but the consequences for oneself. The result is a strategy for guiding one's behavior that is more flexible than the deontologist's rules, but without a dominating concern for consequences.

Some critics of virtue ethics complain that this alleged flexibility actually results in a vague, confusing system, in which one finds no method for obtaining guidance about how to act in specific difficult situations. And it is not clear how one is to balance conflicts between the demands of different virtues in situations of conflict (for example, if the truth would humiliate you, should I be honest or kind?) Some critics also suggest that virtue ethics ultimately turns out to be a theory of self-interest and is thus ethically suspect. It should be noted that virtue ethics has not received as much contemporary attention and development as have consequentialism and deontology, although interest in it seems to be increasing.

More detailed discussion of these basic kinds of ethical theory, along with accounts of some works of their principal proponents, are provided in Appendix I. The foregoing features will suffice to let us continue our exploration of the possibility of special ethical status for professionals.

Ethical Disagreement and Ethical Dilemmas

The distinctions just made can help us to understand the diverse character of ethical disagreement. For example, suppose that two physicians disagree about whether to withdraw life-sustaining care from a patient with severe brain damage. Their disagreement could be due to a number of factors. First, they could be in disagreement about the facts, and such factual disagreement could arise at various levels. For instance, they might agree that patients who never can recover consciousness should be allowed to die, but disagree about the chances that this patient will recover. They would then agree on a general principle (probably a derivative one) but disagree about whether the facts indicate that the principle applies to this case. Or, they might have a factual disagreement at a deeper level. They might, for instance, both agree that everything should be done to minimize the suffering of patients and their families. But one physician may believe that allowing permanently comatose patients to die does relieve the family's suffering, while the other believes that it tends to increase the family's suffering (say, in the form of guilt). Thus, the former believes that such patients should be allowed to die, while the latter believes that they should be kept alive. Here we have disagreement about derivative principles resulting from a broader, more general kind of factual disagreement.

But our physicians could also have a fundamental disagreement, with one thinking that it is a fundamental duty to preserve human life whenever possible, and the other believing that it is most important to reduce suffering as much as possible. They may agree about the facts—how patients' families are affected by allowing death to occur, what this patient's chances are, and so on—but they will disagree about the derivative-level policies that should apply in such cases; thus they will disagree about what should be done in this case.

Care must be taken, then, if we are to understand ethical disagreement well. That there is disagreement about a particular case does not, by itself, tell us whether that disagreement is due to disagreement about the facts, or about the derived principles and values, or about the fundamental values. But disagreement cannot be resolved until it is clear precisely what the disagreement is about. We can also see that the deeper the level of its origin, the more difficult the disagreement will be to resolve. Superficial factual issues are often settled relatively easily, but the sort of factual claim that bolsters general derived values and principles is often more difficult to establish. Also, the more basic a value is, the more difficult it will be to alter it. And since it has not been made clear how fundamental values and principles are to be determined, it is also unclear how disagreement about them should be resolved.

It is important, too, not to be smug about agreement in specific ethical judgments. It is not unusual for people with different fundamental values, emphasizing different sets of facts, to arrive at agreement about particular cases. Perhaps we would be unable to function in society if this were not possible, but such coincidental agreement can mask a great deal of deeper disagreement and mislead a casual observer to anticipate harmonious cooperation where only conflict and argument will occur.

But not all of our ethical conflict involves disagreement between two or more persons. It sometimes happens that we encounter a situation in which some of the values or principles to which we subscribe conflict with one another. Suppose, for instance, that a physician is very deeply committed both to the prevention of suffering and to the preservation of human life. Such a physician, when confronted by the kind of brain-damaged patient previously described, might find that complete fidelity to all her principles is impossible. Some sort of choice is required between prolonging life and relieving suffering. Meeting the requirements of one value or principle is not compatible with meeting the requirements of the other, so that no course of action allows her to proceed without some ethical loss.

Problems of this sort, where every plausible course of action seems to promote some ethical goals only at the cost of others, are called *ethical dilemmas.* They can arise for anyone, professional or not, but certain dilemmas tend to arise repeatedly in certain occupations. Much of the literature on ethical problems in the professions consists of discussion and debate about such ethical dilemmas. Details of many ethical dilemmas are provided in the following chapters, but it is worth briefly considering some general features of these dilemmas here. First, let us consider the ethical dilemma as it arises for one person.

Now, it may happen that in some apparent dilemmas, factual error is involved. That is, the ethical conflict disappears once a person has gathered a more accurate picture of the situation. But such cases really are not ethical dilemmas, strictly speaking. Our concern is with the cases in which there is a genuine conflict among the values to which a single individual subscribes. How can that conflict be resolved? One possibility is that the conflict arises between two or more derivative values or principles that are both derived from the same more fundamental value. In that case, one can try to resolve the dilemma by asking what policy would best serve the more fundamental value, thus bypassing the derivative items in conflict. So, for instance, if one is caught between breaking a promise and telling a lie, and one believes that we should tell the truth and keep our promises because both types of behavior contribute to maximizing good and minimizing harm (a consequentialist kind of outlook), then we might simply ask whether, in this case, it would do more good, or more harm, to keep the promise or to tell the truth, and then do what counts most in terms of our fundamental values. This possibility makes ethical monism seem attractive to a number of students of ethics, because if there is, indeed, only *one* fundamental value, then it should be possible, in principle, to resolve all our ethical dilemmas in this way. On the other hand, if there are several fundamental values or principles and they, or values derived from them, conflict, then it is quite unclear how we should decide which of them is more important. All that is clear is that, somehow, one must decide which of the competing fundamental values has priority.

Ethical dilemmas also arise for groups of persons. In that case, the conflict giving rise to the dilemma will be among values widely held by members of the group, and for many members of the group the dilemma will be a personal one as well, arising within the system of their own personal values. But other members of the group will not see the problem as a personal dilemma, because they don't subscribe to one of the values in conflict, or because they regard it as derivative when others see it as fundamental. Thus the ethical dilemma that confronts a whole group is more complex than the personal dilemma, since it will also be a personal dilemma for some members of the group but it will involve a variety of kinds of ethical disagreement among other members of the group. And if the group admits much variety among its members, then more than one kind of personal dilemma may become involved. That is, different persons with different value systems may discover different personal dilemmas that are related to the focal issue. The larger the group, the more complex the structure of the dilemma becomes, and when an issue acquires the status of a dilemma for a whole nation or society, its structure can achieve staggering complexity. The current collection of issues concerning abortion illustrates one such intractable complex.

ETHICAL ROLES AND PROFESSIONAL ETHICS

Now, at last, we are in a position to examine and clarify the idea of *ethical status*. One's ethical status includes the rights and duties that one has; the ethically significant goods and bads that one might enjoy, suffer, or produce; and those states of character that would count as virtues or vices if one exhibited them. All these factors, from the level of fundamental values and principles through all derivative levels to specific judgments about particular situations, are included, along with considerations of the relative importance of each item in comparison with the others.

One's ethical status, then, is the complete inventory of features of one's place in the ethical scheme of things. From the descriptive point of view, one's ethical status is one's place in the *actual* system of (ethical) values that exists in one's society.[2] From the normative point of view, one's ethical status is the complete structure of values and principles that *should* guide one's conduct and that *should* determine the evaluation of one's character or the ethical significance of events that happen to one. From either point of view,

---

[2] The account one gets of a person's descriptive ethical status will be a function of how narrowly or broadly one interprets the word *society* here.

of course, we will never offer a *complete* account of anyone's ethical status. But, as it turns out, a complete account is not necessary for us to explore the possibility that different persons might have different normative ethical status. Let us then turn to these questions: Is it possible for different people to have different normative ethical status? And if so, what sorts of differences can there be, and why should there be such differences?

Universalizability, Equality, and Ethical Harmony

Ethical theorists have developed three considerations that argue against diversity in normative ethical status. The first of these, which we may call the *universalizability* requirement,[3] is a requirement of logical consistency. The heart of this requirement is the claim that if we make a normative ethical judgment about one situation and justify our judgment by appealing to certain features of that situation, then we must be willing to make a similar judgment about any other situation that exhibits those same features. Or, to put it differently, if we make different normative ethical judgments about two situations, then we must be able to point to some ethically relevant feature(s) present in one of those situations but not in the other.

Suppose, for example, that we believe that it is wrong to perform major surgery on an adult without the use of anesthesia, and we justify our belief by claiming that such a practice would cause unnecessary pain. If we hear that it is routine to perform major surgery on infants without benefit of anesthesia, then we must be prepared either to condemn that practice or to explain why it is significantly different from surgery without anesthesia on adults. Of course, there are a number of differences between the two surgical situations. Adults are older and larger than infants, and are able to express discomfort and protest in ways that infants cannot. And some different surgical equipment and techniques are called for. But these differences will seem ethically irrelevant to most people. On the other hand, if it were claimed that infants are not sufficiently developed to feel pain, then that would be a relevant response; and it would be another relevant response to claim that anesthesia is life-threatening to infants but not to adults. But unless we discover some such relevant differences in the two situations, it would be *irrational* for us to condemn one but not the other.

It is important to note that the universalizability requirement does not tell us whether to condemn or endorse any kind of behavior; it only requires us to be consistent in the way we make and justify our ethical appraisals. It is also important to realize that this requirement leaves room for a great deal of debate about what kinds of differences are ethically relevant; and that disagreement about which values and principles are fundamental generates disagreement about the ethical relevance of various features of situations. Still, this requirement is an important one to meet and reminds us that if we want to claim that the ethical status of some people differs from that of others, then we must be prepared to point out ethically relevant reasons for the difference.

[3] A clear account of universalizability is given in R. M. Hare's *Freedom and Reason* (Oxford: Clarendon Press, 1963).

The second consideration we must keep in mind, which we can call the requirement of *equality*, is a normative one. It is a widely (although not universally) accepted ethical principle that in a just society, the distribution of burdens and benefits should be roughly equal—that discrimination against or in favor of some persons is ethically wrong. Thus, if we wanted to claim that the normative ethical status of some people differs from that of others, then we would need to be able to show that the difference did not result in some seriously unequal distribution of burdens and benefits or in some form of discrimination. And, in particular, if we claim that professionals are entitled to treat their clients, or their colleagues, or any other class of people differently than nonprofessionals should, then we will need to show that we are not advocating some form of discrimination or inequity. It is important to emphasize that it is not being claimed here that we would be *irrational* or *inconsistent* if we advocated inequitable differences in normative ethical status. Instead, the claim is that we would be making an ethical mistake ourselves—that we would be *unjust*. Such injustice could be justified only (if at all) by showing that the injustice itself results in ethical gains of such importance that it is a reasonable ethical price to pay to achieve those gains. Those who regard equality as a *fundamental* ethical value are, of course, less likely to believe that such a justification can be found than are those who believe that equality has derivative status.

The third consideration to be introduced here can be called the requirement of *harmony*. Many people, in discussing normative ethics, assume that if we all somehow understood our rights and duties and acted precisely as we should, then our actions would all fit together in one compatible, harmonious whole. The alternative view would be that our real, normatively authentic duties and rights can arise in ways that lead to conflict, so that if I am to do what I am ethically required to do, I must act in a way that will prevent you from doing what you are ethically required to do.[4] Troublesome cases are not difficult to find. Is it the real duty of soldiers in opposing armies to prevent one another from succeeding? Is it the real duty of lawyers on opposing sides of the same case to try with all their skill to win? Is it the real duty of the physician to keep confidential information that it is the real duty of an attorney in a civil suit to discover, and the real duty of a journalist to make public? Or, if we all understood our roles, would our efforts all become cooperative? It seems clear, at least, that the greater the diversity we allow in the ethical status of different persons, the greater the risk we run of ethical disharmony as a result. And, thus, if we are inclined to think that the *right* ethical system must be harmonious, we may be reluctant to admit much variation in ethical status.

In the light of the three preceding considerations, then, can there be any variation in ethical status? Or are we all subject to precisely the same duties, entitled to precisely the same rights, subject to precisely the same set of ethically pertinent goods and harms, and able to be virtuous or vicious in precisely the same ways?

No one denies some difference in the ethical status of individuals. At the level of specific duties, rights, goods, and so on, there must be some

---

[4] An interesting and compact argument for ethical harmony can be found in William H. Baumer's "Indefensible Impersonal Egoism," *Philosophical Studies*, vol. 18, 1967.

variation. For example, *I* may have a duty to clean up the glass on my kitchen floor, but *you* don't have that duty. And, even though we all should keep our promises, if Ames promises to help Jones on moving day, and Beasley does not make such a promise, then Ames has a specific duty or obligation that Beasley does not have. In the details of our daily lives, as a result of what we do and what others do involving us, we acquire and shed specific "bits" of our ethical status.

Moreover, many of us seem to believe that there are legitimate differences in ethical status at a *general* level. For example, we may believe that the needy have a lesser obligation to perform community service than the wealthy. Or we may believe that adults have an ethical (not just legal) right to political participation, while children have no such right. In many cases, this diversity in ethical status will appear only at the level of derivative values and principles, so that it can be maintained that all persons share the same system of fundamental values and principles, but that various factual differences among us justify diverging derivative ethical status. For such a position to be correct, of course, the factual differences involved must be ethically relevant and consistently treated. And where some serious inequities seem to result from the alleged differences in ethical status, it should be possible to show that they are justified by ethical gains for which they are the means, or from which they are the unavoidable by-product. And again, if we take ethical harmony to be an important requirement, then no derivative-level differences in ethical status could be accepted that produced conflicting duties for different persons.

These requirements not may be easy to meet. For instance, it is often claimed that children are less rational or reflective than adults, or less experienced and less practical, and that that is why they have no right to political participation. But are we really prepared to universalize such a judgment? If so, shouldn't we claim that irrational, naive, and impractical adults should also be barred from political involvement? Few persons who advocate this difference in the ethical status of children and adults are inclined to accept this further differentiation in the ethical status of adults.

Finally, some will advocate a radical sort of diversity in ethical status, so that different persons are thought to be subject to different *fundamental* values or principles. For example, at least some people who argue for a substantial difference in the ethical status of members of different races seem to take this radical approach. Where differences in ethical status are thought to run this deep, it is not surprising that other differences appear at the derivative level as well, and the problems of meeting the requirements of universalizability, equality, and harmony are likely to be formidable. In addition, the problem of understanding how *anyone* is subject to fundamental values and principles becomes more pressing, since there is a need to explain why different persons are subject to different fundamental values or principles.

Ethical Roles

An ethical role can be defined in terms of three sets of considerations. First, we must be able to identify a specific function, office, or position that may be acquired (the role). Second, the ethical status of persons in this identified role must differ in some systematic way from the ethical status of persons not in the role. Systematic differences must be deeper than the specific differences we have as a result of leading our personal lives. What we require here is some derivative or fundamental value, or complex of values, that applies in the same way to everyone in the role and does not apply in that way to anyone not in the role. Third, this ethical status peculiar to occupants of the role must arise from, be based upon, or depend upon the characteristics that essentially define the role.

One possible example we might consider is the *parental* role. It is widely believed that the duties and rights of parents toward their own children differ significantly from the rights and duties of adults toward children in general. For example, we may believe that every adult has a duty to be protective toward any child. But we expect such protectiveness to be dispensed fairly. On the other hand, parents are widely thought to be at least entitled, and perhaps even ethically obligated, to discriminate in favor of their own children. A father who refuses to provide his own children with an education in order to finance health care for orphans he has never met is likely to be subjected to ethical criticism. Such criticism would not be directed at a father who refuses to finance the education of his children in order to provide basic health care *for them.* Similar views are held regarding the special ethical roles of friends, or of neighbors, or of compatriots. And, of course, for each of these roles there are critics who maintain that no special ethical role should be acknowledged. Typically, such critics challenge the claim that there is anything essential to the role in question that could justify the special ethical status associated with it. Such role distinctions, it is often argued, promote disharmony, are inequitable, and are based either on inconsistent appeals to defining characteristics of the role or on characteristics that simply are not ethically relevant.

We are now able to reformulate our opening question about the special ethical status of professionals. What we want to know is whether there are *professional ethical roles.* Or, more completely, we want to know whether there are occupations whose defining characteristics provide the basis for one or more distinct ethical roles for anyone pursuing one of those occupations.[5]

As we have seen, one response to this question will be negative. Some people will argue that professionals are subject to the same fundamental and derivative values as anyone else, and that their conduct should be evaluated precisely as anyone else's should. Because of their special expertise and interests, professionals may develop more *specific* rights and duties of certain kinds than a layperson would develop, but we have no need to appeal to a role ethic to explain that. We should note that such a position will tend to protect professionals from claims that they have extraordinary duties to their clients or to the public, but it will also prevent professionals from claiming extraordinary immunities from the requirements of ordinary ethical conduct.

At the other extreme, some will claim that the life of the professional is so different from ordinary life that even the fundamental ethical status of professionals differs from that of nonprofessionals. Some artists seem to have claimed that the importance of their art transcends the demands of ordinary

[5] For an extended discussion of professional ethical roles, see Alan H. Goldman's *The Moral Foundations of Professional Ethics* (Totowa, N.J.: Rowman and Littlefield, 1980).

morality and imposes a "higher" ethic on them. And it may be that in a number of professions there are persons who view their entrance into the profession as a kind of transformation—a response to a calling or vocation that literally turns them into different persons with fundamentally different ethical roles. When such claims are clearly announced, they are usually not well received. Ordinary persons tend to be skeptical about the alleged distinction between transcendence of their ethical ideals and violation of them. But, of course, our concern is with the correctness of such claims rather than with their popularity.

Between these two extremes lie a variety of more "moderate" accounts of professional role ethics. What these accounts have in common is that they all focus on derivative-level differences between the ethical status of various professionals and the ethical status of nonprofessionals. The crucial problem for such moderate accounts is to determine which essential features of a profession justify deriving role-special values and principles from the common fundamental values and principles shared with other professions and with nonprofessionals. Considerations of universalizability, equality, and ethical harmony play an important part. An even more important part is played by the choice of fundamental values and principles that each ethical theorist makes. While we cannot review all the possible variations on this theme, it is possible to outline certain very general tendencies.

When the emphasis is on consequential fundamental values, the natural tendency is to consider the impact of a profession on the promotion of good and the prevention of evil. In that case, special duties or rights will be assigned to professionals if it appears that doing so will result in more good or less harm than any competing assignment of duties or rights. For example, such an argument might be offered to support the claim that physicians have a special duty of *confidentiality*. As they deal with patients, physicians often gather very personal and sensitive information. That information could be of great importance to other people, and a layperson who happened to have the information might feel a strong sense of obligation to reveal it to those people. But, so the argument goes, the physician must not reveal the information without the patient's permission. If patients knew or even suspected that physicians might reveal embarrassing or compromising information about them, they would be reluctant to seek medical help or to give sensitive information that could facilitate diagnosis and treatment. Thus, a policy of confidentiality increases the number of people who are willing to seek medical help when they need it and improves the quality of that help. Even though such a policy may result in occasional harm, then, that harm is outweighed by the good generated by the policy. Of course, no such considerations apply to the ordinary person, so we see here consequential reasons for thinking that physicians and laypersons have different duties in handling sensitive information. It is worth noting the rather extensive and complex body of information required for such an argument to succeed: What would we have to know in order to be sure that more good is done by requiring confidentiality than would be done by requiring disclosure of critical information?

Emphasis on deontological fundamental principles may generate a variety of approaches to professional ethical roles. If the primary concern is with individual liberties, the professional may be presented as simply another citizen pursuing a chosen occupation in a capitalistic society, who is free to accept or reject clients, or to choose conditions of practice, and so on. Such an approach is unlikely to specify a distinct ethical role for the professional. On the contrary, it usually represents the professional as a person with only those rights and duties that we all share or that arise from the conduct of one's private life.

On the other hand, if the emphasis is on the rights of those in need of professional service, then moderate accounts may be developed that assign some special obligations to professionals. It might be argued, for instance, that everyone has a right to basic health care or to legal representation. And such rights may impose obligations on the rest of us to do what we can to meet those needs. But most of us can do little, since meeting these needs requires expertise. Thus, while professionals and laypersons share duties to respond to everyone's basic needs, the layperson's response will take forms such as political and financial support for social policy that responds to such needs. The professional, on the other hand, will have much more demanding derivative duties to see that services are provided to those in need in as fair a manner as possible.

Of course, not every deontologist begins with rights. If the fundamental emphasis is on duties or obligations, certain kinds of *contractual* approaches to professional ethics can be developed. For example, it may be argued that professionals agree to undertake certain special responsibilities when they enter their professions. And the fundamental duty to keep one's agreements then produces special duties for every member of such professions. The existence of professional oaths and codes of ethics, as well as uniform standards of conduct and practice throughout a profession, contribute to the plausibility of such accounts.

Yet another deontological position rests on the obligations that professionals may have as a result of their debt to society. The education and training required by professionals would be virtually impossible to obtain were it not for supporting public policies and investments of large amounts of public funds. Few who enter the professions could afford to pay the actual cost of their education; and without public support, the institutions in which that education takes place would not exist. It may be argued, then, that professionals are responsible to the public for their very existence and are thus obligated to take up a role that is defined by public will. Thus, professional roles may be at least partly definable by legislation and administrative decision. When private individuals did arrange for and pay for their own training, such an argument might not have seemed plausible. Now, public involvement in virtually every aspect of education makes the argument more interesting.

Still other approaches to professional roles result from an emphasis on virtues and vices. If it is held that there is a single ideal human nature that every virtuous person should try to achieve, few deep-level professional role distinctions are likely to be acknowledged. The expertise a professional possesses may offer somewhat special means for cultivating or exhibiting virtue, but we would not expect the behavior of the virtuous professional to deviate greatly from the behavior of any other virtuous person. On the other hand, if it is possible for different people to have different normatively valid ideals, and especially if one's ideals can be determined by an act of commitment or dedication, then the virtuous professional might be regarded as quite different from the virtuous layperson or from virtuous members of other professions.

It seems clear that some persons, on entering a profession, do commit or dedicate themselves to a kind of life and practice that they regard as distinct from everyday life. The character of these commitments can vary greatly from one profession to another, or even within a single profession. Some commitments are made to the service of clients or society. In that case, the virtuous professional will be the one who excels at meeting the needs of clients or society. But commitments can be made to other things—for instance, to excellence in the skills that the professional practices. The importance of such differences in commitment can be seen if we consider the case of a demanding, brilliant piece of surgical work done on a patient who could not possibly benefit from it. The practice of professional skills is superior; the service to the patient is inferior. On the view we are considering, the character of one's commitments might determine whether it is an exercise of professional virtue or not.

In all the approaches to professional ethics just sketched, the professional's role is derived from the fundamental values and principles that one believes are correct. But there is also an approach that deliberately attempts to avoid selecting any particular set of fundamental values. In this approach, a fictitious *social contract* is described. In contrast to the deontological contract just discussed, this is not an agreement that any actual persons are supposed to have made; rather, it is the imaginary agreement that well-informed, unbiased, rational persons *would* make if they were asked to design a society or some smaller set of its institutions. The strategy is to make no assumptions at all about fundamental values. Indeed, we may even assume that the parties to our fictitious contract subscribe to different values. But if they really are (very) well-informed, unbiased, and rational, must not whatever set of institutions they work out be at least fair and just? And if those institutions distinguish special roles for certain professions, or if they deny such roles, then we might succeed in identifying a normatively correct professional ethic without having had to resolve the vexing question about fundamental values and principles.

This proposal has received a great deal of attention, both favorable and unfavorable.[6] Several attempts have been made to work out its significance for professional ethics, but the results do not show great uniformity. Critics wonder how we, who are not very well informed, unbiased, or rational, could know what agreement these fictitious individuals would make; and they suspect that what the social-contract theorist regards as a rational, unbiased choice is instead merely a reflection of that theorist's own set of fundamental values. Furthermore, they ask, even if we could discover in this way what the professional's role should be in an ideal, just society, can we be sure that the same role would be appropriate in the far-from-ideal and not entirely just society that actually confronts us?

---

[6] John Rawls has presented the most widely known contemporary social-contract account in *A Theory of Justice* (Cambridge, Mass.: Harvard University Press, 1974–1975). See Appendix I for some discussion of his views.

CONCLUDING REMARKS

We can see that the question of whether professionals have special ethical roles is a complex one. The way in which we respond will depend upon (1) what features of an occupation we believe make it a profession; (2) what features of a specific profession we think are essential to its identity; (3) the normative values and principles we take to be fundamental, and their relationship to the essential features of a profession; (4) our beliefs about many facts concerning the requirements and effects of practicing a profession in a certain way, including impact on clients, colleagues, society, and self; and (5) the values and principles we believe can be derived from (2), (3), and (4).

There is disagreement about all of these items and thus about who the professionals are, what they should be doing, and, indeed, whether they should exist at all. There is uncertainty about which situations really are ethical dilemmas for individual professionals and how those situations should be managed. And there is corresponding uncertainty about how clients, institutions, employers, and society should react to and interact with professionals and their professions. While we have explored some aspects of these difficult normative questions here, we have resolved none of them.

Subsequent chapters provide more detailed consideration of specific subdivisions of our general problem. Chapter 2 treats the relationships between professionals and their clients; Chapter 3 examines the relationships among professionals and their employers, employees, and sheltering institutions. Questions of the just and fair distribution of professional services are taken up in Chapter 4, and Chapter 5 explores the problem of deciding who should control, regulate, or oversee professional conduct.

Solutions to the problems raised in these chapters depend upon our answers to the questions just presented, and the disagreement about how to answer these questions will be reflected in disagreement about how best to deal with those problems. But exploring the details of more specific issues and wrestling with the ethical dilemmas connected with them gives us a sharper perspective on the significance of whatever position we are inclined to take on the question of professional ethical roles. Thus, rather than attempting to answer the most general theoretical questions first, and then going on to more specific problems, it is better to consider questions of specific ethical decisions, of derived policies, and of theoretical foundations together. Our grasp of the issues at each level will illuminate our understanding of the rest.

PROFESSIONAL DOMINANCE

Ivan Illich

Illich denounces professionals for maintaining tyrannical and unjustifiable power over laypersons. Central to his argument are the claims that professionals have invented many of the needs that they claim to serve, and that the degree of technical expertise required to serve real need is vastly overrated. In addition, Illich accuses professionals of usurping our authority to make our own decisions about our personal lives.

Let us first face the fact that the bodies of specialists that now dominate the creation, adjudication, and satisfaction of needs are a new kind of cartel. And this must be recognized in order to outflank their developing defenses. For we already see the new biocrat hiding behind the benevolent mask of the physician of old; the pedocrat's behavioral aggression is shrugged off as the overzealous, perhaps silly care of the concerned teacher; the personnel manager equipped with a psychological arsenal presents himself in the guise of an old-time foreman. The new specialists, who are usually servicers of human needs that their specialty has defined, tend to wear the mask of love and to provide some form of care. They are more deeply entrenched than a Byzantine bureaucracy, more international than a world church, more stable than any labor union, endowed with wider competencies than any shaman, and equipped with a tighter hold over those they claim than any mafia.

The new organized specialists must, first, be carefully distinguished from racketeers. Educators, for instance, now tell society what must be learned and write off what has been learned outside school. By this kind of monopoly, which enables tyrannical professions to prevent you from shopping elsewhere and from making your own booze, they at first seem to fit the dictionary definition of gangsters. But gangsters, for their own profit, corner a basic necessity by controlling supplies. Educators and

doctors and social workers today—as did priests and lawyers formerly—gain legal power to create the need that, by law, they alone will be allowed to serve. They turn the modern state into a holding corporation of enterprises that facilitate the operation of their self-certified competencies.

Legalized control over work has taken many different forms: soldiers of fortune refused to fight until they got the license to plunder; Lysistrata organized female chattels to enforce peace by refusing sex; doctors in Cos conspired by oath to pass trade secrets only to their offspring; guilds set the curricula, prayers, tests, pilgrimages, and hazings through which Hans Sachs had to pass before he was permitted to shoe his fellow burghers. In capitalist countries, unions attempt to control who shall work what hours for what pay. All these trade associations are attempts by specialists to determine how their kind of work shall be done and by whom. But none of these specialists are professionals in the sense that doctors, for instance, are today. Today's domineering professionals, of whom physicians provide the most striking and painful example, go further: They decide what shall be made, for whom, and how it shall be administered. They claim special, incommunicable knowledge, not just about the way things are and are to be made, but also about the reasons why their services ought to be needed. Merchants sell you the goods they stock. Guildsmen guarantee quality. Some craftspeople tailor their product to your measure or fancy. Professionals, however, tell you what you need. They claim the power to prescribe. They not only advertise what is good but ordain what is right. Neither income, long training, delicate tasks, nor social standing is the mark of the professional. Their income can be low or taxed away, their training compressed into weeks instead of years; their status can approach that of the oldest profession. Rather, what counts is the professional's authority to define a person as client, to determine that person's need, and to hand that person a prescription which defines this new social role. Unlike the hookers of old, the modern professional is not one who sells what others give for free, but rather one who decides what ought to be sold and must not be given for free.

There is a further distinction between professional power and that of other occupations: Professional power springs from a different source. A guild, a union, or a gang forces respect for its interest and rights by a strike, blackmail, or overt violence. In contrast, a profession, like a priesthood, holds power by concession from an elite whose interests it props up. As a priesthood offers the way to salvation in the train of an anointed king, so a profession interprets, protects, and supplies a special this-worldly interest to the constituency of modern rulers. Professional power is a specialized form of the privilege to prescribe what is right for others and what they therefore need. It is the source of prestige and control within the industrial state. This kind of professional power could, of course, come into existence only in societies where elite membership itself is legitimated, if not acquired, by professional status: a society where governing elites are attributed a unique kind of objectivity in defining the moral status of a lack. It fits like a glove the age in which even access to parliament, the house of commons, is in fact limited to those who have acquired the title of master by accumulating knowl-

edge stock in some college. Professional autonomy and license in defining the needs of society are the logical forms that oligarchy takes in a political culture that has replaced the means test by knowledge-stock certificates issued by schools. The professions' power over the work their members do is thus distinct in both scope and origin.

Toward Professional Tyranny

Professional power has also, recently, so changed in degree that two animals of entirely different colors now go by the same name. For instance, the practicing and experimenting health scientist consistently evades critical analysis by dressing up in the clothes of yesterday's family doctor. The wandering physician became the medical doctor when he left commerce in drugs to the pharmacist and kept for himself the power to prescribe them. At that moment, he acquired a new kind of authority by uniting three roles in one person: the sapiential authority to advise, instruct, and direct; the moral authority that makes its acceptance not just useful but obligatory; and the charismatic authority that allows the physician to appeal to some supreme interest of his clients that outranks not only conscience but sometimes even the *raison d'état.* This kind of doctor, of course, still exists, but within a modern medical system he is a figure out of the past. A new kind of health scientist is now much more common. He increasingly deals more with cases than with persons; he deals with the breakdown that he can perceive in the case rather than with the complaint of the individual; he protects society's interest rather than the person's. The authorities that, during the liberal age, had coalesced in the individual practitioner in his treatment of a patient are now claimed by the professional corporation in the service of the state. This entity now carves out for itself a social mission.

Only during the last twenty-five years has medicine turned from a liberal into a dominant profession by obtaining the power to indicate what constitutes a health need for people in general. Health specialists as a corporation have acquired the authority to determine what health care must be provided to society at large. It is no longer the individual professional who imputes a "need" to the individual client, but a corporate agency that imputes a need to entire classes of people and then claims the mandate to test the complete population in order to identify all who belong to the group of potential patients. And what happens in health care is thoroughly consistent with what goes on in other domains. New pundits constantly jump on the bandwagon of the therapeutic-care provider: educators, social workers, the military, town planners, judges, policemen, and their ilk have obviously made it. They enjoy wide autonomy in creating the diagnostic tools by which they then catch their clients for treatment. Dozens of other need-creators try: International bankers "diagnose" the ills of an African country and then induce it to swallow the prescribed treatment, even though the "patient" might die; security specialists evaluate the loyalty risk in a citizen and then extinguish his private sphere; dog-catchers sell themselves to the public as pest-controllers and claim a monopoly over the lives of stray dogs. The only way to prevent the escalation of needs is a fundamental, political exposure of those illusions that legitimate dominating professions.

Many professions are so well established that they not only exercise tutelage over the citizen-become-client but also determine the shape of his world-become-ward. The language in which he perceives himself, his perception of rights and freedoms, and his awareness of needs all derive from professional hegemony.

The difference between craftsman, liberal professional, and the new technocrat can be clarified by comparing their typical reactions to people who neglect their respective advice. If you did not take the craftsman's advice, you were a fool. If you did not take liberal counsel, society blamed you. Now the profession or the government may be blamed when you escape from the care that your lawyer, teacher, surgeon, or shrink has decided upon for you. Under the pretense of meeting needs better and on a more equitable basis, the service professional has mutated into a crusading philanthropist. The nutritionist prescribes the "right" formula for the infant and the psychiatrist the "right" antidepressant, and the schoolmaster—now acting with the fuller power of "educator"—feels entitled to push his method between you and anything you want to learn. Each new specialty in service production thrives only when the public has accepted and the law has endorsed a new perception of what ought not to exist. Schools expanded in a moralizing crusade against illiteracy, once illiteracy had been defined as an evil. Maternity wards mushroomed to do away with home births.

Professionals claim a monopoly over the definition of deviance and the remedies needed. For example, lawyers assert that they alone have the competence and the legal right to provide assistance in divorce. If you devise a kit for do-it-yourself divorce, you find yourself in a double bind: If you are not a lawyer, you are liable for practicing without a license; if you are a member of the bar, you can be expelled for unprofessional behavior. Professionals also claim secret knowledge about human nature and its weaknesses, knowledge they are also mandated to apply. Gravediggers, for example, did not become members of a profession by calling themselves morticians, by obtaining college credentials, by raising their incomes, or by getting rid of the odor attached to their trade by electing one of themselves president of the Lion's Club. Morticians formed a profession, a dominant and disabling one, when they acquired the muscle to have the police stop your burial if you are not embalmed and boxed by them. In any area where a human need can be imagined, these new disabling professions claim that they are the exclusive wardens of the public good.

Professions as a New Clergy

The transformation of a liberal profession into a dominant one is equivalent to the legal establishment of a church. Physicians transmogrified into biocrats, teachers into gnosocrats, morticians into thanatocrats, are much closer to state-supported clergies than to trade associations. The professional as teacher of the current brand of scientific orthodoxy acts as theologian. As moral entrepreneur, he acts the role of priest: He creates the need for his mediation. As crusading helper, he acts the part of the missionary and hunts down the underprivileged. As inquisitor, he outlaws the unorthodox—he imposes his solutions on the recalcitrant who refuse to recognize that they are a problem. This multifaceted investiture with the task of relieving a specific inconvenience of man's estate turns each profession into the analogue of an established cult. The public acceptance of domineering professions is thus essentially a political event. The new profession creates a new hierarchy, new clients and outcasts, and a new strain on the budget. But also, each new establishment of professional legitimacy means that the political tasks of lawmaking, judicial review, and executive power lose more of their proper character and independence. Public affairs pass from the layperson's elected peers into the hands of a self-accrediting elite.

When medicine recently outgrew its liberal restraints, it invaded legislation by establishing public norms. Physicians had always determined what constituted disease; dominant medicine now determines what diseases society shall not tolerate. Medicine has invaded the courts. Physicians had always diagnosed who was sick; dominant medicine, however, brands those who must be treated. Liberal practitioners prescribed a cure; dominant medicine has public powers of correction: It decides what shall be done with or to the sick. In a democracy, the power to make laws, execute them, and achieve public justice must derive from the citizens themselves. This citizen control over the key powers has been restricted, weakened, and sometimes abolished by the rise of churchlike professions. Government by a congress that bases its decisions on expert opinions of such professions might be government for, but never by, the people. This is not the place to investigate the intent with which political rule was thus weakened; it is sufficient to indicate the professional disqualification of lay opinion as a necessary condition for this subversion.

Citizen liberties are grounded in the rule that excludes hearsay from testimony on which public decisions are based. What people can see for themselves and interpret is the common ground for binding rules. Opinions, beliefs, inferences, or persuasions ought not to stand when in conflict with the eyewitness—ever. Expert elites could become dominant professions only by a piecemeal erosion and final reversal of this rule. In the legislature and courts, the rule against hearsay evidence is now, *de facto*, suspended in favor of the opinions proffered by the members of these self-accredited elites.

But let us not confuse the public use of expert factual knowledge with a profession's corporate exercise of normative judgment. When a craftsman, such as a gunmaker, was called into court as an expert to reveal to the jury the secrets of his trade, he apprenticed the jury to his craft on the spot. He demonstrated visibly from which barrel the bullet had come. Today, most experts play a different role. The dominant professional provides jury or legislature with his fellow initiate's opinion rather than with factual evidence and a skill. He calls for a suspension of the hearsay rule and inevitably undermines the rule of law. Thus, democratic power is ineluctably abridged.

The Hegemony of Imputed Needs

Professions could not have become dominant and disabling unless people had been ready to experience as a lack that which the expert imputed to them as a need. Their mutual dependence as tutor and charge has become resistant to analysis because it has been obscured by corrupted language. Good old words have been made into branding irons that claim wardship for experts over home, shop, store, and the space or ether between them. Language, the most fundamental of commons, is thus polluted by twisted strands of jargon, each under the control of another profession. The disseizin of words, the depletion of ordinary language and its degradation into bureaucratic terminology, parallel in a more intimately debasing manner that particular form of environmental degradation that dispossesses people of their usefulness unless they are gainfully employed. Possible changes in design, attitudes, and laws that would retrench professional dominance cannot be proposed unless we become more sensitive to the misnomers behind which this dominance hides. . . .

Used as a noun, "need" is the individual offprint of a professional pattern; it is a plastic-foam replica of the mold in which professionals cast their staple; it is the advertised shape of the brood cells out of which consumers are produced. To be ignorant or unconvinced of one's own needs has become the unforgivable antisocial act. The good citizen is one who imputes standardized needs to himself with such conviction that he drowns out any desire for alternatives, much less for the renunciation of needs.

When I was born, before Stalin and Hitler and Roosevelt came to power, only the rich, hypochondriacs, and members of elite unions spoke of their need for medical care when their temperatures rose. Doctors then, in response, could not do much more than grandmothers had done. In medicine the first mutation of needs came with sulfa drugs and antibiotics. As the control of infections became a simple and effective routine, drugs went more and more on prescription. Assignment of the sick-role became a medical monopoly. The person who felt ill had to go to the clinic to be labeled with a disease name and to be legitimately declared a member of the minority of the so-called sick: people excused from work, entitled to help, put under doctor's orders, and enjoined to heal in order to become useful again. Paradoxically, as pharmacological technique—tests and drugs—became so predictable and cheap that one could have dispensed with the physician, society enacted laws and police regulations to restrict the free use of those procedures that science had simplified, and placed them on the prescription list.

The second mutation of medical needs happened when the sick ceased to be a minority. Today, few people eschew doctors' orders for any length of time. In Italy, the United States, France, or Belgium, one out of every two citizens is being watched simultaneously by several health professionals who treat, advise, or at least observe him or her. The object of such specialized care is, more often than not, a condition of teeth, womb, emotions, blood pressure, or hormone levels that the patient himself does not feel. Patients are no more in the minority. Now, the minority are those deviants who somehow escape from any and all patient-roles. This minority is made up of the poor, the peasants, the recent immigrants, and sundry others who, sometimes on their own volition, have gone medically AWOL. Just twenty years ago, it was a sign of normal health—which was assumed to be good—to get along without a doctor. The same status of nonpatient is now indicative of poverty or dissidence. Even the status of the hypochondriac has changed. For the doctor in the forties, this was the label applied to the gate-crashers in his office—the designation reserved for the imaginary sick. Now, doctors refer to the minority who flee them by the same name: Hypochondriacs are the imaginary healthy. To be plugged into a professional system as a lifelong client is no longer a stigma that sets apart the disabled person from citizens at large. We now live in a society organized for deviant majorities and their keepers. To be an active client of several professionals provides you with a well-defined place within the realm of consumers for the sake of whom our society functions. Thus, the transformation of medicine from a liberal consulting profession into a dominant, disabling profession has immeasurably increased the number of the needy.

At this critical moment, imputed needs move into a third mutation. They coalesce into what the experts call a multidisciplinary problem necessitating, therefore, a multiprofessional solution. First, the proliferation of commodities, each tending to turn into a requirement, has effectively trained the consumer to need on command. Next, the progressive fragmentation of needs into ever smaller and unconnected parts has made the client dependent on professional judgment for the blending of his needs into a meaningful whole. The auto industry provides a good example. By the end of the sixties, the advertised optional equipment needed to make a basic Ford desirable had been multiplied immensely. But contrary to the customer's expectations, this "optimal" flim-flam is in fact installed on the assembly line of the Detroit factory, and the shopper in Plains is left with a choice between a few packaged samples that are shipped at random: He can either buy the convertible that he wants but with the green seats he hates, or he can humor his girlfriend with leopard-skin seats at the cost of buying an unwanted paisley hardtop.

Finally, the client is trained to need a team approach to receive what his guardians consider "satisfactory treatment." Personal services that improve the consumer illustrate the point. Therapeutic affluence has exhausted the available lifetime of many whom service professionals diagnose as standing in need of more. The intensity of the service economy has made the time needed for the consumption of pedagogical, medical, and social treatments increasingly scarce. Time scarcity may soon turn into the major obstacle to the consumption of prescribed, and often publicly financed, services. Signs of such scarcity become evident from one's early years. Already in kindergarten, the child is subjected to management by a team made up of such specialists as the allergist, speech pathologist, pediatrician, child psychologist, social worker, physical-education instructor, and teacher. By forming such a pedocratic team, many different professionals attempt to share the time that has become the major limiting factor to the imputation of further needs. For the adult, it is not the school but the workplace where the packaging of services focuses. The personnel manager, labor educator, in-service trainer, insurance planner, consciousness-raiser find it more profitable to share the worker's time than to compete for it. A need-less citizen would be highly suspicious. People are told that they need their jobs not so much for the money as for the services they get. The commons are extinguished and replaced by a new placenta built of funnels that deliver professional services. Life is paralyzed in permanent intensive care. . . .

The disabling of the citizen through professional dominance is completed through the power of illusion. Hopes of religious salvation are displaced by expectations that center on the state as supreme manager of professional services. Each of many special priesthoods claims competence to define public issues in terms of specific serviceable problems. The acceptance of this claim legitimates the docile recognition of imputed lacks on the part of the layman, whose world turns into an echo-chamber of needs. The satisfaction of self-defined preference is sacrificed to the fulfillment of educated needs. This dominance of engineered and managed needs is reflected in the skyline of the city: Professional buildings look down on the crowds that shuttle between them in a continual pilgrimage to the new cathedrals of health, education, and welfare. Healthy homes are transformed into hygienic apartments where one cannot be born, cannot be sick, and cannot die decently. Not only are helpful neighbors a vanishing species, but also liberal doctors who make house calls. Workplaces fit for apprenticeship turn into opaque mazes of corridors that permit access only to functionaries equipped with "identities" in mica holders, pinned to their lapels. A world designed for service deliveries is the utopia of citizens turned into welfare recipients.

The prevailing addiction to imputable needs on the part of the rich, and the paralyzing fascination with needs on the part of the poor, would indeed be irreversible if people actually fitted the calculus of needs. But this is not so. Beyond a certain level of intensity, medicine engenders helplessness and disease; education turns into the major generator of a disabling division of labor; fast transportation systems turn urbanized people for about one-sixth of their waking hours into passengers, and for an equal amount of time into members of the road gang that works to pay Ford, Exxon, and the highway department. The threshold at which medicine, education, and transportation turn into counterproductive tools has been reached in all the countries of the world with per capita incomes comparable at least to those prevalent in Cuba. In all countries examined, and contrary to the illusions propagated by the orthodoxies of both East and West, this specific counterproductivity bears no relation to the kind of school, vehicle, or health organization now used. It sets in when the capital intensity of the production process passes a critical threshold.

Our major institutions have acquired the uncanny power to subvert the very purposes for which they were originally engineered and financed. Under the rule of our most prestigious professions, our institutional tools have as their principal product paradoxical counterproductivity— the systematic disabling of the citizenry. A city built around wheels becomes inappropriate for feet, and no increase of wheels can overcome the engineered immobility of such cripples. Autonomous action is paralyzed by a surfeit of commodities and treatments. But this does not represent simply a net loss of satisfactions that do not happen to fit into the industrial age. The impotence to produce use-values ultimately renders counterpurposive the very commodities meant to replace them. The car, the doctor, the school, and the manager are then commodities that have turned into destructive nuisances for the consumer, and retain net value only for the provider of services.

Why are there no rebellions against the coalescence of late industrial society into one huge disabling service-delivery system? The chief explanation must be sought in the illusion-generating power that these same systems possess. Besides doing technical things to body and mind, professionally attended institutions function also as powerful rituals which generate credence in the things their managers promise. Besides teaching Johnny to read, schools also teach him that learning from teachers is "better" and that without compulsory schools, fewer books would be read by the poor. Besides providing locomotion, the bus just as much as the sedan reshapes the environment and puts walking out of step. Besides providing help in avoiding taxes, lawyers also convey the notion that laws solve problems. An ever-growing part of our major institutions' function is the cultivation and maintenance of . . . illusions which turn the citizen into a client to be saved by experts.

PHYSICIANS VERSUS LAWYERS: A CONFLICT
OF CULTURES

Daniel M. Fox

This is an examination, from a physician's perspective, of ways in which the aims and methods of physicians and lawyers differ. Fox identifies five major areas of disagreement: the nature of authority, proper methods for resolving conflict, the relative importance of procedure as opposed to substance in a dispute, the method by which to evaluate risk, and the legitimacy of solving problems politically rather than by appeal to objective evidence.

The AIDS epidemic raises problems of public health policy that require physicians and lawyers to work together as never before. They must collaborate, for example, in safeguarding the privacy of persons with AIDS when their names are reported to public health agencies. Together, the two professions must assess what information is needed to monitor the epidemic, to assist science, and to protect people who have not become seropositive, and then develop strategies to preserve some privacy for persons with the disease.[1]

Working collaboratively is no easy task for professions that have fundamentally different conceptions of their roles and their prerogatives and that increasingly regard each other as antagonists. Thus, even as the AIDS epidemic provides an opportunity for cooperation, it provides new occasions for conflict between members of the legal and medical professions. If we are to move in the direction of cooperation rather than conflict, we must understand the roots of the antagonism between the professions and the contemporary forces that threaten to deepen it.

I have observed the antagonism of physicians toward lawyers during fourteen years as a faculty member and senior manager

of an academic health center—a teaching hospital and five professional schools—that is a unit of a large state university. This experience has no doubt given me a limited view of both professions. The lawyers I have observed are either public employees or private counsel retained to assist them. The physicians I work with are clinicians and scientists who are full-time faculty members at a medical school. I have recently observed physicians and lawyers concerned about AIDS while doing research on issues of public policy raised by the disease and coediting a special issue of a journal addressing the public context of the epidemic.

I oversimplify [here] the relationship between physicians and lawyers in order to examine the conflict between them. In particular, I emphasize physicians' antagonism to lawyers, rather than lawyers' role in the conflict. In part I do this because I have little first-hand knowledge concerning lawyers' unguarded opinions about physicians. But it is also because—the negligence bar aside—I suspect that most lawyers are not normally antagonistic toward physicians. Physicians, on the other hand, believe they are being taken advantage of by lawyers who do not understand medicine or value it properly. They are, moreover, mortified because the conflict is usually displayed in public settings controlled by lawyers—court

---

[1] Gostin, *The Future of Communicable Disease Control: Toward a New Concept of Public Health Law*, 64 Milbank Quarterly, Supplement I, at 79 (1986).

From Daniel M. Fox, "Physicians versus Lawyers: A Conflict of Cultures," in *AIDS and the Law,* ed. Harlon L. Dalton, et al. (New Haven: Yale University Press, 1987). Reprinted by permission of Yale University Press.

proceedings and legislative hearings. To be sure, not all physicians fall within the terms of my analysis. Some of them enjoy a role analogous to barracks or jailhouse lawyers. A few even study the law. Others relish it: I know an eminent physician, for example, who is fond of quoting in his administrative work aphorisms about the law he learned from his late father. Moreover, as I will describe at the end of the discussion, some physicians and lawyers are in fact collaborating on issues pertaining to AIDS.

The conflict between physicians and lawyers, though is rooted in the modern history of the two professions, has become more intense in recent years as the authority most people accord to physicians has diminished. Some physicians accuse lawyers of helping to undermine public confidence in them by mindlessly pursuing malpractice litigation. Many attribute their rising premiums for malpractice insurance to the work of greedy and unscrupulous lawyers. Others assert that so-called "defensive medicine," ordering marginally useful tests and therapies to avoid being sued, has helped to increase the cost of medical care. Physicians often blame lawyers for the mass of regulations that burden them. In an astonishing display of professional bigotry, the new president of the Association of American Medical Colleges told a medical school graduating class in June 1986, "We're swimming in shark-infested waters where the sharks are lawyers."[2]

Events during the AIDS epidemic have reinforced physicians' irritation with lawyers. Many physicians are offended that decisions about whether particular children with AIDS can attend school are made by judges after argument by lawyers. They are dismayed when an official of the U.S. Department of Justice issues a ruling about discrimination against persons with AIDS in the workplace that ignores medical opin-ion. Even though physicians disagree among themselves about precisely who is at risk of getting AIDS, they condemn lawyers who argue on behalf of their clients that any conceivable risk is intolerable. They routinely curse the politicians and even the public health officials who debate laws or issue regulations that, in their view, interfere with the practice of medicine; an instance in point is the guidelines for AIDS treatment centers in New York State, which require hospitals to designate a unit for AIDS patients.

Physicians are often grateful to the lawyers who defend them against lay intruders into the practice of medicine. For instance, I heard no complaints about the lawyers who defended the State University of New York, my employer, against the Right-to-Life movement and the federal government in the Baby Jane Doe case in 1983 and 1984. Occasionally, however, physicians would recall, in vexed tones, that lawyers had caused the problem in the first place—notably A. Lawrence Washburn, a free-lance Right-to-Lifer, and the attorneys who advised the Department of Health and Human Services that Section 504 of the Rehabilitation Act of 1973 applied to disabled newborns.

The antagonism many physicians feel toward lawyers is the result of fundamental disagreement about five issues: the nature of authority, how conflict should be resolved, the relative importance of procedure and substance, the nature and significance of risk, and the legitimacy of politics as a method of solving problems.

This disagreement began in the early nineteenth century, when physicians and lawyers began to make very different assumptions about the sources of useful knowledge and the nature of authority. Until then, elite lawyers, physicians, and clergy shared knowledge and values derived from a common education in classical languages and history and in moral and natural philosophy. As knowledge became more specialized in the nineteenth century,

---

[2] *196 New Doctors Are Told of Problems Awaiting Solutions,* N.Y. Times, June 3, 1986, at A2 (quoting Dr. Robert G. Petersdorf).

the basis of physicians' expertise became the experimental sciences that had emerged from *natural* philosophy—anatomy, biochemistry, microbiology, pharmacology, physiology, and experimental pathology. Lawyers, in contrast, derived their expertise from the disciplines that emerged from the old *moral* philosophy—notably history, philosophy, economics, and politics—as well as from the traditions of the law itself.[3]

This difference in the sources of knowledge of the two professions became, by the middle of the nineteenth century, the basis of divergent views of authority. Lawyers held that authority derived from the law and its institutions—that is, from texts and how they were interpreted by opposing counsel and by judges. Authority, like knowledge, was, for lawyers, cumulative and as contingent on the interplay of people and events as it was constrained by logic, precedent, and values. Lawyers *made* law—as litigators, judges, and legislators. The law was what lawyers, following the rules of their profession and conscious of the dominant values of their society, said it was.

Physicians, on the other hand, derived authority from their command of increasingly effective technologies for diagnosis and treatment that were based on science. Unlike lawyers, who made law, scientists *discovered* the laws that, they presumed, governed nature. To most scientists, arguments about the relationship between laws of nature and social arrangements interfered with experiment and observation. For them, the old tests of discredited science were impediments to progress. Although some aspects of physicians' clinical acumen were cumulative, their command of science and the technology derived from it was the antithesis of reliance on precedent. Authority reposed in individual physicians, armed with the latest knowledge,

and not in precedent or in institutions. Lawyers were officers of the court. In sharp contrast, physicians were formally aloof from hospitals; they were accorded the privilege of practicing in them by lay trustees. These contrasting views of authority have persisted to the present.

To most physicians, adversarial proceedings are an ineffective and irrational method for resolving conflict. Where Anglo-American lawyers presume that a person accused of a crime is innocent until proven guilty in a court of law, physicians believe it is dangerous to make any presumption before examining evidence. Similarly, most physicians do not understand the history or the logic of lawyers' claim that formalized conflict between plaintiffs and defendants in a courtroom or around a table resolves disagreements with reasonable equity and preserves social peace.

Physicians are trained to rely on two methods of addressing conflicts about data and their interpretation. The first method is the assertion of authority from the top of a hierarchy in which power is derived from knowledge. The second method is peer review—discussion to consensus among experts of roughly equal standing and attainment. Both methods, the hierarchical and the consensual, rest on the assumption that truth is best determined by experts.

Hierarchical authority characterizes medical education, clinical decision-making in teaching hospitals, and the presumed relationship between the authors of papers in the most prestigious journals and their readers. A principal goal of medical education is to inculcate lifelong habits of deference to superior knowledge and experience. On the other hand, most academic physicians use consensus to resolve conflicts about scientific findings and the appropriateness of particular methods of diagnosis and treatment. Moreover, outside academic medicine, consensus is more important than deference to authority. According to recent studies, for example,

[3] For sources about the impact of the divergence between natural and moral philosophy on medicine and the social sciences, see D. Fox, *Economists and Health Care* (1979).

physicians' decisions about the indications for particular surgical procedures and appropriate lengths of hospital stays vary from one geographic area to another.[4]

Courtroom procedure violates what most physicians believe about how conflicts ought to be resolved. The role of juries particularly appalls them. It is difficult for anyone trained in medicine to comprehend how people without expertise can determine guilt or innocence, fault, or liability—especially when a professional is accused of negligence. Physicians are also bewildered by judges' behavior. They are amazed that the person with the authority to interpret the law asks questions of witnesses and makes comments that seem to reveal personal opinions, and they are confused when the personal opinions and the result don't match. For example, during the recent suit brought by parents in Queens, New York, to prevent a child with AIDS from attending school, some physicians, like some journalists, were surprised by the apparent contradiction between the judges' comments during the proceeding and his decision. In addition, the notion that one set of rules governs the character and admissibility of evidence and another the interpretation of law is foreign to people who are unfamiliar with legal institutions.

Least comprehensible of all to physicians is the role of counsel. Most physicians do not believe that an individual's interest can be served by making the best possible legal case on his or her behalf. Like lawyers, physicians have a privileged, confidential relationship with the individuals who engage their services. Unlike lawyers, however, they diagnose and treat, rather than defend, these people, whom they call patients. Physicians disdain the use of the word *client* by lawyers, or social workers,

or by some nurse practitioners because it connotes advocacy rather than an obligation to act honorably. Many physicians assert that lawyers are often too willing to distort evidence, or just take it out of context, to make the best case for their clients. Moreover, they accuse lawyers of being too willing to meddle in physicians' areas of expertise for the sake of a fee.

I have observed this aspect of the conflict between physicians and lawyers whenever allegations are made of cheating by medical students or of erratic or unethical behavior by physicians. Those who are accused almost always retain a lawyer, which incenses the members of the faculty or the medical staff of the hospital who are obligated to address the incident. To them, peer review is the proper way to determine facts and remedy errors. Moreover, the best remedies are, they believe, either exoneration, expulsion from the institution, or medical treatment. The concept of a settlement violates their values. As one of my colleagues once said with some disgust, "This is not a legal case; it is the case of an impaired physician."

Efforts to explain the purpose of adversarial proceedings to physicians rarely succeed. Yet physicians are no more ignorant of the law than most other Americans. They may know even more about legal institutions than most people as a result of their general education and personal experience. Like most nonlawyers, however, they do not truly comprehend what the rules of evidence are meant to accomplish. Nor do physicians understand the role of such central legal ideas as precedent, procedure, and legislative intent.

The convention that law, like history, is written in words rather than in unfamiliar symbols, formulae, or diagrams creates an illusion of communicability, but the law is just as difficult for outsiders to comprehend as medical science or mathematics. That is because the words—the letter of the law—represent only a fraction of what lawyers mean by "the law." The words derive much

[4] For physicians' views of hierarchy and peers and their relationship to public policy, see D. Fox, *Health Policies Health Politics: The Experience of Britain and America, 1911–1965* (1986). For small area variation in medical practice, see the many papers of John Wennberg, in the *New England Journal of Medicine* and other publications.

of their meaning from such considerations as: what those who enacted the provision (in which the words appear) meant to convey by the words; more broadly, what they were seeking to accomplish; the presence or absence of conflicting goals that need to be harmonized; how the words to be interpreted fit within the overall structure of the enactment; lessons drawn from earlier attempts to interpret the same or similar language used in the same or a similar context; the doctrinal consequences that flow from each plausible interpretation; the practical consequences; the existence or nonexistence of stable business or social arrangements based on a particular interpretation; and the imperatives of the institutions through which the law operates.

Even more incomprehensible to physicians than the vagaries of textual interpretation is the fact that law, lawyers, and legal institutions are every bit as much committed to employing the right process as to arriving at the right outcome. Lawyers' attachment to procedure, sometimes to the seeming detriment of substance, is the third issue that fundamentally divides the medical and legal professions.

Physicians find it difficult to appreciate, even after detailed explanation, why a case has been dismissed because a defendant's rights were violated or why a verdict was overturned because of a violation of procedure. Physicians value results over process. Even if they are admirably attentive to their patients as persons they are often irritated by fervent advocates of patients' rights. For many of them the central question is not whether a patient's autonomy was respected but whether the best possible medical care was provided. Due process is, at best, a vague memory from high school about the Fourteenth Amendment to the Constitution. Physicians usually associate the phrase with legal interference with proper treatment; with, for instance, cases in which consent must be obtained for blood transfusions for minor children of Jehovah's Witnesses or for surgery on long-term patients in state mental hospitals.

Equally incomprehensible to physicians is the approach lawyers sometimes take to risk assessment. Physicians contrast their own sophisticated view of risk to what they consider the simplistic definition used by lawyers. For physicians, risk is inherent in every activity, including every medical procedure. Their primary concern is relative risk—that is, the balancing of risk and benefit in the best interests of patients or (in environmental cases) of people who come in contact with the environmental hazard. Physicians often accuse lawyers—who, they insist, should know better—of advocating, on behalf of clients, concepts of risk held by the most frightened or uneducated members of the lay public. Just as physicians generally uphold the law, many of them argue, lawyers have an obligation to insist that because risks are inherent in life they must always be compared to other risks, not to the impossible ideal of certainty.

To be sure, there are competing views of risk within medicine. For example, at the trial in Queens, New York, in which parents sought to exclude a child with AIDS from attending school with their children, three distinct medical views of risk were displayed: the epidemiological, the clinical, and the laboratory-based. The epidemiologists testified that a low level of risk was not sufficient cause to exclude the child from school and that according to current knowledge, the plaintiff's children were at greater risk of accidents on the way to school than they were of acquiring antibodies to the AIDS virus, much less the disease itself. However, a witness who was a laboratory scientist testified very differently: A risk that had not been ruled out by scientists could not be dismissed. The views of most of the clinicians fell in between: Patients should guard against any demonstrated risk, no matter how low.

The physicians, unlike the lawyers for either the plaintiffs or the city, testified to their professional opinions. The lawyers for each side, in contrast, represented their clients' standards for how much risk was tolerable. Lawyers for the city advocated the epidemiological view of risk. The plaintiff's lawyers insisted that the Board of Education should keep children with AIDS out of school as long as any other children might be at risk of harm. A recent analysis of the testimony in the case concluded that, "The school board and the judge proceeded as if a single counterexample to the usual transmission patterns would destroy the city's case."[5]

Statements outside the courtroom also exemplified the different roles of physicians and lawyers. Physicians are troubled by conflicts between their personal anxieties and professional opinion. When interviewed by reporters, at least two of them, witnesses for the city, acknowledged that, as parents, they would worry about sending their children to a classroom attended by a child with AIDS. Some lawyers may have similar anxieties but they are not a source of conflict; their professional obligation is to represent their clients. A few weeks after the trial in Queens, the counsel for the plaintiffs irritated many participants in a conference of health professionals when he said that he did not know whose definition of risk he personally supported. To physicians and other health professionals, it was unconscionable for him to advocate a definition of risk simply because it was his client's point of view. (Lawyers' personal opinions about risk may be influential in settings where they do not represent clients in litigation—when, for example, they work in regulatory agencies or legislatures. But that is beyond [our] scope [here].)

The final area of profound disagreement between physicians and lawyers is the role and uses of politics. For lawyers, politics is a normal and essential aspect of professional life. Most physicians, in contrast, hold that politics is intrusive, a distraction from more important matters. Lawyers write or seek to influence laws and regulations as an extension of their other professional roles. Most physicians consider these activities to be so distasteful that, when they are unavoidably caught up in them, they behave petulantly. Even masters of medical politics often claim to be apolitical.

Most physicians are actually ambivalent about politics. On the one hand, they regard political activities as wasteful and undignified. On the other, they use politics, often successfully, to press their collective interests. This ambivalence has made them difficult allies in most of the public debates about health policy in this century. There is no reason to expect most of them to behave differently in issues relating to AIDS, even if what is at stake is protecting their patients' rights to insurance, employment, or housing.

The AIDS epidemic, then, will probably reinforce physicians' antagonism to lawyers, because it is rooted in fundamentally different assumptions about knowledge and authority. It has been reinforced by countless anecdotes and often by personal experience. Most physicians will continue to grumble about lawyers while they rely on them for defense against intrusions in medical practice.

But I have also observed a different relationship between some physicians and some lawyers during the AIDS epidemic. An unusual number of physicians are working collegially with lawyers. Physicians who treat substantial numbers of AIDS patients occasionally say they are impressed by lawyers' efforts to keep them in school or at work and to protect their entitlement to fringe benefits and public funds. Many physicians understand that this may be the first epidemic in this century in which lawyers can do as much for victims as doctors—and maybe more.

This collaboration of physicians and lawyers is certainly not occurring everywhere. Even within the federal government, there

[5] Nelkin & Hilgartner, *Disputed Areas of Risk: A Public School Controversy Over AIDS.* 64 Milbank Quarterly, Supplement I, at 117 (1986).

is conflict between the Public Health Service and the Department of Justice about the risk of transmitting AIDS in the workplace. Similar conflict, or at least mutual incomprehension, is most likely occurring in many states.[6]

A major reason for the collaboration, where it occurs, is that AIDS is the first major infectious disease in more than half a century that is beyond the reach of medical science. The present relative helplessness of physicians recalls epidemics of the past—during the centuries before there were antibiotics and reliable vaccines.

Another reason—and one that emphasizes the central argument of this essay— is that many of the physicians who are

[6] For a review of the history of policy for AIDS, see Fox, *AIDS and the American Health Polity: The History and Prospects of a Crisis of Authority,* 64 Milbank Quarterly, Supplement I, at 7 (1986).

deeply involved in the AIDS epidemic were not particularly antagonistic to lawyers in the past. To describe the dominant medical attitude of antagonism to lawyers, I necessarily oversimplified the attitudes of the medical profession. However, within medicine there have always been people who understood perfectly well the purposes and practices of lawyers. Many of these physicians have been, in some significant way, marginal within medicine. These marginal physicians include those who chose careers in public health but also clinicians who pride themselves on being liberally educated intellectuals and, of course, those who are openly gay. Sadly, the collaboration of these physicians with lawyers on issues raised by the AIDS epidemic will most likely increase their marginality. For most physicians, encounters with lawyers remain occasions for impatience or anger.

THE THEORY OF PROFESSIONS: STATE OF THE ART

Eliot Freidson

After presenting a brief history of attempts to define the nature of a profession, Freidson considers a number of factors that have prevented agreement about the definition. He argues that the concept of a profession is a folk concept, *which varies according to who is employing it and the function it is intended to serve. Approaches to the definition of this folk concept are discussed, along with the significance of Freidson's view for those interested in professionalizing their occupations.*

The Problem of Definition

Much debate, going back at least as far as Flexner (1915), has centered around how professions should be defined—which occupations should be called professions, and by what institutional criteria. But while most definitions overlap in the elements, traits or attributes they include, a number of tallies have demonstrated a persistent

lack of consensus about which traits are to be emphasized in theorizing (Millerson 1964, p. 5). No small part of the criticism of the traditional literature on the professions has been devoted to pointing out a lack of consensus. Because we seem to be no nearer consensus than we were in 1915, and because usage varies substantively, logically and conceptually (Freidson 1977),

From Eliot Freidson, "The Theory of Professions: State of the Art" in *The Sociology of the Professions,* ed. Robert Dingwall and Philip Lewis (New York: St. Martin's Press, 1983). Reprinted by permission of St. Martin's Press.

some analysts have given the impression of condemning the very practice of seeking a definition. But surely such condemnation is inappropriate. In order to think clearly and systematically about anything, one must delimit the subject-matter to be addressed by empirical and intellectual analysis. We cannot develop theory if we are not certain what we are talking about.

One method of attempting to solve the problem of definition has been to deprecate the value of defining the characteristics of professions as "inherently distinct from other occupations" (Klegon 1978, p. 268) and to urge instead discussing the process by which occupations claim or gain professional status. The outcome of such a position, however, is to avoid entirely any *conscious* definition while in fact covertly advancing an implicit and unsatisfactorily vague definition of a profession as an occupation that has gained professional status. What is professional status? How does one determine when it does and when it does not exist? What are its characteristics?

A closely related suggestion is to shift focus from a "static" conception of profession as a distinct type of occupation to the process by which occupations are professionalized (Vollmer and Mills 1966). However, as Turner and Hodge (1970, p. 23) and Johnson (1972, p. 31) have correctly noted, an emphasis on process rather than structure, on professionalization rather than on the attributes of professions, does not really solve the problem of definition. To speak about the process of professionalization requires one to define the direction of the process, and the endstate of professionalism toward which an occupation may be moving. Without *some* definition of profession the concept of professionalization is virtually meaningless, as is the intention to study process rather than structure. One cannot study process without a definition guiding one's focus any more fruitfully than one can study structure without a definition.

In all, the issue of definition for a theory of professions cannot be dealt with profitably either by denial or by avoidance. A word with so many connotations and denotations cannot be employed in precise discourse without definition. One can avoid the issue of definition only if one adopts the patently anti-analytical position that all occupations—whether casual day-labor, assembly-line work, teaching, surgery or systems analysis—are so much alike that there is no point in making distinctions of any kind among them. That there are no differences of any analytic importance must be firmly denied.

Given the necessity of definition, one may note that the character of an adequate definition must be such as to specify a set of referents by which the phenomenon may be discriminated in the empirical world—that is, specifying attributes, traits or defining characteristics. Unfortunately, there has been a tendency in the recent critical literature to confuse the act of specifying defining characteristics with the particular characteristics specified by earlier writers. One can criticize a definition because of the analytically and empirically ambiguous traits it singles out (Freidson 1970a), or because its traits have no systematic interrelations and no theoretical rationale (Johnson 1972). But it is not the fact that a definition is composed of traits or attributes that can be justifiably criticized.

In all, then, it would seem that in the present state of the art of theorizing about professions, recent comments on the issue of definition miss the mark. The definitional problem that has plagued the field for over half a century is not one created by squabbling pedants, to be solved by eschewing definition entirely. Nor is the problem created by the adoption of a static "structural" or "functional" approach, to be solved by a "process" or "conflict" approach. Nor is the problem created by including traits or attributes in a definition. The problem, I suggest, lies much deeper than that. It is created by attempting to treat profession as if it were a generic concept rather than a changing historic concept, with particular roots in an industrial nation strongly influenced by Anglo-American institutions.

The Parochialism of the Institutional Concept of Profession

In order to elaborate my argument about the nature of the concept of profession, it is necessary first of all to emphasize the difference between two very different usages which are sometimes confused. First, there is the concept of profession that refers to a broad stratum of relatively prestigious but quite varied occupations whose members have all had some kind of higher education and who are identified more by their educational status than by their specific occupational skills. Second, there is the concept of profession as a limited number of occupations which have particular institutional and ideological traits more or less in common. It is only this second concept which allows us to think of 'professionalism' as, in Johnson's terms, a way of organizing an occupation (Johnson 1972, p. 45). It represents much more than only a status, for it produces distinctive occupational identities and exclusionary market shelters (cf. Parkin 1979) which set each occupation apart from (and often in opposition to) the others.

Furthermore, the two differ markedly in their relevance to present-day industrial societies. The concept of profession as a very broad, educated stratum has been applied without much difficulty to all industrial nations (for example, Ben-David 1977, p. 30). But it refers to a much more general and vague phenomenon than does the institutional concept of profession as a distinctive form of organized occupation. The major theoretical writings on the professions have all addressed themselves to professions in this second sense—as a fairly limited number of occupations which share characteristics of considerably greater spec-

ificity than higher education alone, and which are distinctive as separate occupations. Their members conceive of themselves by their occupation first and by their "class," if at all, only second. It is precisely this institutional concept of profession which is very difficult to apply to the entire range of occupations in the "professional stratum" of any industrial nation, or even to those middle-class occupations in Europe which would, in Anglo-American nations, be considered professions in the more narrow sense.

Occupations called professions in English have had a rather special history. As we all know, the medieval universities of Europe spawned the three original learned professions of medicine, law and the clergy (of which university teaching was part). Elliott (1972, pp. 14, 32) has suggested the term "status professions" for them, pointing out quite accurately their marked difference from the recent "occupational professions."

As the occupational structure of capitalist industrialism developed during the nineteenth century in England, and then later in the United States, terminological consensus became greatly confused by the efforts of newly reorganized or newly formed middle-class occupations to seek the title of "profession" because it was connected with the gentlemanly status of the traditional learned professions (Reader 1967; Larson 1977). While there were very important differences between the two nations, they had in common a comparatively passive state apparatus with a strong but by no means unambivalent *laissez-faire* philosophy, and a small civil service.

Occupations seeking a secure and privileged place in the economy of those countries could not do more than seek state support for an exclusionary shelter in the open market where they had to compete with rival occupations. They had to organize their own training and credentialing institutions, since the state played a passive role in such affairs. Unlike other countries, the title "profession" was used to establish the status of successful occupations; it became part of the official occupational classification scheme in the United States and in England, expanding its coverage slowly by including more occupations in the same category, with the same title, as the original status professions of the medieval universities (cf. Reader 1967, pp. 146–66, 207–11). Gaining recognition as a "profession" was important to occupations not only because it was associated with traditional gentry status, but also because its traditional connotations of disinterested dedication and learning legitimated the effort to gain protection from competition in the labor market. Given *laissez-faire* philosophy, only quite special excuses could justify the state-sanctioned creation of a market shelter. The ideologies of special expertise and moral probity provided by the traditional concept of status profession, sustained by ostensibly supportive occupational institutions, provided just such a basis for legitimating protection from the winds of occupational competition.

In England and the United States, the tendency was for each occupation to have to mount its own movement for recognition and protection. Its members' loyalties and identities were attached to their individual occupation and its institutions. The situation was rather different in Europe, where the state was much more active in organizing both training and employment. The traditional status professions maintained their occupational distinctions as they reorganized their corporate bodies, but the new, middle-class occupations did not seek classification as "professions" to gain status and justify a market shelter: such an umbrella title imputing special institutional characteristics to them is not employed to distinguish them (cf. Hughes 1971, pp. 387–8). Rather, their status and security are gained by their attendance at state-controlled, elite institutions of higher education which assures them of elite positions in the civil service or other technical-

managerial positions. In nineteenth-century Russia and Poland, merely to be a graduate of a *gymnasium* was what was important, not one's occupation (Gella 1976). In Germany, what was important was to be a university graduate, an *Akademiker* (Rueschemeyer 1973b, pp. 63–122; Ringer 1979, p. 411). In France, one's fortunes flowed from attending one of the *grandes écoles* (for example, Ben-David 1977, pp. 38–46). Primary identity was not given by occupation, but by the status gained by elite education no matter what the particular specialty. As Ben-David noted for France,

the technically competent . . . whom the [*grandes écoles*] system was . . . designed to produce . . . do not primarily identify themselves by their professional qualifications, but by their employment. If they are in private practice, they tend to consider themselves part of the *bourgeois entrepreneur* class, and if they are salaried, they consider themselves officials of a certain rank, rather than chemists or engineers. (Ben-David 1977, p. 46).

This is a far cry from Anglo-American professions, which gain their distinction and position in the marketplace less from the prestige of the institutions in which they were educated than from their training and identity as particular, corporately-organized occupations to which specialized knowledge, ethicality and importance to society are imputed, and for which privilege is claimed.[1]

It is thus not without justice that professionalism has been called "the British disease" (Fores and Glover 1978, p. 15), though I would prefer to call it an "Anglo-

---

[1] The evidence is overwhelming that *within* any given profession, differential life-chances are strongly influenced by the prestige of the educational institution from which one receives one's credentials. Thus, I do *not* mean to imply that in Anglo-American countries elite institutions of higher education play no part in occupational careers. I am arguing only that in English-speaking countries, occupational identity and commitment are considerably more developed than identity as an elite educated class or trans-occupational technical-managerial stratum. Thus, the institutional concept of profession is more relevant to them than to European nations.

American disease." Nor is it an accident that the theoretical literature on the professions is almost wholly Anglo-American, European reviews and use of the Anglo-American literature notwithstanding (Maurice 1972, pp. 213–25). All in all, I would argue that as an institutional concept, the term "profession" is intrinsically bound up with a particular period of history and with only a limited number of nations in that period of history.

The Inevitability of Apologetics and Polemics

If we grant the concrete, historically bound character of the term, we can better understand some of the other controversies surrounding definition in the recent literature. Metatheoretical critiques have frequently noted that earlier writings on the professions created definitions which were reflections of what spokesmen for Anglo-American occupations seeking social recognition as professions say about themselves (Freidson 1970a, pp. 77–84; Gyarmati 1975, pp. 629–54). Roth (1974, p. 17) put this criticism very forcefully: "Sociologists . . . have become the dupe of established professions (helping them justify their dominant position and its payoff) and arbiters of occupations on the make." The implication of such criticism is that theorizers should in some sense strive to create a definition which does not reflect the interests of the groups it attempts to delineate, that their definition should be more detached in its perspective. However, because of the very nature of the concept, one cannot avoid its intrinsic connection with the evaluative social processes which create it.

For the professions, the issues for commentary and analysis are determined more or less by the national history of the term itself, and by the usage of that term both by members of particular occupations and by members of other groups in Anglo-American society. Given the historical fact

that the term is a socially valued label, with the possibility of social, economic, political or at the very least symbolic rewards accruing to those so labeled, it seems inevitable both that disagreement about its application to particular persons or occupations will exist, and that disagreement will exist about the propriety of the special rewards accruing to those to whom it is applied. Because of the nature of the concept, *any* enterprise of defining and analyzing it is inevitably subject to the possibility of being employed to direct the assignment and justification of rewards to some, and the withholding of rewards from others.

It follows, therefore, that those whom Roth described as "dupes" sustain the positions both of established professions and those attempting to gain their success by emulating them. It also follows, however, that those, including myself and Roth, who undertake highly critical evaluations of others' definitions and analyses, also serve as "dupes," though of different agents— "dupes" both of managerial programs of deskilling and proletarianizing professional work, and of working class movements aimed at reducing pay differentials and barriers to entry into "professional" jobs. Both sets of writers, while differing in substance, do not differ in intellectual approach to the concept. The watershed of the scholarly literature that I noted as occurring in the 1960s was a watershed in changing social sympathy and substantive interest, but marked no break with the earlier preoccupation of adjudicating the application of the label and its rewards. Perhaps that is why there have not been any coherent advances in theorizing in spite of the marked change in the tone of the literature—because the *basis* for theorizing has not changed.

The Phenomenology of Profession

If "profession" may be described as a folk concept, then the research strategy appropriate to it is phenomenological in character. One does not attempt to determine what profession is in an absolute sense so much as how people in a society determine who is a professional and who is not, how they "make" or "accomplish" professions by their activities, and what the consequences are for the way in which they see themselves and perform their work. This is not, however, a simple undertaking, for we cannot realistically assume that there is an holistic folk which produces only one folk concept of profession in societies as complex as ours. There must be a number of folk and thus a number of folk concepts. Surely it seems likely that rather different concepts of profession would be advanced by occupations seeking the rewards of a professional label than by other occupations attempting to preserve the rewards they have already won, or by sets of employers or clients seeking to control the terms, conditions and content of the jobs they wish done, or by government agencies seeking to create a systematic means by which to classify and account for the occupations of the labor force, or by the general public. Indeed, the very fact of such a variety of group interests and perspectives may be seen to be responsible for the variety of conceptions of profession advanced, each to its own appreciative audience, responsible for the dissensus characteristic of the usage and concrete occupational referents of the term. Is there, however, one of those perspectives which can be said to be authoritative? Are there others which can be said to be invalid or unimportant?

Many recent critics of the literature on professions seem to feel that it is somehow inappropriate for sociologists to make their own pronouncements about the essence of the concept of profession, and thus to serve as arbiters or dupes. Some urge that sociologists should instead study how other members of society employ the concept without projecting their own conceptions. In a well-reasoned statement, Dingwall (1976, pp. 331–49) recently suggested that rather than define professions by fiat, sociologists would do better to devote themselves to the study and explication of the way ordinary members of particular occupations invoke and employ the term during the course of their everyday activities, to study how such members "accomplish" profession independently of sociologists' definitions. However, unlike most critics, who are content with exhortation alone, Dingwall goes on to present data from an interesting study of his own which took that advice seriously. But my reading of his study indicates that such accomplishment on the part of the members of one occupation cannot fail to include taking into account the conceptions of members of other occupations with whom interaction takes place, and negotiating with them some workable agreement on usage and the activities and relationships it implies. Nonetheless, even that is not enough: among the groups which have to be taken into account are the very sociologists who define profession by fiat, since they, too, are members of the phenomenological world of occupations.

Sociologists are part of social life, and they produce some of the symbolic resources employed by other members of their society, most especially when they play the deliberately accessible role of commenting on and analyzing contemporary social issues. In their way, serving in their special role of intellectual, sociologists accomplish profession as much as do the occupations they discuss. Even without efforts at disseminating their analyses widely by popularization, the esoteric, specialized work of sociologists is sought out by others and, if not taken as authoritative, then at least considered worth thinking about. Perhaps most consequentially for the actual process of professionalization, some sociological formations are employed in part as rationale and justification for the creation of the official occupational categories by which modern governmental and corporate agencies sort and classify occupa-

tions with an eye to justifying job requirements, perquisites and wage differentials
(Scoville 1965; Désrosières n.d.; Davies
1980b). Those official categories, or titles,
and the criteria by which they are constituted, pose critical contingencies for the
rewards available to an occupation, including the status of "profession."

If they are to succeed in their attempt
to gain the official title of profession, it is
not enough that occupations accomplish
profession interpersonally, negotiating their
daily tasks with the others with whom they
work. Both the limits and the substance of
negotiation are in part given in advance.
Only after getting jobs of a given character
can the members of an occupation negotiate profession with other workers. In order to obtain the jobs which provide the
resources for negotiation, both the institutional characteristics of an occupation,
and such characteristics of its members as
their formal education, must conform to
official criteria of profession. Cosmetic
changes on the institutional face which an
occupation presents to the world may not
be enough for official recognition. The
everyday world of the ordinary members
of a striving occupation may also have to
change, taking on some of the appearances
that sociologists have specified as intrinsically professional, albeit by fiat (Hughes
1971, p. 339). Thus, how everyday members accomplish profession through their
activities may be in part influenced by how
sociologists accomplish profession as a concept, and by how official agencies accomplish profession as an administrative category.

What profession is phenomenologically,
then, is not determined solely by members
of occupations performing work in a way
that leads others to respond to them as
professionals. There are a number of different perspectives and performances, no
one of which may be thought to be better
grounded, phenomenologically, than any
other. Some, however, are more consequential than others, if only because they

are attached to positions in which it is
possible to exercise substantial political and
economic power of far-ranging significance. While these may not be authoritative in any epistemological sense, they might
be taken to be authoritative in a pragmatic
sense of setting the political and economic
limits within which everyday professional
work can go on, and of providing the political and economic resources without
which some circumstances and opportunities for work cannot take place.[2] Though
such pragmatically authoritative "definitions" are themselves negotiated and
changed by the efforts of organized occupational groups and other agencies, and
thus are not so rigid and stable as the terms
"official" and "formal" imply, they cannot
be dismissed as somehow less legitimate
than those of the participants in everyday
work.

So, too, may the work of sociologists be
viewed. As researchers and consultants in
everyday work-settings, and as researchers
and theorists whose work is examined and
consulted by those formulating the legal
and economic parameters of the marketplace, sociologists also are legitimate participants. They can no more avoid creating
definitions, if only implicitly, than can other
participants. The fact of advancing definitions cannot be much of an issue in comparison to the choice of particular interests
to advance in the social process of definition. But even there, the diversity of
emphases and interests in the sociological
literature implies a variety of choices. It
also implies that the prospects for unan-
imity in the future are rather poor. How,
then, can the state of the art be advanced?

---

[2] In the United States there are considerable advantages
attached to being in an occupation that has been officially
recognized as a profession. Needless to say, when it is employed as a legal and administrative category, "profession"
must be defined in such a way as to allow practical discrimination among occupations and occupational roles by those
administering the law. The legal status and definition of
professions in tax, immigration, labor and other bodies of
law (including the rules of evidence) simply beg for thorough
investigation and analysis.

Beyond the Folk Concept

One way of attempting to resolve the problem of defining and theorizing coherently about professions in institutional terms lies in asserting the role of the sociologist as an especially authoritative analyst who is free to forsake ordinary usage in favor of his own more precise and "scientific" abstractions. Even though sociologists in such a role cannot claim to be independent of their time and place, they can nonetheless attempt to create abstract concepts which are applicable to more than what is to be found in their time and place. Such an attempt has in fact been made by some of the more theoretically inclined writers on the professions. Remaining concerned with analyzing historic professions, they have abandoned the effort to delineate all the traits that professions have in common and attempted instead to emphasize a parsimonious set of circumstances which have analytic importance in themselves and with which other institutional characteristics can be connected systematically (Goode 1969, pp. 266–313; Freidson 1970a, pp. 71–84; Johnson 1972, pp. 37–47).

Interesting as those efforts may be, however, they have been too compromised to be successful. They are, as Becker (1970, p. 91) noted, no longer faithful to the folk concept insofar as they abstract and select from it. But at the same time they have stopped short of creating fully abstract concepts which go beyond the folk concept. If those efforts were to be really abstract and "scientific," then their conceptualization would have to be tested by examining all occupations known to have the postulated critical traits of trust, autonomy, collegial control or whatever, but instead, only the occupations called professions are referred to by such writers. Were they to go beyond the folk concept, no longer would they be addressing professions as such so much as occupations in general. That is the crux of the matter.

I do not believe that it is possible to move beyond the folk concept of profession without forsaking one's preoccupation with professions (Turner and Hodge 1970, p. 33). In order really to move beyond the folk concept one must ask on the grounds of some reasoned theoretical stance what the features are by which one may usefully and consequentially distinguish among occupations in general and the processes through which they develop, maintain themselves, grow and decline. On the basis of such features one could distinguish theoretically significant groupings or types of occupations and occupational processes by which historically defined occupations, including professions, could be classified and understood. Since theoretical salience is the issue, and not the historic Anglo-American professions as such, no attempt would be made to create a class into which would fit all the occupations that are called professions. By the nature of the enterprise, no attempt *need* be made. The "essence" of profession ceases to be an issue. One's conceptualization would be evaluated for its capacity to order and guide the explanation of the circumstances of a variety of historical occupations, no matter how they happen to be labeled by one audience or another in a particular country and at a particular time.

Liberated from the concept of profession by such an approach, one is also liberated from the grotesque dichotomy, or continuum, by which an ideal type or model of "profession" is used to order *all* occupations. Since virtually all occupations do not come close to conforming to that model, the whole rich variety is reduced to being merely non-professions, defined negatively and emptily as lacking professional characteristics. When one goes beyond the folk concept and attempts to conceptualize the variety of occupations *among* which are to be counted the historic professions, one is in a position to formulate a considerably more flexible set of concepts about occupations that would go far to remedy the present conceptual poverty that stems from the use of such a parochial and simplistic dichotomy or continuum.

Pursuing the Folk Concept

The theoretical program which takes us beyond the folk concept deliberately replaces the task of developing a theory of professions with the task of developing a more general and abstract theory of occupations by which one can analyze the historic professions as well as other occupations in the same conceptual terms, but without assuming that those professions necessarily represent a single, generic type of occupation. But this does not mean that there is no future at all for a theory of professions. The future of a theory of professions seems to lie in adopting a different strategy. Whereas a theory of occupations would be concerned with developing a genuinely abstract theory which attempts to be exhaustive in its applicability, a theory of professions, relieved of the task of broad generalization, would attempt instead to develop better means of understanding and interpreting what is conceived of as a concrete, changing, historical and national phenomenon. The future of profession lies in embracing the concept as an intrinsically ambiguous, multifaceted folk concept, of which no single definition and no attempt at isolating its essence will ever be generally persuasive. Given the nature of the concept, such a theory is developed by recognizing that there is no single, truly explanatory trait or characteristic—including such a recent candidate as "power"—that can join together all occupations called professions beyond the actual fact of coming to be called professions. Thus, profession is treated as an empirical entity about which there is little ground for generalizing as an homogeneous class or a logically exclusive conceptual category. The task for a theory of professions is to document the untidiness and inconsistency of the empirical phenomenon and to ex-

plain its character in those countries where it exists. Such a theory would have, I believe, two major tasks.

First, such a theory should be able to trace and explain the development and significance of the use of the title in Anglo-American societies. Such a task is aided, but not accomplished, by the chronology of usage which the invaluable *Oxford Unabridged Dictionary* provides. A chronology, however, does not tell us why usage developed as it did in English-speaking countries, as opposed to those which have the same root in their vocabularies, but which use the noun form to denote occupations in general and requires an adjective like "liberal," "free" or "learned" to denote a particular type of occupation. Furthermore, a chronology of usage does not tell us how and why particular occupations came to be labeled professions by their members and recognized as such by others; how and why official classifications employing the term developed; why the occupations so classified changed over time; or what the consequences were of membership in such classifications for both the organized occupation and its members. Some small movement toward the development of a theory of occupational nomenclature has begun (Scoville 1965; Katz 1972; Désrosières n.d.; Sharlin 1979), as has some modest effort to analyze the development of the official title of profession in English-speaking countries (cf. Reader 1967; Davies 1980b) but a great deal more must be done before we are in a position to dignify what we know by calling it a theory.

In contrast to investigating the nature of the official title itself, a great deal has already been done to investigate the special privileges of organized occupations which have gained official recognition as professions. In addition, numerous field studies have investigated the problems that the members of those occupations have at work in negotiating with administrators, other occupations, and clients for the prerogatives of the title. The former body of studies tells us about the consequences of official, legal use of the title, while the latter tells us how the title is negotiated and accomplished in everyday work life. As a number of critics have noted correctly, however, a disproportionate number of those studies is addressed to health-related occupations that claim the title. Advances in theorizing about the title and its use positively require the close study of many more occupations in other industries.

While the first task is concerned primarily with analyzing the title "profession" as a socio-political artifact, the second task is concerned primarily with analyzing in some detail the occupations to which the title has been applied. In the spirit of the distinction between a sociology of occupations and a sociology of professions, it follows that the thrust of such a task is to be concerned with the role of the title in the aspirations and fortunes of those occupations claiming it, and not with some quality or trait that all occupations claiming the title may share. The strategy of analysis, therefore, is particular rather than general, studying occupations as individual empirical cases rather than as specimens of some more general, fixed concept.

As individual cases, the question becomes how the quest for the classification in official categories and, on occasion, for legal status as a profession interacts with the development of the occupation's corporate organization and influences its position in the polity and the labor market, its division of labor, and its members' positions in the concrete settings where they work. But while virtually all occupations called professions (as well as others rarely so called) may be classified as such in labor force or census categories, rather few have the legal status of professions. In the selection of individual occupations for study, therefore, loose recognition as a profession by the general public, and even the occupation's own claim (so long as it is taken seriously by some consequential audience) may be employed to locate cases. Thus,

not only traditionally accepted doctors, lawyers and professors, but also engineers, pharmacists, social workers, schoolteachers, librarians and many more to which the title is attached by some audiences but not others, can all be appropriate cases for analysis no matter how they might otherwise differ or fail to conform to various definitions.

The outcome of such a program would be at the very least to add to our knowledge about a number of occupations, knowledge which would be all the richer for its emphasis on the special characteristics of each rather than on the comparatively little they share that corresponds to some simplistic model or ideal type. As important would be the consequence of forsaking the equally simplistic but less formally or self-consciously stated assumptions of recent emphases on "professionalization"—that occupational movements for professionalization are necessarily oriented toward change and mobility, for example, rather than toward stability and security. By expanding the universe of occupations on which we have detailed and systematic data, and by analyzing them as individual, historic cases, we could establish the ground for catholic comparisons that we lack at present. Such a foundation would go far toward portraying the variety of contexts and inconsistencies intrinsic to the notion of profession, as well as the varied role of the notion in the fortunes of a number of occupations and their members in English-speaking societies. Such a portrait is certain to be richer and more varied than that abstract essence toward which the traditional literature aimed, but in being so, it is likely to be more faithful to reality.

The Obligation of Definition

In conclusion, it is incumbent on me to address the problem of definition with which this paper began. It should be clear by now that I do not think the problem can be solved by struggling to formulate a single definition which is hoped to win the day. The concrete, historical character of the concept and the many perspectives from which it can legitimately be viewed and from which sense can be made of it, preclude the hope of any widely-accepted definition of general analytic value.

It is precisely because of the lack of any solution to the problem that I feel that serious writers on the topic should be obliged to display to readers what they have in mind when the word is used—that is, to indicate the definition upon which their exposition is predicated and, for even greater clarity, examples of the occupations they mean to include and those they mean to exclude. Provided with such guidance, readers will then be in a position to judge whether X is really talking about the same thing as Y. If X means to refer only to those few occupations recognized by almost everyone as professions, possessing very high prestige and a genuine monopoly over a set of widely demanded tasks, while Y means to refer as well to occupations which try to ameliorate their low prestige and weak economic position by referring to themselves as professions, then each is talking about incomparable categories and both the writers and their readers should be aware of the fact.

The same obligation should be recognized by those who write about "professionalization," though clarity is more difficult because of the processual character of the concept. Even if one defines the traits constituting the end-point toward which the process is assumed to be headed, how many of those traits, and in what degree, must an occupation display before it makes sense to talk of it as involved in a process of professionalization rather than in a process of merely improving its economic or status position? If it does not make sense to talk of the professionalization of labor in general as the terms and conditions of its work improve over time, what characteristics must exist before it *does* make sense to do so? Must one use the term only retrospectively to label the process by which present-day professions have attained their position? Is there a distinctive difference between professionalization in particular and the collective efforts of occupations in general to improve their job security, working conditions, income and prestige? No doubt on these issues, as on those connected with defining profession, writers will differ, but they are unlikely to be able to debate the relative virtues of those differences if they are not self-conscious about what they are. It is precisely because differences are inevitable that their specification should be an obligation for the writer and a requirement of the writer by the reader. Such an obligation may not increase consensus, but it would certainly increase the clarity and precision of a body of literature whose status has been vague and chaotic for too long.

References

BECKER, H. S. (1970) "The Nature of a Profession," in H. S. Becker, *Sociological Work* (Chicago: Aldine).

BEN-DAVID, J. (1977) *Centers of Learning: Britain, France and the United States* (New York: McGraw-Hill).

DAVIES, C. (1980b) "Making Sense of the Census in Britain and the USA," *Sociological Review*, 28.

DÉSROSIÈRES, A. (n.d.) "Elements pour l'histoire des nomenclatures socio-professionelles," in F. Bédarida et. al., *Pour un Histoire de la Statistique*, Vol. 1 (Paris: Institut National de la Statistique et des Études Économiques), pp. 155–94.

DINGWALL, R. (1976) "Accomplishing Profession," *Sociological Review*, 24, pp. 331–49.

ELLIOTT, P. (1972) *The Sociology of the Professions* (London: Macmillan).

FLEXNER, A. (1915) "Is Social Work a Profession?" in *Studies in Social Work*, no. 4 (New York: New York School of Philanthropy).

FORES, M. AND I. GLOVER (1978) "The British Disease: Professionalism," *The Times Higher Education Supplement* (24 Feb.), p. 15.

FREIDSON, E. (1970a) *Profession of Medicine: A Study of the Sociology of Applied Knowledge* (New York: Dodd, Mead and Co.).

FREIDSON, E. (1977) "The Futures of Professionalisation," in M. Stacey, M. E. Reid, R. Dingwall and C. Heath (eds), *Health and the Division of Labour* (London: Croom Helm), pp. 14–38.

GELLA, A. (1976) "An Introduction to the Sociology of the Intelligentsia," in A. Gella (ed.), *The Intelligentsia and the Intellectuals: Theory, Method and Case Study* (London: Sage).

GOODE, W. J. (1969) "The Theoretical Limits of Professionalization," in A. Etzioni (ed.), *The Semi-Professions and Their Organization* (New York: Free Press), pp. 266–313.

GYARMATI, G. (1975) "Ideologies, Roles and Aspirations. The Doctrine of the Professions: The Basis of a Power Structure," *International Social Science Journal*, 27, pp. 629–54.

HUGHES, E. C. (1971) *The Sociological Eye* (Chicago: Aldine).

JOHNSON, T. J. (1972) *Professions and Power* (London: Macmillan).

KATZ, M. B. (1972) "Occupational Classification in History," *Journal of Interdisciplinary History*, 3, pp. 63–88.

KLEGON, D. A. (1978) "The Sociology of Professions: an Emerging Perspective," *Sociology of Work and Occupations*, 5, pp. 259–83.

LARSON, M. S. (1977) *The Rise of Professionalism: A Sociological Analysis* (London: University of California Press).

MAURICE, M. (1972) "Propos sur la Sociologie des Professions," *Sociologie du Travail*, 13, pp. 213–25.

MILLERSON, G. (1964) *The Qualifying Associations* (London: Routledge and Kegan Paul).

PARKIN, F. (1979) *Marxism and Class Theory* (New York: Columbia University Press).

READER, W. J. (1967) *Professional Men: The Rise of the Professional Classes in Nineteenth Century England* (New York: Basic Books).

RINGER, F. K. (1979) "The German Academic Community," in A. Oleson and J. Voss (eds), *The Organization of Knowledge in Modern America 1860–1920* (Baltimore: Johns Hopkins University Press).

ROTH, J. (1974) "Professionalism: the Sociologist's Decoy," *Sociology of Work and Occupations*, 1, pp. 6–23.

RUESCHEMEYER, D. (1973b) *Lawyers and Their Society. A Comparative Study of the Legal Profession in Germany and in the United States* (Cambridge, Mass: Harvard University Press).

SCOVILLE, J. G. (1965) "The Development and Relevance of U.S. Occupational Data," *Industrial and Labour Relations*, 19, pp. 70–9.

SHARLIN, A. (1979) "From the Social Study of Mobility to the Study of Society," *American Journal of Sociology*, 85, pp. 338–60.

TURNER, C. AND M. N. HODGE (1970) "Occupations and Professions," in J. A. Jackson (ed.), *Professions and Professionalisation* (Cambridge: Cambridge University Press).

VOLLMER, H. W. AND D. J. MILLS (eds.) (1966) *Professionalization* (Englewood Cliffs, N.J.: Prentice-Hall).

PROFESSIONALIZATION: THE INTRACTABLE PLURALITY OF VALUES

Lisa H. Newton

Newton discusses some of the difficulties involved in trying to define the nature of a profession and then explores the relationship between a profession and the society that harbors it. She argues that there are at least three ways in which an occupation can grow into a profession: engaging in a skilled, perennial activity; developing a service for which a market exists; or providing help to other individuals. With this account of professionalization for a basis, she develops a broadly inclusive concept of a profession.

Any account of the professions, and of the role played by professions in the larger society, must meet two criteria: It must include the salient characteristics of professions, even the characteristics apparently in conflict; and it must make logical and moral sense of the substantial rights and responsibilities assigned to them. The two features most publicly associated with professionalism, by any profession's own declaration at least, are maximal compe- tence in a certain area of knowledge or skill, and a moral commitment to the public good in that area; these features may be treated as the individually necessary and jointly sufficient conditions to justify "professionalization," i.e., *the social award of a legitimate monopoly of practice in that area to the organized profession.* A third prominent feature of some professions is the commitment on the part of individual professionals to the welfare and interests of in-

From Lisa H. Newton, "Professionalization: The Intractable Plurality of Values," in *Profits and Professions*, ed. Wade L. Robison, et al. (Clifton, N.J.: Humana Press, 1983). Reprinted by permission.

dividuals in their charge—clients, patients, students, or parishioners—even when (as in certain cases of maintenance of "confidentiality") protection of such interests is contrary to the public good and thus apparently derogates from the "public service" commitment above. This feature too can be integrated into the larger picture of the common good as productive of social welfare in the long run. By reassuring the public that confidences will be respected, such a provision increases public trust in the profession and encourages the public to resort to professionals in time of need. There is also a fourth characteristic of most professions: The professionals seem to be able to command very large fees. This feature can be justified as a benefit of legal monopoly. For example, remuneration is one more inducement to the profession to adhere to the set of rules identified as its "professional ethic," general adherence to which will benefit the society as a whole: If the ethic is substantially violated the monopoly will be withdrawn and the benefit will be lost. The first criterion is well met by this account; the second is satisfied in the assumption that the specific moral commitment of any profession fits an area of social concern or need: There must be a match between the service that the profession is qualified to provide and an area of public need that would be very difficult to provide for through ordinary public facilities. Such a close fit between professionally offered service and demand—conjoined with the requirements that provision of the service entail lengthy training in esoteric skill and knowledge, that the providers offering the service can validate claims to competence in it, and that they have publicly committed themselves to use their skills only for the public good—justifies entrusting that area of social need to the providers of that service.

Given the characteristics of a profession, and the account that rationalizes them, it would seem to follow immediately that a profession could be held responsible for professional practice only as a whole, i.e., collectively. For professionalization, social legitimation of monopoly of practice in the area of maximal competence, is certainly an assignment of responsibility in any of Kurt Baier's[1] senses of "responsibility": It is an assigned *task* in an area of concern, for performance of which the profession is henceforth publicly *accountable*, mishaps in which will indicate professional *culpability*, and for which mishaps the professionals may very well be held *liable*. But to whom, or what, is the professional *answerable*, to complete Baier's list of senses of "responsible"? Not to the individual client or patient, by definition: The designation of a profession implies the incompetence of the layman to judge professional performance. The only superior to which a professional could be answerable is the state itself that granted professional status, and he or she is answerable there only through the profession as a whole, to which that status was actually granted. (The state, of course, has no more professional competence than any layman; it can call the profession to account not by virtue of superior expertise, but by virtue of its inalienable sovereignty over all areas of social concern. The state simply cannot assign any area of public action, welfare, or responsibility to any private group irrevocably; the consent of the people to the government cannot be construed to permit permanent loss of popular sovereignty in any category. Ultimately, the state *must* say whether the public is being properly served, so all who claim to serve the public must report to it.) It would follow that the professional must consider himself primarily responsible, not to the desires of his clients nor to the immediate demands of the larger society, but to his own professional ethic. It is the function of that ethic to spell out the obligation of the profession

[1] Kurt Baier, "Guilt and Responsibility" in *Individual and Collective Responsibility*, P. French, ed. (Cambridge, Mass.: Schenkman Pub. Co., 1972), pp. 35–61.

as a whole to the society as a whole—and it is the philosophers' job, perhaps, as members of that society particularly well-trained for such things, to keep these "professional ethics" under careful surveillance, to ensure that they do in fact serve the public interest.

In some respects, however, this account fails to explain certain attitudes and current practices of professionals, also certain of our attitudes and current practices with regard to them. Paying attention to these areas of discrepancy may serve to illuminate other possibilities for coming to grips with a surprisingly complex social phenomenon. To begin with the last point, it should be noted that we do not in fact hold professionals *collectively* accountable for professional performance, nor is it clear that we could if we wanted to. In fact we permit laymen to bring lawsuits against professionals alleging malpractice—alleging, that is, professional incompetence, as opposed to simple negligence. To be sure "expert testimony," support from other professionals of the same sort, is solicited by the plaintiff's lawyers in such cases; still, the suit originates with a layman's flat-out judgment that the professional did not know what he or she was doing, and terminates with a lay jury's verdict on that judgment. Both would be inappropriate in a context where the delegation of social responsibility, including the award of the monopoly of practice, had been to a profession collectively, and where that delegation has been justified by acknowledgment of a monopoly of competence in the field. The completion of "professionalization" would entail legal restraints on such private actions, permitting only professional review of complaints of inadequacy of professional performance. What would be the effect of establishing such unprecedented legal immunities, especially for groups already under suspicion of overprivilege, upon the already fragile morale of an envious and conflict-ridden populace? Would any attempt to secure sole jurisdiction of profes-

sional review boards be well-advised in this era of consumerism?

Second, there is the difficulty that professional organizations have at present only very limited authority in their own fields of practice. I do not know how many practicing philosophy professors belong to the American Philosophy Association. I suspect that the proportion is not large, and that it would drop precipitously if the APA tried to exercise any authority over its membership. To be quite frank, I have difficulty *imagining* the APA exercising authority; I cannot conceive what form such exercise might take. The bare possibility of such exercise, prescinding from questions of acceptability, would require a radical redistribution of educational power, a centralization of academic functioning that is at least unprecedented and probably unconstitutional. And how could the legitimate authority of an academic professional organization be reconciled with the profession's ruling value, academic freedom? Of course, the academic profession, especially the philosophical sector of it, may be a poor prototype for a profession. But even the medical profession, which presents such a monolithic appearance to outsiders, claims only 50% membership in its own noisy and opinionated professional organization, the American Medical Association; that proportion is, apparently, decreasing. And a complete account of the professions certainly ought to be able to handle the academic profession.

At present, then, we simply cannot address the professions as we address incorporated businesses, viz., as legal, if fictional, individuals. And as Richard DeGeorge has pointed out, the major area of *collective* responsibility that we now recognize, viz., corporate responsibility, is collective only from a point of view internal to the corporation: we hold a corporation responsible for a social task (e.g., supplying water in a certain district) *as an individual,* and it is by virtue of the assignment of *individual* responsibility to this fictive individual-ual that we can speak intelligibly of the *collective* responsibility of the members of the firm to carry out the task.[2] It is this corporative model of responsibility assumption that seems to dominate the account of professionalization presented above, and that account is therefore presented with some problems by the comparative disorganization of the professions. The completion of professionalization on this model will require much more powerful and inclusive professional organizations; they would have to be capable of assuming liability for actions undertaken by their members, who would answer to their organizations alone for performances within the definition of professional practice. Should the development of such organizations be encouraged, at least for professions where no theoretical difficulties attend legitimization?

Several arguments against encouraging such organizations come immediately to mind. The object of professionalization is supposedly to serve the public interest, but the professionals of our experience seem to recognize many interests as legitimate, only some of which dovetail with the public good at any given time. Sets of professional goods that seem above to fit together neatly—personal profit, the cultivation of expertise, the protection of the individual client, and service to the public in a specialized capacity—do not always seem to work together in fact. Indeed, the most common popular judgment on the professions is that they tend to pursue one of the first three sets of goods to the exclusion of the others and of the fourth. Thus, the most common accusation leveled at professions is (1) that they are greedy, that the first priority of their professional practice is the resulting extrinsic reward of money, prestige, or power; their professional organizations simply function to protect their income

potential. And if their pursuit of the dollar is cause for suspicion, their (2) pursuit of the aesthetic delights of expertise in their own professional art is simply infuriating. Nothing can raise a hospital patient's blood pressure faster than being treated as an "interesting case," an object of eager curiosity to hosts of interns and subject of fascinated experimentation for the attending physicians. Their enthusiasm over a magnificent opportunity to refine the art of medicine quite escapes the poor patient, who soon comes to resent being treated as irrelevant to the proceedings and less valuable than his disease. Will they keep him sick in order to continue studying him? And even when the professional's practice is very clearly oriented to the interests of the individual who has requested his professional services, (3) it is not clear that service to those interests is service to the society. We are reminded of the Mafia lawyers who energetically track down every thread of constitutional right that might help their unsavory clients, all for the purpose of defeating the public interest in putting criminals behind bars. Professionals seem to have commitments all over the place, in constant conflict with each other as well as with us. The unified ethical content suggested by their published ethics does not seem to be reflected in the world of practice nor in the official acts of the professional associations. It would appear that the protection of the public, then, requires that we continue to hold professionals individually accountable to that public (via lawsuit if necessary) and refrain from granting even more legal powers and immunities to the profession as a whole or to any organization within it, at least as presently structured. The sort of structural modifications that would be required by the public interest may be deduced from the discussion so far: Each professional would have to be required to belong to his professional association, the association would have to be, like any corporation, prepared to assume financial liability for

[2] Richard T. DeGeorge, "Moral Responsibility and the Corporation," read at a conference on Collective Responsibility in the Professions, Dayton, Ohio, October 27, 1978.

malpractice or misfeasance, and a network of professional ombudsmen would have to be maintained, to mediate lay complaints and collective responsibilities. And such modifications seem far in the future.

By way of summary of the present section to this point: Against the neat and plausible account of professions and professionalization suggested at the outset, I have held that current attitudes and practices of and towards professionals fail to bear it out, and that the professions are far more disorganized, ethically and legally, than the attribution of collective responsibility and rights will permit.

One more failure should be mentioned as similarly significant in our investigation of this account of the professions. There are identifiable social needs, and there are professions serving them; but there does not appear to be any one-to-one correspondence between profession and need. To be sure, the ABA proclaims the legal profession "guardians of the Rule of Law," but the thrust of the legal profession seems to be much more toward the settlement of disputes, and it is from that need that lawyers are wont to trace their own origins. Guardianship of the law was traditionally assigned to statesmen, who despised the litigious sorts who represented clients in lawsuits; but the profession of "statesman" seems to have been lost in the development of the democracies. "Health care" also is a societal need, but the professional picture here is even more blurred. The profession of medicine is not the only profession interested in health care; it is not interested in all aspects of health care, and *is* interested in subjects (especially in medical research) that are only indirectly involved with protecting the health of the people of the society. The nursing profession, meanwhile, which is in constant, if subdued, conflict with the medical profession over jurisdictions of health care, regards its medically oriented work as continuous with its work in caring for people who have no health problems at all. The lab-

oratory work that is directed to health care—from the biochemist's experimentation with inhibitors of enzymes to the technician's run of standard serum tests—is continuous with laboratory work dedicated to the development of more salable toothpaste. In short, the picture of professional health care is not one of a profession internally *dedicated* to the care of the people's health and assuming publicly the moral responsibility for that care. It is, rather, one of disparate preexistent professions *recruited* by the society to serve a perceived need, once the need was perceived, and only reluctantly working together on the assigned tasks. The same picture emerges in other professional areas: As the profession of "statesman" had disappeared, its expertise discredited in populist revolts, the profession of law was recruited to fill the breach; it has not done so very successfully.[3] More successful was the recruitment of the physicists in the second and third quarters of this century. The profession has been around, discussing the abstruse qualities of basic matter, for centuries; when military exigency suddenly required the development of highly sophisticated nuclear explosives and the rockets to deliver them, a whole profession moved easily into the task, putting together whole new industries, not to mention perfectly dreadful military capabilities, virtually overnight. Basic research now seems to be less useful to the government, and physics is retreating from a central position of social significance back to the academic place it once occupied. Nowhere along the line, in its brief period of national limelight, did the profession announce any professional dedication to public service. Rather, the

[3] As Monroe Freedman points out in *Lawyers' Ethics in an Adversary System* (Indianapolis and New York: Bobbs-Merrill, 1975), portions of the professional ethic of law may be flatly incompatible with pursuit of the public interest, not just potentially but actually and always. See Stephen Toulmin, "The Meaning of Professionalism: Doctor's Ethics and Biomedical Science" in *Knowledge, Value and Belief,* H. T. Engelhardt, Jr., and D. Callahan, eds. (Hastings-on-Hudson, New York: Hastings Center, 1977), 264–68.

profession had the expertise, knew where experts could be found and how to train more of them; and that expertise, whose existence predated the social need for it, was all that was required of them.

What we have, in short, in the relation between our professions and the state, is a highly fluid situation. Professions arise and disappear without public trust or social responsibility playing any particular part in their fate; they are recruited, singly or in groups, to assume a social responsibility more or less fitted to their talents, dismissed when the need is gone or a better solution to the problem is found, all without changing their nature as professions. How is it then, that professions exist, prior and posterior to social need, only partially and badly organized in professional associations, able somehow in this disorder to assume and carry on societal responsibilities when required to? A sketch of an answer to that question will constitute, in effect, another account of professionalization.

This account of professionalization might begin, not with the notion of a "societal need," but with that of a "perennial activity." The inception of a profession would be found in the existence of a skilled activity—one in which expertise can be cultivated, if its practitioners desire to cultivate it—that some people will always take up, without reference to extrinsic motivations or rewards beyond the natural end of the activity. One class of perennial activities would be those enjoyable for their own sake. We are all familiar with this class, or we ought to be, for philosophical inquiry is one of them. Gambling is another, and the performing arts provide as many more examples. A second class of perennial activities would include those addressed to obvious and recurrent human need: cooking, or gardening, or healing the sick, or seeking (or preventing) the intervention of the deity to further human goods. In each of these activities, the art or skill may be cultivated for its own sake,

i.e., for the sake of that simple and universal human satisfaction of doing something very well indeed. In most of them, practitioners will enjoy and profit from each other's company for purposes of exchanging information and practicing new techniques. In most of them, structured associations may (but need not) arise, to keep the like-minded practitioners in touch with each other and with the state of the art, eventually to formulate standards of excellence for the enterprise, perhaps to arrange conventions, contests, and prizes to encourage the attainment of higher levels of skill in practice, perhaps where relevant, to circulate literature of interest to the field. We have now "amateur" societies dedicated to philately, mycology, and organic gardening, not to mention scientology and theosophy, which differ from groupings of the learned professions only in that there is insufficient private or public demand for their skills to make any widespread practice profitable.

The beginnings of a profession might be here, then, in any skilled activity. The next logical step would be the one implicit in the last distinction above: to attempt to find a market for the skill, so that the practitioners would not be compelled to hold down jobs in addition to their chosen practice. In ordinary parlance, it is this step into "full-time," paid, status that makes the "professional"; Stephen Toulmin makes it his first criterion of professionalization that "Professionals engage in their chosen activities 'for a living' rather than 'for fun'—as amateurs or dilettantes."[4] Nothing about a commitment to public service is entailed here. If a charitable organization, for instance, decides that it needs much more money than it is getting by having its own members pass the hat, it may decide to hire a "professional" fund raiser, one who will charge the organization for his services, as an investment. In this case, "professional" means specifically

---

[4] Toulmin, *op. cit.*, p. 256.

"for hire," "personal-gain-oriented," in contrast to a pure public service orientation. For some professions, moreover, the orientation to the sale of professional services seems to be the defining mark of "membership" in the profession. In the case of the oldest of all the professions, for example, the activity that characterizes professional performance is certainly enjoyable in itself, but could never serve as a basis for group identity when carried on in an amateur status. It is specifically the decision to engage in the activity "full time," for pay, that creates the orientation toward the development of excellence in the art.

A profession crystallized, primarily or otherwise, around the common objective of personal gain might also find it worthwhile to create a professional organization to further the ends of the profession. Of all the varieties of association in our society, as a matter of fact, the most common seems to be of persons who earn their living in the same way, the labor unions being the prime example. Unions (and their relatives with other names) can keep track of markets and help the members sell their services at the highest possible price. They can ensure that members who have halted work temporarily in order to concentrate on efforts to secure higher remuneration will not be replaced, and their protest rendered useless, by similarly trained professionals. With the large numbers of an entire profession to back them up, unions can engage in political lobbying and public campaigns to secure legislation favorable to the profession, and so forth. But note that here again, the profession is not required to organize to establish its identity.

We have, then, two candidates for the essence of "professionalism," two possible *raisons d'être* for a profession: It can exist for the sake of excellence in the practice, or it can exist for the sake of profit for the practitioners. A third possible motivating principle overlaps with the first: The point of the activity might be the direct service rendered to identifiable others. The qualifiers "direct" and "identifiable" rule out professions in, e.g., scientific research, which may very well obtain information useful to someone somewhere in the long run, but whose criteria for excellence do not include reference to that use. A service orientation in a profession would originate in the clear and urgent need of another human being, to which we respond, in compassion, by offering help. Perhaps the best examples of such help should not be taken from the overworked and complicated files of the medical profession, but from those of much more recent health care and other "helping" professions: the geriatric nurses who staff nursing homes and homes for the elderly, the specialized pediatric staff who administer the schools for retarded and handicapped children, the funeral directors, social workers, family counselors, career advisors, and marriage consultants. What all these professions have in common is that until relatively recently, the helping function they perform was carried on completely by amateurs, perhaps slightly assisted by religious functionaries (whose duties, as originally understood, had very little to do with "pastoral" work, but emphasized almost exclusively the work of mediation between God and man). As the society becomes larger, more urbanized, specialized, and anonymous, not to mention richer, interpersonal functions increasingly migrate out of family and amateur purview into the realm of newly specialized expertise.

A peculiar feature of this type of professional practice, the feature that sets it off from the others and gives it moral direction, is the unique psychological and moral bond that normally forms between the professional and the individuals within his professional charge. Both aspects of this peculiar bond arise from the fact that in the situation of practice, the practitioner–client encounter, the professional is by definition, relative to the client, healthy, strong, knowledgeable, confident, and in control of the situation; the client is sick, weak, ignorant, frightened, and helpless. Prate as we will about the "autonomy" of the client, the fact remains that the client, at least at the outset of the relationship, must be passive and trusting, while the professional is the trusted agent. One moral bond, beyond the ordinary one obtaining in human relationships, is immediately generated: The client is terribly vulnerable, the professional has it easily within his or her power to take advantage of the client's helplessness for personal profit, and therefore the professional is under obligation not to do that. Beyond this prohibition, it may be, as is sometimes claimed, that positive responsibility is generated where the serious need for attention encounters the capacity to meet that need. I am not sure such a positive obligation could be established. If it can be, it is worth noting that this imperative, like the prohibition of harm, is generated merely by the inequality of the positions of professional and client, and by the situation of initial consultation, in which the individual approaches the professional for advice on *whether to assume* the role of "client"—prior to any contract, or to the establishment of any "professional–client" relationship that might be governed by law or professional ethics.

The psychological aspect of this bond, when present, stems from what Hume would call the natural sympathy among human beings. Seeing the need, and the helplessness, of another, and possessing the means to help, we are immediately moved to provide it. A more common way of describing the same phenomenon would be to say that the need, helplessness, and trust in us of another human arouses our parental feelings ("maternal instinct") and that we are naturally moved to protect and nurture that human. The generic name of this impulse is "love"; and so we can say that teachers, quite simply and innocently, come to love their students, physicians their patients, priests their flock, and nurses the persons in their charge. This curious and profound relationship gives a distinctive direction to professions where one-to-one practice is appropriate. From the moral aspect emerges the professional's obligation to protect the client from the dangers of professional performance at least, and from other dangers in his professional competence to combat; from the psychological aspect emerges a likelihood that the professional will in fact act protectively if a client is threatened by anything, including the larger society; and from the inarticulate combination of the two emerges the view that the professional has the right and duty to set aside the demands of any party, including the larger society, in the interests of protecting his client.

As these professions derive, primarily or otherwise, from the need of those they serve, their clients, the emphasis of a professional organization might well reflect that derivation in a high degree of "client-centered" concern. We would expect norms of professional conduct to be frankly based on the success of such conduct in providing help for individuals; we would expect these norms to encourage, in the professional, attitudes of protectiveness and support for clients, and to evaluate technical developments in the field by their immediate practical usefulness in helping clients. We would expect the professional organization to engage in political activities on behalf of client groupings, not groupings of professionals. Expecially where a newly professionalized service is carried on for pay, we would look for such professional organizations to set up stern criteria for membership, to exercise vigilance against "quacks" and other false practitioners seeking to victimize clients for profit, and to encourage legislation regulating the industry in which the profession does its work. Again, although such an organization would be highly useful in fulfilling professional tasks, it is not necessary; the help can be administered all the same without it.

On this account of professionalization, then, there are at least three possible routes to professional status prior to direct contact with the larger society: engagement in a perennial activity, development of a service for which a market exists, and provision of help to other individuals. Minimally, any profession, to be called by that name, must exhibit some degree of the first two characteristics: There must be an identifiable skilled activity that constitutes professional practice (including, as a necessary condition, some means of transmitting the "state of the art" to new generations of practitioners,) and the practice must be carried on for pay, "full time." Beyond that minimum, variety is the rule; a profession may exhibit only one professional form, pursue only one of the three possible goods; it may pursue one primarily and include the others as subsidiary goals; or it may, like the medical profession in its more exciting moments, exhibit all three pursuits in apparently equal proportion and noticeable conflict. Similarly, professional organizations, where they exist, may attempt, like the American Medical Association, to speak for all the goals of the profession, and so reflect, in their own internal conflicts and changes of direction, the failure of consensus in the profession as a whole. Or a profession may maintain, quite unofficially but quite effectively, a multiplicity of associations for its multiple pursuits. My own campus is not organized, but I have colleagues elsewhere who belong simultaneously to the American Philosophical Association (through which they advance the art of philosophy), the American Association of University Professors (to keep an eye on the teaching situation, with regard to academic freedom, "teacher evaluation" techniques, and so on), and a local affiliate of the AFL-CIO (to show up at contract time and protect their jobs and incomes.) The functions are not clearly divided among the associations even when all are simultaneously available, you will note; in this field, *nothing* is clearly divided.

Out of this conflict-filled background, how does it happen that professions can take on roles of tremendous social responsibility? For in the three possible commitments so far, the public good does not find a place; and even if a commitment to the public could be generated, the presence of the other three in some proportion would make perfect adherence to the commitment highly unlikely. Toulmin suggests,[5] and the suggestion is certainly plausible, that the profession's commitment to render service to the public is best understood as one major term of a "contract" between the society and the profession. Perceiving a social need, and the profession's competence to handle it, the society negotiates a deal with the profession: The society will confer the benefits and privileges of legal monopoly upon the group in return for a promise of public service, i.e., a promise to carry on professional practice in accordance with high standards of performance, for the public good. (Toulmin assumes that the deal is actually made between a legislative body and a professional guild or organization. This need not be the case; the legislature may simply announce that henceforth, all individuals who would call themselves "professionals" of a certain type must announce their willingness to adhere to a publicly promulgated code of ethics embodying the obligation to public service, in return for which the law will protect them in a quasimonopoly situation.) To hold up its end of the deal, the profession incorporates its terms into its ethical fabric in some public way, typically issuing a professional ethic in which its preeminent willingness and sole competence to serve the people is set forth with maximum eloquence. This is why the codes emphasize public service to such a great extent: Public service is the last professional commitment, not the first; it is the most doubtful of the profession's commitments, the one questioned most by its own members as well as by the society at large.

[5] *Op. cit.* pp. 256, 258.

Now we have come full circle: The link between the profession and the larger society is recent, questionable, and inessential to the existence of either, but is of great benefit to the profession and eminently worth keeping. The writing of an eloquent and public-spirited "professional ethic" upon the formation of the link serves to explain and justify, to the general public, the conferral of privileges on the profession, even as it serves to reassure the legislature of professional trustworthiness, and convey the terms of the contract to the present and future members of the profession. The profession presents its ethic as a moral justification of its monopoly, and the public can justifiably hold a profession to that ethic to ensure that its needs will be met.

With this account of the professions, however—a variant of "social contract" theory, if we may refer to the original account as a "social generation" theory— the relationship between profession and society is shown to be a dynamic one, and additional options available for the profession and for the public come into focus. For instance, it becomes clear that a profession can refuse a public contract, if it finds any terms of public service unacceptable in light of its other commitments; various of the fine and performing arts have, on occasion, discussed the advisability of such refusal. For another instance, it becomes clear that the society can rearrange its contracts with the professions, to ensure a closer fit between professional directions and social need, without incurring the need for radical restructuring in those professions. A suggestion could be made, in illustration of this point, that the medical profession simply be dismissed as caretaker of public health, to be replaced by the nursing profession (or alternatively, by a separate group of "public health professionals"). Should that suggestion be implemented, medicine would continue to be practiced as before, as far as the treatment of individual patients is concerned; but authorization for treatment, third-party payments, hospital admissions, and so on would all be routed through the new social contractor. On the "social generation" account, such rearrangement would have to be called "deprofessionalization," which sounds much more drastic than the minimal adjustments that would actually be entailed by such a change. One virtue of the "social contract" account, then, is that it calls attention to the flexibility of the undertakings we have with and as professionals, and the range of possible relationships among which the public and the profession may choose.

Another virtue of the account, I will say by way of conclusion, is the legitimacy it provides for the preservation of a plurality of logically independent and potentially conflicting goods. The structure of a profession in fact permits and encourages conflicting pursuits, as noted; and this is its major strength, for the conflict reflects the genuine irreducibility of value orientations. It is dubious, as Thomas Nagel says, "that all value rests on a single foundation or can be combined into a unified system, because different types of values represent the development and articulation of different points of view, all of which combine to produce decisions."[6] The various possible conceptual origins of professions that I have tried to articulate in the foregoing are the developmental origins of such contrasting "points of view"; priorities must be assigned among these perspectives for individual decisions in conflict situations, but as general principles they retain their independent validity.

The value of the professions, then, for any advanced society, is not only that they perform social services on occasion, or assume responsibility for an area of social concern. It is also that, whether or not currently engaged in social service, they retain their nature as articulators of values.

[6] "The Fragmentation of Value," in *Knowledge, Value and Belief, op. cit.*, p. 290.

Even more, that in articulating and protecting potentially conflicting values, they truthfully reflect a moral universe that does not seem to be entirely coherent and that finds its best institutional expression in the permanent (and quarrelsome) coexistence of a plurality of institutional goods.

RIGHTS AND ROLES

Charles Fried

Fried considers the criticism that professionals' commitments to their own clients may lead to an unjust distribution of professional services, or even (especially in the case of lawyers) deliberate attempts by the professional to defeat the claims of those who are most in need, or who are in the right. Taking individual liberties to be fundamental, he argues against the idea that professionals have a special obligation to prevent or compensate for such inequities, and he argues for the professional's right to practice in ways that may sometimes produce such inequities.

The traditional conception of the doctor's or lawyer's role poses two sorts of problems. One problem is similar for both professions: Doctors and lawyers are said to owe a duty of loyalty to their clients, a loyalty which in its usual interpretation requires taking the medical or legal interests of that client more seriously than the interests of others in similar or greater need, more seriously, indeed, than formulas of either efficiency (utility, maximization) or fairness (equality?) would require or even permit. Viewing the doctor's or lawyer's time as a scarce resource, therefore, the conception of professional loyalty requires individual professionals to distribute this scarce resource in ways that may very well be incompatible with their fairest or most efficient use. The second problem is peculiar to the legal profession. Both doctors and lawyers have clients, but the clients of doctors are not ordinarily viewed as having adversaries—at most they may have competitors for medical resources. Lawyers, by contrast, often serve their clients by assisting them in defeating the claims and interests of other persons whose needs may be greater and whose causes may be more just.

The classic statement of the traditional conception of a lawyer's loyalty to his client was formulated by Lord Brougham:

An advocate, in the discharge of his duty, knows but one person in all the world, and that person is his client. To save that client by all means and expedients, and at all hazards and costs to other persons, and, among them, to himself, is his first and only duty; and in performing this duty he must not regard the alarm, the torments, the destruction which he may bring upon others. Separating the duty of a patriot from that of an advocate, he must go on reckless of consequences, though it should be his unhappy fate to involve his country in confusion. (*The Trial of Queen Caroline*, ed. J. Nightingale [London: Albion Press, 1821], vol. 2, p. 8.)

Thus the lawyer's professional role may entail not only unduly favoring his client—an apparent violation of the principle of fair shares and of the positive rights of others—but also actually harming others, the client's adversaries, thus apparently violating these adversaries' negative rights. The demands of fairness and efficiency would seem to be satisfied only if doctors

From Charles Fried, *Right and Wrong* (Cambridge, MA: Harvard University Press, 1978). Reprinted by permission of the publisher.

and lawyers were obliged or felt obliged to function for the common good alone—that is, in an essentially bureaucratic mode, servicing the population in the same way that a maintenance crew services the capital equipment of an enterprise: seeking at all times to maximize output, minimize costs, repairing where efficient, amortizing, and allowing for replacement on the same grounds. The idea of loyalty to a client would be as inappropriate as loyalty on the part of a mechanic to the machines he services. The loyalty is to the enterprise and exactly so much care is devoted to a particular part as the whole demands.

An immediate objection to this conception is that the loyalty of the professional to his client seems to be part of the very good which is being provided, just as loyalty is part of the indivisible good of friendship. A patient may not expect that his doctor will minister to every whim, but he does expect that when he does come under the doctor's care the doctor will act in the patient's interest. (And this is as true in a state-financed system such as the British National Health Service as it is in the supposedly private system obtaining in the United States.) To be sure, a doctor cannot procure resources without limit, but a patient expects his doctor to do his best for him with what is available and not to omit or choose therapies on the grounds of what is best for society. It might be best for society if all nonproductive members expired quickly and costlessly, but it is not part of the doctor's role to procure that result.

It is even more difficult to conceive clearly what it would mean for a lawyer to govern his professional conduct not by the interests of his client but by the principles of distributive justice and social efficiency. The lawyer assists his client in respect to his legal position vis-à-vis the collectivity and others. There is by hypothesis a best arrangement of social interests, and the lawyer perhaps should seek to bring about that arrangement, irrespec-

tive of whether his efforts further his client's interests. This conception was expressed by the professors of the University of Havana law faculty: "The first job of a revolutionary lawyer is not to argue that his client is innocent, but rather to determine if his client is guilty and, if so, to seek the sanction which will best rehabilitate him" (Harold Berman, "The Cuban Popular Tribunals," *Columbia Law Review* 69 [1969]: 1341). The same conclusion was reached by a Bulgarian lawyer defending a client against a charge of treason: "In a Socialist state there is no division of duty between the judge, prosecutor and defense counsel . . . The defense must assist the prosecution to find the objective truth in the case" (John Kaplan, *Criminal Justice: Introductory Cases and the Materials* [New York: Foundation Press, 1973], pp. 264–65). In this view, then, a client coming to a lawyer is like a citizen making a request of a government agency: The bureaucrat owes him no special duty but must treat the client with impartiality and an eye solely to advancing the public interest.

Now I shall argue that the traditional conception of professional loyalty is sound and practical. It offers a form of life and work which a just society must permit and a morally sensitive person may confidently adopt. It is my thesis that if a lawyer *in a reasonably just society* gives good and faithful counsel, then he fulfills his role well and that role itself is a good one. Indeed, a good lawyer is a good man, and the fact that he chooses his clients among those who can pay the most or whose cases involve travel and excitement does not vitiate that conclusion. So too the doctor who serves his patients with skill and devotion is a good man, however he chooses those patients. To be sure those who devote their time to the unfortunate and downtrodden approach heroism or sainthood, but that is another matter.

The analogy of professional roles to the concept of friendship is striking. In both cases one person assumes the interests of another. To be sure, the range of interests (medical, legal) is much more sharply defined in the professional case, yet within that range there obtain similar notions of loyalty and personal care even in the face of the competing claims of the larger collectivity.[1] Indeed, we may even discern the same (inadequate) arguments—rule-utilitarianism being the most frequent example—brought into play to show that traditional professional loyalty is conducive to efficiency and fair distribution after all. I have argued that respect for individual personality requires that we recognize not only a legal but a moral privilege to confer some benefits on friends and relations just according to inclination, without regard to fairness or efficiency. What we do thus is, after all, good in itself and the resources we spend are ours to spend. I now suggest that the lawyer who assists a client in a lawsuit full of spite or a doctor who tends the hearts and entrails of the sedentary rich is a good man, just as the good friend is a good man, a man who has chosen a good and useful life.

Why not? Is it because the analogy to friendship is imperfect in a number of ways? Professional relations are one-sided in ways that friendship should not be, since the client owes no reciprocal loyalty to his doctor or lawyer. Further, the professional generally demands payment for his services, although the relation is understood to have the same contours whether undertaken from love of humanity, love of a cause, or plain greed. Finally, these are public professions and so it might seem that they may be socialized like other aspects of public economic life. And yet,

despite these differences, I believe the analogy to friendship is illuminating because, as in the case of friendship, an ultimate legal and moral discretion to enter into these relations and show loyalty within them must be allowed.

Consider the case of the doctor. Surely it would violate both negative rights and the notion of personal liberty in the bestowal of friendship to forbid a doctor from doing good to whomever he chose so long as he used his own time and resources. Now, there is a large problem about the resources (medicines, hospital beds, and so on), but the point is that all of the doctor's *time* is his own, because *everybody's* time is his own. But it will be objected that the doctor's time is valuable; there is so much good he might do if it were best used. Maybe, and yet I have argued that your right to your own time (to yourself, indeed) may not depend on how valuable you are to others. Nor can it be the case that you are less free because you choose to use your time helping people than if you had chosen to spend it playing cards. And finally, it is hard to see why your liberty in respect to your own time is lessened because you accept a fee for the good you do—provided you pay the taxes due on that fee. True, you might be doing so much more good elsewhere, but that, I have argued, may not be the basis of compulsion exercised upon the person of anyone, for no one owes his person or efforts to the common good—we all owe only a fair share of objective resources. If doctors may be drafted to serve the common good, why then not draft persons to *become* doctors (or hairdressers) if that is what efficiency requires? This is a path we should not even begin to travel.[2]

---

[1] The professional relation is cooler, but this is only a function of its being focused on the particular interests in question. There can still be passion in respect to the interest. Moreover, it is important to the kind of "friendship" which a doctor or lawyer bears that he be able to abstract from the other, irrelevant aspects of his client's life plan, so that being indifferent to them, he is not responsible for them. That is why the doctor who cures a criminal is not implicated in his depredations any more than is the lawyer who procures the criminal's acquittal in a fair trial by legal means.

[2] This argument should not be taken to prove too much. In particular, it does not at all show that the state may not choose to run a comprehensive system of free or subsidized health care. I express no view on socialist enterprise in general or socialized medicine in particular. I argue only that whether or not the state should own the means of production, a man's talents and labor are not social resources. They are his own. So the community is morally free to

This is the case for recognizing a *right* to practice medicine on traditional lines of loyalty to one's patients and to choose those patients as one wills. But I have asserted that to cure the sick and to show loyalty and personal care is a *morally* good life, no matter who it is one cares for or how the patients are chosen. And why is it not a good life? One is doing good and by hypothesis is neither harming others nor depriving them of anything to which they are entitled. No doubt to seek out the neediest and most neglected is a nobler way of life still. But it is just my argument that to be a good man you do not have to be the best possible man you might be.

The case of the lawyer is somewhat different. I put aside for the moment the harm the lawyer may do as he assists his client against adversaries. Still, illness is a natural fact, while the legal difficulties in which the lawyer gives his aid are themselves the product of organized society. So why may not organized society control both the content of the lawyer-client relation and the basis on which clients are chosen? But it is a total nonsequitur to make the passage from the law's conventional nature to a social right to require that lawyers render legal service only when, how, and to whom it is efficient to do so. On the contrary, precisely because of the conventional nature of legal institutions, society is bound to permit legal advice to be given according to the traditional model: by lawyers who feel bound to serve loyally (within the law) the interests of their clients, clients chosen in any way the lawyer wishes.

The argument is a straightforward corollary of the general thesis about rights, that society is bound to respect individual rights even if it is socially inefficient to do so, even if fair distribution would be advanced by overriding rights. Now, a lawyer advises his client about what his rights are

and assists him in exercising those rights (by bringing and defending lawsuits, drafting instruments, and so on). Moreover, among the rights that an individual has is the right not to be subjected to legal constraints except in accordance with duly enacted and applied rules of law—this is the principle of the rule of law. Thus in a reasonably just society it may be the case that distributive justice would be advanced if the tax laws were amended to tax capital gains as ordinary income or to forbid the deduction of interest on home mortgages, but until the law is so amended every citizen has the perfect right to use these tax advantages in determining his legal debt to society. And it would be an obvious violation of right to tax anyone *as if* the law had been amended just because it should be amended. Similarly, the right to freedom of speech includes the right to say many things it would be more efficient, more agreeable and decent not to say, but the right would be no right at all if society could restrict speech on that basis. But if society must allow individuals to exercise their rights whether or not that exercise accords with efficiency or an ideal of fairness, then it follows that society must also allow individuals to learn what their rights are and to assert those rights. Moreover, since society may not restrict the assertion of rights on grounds of efficiency, it follows that it may not restrict access to those who would advise and assist in their assertion on such grounds. If society may not forbid the use of a legal tax deduction just because it is inefficient, it also may not forbid a client's finding out about the loophole or a lawyer's telling him about it. In short, it is as inadmissible to restrict, on grounds of social policy, seeking and giving help regarding the assertion of rights as it is to use social policy to restrict those rights themselves.

Nothing I have said argues, however, that society is also obliged to *furnish* legal assistance on the traditional model to all who desire it or that the traditional model

---

operate a health service and hire physicians. But it would violate rights to make such a state enterprise the only way in which persons may receive or confer medical benefits upon each other.

should have the monopoly it now enjoys in providing legal services. As with medicine, citizens or the government acting on their behalf may find it cheaper and more efficient to provide legal services and hire lawyers whose loyalties are those of functionaries: they serve the efficient functioning of a larger abstract entity. Like military doctors, lawyers in such organizations would take only those cases deemed worth taking and pursue only those defenses worth pursuing on some organizational criteria. Provided the clients are not deceived, I see no objection to this. It would in all likelihood provide cheaper service and distribute it more fairly than the individualized mode which prevails at least in theory today. I argue only that neither lawyers nor clients may be *compelled* to operate within this bureaucratic model. If the bureaucratic model is cheaper and generally satisfactory, the traditional conception may all but die out. But recognizing this alternative is very different from restricting the right of lawyers and clients to operate in the traditional mode if they wish.

It may be an exercise of right, but is it good to advise rich clients about minimizing their taxes or to defend a vicious criminal? For I readily concede that a man who enjoys—even legally—more than his fair share is himself morally obliged to give to others, just as the criminal is morally obliged to accept, not resist, punishment. Now, while it may be morally wrong for the client to exercise his legal rights in such cases, the moral privilege of the lawyer to assist such clients derives from the theorem that it is morally right that people have legal rights. It is a morally good system of law which recognizes a privilege against self-incrimination, even though it may be morally wrong for an individual to invoke the privilege to prevent his own just punishment. In counseling the rich man or the criminal, the lawyer draws his moral justification not by reference to the ultimate exercise of autonomy which the client's right leaves the client (that exercise,

I concede, may be bad) but from the good that inheres in the client's having the right, the autonomy, to make this choice. Once again, intention is crucial. The lawyer's activity is good because he intends to assist his client in exercising his rights; the lawyer does not intend the ultimate harm the client may do by exercising those rights. The lawyer's role is crucial. It insulates the lawyer from implication in that ultimate effect of the exercise of his client's rights. What the lawyer does intend, it is right to intend.[3]

Thus one who makes a life's work out of relieving the particular legal or medical needs of particular people and adopts as the regulative principle of his activity loyalty to the particular person before him acts not only justly but well. Nor does it matter that this activity provides a living as well as a way of life. For the relationship one assumes has the same quality, whatever the reason—pay, ambition, curiosity, excitement, pity, indignation—one may have had for assuming it. All this may seem just too pat and comfortable. It leaves out of account the individual's duty to the collectivity—whether he acts in a professional role or simply as a citizen. It leaves out of account his duty to help people who are not his friends, relations, or clients. And for the lawyer who helps his client to do moral wrong by asserting his legal rights, it leaves out of account the duty not to harm other people. . . .

The principal objection to the traditional conception of professional loyalty re-

[3] A difficult problem is presented when the lawyer's advice will be used not to exercise (perhaps in an undesirable way) legal rights, but to violate the law. A famous example is the lawyer who described the details of the defense of temporary insanity to his client—who had just admitted killing his wife—knowing (and perhaps intending) that the client would concoct a story to place himself within that defense. My argument does not cover such cases, since the lawyer is assisting his client in committing a fresh crime (perjury) and in defeating the legal system instead of assisting him to exercise legal rights. The client has no legal right to lie or to escape conviction by a perjured defense. The abuse of legal process to delay just claims by an opposing party falls by the same argument, as does the use of devices such as discovery or postponement of trial for purposes of delay.

lates to its systematic social effects. Is the traditional conception really tolerable if it means that the poor or those living in rural areas are deprived of medical or legal services? Is it really tolerable if it means that those who already enjoy power can perpetuate their privileges by monopolizing the best legal talent? Is the individual practitioner absolved from caring about these implications of his choices? . . . The availability of medical or legal services is indeed a matter of social concern, and therefore policy-makers, legislators, voters, and administrators must attend to that matter. They must decide what a fair distribution of medical or legal services would look like, and then they must seek to implement their conclusions, using whatever political, economic, or other incentives are available to them. That is their job. That is their obligation. The obligation of the individual providers of medical or legal services is, however, a different one. They are quite free in their choice of client, although once the client is chosen they are tied to the client by iron bonds of loyalty.

There is no anomaly here. Bureaucrats and government officials work to create a situation in which the correct distribution of medical care will come about as a result of the choices of doctors and their patients. If the criterion for the just distribution of benefits and burdens in the society is, say, equality, then the social system would have to put enough purchasing power in the hands of prospective patients and clients to attract the necessary number of persons into the profession. On the other hand, if the social system were wedded to a criterion not of equality but of a decent minimum, then once again redistribution would take place up to that point where the poorest sector of the society would be able to command decent medical and legal services along with other necessities of life. Individual doctors or individual lawyers would continue to choose their clients according to whatever inclinations move them. With reasonably free entry into the professions,

the normal desire to make a useful, interesting living should deliver the requisite number of doctors and lawyers to the marketplace.

Now, in structuring a system of health or legal services, government officials must respect the constraints of right and wrong. . . . They may not make the system work by simply drafting doctors or lawyers and telling them what to do, to whom, and when—as, for instance, if they compelled the professionals to show less care for their individual clients or to breach duties of confidentiality or loyalty. On the other hand, a doctor can only use such external resources—medicines, hospital beds, appliances—as are available, and if these are socially rationed, it is no part of his loyalty to his patient to seek to circumvent the system by going into the black market or trying to jump the queue. Furthermore, although a just society must allow the traditionally conceived principles of professional loyalty to exist, it need not give them a monopoly on the delivery of legal and medical services. It may be that some individuals would prefer to spend their money on cheaper, more efficient, but less personally oriented delivery systems. That too should be their right.

It is said that the medical profession has a special responsibility for the health of society just as the legal profession does for justice. This has often been thought to entail a requirement that individual doctors and lawyers should give some of their time to care for the poor. In a just society this would not be a serious issue; for, as I have argued, it is the job of the society as a whole to assure that its citizens can afford a decent standard of living, and the task of providing the components of that standard should not fall specially on those who happen to provide necessities, whether they be doctors or grocers or plumbers. So this professional obligation must be understood differently, as a special obligation to work for these just social arrangements. It is quite clearly an entailment of my theory of positive rights that we all have a corresponding positive duty to work for the establishment of a regime in which people's right to their fair share will be accorded. This does not, however, mean that any individual must give up his property as if a general scheme existed when it does not. One is not obliged to emulate St. Francis by impoverishing himself in order to relieve a misery which he did not create and which all should share in alleviating. Similarly, it is not enough to emulate John D. Rockefeller, Sr., by giving out dimes to poor people, on the theory perhaps that this is all that any one person's share of a grossly excessive fortune would amount to. The obligation is a social obligation which is discharged by working socially—specifically, politically—for the establishment of just social institutions which will procure a fair share *from* and *to* everyone. This obligation to work for just institutions is the most particular devolution of the bureaucratic function. It is the sense in which we are all bureaucrats, the sense in which we are all responsible for realizing the abstract principles of justice.

The lawyer accordingly has a moral obligation to work for the establishment of just institutions generally, but entirely the wrong kinds of conclusions have been drawn from this proposition. Some more fervent critics of the profession have put forward a conception of the lawyer as a kind of anointed priest of justice—a high priest whose cleaving to the traditional conception of the lawyer's role opens him to the charge of apostasy. But this is wrong. In a democratic society, justice has no anointed priests. (It is a priesthood of all believers.) Every citizen has the same duty to work for the establishment of just institutions, and the lawyer has no special moral responsibilities in that regard. To be sure, the lawyer like any citizen, must use all his knowledge and talent to fulfill that general duty of citizenship, and this may mean that there are special perspectives and opportunities for him.[4]

There is a special difficulty when, in the context of a generally just social system, particular individuals fall through the cracks, as it were, of a well-designed system. Who is going to catch them? The bureaucrat, by hypothesis, cannot, since it is through the cracks of his well-devised system that the particular person has fallen. Does not the doctor or lawyer have an obligation at least in such a case to aid the anomalous person in need, while retaining his own general freedom? A good example of this is the unsavory criminal defendant whom nobody wants to represent. There may be money for that person's defense, so that is not the problem. The legal profession has long affirmed a duty of individual lawyers to accept assignment to such cases—indeed, a duty to accept such cases without assignment if a particular

[4] Regulations forbid qualified and financially responsible persons and bodies, such as banks, insurance companies, title companies, or real estate brokers, from supplying routine legal services which lawyers (or rather their secretaries and automatic typewriters) provide at high cost. There are also regulations prohibiting advertising by lawyers (recently declared unconstitutional) and limiting prepaid group legal services. All of these regulations are justified by the legal profession as necessary to protect the public and to maintain professional standards. In my view, such arguments are hypocritical or self-deluding rationalizations for what is essentially an anticompetitive conspiracy in restraint of trade. (The arguments are almost identical to those used by opticians, pharmacists, and funeral directors—with transparently self-serving motives.) It is no surprise that critics of the legal profession take it at its pompous word, and seek to fasten on it duties commensurate with its moralizing pretensions.

Unfortunately, many lawyers identify themselves with their clients' causes, rather than simply giving legal advice and performing legal services. To submit the most favorable legal argument on behalf of a client is one thing, to profess belief in it and to advocate it personally in extralegal contexts is quite another. Lawyers in the United States—unlike English barristers—too often consider it good business to identify personally and totally with their clients. Lawyers who represent unions will not represent management, and vice versa. There is a defendants' and a plaintiffs' antitrust, malpractice, and personal accident bar engaged in intense public relations and lobbying efforts. Lawyers for liquor companies feel they must drink and lawyers for tobacco companies feel they must smoke. In this sorry state of affairs—which is not justified by my argument—it is reasonable to judge the lawyer by the causes with which he chooses to identify himself. So here, too, the lack of discretion and of professional austerity makes lawyers fair game for the moralizing criticisms which I am seeking to refute.

lawyer knows that a person in great legal need may otherwise go unrepresented. I think we can accept such an individual obligation without compromising the two-tier system I have been developing. It is after all a special case of the duty of beneficence. By hypothesis the situations will be anomalous, so that the imposition of such an obligation will not compromise the general principle of the professional's right to choose his own client. Indeed, by recognizing such an obligation in rare instances, a certain independence of the lawyer might be affirmed, since it is thereby shown that the professional does not necessarily choose his case because of an unprofessional attachment to a client's cause.
. . .

. . . Doctors, lawyers, and friends are good men and lead good lives if they fulfill their obligations of justice to society as a whole—obey the law, work for the furtherance of just institutions—and take wise and faithful care of their clients and friends. They are at liberty to construct their lives out of what personal scraps and shards of motivation their inclination and character suggest—idealism, greed, curiosity, love of luxury, love of adventure or knowledge—as long as they do indeed give wise and faithful counsel. There are those who may wish to give greater coherence to these elements of motivation and to live out their lives in closer connection with the general well-being of humanity. And we can recognize the perfection of such an attitude without at all denying the moral sufficiency of doing justice and doing such good as one chooses. That much freedom—moral and political—must be left us. It is the task of the social system as a whole to work for the general conditions under which everyone will benefit in fair measure from the true performance of doctors, lawyers, teachers, musicians, and friends. But I would not see the integrity of those roles or the sanctity of the self undermined in the name of the common good.

Those who argue for a different attitude, one in which we are all servants of the greatest good, like to remind us of the sacrifices and impersonality evoked by wartime, by catastrophes and famine. Now, I am willing to admit that emergencies create their own morality in which the rights and obligations of everyday life are loosened or altogether dispensed with. But it is a mistake to generalize from such contexts and to use them as the intellectual basis from which the total structure of our moral life is derived. On the contrary, the only thing that makes special principles tolerable for emergencies is just the fact that emergencies are extraordinary. It is when the general long-term situation of society is made to correspond to a continuing catastrophe that morality, civilization, and everything specially human are undermined. And there can be no doubt that my approach is less "efficient" than one in which each person acts or is forced to act as if he were responsible for the system as a whole. But such theoretically homogeneous systems would be sure to obliterate crucial aspects of a total, rich, human, moral life. We must resist even those idealists who would draft us only temporarily in order that their millennium may come sooner. After all, the millennium may never come, and then where would we be?

THE TRIPLE CONTRACT: A NEW FOUNDATION FOR MEDICAL ETHICS

Robert M. Veatch

Veatch argues that a professional's role in a society can be determined only on the basis of a common set of fundamental values and principles acceptable to the whole society. He urges the use of a hypothetical social contract to determine what these values and principles should be. Repeated applications of contractual reasoning are employed to establish the role of a single profession (in this case, medicine) within such a society and the role of the individual professional interacting with the individual client.

Prosenjit Poddar was a student at the University of California at Berkeley. He participated in folk dancing classes at the school, where he met and fell in love with Tatiana Tarasoff. Rejected by Ms. Tarasoff, Poddar fell into a deep depression resulting in declining health and neglect of his studies. In August 1969 he sought treatment as a voluntary outpatient at Cowell Memorial Hospital, a university-affiliated facility. According to the eventual legal complaint against him, it is alleged that he confided to Dr. Lawrence Moore, a psychologist at the hospital, that he was going to kill an unnamed girl, readily identifiable as Tatiana, when she returned from spending a summer in Brazil. Dr. Moore, with the concurrence of two psychiatrists, decided that Poddar should be committed for observation to a mental hospital.

He wrote a letter of diagnosis to the campus police requesting that they detain Poddar for emergency psychiatric evaluation. They did so, but released Poddar when he appeared rational and promised to stay away from Tatiana. On October 27, 1969, Poddar killed Tatiana Tarasoff, two months after confiding his intention to do so to Dr. Moore.

The central issue in the court case was whether a health professional, a psychiatrist or psychotherapist, has a duty to warn an intended victim in cases such as this. . . .

Whether the people who are in danger will be benefited more by the keeping or breaking of a confidence is an empirical question. There is also a question of principle, however. If it turns out that the patient would benefit more by keeping the confidence, but others would benefit more by breaking it, should the therapist break the confidence or keep it? Is he or she to compromise the commitment to the patient in order to serve society? This is the issue over which the court and the professional society disagreed. Our question is: To what extent should the court let a professional group's commitment to patient confidentiality influence its decision on the duty of the therapist?[1] . . .

If we are going to cut through the apparent cultural relativism of the endless list of possible principles for medical ethics, we are going to have to seek a universal or absolutist basis for a medical ethics. It will not do to have one set of basic principles about what the physician should do in a particular case held by one religious or professional group and another set of principles held by another group about what the same physician should do in the same situation. Above all, we need a common framework, acceptable to both lay people and professional, within which to decide what is ethically acceptable medical practice.

[1] Based on Tarasoff v. Regents of University of California. Supreme Court of Calif. Sup., 131 Cal. Rptr. 14 (July 1, 1976); see also Dennis W. Daley, "Tarasoff and the Psychotherapist's Duty to Warn," *San Diego Law Review* 12 (1975):932–51; Joseph Al Latham, "Torts—Duty to Act for Protection of Another—Liability of Psychotherapist for Failure to Warn of Homicide Threatened by Patient," *Vanderbilt Law Review* 28 (1975):631–40; and Howard Gurevita, "Tarasoff: Protective Privilege Versus Public Peril," *American Journal of Psychiatry* 134 (March 1977):289–92.

This condition of universal applicability is so central to ethics that it is often incorporated into the very notion of what ethics means. When someone claims that a particular behavior in a particular circumstance is unethical, he is making a claim that he believes should be accepted in principle by everybody. To the extent that people do not accept it, they either have misunderstood the facts, are thinking of a somewhat different circumstance, or have made an error in moral judgment. A claim that a particular behavior is ethical thus comes to more than a matter of mere taste or preference. We think it is a matter worth fighting about when we talk of whether a particular physician in Japan ought to collaborate in a murder or whether a particular psychotherapist ought to disclose a confidence to an identified potential victim. On the other hand, we tend not to care whether the Japanese prefer raw fish to pizza; that is a matter of taste. Ethical questions are basic. If we label the claim ethical, rather than merely preferential, we are making a judgment within a framework that we take to be applicable to all. . . .

We now have several approaches to the discovery or generation of a universally applicable framework for morally structuring a society, and they are not so different from each other as they originally appeared. In the end, they all turn on some notion of reasonable people coming together, attempting to approximate the moral point of view, in order to contract to or at least agree on a framework. Some would hope to discover the content of the original covenant between God and man, others to discover what an ideal observer—if such an observer existed—would approve of. These two groups should have very little separating them methodologically in the task of generating a common framework. Their product in either case might be called the basic social contract. Still others would see themselves as reasonable people coming together collectively to use their rational processes in discovering the moral order. All of these groups are engaged in contracting; all concede that real, finite people can only approximate the moral point of view required of them and that the real moral order would be the one acknowledged by a hypothetical group of contractors who are capable of perfect knowledge and of perfectly taking the moral point of view.

The term *contract* is used guardedly, since for some it means a basic social contract only epistemologically because another earlier and more fundamental contract between God and man precedes it. For others it is a basic social contract only epistemologically because it is the best way to approximate what an ideal observer would approve or what reason would require. An ethic rooted in a social contract is, with these emendations, not at odds with the view that the moral order can be discovered. Hobbes and Locke may not have been able to reconcile natural law theory with their contract theory, but modern man certainly can.

Moreover, the model of contractors trying to discover the moral order is not very different from the one where contractors create or invent the moral framework. Both approaches require acknowledgment of man's real, finite limits and of an impartial point of view. They also include full and equal consideration of everybody's interests.

In the case of the moral-framework creators, real people come together with the task of inventing the basic principles constitutive of their society. They will be successful to the extent that they respect each person's liberty and treat everybody's interests equally. Fallible humans, they attempt to mimic a hypothetical contract that would have been drawn by those who could meet completely the conditions of the moral point of view. In the other case, real people come together because they have the task of discovering the basic principles constitutive of their society. They will be successful to the extent that they take an impartial point of view, becoming an approximation of the ideal observer or the ideal rational agent. Also fallible humans, they attempt to mimic a hypothetical contract that would be drawn by those who can completely meet the imposed conditions.

Is there any reason why real people coming together to establish or reaffirm the most fundamental principles and practices of their society should disagree if they are working from these various perspectives? There are at least two quite different reasons why people seeking the moral framework use the heuristic device of thinking of themselves as impartial contractors. For one group it is a very sophisticated technique based on enlightened self-interest. For the other, it is the best epistemological tool it has for discovering the moral order. For the former group the principles are agreed to because they reflect self-interest; for the latter it does not make much sense to ask why they are agreed to, they simply are. (Reason dictates so, or the moral sense perceives them so. To ask why people should agree to the basic moral framework makes no more sense than to ask why objects should act according to the laws of gravity or why two plus two should equal four. It is simply the way of the universe, according to the combined wisdom of our best powers of perception and/or reason.)

There is, thus, a moral community constituted symbolically by the metaphor of the contract or covenant. There is a convergence between the vision of people coming together to discover a preexisting moral order—an order that takes equally into account the welfare of all—and the vision of people coming together to invent a moral order that as well takes equally into account the welfare of all. The members of the moral community thus generated are bound together by bonds of mutual loyalty and trust. There is a fundamental equality and reciprocity in the relationship, something missing in the philanthropic condescension of professional code ethics. . . .

We are working gradually toward the solution of Dr. Moore's problem. We have the source of a framework within which we can begin to determine whether society should be structured with practices and principles that induce a psychotherapist to disclose a patient's confidence under certain circumstances. Before we have an answer, however, we shall need to know what the basic content of the social contract is; that is, we need to know substantively what the basic principles and practices for the society ought to be.

This is not to say that those basic principles, if known, could tell us for certain what Dr. Moore should do; basic principles are very general. We may need to develop further rules, guidelines, or rights claims that specify how to move from the most general principles to the specific case. We may also need to know whether there are special role-specific duties that might lead to a different obligation regarding confidentiality for a health professional or a psychotherapist than for citizens not in those roles.

It seems clear that both the articulation of the moral rules and the spelling out of role-specific duties for professionals will have to be derived from the basic social contract. . . .

The Contract Between Society and a Profession

In Dr. Moore's case we are not so much interested in the general question of whether a person outside a professional relationship should disclose potentially lifesaving confidential information as in the more specific question of whether a person in the role of a health professional should disclose the confidence. For this particular medical ethical problem, we shall have to understand how health professionals might have special obligations and privileges not applicable to other members of the society.

There are, of course, other roles in society that require specific duties, but in all three of the cases we have presented thus far—that of the physician asked for information on killing, that of a professional association's right to limit advertising, and that of a psychotherapist's dilemma on disclosure of useful information—the problems concern the special duties of medical professionals. Likewise, lay people, when interacting with professionals, have special, role-specific duties that do not apply when they interact with nonprofessionals. These might include not only special duties of keeping appointments and paying bills, but others, such as disclosure of one's personal life situation or plans, that are not normally disclosed socially. The patient's special duties often relate to reporting symptoms honestly.

I have already conceded that there may be such role-specific duties, but I have argued that they cannot exist simply because a profession itself imposes them or alleges it alone possesses the ability to know what is ethical for professionals or patients. If the possibility, indeed the necessity, exists then that in certain circumstances professionals and patients will have obligations not shared by those in other roles, where can such duties come from? If they are moral duties, as we have developed that term, they must derive at least indirectly from the basic social contract. . . .

The second contract will be generated within the context of the more basic social contract. Therefore, it will be limited by the principles of that contract. The basic social contract will tell us what the fundamental ethical principles for the society are: those that would be agreed to if the contractors treated the interests of all as equal; if, in Rawls's term, they assumed the veil of ignorance. Since real people cannot fully assume this ideal status, the contract is hypothetical. Real contractors must attempt to approximate this moral point of view in order to invent or discover the basic principles.

In the same fashion, if members of a society (including professionals) want to de-termine the special duties of those in a specific role, such as nurses, pharmacists, physicians, or patients, the same tension between an ideal vantage point and man's limited reality would be apparent. The ethically appropriate special duties are those that would be agreed to by ideal, disinterested observers taking the moral point of view. In the real, finite world, the best we can do is approximate that hypothetical contractual position. The actual contract between the profession and society, therefore, to the extent it attempts to articulate a morality for the professional and lay roles, will, at best, approximate the ideal. Still, the actual contract can attempt to formulate an understanding of the role-specific duties within the framework of the basic social contract.

The relationship will be a complex one, however. For example, if it turns out that one of the principles of the basic social covenant is a principle of equity establishing what is a fair distribution of resources in, say, health planning, then any social contract between a profession and a society would have to be in accord with that principle of equity. Exactly how that requirement is met, however, is open to further discussion between the society and the profession. It might turn out that representatives of the profession and the public agree that individual practitioners, in the normal course of their day-to-day practice of medicine, should not be responsible for equitable allocation of health resources. Perhaps the profession as a whole would be given that responsibility, with society exerting its continuing influence by specifying what kinds of physicians be licensed and where those physicians may practice. The result would be a special exemption for the individual practitioner from the general duty of equity because society has determined that that duty can be met more effectively at a broader level. Both sides gain as well because the individual practitioner in the context of his patient–physician relationships is unburdened of the worry that someone else somewhere in the world may have a claim of equity on his services.

This second contract, the one between the profession and society, may provide a basis for resolving Dr. Moore's problem about whether to disclose his knowledge of Prosenjit Poddar's intent to the Tarasoff family. There are, in this situation, good reasons why society might want to have the confidences broken. It might, therefore, agree to a general duty to warn. There are also good reasons why a society might in general want to seal confidences between people, and particularly good reasons why it might want people in certain roles to keep confidence.

The lawyer, for example, might further a system of justice in the long run by keeping confidence rather than disclosing his client's guilt. Society tends to believe that, within limits, defense attorneys should have that "privilege," and it grants such an exemption in its contract with the legal profession. In fact, nondisclosure is a duty, even though society could conceivably gain in the short run from the disclosure.

Likewise, society might plausibly see that health professionals, particularly psychotherapists, could contribute most, on balance, if they were under a special obligation to keep confidences. Such an exemption, for example, might encourage a dangerous patient to remain in therapy, thus minimizing the long-term risk to others. Society might establish a special set of duties and exemptions for psychotherapists in the area of confidentiality. On the other hand, society would almost certainly want to place some limits on the principle of confidentiality. If Dr. Moore faced a patient carrying several loaded revolvers and confessing to a plan to immediately murder a large number of people, it seems likely that many members of the society would draw the line—in a case like this, they would conclude, there is a limit to that special exemption from the duty to warn. (In fact, there may be a more stringent

duty in this case to make the risk known because a trained professional might be in a better position to evaluate the individual's real intentions.) Exactly where the limits of the exemption come and when the special duties begin is probably arbitrary. Society and the profession may both have views on exactly where these lines should be drawn; agreement by all that a clear line should be drawn at this point is probably more important than that it be drawn at any one precise spot.

It should now be clear why a professional group's unilateral declarations on Dr. Moore's duty of confidentiality should not be definitive in deciding what his moral (or legal) duty is. The members of society have a legitimate stake in articulating both the role-specific duties of the health care professional and the reciprocal duties of the patient. They will (or they should) incorporate those duties into the contract made with the professional at the time of licensure. That contract, in turn, should reflect as accurately as possible the one that would be agreed to by our ideal, hypothetical contractors. The health professions (or any other profession) should participate in the decision, setting out the content of this second contract, but should not unilaterally set the terms. In the end, society will outline its terms for granting the privileges of licensure. If the members of the profession (and new members coming up for licensure) are so offended morally (or any other way) by the terms, they can refuse to complete the agreement. If necessary, society will reformulate its understanding of the character of both the professional and the lay roles, taking into account the profession's own understanding of those roles until such time as there is an adequate meeting of the minds.

If the morality of a professional role is linked to this second social contract (which itself is linked to the rights and responsibilities that society grants to the professional along with licensure), then one major problem confronts us. Are the terms of the second contract spelled out once and for all at the time of licensure? If so, our understanding of the professional's moral obligation is fixed in perpetuity at the time he or she is licensed. There is then no room for rethinking the content of the unique moral obligations of the professional, no room for society to readjust its expectations of the professional, and no chance of the professional making a case for reformulation. In short, there is no chance to bring the real second contact into line with what the hypothetical ideal contractors would promise. It thus seems likely that both sides would want the right to renegotiate from time to time, to make more refined attempts at summarizing what the ideal moral relationship is.

One way to adjust our social understanding of the professional's moral obligation may be through reformulation at the time new people enter the professional role. As with the traditional Hippocratic physician, young medical students will be presented (at least figuratively) the moral framework of their anticipated new role, be socialized into that framework, and either accept or reject the moral stipulations accompanying it. This means that if society develops a new understanding of what it thinks ought to be the moral conditions, the role-specific duties, and the practice of a profession, such a shift would gradually be introduced so that over a generation a new understanding of the morality of the role would be established.

An alternative is to place limits on the length of time of licensure. Renewed negotiation could take place, every five years. At that time, if society wanted to change its understanding of the conditions under which confidences had to be disclosed, it could do so at this periodic renegotiation. The profession also would have a chance to articulate its understanding of the duty of the professional and a new bargain would be struck. Insofar as this is moral bargaining, the moral point of view would be taken. All contractors would ask what the

role-specific duties should be for, say, psychotherapists; for example, they would try to imagine that they did not know whether they were to be therapists, future patients with homicidal tendencies, future lovers of mentally deranged patients with homicidal tendencies, or merely bystanders.

This approach has the added advantage of allowing reformulation of the lay person's role-specific duties in relationships with a professional. Periodically, we as a society might become convinced that we can articulate a better approximation of the ideal social contract between the profession and the society, specifying more appropriately the moral structure of both lay and professional roles.

We still have not really addressed what the content of the professional's duty should be when faced with the question of keeping confidences or any other problem. We now have a framework, however, for understanding how the question can be asked. The framework is in principle accessible to all and is perceived by all as morally legitimate.

The Contract Between Professionals and Patients

At this point we have a framework of a basic social contract by which we can understand what it means to affirm a basic set of ethical principles. Within that basic social contract we also have a framework for generating a set of role-specific duties regarding relations between professionals and lay people via the mechanism of a second social contract. The result will be a general moral framework for the society and a more narrowly formulated moral framework for lay and professional roles.

In a liberal society, these two contracts will not fix all the dimensions of a social choice. There will be points on which the original social contractors would be indifferent; these would be left as matters of taste or preference or personal beliefs and values. Likewise, it can be assumed that lay and professional options for action will not be rigidly determined by the second contract. Professional and lay person will retain some discretion for acting according to his or her personal beliefs and values. Those decisions will have to be in accord with the two contracts, but substantial latitude will remain—for example, to practice surgery or psychiatry, to opt for high risk-high gain options or low risk-low gain ones, to treat aggressively or conservatively, to emphasize prevention or therapy, and so forth.

At the same time, patients in interactions with the professional will have a range of views about these same variables. Some of the variables may be universally recognized as matters of life-style preference or taste. Others may possibly be perceived as moral matters.

It is at first puzzling to understand how matters that are moral could stand outside the moral principles growing out of the basic social contract and the second contract. Several reasons can be offered. First, some questions may not be considered by all to be matters of morality. Card playing, contraception, and the use of narcotics for pain control are all ambiguously regarded issues. Some see them as issues of morality, others as mere matters of prudence or preference.

Second, some of the residuum may actually include matters of morality—those that would be resolved by the principles agreed upon by social contractors taking the moral point of view. But it is possible that one of the principles would itself be a principle of liberty, permitting individual discretion in interpreting the ethical principles for action and even permitting limited departures from what is moral in the name of individual choice. At the very least, the principle of liberty is likely to leave room for individual discretion in understanding how the basic principles apply to the individual case.

From these sources it is quite possible that some choices within a social contract framework, even moral ones, will remain

for individual practitioners and individual lay people. Both practitioner and lay person should have the right to make such choices based on their own beliefs and values as well as their understanding of the implications of the social contract for specific medical ethical problems. If lay persons are given complete authority for specifying the framework of the lay–professional relationship (within the bounds of the first two contracts), the professional loses all sense of being an autonomous agent with the right to make moral and other value choices. If, on the other hand, the professional is given complete authority to specify the terms of the relationship, the lay person is similarly disenfranchised and dehumanized. The solution seems to be that a third contract or covenant be negotiated between the professional and the lay person. (Here and elsewhere I use these terms to refer either to individuals or to groups. The professional may be a professional team: a group practice with physicians, nurses, social workers, and other health professionals or a Health Maintenance Organization. The lay person may be a couple, a family, or even a whole community.[2])

This contract or covenant between the professional and the lay person would fill the gaps—it would stipulate the belief system, the residuum of moral values, the specific understanding of how basic ethical principles apply to specific problems, and lifestyle preferences that will constitute the basis of the specific relationship. For example, some professional–lay relationships might be established with the agreement that certain kinds of treatment for the terminally ill are not appropriate. The more basic social contract and the secondary professional contract probably would establish certain broad rights to have or refuse treatment. They can never, however,

---

[2] See Robert M. Veatch, *Value-Freedom in Science and Technology* (Missoula, Montana: Scholars Press, 1976), pp. 52–54, for a fuller account of the claim that lay and professional actors are often more appropriately thought of as groups rather than individuals.

specify in any detail what the trusting, harmonious relationship will be at the individual level. If professional and lay persons can agree ahead of time on some of the constitutive elements of that relationship, neither will be forced into the intolerable situation of having to choose between violating one's conscience and violating the conscience of the other party.

Probably the basic social contract and the contract between the professional and society also will specify some broad right for patients to have access to certain kinds of information. State laws and court cases are currently clarifying that right in law. It seems reasonable to believe, however, that all professionals and lay persons will not reach exactly the same conclusion on precisely what information should be transmitted or how it should be done. Within the limit of the first two contracts, individual professionals and lay persons should develop a clear understanding of this right of access in their particular relationship. Will it include a right to the actual documents or only the information in them? Will it include psychological information or only organic medical information? Will it cover information that physicians sincerely believe will not be in the patient's interest to know? Some of these questions will probably be answered in the first two contracts, but a range of discretion is likely to remain. That should be specified in the third contract, the contract between the professional and the lay person, within the bounds of the earlier, broader contracts.

Medical institutions have begun to articulate a moral identity—a set of beliefs and values—that can be the professional starting point for this third social contract. The clearest present-day example is the hospice, where a philosophical stance about important matters of belief and world view is articulated more or less explicitly. Lay people know (or should know) when they choose to enter a relationship in such an institution that certain attitudes prevail about aggressive intervention and so-called "extraordinary" measures.

Likewise, lay people have begun to cluster in groups around the sets of values and beliefs that they consider crucial, that they want to incorporate into their lay–professional relationships. We see this happening in feminist health collectives as well as in certain religious groups.

It would seem wise for small "sectarian" groups sharing a common ideology of health care to come together. They could include both lay people and professionals holding a common moral, philosophical, theological, or ideological framework. Christian Science, Jehovah's Witnesses, Seventh Day Adventists, holistic health centers, and Oral Roberts's medical complex in Tulsa are the ideal models of this, even if they have not chosen the right system of beliefs and values. Lay people and practitioners in such a community would share a common framework. They might share a common story, history, or world view—an option that Stanley Hauerwas recently suggested ought to be the basis for articulating opposition to abortion.[3] No one then would be foolish enough to select a health professional or accept a patient without a common understanding of beliefs and values adequate to the circumstances. A health collective could not organize around a commitment to extensive use of heroin; to active, intentional mercy killing; or to extend parents and physicians the right to work together to withhold safe, simple, and sure treatments from children even if they were convinced these were important. They could, however, organize around commitments that are within the constraints of the first two contracts.

Conclusion

The result, finally, is what I have called a triple-contract theory of medical ethics. The first contract specifies the basic content of an ethical system. It is what con-

[3] Stanley Hauerwas, "Abortion: Why the Arguments Fail," *Hospital Progress* 61 (January 1980):38–47.

tractors taking the moral point of view (the outlook that other people's welfare is considered on the same scale as one's own) would invent or discover or have revealed to them as the basic ethical principles for society. Real humans, being finite, can only approximate this hypothetical condition, but it is the best system we have for knowing the basic content of an ethical system. It is a system usable by those who are convinced that morality is objective and absolute (whether they derive their ethical theory from a theological system, attempt to determine the ethical principles by use of reason, or believe they can use the moral sentiments to discover them). It is also usable by those who are convinced that morality is subjective. (They would see real people coming together assuming the moral point of view for more practical purposes of trying to reach an agreement on a system that would lead to joint harmonious survival.) I find it hard to discover what differences in principle would result, what differences in content of the social contract could be expected from these approaches that appear to be so different. In either case, a set of basic principles for organizing society will emerge. The inventors should have no problem with those who approach morality believing they are pursuing something that is objective. If anything, it will give their fellow contractors an added incentive to be fair in assuming the moral point of view. On the other hand, the discoverers should not be overly troubled by those among their fellows who think they are only inventing an ethic. Assuming the inventors take the moral point of view, they should be in roughly the same position as those who set out to discover a morality. From the point of view of those who believe ethical principles are there for hu-

mans to discover or have revealed to them—for those who believe they are in the created order, in nature, in reason, or in the empirical reality—it should not be surprising if the inventors come up with the set of principles that the discoverers believe actually exists. They might feel sorry for the inventors, believing they do not understand the true basis of the apparently subjective conclusions. If the inventors think they have created the basic principles, it may tell on their character; it may lead to a false sense of pride and anthropocentrism, but it should not affect the content. If those principles turn out to be there for the discovering, however, it would not be surprising if the inventors find them or at least some approximation of them. From either approach, a set of principles will be articulated that will constitute the foundation for a morality.

Once that basic social contract articulates these fundamental principles, a second contract, one between the society and a profession, can then spell out (again from the moral point of view) the special role-specific duties regarding interactions between lay people and professionals. The only limit of that second contract will be that as a whole it cannot contravene the morality of the prior, more basic, social contract.

Finally, within the context of these two contracts, individual professionals and lay persons (or the groups that function as individual units) have the opportunity to spell out further the terms, moral and otherwise, of their relationship. The result is a triple-contract theory of medical ethics, one that in principle is accessible to all and applicable to all. We are left only with the problem of what the content of these various contracts will be.

THE PRIMACY OF THE ACT OF PROFESSION

Edmund D. Pellegrino

Pellegrino argues for a special role ethic for the healthcare professions. This ethic is based on two sets of considerations: the characteristics of those who need the healthcare professional's expertise and the nature of the commitment made by such professionals when they enter their professions. He suggests that similar analysis of other kinds of need and entry commitments could establish proper ethical roles for other professions.

Is a commonly accepted code of professional morality possible in a democratic, morally pluralistic society? Are there philosophically justifiable obligations that bind all who profess medicine, or more generally, all who profess to heal? Can obligations be derived that are prior to, and independent of, the particular positions physicians or patients may take on the specific medical moral dilemmas of the day? In short, is it possible to reconstruct a professional morality more suited to contemporary requirements than the Hippocratic ethic?

. . . Today codes of professional ethics are less universally accepted, narrower in the obligations they assume, more legalistic and cautious in tone, and more centered on scientific competence than humane considerations. While the special obligations to protect the subjects of human investigation have been recognized, little attention has been paid to the moral agency of patients in the more mundane and more multitudinous daily interactions with physicians. Even scantier notice is given to the physician's social responsibilities and their potential conflicts with his responsibilities to individual patients.

Two alternatives seem open at present: One is to abandon the possibility of a common set of higher moral principles and return to the simpler and less demanding ethics of a craft. This was the model of the early Greek physician; it assures at least the promise of competence, a promise which should survive even in a morally pluralistic society. The other alternative is to seek a philosophical reconstruction of professional ethics, one derived from the natures of medicine and medical acts and their interrlationships in the act of healing.

This essay takes the second alternative and seeks a foundation for medical morality—some irreducible source which can define the moral conduct of the human relationships specific to medical activity. This foundation should be prior to, and compatible with, a fairly wide range of value systems insofar as specific moral dilemmas are concerned. It should also be susceptible to expansion, enrichment, and illumination by additional obligations derived from theologically or humanistically based value systems. In short, this essay seeks a basis for professional ethics which defines the normative guidelines which must, of necessity, bind all who profess to heal.

While medicine and the physician will be used as the illustrations, the principles we derive are intrinsic to the professional activity of all health professionals—nurses, dentists, optometrists, allied health workers, psychologists, social workers, pharmacists, and podiatrists. Indeed, they could form the basis for a single common code of ethics for all the "healing" professions. . . .

From Edmund A. Pellegrino, "Toward a Reconstruction of Medical Morality: The Primacy of the Act of Profession and The Fact of Illness," *The Journal of Medicine of Philosophy*, vol. 4, no. 1 (1979), 32–56. Reprinted by permission.

My inquiry will advance in three stages. First, the traditional sources for professional morality are examined and found wanting: then a philosophical basis for professional ethics is proposed based on the relationships of the act of profession, the act of medicine, and the fact of illness; finally, the obligations which derive from these relationships are outlined briefly.

Sources of Medical Morality

All codes of medical ethics reflect certain implicit philosophical assumptions: about the nature of medicine, the patient–physician relationship, and the good life. These assumptions dictate what is right conduct for both the physician and the patient. They give rise, therefore, to at least three constantly interacting levels of moral decision: what is right conduct for the physician qua physician and for the patient qua patient, what is right conduct for physician and patient as good persons irrespective of their situations as physician or patient, and the conjunction of these two levels in a third—determining right conduct in a specific moral dilemma.

The first level is that of professional morality properly speaking, and is the focus of this essay. The second is more properly the realm of general moral philosophy, and the third comprises the agenda of biomedical ethics as it is usually construed today. All three are closely intermingled in any medical decision or act and are disentangled with difficulty.

. . . This essay attempts to establish a philosophical framework for professional ethics based on three phenomena specific to medicine: the fact of illness, the act of profession, and the act of medicine. The interrelationships of these three phenomena are sufficiently unique to medicine to constitute a specific and unique kind of human relationship which ought to be conducted in certain specific ways to be morally defensible.

The Fact of Illness

Medicine and physicians exist because humans become ill. Illness is a subjective state, one in which a human being detects some change, acute or chronic, in his/her mode of existence based in anxiety about the functions of body or mind. Illness may or may not be associated with demonstrable pathology. What is crucial to being ill is the perception of an altered state of existence, one in which the patient interprets some symptom or sign as an indication that he/she is no longer "healthy," according to the patient's own definition of that fluid and multi-interpretable word.

A person who arrives at the conclusion that he/she is "ill" becomes a patient—one who bears some disability, some deficiency or concern, one who is no longer "whole," one who perceives special limits on his or her accustomed activity.

The person who becomes a patient suffers what is nothing less than an ontological assault. In our usual state we see ourselves identified with our bodies, facing the world and acting on it in essential unity. In illness the body is interposed between us and reality—it impedes our choices and actions and is no longer fully responsive. The body stands opposite to the self. Instead of serving us, we must serve it. It intrudes on our existence rather than enhancing or enriching it. We can no longer use it for transbodily purposes.

With this assault on the ontological unity of body and self, illness erodes the image we have fashioned of ourselves over the years. That image harmonizes our deficiencies and our strong points; we carefully and laboriously protect and refurbish it; we delicately balance it against the external exigencies of human life. Illness forces a reappraisal and that poses a threat to the old image; it opens up all the old anxieties and imposes new ones—often including the real threat of death or drastic alterations in life-style.

This ontological assault is aggravated by the loss of most of the freedoms we identify as peculiarly human. The patient is no longer free to make rational choices among alternatives. He lacks the knowledge and the skills necessary to cure himself or gain relief of pain and suffering. In many illnesses, the patient is not even free to reject medicine, as in severe trauma or other overwhelming acute emergencies. Voluntarily or not, the patient is forced to place himself under the power of another person, the health professional, who has the knowledge and the skills which can heal— but also harm. This involuntary need grounds the axiom of vulnerability from which follows the obligations of the physician.

When a person becomes "ill," he is therefore in an exceptionally vulnerable state, one which severely compromises his customary human freedoms to use his body for transbodily purposes, to make his own decisions, to act for himself, and to accept or reject the services of others. The state of being ill is therefore a state of "wounded humanity," of a person compromised in his fundamental capacity to deal with his vulnerability.

How unique is the state of illness? Is not vulnerability a common condition in many other human situations? After all, the prisoner is deprived of freedom and civil rights; the poor and the socially outcast are constrained even in the most mundane matters of life; none of us is totally "free"; we must all conform to some set of social conventions. But in none of these situations is our capacity to deal with our vulnerability so impaired as in illness. We feel, usually, that we can cope with almost all of the other states of vulnerability if we have our "health." After all, we perceive health as a means toward freedom and other primary values. We ask only to be released from prison, given a job or money, and if we are healthy, we can rebuild our humanity and the integrity of our person. In illness, none of these things will help.

Our essential mechanisms for coping with all other existential exigencies are compromised; we face the threat of loss of life itself, or we are suddenly asked to live a life which appears not worth living.

There is, therefore, a special dimension of anguish in illness. That is why healing cannot be classified as a commodity, or as a service on a par with going to a mechanic to have one's car fixed, to a lawyer for repair of one's legal fences, or even to a teacher for repair of one's defects in knowledge. The teacher–student, lawyer–client, serviceman–customer relationships have some of the elements of the physician–patient relationship. There is in them an inequality of knowledge and skill, and one person seeks assistance from another who professes to provide it. What is different is the unique ontological assault of illness on the body–self unity, and the primacy of the freedom to deal with all other life situations which illness removed. Without denying the analogy with, let us say, the lawyer–client relationship, it would be difficult to argue that the degree of injury to our humanity and the kind of injury we suffer in litigation are identical in their existential consequences to being ill.

The Act of Profession

In the presence of a patient in the peculiar state of vulnerable humanity which is illness, the health professional makes a "profession." He or she "declares aloud" that he has special knowledge and skills, that he can heal, or help, and that he will do so in the patient's interest, not his own. According to the *Oxford English Dictionary*, the etymology of the word "profession"— from the verb *profiteri*, to declare aloud or publicly—is closer to the meaning of the act than more recent formulations. That is what entering a profession means—not simply becoming a member of a defined group with a common education, standards of performance, and a common ethic. These are all secondary conditions of the central act of profession, which is an active, conscious declaration, voluntarily entered into and signifying willingness to assume the obligations necessary to make the declaration authentic.

All health professionals make this act of profession publicly when they accept a degree at graduation, when they take the oath of their profession, and, most important, every time they present themselves to a patient in need who seeks their assistance in healing. They make the act of profession implicitly, but nonetheless undeniably. The expectation is thus induced in the ill person that the declaration will be true and authentic, that the professional's knowledge and skill are genuine, and that the professional's concern for the patient's interests will be truly exercised.

Medicine is, of course, not alone in making an act of profession which invites specific expectations of performance. Lawyers, teachers, and ministers similarly declare a special competence and its use in the interests of those who seek their aid. Their clients also lack something they need. Like the patient, they too are vulnerable to varying degrees. The ethics of each profession rests on the authenticity of its claim—the physician's claim to restore health, the lawyer's to seek justice, the teacher's to redress ignorance, and the minister's to teach the way of salvation.

The act of profession is a promise made to another person, who is in need and therefore existentially vulnerable. The relationship between the professional and those he or she serves is characterized by an inequality in which the professional holds the balance of power. All the usual ethical obligations of making and keeping promises apply, but with a difference—the inequality of power poses special obligations on the person who professes. The professional–client relationship is not simply a contract between equals in which each party can negotiate in his own interest, since one part is not free *not* to negotiate. Medicine, law, teaching, and the ministry do not supply products in the usual legal and commercial sense.

Each profession fulfills the promise inherent in its act of profession by a specific action which identifies that profession. This central act is the vehicle of authenticity and the bridge which joins the need of the one seeking help with the promise of the one professing to help. We can examine that central act only for medicine, though analogous analyses are applicable to other professions.

The Central Act of Medicine

A patient in need who consults a physician wants to know what is wrong, what can be done about it, and what should be done. . . . These three questions, and the subjects of questions which contribute to answering them, taken together constitute the anatomy of clinical judgment previously developed. The final question—what should be done?—is the major focus of the patient's attention and the end toward which the whole process must be directed. It eventuates in a recommended action. While all the other questions leading to it can be reopened, the recommended action is, once taken, irretrievable.

The end of medicine, formally considered, is therefore a right and good healing action taken in the interests of a particular patient. All the science and art of the physician converge on the choice: among the many things that can be done, that which should be done for this person in this particular situation of life. It is a choice of what is right in the sense of what conforms scientifically, logically, and technically to the patient's needs and a choice of what is good, what is "worthwhile" for this patient. The recommended action intermingles technical and moral dimensions which may not always be immediately reconcilable.

This culmination in a right and good healing action is what constitutes medicine qua medicine. Diagnosis and therapeutics singly and together serve this end. The physician acts as physician only when he particularizes the conclusions about what is wrong and what can be done in a decision about what ought to be, must be, may be, or should not be done for this patient, here and now.

The patient expects the end of medicine to be an action which is right and good for him. This is the promise he perceives in the act of profession, collectively from organized medicine, and singularly from his personal physician or physicians. It is what he expects also from medical and health organizations—the team, the hospital, or the agency.

The medical act combines technical and moral decision making in a way which makes it a moral enterprise of a special kind. Each medical decision involves the complicated interplay of several value sets—those of the physician, of the patient, and of society. In a pluralistic society, these value sets may differ sharply from each other. The possibilities of conflict in the conception of the good between physician and patient are many. A very special problem in medical decision making is how to resolve these conflicts in a morally defensible way.

For the conflicts of values occur in a relationship of inequality inherent in the vulnerability of the patient, as we have outlined it above. The assault of illness on the usual freedoms of the human being presents an immediate and present danger that the patient's values might be violated or that the physician may confuse technical with moral authority. The patient's moral agency is at risk, and a special obligation of the act of profession is to protect that moral agency while treating the patient.

By virtue of his act of profession, the physician raises specific expectations and thus voluntarily assumes certain specific obligations. It is these obligations, as well as those of the patient to the physician, which we shall examine next.

Obligations Arising from the Special Nature of the Patient–Physician Relationship

The obligations which arise from the construal of the patient–physician relationship outlined here could form the philosophical basis for a professional ethic—one which would bind the physician regardless of the position he might take on any of the specific moral dilemmas of medicine. A cursory examination of these obligations can illustrate the primacy of the acts of profession and medicine taken in the face of the fact of illness.

Let it be clear that no new moral principles need be elaborated. The well-adopted moral principles of truth telling and promise keeping, as well as the principles of no harm and vulnerability, will suffice, but modulated by those special existential circumstances which define the relationship of one needing to be healed confronting one professing to heal. The same principle would apply by analogy to the lawyer–client, teacher–student, minister–subject relationships, each modified by the specific expectations generated by the act of profession each makes when a patient or client is confronted seeking assistance.

To begin with, the act of medical profession is inauthentic and a lie unless it fulfills the expectation of technical competence. If the special knowledge upon which the act of profession is based is wanting, then the whole relationship begins with a lie. The decision may even fortuitously turn out to be the "right and good" one for the patient, but if it does, it is based on chance, not knowledge. The patient has been deceived into believing the advice he received is the fruit of the physician's competence. The far greater likelihood is that the incompetent physician will not make the right or good decision. Then he becomes worse than a quack. The latter at least follows a system which makes no claim to being scientific, while the incompetent physician enshrouds his ignorance in a mantle of science.

The moral obligation to be competent is a lifelong one and an affair of daily concern. It begins with a sound medical education and house staff training, and goes on to a dedication to continuing education, a willingness to subject his decisions to peer review, an openness to criticism by one's colleagues, a willingness to confess ignorance or error to the patient, and a concentrated and sustained effort to deepen one's clinical craftsmanship. Competence, then, is a moral imperative, and a clear statement of that fact together with its fullest implications should be an essential element in any professional code. Competence is explicitly required by the first four principles of the latest revision of the AMA code. It is equated therein with "scientific" medicine. Such a formulation is correctly applicable to the technical steps involved in diagnosis, prognosis, and therapeutics. It includes also the art and skill needed to perform the recommended procedures safely and with a minimum of discomfort.

But in the complex anatomy of clinical judgment, competence is a necessary, but not sufficient, condition of a moral medical transaction and an authentic act of profession. Competence must itself be shaped by the end of the medical act—a right and good healing action for a particular patient. Competence must be employed in the best interest of the patient, and wherever possible that interest must conform with the patient's values and sense of what it is to be healthy.

Technically correct conclusions may not necessarily be in the patient's best interest when that interest is defined in the patient's terms, for example, abortion for a Catholic, transfusion for a Jehovah's Witness, prolonging life in someone prepared to die, or "letting" another die who wants to live what may seem to the physician an unsatisfying life. A scientifically correct medical conclusion, its "oughtness," can

range from "must," "should," "may," "need not," or "must not," depending upon the interacting moral agencies of patient and physician.

The physician has a special moral obligation to assure and facilitate the patient's moral agency, especially in the light of the patient's special vulnerability. To assure a fully participatory moral agency, the physician must repair to the extent possible the wounded humanity and state of inequality of the sick person. He does so only in part by curing, or containing, illness or relieving pain and anxiety. These must be complemented by disclosure of the information necessary for valid choice and genuine consent and by guarding against manipulation of choice and consent to accommodate to the physician's personal or social philosophy of the good life.

A first requirement, therefore, is to remedy the patient's information deficit as completely as possible. Information must be clear and understandable and in the patient's language. He must know the nature of his illness, its prognosis, the alternative modes of treatment, their probable effectiveness, cost, discomfort, side effects, and the quality of life they may yield. Disclosure must include degrees of ignorance as well as knowledge and the physician's own limitations.

The physician who is conscious of the special nature of his act of profession will not easily excuse himself from the obligation of disclosure on the grounds that the patient cannot understand or will be harmed by the information. There are few, if any, evidences that such knowledge is deleterious, the Hippocratic warnings to the contrary. Indeed, in those rare instances where the matter has been studied, informed patients show a lower anxiety and complication rate than the uninformed.

Reducing the inequality in information between patient and physician is essential in obtaining a morally valid consent which is the vehicle for expression of the patient's moral agency. More is required than the minimal conditions of a legally valid consent, which is, after all, guarantee against the grosser violations of the patient's right to decide. A morally valid consent moves closer to the realization of both senses of the word " con-sent" (Latin: *consentire*), to feel and to know something together. Patient and physician, therefore, must each feel he knows and understands the available facts, and each must feel he is truly part of the decision making.

When the patient cannot participate in the decision, the physician must deal with the patient's surrogate—the family, guardian, or the court. The obligations to respect the patient's value system are the same. When dealing with surrogates, however, an additional obligation is imposed, and that is to be sure that they do in fact have the patient's interests at heart. In the case of the unconscious patient or the child, the physician must assure himself that the surrogate, parent or family, does not unconsciously wish the patient's demise.

This state of feeling and knowing together places the actual locus of decision making somewhere between physician and patient, and not really with one or the other. As in any relationship between humans, medical or otherwise, obtaining consent requires persuasion, a mutual accommodation of wills. It is extremely difficult to set limits on the degree to which manipulation of consent is morally permissible. It is important for this essay only to indicate that the physician must be alert to those subtle choices of words, nuances of emphasis, or body language which tip the patient's consent in the direction of what the physician feels is "good." It is unrealistic to expect even the most ethically sensitive physician not to wish the patient would make certain choices. In some cases some degree of persuasion may even be ethically obligatory.

No set of rules could encompass all the subtle complexities of even the most ordinary relationship between two persons, much less the special dimensions peculiar to the medical transaction in which one person in special need seeks the assistance of another who professes to help. The morality of clinical judgment goes well beyond the merely technical and scientific probity of the craft.

There are times when the physician can and should exert moral agency for the patient and make the value choice in his behalf. One instance would be when the patient or family request him to do so even after the physician has attempted to provide the necessary information and has taken all pains to be clear and unequivocal about the choices. Some patients and families are either emotionally or educationally ill-equipped to deal with such difficult decisions. They may then ask the physician to "decide." The physician then has a mandate to assume moral agency, and it would be a failure of the authenticity of his act of profession not to say what should be done. The same applies when the situation is of such an urgent nature that to consult the patient or even his or her family would be impossible or would delay emergency treatment. In the operating and emergency rooms, the intensive-care and coronary-care units, the obligations we have stressed must be drastically modified because the patient's interest itself overrides even these fundamental requirements of medical morality. The retrospective examination of how, for what reasons, and according to what value sets the decisions were made is an essential antidote to overzealous assumption of moral authority even in emergency situations.

Here, too, a caveat is in order. For the physician to say simply that he would treat the patient as he would treat himself or a member of his family is morally unsound. This misinterpretation of the golden rule would only reopen the possibiity of overriding the patient's wishes. The golden rule in medical decisions is to be observed rather differently: We should so act that we accord the patient the same opportunity to express or actualize his own view of what he considers worthwhile as we would desire for ourselves. This latter interpretation of the golden rule is fully consistent with the view of authenticity of the act of profession we have developed in this essay.

What obligations of this type require is a combination of conscious advertence to the meanings of the three elements—the fact of illness, the act of profession, and the act of medicine—with compassion. We do not think this has to involve the *iatrike philia,* the love of which Pedro Lain-Entralgo speaks as the fundamental link in his superb phenomenological study of the physician–patient relationship. It does require the capacity to "feel with" the patient something of the existential situation he is experiencing in the condition of illness, whether it is somatic or physical in origin. Not to be able to feel something of the patient's anguish and anxiety before the ontological assault of illness is to rely on only a rational adumbration of the obligations which inhere in the act of profession. But even this is superior to the more traditional conception of the physician as benevolent agent of both technical and moral decision making who decides what is "best" for the patient.

Many aspects of the physician's obligations which could be derived from the philosophy of the medical transaction proposed here have not been touched upon. Those chosen are meant to be illustrative, and not comprehensive. We have not discussed, for example, how to resolve conflicts in values between physician and patient, between the physician's social and patient responsibilities, the obligations of the profession as a corporate whole, or the applicability of these principles when the physician functions in a collectivity as a member of a team, or an institution.

Also, on this view, there is a set of obligations which would bind the patient so that we can begin to develop an ethics of the "good" patient. If the physician construes his act of profession as a promise of a special kind given under special conditions, and if the patient understands it that way, then the patient incurs certain obligations as well. He must be truthful in the information he gives the physician; he must avoid manipulating the physician in consent; he must follow recommendations mutually agreed upon faithfully; he must educate himself sufficiently to comprehend the facts disclosed to him, and take the trouble to be sure he does understand; he must not consult another physician without informing his medical attendant unless he suspects dishonesty or malpractice. Further, he is partially obligated, by the fact that he is a member of the human race, to participate in reasonable experiments which are either aimed at healing his disease (therapeutic) or at discovering possible cures for this disease for others (nontherapeutic), provided the other rules for professional behavior are followed. We say "partially obligated" because the vulnerability of the patient excuses him from any absolute obligation.

The principle of autonomy and the principle of partial obligation enunciated above represent almost a classic example of the possible clash between two goods. On the one hand, the person who is ill is clearly given the opportunity and the freedom to attend to his needs for healing, a value which takes precedence over any altruism to be demanded of him. However, the ill person is also a member of the human race and has obligations to help foster the understanding of the disease so that either he or others might benefit.

The patient, in short, in the relationship we have described, owes the physician the same respect for his values and cannot demand that the physician violate them even when the patient might benefit. The patient cannot ask his physician to practice deception with insurance companies and governmental agencies. In sum, even though the vulnerability imposed by illness makes the patient more vulnerable, the tyranny of the patient is as wrong as the tyranny of the physician.

This construal of the patient–physician relationship calls, therefore, for mutual respect and compassion, even though it involves one person who is less free and more vulnerable. That is why the relationship cannot be regarded as a contract or even a covenant. It is not an agreement between two parties more or less equal, more of less free, who can negotiate terms for the delivery of some service or commodity. Medical care is not a commodity one may choose as freely as one chooses automobiles or television sets.

What we propose is a mutually binding set of obligations, predicated upon a special kind of human interaction and deriving its morality from the empirical realities in the relationship which specify it among human relationships. These specifications could be the basis for a philosophically justifiable statement of principles—a code—common to all physicians, indeed to all healers. If their implications are expanded, we can even hope for a more general code applicable to all the health professions at least in part since all health professionals make an act of profession in the sense we have defined it here.

The post-Hippocratic reconstruction of professional ethics is therefore possible. We need not return to the ethics of the good craftsman, as in our Greek beginnings. We can instead extend and build upon the idea of Scribonius Largus and Panaetius that there is an ethic specific to each profession, based in the nature of that profession, and philosophically justifiable.

LAWYERS AS PROFESSIONALS: SOME MORAL ISSUES

Richard A. Wasserstrom

Lawyers are often accused of treating their clients and the rest of society in ways that are either immoral or amoral. In evaluating these accusations, Wasserstrom carefully considers a number of arguments for and against the existence of special ethical roles for professionals in general, and for lawyers in particular. He urges that, rather than accepting special ethical roles that result in less-than-humane practice, we seriously consider cautious moves toward deprofessionalization.

In this [selection] I examine two moral criticisms of lawyers which, if well-founded, are fundamental. Neither is new but each appears to apply with particular force today. Both tend to be made by those not in the mainstream of the legal profession and to be rejected by those who are in it. Both in some sense concern the lawyer–client relationship.

The first criticism centers around the lawyer's stance toward the world at large. The accusation is that the lawyer–client relationship renders the lawyer at best systematically amoral and at worst more than occasionally immoral in his or her dealings with the rest of mankind.

The second criticism focuses upon the relationship between the lawyer and the client. Here the charge is that it is the lawyer–client relationship which is morally objectionable because it is a relationship in which the lawyer dominates and in which the lawyer typically, and perhaps inevitably, treats the client in both an impersonal and paternalistic fashion.

To a considerable degree these two criticisms of lawyers derive, I believe, from the fact that the lawyer is a professional. And

From Richard A. Wasserstrom, "Lawyers as Professionals: Some Moral Issues," *Human Rights,* vol. 5, no. 1 (1975), 1–24. Reprinted by permission.

to the extent to which this is the case, the more generic problems I will be exploring are those of professionalism generally. But in some respects, the lawyer's situation is different from that of other professionals. The lawyer is vulnerable to some moral criticism that does not as readily or as easily attach to any other professional. And this, too, is an issue that I shall be examining.[1]

Although I am undecided about the ultimate merits of either criticism, I am convinced that each is deserving of careful articulation and assessment, and that each contains insights that deserve more ac-

[1] Because of the significance for my analysis of the closely related concepts of a profession and a professional, it will be helpful to indicate at the outset what I take to be the central features of a profession.

But first there is an ambiguity that must be noted so that it can be dismissed. There is one sense of "professional" and hence of "profession" with which I am not concerned. That is the sense in which there are in our culture, professional athletes, professional actors, and professional beauticians. In this sense, a person who possesses sufficient skill to engage in an activity for money and who elects to do so is a professional rather than, say, an amateur or a volunteer. This is, as I have said, not the sense of "profession" in which I am interested.

I am interested, instead, in the characteristics of professions such as law, or medicine. There are, I think, at least six that are worth noting.

(1) The professions require a substantial period of formal education—at least as much if not more than that required by any other occupation.

(2) The professions require the comprehension of a substantial amount of theoretical knowledge and the utilization of a substantial amount of intellectual ability. Neither manual nor creative ability is typically demanded. This is one thing that distinguishes the professions both from highly skilled crafts—like glassblowing—and from the arts.

(3) The professions are both an economic monopoly and largely self-regulating. Not only is the practice of the profession restricted to those who are certified as possessing the requisite competencies, but the questions of what competencies are required and who possesses them are questions that are left to the members of the profession to decide for themselves.

(4) The professions are clearly among the occupations that possess the greatest social prestige in the society. They also typically provide a degree of material affluence substantially greater than that enjoyed by most working persons.

(5) The professions are almost always involved with matters which from time to time are among the greatest personal concerns that humans have: physical health, psychic well-being, liberty, and the like. As a result, persons who seek the services of a professional are often in a state of appreciable concern, if not vulnerability, when they do so.

(6) The professions almost always involve at their core a significant interpersonal relationship between the professional, on the one hand, and the person who is thought to require the professional's services: the patient or the client.

knowledgment than they often receive. My ambition is, therefore, more to exhibit the relevant considerations and to stimulate additional reflection, than it is to provide any very definite conclusions.

I

As I have indicated, the first issue I propose to examine concerns the ways the professional–client relationship affects the professional's stance toward the world at large. The primary question that is presented is whether there is adequate justification for the kind of moral universe that comes to be inhabited by the lawyer as he or she goes through professional life. For at best the lawyer's world is a simplified moral world; often it is an amoral one; and more than occasionally, perhaps, an overtly immoral one. . . .

As I have already noted, one central feature of the professions in general and of law in particular is that there is a special, complicated relationship between the professional, and the client or patient. For each of the parties in this relationship, but especially for the professional, the behavior that is involved is, to a very significant degree, what I call role-differentiated behavior. And this is significant because it is the nature of role-differentiated behavior that it often makes it both appropriate and desirable for the person in a particular role to put to one side considerations of various sorts—and especially various moral considerations—that would otherwise be relevant if not decisive. Some illustrations will help to make clear what I mean both by role-differentiated behavior and by the way role-differentiated behavior often alters, if not eliminates, the significance of those moral considerations that would obtain, were it not for the presence of the role.

Being a parent is, in probably every human culture, to be involved in role-differentiated behavior. In our own culture, and once again in most, if not all, human cultures, as a parent one is entitled, if not obligated, to prefer the interests of one's own children over those of children generally. That is to say, it is regarded as appropriate for a parent to allocate excessive goods to his or her own children, even though other children may have substantially more pressing and genuine needs for these same items. If one were trying to decide what the right way was to distribute assets among a group of children all of whom were strangers to oneself, the relevant moral considerations would be very different from those that would be thought to obtain once one's own children were in the picture. In the role of a parent, the claims of other children vis-à-vis one's own are, if not rendered morally irrelevant, certainly rendered less morally significant. In short, the role-differentiated character of the situation alters the relevant moral point of view enormously.

A similar situation is presented by the case of the scientist. For a number of years there has been debate and controversy within the scientific community over the question of whether scientists should participate in the development and elaboration of atomic theory, especially as those theoretical advances could then be translated into development of atomic weapons that would become a part of the arsenal of existing nation states. The dominant view, although it was not the unanimous one, in the scientific community was that the role of the scientist was to expand the limits of human knowledge. Atomic power was a force which had previously not been utilizable by human beings. The job of the scientist was, among other things, to develop ways and means by which that could now be done. And it was simply no part of one's role as a scientist to forego inquiry, or divert one's scientific explorations because of the fact that the fruits of the investigation could be or would be put to improper, immoral, or even catastrophic uses. The moral issues concerning whether and when to develop and use nuclear weapons were to be decided by others; by citizens and statesment; they were not the concern of the scientist *qua* scientist.

In both of these cases it is, of course, conceivable that plausible and even thoroughly convincing arguments exist for the desirability of the role-differentiated behavior and its attendant neglect of what would otherwise be morally relevant considerations. Nonetheless, it is, I believe, also the case that the burden of proof, so to speak, is always upon the proponent of the desirability of this kind of role-differentiated behavior. For in the absence of special reasons why parents ought to prefer the interests of their children over those of children in general, the moral point of view surely requires that the claims and needs of all children receive equal consideration. But we take the rightness of parental preference so for granted, that we often neglect, I think, the fact that it is anything but self-evidently morally appropriate. My own view, for example, is that careful reflection shows that the *degree* of parental preference systematically encouraged in our own culture is far too extensive to be morally justified.

All of this is significant just because to be a professional is to be enmeshed in role-differentiated behavior of precisely this sort. One's role as a doctor, psychiatrist, or lawyer alters one's moral universe in a fashion analogous to that described above. Of special significance here is the fact that the professional *qua* professional has a client or patient whose interests must be represented, attended to, or looked after by the professional. And that means that the role of the professional (like that of the parent) is to prefer in a variety of ways the interests of the client or patient over those of individuals generally.

Consider, more specifically, the role-differentiated behavior of the lawyer. Conventional wisdom has it that where the attorney–client relationship exists, the point of view of the attorney is properly different—and appreciably so—from that which would be appropriate in the absence of the attorney–client relationship. For where the attorney–client relationship exists, it is often appropriate and many times even obligatory for the attorney to do things that, all other things being equal, an ordinary person need not, and should not, do. What is characteristic of this role of a lawyer is the lawyer's required indifference to a wide variety of ends and consequences that in other contexts would be of undeniable moral significance. Once a lawyer represents a client, the lawyer has a duty to make his or her expertise fully available in the realization of the end sought by the client, irrespective, for the most part, of the moral worth to which the end will be put or the character of the client who seeks to utilize it. Provided that the end sought is not illegal, the lawyer is, in essence, an amoral technician whose peculiar skills and knowledge in respect to the law are available to those with whom the relationship of client is established. The question, as I have indicated, is whether this particular and pervasive feature of professionalism is itself justifiable. At a minimum, I do not think any of the typical, simple answers will suffice.

One such answer focuses upon and generalizes from the criminal defense lawyer. For what is probably the most familiar aspect of this role-differentiated character of the lawyer's activity is that of the defense of a client charged with a crime. The received view within the profession (and to a lesser degree within the society at large) is that having once agreed to represent the client, the lawyer is under an obligation to do his or her best to defend that person at trial, irrespective, for instance, even of the lawyer's belief in the client's innocence. There are limits, of course, to what constitutes a defense: A lawyer cannot bribe or intimidate witnesses to increase the likelihood of securing an acquittal. And there are legitimate questions, in close cases, about how those limits are to be delineated. But, however these matters get resolved, it is at least clear that it is thought both

appropriate and obligatory for the attorney to put on as vigorous and persuasive a defense of a client believed to be guilty as would have been mounted by the lawyer thoroughly convinced of the client's innocence. I suspect that many persons find this an attractive and admirable feature of the life of a legal professional. I know that often I do. The justifications are varied and, as I shall argue below, probably convincing.

But part of the difficulty is that the irrelevance of the guilt or innocence of an accused client by no means exhausts the altered perspective of the lawyer's conscience, even in criminal cases. For in the course of defending an accused, an attorney may have, as a part of his or her duty of representation, the obligation to invoke procedures and practices which are themselves morally objectionable and of which the lawyer in other contexts might thoroughly disapprove. And these situations, I think, are somewhat less comfortable to confront. For example, in California, the case law permits a defendant in a rape case to secure in some circumstances an order from the court requiring the complaining witness, that is the rape victim, to submit to a psychiatric examination before trial.[2] For no other crime is such a pretrial remedy available. In no other case can the victim of a crime be required to undergo psychiatric examination at the request of the defendant on the ground that the results of the examination may help the defendant prove that the offense did not take place. I think such a rule is wrong and is reflective of the sexist bias of the law in respect to rape. I certainly do not think it right that rape victims should be singled out by the law for this kind of special pretrial treatment, and I am skeptical about the morality of any involuntary psychiatric examination of witnesses. Nonetheless, it appears to be part of the role-differentiated

---

[2] *Ballard v. Superior Court*, 64 Cal. 2d 159, 410 P.2d 838, 49 *Cal. Rptr.* 302 (1966).

obligation of a lawyer for a defendant charged with rape to seek to take advantage of this particular rule of law—irrespective of the independent moral view he or she may have of the rightness or wrongness of such a rule.

Nor, it is important to point out, is this peculiar, strikingly amoral behavior limited to the lawyer involved with the workings of the criminal law. Most clients come to lawyers to get the lawyers to help them do things that they could not easily do without the assistance provided by the lawyer's special competence. They wish, for instance, to dispose of their property in a certain way at death. They wish to contract for the purchase or sale of a house or a business. They wish to set up a corporation which will manufacture and market a new product. They wish to minimize their income taxes. And so on. In each case, they need the assistance of the professional, the lawyer, for he or she alone has the special skill which will make it possible for the client to achieve the desired result.

And in each case, the role-differentiated character of the lawyer's way of being tends to render irrelevant what would otherwise be morally relevant considerations. Suppose that a client desires to make a will disinheriting her children because they opposed the war in Vietnam. Should the lawyer refuse to draft the will because the lawyer thinks this a bad reason to disinherit one's children? Suppose a client can avoid the payment of taxes through a loophole only available to a few wealthy taxpayers. Should the lawyer refuse to tell the client of a loophole because the lawyer thinks it an unfair advantage for the rich? Suppose a client wants to start a corporation that will manufacture, distribute and promote a harmful but not illegal substance, e.g., cigarettes. Should the lawyer refuse to prepare the articles of incorporation for the corporation? In each case, the accepted view within the profession is that these matters are just of no concern to the lawyer *qua* lawyer. The lawyer need not of course

agree to represent the client (and that is equally true for the unpopular client accused of a heinous crime), but there is nothing wrong with representing a client whose aims and purposes are quite immoral. And having agreed to do so, the lawyer is required to provide the best possible assistance, without regard to his or her disapproval of the objective that is sought.

The lesson, on this view, is clear. The job of the lawyer, so the argument typically concludes, is not to approve or disapprove of the character of his or her client, the cause for which the client seeks the lawyer's assistance, or the avenues provided by the law to achieve that which the client wants to accomplish. The lawyer's task is, instead, to provide that competence which the client lacks and the lawyer, as professional, possesses. In this way, the lawyer as professional comes to inhabit a simplified universe which is strikingly amoral—which regards as morally irrelevant any number of factors which nonprofessional citizens might take to be important, if not decisive, in their everyday lives. . . .

One difficulty in even thinking about all of this is that lawyers may not be very objective or detached in their attempts to work the problem through. For one feature of this simplified, intellectual world is that it is often a very comfortable one to inhabit. . . .

But there is, of course, also an argument which seeks to demonstrate that it is good and not merely comfortable for lawyers to behave this way.

It is good, so the argument goes, that the lawyer's behavior and concomitant point of view are role-differentiated because the lawyer *qua* lawyer participates in a complex institution which functions well only if the individuals adhere to their institutional roles.

For example, when there is a conflict between individuals, or between the state and an individual, there is a well-established institutional mechanism by which to get that dispute resolved. That mechanism is the trial in which each side is represented by a lawyer whose job it is both to present his or her client's case in the most attractive, forceful light and to seek to expose the weaknesses and defects in the case of the opponent.

When an individual is charged with having committed a crime, the trial is the mechanism by which we determine in our society whether or not the person is in fact guilty. Just imagine what would happen if lawyers were to refuse, for instance, to represent persons whom they thought to be guilty. In a case where the guilt of a person seemed clear, it might turn out that some individuals would be deprived completely of the opportunity to have the system determine whether or not they are in fact guilty. The private judgment of individual lawyers would in effect be substituted for the public, institutional judgment of the judge and jury. The amorality of lawyers helps to guarantee that every criminal defendant will have his or her day in court.

In addition, of course, appearances can be deceiving. Persons who appear before trial to be clearly guilty do sometimes turn out to be innocent. Even persons who confess their guilt to their attorney occasionally turn out to have lied or to have been mistaken. The adversary system, so this argument continues, is simply a better method than any other that has been established by which to determine the legally relevant facts in any given case. It is certainly a better method than the exercise of private judgment by any particular individual. And the adversary system only works if each party to the controversy has a lawyer, a person whose institutional role it is to argue, plead and present the merits of his or her case and the demerits of the opponent's. Thus if the adversary system is to work, it is necessary that there be lawyers who will play their appropriate, professional, institutional role of representative of the client's cause.

Nor is the amorality of the institutional role of the lawyer restricted to the defense of those accused of crimes. As was indicated earlier, when the lawyer functions in his most usual role, he or she functions as a counselor, as a professional whose task it is to help people realize those objectives and ends that the law permits them to obtain and which cannot be obtained without the attorney's special competence in the law. The attorney may think it wrong to disinherit one's children because of their views about the Vietnam war, but the attorney's complaint is really with the laws of inheritance and not with his or her client. The attorney may think the tax provision an unfair, unjustifiable loophole, but once more the complaint is really with the Internal Revenue Code and not with the client who seeks to take advantage of it. And these matters, too, lie beyond the ambit of the lawyer's moral point of view as institutional counselor and facilitator. If lawyers were to substitute their own private views of what ought to be legally permissible and impermissible for those of the legislature, this would constitute a surreptitious and undesirable shift from a democracy to an oligarchy of lawyers. For given the fact that lawyers are needed to effectuate the wishes of clients, the lawyer ought to make his or her skills available to those who seek them without regard for the particular objectives of the client. . . .

While not wholly convinced by a response such as the above, I am prepared to accept it because the issue at hand seems to me to be a deeper one. . . .

As I indicated earlier, I do believe that the amoral behavior of the *criminal* defense lawyer is justifiable. But I think that justification depends at least as much upon the special needs of an accused as upon any more general defense of a lawyer's role-differentiated behavior. As a matter of fact I think it likely that many persons such as myself have been misled by the special features of the criminal case. Because a deprivation of liberty is so serious, because the prosecutorial resources of the state are so vast, and because, perhaps, of a serious skepticism about the rightness of punishment even where wrongdoing has occurred, it is easy to accept the view that it makes sense to charge the defense counsel with the job of making the best possible case for the accused—without regard, so to speak, for the merits. This coupled with the fact that it is an adversarial proceeding succeeds, I think, in justifying the amorality of the criminal defense counsel. But this does not, however, justify a comparable perspective on the part of lawyers generally. Once we leave the peculiar situation of the criminal defense lawyer, I think it quite likely that the role-differentiated morality of the lawyer is almost certainly excessive and at times inappropriate. That is to say, this special case to one side, I am inclined to think that we might all be better served if lawyers were to see themselves less as subject to role-differentiated behavior and more as subject to the demands of the moral point of view. In this sense it may be that we need a good deal less rather than more professionalism in our society generally and among lawyers in particular.

Moreover, even if I am wrong about all this, four things do seem to me to be true and important.

First, all of the arguments that support the role-differentiated amorality of the lawyer on institutional grounds can succeed only if the enormous degree of trust and confidence in the institutions themselves is itself justified. If the institutions work well and fairly, there may be good sense to deferring important moral concerns and criticisms to another time and place, to the level of institutional criticism and assessment. But the less certain we are entitled to be of either the rightness or the self-corrective nature of the larger institutions of which the professional is a part, the less apparent it is that we should encourage the professional to avoid direct engagement with the moral issues as they arise.

And we are, today, I believe, certainly entitled to be quite skeptical both of the fairness and of the capacity for self-correction of our larger institutional mechanisms, including the legal system. To the degree to which the institutional rules and practices are unjust, unwise or undesirable, to that same degree is the case for the role-differentiated behavior of the lawyer weakened if not destroyed.

Second, it is clear that there are definite character traits that the professional such as the lawyer must take on if the system is to work. What is less clear is that they are admirable ones. Even if the role-differentiated amorality of the professional lawyer is justified by the virtues of the adversary system, this also means that the lawyer *qua* lawyer will be encouraged to be competitive rather than cooperative; aggressive rather than accommodating; ruthless rather than compassionate; and pragmatic rather than principled. This is, I think, part of the logic of the role-differentiated behavior of lawyers in particular, and to a lesser degree of professionals in general. It is surely neither accidental nor unimportant that these are the same character traits that are emphasized and valued by the capitalist ethic—and on precisely analogous grounds. Because the ideals of professionalism and capitalism are the dominant ones within our culture, it is harder than most of us suspect even to take seriously the suggestion that radically different styles of living, kinds of occupational outlooks, and types of social institutions might be possible, let alone preferable.

Third, there is a special feature of the role-differentiated behavior of the lawyer that distinguishes it from the comparable behavior of other professionals. What I have in mind can be brought out through the following question: Why is it that it seems far less plausible to talk critically about the amorality of the doctor, for instance, who treats all patients irrespective of their moral character than it does to talk critically about the comparable amorality of the lawyer? Why is it that it seems so obviously sensible, simple and right for the doctor's behavior to be narrowly and rigidly role-differentiated, *i.e.,* just to try to cure those who are ill? And why is it that at the very least it seems so complicated, uncertain, and troublesome to decide whether it is right for the lawyer's behavior to be similarly role-differentiated?

The answer, I think, is twofold. To begin with (and this I think is the less interesting point) it is, so to speak, intrinsically good to try to cure disease, but in no comparable way is it intrinsically good to try to win every lawsuit or help every client realize his or her objective. In addition (and this I take to be the truly interesting point), the lawyer's behavior is different in kind from the doctor's. The lawyer—and especially the lawyer as advocate—directly says and affirms things. The lawyer makes the case for the client. He or she tries to explain, persuade and convince others that the client's cause should prevail. The lawyer lives with and within a dilemma that is not shared by other professionals. If the lawyer actually believes everything that he or she asserts on behalf of the client, then it appears to be proper to regard the lawyer as in fact embracing and endorsing the points of view that he or she articulates. If the lawyer does not in fact believe what is urged by way of argument, if the lawyer is only playing a role, then it appears to be proper to tax the lawyer with hypocrisy and insincerity. To be sure, actors in a play take on roles and say things that the characters, not the actors, believe. But we know it is a play and that they are actors. The law courts are not, however, theaters, and the lawyers both talk about justice and they genuinely seek to persuade. The fact that the lawyer's words, thoughts, and convictions are, apparently, for sale and at the service of the client helps us, I think, to understand the peculiar hostility which is more than occasionally uniquely directed by lay persons toward lawyers. The verbal,

role-differentiated behavior of the lawyer *qua* advocate puts the lawyer's integrity into question in a way that distinguishes the lawyer from the other professionals.[3]

Fourth, and related closely to the three points just discussed, even if on balance the role-differentiated character of the lawyer's way of thinking and acting is ultimately deemed to be justifiable within the system on systemic instrumental grounds, it still remains the case that we do pay a social price for that way of thought and action. For to become and to be a professional, such as a lawyer, is to incorporate within oneself ways of behaving and ways of thinking that shape the whole person. It is especially hard, if not impossible, because of the nature of the professions, for one's professional way of thinking not to dominate one's entire adult life. . . .

The nature of the professions—the lengthy educational preparation, the prestige and economic rewards, and the concomitant enhanced sense of self—makes the role of professional a difficult one to shed even in those obvious situations in which that role is neither required nor appropriate. In important respects, one's professional role becomes and is one's dominant role, so that for many persons at least they become their professional being. This is at a minimum a heavy price to pay for the professions as we know them in our culture, and especially so for lawyers. Whether it is an inevitable price is, I think, an open question, largely because the problem has not begun to be fully perceived as such by the professionals in general, the legal profession in particular, or by the educational institutions that train professionals.

II

The role-differentiated behavior of the professional also lies at the heart of the second of the two moral issues I want to

---

[3] I owe this insight, which I think is an important and seldom appreciated one, to Leon Letwin.

discuss, namely, the character of the interpersonal relationship that exists between the lawyer and the client. As I indicated at the outset, the charge that I want to examine here is that the relationship between the lawyer and the client is typically, if not inevitably, a morally defective one in which the client is not treated with the respect and dignity that he or she deserves. . . .

One way to begin to explore the problem is to see that one pervasive, and I think necessary, feature of the relationship between any professional and the client or patient is that it is in some sense a relationship of inequality. This relationship of inequality is intrinsic to the existence of professionalism. For the professional is, in some respects at least, always in a position of dominance vis-à-vis the client, and the client in a position of dependence vis-à-vis the professional. To be sure, the client can often decide whether or not to enter into a relationship with a professional. And often, too, the client has the power to decide whether to terminate the relationship. But the significant thing I want to focus upon is that while the relationship exists, there are important respects in which the relationship cannot be a relationship between equals and must be one in which it is the professional who is in control. As I have said, I believe this is a necessary and not merely a familiar characteristic of the relationship between professionals and those they serve. Its existence is brought about by the following features.

To begin with, there is the fact that one characteristic of professions is that the professional is the possessor of expert knowledge of a sort not readily or easily attainable by members of the community at large. Hence, in the most straightforward of all senses the client, typically, is dependent upon the professional's skill or knowledge because the client does not possess the same knowledge.

Moreover, virtually every profession has its own technical language, a private terminology which can only be fully understood by the members of the profession. The presence of such a language plays the dual role of creating and affirming the membership of the professionals within the profession and of preventing the client from fully discussing or understanding his or her concerns in the language of the profession.

These circumstances, together with others, produce the added consequence that the client is in a poor position effectively to evaluate how well or badly the professional performs. In the professions, the professional does not look primarily to the client to evaluate the professional's work. The assessment of ongoing professional competence is something that is largely a matter of self-assessment conducted by the practising professional. Where external assessment does occur, it is carried out not by clients or patients but by other members of the profession, themselves. It is significant, and surely surprising to the outsider, to discover to what degree the professions are self-regulating. They control who shall be admitted to the professions and they determine (typically only if there has been a serious complaint) whether the members of the profession are performing in a minimally satisfactory way. This leads professionals to have a powerful motive to be far more concerned with the way they are viewed by their colleagues than with the way they are viewed by their clients. This means, too, that clients will necessarily lack the power to make effective evaluations and criticisms of the way the professional is responding to the client's needs.

In addition, because the matters for which professional assistance is sought usually involve things of great personal concern to the client, it is the received wisdom within the professions that the client lacks the perspective necessary to pursue in a satisfactory way his or her own best interests, and that the client requires a detached, disinterested representative to look after his or her interests. That is to say, even if the client had the same knowledge or competence that the professional had, the client would be thought to lack the objectivity required to utilize that competency effectively on his or her own behalf.

Finally, as I have indicated, to be a professional is to have been acculturated in a certain way. It is to have satisfactorily passed through a lengthy and allegedly difficult period of study and training. It is to have done something hard. Something that not everyone can do. Almost all professions encourage this way of viewing oneself; as having joined an elect group by virtue of hard work and mastery of the mysteries of the profession. In addition, the society at large treats members of a profession as members of an elite by paying them more than most people for the work they do with their heads rather than their hands, and by according them a substantial amount of social prestige and power by virtue of their membership in a profession. It is hard, I think, if not impossible, for a person to emerge from professional training and participate in a profession without the belief that he or she is a special kind of person, both different from and somewhat better than those nonprofessional members of the social order. It is equally hard for the other members of society not to hold an analogous view of the professionals. And these beliefs surely contribute, too, to the dominant role played by a professional in any professional–client relationship.

If the foregoing analysis is correct, then one question that is raised is whether it is a proper and serious criticism of the professions that the relationship between the professional and the client is an inherently unequal one in this sense.

One possible response would be to reject the view that all relationships of inequality (in this sense of inequality) are in fact undesirable. Such a response might claim, for example, that there is nothing at all wrong with inequality in relationships as long as the inequality is consensually imposed. Or, it may be argued, this kind of inequality is wholly unobjectionable because it is fitting, desired, or necessary in the circumstances. And, finally, it may be urged, whatever undesirability does attach to relationships by virtue of their lack of equality is outweighed by the benefits of role-differentiated relationships.

Another possible response would be to maintain that all human relationships of inequality (again in this sense of inequality) are for that reason alone objectionable on moral grounds—any time two or more persons are in a relationship in which power is not shared equally, the relationship is on that ground appropriately to be condemned. This criticism would solve the problem by abolishing the professions.

A third possible response, and the one that I want to consider in some detail, is a more sophisticated variant of the second response. It might begin by conceding, at least for purposes of argument, that some inequality may be inevitable in any professional–client relationship. It might concede, too, that a measure of this kind of inequality may even on occasion be desirable. But it sees the relationship between the professional and the client as typically flawed in a more fundamental way, as involving far more than the kind of relatively benign inequality delineated above. This criticism focuses upon the fact that the professional often, if not systematically, interacts with the client in both a manipulative and a paternalistic fashion. The point is not that the professional is merely dominant within the relationship. Rather, it is that from the professional's point of view the client is seen and responded to more like an object than a human being, and more like a child than an adult. The professional does not, in short, treat the client like a person; the professional does not accord the client the respect that he or she deserves. And these, it is claimed, are without question genuine moral defects in any meaningful human relationship. They are, moreover, defects that are capable of being eradicated once their cause is per-

ceived and corrective action taken. The solution, so the argument goes, is to "de-professionalize" the professions: not do away with the professions entirely, but weaken or eliminate those features of professionalism that produce these kinds of defective, interpersonal relationships.
. . .

Now one can, I think, respond to the foregoing in a variety of ways. One could, to begin with, insist that the paternalistic and impersonal ways of behaving are the aberrant rather than the usual characteristics of the lawyer–client relationship. One could, therefore, argue that a minor adjustment in better legal education aimed at sensitizing prospective lawyers to the possibility of these abuses is all that is required to prevent them. Or, one could, to take the same tack described earlier, regard these features of the lawyer–client relationship as endemic but not as especially serious. One might have a view that, at least in moderation, relationships having these features are a very reasonable price to pay (if it is a price at all) for the very appreciable benefits of professionalism. The impersonality of a surgeon, for example, may make it easier rather than harder for him or for her to do a good job of operating successfully on a patient. The impersonality of a lawyer may make it easier rather than harder for him or for her to do a good job of representing a client. The paternalism of lawyers may be justified by the fact that they do in fact know better— at least within many areas of common concern to the parties involved—what is best for the client. And, it might even be claimed, clients want to be treated in this way.

But if these answers do not satisfy, if one believes that these are typical, if not systemic, features of the professional character of the lawyer–client relationship, and if one believes, as well, that these are morally objectionable features of that or any other relationship among persons, it does look as though one way to proceed is to "deprofessionalize" the law—to weaken, if not excise, those features of legal professionalism that tend to produce these kinds of interpersonal relationships.

The issue seems to me difficult just because I do think that there are important and distinctive competencies that are at the heart of the legal profession. If there were not, the solution would be simple. If there were no such competencies—if, that is, lawyers didn't really help people any more than (so it is sometimes claimed) therapists do—then no significant social goods would be furthered by the maintenance of the legal profession. But, as I have said, my own view is that there are special competencies and that they are valuable. This makes it harder to determine what to preserve and what to shed. The question, as I see it, is how to weaken the bad consequences of the role-differentiated lawyer–client relationship without destroying the good that lawyers do.

Without developing the claim at all adequately in terms of scope or detail, I want finally to suggest the direction this might take. Desirable change could be brought about in part by a sustained effort to simplify legal language and to make the legal processes less mysterious and more directly available to lay persons. The way the law works now, it is very hard for lay persons either to understand it or to evaluate or solve legal problems more on their own. But it is not at all clear that substantial revisions could not occur along these lines. Divorce, probate, and personal injury are only three fairly obvious areas where the lawyers' economic self-interest says a good deal more about resistance to change and simplification than does a consideration on the merits.

The more fundamental changes, though, would, I think, have to await an explicit effort to alter the ways in which lawyers are educated and acculturated to view themselves, their clients, and the relationships that ought to exist between them. It is, I believe, indicative of the state of legal education and of the profession that there has been to date extremely little self-conscious concern even with the possibility that these dimensions of the attorney–client relationship are worth examining—to say nothing of being capable of alteration. That awareness is, surely, the prerequisite to any serious assessment of the moral character of the attorney–client relationship as a relationship among adult human beings.

I do not know whether the typical lawyer–client relationship is as I have described it; nor do I know to what degree role-differentiation is the cause; nor do I even know very precisely what "deprofessionalization" would be like or whether it would on the whole be good or bad. I am convinced, however, that this, too, is a topic worth taking seriously and worth attending to more systematically than has been the case to date.

SUGGESTED READINGS

BAYLES, MICHAEL D. *Professional Ethics.* Belmont, Calif.: Wadsworth, 1981.

BEAUCHAMP, TOM L. *Philosophical Ethics.* New York: McGraw-Hill, 1982.

CAMENISCH, PAUL F. *Grounding Professional Ethics in a Pluralistic Society.* New York: Haven, 1983.

CALLAHAN, JOAN C. (ed.) *Ethical Issues in Professional Life.* New York: Oxford, 1988.

FLORES, ALBERT. *Professional Ideals.* Belmont, Calif.: Wadsworth, 1988.

FREEDMAN, BENJAMIN. "A Meta-Ethics for Professional Morality." *Ethics* 89:1 (1978):1–9.

———. "What Really Makes Professional Morality Different: Response to Martin." *Ethics* 91:4 (1981):626–30.

FREIDSON, ELIOT. *The Professions and Their Prospects.* Beverly Hills, Calif.: Sage Publications, Inc., 1983.

GOLDMAN, ALAN H. *The Moral Foundations of Professional Ethics.* Totowa, N.J.: Rowman & Littlefield, 1980.

HUGHES, EVERETT C. "Professions." *Daedalus* 92,(1963):655–68.

JENNINGS, BRUCE, CAROL LEVINE, AND JOYCE BERMEL (eds). *The Public Duties of the Professions. Hastings Center Report Special Supplement* (February 1987).

MARTIN, MIKE W. "Professional and Ordinary Morality: a Reply to Freedman." *Ethics* 91:4(1981):632–33.

———. "Rights and the Meta-Ethics of Professional Morality." *Ethics* 91:4(1981):619–25.

ROBISON, WADE L., MICAHEL S. PRITCHARD, AND JOSEPH ELLIN (eds). *Profits and Professions.* Clifton, N.J.: Humana Press, 1983.

SHAFFER, THOMAS L. "The Ethics of Dissent and Friendship in the American Professions." *West Virginia Law Review* 88:4(1986):623–66.

SHER, GEORGE (ed.) *Moral Philosophy.* New York: Harcourt Brace Jovanovich, 1987.

VOLLMER, HOWARD M. AND DONALD L. MILLS (eds.) *Professionalization.* Englewood Cliffs, N.J.: Prentice-Hall, 1966.

WILENSKY, HAROLD L. "The Professionalization of Everyone?" *American Journal of Sociology* 70(1964):137–58.

TWO

The Professional–Client Relationship

In the course of their development since the 1960s, most of the disciplines within professional ethics have focused their attention on issues arising within the professional–client relationship. Understood as the ongoing, often quite personal interaction between the individual professional and the individual client, this relationship arises in many contexts: between physician and patient, between attorney and client, and so on. Despite the enormous variety within these individual professional–client relationships, however, certain characteristic dilemmas repeatedly arise: for example, should the physician tell the patient the truth, even if the truth is very grim? May the lawyer reveal what the client says in private, if the lawyer alone discovers that the client is guilty and knows that there is no other way to protect third parties or to see that justice is done? Similar dilemmas arise in many additional professional areas: for instance, how fully ought the stockbroker inform a client about the risks of a particular investment, especially when such risks are difficult to predict? To what extent, if any, may the professor manipulate and coerce the student in certain sorts of learning activities—for instance, with assignments and exams—when it is clearly for the student's own good? What ought the surgeon tell the patient about the risks of a recommended procedure, especially if the surgeon fears that hearing these risks will frighten the patient away from undergoing it? May the architect whose client's intentions are good but whose taste is bad manipulate the client by claiming that certain aesthetic atrocities are ruled out by "structural considerations," or ought the architect design whatever ugly building the client wants? To what extent may the psychologist control the client in therapeutic situations—for instance, in aversive conditioning and behavior modification programs? Each individual relationship between professional and client has its own distinctive features, of course, depending on the personalities of the parties involved, the particular circumstances, and the specific nature of the professional area involved; but moral dilemmas much like these arise repeatedly in all areas of professional practice.

These practical dilemmas themselves raise more general theoretical issues—among them, issues about truth-telling and deception, about confidentiality and harms to third parties, and about client consent and professional authority, to name those we will be discussing here. These are the classic issues of professional ethics, in the sense that they are both the issues with which professional ethics first concerned itself and the issues that have received the most sustained, developed, reflective discussion in the literature of professional ethics. But these issues in turn rest on a single, still more fundamental issue about the nature of the professional–client relationship. This chapter will address these classic issues and the underlying fundamental question, and, by examining three different models of the professional–client relationship, will show how our varying conceptions of the professions and of what it is to be a professional influence our answers to these central questions.

To be sure, traditional explorations within this classic area of professional ethics have envisioned the professional as a single, independent practitioner, interacting with a single, independent client; this one-on-one model, as we will see in Chapter 3, is growing less realistic as the character of the professions changes in the contemporary world. Nevertheless, it is the traditional one-on-one relationship that not only exhibits most vividly the classic problems of professional ethics but that also gives us particularly sharp insight into the central underlying problem of professional ethics, both in traditional relationships and in the group-practice, corporate settings of today's professional world.

THE CENTRAL ETHICAL PROBLEM OF THE PROFESSIONAL–CLIENT RELATIONSHIP

The classic, central problem in professional ethics may be described as that of *control*. Because of the professional's training and expertise and the client's need of the professional's services, the professional and client are in a position of relative inequality with respect to the transaction between them. Thus the central ethical problem arising within the relationship between them involves the duties and obligations of two parties in a relationship of unequal power, and specifically concerns the appropriate assignment of authority or control to each of them. This inequality is endemic and ubiquitous in the professions; indeed, it is universally characteristic of the professional–client relationship and underlies most of the specific problems of truth-telling, confidentiality, and consent with which we will be concerned.

Suppose, for instance, that you are a patient. Your physician has diagnosed your symptoms as characteristic of a malignant condition and tells you to report for a course of radiotherapy and chemotherapy. Is this an order? A recommendation? A suggestion, which you can take or leave? Who controls the situation here—you or your physician? Or suppose you have been arrested with 1½ lbs. of a controlled substance in your car, and your lawyer says you should plead guilty. Is *this* an order, a recommendation, a suggestion? Your stockbroker tells you to sell a stock you've held for 15 years; your political science professor assigns a 20-page paper defending political extremism; your optometrist reminds you that extended-wear contact lenses are now available with your correction; your architect says you should have a steel I-beam in the living-room ceiling of the house you are building and should paint the interior walls a specific slightly blue-hued flat white. Worst of all, your veterinarian says that the time has come to put to sleep the cat you've had for 17 years. Can we understand what the stockbroker says as a recommendation, what the professor says as an order, what the optometrist says as a suggestion, what the architect says as partly order and partly suggestion, and what the veterinarian says as a humane nudge—or are relationships of authority and control in professional–client interactions a good deal more complicated than that? Who gets the last word, the final say, in these relationships anyway? Who is, or should be, in control?

In all of the professions, the professional practitioner has, by virtue of his professional training, a body of specialized knowledge and access to further, developing knowledge in the field, as well as a set of specialized skills which are in part a product of training and in part a product of professional experience gained in practice in the field. Having this knowledge and expertise are part of what it is to be a professional. But this knowledge and expertise give the professional an advantage in power over the client. The client, on the other hand, is in need: He characteristically has neither the specialized knowledge relevant to the matter at hand nor specialized skills in the processes involved; that is why he seeks the services of the professional. Although the client may be more powerful than the professional in a variety of other social contexts, and although the client is furthermore either directly or indirectly the source of the professional's income, the client is nevertheless comparatively powerless with respect to the professional matter at hand. Nor is this inequality occasional or incidental; because the client consults the professional for help in matters that he cannot resolve himself, this inequality is a universal, defining feature of the professional–client relationship.

Sometimes the client's need for professional help is a function of legal restrictions or other policies: the patient cannot write his own prescription, for instance, even if he believes that he can make his own diagnosis. More often, however, the patient's need is the product of his lack of knowledge of the matter at hand. In a society in which legal and policy restrictions often reinforce professional roles, the client's need for professional help is typically a matter both of his own lack of expertise and of legal or policy restriction. But this inequality then gives rise to a number of moral questions: What is, or ought to be, the nature of the relationship between the two parties involved? To whom ought authority over this relationship be assigned? And what does this entail about the duties and obligations of the practitioner and the client, respectively, as they interact within this relationship? These are all components of the central, classic question of control.

American law, recognizing the fundamental inequalities of power with respect to the matter at hand between the professional and the client, and thus tacitly recognizing the moral issues this raises, asserts what is called the *fiduciary* obligation of the professional. This obligation, which requires that the professional remain worthy of the client's trust, prohibits the professional from using her specialized knowledge or skills to, so to speak, "take advantage" of the client. After all, it would be quite easy in most professional situations for the professional to use her advantage in knowledge and expertise to undermine the client's interests. The untrustworthy physician has precisely the sort of technical knowledge and skill that would make it possible to undermine the patient's health; the unscrupulous lawyer could easily worsen the client's legal position; the stockbroker knows how to ruin the client financially; and the professor could sabotage the student's hopes of an education by grading unfairly, for instance, and thus spoiling the student's chances of admission to further study.

The principle of fiduciary responsibility of the professional to the client is intended to protect against abuses of these sorts. However, the principle of fiduciary responsibility, while repeatedly appealed to in the law, is nowhere adequately explicated as a fundamental concept in professional ethics, and nowhere are its consequences for actual professional practice across a variety of fields fully examined. Nor is it evident, with respect to the major issues posed by the professional–client relationship, what observation of the fiduciary principle would in practice require, or what the professional would have to do or refrain from doing in order to remain "worthy of the client's trust." Yet if we do not have an adequate conception of what the relationship between professional and client should be, we have no way of saying when the professional exceeds the obligations imposed by this relationship in a way that is "untrustworthy" or "takes advantage" of the client. Consequently, we must first consider what form the relationship should take.

As a method of doing this, we can consider various "models" of the professional–client relationship. Such models, of which many have been proposed in various professional areas since Robert Veatch's classic analysis of the physician–patient relationship,[1] serve as characterizations of the various ways in which the professional–client relationship can be understood. But these models are not merely descriptive; they can also be understood as normative in character, and as such, they permit us to draw inferences about how professional practice should be conducted—including not only inferences about general theoretical issues like truth-telling, confidentiality, and consent, but also conclusions about specific dilemmas arising within individual professional–client relationships. In this way, different models yield different conclusions about what is "trustworthy" professional practice—that is, practice that honors the professional's fundamental fiduciary obligation to the client.

Models of specific professional–client relationships are sometimes described in terms of other human relationships. So, for instance, we are sometimes told that the physician functions, or should function, like a priest or an engineer or a teacher, that the lawyer should be like a friend, and so on. But without much more detailed analysis, these labels do not tell us very much. In this chapter, instead of appealing to descriptive labels, we will construct three complex, abstract models of the professional–client relationship. One of these is a paternalist model; the second, at the opposite end of the "control" spectrum, is an autonomist model; the third, a hybrid model of consent, falls somewhere between. These models are only three along the broad spectrum of possibilities of control in the professional–client relationship, from complete control by the professional to complete control by the client, but they will allow us to see how adopting one model rather than another has profound consequences for the central issues in professional ethics.

---

[1] "Models for Ethical Medicine in a Revolutionary Age," *The Hastings Center Report* 2:3 June 1972), pp. 5–7.

From these considerations, it is apparent that we are by no means consistent in the background models to which we appeal in considering actual issues in professional ethics. For instance, when we discuss truth-telling, we tend to resort to one of these models; when we consider confidentiality, we typically appeal to quite a different one; and when we address issues in consent, we commonly use another one still. Thus, while clarifying the background models of the professional–client relationship must be the first project in professional ethics, it may not resolve all the issues at hand, and while it is evident as a descriptive matter that we are erratic in our appeals to various professional models, it is by no means clear that normative agreement could be reached about which model is appropriate in all situations. Nevertheless, seeing these descriptive-normative models as they are actually employed in our thinking about issues in professional ethics will go a long way toward explaining why these issues are as difficult as they are.

THE PATERNALIST MODEL AND THE ISSUE OF TRUTH-TELLING

It is often argued that the professions are—and should be—paternalistic in character. Drawing on a characterization of paternalism as interference with a person's liberty of action, or the violation of other moral rules with respect to that person, *for that person's own sake*, it is claimed that in many of the situations that arise in professional practice, it is appropriate for the professional to interfere with the client's liberty or to violate other moral rules— including, among others, not telling him the truth—for his own good. Thus, the paternalist holds, it is appropriate for the professional to control the client (even when the client requests otherwise) because it is the professional who, by virtue of her specialized knowledge and skills, can best protect the client's true interests. The professional is appropriately active; the client is appropriately passive in this relationship, and allows the professional both to decide what is to be done and to carry out the resulting course of action. After all, the client does not have either adequate knowledge about or skills in the matter at hand; that is why he consults the professional in the first place. The client is in *need* of help that he cannot supply for himself; were he to control the way in which the professional provides services or deals with the problem, he could, in his ignorance, do himself still greater harm.

It is important to see that although the professional is assigned control under the paternalist model of the professional–client relationship, this does not permit the professional to treat the client any way she wants. Specifically, the principle of paternalism does not license interference by the professional in the client's liberty that is not for the client's sake; the professional must interfere only when, to the best of her informed, experienced belief, doing so will benefit the client rather than harm him. This rules out the physician who hospitalizes a patient in order to keep the hospital's bed count up, the psychiatrist who insists that a patient continue a course of therapy beyond the point at which it is no longer productive in order to keep his own income arriving, the attorney who urges a client to pursue a suit that may cause the client considerable emotional damage but will make a name for the attorney, and so on. Although these sorts of scenarios are by no means infrequent in the real world, no defensible principle of professional ethics permits them.

Asserting that the client's choices must be controlled for the client's own sake, the paternalist model assigns this control to the professional. The client puts himself in the hands of the professional, and in so doing relies on the professional's fiduciary obligation to the client to protect him from being taken advantage of. Thus, the professional and the client are not to be viewed as at odds, or as opponents, in the paternalist professional–client relationship; although the professional controls the client, it is for the client's own good. Under this model, the professional's directives to the client are best understood as *orders;* they are things that the professional requires the client to do, although of course they are required for the client's own good, and the client is expected (both by the professional and by himself) to obey. Under this model, too, the basis of the professional's directives is clear: It is the client's interests, at least as they are interpreted by the professional. On this model, the client has no obligations to the professional other than to pay the professional's fee; nor does the client have recourse against the professional for invasions of his liberty or for courses of action that he does not accept, except where the client can show that they were not in his interest as the professional perceived it. On this thoroughgoing paternalist model, it is not sufficient moral recourse for the client to show that the professional did something that he, the client, did not want done; provided it was in the client's interests, it was, on this model, the appropriate thing for the professional to do.

Drawing on the classic position articulated by John Stuart Mill, those objecting to this paternalist model of the professional–client relationship insist that the liberty that would be violated by the professional's interferences is far more important than whatever interests of the client would be served. Perhaps the professional can be trusted to act in the interests of the client; but this, they insist, is not enough to compensate for the client's being controlled. To be sure, intervention is warranted to prevent a person from harming others, but *paternalistic* intervention, performed solely for that individual's own sake, is never warranted. "Over himself, over his own body and mind," Mill insists, "the individual is sovereign."[2] Mill believes that it is appropriate to advise a person against acting on choices that will apparently cause him harm, but that it is not appropriate to interfere with his liberty to act as he knowingly and voluntarily chooses. Mill insists that "the only freedom which deserves the name is that of pursuing our own good in our own way, so long as we do not attempt to deprive others of theirs or impede their efforts to obtain it."[3]

Mill intends his doctrine to apply only to persons "in the maturity of their faculties"[4]—that is, persons who are capable of considered, reasoned choice. Paternalistic intervention, he grants, is appropriate in making choices

[2] John Stuart Mill, *On Liberty* (first published, 1859), ed. C. V. Shields (Indianapolis: Bobbs-Merrill, 1956), p. 13.
[3] Mill, *On Liberty,* p. 15.
[4] Mill, *On Liberty,* p. 13.

for children (indeed, the very word *paternalist* is derived from the Latin for *father* and suggests the well-meaning control that parents exercise over their children). Paternalistic intervention is also appropriate, Mill grants, in making choices for mentally ill, retarded, or unconscious persons, for persons rendered temporarily incompetent by injury or illness, and for others whose rationality is impaired. These are persons who are either temporarily or permanently incapable of considered, reasoned choice.

This distinction, between the person whose rational capacities are impaired and the person who is capable of choice, is the basis of the distinction in recent professional-ethics literature between "hard," or "strong," paternalism—that which involves intervention in the choices of a person capable of making her own choices, on the grounds that her own choices will do her harm—and "soft," or "weak," paternalism—intervention on behalf of a person whose reasoning capacities are impaired. Mill wholly rejects the former; he accepts the latter.

Two practical problems attend Mill's distinction. First, it is often difficult to tell whether a client is sufficiently rationally impaired to warrant intervention, or whether the intervention is proposed solely in order to prevent the client from doing himself harm; that is, it is often hard to tell whether a proposed intervention would be a case of "soft paternalism" or of "hard paternalism." Consider, for instance, the attorney's client who insists on testifying in her own behalf at her trial, although it is certain to work to her disadvantage. Is she so driven by anger, outrage, or a desire to get even with the opposing party that her reasoning capacities are impaired, or is she acting on a voluntary, reasoned, maybe principled—though perhaps imprudent—choice? Second, it is not clear whether the paternalizer—in this case, the professional—is the best judge of whether the paternalizee—the client—is impaired. On the one hand, the professional's greater knowledge and skill in the matter at hand may seem to make him the most perceptive judge of whether the client can make rational choices with respect to the matter at hand; on the other, however, this very knowledge and skill may also introduce systematic, professionally entrenched biases into his perception of the client's choices. If the attorney takes winning the case as the value of greatest importance, and the client believes that the opportunity to assert and defend her views is a value outweighing victory, the two may disagree at a profound level about what would constitute harm. According to the paternalist model of the professional–client relationship, however, these two practical problems do not arise: Because the paternalist model accepts both hard and soft paternalism, it is not necessary to distinguish clearly between them. And because it gives the professional authority to prevent a client from making choices, even when they are reasoned choices, that in the eyes of the professional will cause the client harm, it is not troubled by the possibility that the client will perceive these harms differently.

Truth-Telling

The paternalist model of the professional–client relationship may be best illustrated by the classic issue of truth-telling and deception in medicine. (This is not to say that issues concerning truth-telling do not arise in connection with other models, but that they are particularly vivid in the area of medicine.) According to the traditional paternalist view, the physician *ought* to withhold the truth from the patient, or distort information, or directly lie, whenever doing so will serve what the professional understands to be the patient's interests—regardless of the patient's preferences or of any putative "right to know." The classic example concerns whether to tell the truth to a patient who is dying of cancer, and the underlying rationale has elements of both soft and hard paternalist justifications: Not only is the patient, because he is ill, in an impaired condition, but grim news such as this might lead him to make self-harming choices—like resorting to unproven, potentially dangerous drugs like laetrile, or committing suicide—which are not in his interests. Thus the physician is justified, so the paternalist holds, in telling a lie.

Since the pioneering work of Elizabeth Kübler-Ross in communication about death,[5] physicians have largely revised their view that fatal diagnoses should not be disclosed to patients. Indeed, recent research shows that physicians have almost completely reversed their practices in deceiving patients about fatal diagnoses. While in 1961 about 90 percent of a group of physicians surveyed by Donald Oken said that they generally did *not* tell cancer patients about a fatal diagnosis,[6] by 1977, 98% of all physicians surveyed said that they *do* generally disclose such a diagnosis.[7] This does not represent abandonment of the underlying paternalist policy, however; rather, it is a change of view about whether telling the truth about cancer is in the interests of patients. To be sure, some of this change is associated with the significant improvement over the last quarter of a century in the efficacy of cancer treatment; some is associated with legal requirements for research protocols and fear of legal liability; and some is associated with the belief that patient cooperation with a treatment regimen will be greater if the patient understands the nature of his condition. But the most significant change seems to involve an alteration in what physicians believe is in the interests of patients: They now believe that patients need to know the truth about the approach of death so that they can begin to deal with the personal, emotional, and spiritual issues raised by this reality.

But the moral issue of truth-telling in medicine has not disappeared; rather, it has shifted to new ground. Cancer patients are still often not told the full details of their condition; for example, they might not be told that a remission they are currently enjoying will be of predictably limited duration and does not represent a cure. Similarly, patients are rarely given a full picture of the uncertainties in medicine or of the partial, incomplete nature of medical knowledge; indeed, it is asserted, on the contrary, that patients should be encouraged to have confidence and trust in their physicians. And although it is often done not for paternalist reasons, withholding the truth in placebo-controlled clinical trials is a routine feature of medical experimentation—even when the research is of potential therapeutic value to the

---

[5] Elizabeth Kübler-Ross, *On Death and Dying* (New York: Macmillan Publishing Co., 1969).

[6] Donald Oken, "What to Tell Cancer Patients: A Study of Medical Attitudes," *Journal of the American Medical Association* 175(1961), pp. 1120–28.

[7] Dennis H. Novak, Robin Plumer, Raymond L. Smith, Herbert Ochitill, Gary R. Morrow, and John M. Bennett, "Changes in Physicians' Attitudes Toward Telling the Cancer Patient," *Journal of the American Medical Association* 241:9 (March 2, 1979), pp. 897–900.

patient himself and does not benefit only medical science in general. Deception, one might say, is alive and well in contemporary medicine, even if physicians now routinely disclose fatal diagnoses to cancer patients.

The truth-telling issues within the professional–client relationship have been most conspicuous within medicine and the health-related fields, especially psychiatry, counseling, and nursing. Nevertheless, similar issues, although less frequently discussed, arise in many other professional areas as well. Particularly in the law, as in medicine, engineering, and other professional areas in general, the issue of paternalistic deception of clients is entangled with the larger issue of truth-telling per se and with the question of when and under what conditions departures from the truth can be excused in human communication. The issues of *paternalistic* deception of the client loom largest in the medical professions; issues of nonpaternalistic lying to others—judges, juries, tenants of buildings, users of products, and customers in general—loom largest in the legal and commercial professions. Resolving the background issue of whether a paternalist model of the professional–client relationship is to be favored will not resolve the issue of whether deception in general is permissible in a wide range of professional contexts, but it does provide a point of entry to this important, persistently difficult issue.

THE CLIENT-CONTROL MODEL AND THE PROBLEMS OF CONFIDENTIALITY AND THE UNSAVORY CLIENT

At the opposite extreme along the spectrum of control, we find a quite different model of the professional–client relationship, one which assigns the client control both of the professional–client interaction and of the course of action to be undertaken. Variously called the *engineering, agency,* or *contract* model, as well as *client control*, this model might also be labelled the autonomist model, in that it assigns the client an autonomous role. On the opposite, paternalist model, the client assumed an essentially passive role, putting himself, as we have noted, "in the hands of" the professional. On this autonomist, client-control model, by contrast, the client takes an active, controlling role, and the professional functions essentially as an employee of the client—a kind of consultant, technician, or fancy helpmeet to carry out whatever it is that the client wishes done. Authority is vested in the client, according to this model, despite the professional's advantage in knowledge and skill in the matter at hand, for it is the client who determines to what ends the professional's knowledge and skill shall be put. Those values that control the nature of the interaction are to be the client's, not the professional's, and the professional is not to impose her own values on the client's choices.

According to this antipaternalist, client-control model, many features of professional relationships can be seen in a different light. Not only does the locus of control shift from professional to client, but the basis of decisions shifts too, from the professional's perception of the client's interests to the client's own wishes or desires. Consequently, the force of professional directives, which in the paternalist model were best understood as orders, changes accordingly. For instance, if, as the autonomist model requires, the relationship between physician and patient is held to be appropriately controlled not by the physician's commitment to cure the patient, but by the patient's desire to get well, then "doctor's orders" are not really *orders* at all, but expert suggestions which the patient can choose to accept—if he wants to get well—or reject. In other words, "doctor's orders" become hypothetical imperatives, not categorical ones. Similarly, if the attorney is understood to serve the defendant in a criminal action not out of a commitment to protect the defendant's interests by keeping her out of jail or seeing that her sentence is as light as possible, but because he is in the employ of a person who wants to assert her rights, then the client's attempts to control the conduct of her case—say, by putting herself on the stand—take on quite a different light.

Furthermore, professional directives not only no longer function as orders, but they also come with no moral obligation to accept them. What is controlling are the client's desires, even when, in the professional's perception, these run counter to the client's own interests, and the client has no obligation to conform his desires to the professional's perception of his interests. Of course, in most actual cases in professional practice, what the client desires and what the professional takes to be in the client's interests will coincide. In all these cases, the course of action to be undertaken will be the same whether understood according to a paternalist model or a client-control model. What the client wants and what the professional thinks will benefit the client will diverge in some cases, however, and it is in these cases that the interesting ethical issues emerge. Let us look at two forms of these problems.

Confidentiality

Since under the autonomist model the professional–client relationship is held to be controlled by the client, we may ask to what degree the client has rights against the professional, rights that would obligate the professional to act or refrain from acting in certain ways, regardless of the harms or benefits that might be involved. A most striking illustration of this issue is to be found in the problem of confidentiality. Here the question concerns when, if ever, the client has a right to keep the professional from revealing information that the professional has learned within the professional–client relationship. This issue is part of the larger problem, particularly acute under this model, of the way in which the professional ought to act with respect to the client's intentions, wishes, desires, projects, and so on—especially when these intentions are not merely imprudent, as is often the case in paternalist situations, but are perhaps immoral or illegal or both, in that they threaten to bring harm to others as well.

Issues in confidentiality, though ubiquitous among the professions, are particularly pressing in those professions in which (1) there is private, one-on-one contact between the professional and the client and (2) the client's problem is one that could be embarrassing or harmful to him if revealed. Violations of confidentiality in medicine or psychiatry typically pose risks of embarrassment or public stigma for the client; in law, the risks are typically risks of legal penalty. Within organized religion, confidentiality issues arise most prominently in connection with the practice of confession, wherein the minister, priest, or rabbi is privy to the most painful secrets of persons who come to confess their sins. But what makes the problem of confidentiality acute is that in many cases, the matters that the client wishes to keep secret have to do with harms that he has caused or will cause to other persons. Whether it is the psychiatric patient or the religious parishioner who confesses having homicidal thoughts, the professional hearing this confession is faced with a dilemma in protecting both the client and whomever the client may potentially harm.

The strongest autonomist position assigns the client complete control over all information about the client which the professional learns within the professional–client relationship, whether the client intentionally reveals it or not, or the professional learns it from some other source; on this strong view, the professional may reveal it only with the permission of the client. Only psychiatry, as argued (unsuccessfully) by its professional organization in the *Tarasoff* case, and religion, at least in the Catholic Church's doctrine on confessional confidentiality, support a position this strong—that confidentiality ought *never* be violated. Weaker positions, taken by other professions, generally deny any absolute requirement of confidentiality and variously assert that the professional may disclose this information to prevent harm to other persons, to meet legal requirements, to protect the professional, or to protect the client himself.

Thus, in law, the American Bar Association (ABA) code of ethics permits (but does not require) an attorney to disclose a client's plans to injure or murder someone in the future; although (at least originally) opposed by the psychiatric profession, the *Tarasoff* decision appears to impose such an obligation upon psychiatrists who learn of a patient's homicidal plans. Physicians are required to report certain conditions or diseases, with or without the consent of the patient, including certain communicable diseases, venereal diseases, evidence of child abuse, and gunshot wounds. Prison psychiatrists must report knowledge of an inmate's plans to commit future crimes. The ABA code of ethics still permits attorneys to reveal information learned in confidence from their own clients in order to collect their fees.[8] And physicians typically consider it appropriate to reveal confidential information in order to protect a patient from harming himself—if he is contemplating suicide, for example.

Arguments in all the professions against requirements of confidentiality— that is, arguments which hold that the client has no right to control the relationship in this way—typically involve two distinct sorts of claims. First, it is frequently argued that in the modern world of professional practice, strict confidentiality is simply impossible to guarantee. Too many physicians, nurses, and pharmacists, and hospital administrators read a patient's chart in a hospital setting; too many attorneys, law clerks, secretaries, and office managers have access to a legal client's case. Rather than engender the client's expectations of confidentiality, which would then be disappointed, it is argued, it would be better simply to dispose of the notion altogether and acknowledge that confidentiality is something sacrificed in return for contemporary professional services.

---

[8] See Model Rule 1.6(b)(2), in Thomas D. Morgan and Ronald D. Rotunda, *1984 Selected Standards on Professional Responsibility* (Mineola, N.Y.: Foundation Press, 1984), p. 86.

Second, the more pressing philosophical argument holds that in some cases, it is immoral for the professional to maintain confidentiality—regardless of the client's expectations, the agreement that has been reached, and the nature of the professional model. According to this view, the client has no right to control certain kinds of information. These are cases in which the professional comes to know something about the client that involves harms to third parties—past crimes committed, future crimes contemplated, and the like. Thus, in the infamous Lake Pleasant murder case (to be described in the selections which follow), in which the defendant had told his attorney where his victims' bodies were buried, the attorney's withholding of information from one of the murdered women's parents about where their daughter's body could be found clearly compounded an already huge harm to them. Similarly (in a case also discussed in the selections which follow), the Berkeley psychiatrists' maintenance of the confidentiality of Prosenjit Poddar's threats increased the likelihood that Tatiana Tarasoff would be killed, as indeed she was. Here, the argument is that because the information has such enormous negative consequences for the well-being of other persons, the client can have no right against the professional to keep it unrevealed.

A very strong counterargument to this view comes from the professions themselves. It holds that regardless of the severity of the potential harms to third parties, clients must be recognized to control rights of disclosure, for otherwise clients would be unable to avail themselves of professional services in the first place. Assignment of this sort of control is crucial to the proper functioning of at least certain professional services. For example, the psychiatric patient who believes that a psychiatrist will betray his homicidal fantasies to the police will be unable to reveal them in the first place; but if the patient cannot reveal these fantasies, then the psychiatrist cannot treat them. Similarly, the legal client who cannot tell her attorney the details, incriminating though they may be, of the deeds of which she is accused cannot obtain the best legal defense, since the lawyer needs to know *everything* in order to fully analyze the case. But if the lawyer cannot thoroughly analyze the client's case, the legal profession cannot function as it should in providing the defendant with protection of her rights under the law. What is central here, and what is often overlooked in discussions of models of the professional–client relationship, is the claim that unless the client retains control in at least certain areas of the interaction—even where the interests of third parties may be affected—the professional cannot provide professional services, or cannot provide them in an optimal way. The more important and efficacious the services provided by the professions are taken to be, the more weight this argument will seem to hold.

As we see, the locus of authority in the professional–client relationship is not merely a political issue; it is an issue deeply connected with the ways in which the professions actually function. The arguments supporting the client-control view, if drawn to their fullest conclusions, would entail that the paternalist model is unsatisfactory, not just because it is wrong to interfere with a client's liberty, but because paternalist practice must ultimately undermine the proper function of the profession itself. After all, if the client knows in advance that even his most basic wishes may be overruled, he can never fully cooperate in a relationship in which this may occur. Of course, the paternalist will reply that even though the client knows in advance that his choices may be overruled, under the fiduciary principle he is assured that they will be overruled only in his own interests. But the fiduciary principle is itself challenged, and with it the paternalist model altogether, in cases in which the professional seeks to reveal confidential information, or to overrule other client choices, not for the client's sake, but to prevent harm to third parties. Thus, the issue of confidentiality is hardly settled on any of these models; rather, it introduces the deeper question of whether the professional's primary allegiance on any model is to the client, or to third parties or society at large. This issue has already been raised in Chapter 1; it will be considered more fully in Chapter 3, and will be pursued still further in Chapters 4 and 5.

The Unsavory Client

The limited issue of confidentiality can be generalized to the much broader issue of the professional's obligations vis-à-vis client desires or projects that may be illegal or immoral. To what degree, if any, should the professional be required to participate in the client's projects, especially when, according to the client-control model, the professional is viewed as the client's consultant, technician, or employee? If the client's projects are illegal or immoral, may, or should, the professional refuse to provide services? Should the professional provide services with the intention of dissuading the client or subverting the client's projects? Should the professional reveal the client's projects to others?

Under the client-control model, the client's values dictate the goals of the professional activity; the professional's role is to provide technical assistance in realizing these goals. But while the client's and the professional's values will usually coincide, whether in maintaining health, conducting a sound defense in a criminal trial, or designing an aesthetically attractive building, in some cases the professional may perceive the client's goals as tasteless, foolish, or immoral. Under the paternalist model of the professional–client relationship, the professional may intervene to prevent such projects or refuse to agree to participate in them; under the client-control model, however, the problem is very much greater. Under the client-control model, this issue will arise in a great many professional areas—for instance, for the veterinarian whose client insists that an annoying but perfectly healthy pet be put to sleep, for the loan officer whose bank insists on barely legal redlining, and for attorneys asked to protect shady legal enterprises of various sorts.

It is hardly sufficient simply to assert, as the ABA Model Rules have done, that lawyers representing clients do not thereby ascribe to or support the client's goals or aims.[9] In providing services that enable the client to accomplish his goals, the professional *does* thereby support them. Particularly in corporate law, where pursuit of the firm's objectives by attorneys employed by the firm is loyal and zealous, this problem may loom quite large, since the effects of the actions of major corporations on large numbers of persons may be quite pronounced.

---

[9] Model Rule 1.2(b), in Morgan and Rotunda, *op. cit.*, p. 76.

Perhaps because it assigns the professional a comparatively subsidiary role, the client-control model of the professional–client relationship is virtually never favored by professionals or professional institutions themselves, even though some professional codes of ethics do contain provisions assigning the client rights against the professional. Nor are the principal professions characterized by client-control practices, except in limited, specific areas, typically as enforced by the courts. For the most part, rights of clients that are recognized by professionals or professional institutions, and perhaps also enforced by the courts, consist largely of rights to competent, prompt, continuing services, and the like; what are much rarer are assertions of rights on the part of the client to *control* the course of action undertaken by the client with the professional's aid.

THE CONSENT MODEL AND THE ISSUE OF "INFORMED CONSENT"

Lying between the paternalist and the autonomist models on the spectrum of control, the "consent" model may seem to achieve a desirable compromise in the assignment of control to the professional and to the client. On the consent model, the professional designs and directs the course of action engaged in with the client but does not override the client's choices; rather, the professional grants the client the opportunity to consent to, or withhold consent from, the proposed course of action. A variety of such models have been described in the professional-ethics literature, some of them giving slightly more weight to the professional, some to the client; here we will describe a version—at the very midpoint of the spectrum—in which control is most equally shared.

On the consent model, both professional and client retain a substantial basis for control. The client has complete veto power; if consent is withheld, the professional does not act. On the other hand, the professional has very extensive power to shape the nature of the professional action, for it is the professional who initially identifies the nature of the client's problem, designs a course of action for responding to the problem, and proposes this course of action to the client. By thus controlling the agenda, as it were, the professional to a very large extent controls the character of the professional activity. In some circumstances, the professional may propose two or more alternative courses of action among which the client may choose; in the most frequent scenario, however, the professional offers just one option—the one that she takes to be most nearly in the client's interests—and the client is then free to accept this one option or reject it.

On this model, then, the professional's directives are neither orders nor suggestions; they have the force of recommendations and impose on the client some—though not controlling—obligations. They are to be considered seriously and to be rejected only for good reason. The basis of decision, on this model, is a complex one; although the client's desires may seem to be controlling, the only options from which the client may choose are those designed by the professional with the client's interests in mind. This model casts neither client nor professional in a passive, merely advisory role; both take an active part in determining how the client's problem is to be resolved.

In medicine, where this intermediate model has been most fully discussed, it is most fully reflected in practices requiring "informed consent" for both therapeutic and experimental procedures. Thus, for instance, the surgeon recommends to the patient a surgical procedure and describes the risks and benefits involved; the patient is then free either to accept or to decline the procedure. This requirement of informed consent to medical procedures and experimentation is now firmly established in the law.

The consent model is evident in many other professional fields as well. For instance, the stockbroker may propose an investment strategy that, given various facts of the client's financial position, he believes is best for the client; the client may then consent to this recommendation or reject it, depending, for instance, on whether she prefers conservative or high risk–high yield strategies. The minister may exhort a member of his congregation to, say, reform unacceptable behavior or give more to charity, but it remains up to that person whether to accept this recommendation or not.

In law, the ABA Model Rules governing professional conduct officially endorse this consent model and specifically hold that

> A lawyer shall abide by a client's decisions concerning the objectives of representation . . . and shall consult with the client as to the means by which they are to be pursued. . . . In a criminal case, the lawyer shall abide by the client's decision, after consultation with the lawyer, as to a plea to be entered, whether to waive jury trial and whether the client will testify.[10]

This is interpreted to mean that "Both lawyer and client have authority and responsibility in the objectives and means of representation. The client has ultimate authority to determine the purposes to be served by legal representation . . . At the same time, a lawyer is not required to pursue objectives or employ means simply because a client may wish that the lawyer do so."[11] Here, the lawyer recommends and the client accepts or rejects; neither wholly controls the course of events.

Except in emergency situations or cases in which the client is markedly impaired, this consent model, in which the professional is the architect of the course of professional action but requires the consent of the client in order to pursue it, may seem to be a desirable model for professional practice, since it assigns control both to the professional, as the one with specialized knowledge and skills, and to the client, as the one whose desires and interests are at stake. Nevertheless, it has serious problems, problems vividly exhibited by the issue of "informed consent."

Informed Consent

The consent model assumes that the client will be granted the opportunity to give informed consent to the procedure proposed by the professional, and much of the discussion of this issue has concerned ways in which consent

---

[10] Morgan and Rotunda, *op. cit.*, Rule 1.2, pp. 76–77.
[11] *Ibid.*, p. 77.

can fail to meet this standard. There are two principal constraints: Consent must be adequately informed, and it must be voluntary. Breakdowns or failures of the professional–client relationship under this model generally fall into two categories: those in which the professional does not provide the client with adequate information, even though it would be feasible to do so, and those in which the professional manipulates or coerces the client, or allows some other party or factor to do so, so that the client's decision is not really voluntarily made.

Inadequate Information

The consent model of the professional–client relationship posits an obligation on the part of the professional to provide the client with sufficient information to make an informed decision. This obligation requires both that the professional not conceal or withhold relevant information that is available, and that he act to provide for the client as much information as is relevant for rational decision-making. This obligation is, of course, limited by the client's capacity to absorb and understand the information. In medicine, for instance, a patient's capacity to understand may well be limited by an illness that affects alertness or by other factors of mental status, especially depression and fear; in law, the client's capacity may be limited by, for example, a lack of conceptual grasp of legal complexities or of the nature of background law; in accounting or financial management, capacity may be limited by the client's inability to follow complex calculations; and so on. Individual characteristics of particular clients may limit their capacity to absorb information provided by the professional in many sorts of circumstances.

This limitation is not merely a difficulty arising in some circumstances but not in others, however. It is a fundamental limitation inherent in all professional practice. Although it has been discussed most fully in medicine, the problem of the client's capacity to understand information provided by the professional is a problem in *all* the professions, since, by definition, the professions involve access by the professional to a specialized body of knowledge which nonprofessionals in that area lack. This specialized body of knowledge is one which, typically, the professional has spent many years of training to acquire, and it is typically so complex that it cannot easily be reduced to a form that the layperson can undertand, even if that person is a professional in some other field. Furthermore, the client is often caught in emotionally trying, frightening, or urgent circumstances, and these factors further compromise the client's capacity to understand. But if the client cannot understand the information that is relevant to his circumstances, he is, in effect, "impaired" with respect to rational decision-making. Thus we must ask whether it is even possible for a professional to supply the client with enough information to make a *fully* informed decision, or whether the matters with which the professional deals are simply too complex for that.

On the client-control model, this point is of lesser relevance, since under that model the client makes his decisions, using professional directives as suggestions or advice, whether or not he fully comprehends them. On the paternalist model, it is also of lesser—much lesser—relevance, because the client does not have a choice; his decisions are overruled by the professional when the professional takes them to be against his interests. It is only under the consent model that this problem looms so large, because it is only according to this model that understanding between client and professional about a course of action must be reached.

Manipulation and Coercion

The second general area of ethical concern under the consent model has to do with the possibility that the professional may fail to mitigate or account for coercive factors in the client's situation, or may actually engage in deliberate, direct manipulation, undue influence, or coercion of the client. So, for instance, the physician may fail to account for the coercive influences on patients' decisions of such factors as fear of dying or confinement in a hospital, or she may observe, but not attempt to identify or correct, coercive pressures from a patient's family. Similarly, in planning a course of legal action with a client, the defense attorney may fail to account for the coercive effects of fear of losing one's legal rights, threats from other persons, or incarceration on a client who has previously been jailed.

Although some individual practitioners may be quite sensitive to the kinds of circumstances that can prove coercive in various professional settings, fear on the part of clients is a major factor in many kinds of professional situations: The dentist's patient's decisions may be short-sighted because of fear of pain; the veterinarian's client may fear losing a beloved pet; the accountant's client may fear financial ruin; the professor's client—the student—may fear failure and humiliation; and the clergy's client—the churchgoer—may fear ultimate damnation. Such fears are not normally coercive, of course, but in some cases they may lead to the distortion of the client's choices; if this is so, under the consent model it will be the obligation of the professional, where she can detect such fears, to attempt to correct them.

Furthermore, the professional may engage in kinds of activities that are inherently coercive, but that may seem to be necessary in order to accomplish the professional goal at hand. In the field of education, for example, it is not always easy to differentiate teaching or education from manipulative indoctrination. Some strategies of forcibly expanding and changing a student's beliefs—compulsory assignments and tests, for example—appear to be part of what is required to accomplish the goal of education. To attempt to specify precisely what would be required for "informed consent" to a given course of education would prove difficult indeed. Nevertheless, many students do not seem to consent in any very well-informed way to the process of becoming educated, but merely submit themselves to whatever course of study is required for a specific degree.

Similarly, certain techniques of the professional salesperson clearly violate the requirements of informed consent. In "hard-sell" situations, for instance, the consent of the customer to purchase the product is neither fully informed nor genuinely voluntary; the salesperson manipulates the client, using techniques that can be clearly identified, into agreeing to the purchase of an item she would not otherwise have bought. This might seem to show that sales is merely an occupation, not a profession in the central sense of the word; but it should also lead us to consider just how strong the sales component is in ordinary professional practice. Is the encyclopedia salesperson's pitch just a more extreme version of what professionals do all the time to get their clients to cooperate with their strategies? Physicians often claim that they can get their patients to consent to whatever procedures they recommend, if they do the recommending in a persuasive way; but the same might well be true for attorneys, architects, accountants, and others who may need to "sell" their own clients on the services they supply.

Thus, we see that in practice the consent model may be quite problematic indeed. If client "consent" to the professional's activities is neither fully informed nor genuinely voluntary, then the consent model of the relationship between them ceases to be plausible, and what appeared to be a greater sharing of authority is not that at all. Instead of what seemed to be a desirable compromise between the paternalist and autonomist models, what we may have in this case is simply a better-disguised version of the paternalist model, or perhaps a version that, under the fiction of client "consent," accepts the paternalist model's manipulative and coercive strategies, but does not share its concern for the client's interests. This is often said to be particularly common in contemporary medicine, where signatures on "consent" forms are obtained not to record or ensure that the patient really understands and fully consents to the course of action that the physician has proposed, but to protect the physician from legal liability. To be sure, the patient has a legal remedy if he can show that his consent was in fact not fully informed or was not voluntary, but this is a cumbersome procedure and in any case can be used only when the patient can establish that he has been harmed by the procedure performed. On this dim view, the "consent" model is a sham.

But there is a more optimistic view of the consent model as well. According to this view, the interaction between professional and client involves not covert manipulation but mutual conversation; here, the professional provides expertise about technical matters and the client contributes information about her own values and perceptions of the process at hand. Neither party controls the interaction, and the resulting agreement is the product of discussion, mutual criticism and questioning, and continuing dialogue on both sides. It is not that the professional and the client begin as adversaries, working to hammer out a compromise between their competing interests; they begin as co-workers, seeking to better understand what each has to contribute to the project at hand. This is a model of mutual accommodation, in which neither party is in the driver's seat; in fact, the notion of *control* drops out. The client recognizes that the professional must practice within the limits of the professional discipline and in accord with his perceptions of the client's interests; but the professional recognizes that the client's desires are central, even though they may diverge from what he, as a professional, is trained to recognize. This, of course, is a utopian model of professional practice, an ideal that is only sometimes achieved. It is clearly preferable in its distribution of control to either the paternalist or the autonomist models with which it competes. But it is an ideal that is very often corrupted in practice, and the real issue is whether these corruptions of the consent model, because they disguise the distribution of control, are worse than the alternative models themselves.

On the other hand, it may be that partial understanding by the client of the activities that the professional proposes is possible, at least insofar as it involves understanding general considerations although not specific technicalities; the question then remains whether a partial understanding of this sort is adequate in support of the client-consent model.

CONCLUSION

The questions considered here are those that characteristically arise within the traditional, one-on-one professional–client relationship. Such relationships are becoming increasingly uncommon in the contemporary professional world, especially, as we shall see more fully in Chapter 3, as professionals abandon individual practice and are employed by larger professional organizations or firms. Such relationships are also increasingly threatened by the distributive pressures to be considered in Chapter 4, and are reshaped by the self-regulatory mechanisms to be discussed in Chapter 5. Increasing external regulation and cost-attentiveness clearly plays a role as well. But these initial problems of truth-telling and deception, confidentiality, and informed consent remain fundamental problems even as the nature of the professions changes; the problems may just be harder to see in less simple contexts, and harder still to resolve.

Examination of various models of the professional–client relationship has led us to ask which of these models is the most defensible on moral grounds, and whether the corruptions of an ideal model are worse than either of two less satisfactory ones. But this raises a prior question: whether a single model—any one of them—is equally tenable within the varying professions, or whether one model is appropriate for certain professions and a different one is more suitable for others. Traditionally, the paternalist model has been employed in the medical and other treating professions, in which the likelihood of client impairment is particularly high, while the consent model has been appealed to in the consulting professions like engineering, accounting, and law. Indeed, it is quite reasonable to expect greater emphasis on client control in what we might call the discretionary professions—those in which the services provided function as a luxury—than in those in which the client is in acute health- or welfare-jeopardizing need. Even so, no profession, as a whole, unequivocally espouses the client-control model. But the fact that these models have been traditionally accepted and rejected in different ways is hardly sufficient to justify this, and we must ask how we should decide which model is appropriate in which professions in the first place. What about those areas of professional practice that seem to fall on the borders between one and another—forensic medicine, for instance? Do the various models tell us different things about different professions, and is uniform adherence to one or another model even within a profession a desirable thing? These are some of the questions that arise just within the professional–client relationship, even before we consider the issues of professionals within organizations, of professional self-regulation, and of distributive justice in the chapters to follow.

TRUTHTELLING

PATIENT TRUTHFULNESS: A TEST OF MODELS OF THE PHYSICIAN–PATIENT RELATIONSHIP*

Harold Y. Vanderpool and Gary B. Weiss

Using as a test the case of a patient who seems to be lying, Vanderpool and Weiss examine two principal models of the physician–patient relationship: paternalism, and client-control or "agency." They describe the difficulties with both models, concluding that although each illuminates certain features of this relationship, each is also problematic and sometimes immoral. It should be noted that this analysis involves only two, rather than three, models, as in the text introducing this chapter, and the reader may wish to consider whether a third model would overcome the objections noted by Vanderpool and Weiss.

Although truth-telling by physicians has been discussed extensively in recent years in medical ethics literature, little attention has been given to the truthfulness of patients. Are patients always morally obligated to tell their doctors the truth, or might patient truth-telling depend upon the model of the doctor–patient relationship being followed? How should the doctor deal with the patient whose veracity is in question? Or with one whose lack of truthfulness is proven? How should the doctor who is proceeding according to a paternalistic model of the physician–patient relationship deal with these patients? Would the actions of the physician differ if the doctor regards each patient as a free moral agent? Might a scrutiny of issues related to patient truthfulness even cause us to rethink the adequacy of different moral models of the physician–patient relationship? In light of such questions, it is rather remarkable that more attention has not been given to the veracity of patients.

In order to focus this discussion, we will begin with an actual case, the identifying

* References have been deleted without indication.

details of which have been changed to assure anonymity. We shall first use the case to understand the way two prominent models of the doctor–patient relationship differ with respect to handling patients whose veracity is in doubt. On the basis of this analysis and empirical studies respecting both the truthfulness and the accuracy of the information patients convey to doctors, we will then critically evaluate the adequacy of these models.

Case Report

R. B. is a twenty-three-year-old woman who was referred to the hematology clinic because of problems of easy bruisability. Within the past year she had three episodes of significant subcutaneous hematomas due to reportedly minor impacts to her body and extremities. She gave no past medical or family history of a bleeding disorder. She denied the use of any medications. Routine laboratory tests, including platelet count, prothrombin time, and partial thromboplastin time were normal. Measurement of the template bleeding time, however, suggested that an abnormality in platelet function existed. Platelet aggregation studies demonstrated minimal abnormalities, and electron microscopy of the platelets was within normal limits. These results suggested that there might be a drug effect on platelet function as would be seen in a patient who had been taking aspirin. It was possible, however, that the patient had either underestimated the severity of the traumas that were causing her bruises, or she might have some rare platelet abnormality.

R. B.'s case was presented at the hematology clinic conference, and it was agreed that a drug screen was indicated (especially measurement of salicylate levels to exclude aspirin use) before a longer, more complicated diagnostic search should be undertaken. Yet the patient had strongly denied the use of any drugs, including those containing aspirin. She denied this both at initial history taking and prior to the measurement of her bleeding time. How should her doctor proceed?

Case Discussion

The course of action chosen by the doctor hinges upon ethical considerations, which are critically significant for perhaps all medical cases. Is it moral to test R. B.'s truthfulness without her knowledge? If so, should R. B. be told about the test's results? Should this test be charged to her bill? Should she be told that it is being charged to her account? If the doctor proceeds with the option of ordering a drug screen only if R. B. is informed, should her truthfulness be openly questioned by her doctor? Why not take the patient at her word, inform her about the additional laboratory work, family studies, and contacts with researchers that can be initiated, and allow her to choose a diagnostic course of action? Might this course of action somehow compromise a doctor's moral integrity and/or effectiveness as a scientific practitioner? We will demonstrate how each of two prominent ethical models of the doctor–patient relationship legitimates a different course of action with respect to the

care of R. B. We will then focus on some of the limits and inadequacies of these models of the physician–patient relationship, especially the model that presumes that patients must be respected as free moral agents.

Paternalism

The classic model of the physician–patient relationship is the paternalistic or priestly model, principles of which are contained in the ancient Greek oath. The ethical codes of the American Medical Association beginning with its first code of 1847 and including the several revisions of this code through 1957 also reflect this model. Paternalism can be briefly defined as taking an action toward another person without his or her permission and justified by the action's serving the welfare, interests, and/or needs of that person. Since paternalism overrides the commonly held moral principle of the self-determination or autonomy of the individual, it can also be characterized negatively as interfering with a person's liberty of action on the basis of its serving the welfare, interests, or needs of that person. Although this interference is sometimes regarded as coercive, it need not always be viewed as forced upon others.

The logical assumptions of paternalism include, first, that paternalistic actions are usually taken toward others without their knowledge or permission, thus interfering with the extent of their choices as free persons. Second, paternalistic acts are justified as intended for the good or benefit of others. The therapeutic benefit of the patient is the fundamental justification for paternalistic acts within medicine. Indeed, unless the doctor is committed to the medical and health needs of patients, he loses his professional *raison d'être*. Third, as a correlate of point two, paternalism assumes that the doctor is benevolent and will perform only those interventions that are likely to benefit rather than harm patients.

Fourth, paternalism assumes that the person who takes actions toward others without their consent feels qualified to act on their behalf. This correlates with the traditions of medicine in two ways. Medical professionals undergo training in order to possess the knowledge, skill, and judgment that will enable them to benefit sick and injured persons. Medical paternalism also assumes that compared to physicians, patients are relatively uninformed about medical interventions. Patients, especially seriously ill patients, are depicted as physically, emotionally, and socially isolated and threatened, as losing control over their existence, and as unable to reason or think like normal persons. They are therefore described as assuming passive and/or dependent roles *vis-à-vis* medical professionals. Their lack of medical knowledge, compromised emotional states, and/or impaired reasoning abilities are often viewed as obstacles to fully informed consent and as impediments to their being able to exercise their moral rights on an equal level with doctors and other health professionals.

Fifth, the paternalist acts benevolently in another's behalf by obtaining as accurate an assessment of outcomes or consequences as is possible. The consequences weighed include physical pain and pleasure, psychological well-being, and "personal worth" values like confidentiality and privacy. Paternalism thus deals with persons as individuals of value rather than as autonomous moral agents. As a benevolent expert, the physician is thus responsible for arriving at a diagnosis and initiating therapy with a minimal degree of physical, psychological, and personal harm and a maximal degree of good or benefit.

Within the paternalistic model of the physician–patient relationship, truthfulness is a relative moral value that is honored or not honored depending upon an assessment of beneficial and harmful outcomes. The nuances and definitions at play here are complex, encompassing such factors as justifying or not justifying truth-telling depending upon what constitutes "harm" and "benefit," what harms are probable, what the magnitude of these harms is—for example, whether they are reversible or irreversible, and what the probability and magnitude of benefits are. Act utilitarians view honesty as secondary to the physical and/or psychosocial well-being of the patient, while rule utilitarians may view honesty as always or nearly always beneficial—as is presupposed in some medical oaths and codes and not in others. Cases are important to consider partly because they enable us to identify various definitions of harm and benefit and various types of consequentialism within the general category of medical paternalism.

The questions posed earlier with respect to R. B.'s case can be answered within the framework and values of these assumptions of paternalism. We propose that a paternalistic doctor will proceed in the following manner. The test will be ordered as an "ordinary," logical step in the diagnostic work-up of this patient. At this point, the physician assumes that R. B.'s morality and/or inaccurate recall need not interfere with obtaining the diagnosis upon which effective medical benefit depends. In the paternalistic model, patient care is not necessarily dependent upon the veracity of patients.

It is unnecessary for the paternalistic doctor to disturb the patient and risk a rupture in the physician–patient relationship by telling her that her word is not being taken at face-value. While the patient might discover that a separate drug screen has been ordered, and conclude that she is not being trusted, this risk is minimal. If the test is negative, the most likely cause of her medical problems will have been eliminated—a clear benefit. The screening test would be listed as one of numerous tests on her medical chart and as a charge on her bill. Even as the care of R. B. is not dependent upon the accuracy and/or honesty of the information given to the doctor, so also the doctor need not be fully truthful with R. B., because truth-telling *per se* is regarded as secondary to medical benefit.

It is unlikely that charging the drug screen to R. B.'s bill will cause harm or hurt because its chances of being discovered are slim. If R. B. finds out that her word has been doubted and feels insulted, the physician–patient relationship may be adversely affected. The doctor, however, can apologize and explain that many patients do not remember the drugs they take, thereby emphasizing the accuracy of her comments rather than her moral lack of truthfulness.

If, however, the test is positive, the physician has discovered the essential factor behind the patient's easy bruisability. The physician would share the results of this test with the patient, maintaining that one of her tests had indicated that she has been taking a drug (or drugs), and that she must cease taking this drug if she wishes to stop bruising. The physician should not criticize the patient for a lack of veracity, because fear and guilt apparently have little, if any, impact on the compliance of most patients regarding their doctor's recommendations. Indeed, confronting the patient moralistically is likely to frustrate the ultimate aim of paternalistic medical care—the curing of the patient. Rather than resulting in better cooperation, moral rebukes may lead to greater hostility and psychological resistance to recommended therapy.

The Agency Model

The model of the physician–patient relationship that assumes that the patient is a free moral agent derives from a different set of values and gives rise to different approaches and actions by the physician. This model was first generally referred to as the contractual model of the professional–lay relationship and continues to be referred to in this manner because it assumes that doctors and patients make mu-

tual and binding contracts or agreements with each other. However, since the physician–patient relationship differs in a variety of respects from ordinary contractual relationships between buyers and sellers of goods and services, this model is now often referred to either as a covenant model or as a relationship in which patients are their own agents. Those who prefer the term *covenant* wish to avoid certain legalistic or individualistic implications of many contracts, while nevertheless assuming that covenants include both mutual agreements and a respect for each person's self-determining agency. For convenience and in order to register more precisely its moral elements, we will usually refer to this as the agency model, although it can also be called the autonomy or contractual model. We will deal with the common features of the agency model as presented by various authors rather than attempt to compare and contrast differences in emphasis between authors.

The fundamental value of the agency model is the non-consequentialist moral principle that every competent adult is a person who should be respected as a self-determining agent. This moral principle assumes that persons are free to choose different courses of action for themselves and that this freedom is a logical prerequisite of "the existence of a moral community."[1] Mutual respect for the free choices of other persons is logically required if persons are to preserve their freedom without resorting to force or violence. Doctors and patients must therefore relate to each other out of mutual respect for each other's autonomy, rather than use one another as a means toward certain ends.

With respect to patients, moral autonomy is preserved if they are allowed to choose which diagnostic and therapeutic interventions will be performed. They can-

[1] H. Tristram Engelhardt, Jr., "Basic Ethical Principles in the Conduct of Biomedical and Behavioral Research Involving Human Subjects," *Texas Reports on Biology and Medicine* 38 (1979), p. 141.

not make choices and determine their own ends unless they are given truthful and adequate information pertaining to their health needs, unless they comprehend this information, and unless their choices are free from coercion, duress, or rewards that relate intrinsically to the conditions of their personal rights and freedoms. These criteria regarding information, comprehension, and freedom comprise the fundamental ingredients of the process of informed consent. Even as these criteria represent the moral rights of patients in the agency model, so also they represent the moral duties of physicians who relate to patients as autonomous agents.

The agency model also assumes that doctors are self-determining moral agents. As persons with moral rights and duties, doctors cannot perform certain acts (like harming patients) and may be conscientiously opposed to performing others (like abortion). The agency model forbids patients from coercing doctors in these respects. When actions are taken by a patient that interfere with the physician's moral freedom or undermine their mutual agreements, the physician has the right to end the relationship and suggest that the patient seek care elsewhere.

A lack of honesty on the part of either doctor or patient undermines the agency model of the physician–patient relationship because this can limit the freedom of either party and amounts to a using of others for personal ends. The agency model, furthermore, assumes that doctor and patient are to make clear and honest agreements that are mutual and binding until replaced by a new set of binding agreements. Patients and doctors, however, may conceal personal information that is extraneous to their agreements, thus protecting important degrees of privacy and autonomy.

The agency model differs from paternalism in important ways. The prioritizing of the doctor's therapeutic role differs in the paternalistic and agency models. Whereas intended therapeutic benefit is primary in the paternalistic model, it is secondary when patients are respected as self-determining agents. The medical expertise of the doctor is not called into play until it is explicitly consented to by the patient. Of course, patients are free to request that their doctors take over their care and make decisions for them diagnostically and therapeutically. In such instances, however, the agency model assumes that physician and patient agree on the nature and extent of the procedures available to and accepted by the patient. Agreements between persons are contextually specific. Thus, when unforeseen or unexpected changes occur with respect to diagnosis, therapy, or the patient's disease process, a new level of agreement and consent is called for.

In contrast to paternalism, the agency model also assumes that the awareness and reasoning powers of patients are either not compromised to a degree that prevents their making competent decisions concerning their medical care or that a moral and/or legal surrogate will have been secured by the patient. This model requires that the doctor tell the patient or the patient's surrogate in ordinary language what diagnostic and therapeutic procedures are needed, what harms and benefits are likely, and what costs and time constraints are involved. In legal terms, patients are to be told what an "average, reasonable patient" needs to know in order to make a decision.

When the doctor deals with R. B. on the basis of these principles, several actions will be taken. First, the drug screen will not be ordered without the patient's informed consent. This includes a common-sense description of the number, invasiveness, costs, and time-requirements of the tests needed for her diagnosis. Unless R. B. explicitly gives her doctor *carte blanche*, it would be a dishonest rationalization for the doctor to view the drug screen as one of the tests covered under the umbrella of their initial diagnostic agreement. Clearly this screen represents a second phase of her diagnostic workup.

In order to inform R. B. about the additional drug screen and secure her consent, the doctor need not confront her with the possibility that she is lying. Indeed, without express information to the contrary, such a confrontation represents an unwarranted assumption concerning R. B.'s motivations. The physician should rather describe honestly and precisely the results of the diagnostic tests and suggest either that her bruises may be caused by the action of a drug, probably aspirin, on her platelets, or that she has some kind of rare abnormality in platelet function. This gives R. B. the opportunity either to admit that she is taking a drug or to deny again that she is taking anything, including aspirin.

If she admits that she might have been taking one or more drugs, the test could be ordered by the physician if she consents to it. Of course if she says she is taking aspirin, there is no need for the test. If, however, R. B. again denies that she is taking aspirin or any other drug, the doctor's options are either to confront R. B. with the belief that she is lying (or has a poor memory) or to take her at her word and not order the test. Unless the doctor has clear evidence that R. B. is taking aspirin (which is not the case), it is morally wrong for the doctor to presume to know her thoughts and charge her with dishonesty. A charge of dishonesty in this instance intrudes into R. B.'s privacy and unwarrantably questions her right to determine her own course of action. A questioning of her ability to remember the drugs she takes after she has clearly and strongly denied this twice implies that she is stupid and although unlikely, she may well be so personally offended that it will end the doctor–patient relationship. Because R. B.'s drug history must be accepted at face-value and viewed as her chosen course of action, the doctor must give up the possibility of obtaining a drug screen. Even as the free agency of patients allows them to refuse

recommended therapies, so also this freedom to choose can place limits on medical diagnosis.

Having eliminated obtaining a drug screen, the doctor is faced with a moral dilemma. In order to respect R. B.'s free agency, the doctor must present R. B. with a choice either of adjusting to the fact that she bruises easily or of consenting to further diagnostic testing regarding whether and how her bruises might be caused by an unusual platelet disorder. (The expenses and lengthiness of this latter course of action would need to be described as accurately as possible by the physician in order for R. B. to be able to decide whether she wishes additional laboratory work, family studies, and contacts with researchers to be initiated.) The doctor's own moral agency, however, is likely undermined by this preservation of R. B.'s autonomy. Regarding her first choice, the doctor may believe that drug ingestion is causing her easy bruisability and that therefore she does not have to adjust to the fact that she bruises easily. For the reasons outlined above, however, the doctor is unable to be honest with R. B. in this regard.

Depending upon the physician's moral convictions, the second choice offered to R. B. is even more problematic, for the physician is likely to have conscientious moral qualms about proceeding without a more accurate knowledge of R. B.'s drug history. Even though R. B. is willing to choose the expenses, doubtful results, inconveniences, and risks of further medical interventions, the doctor's objections to this option may include any or all of the following moral concerns: a belief that this approach compromises a commitment to perform only those medical procedures that are likely to benefit rather than harm patients; a belief that by compromising diagnostic accuracy the doctor breaks numerous promises to self, teachers, and profession; a conviction that the doctor can help and care for a number of patients in place of the time consumed by R. B.'s problematic workup; a conviction (assuming that R. B. is not personally paying for her treatment) that other parties should not have to pay for an expensive and possibly superfluous diagnostic search. In short, both the ethical convictions and the therapeutic *raison d'être* of the physician may be undermined by a new therapeutic contract with R. B. The physician's moral dilemma is poignant: He is unable both to respect R. B.'s moral autonomy and act in keeping with his own moral convictions and with certain fundamental values of his profession.

Finally, if the physician somehow discovers that R. B. is lying he is fully entitled to end the relationship with R. B. Even as the doctor cannot use the patient as a means toward an end in the agency model, so also the patient is prohibited morally from using the doctor as a means.

Critiques of Paternalism

Having outlined and illustrated the character of each of these models of the physician–patient relationship, which should be followed? This cannot be determined without critically examining the ethical and philosophical assumptions of each model.

An analysis of paternalism gives rise to several serious questions and dilemmas. These include problematic epistemological assumptions related to the harm–benefit analysis required by the paternalistic model, namely, the difficulty of judging which complex sets of harms and benefits will actually suit the personal beliefs and experiences of the patient; ethical problems over limiting the free choice of competent adults; possible abuses associated with justifying means by ends; assumptions that doctors will display degrees of benevolence toward patients that do not correspond with observations of some medical sociologists; and arguments favoring moral autonomy in cultural settings marked by ideological pluralism. In short, logical, moral, legal, social, and cultural perspectives all

call into question fundamental assumptions of the paternalistic model.

In light of these criticisms, paternalism appears to have been discredited. Furthermore, it is widely assumed by the majority of those who write on issues pertaining to medical ethics and law at the present time that critiques of paternalism lend strong support to the agency model. However, since a discrediting of one model does not automatically vindicate another, a critical examination of selected features of the agency model is merited.

Critiques of the Agency Model

In spite of wide acceptance, the agency model has been criticized from several perspectives. It lacks social realism insofar as the contracts or agreements made by doctors and patients cannot be abstracted from the complex social institutions, agencies, and obligations surrounding medical practice. It has been criticized as ethically incomplete; for while its stipulations require that the freedom of patients be respected, these stipulations do not make health care professionals responsible for actively caring for patients or for healing them out of benevolence. The ethics of the agency model also do not address issues of social justice, or call for a nurturing of moral virtues like temperance, compassion, and courage.

Furthermore, it has been argued that the free agency of patients is seriously compromised, if not eroded, by sickness and infirmity. This means that the contractual agreements of many doctors and patients are unequal; and it means that truly informed consent is problematic for those whose rationality and independence are compromised by sickness.

While we believe that each of these criticisms bears some merit and deserves further elaboration and analysis, we will criticize the agency model from another perspective, that is, question whether it is *possible* to construe doctor–patient interactions involving competent adults as mutual moral agreements. . . . The case of R. B. is pertinent as a point of departure because it involves a competent adult in a non-emergency situation—clearly not one of the recognized exceptions to the agency model.

We noted in the case of R. B. that even as the accuracy and truthfulness of the doctor's communication with the patient is essential in order to uphold the moral elements of the agency model, so also the non-deceptiveness of the patient and the accuracy of the information supplied by the patient are of fundamental importance. Inaccurate or false information from doctors betrays the principles inherent to informed consent, undercutting the patient's free moral agency. Deceptive information from patients constitutes a manipulating of doctors as a means toward the patient's ends. Inaccurate information from patients that directly influences diagnosis and therapy (as it must when it is morally offensive to test for it) is antithetical to the doctor's professional roles and perhaps to his moral convictions.

It might be argued that a certain degree of inaccurate or deceptive information from doctors and patients is unavoidable and represents the price of free agency. It might furthermore be thought that the cost of free agency is not great. As a beginning, let us first examine some of the costs or consequences of this non-consequentialist position. We will do this by exploring some of the literature on the unreliability and deceptiveness of patients, an exploration that will quickly take us beyond consequentialist reasoning. We do not imply by this discussion that patients are unreliable and/or immoral compared to doctors.

Empirical studies of the reliability of the data supplied by patients give us the following profile: Patients are often forgetful. They forget between 37% and 54% of the information given by their doctors soon

after leaving the office or clinic.[2] Their forgetfulness and/or ability to remember depend on such factors as their anxiety and the importance patients attribute to the information provided. Attempts to change the total recall of patients are frustrating. The information that is supplied by patients is also highly unreliable. For example, 69% of a group of tuberculosis patients made errors in reporting the drugs they were taking, and 45% of these patients made serious errors;[3] 32% of a patient population reported their diseases inaccurately or incompletely;[4] 28% of another study group erred on the drugs they were taking;[5] and 25% of asthmatics in a study characteristically mislabeled other symptoms as asthma attacks.[6] In incidents of self-poisoning, 55% of a patient group either exaggerated or underestimated the *number* of drugs that they had taken, leading the researcher to conclude that "little reliance can be placed on the patient's history."[7] Insofar as patients regard the information they give to doctors as accurate and certain (as in the case of R. B.), this information, if unreliable, becomes disruptive in the agency model of the doctor–patient relationship. While incorrect information need not destroy the doctor–patient relationship, it is likely to disrupt the outcome.

Studies relating to the degree to which patients falsify information are at least as

[2] P. Lay, "Psychological Studies of Doctor-patient Communications," in S. Rachman, ed., *Contributions to Medical Psychology*, vol. 1 (Oxford, England: Pergamon Press, 1977), pp. 23–24.

[3] A. B. Hecht, "Improving Medication Compliance by Teaching Out-Patients," *Nursing Forum* 13 (1974), pp. 112–29.

[4] W. F. Brady and J. T. Martinoff, "Validity of Health History Data Collected from Dental Patients and Patient Perception of Health Status," *Journal of the American Dental Association* 101 (1980), pp. 642–45.

[5] D. F. Preston and F. L. Miller, "The Tuberculosis Outpatient's Defection from Therapy," *American Journal of the Medical Sciences* 247 (1964), pp. 21–24.

[6] J. A. Dirks and R. A. Kinsman, "Mislabeling of Symptoms by Asthmatics: Frequency and Impact on Management," *Practical Cardiology* 10:4 (1984), pp. 77–81.

[7] N. Wright, "An Assessment of the Unreliability of the History Given by Self-Poisoned Patients," *Clinical Toxicology* 16 (1980), pp. 381–84.

disturbing as those regarding forgetfulness and unreliability. One of the earliest studies of patient truthfulness showed that between 39% and 65% of parents lied to their children's doctors concerning their administering penicillin to their children. These researchers stated that the degree of patient "unreliability" discovered was a "striking finding" in their study.[8] Other studies have borne out the general accuracy of these figures. . . . These data suggest that the case of R. B. represents only the tip of an iceberg.

Studies of non-compliance relate indirectly to patient veracity insofar as non-compliance involves the patients' not keeping tacit and/or explicit promises. Patient non-compliance is extensive. It varies from between 11% and 93% depending upon such factors as disease type, drugs prescribed, family influence, patient satisfaction, and the time frame for taking medications. Non-compliance, like a lack of veracity, can sometimes be serious in terms of harms to patients and misjudgments by doctors. For example, the hypertensive whose condition has not been well-controlled as an out-patient because of failures to comply with recommended therapy may develop severe hypotension when hospitalized and administered all of the medication that he or she was supposedly taking.

These data show that free choice is exceedingly expensive. If doctors take the information supplied by patients at face value and set this above diagnostic testing and accurate therapy—as is often required by the agency model, a large percentage of patients will be misdiagnosed, poorly treated, and sometimes seriously harmed. Furthermore, these misdiagnoses, problematic therapies, and harms would have to be morally acceptable to doctors, whose moral convictions must also be respected according to the agency model. Because

the agency model assumes that neither the patient nor the doctor should be morally coerced (that both have rights of moral choice), the doctor is placed in a moral bind. If doctors are willing to formulate problematic and/or invalid diagnoses, they bear responsibilities for ineffective and/or harmful therapies and must redefine what is now taken to be "responsible" therapy. If they accept the information supplied by patients as normative for diagnosis, they betray a long-standing commitment to scientific accuracy within medicine.

Rather than valuing the often inaccurate or falsified "choices" of patients over what is likely or demonstrably true, doctors might of course openly question their patients' truthfulness and the accuracy of the information supplied by these patients. In order to follow this course, doctors must gather information from patients concerning their degree of honesty or dishonesty (presumably with their consent), or learn how to recognize when patients are falsifying information (an impossible task) or risk offending patients by questioning their accuracy.

In the face of these frustrations and dilemmas, doctors have one other option: They can take the role of moral educators, instructing their patients about the principles of moral agreements, and conducting their practices so as to enhance greater autonomy and freedom. This option, however, smacks of moral elitism, and is even antithetical to the principles of mutual respect. It means that doctors would require patients to consent to certain moral rules before receiving medical care, which would be coercive.

The price of free choice within the agency model encompasses much more than a large number of misdiagnoses and additional expenses. It seriously conflicts with important moral and non-moral values inherent in the practice of modern medicine and leads to fundamental, sometimes unresolvable moral dilemmas for physicians. Such dilemmas over the free agency of

---

[8] A. B. Bergman and R. J. Werner, "Failure of Children to Receive Penicillin by Mouth," *New England Journal of Medicine* 268 (1963), p. 1337.

patients *vis-à-vis* that of doctors makes the agency model not merely "expensive," but impossible as a moral option in numerous circumstances, including those involving informed and competent adult patients.

The Complexities of Doctor–Patient Relating

The variety and complexity of doctor–patient interactions helps explain why these dilemmas and conflicts occur. The literature on patient deceptiveness and non-compliance indicates some of the reasons why patients are not always truthful and do not always keep their promises to doctors. Many patients wish to avoid embarrassment and/or not disappoint their doctors; some wish to obtain narcotics; some are influenced, pro and con, by family obligations, pressures, and beliefs; some feel a need to punish themselves, or deny the seriousness of their illness, or prove their self-reliance, or deny the physician's potency. Some even invent their entire illness. In short, patients interact with doctors out of the complexity of their psychological, social, and existential experiences. They relate to doctors out of their unique, sometimes eccentric definitions of self, out of their several prior and valued "contracts" with others, and out of ordinary human traits such as willfulness, weakness, risk-taking, and a desire for privacy.

The essential features of the agency model often conflict with this rich understanding of doctor–patient interactions. The agency model assumes that the agreements between doctors and patients will not be ethically compromised or undermined by prior and valued relationships, obligations, and habits. Patients, however, frequently do not think of their agreements with doctors as supplanting other commitments and orientations, thereby calling for the degrees of conscientious honesty, information-sharing, and consent required by the agency model. Patients make contingent and relative contracts with their doc-

tors, the character and types of which merit more attention.

Studies dealing with why patients visit doctors also bear on this analysis. Approximately 70% to 90% of patients seeking general ambulatory health care do not present with serious physical disorders, and only 40% of ambulatory patients can clearly be diagnosed for somatic disorders.[9] These figures and a variety of studies indicate that many patients seek out doctors for "non-medical" reasons, including worries over their health status due to common stresses in their lives, a desire for sustenance and social support due to isolation, or a desire for information that will quell anxieties or uncertainties. Patients therefore bring into clinics and hospitals a variety of psychosocial and "psychospiritual" agendas and assume that doctors can and will help them with these issues.

In these "non-medical" circumstances, patients often cannot supply accurate information because they are often unconscious, unclear, or confused about their needs and motives. The nuances and complexities of truth-telling in such circumstances stagger the imagination. The patient often does not know what to be honest about, often endows the physician (through transference) with distorted and/or false attributes and roles, and is understandably unable to separate "medical" needs from an array of past and present life needs and commitments. In order for doctors to treat patients according to the agency model in these circumstances, they would have to secure the informed consent of patients with respect to the medical, quasi-medical, and non-medical interventions that will be utilized and seek to relate how these bear or are likely to bear on the real, perhaps underlying and unconscious needs, motives, and reactions of the patient. Informed consent regarding both diagnosis and therapy in these settings would thus

[9] A. J. Barsky, "Hidden Reasons Some Patients Visit Doctors," *Annals of Internal Medicine* 94 (1981), pp. 492–98.

involve awkward, embarrassing, intrusive, offensive, and possibly harmful communications between doctor and patient. Even then, the truthfulness of doctor and patient alike cannot be assured. Truth and truthfulness as they bear on the health needs of the patient are at best proximately defined, let alone achieved.

To summarize, empirical studies of patient forgetfulness and deception indicate that honesty with doctors is viewed as relative and contingent by many patients, while studies on why patients visit doctors indicate that the dynamics of doctor–patient relationships are so complex and varied that truthful communication is at best approximated. The honesty required for informed consent and mutual contracting within the agency model seems as fully difficult to define, refine, and achieve as accurate harm–benefit analysis is in the paternalistic model. Under ideal circumstances both models are possible, but in the real, complex world of patient behavior and doctor–patient relating, each model fails.

Conclusions

This analysis indicates that the agency model is inherently unrealistic and/or unethical in regard to many, perhaps the majority of medical interventions. Our point is that, taken on its own terms, the agency model frequently does not square with how doctors and patients can, do, and ought to relate to each other. It is therefore untenable to conclude that the agency model is vindicated because the paternalistic model is also problematic and sometimes immoral. Neither model is adequate

for all circumstances, and each is subject to serious philosophical and ethical criticisms.

Having summarized the philosophical and ethical criticisms of paternalism and developed this philosophical critique of the agency model, we are faced with the contructive challenge of determining how doctor–patient relationships should be ethically structured. This analysis shows that medical interventions based on the agency model are possible only when an honest and mutual sharing of all information relevant to each respective intervention occurs between doctor and patient. Even then, such honest sharing should be viewed as approximated rather than fully achieved. This raises intriguing questions as to when, if ever, these conditions are met. We suspect that only a detailed examination of actual cases will be able to determine the extent to which the agency model is both possible and moral.

Given the criticisms of both the paternalistic and agency models, it would be a tragedy for medical professionals to conclude that because neither is fully sufficient and each is seriously flawed, that moral relationships do not count. R. B.'s case is interesting in part because it demonstrates how moral relationships make a difference and profoundly shape the behavior of doctors and patients. Precisely because ethical relationships are important, a continued search for more adequate ways of morally understanding and structuring physician–patient relationships is merited. As our discussion indicates, this search needs to be informed by empirical studies of patient behavior and the multi-faceted dynamics of physician–patient interactions.

LIES TO THE SICK AND DYING*

Sissela Bok

In this selection from her well-known book Lying, *Bok considers whether the physician may withhold the truth from a patient whose prognosis is very grim or fatal. She points out that traditional codes of medical ethics have not prohibited lying, and that strong arguments can be advanced in favor of doing so to protect the patient. However, she argues, a patient has a right to know the truth, and while some exceptions may be justified, the physician should, in general, practice openness in disclosure.*

Deception as Therapy

A forty-six-year-old man, coming to a clinic for a routine physical check-up needed for insurance purposes, is diagnosed as having a form of cancer likely to cause him to die within six months. No known cure exists for it. Chemotherapy may prolong life by a few extra months, but will have side effects the physician does not think warranted in this case. In addition, he believes that such therapy should be reserved for patients with a chance for recovery or remission. The patient has no symptoms giving him any reason to believe that he is not perfectly healthy. He expects to take a short vacation in a week.

For the physician, there are now several choices involving truthfulness. Ought he to tell the patient what he has learned, or conceal it? If asked, should he deny it? If he decides to reveal the diagnosis, should he delay doing so until after the patient returns from his vacation? Finally, even if he does reveal the serious nature of the diagnosis, should he mention the possibility of chemotherapy and his reasons for not recommending it in this case? Or should he encourage every last effort to postpone death?

In this particular case, the physician chose to inform the patient of his diagnosis right away. He did not, however, mention the possibility of chemotherapy. A medical student working under him disagreed; several nurses also thought that the patient should have been informed of this possibility. They tried, unsuccessfully, to persuade the physician that this was the patient's right. When persuasion had failed, the student elected to disobey the doctor by informing the patient of the alternative of chemotherapy. After consultation with family members, the patient chose to ask for the treatment.

Doctors confront such choices often and urgently. What they reveal, hold back, or distort will matter profoundly to their patients. Doctors stress with corresponding vehemence their reasons for the distortion or concealment: not to confuse a sick person needlessly, or cause what may well be unnecessary pain or discomfort, as in the case of the cancer patient; not to leave a patient without hope, as in those many cases where the dying are not told the truth about their condition; or to improve the chances of cure, as where unwarranted optimism is expressed about some form of therapy. Doctors use information as part of the therapeutic regimen; it is given out in amounts, in admixtures, and according to timing believed best for patients. Accuracy, by comparison, matters far less.

Lying to patients has, therefore, seemed an especially excusable act. Some would

---

* References have been deleted without indication.

argue that doctors, and *only* doctors, should be granted the right to manipulate the truth in ways so undesirable for politicians, lawyers, and others. Doctors are trained to help patients; their relationship to patients carries special obligations, and they know much more than laymen about what helps and hinders recovery and survival.

Even the most conscientious doctors, then, who hold themselves at a distance from the quacks and the purveyors of false remedies, hesitate to forswear all lying. Lying is usually wrong, they argue, but less so than allowing the truth to harm patients. . . . In the case of the man mentioned at the beginning of this chapter, some physicians might feel justified in lying for the good of the patient; others might be truthful. Some may conceal alternatives to the treatment they recommend; others not. In each case, they could appeal to the A.M.A. Principles of Ethics. A great many would choose to be able to lie. They would claim that not only can a lie avoid harm for the patient, but that it is also hard to know whether they have been right in the first place in making their pessimistic diagnosis; a "truthful" statement could therefore turn out to hurt patients unnecessarily. The concern for curing and for supporting those who cannot be cured then runs counter to the desire to be completely open. This concern is especially strong where the prognosis is bleak; even more so when patients are so affected by their illness or their medication that they are more dependent than usual, perhaps more easily depressed or irrational.

Physicians know only too well how uncertain a diagnosis or prognosis can be. They know how hard it is to give meaningful and correct answers regarding health and illness. They also know that disclosing their own uncertainty or fears can reduce those benefits that depend upon faith in recovery. They fear, too, that revealing grave risks, no matter how unlikely it is that these will come about, may exercise the pull of the "self-fulfilling prophecy."

They dislike being the bearers of uncertain or bad news as much as anyone else. And last, but not least, sitting down to discuss an illness truthfully and sensitively may take much-needed time away from other patients.

These reasons help explain why nurses and physicians and relatives of the sick and dying prefer not to be bound by rules that might limit their ability to suppress, delay, or distort information. This is not to say that they necessarily plan to lie much of the time. They merely want to have the freedom to do so when they believe it wise. And the reluctance to see lying prohibited explains, in turn, the failure of the codes and oaths to come to grips with the problems of truth-telling and lying.

But sharp conflicts are now arising. Doctors no longer work alone with patients. They have to consult with others much more than before; if they choose to lie, the choice may not be met with approval by all who take part in the care of the patient. A nurse expresses the difficulty which results as follows:

From personal experience I would say that the patients who aren't told about their terminal illness have so many verbal and mental questions unanswered that many will begin to realize that their illness is more serious than they're being told [. . .]

Nurses care for these patients twenty-four hours a day compared to a doctor's daily brief visit, and it is the nurse many times that the patient will relate to, once his underlying fears become overwhelming. [. . .] This is difficult for us nurses because being in constant contact with patients we can see the events leading up to this. The patient continually asks you, "Why isn't my pain decreasing?" or "Why isn't the radiation treatment easing the pain?" [. . .] We cannot legally give these patients an honest answer as a nurse (and I'm sure I wouldn't want to) yet the problem is still not resolved and the circle grows larger and larger with the patient alone in the middle.[1]

[1] Mary Barrett, letter, *Boston Globe*, November 16, 1976, p. 1.

The doctor's choice to lie increasingly involves co-workers in acting a part they find neither humane nor wise. The fact that these problems have not been carefully thought through within the medical profession, nor seriously addressed in medical education, merely serves to intensify the conflicts. Different doctors then respond very differently to patients in exactly similar predicaments. The friction is increased by the fact that relatives often disagree even where those giving medical care to a patient are in accord on how to approach the patient. Here again, because physicians have not worked out to common satisfaction the question of whether relatives have the right to make such requests, the problems are allowed to be haphazardly resolved by each physician as he sees fit.

The Patient's Perspective

The turmoil in the medical profession regarding truth-telling is further augmented by the pressures that patients themselves now bring to bear and by empirical data coming to light. Challenges are growing to the three major arguments for lying to patients: that truthfulness is impossible; that patients do not want bad news; and that truthful information harms them.

The first of these arguments . . . confuses "truth" and "truthfulness" so as to clear the way for occasional lying on grounds supported by the second and third arguments. At this point, we can see more clearly that it is a strategic move intended to discourage the question of truthfulness from carrying much weight in the first place, and thus to leave the choice of what to say and how to say it up to the physician. To claim that "since telling the truth is impossible, there can be no sharp distinction between what is true and what is false" is to try to defeat objections to lying before even discussing them. One need only imagine how such an argument would be received, were it made by a car salesman or a real estate dealer, to see how fallacious it is.

In medicine, however, the argument is supported by a subsidiary point: even if people might ordinarily understand what is spoken to them, patients are often not in a position to do so. This is where paternalism enters in. When we buy cars or houses, the paternalist will argue, we need to have all our wits about us; but when we are ill, we cannot always do so. We need help in making choices, even if help can be given only by keeping us in the dark. And the physician is trained and willing to provide such help.

It is certainly true that some patients cannot make the best choices for themselves when weakened by illness or drugs. But most still can. And even those who are incompetent have a right to have someone—their guardian or spouse perhaps—receive the correct information. . . .

The argument which rejects informing patients because adequate truthful information is impossible in itself or because patients are lacking in understanding, must itself be rejected when looked at from the point of view of patients. They know that liberties granted to the most conscientious and altruistic doctors will be exercised also in the "Medicaid Mills"; that the choices thus kept from patients will be exercised by not only competent but incompetent physicians; and that even the best doctors can make choices patients would want to make differently for themselves.

The second argument for deceiving patients refers specifically to giving them news of a frightening or depressing kind. It holds that patients do not, in fact, generally want such information, that they prefer not to have to face up to serious illness and death. On the basis of such a belief, most doctors in a number of surveys stated that they do not, as a rule, inform patients that they have an illness such as cancer.

When studies are made of what patients desire to know, on the other hand, a large majority say that they *would* like to be told of such a diagnosis. All these studies need updating and should be done with larger numbers of patients and non-patients. But they do show that there is generally a dramatic divergence between physicians and patients on the factual question of whether patients want to know what ails them in cases of serious illness such as cancer. In most of the studies, over 80 percent of the persons asked indicated that they would want to be told.

Sometimes this discrepancy is set aside by doctors who want to retain the view that patients do not want unhappy news. In reality, they claim, the fact that patients say they want it has to be discounted. The more someone asks to know, the more he suffers from fear which will lead to the denial of the information even if it is given. Informing patients is, therefore, useless; they resist and deny having been told what they cannot assimilate. According to this view, empirical studies of what patients say they want are worthless since they do not probe deeply enough to uncover this universal resistance to the contemplation of one's own death.

This view is only partially correct. For some patients, denial is indeed well established in medical experience. A number of patients (estimated at between 15 percent and 25 percent) will give evidence of denial of having been told about their illness, even when they repeatedly ask and are repeatedly informed. And nearly everyone experiences a period of denial at some point in the course of approaching death.

But to say that denial is universal flies in the face of all evidence. And to take any claim to the contrary as "symptomatic" of deeper denial leaves no room for reasoned discourse. There is no way that such universal denial can be proved true or false. To believe in it is a metaphysical belief about man's condition, not a statement about what patients do and do not want. It is true that we can never completely understand the possibility of our own death, any more than being alive in the first place.

But people certainly differ in the degree to which they can approach such knowledge, take it into account in their plans, and make their peace with it.

Montaigne claimed that in order to learn both to live and to die, men have to think about death and be prepared to accept it.[2] To stick one's head in the sand, or to be prevented by lies from trying to discern what is to come, hampers freedom—freedom to consider one's life as a whole, with a beginning, a duration, an end. Some may request to be deceived rather than to see their lives as thus finite; others reject the information which would require them to do so; but most say that they want to know. Their concern for knowing about their condition goes far beyond mere curiosity or the wish to make isolated personal choices in the short time left to them; their stance toward the entire life they have lived, and their ability to give it meaning and completion, are at stake. In lying or withholding the facts which permit such discernment, doctors may reflect their own fears (which, according to one study,[3] are much stronger than those of laymen) of facing questions about the meaning of one's life and the inevitability of death.

Beyond the fundamental deprivation that can result from deception, we are also becoming increasingly aware of all that can befall patients in the course of their illness when information is denied or distorted. Lies place them in a position where they no longer participate in choices concerning their own health, including the choice of whether to be a "patient" in the first place. A terminally ill person who is not informed that his illness is incurable and that he is near death cannot make decisions about the end of his life: about whether or not to enter a hospital, or to have surgery; where and with whom to spend his last days; how to put his affairs in order—these

---

[2] Michel de Montaigne, *Essays*, Book 1, Chapter 20.
[3] Herman Feifel et al., "Physicians Consider Death," *Proceedings of the American Psychoanalytical Association*, 1967, pp. 201–2.

most personal choices cannot be made if he is kept in the dark, or given contradictory hints and clues.

It has always been especially easy to keep knowledge from terminally ill patients. They are most vulnerable, least able to take action to learn what they need to know, or to protect their autonomy. The very fact of being so ill greatly increases the likelihood of control by others. And the fear of being helpless in the face of such control is growing. At the same time, the period of dependency and slow deterioration of health and strength that people undergo has lengthened. There has been a dramatic shift toward institutionalization of the aged and those near death. (Over 80 percent of Americans now die in a hospital or other institution.) . . . The growing fear, if it is not of the moment of dying nor of being dead, is of all that which now precedes dying for so many: the possibility of prolonged pain, the increasing weakness, the uncertainty, the loss of powers and chance of senility, the sense of being a burden. This fear is further nourished by the loss of trust in health professionals. In part, the loss of trust results from the abuses which have been exposed—the Medicaid scandals, the old-age home profiteering, the commercial exploitation of those who seek remedies for their ailments; in part also because of the deceptive practices patients suspect, having seen how friends and relatives were kept in the dark; in part, finally, because of the sheer numbers of persons, often strangers, participating in the care of any one patient. Trust which might have gone to a doctor long known to the patient goes less easily to a team of strangers, no matter how expert or well-meaning. . . .

The reason why even doctors who recognize a patient's right to have information might still not provide it brings us to the third argument against telling all patients the truth. It holds that the information given might hurt the patient and that the concern for the right to such information

is therefore a threat to proper health care. A patient, these doctors argue, may wish to commit suicide after being given discouraging news, or suffer a cardiac arrest, or simply cease to struggle, and thus not grasp the small remaining chance for recovery. And even where the outlook for a patient is very good, the disclosure of a minute risk can shock some patients or cause them to reject needed protection such as a vaccination or antibiotics.

The factual basis for this argument has been challenged from two points of view. The damages associated with the disclosure of sad news or risks are rarer than physicians believe; and the *benefits* which result from being informed are more substantial, even measurably so. Pain is tolerated more easily, recovery from surgery is quicker, and cooperation with therapy is greatly improved. The attitude that "what you don't know won't hurt you" is proving unrealistic; it is what patients do not know but vaguely suspect that causes them corrosive worry.

It is certain that no answers to this question of harm from information are the same for all patients. If we look, first, at the fear expressed by physicians that informing patients of even remote or unlikely risks connected with a drug prescription or operation might shock some and make others refuse the treatment that would have been best for them, it appears to be unfounded for the great majority of patients. Studies show that very few patients respond to being told of such risks by withdrawing their consent to the procedure and that those who do withdraw are the very ones who might well have been upset enough to sue the physician had they not been asked to consent beforehand. It is possible that on even rarer occasions especially susceptible persons might manifest physical deterioration from shock; some physicians have even asked whether patients who die after giving informed consent to an operation, but before it actually takes place, somehow expire because of the information given to them. While such questions are unanswerable in any one case, they certainly argue in favor of caution, a real concern for the person to whom one is recounting the risks he or she will face, and sensitivity to all signs of distress.

The situation is quite different when persons who are already ill, perhaps already quite weak and discouraged, are told of a very serious prognosis. Physicians fear that such knowledge may cause the patients to commit suicide, or to be frightened or depressed to the point that their illness takes a downward turn. The fear that great numbers of patients will commit suicide appears to be unfounded. And if some do, is that a response so unreasonable, so much against the patient's best interest that physicians ought to make it a reason for concealment or lies? Many societies have allowed suicide in the past; our own has decriminalized it; and some are coming to make distinctions among the many suicides which ought to be prevented if at all possible, and those which ought to be respected.

Another possible response to very bleak news is the triggering of physiological mechanisms which allow death to come more quickly—a form of giving up or of preparing for the inevitable, depending on one's outlook. . . . Such a response may be appropriate, in which case it makes the moments of dying as peaceful as those who have died and been resuscitated so often testify. But it may also be brought on inappropriately, when the organism could have lived on, perhaps even induced malevolently, by external acts intended to kill. . . .

It is not inconceivable that unhappy news abruptly conveyed, or a great shock given to someone unable to tolerate it, could also bring on such a "dying response," quite unintended by the speaker. There is every reason to be cautious and to try to know ahead of time how susceptible a patient might be to the accidental triggering—however rare—of such a response. . . .

When, on the other hand, one considers those who are already near death, the "dying response" may be much less inappropriate, much less accidental, much less unreasonable. . . . Modern medicine, in its valiant efforts to defeat disease and to save lives, may be dislocating the conscious as well as the purely organic responses allowing death to come when it is inevitable, thus denying those who are dying the benefits of the traditional approach to death. In lying to them, and in pressing medical efforts to cure them long past the point of possible recovery, physicians may thus rob individuals of an autonomy few would choose to give up. . . .

Apart from the possible harm from information, we are coming to learn much more about the benefits it can bring patients. People follow instructions more carefully if they know what their disease is and why they are asked to take medication; any benefits from those procedures are therefore much more likely to come about. Similarly, people recover faster from surgery and tolerate pain with less medication if they understand what ails them and what can be done for them.

Respect and Truthfulness

Taken all together, the three arguments defending lies to patients stand on much shakier ground as a counter-weight to the right to be informed than is often thought. The common view that many patients cannot understand, do not want, and may be harmed by, knowledge of their condition, and that lying to them is either morally neutral or even to be recommended, must be set aside. Instead, we have to make a more complex comparison. Over against the right of patients to knowledge concerning themselves, the medical and psychological benefits to them from this knowledge, the unnecessary and sometimes harmful treatment to which they can be subjected if ignorant, and the harm to physicians, their profession, and other patients from deceptive practices, we have to set a severely restricted and narrowed paternalistic view—that *some* patients cannot understand, *some* do not want, and *some* may be harmed by, knowledge of their condition, and that they ought not to have to be treated like everyone else if this is not in their best interest.

Such a view is persuasive. A few patients openly request not to be given bad news. Others give clear signals to that effect, or are demonstrably vulnerable to the shock or anguish such news might call forth. Can one not in such cases infer implied consent to being deceived?

Concealment, evasion, withholding of information may at times be necessary. But if someone contemplates lying to a patient or concealing the truth, the burden of proof must shift. It must rest, here, as with all deception, on those who advocate it in any one instance. They must show why they fear a patient may be harmed or how they know that another cannot cope with the truthful knowledge. A decision to deceive must be seen as a very unusual step, to be talked over with colleagues and others who participate in the care of the patient. Reasons must be set forth and debated, alternatives weighed carefully. At all times, the correct information must go to *someone* closely related to the patient.

The law already permits doctors to withhold information from patients where it would clearly hurt their health. But this privilege has been sharply limited by the courts. Certainly it cannot be interpreted so broadly as to permit a general practice of deceiving patients "for their own good." Nor can it be made to include cases where patients might calmly decide, upon hearing their diagnosis, not to go ahead with the therapy their doctor recommends. Least of all can it justify silence or lies to large numbers of patients merely on the grounds that it is not always easy to tell what a patient wants.

For the great majority of patients, on the contrary, the goal must be disclosure, and the atmosphere one of openness. But it would be wrong to assume that patients can therefore be told abruptly about a serious diagnosis—that, so long as openness exists, there are no further requirements of humane concern in such communication. . . . Above all, truthfulness with those who are suffering does not mean that they should be deprived of all hope: hope that there is a chance of recovery, however small; nor of reassurance that they will not be abandoned when they most need help.

Much needs to be done, however, if the deceptive practices are to be eliminated, and if concealment is to be restricted to the few patients who ask for it or those who can be shown to be harmed by openness. The medical profession has to address this problem. Those who are in training to take care of the sick and the dying have to learn how to speak with them, even about dying. . . .

LYING IN THE LAW*

Kenneth Kipnis

Commenting on law as a profession in which there is extended direct contact between professional and client, as there also is in medicine, Kipnis examines situations in which the attorney is institutionally permitted—and sometimes encouraged—to lie. Kipnis describes the degree to which legal practice is permeated with deception, some of it paternalistic though much of it not, despite law's professed search for truth. He offers solutions to specific dilemmas, including lying to a judge, by recommending certain changes in customary legal practice.

In the criminal law, ethical problems can begin with the decision to represent. For every accused rapist, murderer, kidnapper, and extortionist; for every felon who is apprehended and brought to trial, there is an attorney endeavoring to clear the client of the charge. No matter how diabolically corrupt the defendant, no matter how fiendishly loathsome the offense, the attorney's professional responsibility will likely be to try to soften the judgment and mitigate the sentence as much as possible. . . .

. . . Some might compare the attorney to the driver of the getaway car at a bank robbery. In removing the robbers from the scene of their crime, the driver does what he can to see to it that the criminals do not pay for their wrongdoing. How, one might wonder, is the attorney's "professional responsibility" any different? Though the suspects have been apprehended, the lawyer seems equally to assist wrongdoers in evading the just consequences of their actions. While the lawyer and the driver may be different in the eyes of the law, are they ethically distinguishable?

Let us look at questions of complicity as they might emerge in the course of a criminal case. Rodney Soames, the potential client, tells his attorney that he has committed the rape with which he has been charged. Following the crime, the victim,

a Miss Margaret Gregor, called the police and gave them a rough description of her assailant. Among other things, he was said to be wearing a red and white striped sweater. Within forty-five minutes of the attack, Soames, wearing such a sweater, was spotted in the neighborhood and taken into custody. The following day Miss Gregor, a high-strung, emotionally distraught young woman, picked him out of a lineup. Except for saying that he was on his way to a friend's house and that he wanted to talk to a lawyer, Soames has told the police nothing. He is twenty-five, single, and steadily employed as a stock clerk.

Clearly one question that may arise is whether the attorney can properly take this client's case, undertaking to represent him as his advocate in the anticipated criminal proceedings. It is true that the attorney, if she accepts the case, will be "helping a rapist." But it is important here to distinguish between two senses in which one can help a wrongdoer. If what one does is to help a wrongdoer commit a wrongdoing, then one is clearly complicitous. But there are lots of ways in which one can "help a wrongdoer" that do not involve complicity in wrongdoing. If a convicted axe-murderer asks me for the time of day, I do not come to share in any guilt if I show him my watch. The same axe-murderer

* Footnotes have been deleted without indication.

From Kenneth Kipnis, *Legal Ethics,* © 1986, pp. 81–95. Reprinted by permission of Prentice-Hall, Inc., Englewood Cliffs, N.J.

has a right to send a postcard and, accordingly, to have the assistance of officers of the postal service. Not only is it permissible for an officer of the postal service to give effect to the criminal's decision to mail the card; it would be manifestly improper for the official to refuse to do so. What needs to be shown is not that the attorney assists a rapist, but rather that she assists the rapist in doing something that is wrong. What is it, exactly, that the attorney will be doing for the rapist as the proceedings get under way? Only as we assess what is involved in legal advocacy on behalf of the guilty can we address the question of whether the attorney has overstepped the bounds of the ethical.

As the proceedings commence, the attorney's responsibility will be to see to it that her client, even if he is guilty, gets that to which the law entitles him. The Constitution guarantees to criminal defendants, regardless of their culpability, such important protections as the right to counsel, the right to due process, the right to present evidence on their own behalf, the right to cross-examine witnesses, the right to a public trial by jury, the right to appeal to the state for that which is guaranteed as a matter of law. In complex legal systems such as ours, this respect for the dignity of the defendant cannot be secured without skilled legal assistance. There are rules that the community sets for itself before it can properly punish one of its members, rules that secure for all of us a right to a fair hearing before the verdict is spoken. The defense attorney's job is, in the first place, to see to it that the community honors its own rules and, in the second place, to see to it that the court gets a chance to hear what can be said on the defendant's behalf.

It should be remembered that, in criminal proceedings, lawyers are virtually never in a position to do anything directly for their clients. Rather they request that certain things be done, they advance arguments, they petition. The ultimate disposition is always in the hands of another:

the judge, the prosecutor, the jury, the appeals court, the warden, the governor. This is not to say that lawyers bear no responsibility for what these others do. Some responsibility is there. But it does serve to remind us that the petitions of legal representatives are but a part of a much larger decision-making apparatus involving judges, juries, prosecutorial adversaries, and a huge and complex body of law. The defense attorney's job is to see to it that that machine does not dishonor the community's own standards of fairness.

At the moment the chief problem is the arraignment. The client will appear before the judge to enter a plea of "guilty" or "not guilty." (No one is "innocent" in the American legal system.) Procedurally, the entry of the plea is the first formal step a defendant takes in the criminal process. If he pleads "guilty" to the facts, trial is essentially waived and all that remains is the sentencing. On the other hand, if he pleads "not guilty," then, unless the plea is later changed, the state will be "put to its proof" in the forum of a criminal trial. The prosecutor may be obliged to prove beyond a reasonable doubt that the defendant committed the crime for which he is charged. But now, since neither has looked at the state's evidence, it is not clear to the client or the attorney whether the prosecutor can meet the burden of proof. A crossroads has been reached and the attorney must make her first ethical decision: Should she assist the client in entering a plea of "not guilty"?

Perhaps the first answer that comes to mind begins with the observation that, since in this case to plead "not guilty" is to lie, and since it is wrong to lie, the defendant is prohibited from entering a plea of "not guilty." The rapist ought to plead "guilty" to the charge; after all, he committed the crime. Because it is wrong to lie—wrong knowingly to deny what is true—he should " 'fess up" and tell the truth. Accordingly, if what the lawyer and the client jointly undertake to do is to lie, it would seem that they are partners in wrongdoing at the very outset of the criminal process.

But is the rapist ethically culpable for a lie told in entering his plea of "not guilty"? Some would protest that a plea of guilty is not really an assertion at all. Rather it is more like what the starter does at a footrace in calling "Ready, set, go!" What the starter says, it can be argued, is not something that can be true or false. Rather it is a signal that certain things that it would be pointless or improper to do prior to the signal—running toward the finish line, for example—have now become appropriate. In a similar way the doctor's pronunciation of death is a signal that that which used to be the body of a person can now be treated as a corpse. Likewise a plea of "not guilty" signals that the charges will be contested and that a date for a formal trial must be set. The plea is therefore a move in a game, a mere legal formality, carrying none of the weight of a dishonest protestation of innocence.

But this rejoinder won't do. While it is true that the plea signals the applicability of certain procedures, it is equally true that the procedures have their applicability specifically because the defendant has denied committing the crime. The trial can occur precisely because there is disagreement (contradictory assertions) on the issue of whether or not the defendant committed the crime. As a society, we are committed to the principle that only the guilty should be punished. The defendant's guilt is the very reason for punishment. Since there are only two ways in which guilt can be adjudicated—either a guilty plea is accepted, usually before trial, or there is a verdict of "guilty" at trial—the terms "guilty" and "not guilty" do carry weight as assertions. To enter a plea of "not guilty" is to declare publicly "I didn't do it." If the declaration is false, we must regard the defendant as having lied. That a plea also serves as a key move in the criminal process does not entail that it cannot count as an assertion.

Some might protest that the plea cannot be counted as a culpable lie because it is not entered under oath. But while it is true that perjury, to be a crime, requires that the false assertion be one which is made under oath, it is not the case that nonperjurious dishonesty is innocent. The perjuror, it seems, lies twice: once in promising to tell the truth and a second time in the lie itself. The solemnity of the oath may also contribute to the culpability of the offense. But while we may have more reason to condemn the perjuror (who lies twice), we surely have some reason to be critical of those who lie, but less often.

Perhaps it can be argued that the plea of "not guilty" should not be condemned because, while the assertion is false (and known by the asserter to be false), it is not likely to produce false beliefs among those who hear it. An actor in a play may deliver the line "It is raining outside," but no one in the audience forms beliefs about the weather on that basis. While what he says may be false and, indeed, known to be false, the actor avoids culpability simply because no members of the audience can be expected to form false beliefs on the basis of what he says. Likewise, with the false plea of "not guilty," it may be equally unlikely that minds will be changed. The prosecutor, one supposes, has assembled evidence in support of the charge and has formed a responsible judgment that the defendant did indeed commit rape. When the defendant says "not guilty," it is not as if the prosecutor will sheepishly apologize for his mistake and drop charges. What we have when a plea of "not guilty" is entered is not so much a reason to form a judgment as a reason to withhold judgment until all the evidence has been weighed. Perhaps the false plea of "not guilty" is excusable just as the actor's false assertion is.

Still, it may be that the reason few take such protestations of innocence seriously is that we have come to expect defendants to enter pleas of "not guilty" in spite of guilt. Since we "know" that guilty defendants will often lie about their involvement in crime—to avoid punishment if for no other reason—they will not be credited when they declare their innocence. We do not exculpate known or suspected liars on the grounds that they cannot get away with their deception. If the reason why we don't believe defendants' assertions that they are not guilty is that we almost always have reason to believe they are lying, then the fact that we are not misled by their lies is not a reason for excusing the lies. It would thus appear that, even though no one is misled, a lie is told; and, insofar as lying is wrong, the defendant commits just such a wrong in his lie whether or not he succeeds in misleading others.

But is it clear that lying is always wrong? Cases readily come to mind in which, if we are not certain that a lie is justifiable, we are at least less than certain that it is wrong. Other important values can sometimes compete with honesty. An aunt asks us what we think of her hat. Must we speak our minds freely regardless of the effect on her sensibilities? Isn't it permissible, under the circumstances, to pretend? Absolutist positions on this issue are not uniformly persuasive. The standard philosophers' example involves a murderer who asks you if his erstwhile victim is at home. You saw your neighbor enter his house only moments earlier. It would appear that you should have both a right not to contribute to the enterprise of the killer and another right not to be threatened for refusing assistance. If, under the circumstances, the only way to secure these two rights is to lie, then perhaps the lie can be excused. Perhaps you can ethically lie to the murderer without incurring moral blame.

The correlative issue that emerges in the case of the criminal defendant's plea involves the obligation to assist officials in bringing oneself to justice. While the rapist cannot be excused from his crime, is he culpable as well for not cooperating with the officers of the criminal justice system in their effort to deprive him of his liberty? I think this is a difficult question. In part, the Fifth Amendment restriction on being compelled to testify against oneself is evidence of some sensitivity to the complexity of the moral issues here. At a minimum, if the defendant has other obligations that will be compromised by prolonged imprisonment—a condition that will likely be satisfied if he has any positive obligations at all—those obligations must be placed in the balance before we can judge whether the accused is culpable for not publicly acknowledging his guilt. If we suspect that the punishment meted out for the crime will be excessive or that the act, though criminal, was not a wrongdoing, then these considerations should also give us pause before we condemn anyone for hesitating before submitting to punishment. Moreover, loss of liberty is such a serious consequence that it may be necessary generally to excuse those who are not eager to embrace it. The point is that it can be a difficult moral question whether or not lying is permissible to avoid punishment. While we may revere the virtuous George Washington for confessing that he cut down the cherry tree, there may not always be an overriding duty to declare publicly one's wrongdoings when asked to do so. It may not be reasonable to expect everyone to measure up to George Washington's standard, especially when the punishment meted out is so much greater than the one he faced. Because of the consequences he faces if he confesses, it does not seem certain that the rapist is morally prohibited from falsely denying guilt. And if we cannot say confidently that, all things considered, the rapist is morally obligated to confess his crime, then we cannot say confidently that the lawyer is unethical in assisting the rapist in entering a plea of "not guilty." Of course the lawyer does not herself lie in entering the plea on her client's behalf: "Your Honor, my client enters a plea of 'not guilty.'" It is worth observing that some legal systems—the system in the Federal Republic of Germany, for example—function without allowing for a "guilty" plea. There, the defense attorney's job is always to present the defense.

Concerting a False Defense

Let us suppose then that Rodney Soames will now stand trial for the crime of rape. The prosecution's chief witness is the victim, who claims to have gotten a good look at her assailant. She has told the police that the rapist wore a red and white striped sweater. Your client was picked up wearing such a sweater and was still wearing it when the victim identified him in the lineup. Such sweaters are currently popular attire; hundreds have been sold in the city. The young woman's identification may have been influenced by the fact that the distinctive sweater was not worn by any of the others in the lineup. Your client has shared with you the details of the rape and has told you that he was convicted on an assault charge eighteen months earlier in another state. The prosecution's case seems weak. There is the matter of the sweater, and, because of darkness in the woman's apartment where the rape took place and problems with the young woman's eyesight, the victim may not be a credible witness. There are no other witnesses.

In discussions with your client, you tell him that because the punishment for rape has recently been set quite high, juries have been reluctant to convict. However, they do seem to take a dim view of defendants who are unwilling to take the stand to give their version of what happened. Your client decides to try to lie his way to an acquittal, taking the stand and claiming that he has been incorrectly identified as the rapist; he was just innocently walking from his home to a friend's house when he was arrested by the police. Thinking that he stands a good chance of being believed by the jury, he wants to take the stand and lie under oath, thus committing the crime of perjury.

Because of an air of innocence and believability about him, it seems to you that he is quite likely to get away with it. (Do you tell him this?) Though you have neither suggested nor encouraged perjury, he has come to his decision on the basis of the facts, opinions, judgments, and observations that his lawyer shared with him. He has been apprised of the punishment for perjury but elects to take his chances. How ought the defense attorney to deal with a client who intends to commit perjury?

If one looks back on what has happened, it may seem that the problem is rooted in the attorney's knowing too much. It is a widespread view that a criminal lawyer can better serve the client if he or she *doesn't* know what happened. Problems of complicity can be avoided if attorneys artfully arrange their relationship with the client to "preserve deniability" of knowledge concerning the offense. The classic statement of this approach is in Robert Traver's novel *Anatomy of a Murder.*[1] The lawyer is interviewing a client who is accused of first-degree murder.

I paused and lit a cigar. I took my time. I had reached a point where a few wrong answers to a few right questions would leave me with a client—if I took his case—whose cause was legally defenseless. Either I stopped now and begged off and let some other lawyer worry over it or I asked him the few fatal questions and let him hang himself. Or else, like any smart lawyer, I went into the Lecture. I studied my man. . . . He apparently did not realize how close I had him to admitting that he was guilty of first degree murder. . . . The man was a sitting duck. . . .

And what is the Lecture?

The Lecture is an ancient device that lawyers use to coach their clients so that the client won't quite know he has been coached and his lawyer can still preserve the face-saving illusion that he hasn't done any coaching. For coaching clients, like robbing them, is not only frowned

[1] Robert Traver, *Anatomy of a Murder* (New York: St. Martin's Press, Inc., 1958): pp. 32–35.

upon, it is downright unethical and bad, very bad. Hence the Lecture, an artful device as old as the law itself, and one used constantly by some of the nicest and most ethical lawyers in the land.

The lawyer in the novel informs his client that if the facts are as he has stated them, there is no legal defense and he will probably be electrocuted. But, he goes on, if the client acted in a blind rage, there is a possibility of saving his life. He suggests that his client think it over. Not surprisingly, the client soon "recollects" the rage.

"Who, me? I didn't tell him what to say," the lawyer can later comfort himself. "I merely explained the law, see." It is a good practice to scowl and shrug here and add virtuously: "That's my duty, isn't it?"

But the cultivation and protection of the lawyer's ignorance are not consistent with the obligation of a counselor to get the facts. In its Standards Relating to the Defense Function, the American Bar Association condemns "the tactic, occasionally advocated by unscrupulous lawyers . . . of advising the client at the outset not to admit anything to the lawyer which might handicap the lawyer's freedom in calling witnesses or in otherwise making a defense." It is not just a question of what the attorney knows but, equally important, what the attorney should know. If . . . counseling requires that attorneys try to find out what happened, they fail in their obligations as counselors if, preserving deniability, they ask the client not to tell them anything. Excessive concern for clean hands may therefore do more damage to professional integrity than excessive concern for the client. This is because lay clients cannot be expected to make judgments about which facts will help them and which ones will not.

In any event, Rodney Soames has already told his lawyer that he did it. What is the attorney's obligation now?

One option is to abandon the client. To put your client on the stand and build on his perjured testimony is to carry zealous advocacy too far. How would abandonment work? In criminal procedures, the bond between the attorney and the client can often be similar to that of a marriage: The court's permission must be obtained before the lawyer–client relationship can be dissolved. And, as with divorce, there may have to be good grounds for severing the tie. The attorney can go to the judge and ask to be removed from the case. Since getting a new attorney will take the court's time—justice delayed is justice denied—the judge will want to know the reasons. It is here that the attorney may face an insuperable difficulty. For she cannot explain her request by saying "My client wants to perjure himself on the witness stand" without letting the judge know that Rodney Soames is guilty. Apart from the violation of confidentiality, Soames cannot be expected to receive a fair trial in a courtroom dominated by a judge who has been told by the defendant's own attorney that the defendant intends to lie under oath about what he did.

Maybe she can hint at the reason without disclosure. "Your Honor, I have an ethical problem with my client." But in practice this ends up being just as bad, for the words themselves are a clanging bell to experienced judges who will then be alert to what is going on. They will know what the lawyer is saying just because they know what the lawyer is unable to say.

In fact, even if we suppose that the attorney is able to withdraw from representation without compromising the judicial proceedings, that won't solve the problem either. For, knowing now how the game is played, the "innocent" and believable Mr. Soames will not make the mistake of telling the next attorney the truth.[2]

---

[2] The second attorney would know if, as a condition of representation, he or she secures from Soames a waiver of confidentiality as regards communications from the first attorney. The first attorney could thus be required *by Soames*, her former client, to disclose all she knew to subsequent attorneys working on the same matter. The first attorney

The second attorney will rise in court to build on perjured testimony. However, he will not realize that that is what he is doing. And even if we were to require attorneys with "ethical problems" to resign and disclose the defendant's perjurious intentions to all subsequent lawyers, there would still be an uneliminable dilemma. For either some (unethical?) attorney will go forward to defend the perjurious Soames, thus perpetrating a fraud upon the court, or, if the bar is sufficiently "upright," no attorney will. If the former, we are back where we started; with his lawyer's assistance, Soames will get to present his perjurious case. But now suppose no lawyer will represent him. Let us suppose that all the lawyers who would have represented him have been disbarred. In that case, Soames cannot receive a fair trial, because the proceedings will not be fair in the absence of such legal representation. Because legal representation is required for a trial to be fair, and because no lawyer will represent Soames, the state cannot offer Soames a fair trial. Moreover, since, by its own rules, the state cannot properly punish people unless it offers them a fair trial; and since, because of a legal profession that refuses to defend Soames, the state cannot offer Soames the fair trial to which he is entitled, *the state cannot properly punish this rapist.* The ethics of the legal profession should not make it impossible for the state to punish the guilty. This is an equally unacceptable result.

Building on Perjured Testimony

So what is it like to build on perjured testimony? In the first place the attorney should work to discourage her client from committing the crime of perjury. She should

tell him of the possibility that he will be found out and, if so, what the punishment is likely to be. She should advise him not to proceed with his plan. If she is unsuccessful in dissuading him, she may not then assist in the fabrication of his story. She may not suggest how the lie should be told. It would seem, however, to be acceptable to warn the client that some particular aspect of his story may permit the prosecutor to undermine his credibility upon cross-examination. But the lie itself must be the client's handiwork. At this stage, all the attorney owes to the client is the advice not to commit perjury and the assessment of what may happen if the defendant goes ahead anyway and lies under oath.

The attorney will have to put Soames on the witness stand and let him speak. Obviously the questions that she asks her client must not signal in any way that the testimony is perjured. She may not sit back, for example, and ask him merely to tell his story if that is not how she would treat a truthful witness. Nor should she question her client in a way that might expose the perjury: That is the responsibility of the prosecutor. As Monroe Freedman has put it:

. . . the criminal defense attorney, however unwillingly in terms of personal morality, has a professional responsibility as an advocate in an adversary system to examine the perjurious client in the ordinary way and to argue to the jury, as evidence in the case, the testimony presented by the defendant.[3]

This posture has attracted critics. For example, Sissela Bok takes issue with Freedman in her book *Lying:*

If, that is, a lawyer has a client who lies to the court and thus commits perjury, Professor Freedman holds that his defense lawyer has the professional responsibility to ask questions which do not contest this testimony and even to use the false testimony in making the best case for

---

could also have a professional obligation to prevent former clients from defrauding and/or otherwise implicating in wrongdoing other subsequent attorneys who would not be aware of client deception. Such disclosure to a fellow officer of the court, solely to prevent a colleague from being unknowingly implicated in wrongdoing, is not a breach of professional ethics. Of course the disclosure should not go beyond second attorney(s).

[3] Monroe H. Freedman, *Lawyers' Ethics in an Adversary System* (Indianapolis: The Bobbs-Merrill Company, Inc., 1975), pp. 40–41.

the client to the court officers and the jury. That this can involve lying is beyond doubt. Nor is there serious doubt that such instances are not rare in actual practice. Yet perjury has traditionally been more abhorred than other lying. How is it, then, that it has come to be thus defended, albeit by a minority of commentators? Defended, moreover, not just as a regrettable practice at times excusable, but actually as a *professional responsibility.*[4]

In the first place, it should be plain that while perjury—lying under oath—would be committed by the client, it cannot be committed by the client's attorney, since, unless counsel takes the stand as a witness, what the lawyer says to the court is not spoken under oath. So Freedman cannot be said to advocate that lawyers commit perjury. Still, Bok suggests that, in endeavoring to make the best case for a perjurious client, a lawyer guided by commentators such as Freedman will lie in adverting to the testimony of the lying witness. Lies told to the court seem to be culpable, and Bok takes attorneys like Freedman to task for advocating such mendacity on the part of defense attorneys. But is mendacity a necessary part of responsible advocacy in cases such as this one?

In the Code of Professional Responsibility (Ethical Consideration 7–24) is contained the following admonition:

In order to bring about just and informed decisions, evidentiary and procedural rules have been established by tribunals to permit the inclusion of relevant evidence and argument and the exclusion of all other considerations. The expression by a lawyer of his personal opinion as to the justness of a cause, as to the credibility of a witness, as to the culpability of a civil litigant, or as to the guilt or innocence of an accused is not a proper subject for argument to the trier of fact. It is improper as to factual matters because admissible evidence possessed by a lawyer should be presented only as sworn testimony. It is improper as to all other matters because, were the rule otherwise, the silence of

a lawyer on a given occasion could be construed unfavorably to his client. However, a lawyer may argue, on his analysis of the evidence, for any position or conclusion with respect to any of the foregoing matters.

In the related Disciplinary Rules lawyers are warned that, in representing a client, a lawyer shall not "knowingly make a false statement of law or fact" (DR 7-102 [A][5]); and, even more strongly, in appearing in a professional capacity before a tribunal, neither shall an attorney assert "personal knowledge of the facts in issue, except when testifying as a witness" (DR 7-106 [C][3]). What this means is that if there is some matter of fact that is to be determined by the court, lawyers involved in the case are prohibited from expressing as their own beliefs or as things known to them any personal statements concerning that matter. Not only are lawyers prohibited from lying on behalf of their clients: They have been traditionally *prohibited as well from asserting what they know to be true.*

In these passages the code is making an important and easily overlooked distinction between, on the one hand, advancing, on the basis of evidence presented to the court, an argument for conclusions that the attorney knows to be false, and, on the other hand, asserting the truth of those conclusions. If one studies the "assertions" of skilled attorneys, one will readily note the prevalence of such expressions as "I ask the jury to consider that . . ." or "I submit that . . ." or "The conclusion that must be drawn from this evidence is that . . .," and so on. In criminal defense work, the task of the advocate is not, as Bok seems to suppose, convincingly to assert that the defendant is innocent: It is rather to present arguments for acquittal on the basis of the evidence presented to the court. Thus, in her summation, the argument presented by Soames's defense attorney could go as follows:

"As the jury in this case it is your solemn responsibility to reach a verdict. You have

[4] Sissela Bok, *Lying: Moral Choice in Private and Public Life* (New York: Pantheon Books, 1978), pp. 167–168.

heard Rodney Soames tell his story, a story that the prosecution has been unable to refute. You must now ask yourselves whether you believe the defendant's clear explanation of what took place on that fateful afternoon, or whether you will accept the judgment of an emotionally distraught rape victim, rightly angered by the sexual assault committed upon her person, enraged at the man in the red and white striped sweater whom she dimly saw, without her glasses, in the shadows of her darkened apartment. You must ask yourselves whether, when she identified Rodney Soames in the police lineup only hours after her assault, she saw her assailant or saw merely an innocent bystander whose only mistake was to go to his job on that day dressed in the wrong clothes.

"Rape is a terrible offense, and the punishment for it is properly very severe. For that reason great care must be taken before tarring this young man with that broad brush. While it is true that the man who raped Margaret Gregor deserves to be punished, I submit that it is equally true that the prosecution has not proved that Rodney Soames is that man. I ask that, in issuing your verdict in this case, you tell the prosecutor and the police that, before they put anyone through the ordeal of a criminal trial, they make sure they can support their accusations with hard evidence. I ask that you find the defendant not guilty."

A careful reading of the lawyer's summation to the jury will not disclose any lies told by her to the court. Still, what Soames's lawyer says to the jury is, in a sense, wholly misleading. Soames has raped Margaret Gregor and his defense attorney knows it. She is arguing that the jury should form the judgment that Soames is not guilty when in fact she knows he is. In *ordinary discourse* when someone presents powerful arguments for the conclusion P (where P is some proposition), listeners are typically entitled to assume that the speaker believes P. At the least, listeners are entitled to feel wronged if they find out later on that the speaker knew all along that P was false. They are entitled to feel wronged even if line-by-line scrutiny of what was said fails to disclose a single materially false statement. It is not that lawyers lie; it is that, in this special way, they are dishonest.

But the problem with this criticism of defense attorneys is that it fails to take into account the degree to which language in a criminal trial differs from ordinary discourse. The jury in a criminal trial is not supposed to be taking what the defense attorney says as an assertion that the client is innocent. As has been noted earlier, what the attorney believes is irrelevant. Rather, the issue is whether or not the evidence adduced at trial supports, beyond a reasonable doubt, the proposition that the defendant committed the crime with which he has been charged. If juries and others are misled, it is not because defense attorneys are dishonest. It is rather because the required conventions of criminal defense work are insufficiently understood. Bok suggests (pp. 171–73) that judges should warn juries about this. Perhaps it is advisable that judges generally instruct those in the court that, if defense attorneys are unable to dissuade clients from lying under oath, they may be required knowingly to build upon perjured testimony. Judges should make it clear that, in undertaking to represent their clients, defense attorneys are not guaranteeing the truthfulness of what defendants say in court. And neither are defense attorneys supposed to let their personal beliefs about the client's guilt or innocence affect the manner in which they discharge their obligations of advocacy. Instructions such as these would seem ample to blunt criticisms of dishonesty.

Lying to the Judge

Having heard the arguments and the evidence, the jury finds Soames guilty of the crime of rape. In the interests of expediting sentencing, the judge asks Soames's attorney whether her client has any prior convictions. If Soames has no prior convictions, then it would seem appropriate for defense counsel to disclose this. To delay the proceedings might be to antagonize the judge. You don't want the judge to be deciding your client's punishment when he is angry at the defense. But, as we noted earlier, Rodney Soames was convicted eighteen months earlier on an assault charge in another state. And more to the point, the judge's question is completely improper. Other officers of the judicial system should have provided that information to the court in the form of a presentence report. The judge should not be relying on the defense attorney for information that may damage her client's cause.

At this stage four responses are possible. The attorney can answer the question truthfully: "Yes, your honor, my client was convicted on an assault charge." But here there is a betrayal of the client. Damaging confidential information is revealed to the court. The lawyer is no longer working for the client but for the court against the client. In the light of the arguments reviewed earlier on confidentiality in the criminal process, this answer seems unacceptable.

The attorney can refuse to answer the question. "Your honor, that is an improper question." Unfortunately, this answer may be equivalent to the first. If attorneys generally answer such improper questions when truthful answers will further the interests of their clients and refuse to answer them when the truth will damage those interests, then the judge will know (or at least have good reason to believe) that the client has a criminal record. The betrayal occurs as surely as if the attorney had spoken up directly.

A third response is to finesse the question. When asked, "Does your client have any prior convictions?" the quick-witted defense attorney can answer, "None that

I can say, your honor." While judges may conceivably be misled once or twice by this dodge (and even this is unlikely), almost certainly the only one fooled will be the client. Experienced judges will be familiar with the gambit. The criticisms of the first two responses apply equally to this third.

The final response is to lie. "Your honor, my client has no criminal record." The justification for such deception is premised on the propositions that (1) the judge has no right that defense counsel provide him with this information; that (2) the information the judge is requesting is information that the attorney is obligated not to disclose; and that (3) all nondeceptive responses will have the practical effect under the circumstances of disclosing to the judge the very information that the judge is not entitled to receive from the attorney and that the attorney is obligated not to disclose. Under the circumstances it would appear to be obligatory for the attorney to lie to the judge.

But it may be unwise to hasten to this conclusion. For lying can be justified only if attorneys in general freely answer improper questions *when truthful answers are in the interests of their clients.* While it may not be open to Soames's defense attorney to see to it that all lawyers abide by a nondisclosure rule here, whether it serves their clients' interests or not, it is open to the legal profession to make such a determination. Suppose that the standard answer to such questions were something like this: "Notwithstanding whether or not my client has a criminal record, as a member of the legal profession I will face disciplinary proceedings if I proffer an answer to your inquiry. I respectfully ask that you withdraw the question without prejudice to my client." If attorneys routinely respond in this way, the case for deception cannot be made. The rule here is that if it is improper for attorneys truthfully to answer questions when the truth will hurt a client, it is equally improper to answer when the truth will help. This principle sets an important limit to zealous advocacy.

JOURNALISTIC DECEPTION

Deni Elliott

The journalist's "client" is the newspaper-reading, television-watching public. In this article, Elliott asks whether deceptive strategies may be used to serve this public's interests, even though the public may disapprove of the use of such techniques. Elliott considers four kinds of journalistic deception and poses a set of questions illuminating the moral issues they raise.

Deception is a red flag word among journalists these days. Some editors avoid discussions about deception by saying that their staffs are clean—they have company policies never to deceive. Other editors, perhaps more honest, admit that their reporters use deception occasionally to get a story and hold up dramatic, often self-serving stories, to illustrate how the technique is sometimes worth it. . . .

There is . . . something strangely inconsistent about the notion of journalists deceiving people. Story subjects, sources and readers alike trust journalists. They trust that journalists will listen carefully, interpret fairly and print accurately. If it were not for this public trust in the practice of journalism, the journalistic product would not sell. There would be no audience. If not for public trust, story subjects and sources would not give needed interviews. When they deceive, journalists play havoc with the very trust they need to maintain their business.

Yet, journalists do deceive and probably deceive on an almost daily basis. . . . Deception occurs every time that a reporter feigns ignorance to encourage a source to open up. The reporter pretends that she/he doesn't know information which may influence what the source says.

Now, this sort of deception is obviously different from a reporter who works as an aide in a nursing home for the purpose of getting a story, but these deceptive practices differ in degree, not kind. These examples mark points at either end of a deception continuum. The lack of full disclosure on the part of the interviewing reporter is the least serious; the masquerading in the nursing home is the most serious.

Here, I will discuss four different degrees of deception: primary lack of identification, passive misrepresentation, active misrepresentation, and masquerading. They are not equally wrong. They require different justifications for avoidance and for use. An analysis of different degrees of deception may help journalists become more careful in using the difficult-to-avoid lower level deceptive techniques and more judicious in avoiding the higher levels.

A low level of deception, and one common in many student and professional news organizations, is what I'll call primary lack of identification. Here, the journalist declines to identify him/herself at the very start of checking out a potential story.

The journalist may be following up a tip in going out to a store to ask to see an appliance advertised at an unbelievably low price. The reporter may call a firm and ask if the owner will be in and then go out for an interview which might be impossible to get otherwise. The reporter might go to a rental office and ask if there are apartments available, approaching the rental agent in his/her honest identity of being a student, a black, Hispanic, but with-

From Deni Elliott, "The Consequences of Deception in Journalism," in National Ethics Committee, Society of Professional Journalists, Sigma Delta Chi, *1984–85 Journalism Ethics Report*, pp. 14–15. Reprinted by permission.

out the adjunct identification of a journalist.

No active lie is at work in any of these situations. But, simply presenting oneself without disclosure of the journalistic role is a form of deception. The journalist is concealing that identity because she/he understands that the journalistic role might get in the way.

The primary level of investigation sets this misrepresentation as a low level type of deception. Supposedly, the journalist might have happened upon the same information when truly being 'off the job.' She/he is not acting in any way that is different from a normal consumer. This form of deception is acceptable if the reporter is doing no more than checking out the possibility of a story. If there is no story, the investigation is dropped. It is morally permissible, but not obligatory, for the journalist to tell the merchant that she/he was checking out a lead. No information was used in print. No privacy was violated in the process. No relationship is fostered by the journalist. The potential story subject is not acting in any way different from the public actions expected. No story is printed.

It is obligatory for the journalist to provide proper identification before the investigation proceeds past this point and certainly before any information is recorded for publication. When a source of story subject is talking for publication, she/he has a right to know that this is the case. People may react differently for publication from their general actions, even from their general public actions. . . .

A mark further up the deception scale, passive misrepresentation, differs in intent from the point of primary lack of identification. Passive misrepresentation occurs when the reporter is collecting facts for publication, often when the reporter attends an open meeting or lecture, when the participants don't realize that there is media coverage. Again, the notion that a person's public self may be different from

the self presented for publication is essential here. Passive misrepresentation becomes an ethical issue when it's clear to the reporter that the story subject does not know that a reporter is present. The reporter is misrepresenting him/herself in not making the fact known.

Imagine a meeting of students discussing gay rights, or a meeting where women are discussing the horrors of being victims of sexual assault. Persons who speak at these gatherings may assume that they are discussing topics which will be understood and appreciated by those attending the meeting. The speakers might be more protective of what they say if they know it is "on the record." They may prefer that their names not be used. They may well feel damaged and betrayed when they unexpectedly read their statements in the paper.

Ethically, the reporter is obliged to provide journalistic identification as quickly as possible. Even if the reporter did not start out intending to deceive, it is unfair to wield the power of the press with no sensitivity to the expectations of persons attending the meeting. The press has a responsibility to protect those they encounter just as the most powerful party in any power relationship incurs special obligations. . . .

Active misinterpretation, the next mark up the deception scale, is an even more serious form of deception because now the reporter is doing more than collecting information with the intention of publication. Now, the reporter is actively making the story subjects or sources think that she/he is a supporter or sympathizer to gain information. Active misrepresentation can exist even if the reporter identifies him/herself as a journalist. Insincere empathy creates a serious deception. The reporter is going out of his/her way to elicit trust that goes beyond the normal social interchange.

A particularly insidious story comes to mind. In one case, a reporter was planning to show how lack of parental support results in teenage suicides and suicide attempts. The parents she interviewed knew only that the reporter was researching a story on the tragedy of teenaged suicide. The reporter empathized with the parents about the personal loss and guilt. She elicited enough trust so that parents told her details about the suicide victims' troubled lives. The reporter then wrote an article using the information provided to illustrate how the parents' actions or inactions had lead to the children's deaths. The parents, of course, had not been given the chance to respond to this hypothesis since they were not told the true purpose of the interviews. . . .

Masquerading, which falls at the far end of the deception continuum, is the most serious form of deception. When a reporter masquerades, she/he role plays, becomes something she/he is not for the sole purpose of getting a story. The reporter pretends to be an aide in a nursing home, a pet owner approaching the humane society with a sick animal, a recently transferred high school student, a woman considering an abortion. In reality, the journalist is not at all the role being played. "Undercover Reporter at Middleton High School" and similar stories are dramatic. But, the undercover "discovery" that students are smoking dope between classes pales against the serious lack of trust that the unwilling story subjects and the readers feel for the newspaper that uses such tactics. . . .

No matter how good the resulting story, the insidious nature of the information-gathering will not be soon forgotten by readers or by those taken in. This great harm can only be balanced by equally great benefit. It won't do to call the information "important." "Importance" is a vague notion and has been used too often to excuse journalistic excess. Careful consideration, as suggested by the following list of questions, can help editors and reporters decide if the information is worth pursuing through higher level deceptive means.

1. Why do the readers need this information?
2. Would your readers support your information gathering technique even if the story you hope to find isn't there? This question is important because you probably have little solid information or you wouldn't be using the deceptive technique in the first place. If you have enough solid information, the story could be written without undercover work. Whether the reporter finds what she/he hopes or not, public response is the most important consequence to consider.
3. Have you exhausted all other means for obtaining the information?
4. What are your arguments against law enforcement officers doing this undercover work rather than reporters? The result of a law enforcement investigation is likely to harm fewer people than a journalistic undercover investigation. Law enforcement officers are only interested in the persons performing criminal acts. Everyone is vulnerable in a journalistic investigation and anyone in the situation may be unwillingly exposed in the resulting story.
5. Does the reporter understand all of the risks of the assignment (to self and to the practice of journalism in general) and has, she/he been given the chance to turn the assignment down?
6. If the problem is great enough for higher level deceptive practices, what changes are likely to occur through exposure? Is the potential change a great enough benefit to offset the certain damage created in the public trust?

Deception is a dangerous and tempting tool. Reporters and editors should realize the various types of deceptive practices used within the industry and realize that they are all problematic. In deciding to use deception, journalists should keep in mind that the point of view from which to judge the necessity of its use is not from the journalists envisioning a splashy headline. The best point of view is that of the readers and story subjects who will have their trust in the industry put on the line again through use of the technique.

IS BUSINESS BLUFFING ETHICAL?

Albert Carr

Discussing business in a famous, highly controversial piece, Carr insists that certain ubiquitous business practices are exempt from the limitations of ordinary morality. Business "bluffing" by withholding, manipulating, or distorting the truth is not morally wrong, he argues, but involves a "special ethical outlook" which is different from that of the Judeo-Christian religious tradition. Business must be understood as a "game," like poker, Carr insists, and since deception in business is accepted as part of the game, it is not unethical after all.

A respected businessman with whom I discussed the theme of this article remarked with some heat, "You mean to say you're going to encourage men to bluff? Why, bluffing is nothing more than a form of lying! You're advising them to lie!"

I agreed that the basis of private morality is a respect for truth and that the closer a businessman comes to the truth, the more he deserves respect. At the same time, I suggested that most bluffing in business might be regarded simply as game strategy—much like bluffing in poker, which does not reflect on the morality of the bluffer.

I quoted Henry Taylor, the British statesman who pointed out that "falsehood ceases to be falsehood when it is understood on all sides that the truth is not expected to be spoken"—an exact description of bluffing in poker, diplomacy, and business. I cited the analogy of the criminal court, where the criminal is not expected to tell the truth when he pleads "not guilty." Everyone from the judge down takes it for granted that the job of the defendant's attorney is to get his client off, not to reveal the truth; and this is considered ethical practice. I mentioned Representative Omar Burleson, the Democrat from Texas, who was quoted as saying, in regard to the ethics of Congress, "Ethics is a barrel of worms"[1]—a pungent summing up of the problem of deciding who is ethical in politics.

I reminded my friend that millions of businessmen feel constrained every day to say *yes* to their bosses when they secretly believe *no* and that this is generally accepted as permissible strategy when the alternative might be the loss of a job. The essential point, I said, is that the ethics of business are game ethics, different from the ethics of religion.

He remained unconvinced. Referring to the company of which he is president, he declared: "Maybe that's good enough for some businessmen, but I can tell you that we pride ourselves on our ethics. In 30 years not one customer has ever questioned my word or asked to check our figures. We're loyal to our customers and fair to our suppliers. I regard my handshake on a deal as a contract. I've never entered into price-fixing schemes with my competitors. I've never allowed my salesmen to spread injurious rumors about other companies. Our union contract is the best in our industry. And, if I do say so myself, our ethical standards are of the highest!"

He really was saying, without realizing it, that he was living up to the ethical standards of the business game—which are

[1] *The New York Times,* March 9, 1967.

a far cry from those of private life. Like a gentlemanly poker player, he did not play in cahoots with others at the table, try to smear their reputations, or hold back chips he owed them.

But this same fine man, at that very time, was allowing one of his products to be advertised in a way that made it sound a great deal better than it actually was. Another item in his product line was notorious among dealers for its "built-in obsolescence." He was holding back from the market a much-improved product because he did not want it to interfere with sales of the inferior item it would have replaced. He had joined with certain of his competitors in hiring a lobbyist to push a state legislature, by methods that he preferred not to know too much about, into amending a bill then being enacted.

In his view these things had nothing to do with ethics; they were merely normal business practice. He himself undoubtedly avoided outright falsehoods—never lied in so many words. But the entire organization that he ruled was deeply involved in numerous strategies of deception.

Pressure to Deceive

Most executives from time to time are almost compelled, in the interests of their companies or themselves, to practice some form of deception when negotiating with customers, dealers, labor unions, government officials, or even other departments of their companies. By conscious misstatements, concealment of pertinent facts, or exaggeration—in short, by bluffing—they seek to persuade others to agree with them. I think it is fair to say that if the individual executive refuses to bluff from time to time—if he feels obligated to tell the truth, the whole truth, and nothing but the truth—he is ignoring opportunities permitted under the rules and is at a heavy disadvantage in his business dealings.

But here and there a businessman is unable to reconcile himself to the bluff in which he plays a part. His conscience, perhaps spurred by religious idealism, troubles him. He feels guilty; he may develop an ulcer or a nervous tic. Before any executive can make profitable use of the strategy of the bluff, he needs to make sure that in bluffing he will not lose self-respect or become emotionally disturbed. If he is to reconcile personal integrity and high standards of honesty with the practical requirements of business, he must feel that his bluffs are ethically justified. The justification rests on the fact that business, as practiced by individuals as well as by corporations, has the impersonal character of a game—a game that demands both special strategy and an understanding of its special ethics.

The game is played at all levels of corporate life, from the highest to the lowest. At the very instant that a man decides to enter business he may be forced into a game situation, as is shown by the recent experience of a Cornell honor graduate who applied for a job with a large company:

This applicant was given a psychological test which included the statement, "Of the following magazines, check any that you have read either regularly or from time to time, and double-check those which interest you most. *Reader's Digest, Time, Fortune, Saturday Evening Post, The New Republic, Life, Look, Ramparts, Newsweek, Business Week, U.S. News & World Report, The Nation, Playboy, Esquire, Harper's, Sports Illustrated.*"

His tastes in reading were broad, and at one time or another he had read almost all of these magazines. He was a subscriber to *The New Republic*, an enthusiast for *Ramparts*, and an avid student of the pictures in *Playboy*. He was not sure whether his interest in *Playboy* would be held against him, but he had a shrewd suspicion that if he confessed to an interest in *Ramparts* and *The New Republic*, he would be thought a liberal, a radical, or at least an intellectual, and his chances of getting the job, which he needed, would greatly diminish. He therefore checked five of the more conservative magazines. Apparently it was a sound decision, for he got the job.

He had made a game player's decision, consistent with business ethics.

A similar case is that of a magazine space salesman who, owing to a merger, suddenly found himself out of a job:

This man was 58, and, in spite of a good record, his chance of getting a job elsewhere in a business where youth is favored in hiring practice was not good. He was a vigorous, healthy man, and only a considerable amount of gray in his hair suggested his age. Before beginning his job search he touched up his hair with a black dye to confine the gray to his temples. He knew that the truth about his age might well come out in time, but he calculated that he could deal with that situation when it arose. He and his wife decided that he could easily pass for 45, and he so stated his age on his résumé.

This was a lie; yet within the accepted rules of the business game, no moral culpability attaches to it.

The Poker Analogy

We can learn a good deal about the nature of business by comparing it with poker. While both have a large element of chance, in the long run the winner is the man who plays with steady skill. In both games ultimate victory requires intimate knowledge of the rules, insight into the psychology of the other players, a bold front, a considerable amount of self-discipline, and the ability to respond swiftly and effectively to opportunities provided by chance.

No one expects poker to be played on the ethical principles preached in churches. In poker it is right and proper to bluff a friend out of the rewards of being dealt a good hand. A player feels no more than a slight twinge of sympathy, if that, when—with nothing better than a single ace in his hand—he strips a heavy loser, who holds a pair, of the rest of his chips. It was up to the other fellow to protect himself. In the words of an excellent poker player, former President Harry Truman,

"If you can't stand the heat, stay out of the kitchen." If one shows mercy to a loser in poker, it is a personal gesture, divorced from the rules of the game.

Poker has its special ethics, and here I am not referring to rules against cheating. The man who keeps an ace up his sleeve or who marks the cards is more than unethical; he is a crook, and can be punished as such—kicked out of the game or, in the Old West, shot.

In contrast to the cheat, the unethical poker player is one who, while abiding by the letter of the rules, finds ways to put the other players at an unfair disadvantage. Perhaps he unnerves them with loud talk. Or he tries to get them drunk. Or he plays in cahoots with someone else at the table. Ethical poker players frown on such tactics.

Poker's own brand of ethics is different from the ethical ideals of civilized human relationships. The game calls for distrust of the other fellow. It ignores the claim of friendship. Cunning deception and concealment of one's strength and intentions, not kindness and open-heartedness, are vital in poker. No one thinks any the worse of poker on that account. And no one should think any the worse of the game of business because its standards of right and wrong differ from the prevailing traditions of morality in our society.

Discard the Golden Rule

This view of business is especially worrisome to people without much business experience. A minister of my acquaintance once protested that business cannot possibly function in our society unless it is based on the Judeo-Christian system of ethics. He told me: "I know some businessmen have supplied call girls to customers, but there are always a few rotten apples in every barrel. That doesn't mean the rest of the fruit isn't sound. Surely the vast majority of businessmen are ethical. I myself am acquainted with many who adhere to strict codes of ethics based fundamentally on religious teachings. They contribute to good causes. They participate in community activities. They cooperate with other companies to improve working conditions in their industries. Certainly they are not indifferent to ethics." That most businessmen are not indifferent to ethics in their private lives, everyone will agree. My point is that in their office lives they cease to be private citizens; they become game players who must be guided by a somewhat different set of ethical standards.

The point was forcefully made to me by a Midwestern executive who has given a good deal of thought to the question:

"So long as a businessman complies with the laws of the land and avoids telling malicious lies, he's ethical. If the law as written gives a man a wide-open chance to make a killing, he'd be a fool not to take advantage of it. If he doesn't, somebody else will. There's no obligation on him to stop and consider who is going to get hurt. If the law says he can do it, that's all the justification he needs. There's nothing unethical about that. It's just plain business sense."

This executive (call him Robbins) took the stand that even industrial espionage, which is frowned on by some businessmen, ought not to be considered unethical. He recalled a recent meeting of the National Industrial Conference Board where an authority on marketing made a speech in which he deplored the employment of spies by business organizations. More and more companies, he pointed out, find it cheaper to penetrate the secrets of competitors with concealed cameras and microphones or by bribing employees than to set up costly research and design departments of their own. A whole branch of the electronics industry has grown up with this trend, he continued, providing equipment to make industrial espionage easier.

Disturbing? The marketing expert found it so. But when it came to a remedy, he could only appeal to "respect for the golden rule." Robbins thought this a confession of defeat, believing that the golden rule, for all its value as an ideal for society, is simply not feasible as a guide for business. A good part of the time the businessman is trying to do unto others as he hopes others will *not* do unto him.[2] Robbins continued:

"Espionage of one kind or another has become so common in business that it's like taking a drink during Prohibition—it's not considered sinful. And we don't even have Prohibition where espionage is concerned; the law is very tolerant in this area. There's no more shame for a business that uses secret agents than there is for a nation. Bear in mind that there already is at least one large corporation—you can buy its stock over the counter—that makes millions by providing counterespionage service to industrial firms. Espionage in business is not an ethical problem; it's an established technique of business competition."

"We Don't Make the Laws"

Wherever we turn in business, we can perceive the sharp distinction between its ethical standards and those of the churches. Newspapers abound with sensational stories growing out of this distinction:

We read one day that Senator Philip A. Hart of Michigan has attacked food processors for deceptive packaging of numerous products.[3]

The next day there is a Congressional to-do over Ralph Nader's book, *Unsafe At Any Speed*, which demonstrates that automobile companies for years have neglected the safety of car-owning families.[4]

Then another Senator, Lee Metcalf of Montana, and journalist Vic Reinemer show in their book, *Overcharge*, the methods by which utility companies elude regulating government bodies to extract unduly large payments from users of electricity.[5]

---

[2] See Bruce D. Henderson, "Brinkmanship in Business," *Harvard Business Review* 45:2 (March-April 1967) p. 49.
[3] *The New York Times*, November 21, 1966.
[4] New York, Grossman Publishers, Inc., 1965.
[5] New York, David McKay Company, Inc., 1967.

These are merely dramatic instances of a prevailing condition; there is hardly a major industry at which a similar attack could not be aimed. Critics of business regard such behavior as unethical, but the companies concerned know that they are merely playing the business game.

Among the most respected of our business institutions are the insurance companies. A group of insurance executives meeting recently in New England was startled when their guest speaker, social critic Daniel Patrick Moynihan, roundly berated them for "unethical" practices. They had been guilty, Moynihan alleged, of using outdated actuarial tables to obtain unfairly high premiums. They habitually delayed the hearings of lawsuits against them in order to tire out the plaintiffs and win cheap settlements. In their employment policies they used ingenious devices to discriminate against certain minority groups.[6]

It was difficult for the audience to deny the validity of these charges. But these men were business game players. Their reaction to Moynihan's attack was much the same as that of the automobile manufacturers to Nader, of the utilities to Senator Metcalf, and of the food processors to Senator Hart. If the laws governing their businesses change, or if public opinion becomes clamorous, they will make the necessary adjustments. But morally they have in their view done nothing wrong. As long as they comply with the letter of the law, they are within their rights to operate their businesses as they see fit.

The small business is in the same position as the great corporation in this respect. For example:

In 1967 a key manufacturer was accused of providing master keys for automobiles to mail-order customers, although it was obvious that some of the purchasers might be automobile thieves. His defense was plain and straightforward. If there was nothing in the law to prevent him from selling his keys to anyone who ordered

them, it was not up to him to inquire as to his customers' motives. Why was it any worse, he insisted, for him to sell car keys by mail, than for mail-order houses to sell guns that might be used for murder? Until the law was changed, the key manufacturer could regard himself as being just as ethical as any other businessman by the rules of the business game.[7]

Violations of the ethical ideals of society are common in business, but they are not necessarily violations of business principles. Each year the Federal Trade Commission orders hundreds of companies, many of them of the first magnitude, to "cease and desist" from practices which, judged by ordinary standards, are of questionable morality but which are stoutly defended by the companies concerned.

In one case, a firm manufacturing a well-known mouthwash was accused of using a cheap form of alcohol possibly deleterious to health. The company's chief executive, after testifying in Washington, made this comment privately: "We broke no law. We're in a highly competitive industry. If we're going to stay in business, we have to look for profit wherever the law permits. We don't make the laws. We obey them. Then why do we have to put up with this 'holier than thou' talk about ethics? It's sheer hypocrisy. We're not in business to promote ethics. Look at the cigarette companies, for God's sake! If the ethics aren't embodied in the laws by the men who made them, you can't expect businessmen to fill the lack. Why, a sudden submission to Christian ethics by businessmen would bring about the greatest economic upheaval in history!"

It may be noted that the government failed to prove its case against him.

Cast Illusions Aside

Talk about ethics by businessmen is often a thin decorative coating over the hard realities of the game:

---

[6] *The New York Times*, January 17, 1967.

[7] Cited by Ralph Nader in "Business Crime," *The New Republic*, July 1, 1967, p. 7.

Once I listened to a speech by a young executive who pointed to a new industry code as proof that his company and its competitors were deeply aware of their responsibilities to society. It was a code of ethics, he said. The industry was going to police itself, to dissuade constituent companies from wrongdoing. His eyes shone with conviction and enthusiasm.

The same day there was a meeting in a hotel room where the industry's top executives met with the "czar" who was to administer the new code, a man of high repute. No one who was present could doubt their common attitude. In their eyes the code was designed primarily to forestall a move by the federal government to impose stern restrictions on the industry. They felt that the code would hamper them a good deal less than new federal laws would. It was, in other words, conceived as a protection for the industry, not for the public.

The young executive accepted the surface explanation of the code; these leaders, all experienced game players, did not deceive themselves for a moment about its purpose.

The illusion that business can afford to be guided by ethics as conceived in private life is often fostered by speeches and articles containing such phrases as, "It pays to be ethical," or "Sound ethics is good business." Actually this is not an ethical position at all; it is a self-serving calculation in disguise. The speaker is really saying that in the long run a company can make more money if it does not antagonize competitors, suppliers, employees, and customers by squeezing them too hard. He is saying that oversharp policies reduce ultimate gains. That is true, but it has nothing to do with ethics. The underlying attitude is much like that in the familiar story of the shopkeeper who finds an extra $20 bill in the cash register, debates with himself the ethical problem—should he tell his partner?—and finally decides to share the money because the gesture will give him an edge over the s.o.b. the next time they quarrel.

I think it is fair to sum up the prevailing attitude of businessmen on ethics as follows:

We live in what is probably the most competitive of the world's civilized societies. Our customs encourage a high degree of aggression in the individual's striving for success. Business is our main area of competition, and it has been ritualized into a game of strategy. The basic rules of the game have been set by the government, which attempts to detect and punish business frauds. But as long as a company does not transgress the rules of the game set by law, it has the legal right to shape its strategy without reference to anything but its profits. If it takes a long-term view of its profits, it will preserve amicable relations, so far as possible, with those with whom it deals. A wise businessman will not seek advantage to the point where he generates dangerous hostility among employees, competitors, customers, government, or the public at large. But decisions in this area are, in the final test, decisions of strategy, not of ethics.

The Individual and the Game

An individual within a company often finds it difficult to adjust to the requirements of the business game. He tries to preserve his private ethical standards in situations that call for game strategy. When he is obliged to carry out company policies that challenge his conception of himself as an ethical man, he suffers.

It disturbs him when he is ordered, for instance, to deny a raise to a man who deserves it, to fire an employee of long standing, to prepare advertising that he believes to be misleading, to conceal facts that he feels customers are entitled to know, to cheapen the quality of materials used in the manufacture of an established product, to sell as new a product that he knows to be rebuilt, to exaggerate the curative powers of a medicinal preparation, or to coerce dealers.

There are some fortunate executives who, by the nature of their work and circumstances, never have to face problems of this kind. But in one form or another the ethical dilemma is felt sooner or later by most businessmen. Possibly the dilemma is most painful not when the company forces the action on the executive but when he originates it himself—that is, when he has taken or is contemplating a step which is in his own interest but which runs counter to his early moral conditioning. To illustrate:

The manager of an export department, eager to show rising sales, is pressed by a big customer to provide invoices which, while containing no overt falsehood that would violate a U.S. law, are so worded that the customer may be able to evade certain taxes in his homeland.

A company president finds that an aging executive, within a few years of retirement and his pension, is not as productive as formerly. Should he be kept on?

The produce manager of a supermarket debates with himself whether to get rid of a lot of half-rotten tomatoes by including one, with its good side exposed, in every tomato six-pack.

An accountant discovers that he has taken an improper deduction on his company's tax return and fears the consequences if he calls the matter to the president's attention, though he himself has done nothing illegal. Perhaps if he says nothing, no one will notice the error.

A chief executive officer is asked by his directors to comment on a rumor that he owns stock in another company with which he has placed large orders. He could deny it, for the stock is in the name of his son-in-law and he has earlier formally instructed his son-in-law to sell the holding.

Temptations of this kind constantly arise in business. If an executive allows himself to be torn between a decision based on business considerations and one based on his private ethical code, he exposes himself to a grave psychological strain.

This is not to say that sound business strategy necessarily runs counter to ethical ideals. They may frequently coincide; and when they do, everyone is gratified. But the major tests of every move in business, as in all games of strategy, are legality and profit. A man who intends to be a winner in the business game must have a game player's attitude.

The business strategist's decisions must be as impersonal as those of a surgeon performing an operation—concentrating on objective and technique, and subordinating personal feelings. If the chief executive admits that his son-in-law owns the stock, it is because he stands to lose more if the fact comes out later than if he states it boldly and at once. If the supermarket manager orders the rotten tomatoes to be discarded, he does so to avoid an increase in consumer complaints and a loss of goodwill. The company president decides not to fire the elderly executive in the belief that the negative reaction of other employees would in the long run cost the company more than it would lose in keeping him and paying his pension.

All sensible businessmen prefer to be truthful, but they seldom feel inclined to tell the *whole* truth. In the business game truth-telling usually has to be kept within narrow limits if trouble is to be avoided. The point was neatly made a long time ago (in 1888) by one of John D. Rockefeller's associates, Paul Babcock, to Standard Oil Company executives who were about to testify before a government investigating committee: "Parry every question with answers which, while perfectly truthful, are evasive of *bottom* facts."[8] This was, is, and probably always will be regarded as wise and permissible business strategy.

For Office Use Only

An executive's family life can easily be dislocated if he fails to make a sharp distinction between the ethical systems of the home and the office—or if his wife does not grasp that distinction. Many a businessman who has remarked to his wife, "I had to let Jones go today" or "I had to

---

[8] Babcock in a memorandum to Rockefeller (Rockefeller Archives).

admit to the boss that Jim has been goofing off lately," has been met with an indignant protest. "How could you do a thing like that? You know Jones is over 50 and will have a lot of trouble getting another job." Or, "You did that to Jim? With his wife ill and all the worry she's been having with the kids?"

If the executive insists that he had no choice because the profits of the company and his own security were involved, he may see a certain cool and ominous reappraisal in his wife's eyes. Many wives are not prepared to accept the fact that business operates with a special code of ethics. An illuminating illustration of this comes from a Southern sales executive who related a conversation he had had with his wife at a time when a hotly contested political campaign was being waged in their state:

"I made the mistake of telling her that I had had lunch with Colby, who gives me about half my business. Colby mentioned that his company had a stake in the election. Then he said, 'By the way, I'm treasurer of the citizens' committee for Lang. I'm collecting contributions. Can I count on you for a hundred dollars?'

"Well, there I was. I was opposed to Lang, but I knew Colby. If he withdrew his business I could be in a bad spot. So I just smiled and wrote out a check then and there. He thanked me, and we started to talk about his next order. Maybe he thought I shared his political views. If so, I wasn't going to lose any sleep over it.

"I should have had sense enough not to tell Mary about it. She hit the ceiling. She said she was disappointed in me. She said I hadn't acted like a man, that I should have stood up to Colby.

"I said, 'Look, it was an either-or situation. I had to do it or risk losing the business.'

"She came back at me with, 'I don't believe it. You could have been honest with him. You could have said that you didn't feel you ought to contribute to a campaign for a man you weren't going to vote for.

I'm sure he would have understood.'

"I said, 'Mary, you're a wonderful woman, but you're way off the track. Do you know what would have happened if I had said that? Colby would have smiled and said, "Oh, I didn't realize. Forget it." But in his eyes from that moment I would be an oddball, maybe a bit of a radical. He would have listened to me talk about his order and would have promised to give it consideration. After that I wouldn't hear from him for a week. Then I would telephone and learn from his secretary that he wasn't yet ready to place the order. And in about a month I would hear through the grapevine that he was giving his business to another company. A month after that I'd be out of a job.'

"She was silent for a while. Then she said, 'Tom, something is wrong with business when a man is forced to choose between his family's security and his moral obligation to himself. It's easy for me to say you should have stood up to him—but if you had, you might have felt you were betraying me and the kids. I'm sorry that you did it, Tom, but I can't blame you. Something is wrong with business!' "

This wife saw the problem in terms of moral obligation as conceived in private life; her husband saw it as a matter of game strategy. As a player in a weak position, he felt that he could not afford to indulge an ethical sentiment that might have cost him his seat at the table.

Playing to Win

Some men might challenge the Colbys of business—might accept serious setbacks to their business careers rather than risk a feeling of moral cowardice. They merit our respect—but as private individuals, not businessmen. When the skillful player of the business game is compelled to submit to unfair pressure, he does not castigate himself for moral weakness. Instead, he strives to put himself into a strong position where he can defend himself against such pressures in the future without loss.

If a man plans to take a seat in the business game he owes it to himself to master the principles by which the game is played, including its special ethical outlook. He can then hardly fail to recognize that an occasional bluff may well be justified in terms of the game's ethics and warranted in terms of economic necessity. Once he clears his mind on this point, he is in a good position to match his strategy against that of the other players. He can then determine objectively whether a bluff in a given situation has a good chance of succeeding and can decide when and how to bluff, without a feeling of ethical transgression.

To be a winner, a man must play to win. This does not mean that he must be ruthless, cruel, harsh, or treacherous. On the contrary, the better his reputation for integrity, honesty, and decency, the better his chances of victory will be in the long run. But from time to time every businessman, like every poker player, is offered a choice between certain loss or bluffing within the legal rules of the game. If he is not resigned to losing, if he wants to rise in his company and industry, then in such a crisis he will bluff—and bluff hard.

Every now and then one meets a successful businessman who has conveniently forgotten the small or large deceptions that he practiced on his way to fortune. "God gave me my money," old John D. Rockefeller once piously told a Sunday school class. It would be a rare tycoon in our time who would risk the horse laugh with which such a remark would be greeted.

In the last third of the twentieth century even children are aware that if a man has become prosperous in business, he has sometimes departed from the strict truth in order to overcome obstacles or has practiced the more subtle deceptions of the half-truth or the misleading omission. Whatever the form of the bluff, it is an integral part of the game, and the executive who does not master its techniques is not likely to accumulate much money or power.

THE MORAL STATUS OF BLUFFING AND DECEPTION IN BUSINESS*

Thomas L. Carson and Richard E. Wokutch

Carson and Wokutch attempt to show the errors in Carr's case for business bluffing, presented in the preceding selection. Self-interest, economic necessity, and benefits to the party deceived are inadequate justifications for lying, they argue, and to claim that business is a "game" is not enough to legitimize the deceptive practices it involves.

In recent years, the legality and morality of many business practices have come under increasing scrutiny. A range of activ- ities involving exaggeration and deception in advertising, selling, and negotiating has been particularly controversial . . . bluffing and other deceptive practices are often profitable and sometimes felt to be eco-

* Footnotes have been deleted without indication.

From Thomas L. Carson and Richard E. Wokutch, "The Moral Status of Bluffing and Deception in Business," *Profits and Professions: Essays in Business and Professional Ethics*, ed. Wade L. Robison, Michael S. Pritchard, and Joseph Ellin (Clifton, NJ: Humana Press, 1983), pp. 141–55. Reprinted by permission.

nomically necessary. . . . We will attempt to determine whether this fact provides any kind of *moral* justification for such practices.

. . . An individual cannot justify lying simply on the grounds that it is in his or her own self-interest to lie. For it is not always morally permissible to do what is in one's own self-interest. I would not be justified in killing you or falsely accusing you of a crime in order to get your job, even if doing so would be to my advantage. Similarly, a businessperson cannot justify lying or deception *simply* on the grounds that they are advantageous (profitable) to the business. This point can be strengthened if we remember that any advantages one gains as a result of bluffing are usually counterbalanced by corresponding disadvantages on the part of others. If I succeed in getting a higher price by bluffing when I sell my house, then there must be someone else who is paying more than might otherwise have been the case.

"Economic necessity" is a stronger justification for lying than mere profitability. Suppose that it is necessary for a businessperson to engage in lying or deception in order to insure the survival of his or her firm. Many would not object to a person stealing food to prevent starvation of his or her family. It would seem that lying in such a situation to get money to buy food or to continue employing workers so that *they* can buy food would be equally justifiable. This case would best be described as a conflict of duties—a conflict between the duty to be honest and the duty to promote the welfare of those for/to whom one is "responsible" (one's children, one's employees, or the stockholders whose money one manages). However, it is extremely unlikely that bankruptcy would result in the death or starvation of anyone in a society that has unemployment compensation, welfare payments, food stamps, charitable organizations, and even opportunities for begging. The consequences of refraining from lying in transactions might still be very unfavorable indeed, involving, for example, the bankruptcy of a firm, loss of investment, unemployment, and personal suffering associated with this. But a firm that needs to practice lying or deception in order to continue in existence is of doubtful value to society. Perhaps the labor, capital, and raw materials that it uses could be put to better use elsewhere. At least in a free market situation, the interests of economic efficiency would be best served if such firms were to go out of business. An apparent exception to this economic efficiency argument would be a situation in which a firm was pushed to the edge of bankruptcy by the lies of competitors or others.

It seems probable to us that the long-term consequences of the bankruptcy of a firm that needs to lie in order to continue in existence would be better or no worse than those of its continuing to exist. Clearly, on this assumption a businessperson cannot justify lying or deception in order to avoid bankruptcy. Because, in that case, the strong presumption against lying and deception is not counterbalanced by any other considerations (the long-term consequences of the firm's going out of business are no worse than those of its continuing to exist). Suppose, however, that the immediate bad consequences of bankruptcy would not be offset by any long-term benefits. In that case it is no longer clear that it would be wrong for a company to resort to lying and deception out of "economic necessity." One can be justified in lying or deceiving to save individuals from harms far less serious than death. I can be justified in lying about the gender of my friend's roommate to a relative or nosey boss in order to protect that friend from embarrassment or from being fired. If the degree of harm prevented by lying or deception were the only relevant factor (and if bankruptcy would not have any significant long-term benefits), then it would seem that a businessperson could easily justify lying and deceiving in order to protect those associated with the business from the harm that would result from the bankruptcy of the firm. There is, however, another relevant factor that clouds the issue. In the case of lying about the private affairs of one's friends, one is lying to others about matters concerning which they have no right to know. Our present analogy warrants lying and deception for the sake of economic survival only in cases in which the persons being lied to or deceived have no right to the information in question. Among other things, this rules out deceiving customers about dangerous defects in one's products—they have a right to this information—but it does not rule out lying to someone or deceiving him/her about one's minimal bargaining position.

We have argued that personal (or corporate) profit is no justification for lying in business transactions and that lying out of "economic necessity" is also morally objectionable in many cases. But what about lying in order to benefit the party being lied to? There are certainly many self-serving claims to this effect. Some have argued that individuals derive greater satisfaction from a product or service if they can be convinced that it is better than is actually the case. On the other hand, an advertising executive made the argument in the recent FTC hearings on children's advertising that the disappointment children experience when a product fails to meet their commercial-inflated expectations is beneficial because it helps them develop a healthy skepticism. These arguments are not convincing and they appear to be smoke screens for actions taken out of self-interest. Deceptive advertising is almost invariably engaged in for reasons of self-interest even though it is conceivable that consumers might benefit from it.

Although lying and deception can sometimes be justified by reference to the interests of those being lied to or deceived, such cases are very atypical in business situations. Successful bluffing almost invariably harms the other party in business

negotiations. The net effect of a successful bluff is that the bluffed party pays more or receives less than would otherwise be the case.

Lying and deception are very common (if not generally accepted or condoned) in business transactions. Bluffing and other deceptive practices are especially common in economic negotiations and bluffing, at least, is generally thought to be an acceptable practice. Does this fact in any way justify bluffing? We think not. The mere fact that something is standard practice or generally accepted is not enough to justify it. Standard practice and popular opinion can be in error. Such things as slavery were once standard practice and generally accepted. But they are and *were* morally wrong. However, the fact that bluffing is common can justify it indirectly. If one is involved in a negotiation, it is very probable that the other parties with whom one is dealing are themselves bluffing. It seems plausible to say that the presumption against lying and deception holds *only* when the other parties with whom one is dealing are not themselves lying or attempting to deceive one. Given this, there is no presumption against bluffing or deceiving someone who is attempting to bluff or deceive you. It should be stressed again that the prevalence of bluffing *per se* is no justification for bluffing oneself. The justification for bluffing a particular individual in a particular situation derives from the fact that he or she is attempting to deceive you on that occasion. The fact that bluffing is so common only means that there are many situations in which it can be justified on these grounds. In fact, there is such a strong presumption for thinking that the other parties will bluff or lie in negotiating settings that one is justified in presuming that they are lying or bluffing in the absence of any special reasons to the contrary, e.g., one's dealing with an unusually naive or scrupulous person.

A further ground on which lying or deceiving in bargaining situations is sometimes held to be justifiable is the claim that the other parties do not have *a right to know* one's true bargaining position. It is true that the other party does not have a right to know one's position, i.e., it would not be wrong for one to refuse to reveal it to that person. But this is not to say that it is permissible to lie or deceive him or her. You have no right to know where I was born, but it would be *prima facie* wrong for me to lie to you about the place of my birth. So, lying and deception in bargaining situations cannot be justified simply on the grounds that the other parties have no right to know one's true position. This is not to deny that, other things being equal, it is much worse to lie or deceive about a matter concerning which the other parties have a right to know than one about which they have no right to know.

As we have argued, there appears to be a personal economic incentive in many cases for lying, bluffing, and deception. We, therefore, cannot rely solely on the marketplace to eliminate these activities.

CONFIDENTIALITY

WHAT'S AN FBI POSTER DOING IN A NICE JOURNAL LIKE THAT?

Willard Gaylin

This classic piece points to the distortions of the function of medicine that would result if violations of physician–patient confidentiality were to be allowed in order to serve the interests of society.

The pages of the *Archives of Dermatology,* with their full-color pictures of exotic skin diseases, are likely to strike the uninformed eye as bizarre and somewhat repellent. But even the best informed must have been startled by page 308 of the February 1972 issue. There, occupying almost the entire page, was an FBI wanted poster!

Appearing under the department heading, "News and Notes," the item looked identical to those appearing in police stations and post offices. But both of those are government agencies, and the *Archives* is an official publication of the American Medical Association. The graffiti that passes unnoticed in a subway station would outrage us if written on the wall of a church.

It seems ironic that the AMA, which has consistently opposed government intrusion into medical matters even where a legitimate public interest has been proved, should now have volunteered the services of organized medicine into a government function—and in an area so alien from the traditional medical mission as tracking down criminals. . . .

The notice, which also appeared in the *Archives of Internal Medicine,* described a 30-year-old woman indicted by a grand jury for "conspiring with another individual" in an act involving the interstate transportation of explosives. The alleged conspiracy violation occurred early in 1970. Along with the usual pictures in various poses, physical description, and biographical material, appeared the statement that she was known to be afflicted with an "acute and recurrent" skin condition. It further elaborates: "The recurrent aspect of this condition could necessitate treatment by a dermatologist." The reason for the FBI's wanting it in the *Archives of Dermatology* now

From Willard Gaylin, "What's an FBI Poster Doing in a Nice Journal Like That?" *Hastings Center Report*, vol. 2 (April 1972), pp. 1–3. Reprinted by permission.

becomes apparent. The reasons for the AMA's willingness to publish it are less immediately evident.

Before even the ethical questions, what is the legal responsibility of the physician reading this? Consultation with a professor of criminal law revealed that there were indeed open questions about liability and responsibility. If he had doubts—what of the average dermatologist?

The implications to the wanted person—who may or may not be a criminal—will also transcend ethical nicety. In this instance a fatal disease is not present—although it well might be in future cases, and it has been indicated that were the condition heart disease, diabetes, glaucoma, acute depression—the wanted notices would be referred to the appropriate journal. They would make it difficult, if not impossible, to get the necessary treatment.

The major question, however, seems to be whether medicine should be encouraged, or even allowed, to be an extension of the police functions of the society. There is no question that if this is seen as as legitimate function of medicine, it would represent a powerful and immense new ally for the police. In the files of physicians across the country are massive case records which would make an invaluable data bank (ready for computerization) of inestimable service in any police tracking function: the drugs one chronically uses, a tendency toward alcoholism, a hidden homosexual activity, proclivity for flirtations or other sexual idiosyncrasies, prescription glasses, specific allergies, dietary requirements, etc.

There is no question that all of this information would facilitate the police functions of the state. But is that the function of medicine? And in facilitating this other function *what would it do to the primary concern of medicine, which is relief of suffering, the treatment of illness, and the saving of life?* What happens to the tradition of confidentiality—so zealously protected over hundreds of years precisely because it has been seen as fundamental to the effective

function of medicine? Such use of the profession by the police would represent the final destruction of the privacy, intimacy, and trust of a therapeutic relationship already seriously eroded.

It is conceivable that *in extremis* an institution must abandon its traditional role. The organized church has often supported the mass killing of war when it seemed essential for the survival of the state.

How are we to decide, however, *when* to violate our usual primary devotion and allegiance to the private person and his well-being, for the public purpose? How are we physicians to differentiate quantitatively amongst the various crimes and conditions of criminality in which we have no training? Are we prepared to assay indictment versus conviction, versus material witness, versus "wanted for questioning"? What are the relevant weights to be placed on conspiracy to blow up a heating system of the Pentagon, versus armed robbery of a bank, versus possession of marijuana, versus massive embezzlement? How do we weigh these public dangers against the health or survival of a patient? Ought we be making these decisions—or should they be left to public decision-making via the normal legislative processes which, for example, now dictates that gunshot wounds demand violation of confidentiality, but by implication of exclusion allows a host of other material the protection of confidentiality? . . .

The man who made the decision stated that he would have no hesitation printing more such posters in the future, without advice or consultation, in whatever medical journals the AMA published, particularly when there was a specific medical potential for assisting the FBI, because *"no questions of medical ethics are involved."*

The assumption that there are "no ethical issues involved" . . . may represent the most distressing aspect of this entire episode. Whether the publication of such material by an official medical journal is "ethical" or "unethical" may be debatable (and should be debated). That major ethical issues are raised, however, is indisputable. It involves such basic traditional questions as confidentiality and trust, private needs versus public rights, professional values versus personal ethics, the special role of the healer and saver of life, and the power of the state.

THE NATURE OF CONFIDENTIALITY IN MEDICINE*

Ian E. Thompson

Writing within the context of the British healthcare system, Thompson provides a background analysis of the issues in confidentiality by examining the nature of privacy, confidence, and secrecy as they arise within the physician–patient relationship.

A Question of Confidentiality

Why is confidentiality so important or valuable in itself? Most of the available professional codes do not answer this question. They assume that the value of confidentiality is self-evident, and do not seriously examine the grounds for maintaining relationships of confidentiality, nor do they provide adequate moral or philosophical justification for doing so.

It is customary to point to the Hippocratic Oath and then to imply that its provisions have governed doctor–patient relationships since the 5th century B.C. For example, the [British Medical Association] BMA handbook on Medical Ethics[1] begins with an appeal to the Oath as a foundation for medical ethics. In a recent statement on confidentiality the Royal College of Psychiatrists asserts:

One of the few provisions of the Hippocratic Oath which has remained unaltered over nearly 3,000 years is that relating to confidentiality:
"And whatsoever I shall see or hear in the course of my profession, as well as outside my profession in my intercourse with men, if it be what should not be published abroad, I will never divulge, holding such things to be holy secrets."

The undertaking is repeated in the Declaration of Geneva:

I will respect the secrets which are confided in me, even after the patient has died.[2]

This appeal to the "3,000 year-old tradition of the Hippocratic Oath" is not historically justified, because the Oath has not been a regular or constant basis of medical practice through the ages. We should remember that the oath originated in what was an esoteric cult, and the obligations of secrecy were as much concerned with protecting trade secrets and maintaining control over initiates as they were concerned with the patient's interest. (It might be remarked in passing that it is always as much in the practitioner's as the patient's interest to maintain relationships of confidentiality, especially in private practice). In fact, the Oath only applied to the Hippocratic School and there were other schools in antiquity without such require-

---

* Some notes have been deleted without indication.

[1] British Medical Association (1974), *Medical Ethics*. London, BMA House, Tavistock Square, pp. 1–2, 13.

[2] *British Journal of Psychiatry* (October 1976), News and Notes: Confidentiality: A Report to Council, Royal College of Psychiatrists.

From Ian E. Thompson, "The Nature of Confidentiality in Medicine," *Journal of Medical Ethics*, vol. 5 (1979), pp. 57–64. Reprinted by permission.

ments. With the establishment of the medieval universities and faculties of medicine, and with the attempts by Roger II of Sicily in 1140 and Frederick II in 1224 to control and regulate healing practices by legislation, new interest in the Oath was shown by certain guilds of physicians. However, its use never became general. It was only during the late eighteenth and early nineteenth centuries, when physicians and surgeons were struggling to achieve recognition as professionals in their own right, that the demand for an explicit code of professional practice became important.[3] The Hippocratic Oath thus came to be adopted as the trademark of the Victorian doctor, as physicians and surgeons buried the hatchet and turned to more subtle forms of internecine conflict. One of the paradoxes faced by modern medicine and one of the reasons why the Hippocratic Oath has had to be qualified by so many other Codes and Declarations, is that modern medicine is built not on secrecy and rites of initiation, but on exoteric scientific knowledge, on free publication and open access to the results of medical research. These developments now compel us to reexamine the grounds for confidentiality.

Is There a Principle of Confidentiality?

The 1974 BMA handbook on Medical Ethics boldly reaffirms the doctor's obligation to maintain secrecy in what appear to be most uncompromising terms:

It is a doctor's duty strictly to observe the rule of professional secrecy by refraining from disclosing voluntarily to any third party, information which he has learned directly or indirectly in his professional relationship with the patient. The death of the patient does not absolve the doctor from the obligation to maintain secrecy.[4]

However, there immediately follow a list of five kinds of exception:

The exceptions to the general principle are:
a. the patient or his legal adviser gives valid consent
b. the information is required by law
c. the information regarding a patient's health is given in confidence to a relative or other appropriate person, in circumstances where the doctor believes it undesirable on medical grounds to seek the patient's consent
d. rarely, the public interest may persuade the doctor that his duty to the community may override his duty to maintain his patient's confidence;
e. information may be disclosed for the purposes of any medical research project specifically approved for such exception by the BMA including information on cancer registration.[5]

What, one might ask, remains of the patient's right to privacy if the doctor's discretion is so large? If it were not in the doctor's own interest to maintain relationships of confidentiality, one wonders if the reaffirmation of the patient's right to privacy would amount to more than pious rhetoric.

It is significant that except in the case of the doctor being required by law to disclose information in court, the other caveats offered serve to emphasize either the autonomy of the medical profession in deciding what is in the common good (in matters relating to Public Health, Medical Research and Health Service Planning), or in emphasizing the doctor's right to independent clinical judgment (in situations where he considers it undesirable to seek the patient's consent to disclose information).

The point at issue is not whether the medical profession should be an autonomous self-regulating body, nor is it a matter of undermining or attacking the doctor's clinical judgment. The question is whether confidentiality is a matter of *principle* or a matter of practical medical expediency. Is

[3] Freidson, E. (1970/75). *Profession of Medicine*, New York: Dodd Mead & Company. Chapter 1.
[4] British Medical Association (1974). *Medical Ethics*, p. 13.

[5] *Ibid.*, p. 13.

there really a "principle of confidentiality" as the BMA asserts? If so, why do more doctors not go to prison rather than divulge professional secrets? Is a person entitled to privacy as a 'right'? In certain circumstances that right is enforceable in a court of law—in the sense that an injured party can seek legal redress for the public disclosure of confidential information. However, what kind of right is it, and what weight should it be given in relation to other rights? Is it an unconditional moral right? Should the privilege of withholding confidential information which applies in [Britain] only to lawyers, and in certain circumstances to priests, be extended to doctors?

These are some of the questions which should be considered if confidentiality is a matter of strict principle rather than conventional and useful practice. In what follows an attempt is made to clarify some of the values on which it might be possible to argue that there is a principle at stake when matters of confidentiality arise. . . .

Privacy: The Scope and Limits of the Right to Privacy

We may all agree that there is an implicit threat to individual liberty in modern increasingly centralized and technocratic societies. These dangers can be seen in modern technological developments such as computer storage of information, techniques of photocopying, and the invasion of personal privacy by the mass media. However, we may still ask: Is there a *right* to privacy? . . .

The "right to privacy" might well be regarded by many as a device of medical/political rhetoric or an impractical ideal, but on logical grounds, if we concede the existence of individual human rights of any kind, then it is almost tautologically self-evident that there must be a "right to privacy" for without it there would be no private individuals to have or exercise those rights. That the individual should be spir-

itually inviolate, in the sense of being protected from the invasion, violation and abuse of his privacy would seem to be the necessary pre-supposition of his possession of any of the other individual human rights claimed for him, *eg*, the right to freedom of speech, freedom of movement and association, freedom of worship, etc. We must, I think, grant the existence of a right to privacy on formal grounds once we concede the existence of personal rights in any form. Since it is not our purpose to dispute that, the question becomes one of interpreting the scope and limits of the right to privacy.

The moral situation in which patient and doctor encounter one another is one which gives to privacy a special value, confidential privacy is inherent in the situation as a moral pre-supposition for at least three reasons:

1. The patient approaches the doctor under duress of fear, pain or need. This means that the patient is inherently vulnerable and disadvantaged in relation to the doctor. The "contract" between them is not a contract as between equals (hence it may be misleading to speak as some sociologists do of patients as "consumers"). The patient is a patient (*ie*, a sufferer), a person who may well be conforming to the sick role, but whose disease has forced him to accept the limitations and obligations of that role as well as its possible advantages. The moral responsibility of the doctor in the first instance is to respect the vulnerability of the "patient"; his privacy in this sense.

2. The fact that the doctor is a member of a consulting and not just scholarly profession means that "patients" come to him in situations which are of their very nature private, in the consulting room or the relative privacy possible in the hospital ward. The contract to enter into the secrecy of a private consultation implies obligations binding really on both parties, especially where the relationship is one of cooperation based on the acceptance of the authority of one party to guide or even direct the performance of unusual acts (*eg*, getting undressed, allowing

examination of intimate parts, disclosing intimate information.)

3. The sharing of intimate information in the activity of truth-telling involves the implicit rules of reciprocal confidence; otherwise the process could not get started. Violation of confidence does not just involve an infringement of a rule of procedure as if it were a game which does not matter crucially (like admissible cheating in poker). It contradicts the possibility of the "game" itself. This is why both parties to a broken confidential relationship feel mortally wounded.

These factors of initial vulnerability, voluntary self-exposure and confidence-sharing create special obligations in the one to whom these gestures of intimacy and private self-revelation are made. We implicitly recognize this when we discourage importunate people from unburdening themselves to us. They not only demand our attention but impose unwelcome obligations on us.

Areas of medicine where respect for the "right to privacy" would appear to be particularly important are psychiatry and reproductive medicine. In psychiatry the issue of privacy is important because of the peculiar vulnerability of the mentally ill, because of the probing nature of psychiatric investigations of people's psycho-sexual behavior and problems of social adjustment, and because of the considerable stigma still associated with mental illness. The information elicited in the course of psychiatric treatment makes the patient extremely vulnerable to both psychological manipulation and criminal blackmail (if the information falls into the wrong hands). In reproductive medicine, in the treatment of gynecological disorders, male infertility and venereal disease, the issue of privacy is important in relation to the prevailing attitudes and feelings of shame about sexual matters. While these may be culture-dependent and culture-specific, nevertheless taboos and feelings of shame are common to all societies in relation to different things for different people, and the right to privacy remains important in relation to these feelings. . . .

Confidence: The Necessary Ground of the Patient–Doctor Relationship or Contract

The second value implicit in confidentiality is confidence itself. This is not just a desirable concomitant of medical practice, but an essential moral prerequisite of the contractual relationship into which patient and doctor enter. . . . A great deal of the efficacy of medicine depends on "the placebo effect," the ability of the doctor to win the confidence and trust of the patient and to maintain it, often for many years.

However, this confidence (*cum-fides*) is not just desirable for its therapeutic benefits, it is an essential pre-supposition of the contract of cooperation in mutual truthfulness into which doctor and patient enter. Whereas privacy is primarily in the patient's interest, confidence is in the mutual interest of the contracting parties. It is the expression of willingness to enter into the contractual relationship, of the patient's willingness to submit to the doctor's authority and of the doctor's willingness to attend to the patient's needs to the best of his ability. The relationship is not established once and for all, and the doctor and patient are involved in an on-going negotiation of the limits of their confidential relationship and the limits of truthfulness or openness in that relationship through a series of symptoms offered by the patient and responses by the doctor.

In the conflict/cooperation underlying doctor–patient interaction, mutual confidence is a necessary prerequisite. Distrust on either side is enough to bring a relationship to an abrupt end. Insofar as confidence in this situation is essential to the functioning of the relationship, implicit respect for mutual confidences is implied. However, the nature, form and limits of that confidentiality may not be specified or explicit and perhaps ought to be negotiated more explicitly.

It is generally maintained, especially by doctors and in the pious or indignant statements issued by their professional associations, that confidentiality is maintained primarily in the patient's interest. This assumption needs to be questioned if we are to get beneath the surface of the public rhetoric and consider more seriously the practical value and moral significance of confidentiality. The secret of the doctor's power over his patient lies precisely in his possession of what is often vital confidential information (at least in the patient's view). Medical pieties about confidentiality might be more convincing if doctors were more candid about the part played in the "management" of patients by the control and selective disclosure of information. It is also evident in the intercollegial and interprofessional dealings of the doctor that the selective disclosure of confidential information is used by the doctor both to assert and maintain control over "his" patients. The making of referrals is obviously a game requiring great skill or art, both when it involves defining limits to responsibility for individual patients, and when it involves "passing the buck." The cruder forms of this exploitation of confidential information to maintain control of patients are perhaps more obvious in a situation of fee-paying private medicine, but they operate none the less in the [National Health Service] NHS too.

To put the issue into perspective it is perhaps necessary to stop and ask: Whose confidences are they, anyway? In a sense the question has a simple answer: They are the patient's confidences and that is why the doctor has no moral right to use confidential information without the consent of the patient or in the patient's interest.
. . .

The situation in modern health care, whether in the USA or the UK is one of increasing involvement of other professionals and paraprofessionals and changing patterns of interprofessional relationships. Whether in the technologically sophisticated areas of hospital medicine, involving many specialties, or in the primary medical care team, there is a situation of increasingly extended confidence.

Whether we go along with this and accept the fact that in the welfare state with a National Health Service there is an inevitable need for the dilution of confidentiality, in the interests of efficient patient care, systematic medical research, effective public health programs and more rational health service planning; or whether we opt for a system which reinforces patients' rights and physician autonomy, say by giving patients their medical records, or reinforcing medical privilege in relation to confidential information, involves not just the moral issue of patients' rights versus public interest, but, more fundamentally, choices about what kind of society we wish to live in. It may well be too, that what is at issue in the present debate about confidentiality concerns the very nature of medicine as a profession: Is medicine to remain a consulting profession based on confidentiality, patient trust and medical autonomy and responsibility?; or is the doctor to become a paid functionary in an impersonal institution where industrial action is compatible with offering medical services to the public?
. . .

There is a public dimension to confidentiality too, the question of the public confidence in the profession. The crisis of identity through which the profession is passing, as well as a possible crisis of confidence in the medical profession expressed by increasingly strident public criticism of doctors, argues the need for the profession to renegotiate its contract with the public if confidence is to be restored. The BMA, in its handbook on Medical Ethics, tends to be rather arrogant about the ethical standards and traditions of medicine and rather dismissive of social work and other professions. However, the present situation in medicine with regard to confidentiality might well be illuminated by consideration of the example of social work.[6]

Because the status of social work as a profession is still disputed and uncertain and because it is notoriously difficult to set limits to the social worker's task and responsibilities, it has proved necessary in practice for social workers to negotiate fairly explicit contracts with their clients. Likewise, because the social worker has to act as a go-between and advocate on behalf of the client in so many situations (as between client and local authority, hospital, police, etc.) and as an agent of the Courts or the hospital in other situations, it has proved necessary for him to negotiate very carefully the bounds of confidentiality in his dealings with clients and on behalf of clients.

Between the extremes of paternalistic and authoritarian medicine, on the one hand, where the doctor decides on the control and appropriate disclosure of information; and the liberal alternative of giving the patient his medical record and treating the patient's right to decide on the limits of confidentiality as sacrosanct, there stands what I would call the social work model. This model has several advantages: It is flexible and adaptable to the needs of different people and patients with different kinds of complaints; it is based on a more open and democratic procedure; it allows due respect for the patient's rights but also leaves scope for the discretion and independent judgement of the doctor. While it does expose the patient to the risk of undue pressure the demand that the limits of confidentiality should be explicitly determined within the confidential relationship itself rather than by external formal rules means that the process ought to be self-regulating and self-correcting, subject only to the demands of accountability before the courts and the laws of

[6] British Association of Social Workers (1971). *Confidentiality in Social Work*, London. Discussion Paper No 1, BASW Publications, The Oxford House, Derbyshire Street, E2 6HG.

libel. It means that the doctor or other professional becomes not simply the patient's representative but also society's representative in representing to the patient the demands of the common good—where the disclosure of confidential information may be of benefit to others besides himself.

All the authorities seem to agree that the traditional safeguards against breaches of confidentiality, which operated fairly successfully in the patient–family practitioner situation, do not work adequately in modern hospitals and increasingly socialized medicine. It is arguable therefore that the mutual interests of patient and doctor could best be served by more open and explicit discussion of the limits of confidentiality (the determination of what bits are confidential and which are not) so that both know where they stand, and by an extension to doctors of the privilege which applies to lawyers when the issue is the disclosure of proscribed bits of information. It is not enough to speculate that patients would object to the disclosure of particular bits of information. The experience of social workers suggests that there is relatively little that clients regard as strictly confidential. Most of what is required for efficient health service planning, medical research, etc. can be obtained, it is suggested, without too much difficulty; but when confidentiality is important it is crucially important, and should be recognized as such. The vital issue is to determine when it is really important, and can only be breached with grave consequences for patient–doctor trust and with damaging consequences for the patient.

Secrecy: The Doctor's Right to Independent Clinical Judgement

In the introduction it was suggested that secrecy should be included among the values implicit in confidentiality. It may well be asked, however, whether secrecy can be regarded as an end in itself or merely as a means to an end. In earlier times when medical and psychiatric knowledge was more insecure, and uncertain of its scientific base, members of the profession relied more explicitly on secrecy. In fact, it might be suggested that the more uncertainty, the more secrecy tends to surround that area of medicine, not only to protect the doctor but to protect the patient from his ignorance.

However, it is arguable that there is and will remain a perennial tension in medicine between the esoteric "cultic" aspect of medicine and the public esoteric and scientific aspect, between the saving, redemptive aspects of medicine and those aspects concerned with knowledge, prediction and control of the disorders of human life. On the one hand, the doctor's secrets, both his knowledge of the mysteries of medicine and his knowledge of the intimacies of his patients' lives, is the secret of his power. On the other hand, it is also the basis of his claim to autonomy in the exercise of his clinical judgement, knowledge and expertise, and familiarity with the needs of his patient. The aura of secrecy also serves to create patient dependence and compliance, defines the boundaries of the sick role and creates the need for appropriate magic, whether in the form of physical procedures or drugs. However it also conveys a residual feeling of suspicion which can erupt into an "anti-clerical" backlash against the whole medical establishment.

Medical science in its public and esoteric character has a double effect on public attitudes. On the one hand, more general education of the public in scientific and medical matters creates pressure towards the democratization of health care, suggests the possible liberation of patients from doctor-dependence and creates the demand for a new contract between the medical profession and the public based on respect for patients' rights. On the other hand, the claim of medicine to be scientific, to be able to discover and explain the causes of disease, to predict and control their consequences, creates the spiral of rising expectations that medicine will be able to cure all humanity's ills. Both tendencies unfortunately often lead to increasing public skepticism . . .

The dialectic of secrecy and openness in medicine is obviously part of the practical situation we have to take into account, but it does not illustrate how secrecy might be regarded as a value in its own right. Part of the difficulty is that we tend to invest secrecy in general with a negative *value*, even implying that it is synonymous with deceit. This is because we tend to apply the paradigm of scientific truth inappropriately to personal relationships, and uncritically accept the rationalist and liberal ideal of openness as the norm of behavior for professional relationships. Science is concerned with the abstract and impersonal relationships of facts and propositions. Medicine, insofar as it is a human science, is concerned with the degrees of truthfulness possible in different kinds of personal relationships. Secrecy and truthfulness stand in a different relationship from truth and falsity, truth and error or truth and deceit. While truth and falsity apply to statements, truth and error to man's practical judgements and actions, truthfulness and deceit apply to the subtle interactions of persons in confidential relationships. . . .

Secrecy is not the enemy of truthfulness but the companion and guardian of truthfulness as we explore the possibilities for truthfulness in a given situation. Secrecy from this point of view has a value because it has an intimate relationship with the determination of the truth in each unique human situation and the expression of truthfulness in personal relationships. . . .

If truthfulness in personal relationships is expressed in terms of "fidelity to the demands of the situation" and "responsibility to other people," then secrecy is intimately involved as a value implicit in truthfulness and deceit is in fact very rare and perhaps best exemplified by the cynic who is determined to "tell the truth and be damned." Finally, there is a common kind of situation in which the rules of ordinary confidentiality may be called in question, the crisis of the confidential relationship involved in the death or suicide of the patient. Death highlights the limits of the doctor's confidence and perhaps underlines for him the fragmentariness of his knowledge and the failure of his art, especially in the case of premature death. However, death also represents something metaphysical which points to the ultimate boundaries of human experience and raises questions about the significance of human life and the meaning of the human condition. As such, it may be that in the face of death, doctor and patient need to re-examine the pre-suppositions of privacy, confidence and secrecy on which the confidential relation is based. Is the intense difficulty and anxiety experienced by doctors in communicating bad prognoses related to their own unwillingness to penetrate the secrets of death with the dying in the kind of truthfulness which involves both fidelity to the demands of this new and unique situation and responsibility to the patient as person faced with a unique and unrepeatable life crisis?

WHERE THE BODIES ARE BURIED: THE ADVERSARY SYSTEM AND THE OBLIGATION OF CONFIDENTIALITY*

Monroe H. Freedman

In this classic article, Freedman considers the dilemmas of confidentiality faced by the attorney who knows that the client has committed the crime of which he is accused. Taking a controversial case as his starting point, Freedman argues that the lawyer should not reveal matters disclosed by the client in confidence, even though this might seem to compound the already grave wrongs committed by the client. Freedman argues that the scrupulous protection of confidentiality is necessary for the effective functioning of the adversary system itself, and that because this system ultimately preserves the dignity of individuals, protection of confidentiality is indispensable even when it might seem to work against the pursuit of truth.

The current lawyer's ethical rule governing confidentiality, Model Rule 1.6, appears in Appendix II.

In a recent case in Lake Pleasant, New York, a defendant in a murder case told his lawyers about two other people he had killed and where their bodies had been hidden. The lawyers went there, observed the bodies, and took photographs of them. They did not, however, inform the authorities about the bodies until several months later, when their client had confessed to those crimes. In addition to withholding the information from police and prosecutors, one of the attorneys denied information to one of the victims' parents, who came to him in the course of seeking his missing daughter.

There were interesting reactions to that dramatic event. Members of the public were generally shocked at the apparent callous-

---

* Some references have been deleted without indication.

From Monroe H. Freedman, *Lawyers' Ethics in an Adversary System* (Indianapolis, IN: Bobbs-Merrill, 1975), pp. 1–8. Reprinted by permission of the author. See also Freedman, *Personal Responsibility in a Professional System* 27 Catholic Univ. Law Rev. 191 (1978).

ness on the part of the lawyers, whose conduct was considered typical of an unhealthy lack of concern by lawyers with the public interest and with simple decency. That attitude was encouraged by public statements by a local prosecutor, who sought to indict the lawyers for failing to reveal knowledge of a crime and for failing to see that dead bodies were properly buried. In addition, the reactions of lawyers and law professors who were questioned by the press were ambivalent and confused, indicating that few members of the legal profession had given serious thought to the fundamental questions of administration of justice and of professional responsibility that were raised by the case.

One can certainly understand the sense of moral compulsion to assist the parents and to give the dignity of proper burial to the victims. What seems to be less readily understood—but which, to my mind, throws the moral balance in the other direction—is the obligation of the lawyers to their client and, in a larger sense, to a system of administering justice which is itself essential to maintaining human dignity. In short, not only did the two lawyers behave properly, but they would have committed a serious breach of professional responsibility if they had divulged the information contrary to their client's interest. The explanation to that answer takes us to the very nature of our system of criminal justice and, indeed, to the fundamentals of our system of government.

Let us begin, by way of contrast, with an understanding of the role of a criminal defense attorney in a totalitarian state. As expressed by law professors at the University of Havana, "the first job of a revolutionary lawyer is not to argue that his client is innocent, but rather to determine if his client is guilty and, if so, to seek the sanction which will best rehabilitate him."[1]

. . .

The emphasis in a free society is, of course, sharply different. Under our adversary system, the interests of the state are not absolute, or even paramount. The dignity of the individual is respected to the point that even when the citizen is known by the state to have committed a heinous offense, the individual is nevertheless accorded such rights as counsel, trial by jury, due process, and the privilege against self-incrimination.

A trial is, in part, a search for truth. Accordingly, those basic rights are most often characterized as procedural safeguards against error in the search for truth. Actually, however, a trial is far more than a search for truth, and the constitutional rights that are provided by our system of justice may well outweigh the truth-seeking value—a fact which is manifest when we consider that those rights and others guaranteed by the Constitution may well impede the search for truth rather than further it. What more effective way is there, for example, to expose a defendant's guilt than to require self-incrimination, at least to the extent of compelling the defendant to take the stand and respond to interrogation before the jury? The defendant, however, is presumed innocent; the burden is on the prosecution to prove guilt beyond a reasonable doubt, and even the guilty accused has an "absolute constitutional right" to remain silent and to put the government to its proof.[2]

Thus, the defense lawyer's professional obligation may well be to advise the client to withhold the truth. As Justice Jackson said: "Any lawyer worth his salt will tell the suspect in no uncertain terms to make no statement to police under any circumstances."[3] Similarly, the defense lawyer is obligated to prevent the introduction of evidence that may be wholly reliable, such as a murder weapon seized in violation of

[1] J. Kaplan, Criminal Justice 265–66 (1973): Berman, *The Cuban Popular Tribunals,* 60 Colum. L. Rev. 1317, 1341 (1969).

[2] Escobedo v. Illinois, 378 U.S. 478, 84 S. Ct. 1758, 12 L. Ed. 2d 977 *passim* (1964).
[3] Watts v. Indiana, 338 U.S. 49, 59, 69 S. Ct. 1347, 93 L. Ed. 1801, 1809 (1949) (separate opinion).

the Fourth Amendment, or a truthful but involuntary confession. . . .

Such conduct by defense counsel does not constitute obstruction of justice. On the contrary, it is "part of the duty imposed on the most honorable defense counsel," from whom "we countenance or require conduct which in many instances has little, if any, relation to the search for truth."[4] The reasons . . . go back to the nature of our system of criminal justice and to the fundamentals of our system of government. Before we will permit the state to deprive any person of life, liberty, or property, we require that certain processes be duly followed which ensure regard for the dignity of the individual, irrespective of the impact of those processes upon the determination of truth.

By emphasizing that the adversary process has its foundations in respect for human dignity, even at the expense of the search for truth, I do not mean to deprecate the search for truth or to suggest that the adversary system is not concerned with it. On the contrary, truth is a basic value, and the adversary system is one of the most efficient and fair methods designed for determining it. That system proceeds on the assumption that the best way to ascertain the truth is to present to an impartial judge or jury a confrontation between the proponents of conflicting views, assigning to each the task of marshalling and presenting the evidence in as thorough and persuasive a way as possible. The truth-seeking techniques used by the advocates on each side include investigation, pretrial discovery, cross-examination of opposing witnesses, and a marshalling of the evidence in summation. Thus, the judge or jury is given the strongest possible view of each side, and is put in the best possible position to make an accurate and fair judgment. Nevertheless, the point that I now emphasize is that in a society that honors the

dignity of the individual, the high value that we assign to truth-seeking is not an absolute, but may on occasion be subordinated to even higher values.

The concept of a right to counsel is one of the most significant manifestations of our regard for the dignity of the individual. No person is required to stand alone against the awesome power of the People of New York or the Government of the United States of America. Rather, every criminal defendant is guaranteed an advocate—a "champion" against a "hostile world," the "single voice on which he must rely with confidence that his interests will be protected to the fullest extent consistent with the rules of procedure and the standards of professional conduct."[5] In addition, the attorney serves in significant part to assure equality before the law. Thus, the lawyer has been referred to as "the equalizer," who "places each litigant as nearly as possible on an equal footing under the substantive and procedural law under which he is tried."[6]

The lawyer can serve effectively as advocate, however, "only if he knows all that his client knows" concerning the facts of the case. Nor is the client ordinarily competent to evaluate the relevance or significance of particular facts. What may seem incriminating to the client, may actually be exculpatory. For example, one client was reluctant to tell her lawyer that her husband had attacked her with a knife, because it tended to confirm that she had in fact shot him (contrary to what she had at first maintained). Having been persuaded by her attorney's insistence upon complete and candid disclosure, she finally "confessed all"—which permitted the lawyer to defend her properly and successfully on grounds of self-defense.

Obviously, however, the client cannot be expected to reveal to the lawyer all

---

[4] *United States v. Wade*, 338 U.S. 218, 258, 18 L. Ed 2d 1149–1175.

[5] American Bar Association, Standards Relating to the Defense Function 145–46 (1971).

[6] *Id.*

information that is potentially relevant, including that which may well be incriminating, unless the client can be assured that the lawyer will maintain all such information in the strictest confidence. "The purposes and necessities of the relation between a client and his attorney" require "the fullest and freest disclosures" of the client's "objects, motives and acts." If the attorney were permitted to reveal such disclosures, it would be "not only a gross violation of a sacred trust upon his part," but it would "utterly destroy and prevent the usefulness and benefits to be derived from professional assistance."[7] That "sacred trust" of confidentiality must "upon all occasions be inviolable," or else the client could not feel free "to repose [confidence] in the attorney to whom he resorts for legal advice and assistance."[8] Destroy that confidence, and "a man would not venture to consult any skillful person, or would only dare to tell his counselor half his case."[9] The result would be impairment of the "perfect freedom of consultation by client with attorney," which is "essential to the administration of justice."[10] . . .

That is not to say, of course, that the attorney is privileged to go beyond the needs of confidentiality imposed by the adversary system, and actively participate in concealment of evidence or obstruction of justice. For example, in the *Ryder* case,[11] which arose in Virginia several years ago, the attorney removed from his client's safe deposit box a sawed-off shotgun and the money from a bank robbery and put them, for greater safety, into the lawyer's own safe deposit box. The attorney, quite properly, was suspended from practice for 18 months. (The penalty might well have been

heavier, except for the fact that Ryder sought advice from senior members of the bench and bar, and apparently acted more in ignorance than in venality.) The important difference between the *Ryder* case and the one in Lake Pleasant lies in the active role played by the attorney in *Ryder* to conceal evidence. There is no indication, for example, that the attorneys in Lake Pleasant attempted to hide the bodies more effectively. If they had done so, they would have gone beyond maintaining confidentiality and into active participation in the concealment of evidence. . . .

It has been suggested that the information regarding the two bodies in the Lake Pleasant case was not relevant to the crime for which the defendant was being prosecuted, and that, therefore, that knowledge was outside the scope of confidentiality. That point lacks merit for three reasons. First, an unsophisticated lay person should not be required to anticipate which disclosures might fall outside the scope of confidentiality because of insufficient legal relevance. Second, the information in question might well have been highly relevant to the defense of insanity. Third, a lawyer has an obligation to merge other, unrelated crimes into the bargained plea, if it is possible to do so. Accordingly, the information about the other murders was clearly within the protection of confidentiality. . . .

It has also been suggested that the attorneys in Lake Pleasant were not bound by confidentiality once they had undertaken to corroborate the client's information through their own investigation. It is the duty of the lawyer, however, to conduct a thorough investigation of all aspects of the case, and that duty "exists regardless of the accused's admissions or statements to the lawyer of facts constituting guilt. . . ."[12] For example, upon investigation, the attorneys in the Lake Pleasant case

[7] Meecham, Agency §2297 (2d ed. 1914).
[8] American Bar Association, Committee on Professional Ethics and Grievances, Opinion 150 (1936), quoting E. Thornton, Attorneys at Law §94 (1914).
[9] Greenough v. Gaskell, 1 Myl. & K. 98, 103, 39 Eng. Rep. 618, 621 (1833) (Lord Chancellor Brougham).
[10] American Bar Association, Committee on Professional Ethics and Grievances, Opinion 91 (1933).
[11] *In re* Ryder, 263 F. Supp. 360 (E.D. Va. 1967).

[12] American Bar Association, Standards Relating to the Defense Function §4.1.

might have discovered that the client's belief that he had killed other people was false, which would have had important bearing on an insanity defense.[13]

In summary, the Constitution has committed us to an adversary system for the administration of criminal justice. The essentially humanitarian reason for such a system is that it preserves the dignity of the individual, even though that may oc-

casionally require significant frustration of the search for truth and the will of the state. An essential element of that system is the right to counsel, a right that would be meaningless if the defendant were not able to communicate freely and fully with the attorney.

In order to protect that communication—and, ultimately, the adversary system itself—we impose upon attorneys what has been called the "sacred trust" of confidentiality. It was pursuant to that high trust that the lawyers acted in Lake Pleasant, New York, when they refrained from divulging their knowledge of where the bodies were buried.

---

[13] The suggestion has also been made that the attorneys might have revealed the information through an anonymous telephone call. I do not believe that the proposal merits serious discussion—that a breach of the client's trust can be legitimated by carrying out the breach in a surreptitious manner.

TARASOFF V. REGENTS OF THE UNIVERSITY OF CALIFORNIA*

Majority Opinion, Justice Mathew O. Tobriner
Concurring and Dissenting Opinion, Justice Stanley Mosk
Dissenting Opinion, Justice William P. Clark

The landmark Tarasoff *case concerns whether psychotherapists treating a patient who threatens to harm someone have a duty to warn the intended victim, even though doing so would violate the relationship of confidentiality with the patient. In the majority opinion, Justice Tobriner argues that the duty to protect society outweighs the importance of a patient's right to privacy and that the therapist must break confidentiality when doing so is essential to protect a threatened victim. In the dissent, however, Justice Clark argues that imposing a duty to warn would impair the effective treatment of the mentally ill, since assurance of confidentiality is essential in psychotherapy. Clark cites three reasons for this view, and concludes that the new duty to warn established by the majority opinion will "cripple the use and effectiveness" of psychotherapy.*

Majority Opinion

On October 27, 1969, Prosenjit Poddar killed Tatiana Tarasoff. Plaintiffs, Tatiana's parents, allege that two months earlier Poddar confided his intention to kill

Tatiana to Dr. Lawrence Moore, a psychologist employed by the Cowell Memorial Hospital at the University of California at Berkeley. They allege that on Moore's request, the campus police briefly detained Poddar, but released him when he appeared rational. They further claim that Dr. Harvey Powelson, Moore's superior,

---

* Some references have been deleted without indication.

then directed that no further action be taken to detain Poddar. No one warned plaintiffs of Tatiana's peril. . . .

Plaintiffs' complaints predicate liability on . . . defendants' failure to warn plaintiffs of the impending danger . . . Plaintiffs admit that defendant therapists notified the police, but argue on appeal that the therapists failed to exercise reasonable care to protect Tatiana in that they did not confine Poddar and did not warn Tatiana or others likely to apprise her of the danger.

Although, under the common law, as a general rule, one person owed no duty to control the conduct of another, nor to warn those endangered by such conduct the courts have carved out an exception to this rule in cases in which the defendant stands in some special relationship to either the person whose conduct needs to be controlled or in a relationship to the foreseeable victim of that conduct . . .

Although plaintiffs' pleadings assert no special relation between Tatiana and defendant therapists, they establish as between Poddar and defendant therapists the special relationship that arises between a patient and his doctor or psychotherapist. Such a relationship may support affirmative duties for the benefit of third persons. Thus, for example, a hospital must exercise reasonable care to control the behavior of a patient which may endanger other persons. A doctor must also warn a patient if the patient's condition or medication renders certain conduct, such as driving a car, dangerous to others.

Defendants contend, however, that imposition of a duty to exercise reasonable care to protect third persons is unworkable because therapists cannot accurately predict whether or not a patient will resort to violence. In support of this argument amicus representing the American Psychiatric Association and other professional societies cites numerous articles which indicate that therapists, in the present state of the art, are unable reliably to predict violent acts; their forecasts, amicus claims, tend consistently to overpredict violence, and indeed are more often wrong than right. Since predictions of violence are often erroneous, amicus concludes, the courts should not render rulings that predicate the liability of therapists upon the validity of such predictions.

The role of the psychiatrist, who is indeed a practitioner of medicine, and that of the psychologist who performs an allied function, are like that of the physician who must conform to the standards of the profession and who must often make diagnoses and predictions based upon such evaluations. Thus the judgment of the therapist in diagnosing emotional disorders and in predicting whether a patient presents a serious danger of violence is comparable to the judgment which doctors and professionals must regularly render under accepted rules of responsibility.

We recognize the difficulty that a therapist encounters in attempting to forecast whether a patient presents a serious danger of violence. Obviously we do not require that the therapist, in making that determination, render a perfect performance; the therapist need only exercise "that reasonable degree of skill, knowledge, and care ordinarily possessed and exercised by members of [that professional specialty] under similar circumstances." . . . Within the broad range of reasonable practice and treatment in which professional opinion and judgment may differ, the therapist is free to exercise his or her own best judgment without liability; proof, aided by hindsight, that he or she judged wrongly is insufficient to establish negligence.

In the instant case, however, the pleadings do not raise any question as to failure of defendant therapists to predict that Poddar presented a serious danger of violence. On the contrary, the present complaints allege that defendant therapists did in fact predict that Poddar would kill, but were negligent in failing to warn.

Amicus [The American Psychiatric Association] contends, however, that even when a therapist does in fact predict that a patient poses a serious danger of violence to others, the therapist should be absolved of any responsibility for failing to act to protect the potential victim. In our view, however, once a therapist does in fact determine, or under applicable professional standards reasonably should have determined, that a patient poses a serious danger of violence to others, he bears a duty to exercise reasonable care to protect the foreseeable victim of that danger. While the discharge of this duty of due care will necessarily vary with the facts of each case, in each instance the adequacy of the therapist's conduct must be measured against the traditional negligence standard of the rendition of reasonable care under the circumstances. . . .

The risk that unnecessary warnings may be given is a reasonable price to pay for the lives of possible victims that may be saved. We would hesitate to hold that the therapist who is aware that his patient expects to attempt to assassinate the President of the United States would not be obligated to warn the authorities because the therapist cannot predict with accuracy that his patient will commit the crime.

Defendants further argue that free and open communication is essential to psychotherapy . . . The giving of a warning, defendants contend, constitutes a breach of trust which entails the revelation of confidential communications.

We recognize the public interest in supporting effective treatment of mental illness and in protecting the rights of patients to privacy and the consequent public importance of safeguarding the confidential character of psychotherapeutic communication. Against this interest, however, we must weigh the public interest in safety from violent assault. . . .

We realize that the open and confidential character of psychotherapeutic dialogue encourages patients to express threats of violence, few of which are ever executed. Certainly a therapist should not be encouraged routinely to reveal such threats; such disclosures could seriously disrupt the patient's relationship with his therapist and with the persons threatened. To the contrary, the therapist's obligations to his patient require that he not disclose a confidence unless such disclosure is necessary to avert danger to others, and even then that he do so discreetly, and in a fashion that would preserve the privacy of his patient to the fullest extent compatible with the prevention of the threatened danger.

The revelation of a communication under the above circumstances is not a breach of trust or a violation of professional ethics; as stated in the Principles of Medical Ethics of the American Medical Association (1957), section 9: "A physician may not reveal the confidence entrusted to him in the course of medical attendance . . . *unless he is required to do so by law or unless it becomes necessary in order to protect the welfare of the individual or of the community.*" (Emphasis added.) We conclude that the public policy favoring protection of the confidential character of patient-psychotherapist communications must yield to the extent to which disclosure is essential to avert danger to others. The protective privilege ends where the public peril begins.

Our current crowded and computerized society compels the interdependence of its members. In this risk-infested society we can hardly tolerate the further exposure to danger that would result from a concealed knowledge of the therapist that his patient was lethal. If the exercise of reasonable care to protect the threatened victim requires the therapist to warn the endangered party or those who can reasonably be expected to notify him, we see no sufficient societal interest that would protect and justify concealment. The containment of such risks lies in the public interest.

Concurring and Dissenting Opinion

I concur in the result in this instance only because the complaints allege that defendant therapists did in fact predict that

Poddar would kill and were therefore negligent in failing to warn of that danger. Thus the issue here is very narrow: we are not concerned with whether the therapists, pursuant to the standards of their profession, "should have" predicted potential violence; they allegedly did so in actuality. Under these limited circumstances I agree that a cause of action can be stated.

Whether plaintiffs can ultimately prevail is problematical at best. As the complaints admit, the therapists *did* notify the police that Poddar was planning to kill a girl identifiable as Tatiana. While I doubt that more should be required, this issue may be raised in defense and its determination is a question of fact.

I cannot concur, however, in the majority's rule that a therapist may be held liable for failing to predict his patient's tendency to violence if other practitioners, pursuant to the "standards of the profession," would have done so. The question is, what standards? Defendants and a responsible amicus curiae, supported by an impressive body of literature . . . demonstrate that psychiatric predictions of violence are inherently unreliable.

. . . I would restructure the rule designed by the majority to eliminate all reference to conformity to standards of the profession in predicting violence. If a psychiatrist does in fact predict violence, then a duty to warn arises. The majority's expansion of that rule will take us from the world of reality into the wonderland of clairvoyance.

Dissenting Opinion

Until today's majority opinion, both legal and medical authorities have agreed that confidentiality is essential to effectively treat the mentally ill, and that imposing a duty on doctors to disclose patient threats to potential victims would greatly impair treatment. Further, recognizing that effective treatment and society's safety are necessarily intertwined, the Legislature has already decided effective and confidential treatment is preferred over imposition of a duty to warn.

The issue whether effective treatment for the mentally ill should be sacrificed to a system of warnings is, in my opinion, properly one for the Legislature, and we are bound by its judgment. Moreover, even in the absence of clear legislative direction, we must reach the same conclusion because imposing the majority's new duty is certain to result in a net increase in violence.

The majority . . . fails to recognize that . . . overwhelming policy considerations mandate against sacrificing fundamental patient interests without gaining a corresponding increase in public benefit.

**POWER AND PARADOX:
CONFIDENTIALITY IN THE MINISTRY***

Karen Lebacqz

In this discussion of a minister's dilemma about confidentiality in counseling a pregnant teenager, Lebacqz employs both rule-based and consequentialist considerations to discern morally relevant features of the situation. She emphasizes the professional's power not merely to respond to the client, but to define reality for her. From this analysis of

* Some footnotes have been deleted without indication.

From Karen Lebacqz, *Professional Ethics: Power and Paradox* (Nashville, TN: Abingdon Press, 1985). (This article is a condensation of two sections of Lebacqz's book; readers should see the extended argument in the full discussion of the book itself.)

professional power, Lebacqz draws the conclusion that the professional must act not merely with beneficence toward the client, but also to liberate the client. In doing so, Lebacqz provides a complex answer to the minister's dilemma of confidentiality.

Ruth is an associate minister serving her first appointment in a suburban church. Like many "associate" ministers, her primary responsibility is the youth group.

A fifteen-year-old high school junior from the group appears at Ruth's office door one day. Obviously upset, the young woman blurts out, "I need to talk to somebody, but you mustn't share this with *anyone*."

Sensing her deep distress, Ruth replies, "Kathy, what happens here in this office is just between us. Please tell me what's troubling you."

Kathy bursts into tears. "I'm pregnant, and I've got to have an abortion. My parents would kill me if they knew. My boyfriend doesn't know and I don't ever want to see him again. I've missed two periods and I don't have enough money to pay for the abortion. Please help me."

This is a true story. . . . .What should Ruth do? Should she help Kathy secure an abortion? Should she lend her money if needed? Should she keep confidence?

Does it make a difference that Kathy is only fifteen? that she is a member of the youth group? that her parents might be opposed to abortion? that Ruth explicitly says the information will not go beyond the walls of the office? Does it make a difference that Kathy divulges this information to Ruth in her office, because of her work with the youth group—in short, in her professional role? Does it make a difference that Ruth is a woman breaking into a profession dominated by men? that her job might be on the line depending on what she decides? that she is an "associate" minister with collegial obligations toward her senior colleague? Does it make a difference that Ruth's job description includes not only youth work but calling and preaching—hence, direct responsibil-

ities toward the adults of the church as well as the youth? . . .

Rules and Reasons

Every code of ministerial ethics includes a provision binding the minister to keep confidence—for example, "The confidential statements made to a minister by his parishioners are privileged and should never be divulged without the consent of those making them."[1] A clear rule governs the professional's behavior and requires her to keep confidence. Ruth was approached in her professional work setting (her office). Kathy is a member of the youth group—a parishioner. It seems clear, then, that Ruth's code of professional ethics applies to the situation. She can point to a rule binding her to keep confidence. . . .

The rule that binds the minister to confidentiality has a specific history. Since the Fourth Lateran Council in 1215, the Catholic Church has required that matters communicated in confession (the sacrament of penance) were to be "under the seal."[2] Strictly speaking, this means that the lips of the priest are sealed forever. No priest can be compelled to divulge anything told to him in the confessional, and any priest who does divulge such a confidence has broken a sacred duty of the priesthood.

In Reformation tradition, confession or penance is not a sacrament. Counseling occurs under more informal circumstances rather than in the formal setting of the confessional. Nonetheless, the practical and theological underpinnings of secrecy remain.[3] Ruth is bound by church tradition

---

[1] The identical statement appears both in the Congregational code and in the Methodist ministers' ethical code. See Harmon, *Ministerial Ethics and Etiquette*, pp. 201, 204.

[2] Bok, *Secrets*, p. 78.

[3] Cf. Robert E. Regan, *Professional Secrecy in the Light of Moral Principles* (Washington, D.C.: Augustinian Press, 1943) and Thomas Joseph O'Donnell, *Morals in Medicine* (Westminster, Md.: Newman Press, 1960), esp. chap. 7.

and theology to respect confidences and not to divulge them.

Indeed, this strong expectation within theological tradition has given rise to some legal protections for priests and ministers. Under the "priest-penitent privilege," many states exempt ministers and priests from divulging confidential information.[4] While their provisions are often restrictive,[5] they serve the function of reinforcing the expectation that ministers will keep confidence.

There are good reasons to have and to maintain this rule. The guarantee of confidentiality encourages penitents to seek the advice, counsel, and mediated pardon that ministers and priests offer. If forgiveness of sins is integral to salvation and if clearing one's conscience is an important step in receiving forgiveness for sins, then this practice is intimately related to the salvific purposes of the church.[6] The rule that binds ministers to confidentiality facilitates a central task of ministry by encouraging parishioners to divulge their troubles and cleanse their spirits. In keeping the rule, the minister ensures that the reputation of ministry in general, and of her own ministry in particular, is maintained so that others who are troubled or anxious will also be encouraged to seek solace or professional counsel. The rule serves a teleological purpose: It encourages good relations between clients and professionals.

Kathy probably chose Ruth to confide in partly because she likes her and trusts her as a person, but partly also because Ruth is a minister—and therefore is expected to keep confidence. The minister is a "safe environment" for the adolescent to share her fears and troubles. This safety exists because of the rule that binds ministers to confidentiality. Ruth might well consider herself bound by the "seal" or duty to keep confidence, for she was acting in her role as minister and received a "penitential" communication from one of her parishioners.

The first reason for following the rule, therefore, would be recognition of the importance of the rule in establishing the practice of ministry and facilitating its goals.

The second reason is avoiding harm. Once such a rule exists and the expectation of confidentiality is ingrained, to break confidence could have disastrous consequences. . . . Kathy has trusted Ruth. She indicates that Ruth is the only person she can trust in this situation. To share the information with someone else might destroy Kathy's ability to trust any adult— or any professional. Following the rule not only facilitates good relations between professional and client, but also prevents harm to the client.

Another reason for keeping confidence is to protect third parties. When Kathy divulges her own secret, she also divulges information about her boyfriend.

Adhering to the rule is also the safest course of action for the minister in some ways. Having rules to govern professional behavior keeps us from reinventing the wheel every time we make a decision. It is difficult to know ahead of time all of the possible consequences of our actions. Rules develop because the human community has found that they facilitate good consequences. . . .

Situation Ethics

And yet, we do not think that promises should always be kept, or confidences never broken. No matter how important the rule

---

[4] Roy D. Weinberg, *Confidential and Other Privileged Communication* (Dobbs Ferry, N.Y.: Oceana Publications, 1967), see esp. chap. 5. See also Lindell L. Gumper, *Legal Issues in the Practice of Ministry* (Birmingham, Mich.: Psychological Studies and Consultation Program, 1981).

[5] Robert L. Stoyles, "The Dilemma of the Constitutionality of the Priest-Penitent Privilege—The Application of the Religion Clauses," *University of Pittsburgh Law Review* 29 (1967): 27–63.

[6] Weinberg, *Confidential and Other Privileged Communication*, p. 2: "The most commonly advanced argument in support of privilege is that it encourages vital interpersonal relationships which might be seriously prejudiced by the prospect of breached confidentiality."

and how strong the reasons for it, we do find justifiable exceptions. It might be wrong to break a promise for trivial reasons, but not in Kathy's very urgent situation. Though the reasons for keeping confidence in professional situations seem binding on the whole, there may be equally strong reasons here for Ruth to contemplate breaking that rule.

First, Kathy is an adolescent. It is not clear that she knows what is best for her. In the panic of the moment, she may not be considering all the important factors. If Ruth has a professional obligation to seek Kathy's good, she might want to ensure a decision made with broader perspective.

Second, there is a question of potential harm to Kathy. Significant harm might be sufficient to outweigh the binding nature of the rule of confidentiality. Suppose Ruth suspects that Kathy's parents would go through a time of anger and grief and would then offer support and assistance to Kathy. Kathy may be cutting off support and help. Perhaps following the rule would be the right thing to do in most cases, but not in the rare case where the minister is quite sure that the adolescent is harming herself. If the pregnancy is getting into the second trimester, there is also the possibility of physical harm from an abortion.

Third, Kathy is still dependent on her parents and has filial obligations to them. Perhaps they have a right to know—either because of their responsibility for Kathy in general, or simply because they are "family" and their destinies are tied together in some way. What happens to Kathy will affect her entire family on some level. Perhaps, then, they have a right to be involved.

Fourth, there is Kathy's boyfriend. The child-to-be is his as well as hers. Though Kathy declares that she hates the sight of him, this does not account for his possible feelings and rights. Nor does it account for his responsibilities. If he is a member of the youth group, then Ruth has a professional relationship to him as well as to Kathy. What should she do about this relationship and about his rights and responsibilities?

Fifth, there is Ruth's colleague. Does the senior minister on the staff have a right to know simply because he is her colleague? Does he need the information to facilitate his ministry to Kathy's parents? If he is not only Ruth's colleague but also her supervisor, he may be ultimately responsible for anything she does. Does he have a right to protect himself professionally—or to supervise Ruth in making a difficult decision that may affect her entire career?

Sixth, there is the church community. Church members might also claim a right to know on grounds that they are "the body of Christ" and that what affects one of them affects them all. They may genuinely want to "share each other's burdens." While legal responses to abortion currently stress privacy, it is not clear that these grounds should receive theological affirmation. What is Ruth's responsibility to the church as a whole?

Finally, there is the fetus—the child-to-be. Kathy is contemplating ending its life. Some would argue that it has a right to life. Should confidence be broken in order to protect this right?

In short, there are other considerations besides the expectation that ministers keep confidence. What if it seems that Ruth could do more good by breaking the rule than by following it? . . .

Ruth's dilemma presents a striking example of the conflict between the rule that binds us in a situation and those aspects of the situation that make us wonder whether adhering to rules is sufficient. Should the rule hold in this case? Or are the other troubling aspects of the case sufficient to outweigh the rules and justify breaking the promise of confidentiality? . . .

But now a crucial question arises. Does it make a difference to be in a professional setting or role? Is Ruth's dilemma about keeping confidence any different because of her position as a minister than it would be if she had been sought out simply as a friend? Is the professional role a morally relevant feature of the situation that should change the outcome of the decision?

Power and Authority

Some have argued that being in a professional role is not relevant. They liken the professional role to the role of a parent or friend. But . . . I think there remains an important structural difference between the professional role of minister and the trusteeships of parents and friends. Professionals practice in an institutional context, girded by laws, social mores, relatively clear role expectations, and groups of other professionals who both support and delimit their spheres. The professional context carries legal and moral sanctions for inappropriate behavior. The existence of explicit codes of morality for professional groups indicates how institutionalized professional practice is.

This institutionalized character leads to a morally relevant difference in assessing the issue of power and vulnerability. As Sissela Bok puts it, confession in institutionalized practices "increases the authority of the listener while decreasing that of the speaker . . ."[7] In sociological language, professionals have not just "power" (the ability to influence my behavior), but "authority" (legitimated and institutionalized power). Professionals represent society and its power in a way that friends do not. "The minister is a physical representation of the whole community of faith, of the tradition, of a way of viewing the meaning of life, . . . and of God."[8] This representative power is called authority. Professionals have authority to put me in jail, to hospitalize me, to excommunicate me, or in other ways to affect significantly the structures of meaning and of freedom in

my life. Their power is both legitimated and institutionalized.

To be sure, parents and friends have power. Both parents and friends may change the structures of freedom of my life: They can call the police or the mental health authorities and ask to have me committed. But the actual hospitalization or confinement requires the stamp of professional approval. This is the stamp of authority—of a societal decision exercised through the persona of the professional. It is not the personal qualities of the professional that give her or him this power over others, but the very status of being a professional. Part of the role definition of professionals includes this representative power on behalf of society—this power that is legitimated into authority and girded by institutions.

Hence, professionals have a symbolic and representative power that goes beyond the interpersonal power of friends. Indeed, some have argued that it is not possible for professionals to be friends with their clients without jeopardizing the professional role. The difference between the professional as trustee and parents or friends as trustees, therefore, lies in the type of power held and the setting in which it is exercised. To be vulnerable in an unequal and unnatural setting and in the face of a structured and institutionalized power is the fate of clients. I believe that this constitutes a morally relevant difference from other forms of trusteeship. Even in circumstances where professional groups become vulnerable to public exposure or criticism, and where the sharing of information is more reciprocal, professionals nonetheless retain a morally relevant form of power over their clients.

The Problematics of Power

The public is sensitive to abuses of power on the part of professionals. A professional who takes advantage of the weakness of a client for personal gain will be labeled "un-

---

[7] Bok, *Secrets*, p. 80.
[8] Switzer, *Pastor, Preacher, Person*, p. 18.

professional" or "unethical." But so long as professional power is exercised within the boundaries defined as legitimate for the profession, society has not—until recently—perceived a problem. The fact that professional power is legitimated and institutionalized has tended to blind us to the importance of the mere existence of that power. Precisely because it is legitimate power—authority—we forget that there is a significant power gap between professional and client. We also forget that it is a type of power that is very difficult for clients to overcome. The vulnerability of client to professional differs from the vulnerability of friend to friend: The professional can not only hurt my feelings, but has legitimated, institutionalized power to make significant changes in my life.

Until a decade ago, for instance, Kathy would have needed the sanction of a professional in order to secure an abortion. Abortions were permitted only in restricted cases. And it was physicians who decided which cases "merited" this medical intervention. Their power over her would have been considerable.

In the current legal climate, Ruth clearly has no power to prevent Kathy from having an abortion. Her authority does not extend this far. Nonetheless, she does have considerable power and authority. She represents the church, and she represents God. She is, as Southard puts it, a "spiritual authority."[9] And as such, she is "an evaluator of behavior, an upholder of standards, a mediator of godly acceptance of judgment."[10] She interprets for Kathy how her pregnancy and contemplated abortion are seen in the eyes of the church and in the eyes of God. She can facilitate or obstruct the abortion—e.g., by giving or withholding money. She can shame Kathy or provide support. As a professional minister, she interprets on behalf of the church the meaning—and consequences—of Ka-

thy's act. Indeed, she will do this wittingly or unwittingly: her actions, as well as her words, will provide an interpretation of the meaning and significance of Kathy's plight. All of this is a legitimate part of her professional authority.

Now suppose Ruth is opposed to abortion and considers it a grave sin that threatens Kathy's salvation. She therefore tells Kathy that she is a sinner, in need of repentance, and that she must not take this course of action. To do so is not an abuse of authority as it is generally understood. Ruth has not sought her own personal gain. She has neither violated confidence nor broken any of the rules of her professional code. She appears to be acting within the legitimate boundaries of her professional relationship. In short, she remains a trustworthy trustee, using her skill and knowledge to secure the legitimate ends of her profession. Is there anything wrong with this?

The traditional view has been that it is only the abuse of power to secure personal ends that requires watching. So long as the professional does not combine personal interests with professional ones, but stays carefully within the boundaries of legitimated professional goals, the existence of the professional's power is not problematic. Hence, the integrity of the professional person—her or his ability to keep personal agendas out of the professional relationship—was considered a sufficient corrective to problems of professional power. . . .

I disagree. The traditional ethic of integrity and faithfulness is not altogether adequate, even for the interpersonal dimension. It fails to take account of the ways in which the social dimension—the representative nature of the power held by professionals—influences the interpersonal arena. It fails to deal with structural problems in the power gap between professional and client. All too many ministers act precisely as Ruth hypothetically does here, using the vulnerability of the client to secure legitimate professional ends. With the best of intentions, and within the boun-

[9] Southard, *Pastoral Authority*, p. 7.
[10] Ibid., p. 8.

daries of professional practice, they impose a definition of reality on the client in ways that are problematic ethically. As Bok puts it, "Institutional practices of self-revelation . . . are also unequalled means for imposing orthodoxy of every kind."[11]

The Power of Definition

Professionals have the power to define reality. And it is this power that makes dependence on individual virtue an insufficient corrective. Professionals profess.
. . .

The profession is not only entrusted by society with maintenance of a cultural heritage, but also begins to redefine and shape that cultural heritage. The profession defines how some aspect of society is to be thought of and how policy is to be formulated around it. Ruth draws on her professional training to define how a teenage pregnancy and the possibility of abortion are to be interpreted. She may take it as a sign of sin and an opportunity to require repentance or increase shame. She may take it as an unfortunate mistake and an opportunity to offer forgiveness. Each of these approaches has been used historically by her professional group; each falls within the legitimate boundaries of authority; and each constitutes a definition of reality. . . . If this is true for all professions generally, it is even more true for clergy. The primary role of clergy is rarely defined as "the social construction of reality" or "defining reality." Yet that is precisely what clergy do. Other professionals offer definitions of reality under the cover of doing something else. . . . The naming of reality is central to the task of ministry. The minister does not simply heal or help or console. She defines reality by offering a new language, a perspective on hidden meanings, a transformation of ordinary symbols, a hope in the midst of seeming hopelessness. Part of the task of the minister is to "speak the truth." This "truth" is the truth formed by theological language and given shape in the community of faith. In "telling the story," clergy are often providing the framework by which our own stories can be judged and interpreted. The social construction of reality is at the heart of the minister's vocation.

Fidelity and the Limits of Professional Power

We want professionals to have power: power to heal, power to litigate, power to set things right with God or nature or other human beings. We purposefully give professionals legitimated power: authority. But with it comes the power to define our needs and problems as well as to respond to them. And with the power of definition comes a significant control over our lives. We want to be able to trust professionals to use this power wisely. And we want them to use it for our own good. But we must not forget that professional definitions of reality are only as good as the state of the art in the profession. What was once a sickness no longer is. What was once a sin no longer is. This suggests that even professional groups have corrected their own previous definitions. Who will watchdog the current definitions? . . .

Once power is understood to be a central and defining characteristic of professions, the question of distribution and use of power becomes a central ethical issue. Liberation and justice become primary ethical obligations for the professional. Traditional professional ethics is not adequate because it does not take sufficiently into account the nature and structure of institutions, or the implications of the power gap between professional and client. Nowhere do traditional codes of professional ethics take adequate account of these ethical obligations. The words *justice* and *liberation* do not appear in professional codes of ethics. And while such codes stress the integrity and trustworthiness of the profes-

[11] Bok, *Secrets*, p. 86.

sional, these concerns are rarely if ever linked with attention to the structures of delivery of professional care. Traditional professional ethics has operated from the base of professional autonomy and from an individualized professional–client relationship, rather than from a base of examination of structural and institutional aspects of the delivery of care. . . .

Recognizing the role of professional power also means that aspects of the situation dealing with the balance of power and the oppression of the client will be crucial. In contrast to the traditional view of professional ethics that stresses the norm of beneficence, this framework suggests that several other norms are central. To be trustworthy Ruth must act on norms of justice and liberation that attend her position as a professional.

Of course, she is also bound by the structures of her professional setting. Not everything that she would like to do may be possible for her. These structures affect the balance of power and hence the possibilities for justice and liberation.

A Prima Facie Case
for Confidentiality

. . . Ruth might begin with the question. How will liberation happen here? This forces her to ask where oppression is happening and what liberation would mean in this situation.

Once the power of the professional is understood, being trustworthy takes on new meaning: It requires seeking a balance of power in which justice emerges. Where a client is vulnerable and lacking power, justice requires that power be shared. Minimally, Kathy's oppression and powerlessness should not be increased.

Given the concern for fidelity and justice that must accompany the professional's role, I think two features of this situation are most important: Kathy is alone, and she is feeling powerless.

Because of these two features, I would argue that Ruth should keep confidence. If Kathy is telling the truth, then Ruth is the only person (at least, the only one in authority) she has told about her plight. She is cut off from her "significant others"—her parents do not know, and she is scared of their reaction; her boyfriend (who may provide a haven from her parents in other circumstances) also does not know. . . . If Kathy is indeed as alone as she seems, and as vulnerable and powerless as that would make her, then Ruth must be concerned about not increasing Kathy's vulnerability and lack of power.

Since knowledge of a secret gives power, Ruth should begin with a strong bias against divulging Kathy's confidence. Minimally, she should not divulge the information where doing so would simply enhance the power of others over Kathy. Moreover, there is good reason to think that no one should be told. Kathy has chosen to place trust in Ruth. To violate that trust might be to plunge Kathy into a state of utter aloneness, to heighten her vulnerability. This is contrary to the duty of the professional to empower the client, not to increase the client's vulnerability.

In short, a primary concern for justice and liberation, coupled with attention to the structures that give professionals power, suggests that Ruth should *not* break confidence. . . . It seems, then, that both the specific rules of professional ethics and the morally relevant factors brought about by attending to the meaning of trustworthiness in a professional setting give Ruth strong prima facie reasons not to break confidence.

Duties to Others

Yet we also saw above that a strong prima facie case in one direction is not alone sufficient to tell us that Ruth does the right thing if she decides not to share Kathy's information with anyone. There are some good reasons here why she might want to divulge what she has learned. She is concerned about Kathy's good, the parents' rights and interests, the boyfriend's rights and responsibilities, her own collegial obligations, her obligations to the congregation as a whole, and the life of the fetus. . . .

Perhaps the most cogent arguments are those having to do with Kathy's parents and her boyfriend. Each is implicated in some ways by Kathy's decision. All are owed general duties of respect and justice, such that their desires should be taken into account and they should be given information about things that significantly impact on their lives. And, indeed, one could argue that if Ruth is also their minister, then she has not only these general duties toward them, but some particular, role-activated duties as well.

Moreover, there are theological reasons that would incline Ruth to involve them in the decision. The commandment "Honor thy father and thy mother" reflects the structural importance of family ties and lineages. . . .

When presenting this case, I have found that ministers often respond, "Well, it depends on who the parents are. If I knew them well, and knew that they would really support Kathy, I might tell them." It *does* depend on who the parents are—and how well the minister knows them. But I want to add a cautioning note. In my experience, a high percentage of young people entering ministry have very positive feelings about their own parents. . . . Ruth should not automatically accept Kathy's negative assessment of her parents' reaction. But Ruth must also be careful lest she read into the situation positive feelings about her own parents *or* value judgments about how parents *should* be. . . .

Yet we are still left with the question whether Ruth has obligations to the parents (or others) strong enough to override the prima facie case for keeping confidence. I think not. While it is true that Ruth has role-specific duties toward all

members of the congregation (including Kathy's parents), she takes on a special obligation when she enters a confidential counseling relationship with Kathy. . . .The positive goal of reconciliation is not sufficient to override those special obligations that require explicit loyalty to Kathy. The professional's *primary* duty is liberation of the client. Reconciliation is a goal, but liberation is a duty. And liberation is not the same as reconciliation. . . .

Much the same could be said for the other communities suggested above: the boyfriend, the church at large, Kathy's friends. Any of these *might* provide a supportive community for Kathy as she goes through her difficult time of decision. Hence, it is tempting to think that they should be involved. However, if the price of involving them is violation of trust—betrayal—or of the demands of justice and liberation, the price is too high and is not something that the professional can do and still consider herself to be a trustworthy trustee. . . .

The Duty to Divulge

Classical theological arguments about keeping secrets permit several instances in which even the professional may—or indeed, should—break confidence. One of these is where there is direct threat to another person.

Such reasoning has recently been carried into the law. . . .*

Is there an analogous situation here? Kathy is contemplating abortion. Should Ruth then break confidence in order to protect the life of the fetus? . . . Under current law, Kathy has a legal right to abortion. Her contemplated act is not illegal, as was the murder of Tatiana Tarasoff. Since Kathy cannot legally be prevented from securing an abortion, breaking confidence will not necessarily result in protecting the life of the fetus. Nor is there

---

* [See the *Tarasoff* case reprinted in this chapter.]

any way to warn the fetus directly. . . .

What Actually Happened

Since this is a real case, some readers are no doubt wondering what actually did happen. The story is an interesting one.

"Ruth" was not personally or theologically opposed to abortion, nor had her denomination taken an explicit stand against it. Nonetheless, she was concerned about the impact of such a decision on the life of "Kathy." She knew that no matter what Kathy decided, she would live with the decision for the rest of her life. That is a heavy burden for an adolescent. Ruth also felt some responsibility toward Kathy's parents, since her position at the church included some general forms of ministry besides youth work. She therefore decided that, if possible, Kathy should tell at least one of her parents.

In this case, a structural problem actually assisted the resolution of the dilemma. Though Kathy had no money, she could secure an abortion under her parents' medical insurance. But this meant that a record of the procedure might enter Kathy's home through an insurance bill or report. Ruth therefore convinced Kathy that it was too risky not to tell her parents—or at least one of them. Kathy finally agreed to tell her mother.

With Ruth present, Kathy shared her plight with her mother. Her mother supported the decision for an abortion, and gave support in general to Kathy. Together, they decided not to tell Kathy's father, for fear of his temper and possible retribution toward Kathy or her boyfriend.

Kathy did finally have an abortion—with her mother at her side. She thus had at least a small community of support—and an important one. Further, Ruth did not break confidence, since Kathy herself divulged her plight.

It sounds like a story with a happy ending, at least from the perspective of Ruth's professional obligations. In some ways, Ruth did what most ministers hearing the case have suggested would be best: Without breaking confidence, she managed to involve the family and provide a supportive community for Kathy.

Yet the story will not end here. . . . Kathy's mother now shares the burden of confidentiality. . . . It is important to remember that anyone with whom confidence is shared takes on an ethical dilemma. . . .

Kathy's life story now includes an abortion. She must reconcile that with her Christian faith. So Ruth's professional obligations are ongoing. . . .

In the real world, we rarely live "happily ever after." Perhaps, as Hauerwas suggests, the crux is to have a story—and an ethical system—strong enough to deal with the truth of human life.[12]

---

[12] Cf. Hauerwas, *Vision and Virtue*, at p. 117: "A Christian ethic is ultimately an ethic of truth or it is neither Christian nor an ethic substantive enough to deal with the human condition."

CONFIDENTIALITY IN SOCIAL WORK: A REAPPRAISAL*

Janet Moore-Kirkland and Karen Vice Irey

In a striking departure from the emphasis on confidentiality characteristic of other professions, Moore-Kirkland and Irey argue that confidentiality is neither essential nor always desirable in the practice of social work. This is because social workers ought not view their clients as isolated individuals, but as people in social environments. Social workers must function within circumscribed social systems, and their objective is focused, not on individual clients with whom they might establish relationships involving confidentiality, but on intervention within a system of relationships and interactions among a number of people. While traditional notions of confidentiality should not be completely discarded, these authors argue, they should not be given their traditional privileged status.

Confidentiality between worker and client has long been regarded as a cornerstone of psychotherapeutic intervention. Despite increased attention in the social work literature to the limits of confidentiality posed by intervention in the context of an agency, legal constraints, and computer technology, the principle of confidentiality between worker and client remains.

Traditionally, confidentiality is regarded as essential to the process of change that takes place through the exclusive relationship between worker and client. . . . The assumption is that people will be reluctant to seek help without a guarantee of confidentiality. The 1977 Delegate Assembly of the National Association of Social Workers affirmed by resolution the social work profession's belief that a "relationship of . . . confidentiality is essential to the helping process" and that a client gives information to the worker "with the expectation that it will be held in confidence."[1]

Threats to confidentiality are generally envisioned as external forces associated with technological and social change, such as computer systems, the courts, and the federal government, which encroach on the privacy shared by the client and worker. These forces call into question not only the use of information gathered by professionals but even the objective paperwork administered by secretaries and clerks. One response of the social work profession to such threats has been to increase pressure for legislation providing coverage for social workers under privileged communication, similar to that afforded to psychiatrists, psychologists, doctors, and lawyers.

Social Context

The confidential relationship between worker and client retains the basic shape imposed by theories of individual psychopathology and change. It conceives of communication as a simple dyadic exchange in which the worker guarantees the privacy of the client. Yet social work claims a unique professional interest in and responsibility to both the individual and society. Theoretical developments in recent years have provided an integrated framework for viewing change in the interactions among various parts of social systems—families,

---

* Some references have been deleted without indication.

[1] "1977 Delegate Assembly Actions," *National Association of Social Workers News*, 22 (July 1977), p. 8.

From Janet Moore-Kirkland and Karen Vice Irey, "A Reappraisal of Confidentiality," © 1981, National Association of Social Workers, Inc. Reprinted with permission, from *Social Work*, vol. 26, no. 4 (July 1981), 319–22.

groups, communities, and organizations—and given more attention to changing relationships among and between systems.

To define confidentiality only in relation to the one-on-one psychotherapeutic process between worker and client places unnecessary limits on social workers. The definition of confidentiality must deal with people in their social environments—the very relationship that social work claims as its unique focus. Social workers cannot view individuals—including individuals in their relationship to workers—apart from the social context.

The issue of confidentiality within a social context is especially acute in rural environments. In small towns and communities, social workers and clients must function not only in therapeutic sessions but also in daily interactions within circumscribed social systems—families, neighbors, schools, and businesses. Although an analysis of confidentiality from a social systems perspective is not unique to rural communities, rural settings provide an opportunity to examine closely a definable social environment and the relationships among various systems in that environment.

Rural communities are characterized by a smaller, more intimate scale of living, one facet of which is that everyone knows everyone else—or at least everyone else's relative. Often, large extended families and complex interrelationships among families exist. For example, the banker may be the client's employer, the social worker's cousin, a member of the county welfare board, and brother of the client's next-door neighbor. Many townspeople may be interrelated by a shared history, such as being the first settlers in the community, and latecomers may be related by other events, such as settling in the community during an oil boom.

The smaller scale of living also means that everyday events in the community, as well as extraordinary ones, are highly visible. Whether a person goes shopping or

sees a social worker, other people in the community will be aware of it. What goes on behind the closed doors of a home is jealously guarded as private, however, even when it also is known to the neighbors and others. The emphasis on "rugged individualism" in rural communities is often shown in people's reluctance to interfere with each other's activities in the home. Alcoholism or child abuse may be ignored for long periods of time as long as it is contained within the home, although others in the community may be aware of it.

People in rural communities are intricately related through family ties, historical events, and high visibility of behavior, all of which affect the relationship between worker and client and call into question whether the helping relationship can truly be a confidential venture. This is also the case in many other social contexts, including closely knit urban communities and residential settings such as correctional facilities and nursing homes. Rather than automatically reacting to defend the cherished principle of confidentiality from certain threats—whether their source is a rapidly changing technological society or the relationships among social systems—the profession must reexamine the traditional concept of confidentiality. Is it an adequate principle of professional practice in terms of its feasibility, effectiveness, and ethics? If not, what standards of professional behavior should safeguard the relationship between worker, client, and the other social systems?

Example

Consider a social work client, Mr. M, whose family has lived in a small town for three generations. His wife's family has lived there even longer. Mr. M's alcoholism is common knowledge in the community, which began to observe the disintegration of Mr. M and his family long before he was sent to a treatment center out of the county. The neighbors sheltered Mr. M's wife when her husband became violent and have occasionally provided financial assistance for the family. Church members and school teachers cluck with concern over the plight of the children and are already predicting that the 12-year-old son, always a problem in school, will turn out "just like his dad." No one can understand— yet everyone speculates—why Mr. M, whose parents are pillars of the community, has turned out this way, though they know that he and his father get along poorly.

Mr. M's neighbors, work associates, and children's teachers all know of his hospitalization and will view his return to the community from the perspective of their own relationship with the family, their own understanding of alcoholism, and their own opinions about the prognosis. These expectations will shape the community's behavior toward Mr. M and toward each family member. These expectations are an integral part of the social context with which Mr. M and his family must cope. His return home is thus a social event, not a private affair, and the question is not *whether* the community knows about the problem but what blend of information and misinformation has evolved. Speculation will fill in the gaps.

Using this example, [let us] examine the traditional principle of confidentiality.

Feasibility. Is a confidential relationship between client and worker feasible in a rural community? The factors that relate the members of a rural community make virtually every act outside the home—and many in the home—publicly recognized events. Mr. M's condition is known by a wide-ranging network of people, and, at least as it impinges on others in the community, the "problem" is certainly not confidential. Even the custom that a confidential relationship necessarily includes the worker's professional colleagues within the social agency is fraught with difficulties when "everyone knows everybody." . . .

Effectiveness. Is it effective to ignore social relationships in small communities and treat a client in isolation? Speck and Atneave suggest that confidentiality may create problems, and they provide a theoretical base of the lack of confidentiality in a therapeutic situation:

A pathological social network owes most of its rigidity and inflexibility to the presence of secrets, collusions and alliances, which must be broken up for change to occur.[2]

Speck and Atneave contend that the contract with the client system and the social network must be based on trust, not confidentiality. How effective will intervention be if the social worker in the example confines treatment to Mr. M, to the marital couple, or even to the family without dealing with the perceptions and behavior of other significant systems in the immediate social environment? To act as if ignorant of the client's interrelationships in the community is to be naive about the very social relationships that may be a source of difficulty for the client.

Ethics. The concept of the interdependence of systems means that change in one part of a system will affect other parts of the system. Knowing this, is it ethical to work exclusively with one member of a social system while consciously excluding from the process of change those who will also be affected?

Suggested Guidelines

The principle of confidentiality should not be discarded. The confidential nature of the therapeutic relationship should not be the single standard, however. An effective approach to dealing with social systems rather than isolated individuals may not be feasible, effective, or even ethical under the traditional concept of confidentiality, although at the same time the client's right

[2] R. Speck and Carolyn Atneave, *Family Networks* (New York: Random House, 1973), p. 154–55.

to privacy must be guarded and honored. Thus, the social worker must know how to balance an effective intervention involving strategic members of the client's social network with effective safeguards to the client's right to privacy.

The traditional notion of confidentiality will not suffice as a professional standard if social workers are to claim a visible, legitimate role as mediators and facilitators among social systems. At the same time, the profession needs workable principles to provide a standard for professional behavior and accountability. The authors propose the following guidelines to help social workers determine what information should be shared, how, and under what conditions.

One guideline is that *the collection of data should be limited and purposeful and that information should be sought only as it relates to a purpose mutually defined by worker and client.* The guideline provided by the Code of Ethics of the National Association of Social Workers—that social workers should respect the privacy of the people they serve—has typically been interpreted to mean that individuals have a right to their own thoughts, desires, and actions and that in sharing these with a social worker, clients do not lose their right of privacy. . . . Clients have the right to determine what they will divulge to the worker based on a realistic understanding of why the information is being sought and how it will be used.

Social workers are trained to be adept at drawing out information from reluctant parties, a skill that is balanced by the assumption that professionals know what information is necessary for the client's benefit. But social workers also have the power to intrude on an individual's privacy. Social workers often summon voluminous information from clients, which workers dutifully record, that may have only peripheral, if any, relevance to clients' needs. One study found that the issue of confidentiality

was most often introduced when a client appeared reluctant to share certain information. The social worker may use the assurance of confidentiality as license to probe indiscriminately for feelings, attitudes, and psychosocial data that may have no relevance to the problem at hand. In so doing, social workers unnecessarily reinforce their image as experts who amass and then decipher large volumes of information about the past, present, and future of clients who may be having difficulty dealing with the here and now. A more immediate danger is that a client's privacy may be unnecessarily exposed to the worker, the worker's colleagues, and staff who may process the information.

Another general guideline is that *the way information will be used should be an explicit part of the contract between worker and client.* If the worker determines that certain information should be shared with other systems, it is both naive and irresponsible to promote the expectation of complete confidentiality. Sharing information is often regarded as an unfortunate breach of the ideal concept of confidentiality. Yet . . . the lack of confidentiality contributes to the effectiveness of network therapy. As channels of communication open within the social network, members experience relief from sharing private burdens and develop trust in one another. . . .

New information and open communication can present an opportunity for the total system—family, neighborhood, and community—to develop new ways of dealing with each of its parts on a realistic basis.

A third guideline is the authors' contention that *the responsible application of the concept of confidentiality demands that when the client system—individual, family, or group— is being adversely affected by misinformation or poor communication, social workers must use their knowledge of the situation to correct the misinformation.* This should be accomplished with the mutual participation of the client and others. The worker may become the facilitator in such a situation to enable the client to correct the problem. . . .

Finally, *social workers need to consider carefully which categories of information are inviolably private, which are essentially public, and which are discretionary.* The public category includes the overt behavior that the community observes. The private category should include attitudinal and historical data that do not have consequences for others in social relationships. The discretionary area is the broadest and must be negotiated carefully with the client in light of the purposes mutually established in the treatment contract.

The traditional notion of confidentiality has been so encumbered with qualifiers that it is often meaningless as a principle of practice and a guide to professional behavior. Social workers can be more effective social brokers and resource agents if they do not automatically claim this traditional standard of confidentiality or rely on an ad hoc criterion of individual professional judgment. Instead, they must recognize and deal assertively with the theoretical and practical problems posed by the social realities of the profession. This new perspective on confidentiality and practice principles may guide social workers toward new standards.

INFORMED CONSENT

THE FUNCTIONS OF INFORMED CONSENT IN HUMAN EXPERIMENTATION*

Alexander Capron

Capron's classic account of informed consent in medical experimentation identifies the underlying rationale for policies requiring informed consent. The first five functions served by informed consent take place within the relationship between the physician-investigator and the patient who is the research subject; the sixth involves the role of consent within the public at large.

A FUNCTIONAL APPROACH TO INFORMED CONSENT

. . . The "informed consent model" of decisionmaking developed here is intended to illustrate and explore the extent and limits of patient-subjects' authority and capabilities as the "beneficiaries" of the new treatments for catastrophic diseases and at the same time as the "means" through which such new treatments are developed.

"Informed consent" is seen not as a highly formalized event through which the physician-investigator insulates himself from liability, but as an ongoing process through which the physician-investigator and patient-subject, along with other relevant participants including the latter's relatives, continually rededicate themselves to their joint endeavor or withdraw from it if they wish. The model attempts to incorporate a realistic view of the limitations and constraints that psychological forces and personal interrelationships place on informed and voluntary decisionmaking.

---

* Some notes have been deleted without indication.

From Alexander Capron, "Informed Consent in Catastrophic Disease Research and Treatment," *University of Pennsylvania Law Review* 123:2 (Dec. 1974), pp. 364–76. Reprinted by permission.

The Functions of Informed Consent
1. To Promote Individual Autonomy

The requirement of informed consent has two parts, both of which must be met before a medical intervention is permissible: first, that sufficient information is disclosed to the patient so that he can arrive at an intelligent opinion, and second, that the patient agrees to the intervention being performed. The latter facet in particular reflects the concern, traditional in western societies, that the autonomy of each person be respected. This principle is embodied in two great branches of the law: contracts and torts. Protection of the patient's autonomy is accomplished by means of a treatment contract between the physician and patient. Even though the terms of such a contract are usually not reduced to writing, its existence is a prerequisite for therapy. . . . As an Illinois appellate court declared in *Pratt v. Davis,*

the free citizen's first and greatest right, which underlies all others—the right to the inviolability of his person, in other words, his right to himself—is the subject of universal acquiescence, and this right necessarily forbids a physician or surgeon, however skillful or eminent, who has been asked to examine, diagnose, advise, and prescribe . . . to violate without permission the bodily integrity of his patient by a major or capital operation, placing him under anaesthetics for that purpose, and operating on him without his consent or knowledge.[1]

The obvious connection between bodily independence and independence of choice does not mean that autonomy serves only to insulate people from each other. On the contrary, autonomy is a value which deserves to be promoted, through a doctrine of informed consent and elsewhere in the law as well, because it encourages better interactions between the patient-subject and others. In protecting his autonomy of choice, the doctrine assures the patient that

[1] Pratt v. Davis, 118 Ill. App. 161, 166 (1905), *aff'd,* 224 Ill. 300, 79 N.E. 562 (1906).

in going to a physician he will not be trapped into decisions which he does not want; the absence of such assurance would increase the inclination to delay seeking medical intervention even for serious conditions. By promoting trust and confidence between patient and physician, informed consent requirements may thus advance rational decisionmaking. Furthermore, autonomy is centrally associated with the notion of individual responsibility. The freedom to make decisions for oneself carries with it the obligation to answer for the consequences of those decisions. The requirement of consent for medical interventions thus serves to remind all the participants of their agreement concerning the procedure and their acceptance of those things which arise from its proper execution.

2. To Protect the Patient-Subject's Status as a Human Being

The "inviolability of one's person," of which the *Pratt* court spoke, goes beyond the philosophical notion of autonomy and reflects a deep-seated feeling about what it means to be "human." Though part of the concern for human beings contained in our culture relates to protecting people physically, part also relates to the respect which is deemed proper for "nonphysical" aspects of humans, such as their power of thought. This mental component of the concept of "humanness" is expressed through the first facet of the informed consent rule: the requirement that the patient be informed. By emphasizing the importance of involving the patient in decisionmaking in a genuine fashion, this facet of the rule gives further recognition to his or her status as a human being. As Margaret Mead has perceptively commented,

To fail to acquaint a subject of observation or experiment with what is happening—as fully as is possible within the limits of the communication system—is to that extent to degenerate him as a full human being and reduce him to the category of dependency in which he is not permitted to judge for himself.[2]

Paul Ramsey has observed that informed consent is an important example of the faithfulness among people that is normative for all moral interaction. "The principle of an informed consent is the cardinal *canon of loyalty* joining men together in medical practice and investigation."[3]

For informed consent to create a true "joint enterprise" . . . between physician-investigator and patient-subject, the latter's right to full information and to give or withhold assent must be scrupulously respected.[4] The partnership of physician-investigator and patient-subject is based on the mutual recognition that the subject, as a human being, retains the authority to determine what will be done to himself and to receive an explanation of all proposed procedures from his professional collaborator. The enterprise in which both are engaged—whether clinical research or ordinary therapy—requires the cooperation of both for its success, or indeed for its very existence. Thus, it is not for the physician, any more than for the patient, to command the other's participation, whether directly or by turning the consenting process into a charade, a symbolic but contentless formality.

The danger always exists that a physician's belief in the potential benefits of a new medical procedure, such as heart transplantation, will subtly erode his willingness to regard his patient as a full partner in the undertaking. This is especially true as medical procedures become increasingly complicated and a corps of specialists, rather than a lone physician, treats a patient for a catastrophic disease. The physician, often a surgeon, who is in charge

of this veritable army, undeniably has the upper hand in the doctor-patient relationship. Indeed, he may be the originator of a new technique which offers a desperate patient a "chance for cure" which he cannot get from any other practitioner. Yet if the patient's authority is seen as being at an end once he takes the step of initiating the relationship—if he is taken as having given a blanket consent to all steps directed by the physician-investigator—not only will his status as a human being be diminished, but rational decisionmaking may be seriously undermined. Having the patient place himself entirely within the physician's hands has been an accepted part of medical ideology, justified by the physician's concern for the patient's well-being and his alleged need for complete freedom to undertake whatever steps are believed necessary to promote it. But the risk is great, especially in experimental medicine, that the patient's abdication of his decisionmaking authority will convert him from an end in himself to a means that can be employed along with others at the physician's command to serve the goal of the procedure, as defined by the physician and his peers. One need not even observe that in clinical research an experiment may succeed without restoring the patient-subject to health, to conclude that the requirement of an ongoing collaboration among the participants, expressed through a process of renewed "informed consents," is needed to protect the human status of all.

3. To Avoid Fraud and Duress

While these humanistic or philosophical aspects of informed consent clearly have practical aspects as well, the requirement serves additional practical functions. One consequence of truly informed consent is to remove, or at least to diminish, the danger of fraud and duress. The legal model of the doctor-patient relationship should, of course, recognize the very real limitations on rationality which serve to undermine the useful force of the informed

---

[2] Mead, *Research with Human Beings: A Model Derived from Anthropological Field Practice*, 98 Daedalus 361, 375 (1969).

[3] P. Ramsey, *The Patient as Person* 5 (1970).

[4] This posture of course does not preclude a patient-subject explicitly instructing his physician not to tell him. He may do so for many reasons, including complete faith in his physician's actions.

consent rule; these are discussed more fully later in this Article. Yet the model constructed by the law of informed consent still has validity: to the extent that the physician-investigator engages the patient-subject in a comprehensive and comprehensible discussion of the proposed treatment, he reduces the likelihood of misleading or overbearing the patient-subject. The danger that the physician will neglect this duty is probably greater in the case of standard therapy than it is for the major interventions which are of concern here. Nevertheless, physician-investigators' understandable desire to avoid discussing difficult and painful matters and incurring the risk of upsetting the patient-subject, as well as the pressures of time and economics which operate in the catastrophic disease context, may tend to undermine careful adherence to the letter of the law.

Without legal intervention, the idea that the treatment contract would be bargained out between equals is somewhat naive; indeed, the patient usually finds himself faced with an agreement which is *à prendre ou à laisser*. In such case, two remedies present themselves: the law can either remove the choice from the hands of the weaker party (in this instance, the patient-subject) or it can attempt to buttress his ability to exercise choice by erecting certain formal requirements of disclosure. Since the former would represent an abandonment of the basic principles of individual freedom, resort to it is usually limited to situations in which a repeated pattern has demonstrated that "as a matter of law" agreements of the type in question are unconscionable, in that they do not result from the unfettered exercise of rational choice. In the doctor-patient context, the trend seems to be toward the second alternative, the establishment of rules of disclosure. . . . Most medical centers have their own "informed consent" forms for patients, and the federal government has issued [requirements] for the protection of human subjects which set forth the elements of informed consent [updated to conform to current regulations]:

1. A statement that the study involves research, an explanation of the purposes of the research and the expected duration of the subject's participation, a description of the procedures to be followed, and identification of any procedures which are experimental;
2. A description of any reasonably foreseeable risks or discomforts to the subject;
3. A description of any benefits to the subject or to others which may reasonably be expected from the research;
4. A disclosure of appropriate alternative procedures or courses of treatment, if any, that might be advantageous to the subject;
5. A statement describing the extent, if any, to which confidentiality of records identifying the subject will be maintained;
6. For research involving more than minimal risk, an explanation as to whether any compensation and an explanation as to whether any medical treatments are available if injury occurs and, if so, what they consist of, or where further information may be obtained;
7. An explanation of whom to contact for answers to pertinent questions about the research and research subjects' rights, and whom to contact in the event of a research-related injury to the subject; and
8. A statement that participation is voluntary, refusal to participate will involve no penalty or loss of benefits to which the subject is otherwise entitled, and the subject may discontinue participation at any time without penalty or loss of benefits to which the subject is otherwise entitled. . . .

. . . No informed consent, whether oral or written, may include any exculpatory language through which the subject or the representative is made to waive or appear to waive any of the subject's legal rights, or releases or appears to release the investigator, the sponsor, the institution or its agents from liability for negligence.[5]

[5] [Capron's original citation of the 1971 regulations has been replaced with the slightly expanded list from the Code of Federal Regulations, 45 CFR 46.116, revised as of March 8, 1983. This regulation also lists a number of additional elements of informed consent appropriate in specialized circumstances.]

Thus, by detailing the obligation of physician-investigators to warn their patient-subjects fully about their rights, such statements increase the likelihood that the informed consent rule will help to avoid intentional and unintentional fraud and duress.

4. To Encourage Self-Scrutiny by the Physician-Investigator

The requirement of disclosure contained in the informed consent rule raises some perplexing problems for a physician working on the frontiers of catastrophic disease treatment. Perhaps foremost among these is the question: How can one make known to patient-subjects the risks and benefits of new and often untried techniques? A partial response to this query is that one can at least be candid with the patient about the unknown nature and experimental status of the treatment offered as well as about the existence of other established methods, inadequate as they may be. Beyond this, however, the physician-investigator has the additional duty of discovering as much as reasonably possible about the new techniques he proposes to employ. At a minimum this would include making a thorough inventory of the risks of such techniques which have been described in the literature by other investigators. In most situations it would also encompass the duty to explore this aspect of the proposed procedure through animal experimentation and the like to uncover risks of any consequence; this duty is reflected in the accepted principle of biomedical research, independent of the law of informed consent, that human trials ought to be undertaken only after a medical innovation has been shown in animal tests to be relatively risk-free, as compared with its potential benefits. Thus, knowledge sufficient to justify the use of an innovative procedure should usually also suffice for the purpose of consent.

Although some risks will remain "unknown," a candid physician-investigator can still involve his subjects in a valid informed consent process. This would be encouraged if consent to "unknown risks" is taken to include only those "unknown risks" of which the subject is made aware. Such a position does not involve a contradiction in terms, for the patient-subject can certainly be informed of the existence of certain risks whose probability and degree cannot be precisely predicted. There are others which the patient-subject cannot be said to have accepted since the investigator did not anticipate them; it may reasonably be assumed that in most cases the latter category would be very small. The consent is nevertheless valid if the person giving it has been alerted to this residual risk in all clinical research; if the risks exceed this small category and should have been anticipated by a prudent physician-investigator, he would be liable for not discovering and disclosing them. A distinction also exists between risks to which it was reasonable to expose a patient-subject and those which were unreasonable. A physician-investigator who proceeded in the latter instance would of course not be able to assert "consent" as a defense to a claim of negligence. Nor does this impose an unjustified limitation on the patient's right to contract as he chooses—even for "unreasonable" procedures to be performed. In a free, liberal society an individual may well have such a right, but the doctrine of informed consent has a more limited frame of reference, which is the physician-patient relationship. The physician's authority is limited to doing those things which professional opinion holds to be of potential benefit to the patient. This limitation thus inheres in the agreement between the parties.

The need to obtain the patient-subject's informed consent thus tends to enhance the scientific validity and the safety of the trials of new medical procedures in man. . . . If, for example, the surgeons engaged in the initial heart transplants had felt they had to give a full explanation of the risks of graft rejection to the proposed cardiac recipients, they might have proceeded more slowly in the light of the rather disheartening results which had been reported in animal trials and in human kidney transplants at that time when immuno-suppressive techniques were still in their infancy.

As useful as the informed consent requirement may be in encouraging professional self-scrutiny and thereby avoiding thoughtless disrespect of patient-subjects, there is no reason to believe that the end result is assured. Indeed, rather than undertake this process, physician-investigators may instead raise arguments over whether their subjects have the capacity to understand what they are told. Yet this is "a displacement from the real issue, which is the dread of an open and searching dialogue between the investigator and his subject. This displacement is caused by the unacknowledged anxiety over making the invitation in the first place."[6] The rules constructed by the law for medical practice and research may thus force the profession to confront this underlying anxiety, or they may themselves be rendered ineffective by these undeniable yet unspoken psychological forces.

5. To Foster Rational Decisionmaking

Thus far emphasis has been placed on the role of informed consent in protecting patients' autonomy from coercion or disrespectful usage. The preceding section, however, has begun to suggest that reliance on consent can also help physician-investigators to carry out their responsibilities more satisfactorily. The beneficial effects of informed consent in promoting rationality of decisionmaking about catastrophic disease treatment and research go beyond

influencing the investigator. The requirement of informed consent symbolizes a commitment to making the process of developing new therapies a joint enterprise. By actively encouraging the biomedical professionals to include the patient-subject in the decisional process, informed consent serves to place him on a plane with the physician-investigator and to involve him as a person in the work—not merely as an object on which it is being performed. For the participants to remain on the same plane requires a commitment that they view each other not only as equally important individuals but also as joint participants in decisionmaking. Accomplishing this will require, beyond a change in attitude, learning how to communicate to patient-subjects those aspects of the proposed research which will allow them to make decisions at least as rationally as they have made others about their lives. . . .

A rule of informed consent congenial to the model of catastrophic disease decisionmaking elaborated here would view patient-subjects as exercising a major influence on the plans of physician-investigators. Thus, they can also become guarantors of their own rights to autonomy and dignity, by exercising a check over the judgment of physicians who all too often may be biased by their strong desire to "conquer disease."

Moreover, there is no objective, "medical" way to determine the proper treatment for an individual, since disease itself is not an objective concept but depends upon the degree of dysfunction experienced under given conditions by each individual. Thus rationality in resource allocation is possible only when the individuals who bear the costs and receive the benefits from the allocation determine the value of the outcomes. The determination whether a particular project will yield returns to science and society in excess of its costs is best made by biomedical researchers and representatives of the collectivity (to the extent that such an issue

---

[6] Jay Katz, *Experimentation with Human Beings* (1972), p. 787, note 71.

is capable of resolution at all). But who, other than the patient-subjects, can determine whether the benefits of a procedure, conventional or experimental, outweigh the burdens that will be imposed on them? If responsibility follows choice in a system of voluntary interactions, the costs of the system will be minimized when the placement of responsibility (with the consequent incentive to avoid harm) determines who shall have authority to exercise choice.

Some physician-investigators have always been acutely aware of the value of the old adage "two heads are better than one." Their commitment to informing and consulting with their patient-subjects has been based on a recognition of the value of intelligent and dedicated partners, be they patients or fellow scientists. A well-informed patient, after all, is more alert to facts about his own condition that may be of great significance to the investigator, and he also feels freer about reporting what he experiences to his physician, without fear of upsetting him or losing his support. Similarly, a "patient-partner" is better able to endure the often arduous period of recuperation. Many physician-investigators recognize the value of such dedication and take the opportunity of medical publication or meetings to give

credit and thanks to their "coadventurers."

6. To Involve the Public

A final function of informed consent in this model looks outside the physician-patient setting to an involvement of the larger society, since the obtaining of consent can be important for a doctor's, or a medical center's, public relations.[7] Informed consent may also function beyond the area of public reputation and serve to increase society's awareness about human research. This phenomenon is particularly noticeable in the area of organ transplantation. The need to obtain consent from large numbers of potential donors for the removal of their kidneys after death has led to an extensive program of information about renal transplant programs. While the motivation for this information campaign was to recruit individual donors, it also enlightened the public at large about a new development in medicine. The general public thereby becomes an informed decisionmaker, able through legislative actions and the like to accelerate, halt, or alter transplant efforts according to its evaluation of the details disclosed.

[7] The reverse is certainly true: a physician who develops the reputation of using his patients as guinea pigs for his studies or medical innovations without their informed consent will be avoided by those who know that reputation.

PATERNALISM AND PARTIAL AUTONOMY*

Onora O'Neill

Writing in response to standard accounts of informed consent, which suppose that a patient's consent to a medical procedure can be both informed and voluntary, O'Neill shows how difficult these conditions are to satisfy in many sorts of real-life medical situations. Human autonomy is "limited and precarious" in many contexts, she argues, and she shows the reasons for its "messy incompleteness," but she also insists that respect for patients requires that medical practice remain sensitive to these issues.

* Some notes have been deleted without indication.

From Onora O'Neill, "Paternalism and Partial Autonomy in Medicine," *The Journal of Medical Ethics* 10 (1984), pp. 173–78. Reprinted by permission.

Autonomous action, understood literally, is self-legislated action. It is the action of agents who can understand and choose what they do. When cognitive or volitional capacities, or both, are lacking or impaired, autonomous action is reduced or impossible. Autonomy is lacking or incomplete for parts of all lives (infancy, early childhood), for further parts of some lives (unconsciousness, senility, some illness and mental disturbance) and throughout some lives (severe retardation). Since illness often damages autonomy, concern to respect it does not seem a promising fundamental principle for medical ethics. Medical concern would be strangely inadequate if it did not extend to those with incomplete autonomy. Concern for patients' well-being is generally thought a more plausible fundamental principle for medical ethics.

But it is also commonly thought implausible to make beneficence the only fundamental aim of medical practice, since it would then be irrelevant to medical treatment whether patients possessed standard autonomy, impaired autonomy or no capacity for autonomous action. All patients, from infants to the most autonomous, would be treated in ways judged likely to benefit them. Medical practice would be through and through paternalistic, and would treat patients as persons only if beneficence so required.

Recurrent debates about paternalism in medical ethics show that the aim of subordinating concern for autonomy to beneficence remains controversial. The group of notions invoked in these debates—autonomy, paternalism, consent, respect for persons, and treating others as persons—are quite differently articulated in different ethical theories. A consideration of various ways in which they can be articulated casts some light on issues that lie behind discussions of medical paternalism.

1. Paternalism and Autonomy in Result-Oriented Ethics

Most consequentialist moral reasoning does not take patients' autonomy as a fundamental constraint on medical practice. Utilitarian moral reasoning takes the production of welfare or well-being (variously construed) as the criterion of right action. Only when respect for patients' autonomy (fortuitously) maximizes welfare is it morally required. Paternalism is not morally wrong; but some acts which attempt to maximize welfare by disregarding autonomy will be wrong if in fact non-paternalistic action (such as showing respect for others or seeking their consent to action undertaken) would have maximized welfare. Only some 'ideal' form of consequentialism, which took the maintenance of autonomy as an independent value, could regard the subordination of autonomy to beneficence as wrong. In utilitarian ethical thinking autonomy is of marginal ethical importance, and paternalism only misplaced when it reflects miscalculation of benefits.

This unambiguous picture is easily lost sight of because of an historical accident. A classical and still highly influential utilitarian discussion of autonomy and paternalism is John Stuart Mill's *On Liberty*. Mill believed both that each person is the best judge of his or her own happiness and that autonomous pursuit of goals is itself a major source of happiness, so he thought happiness could seldom be maximized by action which thwarted or disregarded others' goals, or took over securing them. Paternalists, on this view, have benevolent motives but don't achieve beneficent results. They miscalculate.

Mill's claims are empirically dubious. Probably many people would be happier under beneficent policies even when these reduce the scope for autonomous action. Some find autonomous pursuit of goals more a source of frustration and anxiety than of satisfaction. In particular, many patients want relief from hard decisions and the burden of autonomy. Even when they don't want decisions made for them they may be unable to make them, or to make them well. The central place Mill assigns autonomy is something of an anomaly in result-oriented ethical thought. It is open to challenge and shows Mill's problem in reconciling liberty with utility rather than any success in showing their coincidence.

2. Paternalism and Autonomy in Action-Oriented Ethics

Autonomy can have a more central place only in an entirely different framework of thought. Within a moral theory which centers on action rather than on results, the preconditions of agency will be fundamental. Since autonomy, of some degree, is a presupposition of agency, an action-centered ethic, whether its fundamental moral category is that of human rights, or of principles of obligation or of moral worth, must make the autonomy of agents of basic rather than derivative moral concern. This concern may be expressed as concern not to use others, but to respect them or "treat them as persons," or to secure their consent and avoid all (including paternalistic) coercion.

A central difficulty for all such theories is once again empirical. It is obvious enough that some human beings lack cognitive and volitional capacities that would warrant thinking of them as autonomous. But where autonomous action is ruled out what can be the moral ground for insisting on respect or support for human autonomy? The question is sharply pointed for medical ethics since patients *standardly* have reduced cognitive and volitional capacities.

Yet most patients have some capacities for agency. Their impairments undercut some but not all possibilities for action.

Hence agent-centered moral theories may be relevant to medical ethics, but only if based on an accurate view of human autonomy. The central tradition of debate in agent-centered ethics has not been helpful here because it has tended to take an abstract and inaccurate view of human autonomy. The history of these discussions is revealing.

Enlightenment political theory and especially Locke's writings are classical sources of arguments against paternalism and for respect for human autonomy. Here the consent of citizens to their governments is held to legitimate government action. In consenting citizens become, in part, the authors of government action: The notion of the sovereignty of the people can be understood as the claim that they have consented to, and so authorized, the laws by which they are ruled. In obeying such laws they are not mere subjects but retain their autonomy.

This picture invited, and got, a tough focus on the question "What constitutes consent?" An early and perennial debate was whether consent has to be *express*—explicitly declared in speech or writing—or can be *tacit*—merely a matter of going along with arrangements. In a political context the debate is whether legitimate government must have explicit allegiance, or whether, for example, continued residence can legitimate government action. A parallel debate in medical ethics asks whether legitimate medical intervention requires explicit consent, recorded by the patient's signing of consent forms, or whether placing oneself in the hands of the doctor constitutes consent to whatever the doctor does, provided it accords with the standards of the medical profession.[1]

---

[1] Here U.S. and British practice differ. U.S. legislation and debates often stress the need to secure informed consent from patients (or their guardians). British law holds that "what information should be disclosed, and how and when, is very much a matter of professional judgement," and that "there is no ground in English law for extending the limited

The underlying picture of human choice and action invoked by those who advocate the "informed consent" account of human autonomy is appropriate to a contractual model of human relations. Just as parties to commercial contracts consent to specific action by others, and have legal redress when this is not forthcoming, and citizens consent to limited government action (and may seek redress when this is exceeded), so patients consent to specified medical procedures (and have cause for grievance if their doctors do otherwise). Those who argue that informed consent criteria are not appropriate in medical practice sometimes explicitly reject the intrusion of commercial and contractual standards in medical care.

The contractual picture of human relations is clearly particularly questionable in medicine. We may think that citizenship and commerce are areas where we are autonomous decision-makers, enjoying what Mill would have called "the maturity of our faculties." In these areas, if anywhere, we come close to being fully rational decision-makers. Various well-known idealizations of human rationality—"rational economic man," "consenting adults," "cosmopolitan citizens," "rational choosers"— may seem tolerable approximations. But the notion that we could be "ideal rational patients" cannot stand up to a moment's scrutiny. This suggests that we cannot plausibly extend the enlightenment model of legitimating consent to medical contexts. Where autonomy is standardly reduced, paternalism must it seems be permissible; opposition to medical paternalism appears to reflect an abstract and inaccurate view of human consent which is irrelevant in medical contexts.

doctrine of informed consent outside the field of property rights." See Sidaway v. Board of Governors of the Bethlehem Royal Hospital and the Maudsley Hospital and Others, Law Report, *The Times*, 1984 Feb. 24. However, medical paternalism may be more practiced in the U.S. than it is praised by those who write on medical ethics.

3. The Opacity of Consent: A Reversal of Perspective

However, the same picture might be seen from quite a different perspective. Human autonomy is limited and precarious in many contexts, and the consent given to others' actions and projects is standardly selective and incomplete. *All* consent is consent to some proposed action or project *under certain descriptions.* When we consent to an action or project we often do not consent even to its logical implications or to its likely results (let alone its actual results), nor to its unavoidable corollaries and presuppositions. Put more technically, consenting (like other propositional attitudes) is *opaque.* When we consent we do not necessarily "see through" to the implications of what we consent to and consent to these also. When a patient consents to an operation he or she will often be unaware of further implications or results of that which is consented to. Risks may not be understood and post-operative expectations may be vague. But the opacity of patients' consent is not radically different from the opacity of all human consenting. Even in the most "transparent," highly regulated, contractual arrangements, consent reaches only a certain distance. This is recognized whenever contracts are voided because of cognitive or volitional disability, or because the expectations of the "reasonable man" about the further implications of some activity do not hold up. Medical cases may then be not so much anomalies, with which consent theory cannot adequately deal, as revealing cases which highlight typical limits of human autonomy and consent.

Yet most discussions of consent theory point in the other direction. The limitations of actual human autonomy aren't taken as constraints on working out the determinate implications of respect for autonomy in actual contexts, but often as *aberrations* from ideally autonomous choosing. The rhetoric of the liberal tradition shows this clearly. Although it is accepted that we are discussing the autonomy of "*finite* rational beings," finitude of all sorts is constantly forgotten in favor of loftier and more abstract perspectives.

4. Actual Consent and "Ideal" Consent

There are advantages to starting with these idealized abstractions rather than the messy incompleteness of human autonomy as it is actually exercised. Debates on consent theory often shift from concern with dubious consent actually given by some agent to a proposed activity or arrangement to concern with consent that would hypothetically be given by an ideally autonomous (rational and free) agent faced with that proposal. This shift to hypothetical consent allows us to treat the peculiar impairments of autonomy which affect us when ill as irrelevant: We can still ask what the (admittedly hypothetical) ideally autonomous patient would consent to. This line of thought curiously allows us to combine ostensible concern for human autonomy with paternalistic medical practice. Having reasoned that some procedure would be consented to by ideally autonomous patients we may then feel its imposition on actual patients of imperfect autonomy is warranted. But by shifting focus from what has (actually) been consented to, to what would (ideally) be consented to, we replace concern for others' autonomy with concern for the autonomy of hypothetical, idealized agents. This is not a convincing account of what it is not to use others, but rather to treat them as persons.

If we don't replace concern for actual autonomy with concern for idealized autonomy, we need to say something definite about when actual consent is genuine and significant and when it is either spurious or misleading, and so unable to legitimize whatever is ostensibly consented to. Instead of facing the sharp outlines of idealized,

hypothetical conceptions of human choosing we may have to look at messy actual choosing. However, we don't need to draw a sharp boundary between genuine, morally significant consent and spurious, impaired consent which does not legitimate. For the whole point of concern for autonomy and hence for genuine consent is that it is not up to the *initiator* of action to choose what to impose: It is up to those affected to choose whether to accept or to reject proposals that are made. To respect others' autonomy requires that we make consent *possible* for them, taking account of whatever partial autonomy they may have. Medical practice respects patients' autonomy when it allows patients as they actually are to refuse or accept what is proposed to them. Of course, some impairments prevent refusal or acceptance. The comatose and various others have to be treated paternalistically. But many patients can understand and refuse or accept what is proposed over a considerable range. Given some capacities for autonomous action, whatever can be made comprehensible to and refusable by patients, can be treated as subject to their consent—or refusal. This may require doctors and others to avoid haste and pressure and to counteract the intimidation of unfamiliar, technically bewildering and socially alien medical environments. Without such care in imparting information and proposing treatment the "consent" patients give to their treatment will lack the autonomous character which would show that they have not been treated paternally but rather as persons.

5. "Informed Consent" and Legitimating Consent

There is a long-standing temptation, both in medical ethics and beyond, to find ways in which consent procedures can be formalized and the avoidance of paternalism guaranteed and routinized. But if the ways in which human autonomy is limited are highly varied, it is not likely that any set procedures can guarantee that consent has been given. Early European colonialists who "negotiated treaties" by which barely literate native peoples without knowledge of European moral and legal traditions "consented" to sales of land or cession of sovereignty reveal only that the colonialists had slight respect for others' autonomy. Medical practice which relies on procedures such as routine signing of "consent forms" may meet conditions for avoiding litigation, but does not show concern for human autonomy as it actually exists. Such procedures are particularly disreputable given our knowledge of the difficulties even the most autonomous have in assimilating distressing information or making unfamiliar and hard decisions.

Serious respect for autonomy, in its varied, limited forms, demands rather that patients' refusal or consent, at least to fundamental aspects of treatment, be made possible. The onus on practitioners is to see that patients, as they actually are, understand what they can about the basics of their diagnosis and the proposed treatment, and are secure enough to refuse the treatment or to insist on changes. If the proposal is accessible and refusable for an actual patient, then (but only then) can silence or going along with it reasonably be construed as consent. The notions of seeking consent and respecting autonomy are brought into disrepute when the "consent" obtained does not genuinely reflect the patient's response to proposed treatment.

6. Partial Autonomy, Coercion and Deception

Once we focus on the limited autonomy of actual patients it becomes clear that consent to *all* aspects and descriptions of proposed treatment is neither possible nor required. Only the ideally, unrestrictedly autonomous could offer such consent. In human contexts, whether medical or po-

litical, the most that we can ask for is consent to the more *fundamental* proposed policies, practices and actions. Patients can no more be asked to consent to every aspect of treatment than citizens can be asked to consent to every act of government. Respect for autonomy requires that consent be possible to *fundamental* aspects of actions and proposals, but allows that consent to trivial and ancillary aspects of action and proposals may be absent or impossible.

Treatment undertaken without consent when a patient could have reached his or her own decisions if approached with care and respect may fail in many ways. In the most serious cases the action undertaken uses patients as tools or instruments. Here the problem is not just that some partially autonomous patient couldn't (or didn't) consent, but that the treatment precluded consent even for ideally autonomous patients. Where a medical proposal hinges fundamentally on coercion or deception, not even the most rational and independent can dissent, or consent. Deceivers don't reveal their fundamental proposal or action; coercers may make their proposal plain enough but rob *anyone* of choice between consent or dissent. In deception "consent" is spurious because cognitive conditions for consent are not met; in coercion "consent" is spurious because volitional conditions for consent are not met.

However, some non-fundamental aspects of treatment to which consent has been given may have to include elements of deception or coercion. Use of placebos or of reassuring but inaccurate accounts of expected pain might sometimes be non-fundamental but indispensable and so permissible deceptions. Restraint of a patient during a painful procedure might be a non-fundamental but indispensable and so permissible coercion. But using patients as unwitting experimental subjects or concealing fundamental aspects of their illness or prognosis or treatment from them, or imposing medical treatment and ignoring or preventing its refusal, would always use patients, and so fail to respect autonomy. At best such imposed treatment might, if benevolent, constitute impermissible paternalism; at worst, if non-benevolent, it might constitute assault or torture.

7. Partial Autonomy, Manipulation and Paternalism

Use of patients is an extreme failure to respect autonomy; it precludes the consent even of the ideally autonomous, let alone of those with cognitive or volitional impairments. Respect for partial autonomy would also require medical practice to avoid treatment which, though refusable by the ideally autonomous, would not be refusable by a particular patient in his or her present condition. Various forms of manipulation and of questionable paternalism fail to meet these requirements. Patients are manipulated if they are "made offers they cannot refuse," given their actual cognitive and volitional capacities. For example, patients who think they may be denied further care or discharged without recourse if they refuse proposed treatment may be unable to refuse it. To ensure that "consent" is not manipulated available alternatives may have to be spelled out and refusal of treatment shown to be a genuine option. "Consent" which is achieved by relying on misleading or alarmist descriptions of prognosis or uninformative accounts of treatment and alternatives does not show genuine respect. Only patients who are quite unable to understand or decide need complete paternalist protection. When there is a relationship of unequal power, knowledge or dependence, as so often between patients and doctors, avoiding manipulation and unacceptable paternalism demands a lot.

Avoiding unacceptable paternalism demands similar care. Manipulators use knowledge of others and their weaknesses to impose their own goals; paternalists may not recognize either others' goals, or that they are *others'* goals. Patients, like anyone with limited understanding and capacity to

choose, may be helped by advice and information, and may need help to achieve their aims. But if it is not the patients' but others' aims which determine the limits and goals of medical intervention, the intervention (even if neither deceptive nor coercive) will be unacceptably paternalistic. Handicapped patients whose ways of life are determined by others may not be deceived or coerced—but they may be unable to refuse what others think appropriate for them. This means that patients' own goals, medical and non-medical, and their plans for achieving these, are constraints on any medical practice which respects patients' autonomy. Since return to health is often central to patients' plans, this constraint may require little divergence from the treatment that paternalistic medical practice would select, except that patients would have to be party to fundamental features of their treatment. But where patients' goals differ from doctors' goals—perhaps they value quality of life or avoiding pain or dependence more than the doctor would— respect for the patient requires that these goals not be overridden or replaced by ones the patient does not share, and that the patient's own part in achieving them not be set aside.

Debates on medical paternalism often assume that the goals of medical action can be determined independently of patients' goals. But in action-oriented ethical thinking, morally required goals are not given independently of agents' goals. Paternalism in this perspective is simply the imposition of others' goals (perhaps those of doctors, nursing homes or relatives) on patients. These goals too must be taken into account if we are to respect the autonomy of doctors, nursing homes and relatives. But imposing their goals on patients capable of some autonomy does not respect patients. The contextually sensitive, action-oriented framework discussed here does not reinstate a contractual or consumer-sovereignty picture of medical practice, in which avoiding deceit and coercion is all that respect requires. On the contrary, it insists that judgements of human autonomy must be contextual, and that what it takes to respect human autonomy will vary with context. When patients' partial autonomy constrains medical practice, respect for patients may demand action which avoids not only deceit and coercion but also manipulation and paternalism; but where autonomy is absent there is no requirement that it be respected.

8. Respecting Limited Autonomy

Medical paternalism has been considered within three frameworks. Within a result-oriented framework of the standard utilitarian type it is not only permissible but required that concern for human autonomy be subordinated to concern for total welfare. Within an action-oriented framework that relies on an abstract, "idealizing" account of human autonomy, medical practice is too readily construed as ruling out all paternalism and permitting only treatment that would be consented to by "idealized" autonomous agents. Within an action-oriented framework that takes account of the partial character of human autonomy we can sketch patterns of reasoning which draw boundaries in given contexts between permissible and impermissible forms of paternalism. This account yields no formula, such as the requirement to avoid coercion and deception may be thought to yield for abstract approaches. But the inadequacies of that formula for guiding action when impairment is severe speak in favor of a more accurate and contextual view of human autonomy.

By trying to incorporate concern for actual, partial capacities for autonomous action into an account of respect for patients and medical paternalism we find that we are left without a single boundary-line between acceptable and unacceptable medical practice. What we have are patterns of reasoning which yield different answers for different patients and for different proposals for treatment. One patient can indeed be expected to come to an informed and autonomous (if idiosyncratic) decision; another may be too confused to take in what his options are. A third may be able to understand the issues but too dependent or too distraught to make decisions. Attempts to provide uniform guidelines for treating patients as persons, respecting their autonomy and avoiding unacceptable medical paternalism are bound to be insensitive to the radical differences of capacity of different patients. A theory of respect for patients must rely heavily and crucially on actual medical judgements to assess patient's current capacities to absorb and act on information given in various ways. But it does not follow that "professional judgement" or "current medical standards" *alone* can provide appropriate criteria for treating patients as persons. For if these do not take the varying ways in which patients can exercise autonomy as constraints on permissible treatment, they may institutionalize unjustifiable paternalism. Professional judgment determines what constitutes respect for patients only when guided by concern to communicate effectively what patients can understand and to respect the decisions that they can make.

THE ARCHITECT AND THE CLIENT

William Dean Howells

In this brief passage from his 1885 novel The Rise of Silas Lapham, *Howells portrays an architect manipulating a pair of clients who are building a house into consenting to features that are quite at odds with what they had originally wanted; furthermore, he makes them believe that their choices were both informed and voluntary. Howells's sketch, of course, portrays a fictional situation in an earlier century, when professional relationships and expectations of consent may have been quite different from contemporary ones, but it remains a vivid account of the way in which the professional can be "skillful . . . in playing upon that simple instrument Man."*

When the spring opened Colonel Lapham showed that he had been in earnest about building on the New Land. His idea of a house was a brownstone front, four stories high, and a French roof with an air chamber above. Inside, there was to be a reception room on the street and a dining room back. The parlors were to be on the second floor and finished in black walnut or parti-colored paint. The chambers were to be on the three floors above, front and rear, with side rooms over the front door. Black walnut was to be used everywhere except in the attic, which was to be painted and grained to look like black walnut. The whole was to be very high studded, and there were to be handsome cornices and elaborate centerpieces throughout, except, again, in the attic.

These ideas he had formed from the inspection of many new buildings which he had seen going up, and which he had a passion for looking into. He was confirmed in his ideas by a master builder who had put up a great many houses on the Back Bay as a speculation, and who told him that if he wanted to have a house in the style, that was the way to have it.

The beginnings of the process by which Lapham escaped from the master builder and ended in the hands of an architect are so obscure that it would be almost impossible to trace them. But it all happened, and Lapham promptly developed his ideas of black-walnut finish, high studding, and cornices. The architect was able to conceal the shudder which they must have sent through him. He was skillful, as nearly all architects are, in playing upon that simple instrument Man. He began to touch Colonel Lapham's stops.

"Oh, certainly, have the parlors high studded. But you've seen some of those pretty, old-fashioned country houses, haven't you, where the entrance story is very low studded?"

"Yes," Lapham assented.

"Well, don't you think something of that kind would have a very nice effect? Have the entrance story low studded, and your parlors on the next floor as high as you please. Put your little reception room here beside the door, and get the whole width of your house frontage for a square hall, and an easy low-tread staircase running up three sides of it. I'm sure Mrs. Lapham would find it much pleasanter." The architect caught toward him a scrap of paper lying on the table at which they were sitting and sketched his idea. "Then have your dining room behind the hall, looking on the water."

He glanced at Mrs. Lapham, who said, "Of course," and the architect went on: "That gets you rid of one of those long, straight, ugly staircases"—until that mo-

From William Dean Howells, *The Rise of Silas Lapham* (1885) (New York: New American Library, 1963), pp. 38–42.

ment Lapham had thought a long, straight staircase the chief ornament of a house—"and gives you an effect of amplitude and space."

"That's so!" said Mrs. Lapham. Her husband merely made a noise in his throat.

"Then, were you thinking of having your parlors together, connected by folding doors?" asked the architect deferentially.

"Yes, of course," said Lapham. "They're always so, ain't they?"

"Well, nearly," said the architect. "I was wondering how would it do to make one large square room at the front, taking the whole breadth of the house, and, with this hall space between, have a music room back for the young ladies?"

Lapham looked helplessly at his wife, whose quicker apprehension had followed the architect's pencil with instant sympathy. "First rate!" she cried.

The Colonel gave way. "I guess that would do. It'll be kind of odd, won't it?"

"Well, I don't know," said the architect. "Not so odd, I hope, as the other thing will be a few years from now." He went on to plan the rest of the house, and he showed himself such a master in regard to all the practical details that Mrs. Lapham began to feel a motherly affection for the young man, and her husband could not deny in his heart that the fellow seemed to understand his business. He stopped walking about the room, as he had begun to do when the architect and Mrs. Lapham entered into the particulars of closets, drainage, kitchen arrangements, and all that, and came back to the table. "I presume," he said, "you'll have the drawing room finished in black walnut?"

"Well, yes," replied the architect, "if you like. But some less-expensive wood can be made just as effective with paint. Of course, you can paint black walnut too."

"Paint it?" gasped the Colonel.

"Yes," said the architect quietly. "White, or a little off-white."

Lapham dropped the plan he had picked up from the table. His wife made a little

move toward him of consolation or support.

"Of course," resumed the architect, "I know there has been a great craze for black walnut. But it's an ugly wood; and for a drawing room there is really nothing like white paint. We should want to introduce a little gold here and there. Perhaps we might run a painted frieze 'round under the cornice—garlands of roses on a gold ground—it would tell wonderfully in a white room."

The Colonel returned less courageously to the charge. "I presume you'll want Eastlake mantel shelves and tiles?" He meant this for a sarcastic thrust at a prevailing foible of the profession.

"Well, no," gently answered the architect. "I was thinking perhaps a white marble chimneypiece, treated in the refined Empire style, would be the thing for that room."

"White marble!" exclaimed the Colonel. "I thought that had gone out long ago."

"Really beautiful things can't go out. They may disappear for a little while, but they must come back. It's only the ugly things that stay out after they've had their day."

Lapham could only venture very modestly, "Hard-wood floors?"

"In the music room, of course," consented the architect.

"And in the drawing room?"

"Carpet. Some sort of moquette, I should say. But I should prefer to consult Mrs. Lapham's taste in that matter."

"And in the other rooms?"

"Oh, carpets, of course."

"And what about the stairs?"

"Carpet. And I should have the rail and banisters white—banisters turned or twisted."

The Colonel said under his breath, "Well, I'm dumned!" but he gave no utterance to his astonishment in the architect's presence. When he went at last—the session did not end till eleven o'clock—Lapham said, "Well, Pert, I guess that fellow's fifty years behind, or ten years ahead. I wonder what the Ongpeer style is?"

"I don't know. I hated to ask. But he seemed to understand what he was talking about. I declare, he knows what a woman wants in a house better than she does herself."

"And a man's simply nowhere in comparison," said Lapham. But he respected a fellow who could beat him at every point, and have a reason ready, as this architect had; and when he recovered from the daze into which the complete upheaval of all his preconceived notions had left him, he was

in a fit state to swear by the architect. It seemed to him that he had discovered the fellow (as he always called him) and owned him now, and the fellow did nothing to disturb this impression. He entered into that brief but intense intimacy with the Laphams which the sympathetic architect holds with his clients. He was privy to all their differences of opinion and all their disputes about the house. He knew just where to insist upon his own ideas, and where to yield. He was really building several other houses, but he gave the Laphams the impression that he was doing none but theirs.

ENGINEERING AND INFORMED CONSENT: AN EXCHANGE

Mike W. Martin, Roland Schinzinger, and Thomas A. Long

In the following three selections, Martin, Schinzinger, and Long discuss whether engineers are morally obliged to obtain informed, voluntary consent from those whom their decisions affect and upon whom they impose risks. In the first selection, Martin and Schinzinger argue that morality requires that the consent of the public be obtained. This means both that the public must know about the risks—so that its consent is informed—and that there be alternatives available to the proposed engineering project, so that its consent is voluntary. Long replies in the second selection that this is impossible, since the engineer, unlike the physician or attorney, does not stand in a personalized relationship with the client. Hence, he concludes, informed consent is morally unnecessary. In the third selection, Martin and Schinzinger reply to Long's claims, showing how the problems of identifying those who should be asked for consent, of obtaining proxy consent, and of diverse responses among groups of individuals can be overcome. They continue to insist that the notion of informed consent has ready applicability even to large-scale engineering projects.

ENGINEERING AS SOCIAL EXPERIMENTATION
(Martin and Schinzinger)

All products of technology have some potential dangers, and thus engineering is an

inherently risky activity. In order to underscore this fact and help in exploring its ethical implications, we suggest that engineering should be viewed as an experimental process. It is not, of course, an experiment conducted solely in a laboratory under controlled conditions. Rather,

From Mike W. Martin and Roland Schinzinger, *Ethics in Engineering* (New York: McGraw-Hill, 1983), pp. 55–61. Reprinted by permission.

it is an experiment on a social scale involving human subjects.

Experimentation is commonly recognized to play an essential role in the design process. Preliminary tests or simulations are conducted from the time it is decided to convert a new engineering concept into its first rough design. Materials and processes are tried out, usually employing formal experimental techniques. Such tests serve as the basis for more detailed designs, which in turn are tested. At the production stage further tests are run, until a finished product evolves. The normal design process is thus iterative, carried out on trial designs with modifications being made on the basis of feedback information acquired from tests. Beyond those specific tests and experiments, however, each engineering project taken as a totality may itself be viewed as an experiment.

Several features of virtually every kind of engineering practice combine to make it appropriate to view engineering projects as experiments. First, any project is carried out in partial ignorance. There are uncertainties in the abstract model used for the design calculations; there are uncertainties in the precise characteristics of the materials purchased; there are uncertainties about the nature of the stresses the finished product will encounter. Engineers do not have the luxury of waiting until all the relevant facts are in before commencing work. At some point theoretical exploration and laboratory testing must be bypassed for the sake of moving ahead on a project. Indeed, one talent crucial to an engineer's success lies precisely in the ability to accomplish tasks with only a partial knowledge of scientific laws about nature and society.

Second, the final outcomes of engineering projects, like those of experiments, are generally uncertain. Often in engineering it is not even known what the possible outcomes may be, and great risks may attend even seemingly benign projects. A reservoir may do damage to a region's social fabric or to its ecosystem. It may not even serve its intended purpose if the dam leaks or breaks. An aqueduct may bring about a population explosion in a region where it is the only source of water, creating dependency and vulnerability without adequate safeguards. An aircraft may become a status symbol which ultimately bankrupts its owners. A special-purpose fingerprint reader may find its main application in the identification and surveillance of dissidents by totalitarian regimes. A nuclear reactor, the scaled-up version of a successful smaller model, may exhibit unexpected problems which endanger the surrounding population, leading to its ultimate shut-down at great cost to owner and consumers alike. A hair dryer may expose the unknowing or unwary user to lung damage from the asbestos insulation in its barrel.

Third, effective engineering relies upon knowledge gained about products both before and after they leave the factory—knowledge needed for improving current products and creating better ones. That is, on-going success in engineering depends upon gaining new knowledge, just as does on-going success in experimentation. Monitoring is thus as essential to engineering as it is to experimentation in general. To monitor is to make periodic observations and tests in order to check for both successful performance and unintended side effects. But since the ultimate test of a product's efficiency, safety, cost-effectiveness, environmental impact, and aesthetic value lies in how well that product functions within society, monitoring cannot be restricted to the development or testing phases of an engineering venture alone. It also extends to the stage of client use as well. Just as in experimentation, both the intermediate and final results of an engineering project deserve analysis if the correct lessons are to be learned from it. . . .

To be sure, engineering differs in some respects from standard experimentation. Some of those very differences help to highlight the engineer's special responsibilities. And exploring the differences can also aid our thinking about the moral responsibilities of all those engaged in engineering.

One great difference is that of experimental control. In a standard experiment this involves the selection, at random, of members for two different groups. The members of one group receive the special, experimental treatment. Members of the other group, called the *control group,* do not receive that special treatment although they are subjected to the same environment as the first group in every other respect.

In engineering this is not the usual practice, unless the project is confined to laboratory experimentation, because the experimental subjects are humans out of the range of the experimenter's control. Indeed, clients and consumers exercise most of the control because it is they who choose the product or item they wish to use. This makes it impossible to obtain a random selection of participants from various groups. Nor can parallel control groups be established based on random sampling. Thus no careful study of the effects of changing variables on two or more comparison groups is possible, and one must simply work with the available historical and retrospective data about various groups which use the product.

This suggests that the view of engineering as a social experiment involves a somewhat extended usage of the concept of experimentation. Nevertheless, "engineering as social experimentation" should not be dismissed as a merely metaphorical notion. There are other fields where it is not uncommon to speak of experiments whose original purpose was not experimental in nature and which involve no control groups.

For example, social scientists monitor and collect data on differences and similarities among existing educational systems that were not initially set up as systematic experiments. In doing so they regard the current diversity of systems as constituting what has been called a "natural experiment" (as opposed to a deliberately initiated one). Similarly, we think that engineering can be appropriately viewed as just such a "natural experiment" using human subjects, despite the fact that most engineers do not currently consider it in that light.

Viewing engineering as an experiment on a societal scale places the focus where it should be: on the human beings affected by technology. For the experiment is performed on persons, not on inanimate objects. In this respect, albeit on a much larger scale, engineering closely parallels medical testing of new drugs and techniques on human subjects.

Society has recently come to recognize the primacy of the subject's safety and freedom of choice about whether to participate in medical experiments. Ever since the revelations of prison and concentration camp horrors in the name of medicine, an increasing number of moral and legal safeguards have arisen to ensure that subjects in experiments participate on the basis of informed consent.

But while current medical practice has increasingly tended to accept as fundamental the subject's moral and legal rights to give informed consent before participating in an experiment, contemporary engineering practice is only beginning to recognize those rights. We believe that the problem of informed consent, which is so vital to the concept of a properly conducted experiment involving human subjects, should be the keystone in the interaction between engineers and the public. We are talking about the *lay public.* When a manufacturer sells a new device to a knowledgeable firm which has its own engineering staff, there is usually an agreement regarding the shared risks and benefits of trying out the technological innovation.

Informed consent is understood as including two main elements: knowledge and voluntariness. First, subjects should be given not only the information they request, but all the information which is needed for making a reasonable decision. Second, subjects must enter into the experiment without being subjected to force, fraud, or deception.

The mere purchase of a product does not constitute informed consent, any more than does the act of showing up on the occasion of a medical examination. The public and clients must be given information about the practical risks and benefits of the product in terms they can understand. Supplying complete information about the product is neither necessary nor in most cases possible. In both medicine and engineering there may be an enormous gap between the experimenter's and the subject's understanding of the complexities of an experiment. But while this gap most likely cannot be closed, it should be possible to convey all pertinent information needed for making a reasonable decision about whether to participate or not.

An engineer cannot succeed in providing essential information about a project or product unless there is cooperation by management and a receptivity on the part of those who should have the information. Management is often understandably reluctant to provide more information than current laws require, fearing disclosure to potential competitors and exposure to potential lawsuits. Moreover, it is possible that, paralleling the experience in medicine, clients or the public may not be interested in all of the relevant information about an engineering project, at least not until a crisis looms. It is important nevertheless that all avenues for disseminating such information be kept open and ready.

The matter of informed consent is surfacing indirectly in the current debate over acceptable forms of energy. Representatives of the nuclear industry can be heard expressing their impatience with critics who worry about reactor malfunction while engaging in statistically more hazardous activities such as driving automobiles and smoking cigarettes. But what is being overlooked by those representatives is the often-found human readiness to accept risks voluntarily undertaken as in daring sports, even while objecting to involuntary risks resulting from activities in which the individual is neither a direct participant nor a decision maker. In other words, we all prefer to be the subjects of our own experiments rather than those of somebody else. When it comes to approving a nearby oil drilling platform or a nuclear plant, affected parties expect their consent to be sought no less than it is when a doctor contemplates surgery. . . .

INFORMED CONSENT AND ENGINEERING (Long)

. . . Martin and Schinzinger believe that the "problem of informed consent . . . should be the keystone in the interaction between engineers and the . . . *lay* public." Engineering must seek to foster more openness with and participation by both clients and the public at large. To see engineering in this way—as social experimentation—is to emphasize the broad *moral* dimensions of a profession whose purpose is to provide "useful technological products within the bounds of safety considerations." It is these moral dimensions which are thought to require informed consent.

Viewing engineering as social experimentation in no way guarantees a conceptual foothold for informed consent. . . . Most of the recent literature on this topic has grown out of reflection on conceptual and ethical issues surrounding the physician–patient relationship and medical experimentation. This being so, I propose to

From Thomas A. Long, "Informed Consent and Engineering," *Business and Professional Ethics Journal* vol. 3, no. 1 (Fall 1983), 59–66. Reprinted by permission.

use medical practice as the model for our understanding of these issues, and I wish to explore some basic questions that must be faced when it is urged that informed consent become a requirement for engineering practice.

. . . If consent is to be "informed," then it must rest on the possession of adequate information, that is, all and only that information that a rational person would want to have. This is not sufficient, however, for if the consent is to be genuine, it must be given without coercion and by someone who is competent to do so. In this sense, informed consent is the result of a process of consultation and discussion, and although the quasi-ritualistic signing of a document at the end of this process may be necessary, the mere existence of a signed and witnessed document in no way guarantees informed consent.

The moral importance of informed consent in medicine arises from a value judgment made in light of a few facts. First, there is the fact that medical treatment always involves some risk, and this is especially true when the therapy is experimental in nature. Second, patients, who also may be therapeutic subjects, usually do not possess much (if any) pertinent medical knowledge; they are at an *epistemic* disadvantage vis-à-vis physicians. But these two facts alone are not sufficient to generate a demand for informed consent procedures. What more is needed is a value judgment [that] *autonomy* is to be respected and encouraged. Put succinctly, it is the belief that persons *ought* to have as much control over their lives as is consistent with respect for others. So understood, autonomy is a value-ideal that informs the liberal political tradition and its early invocation is the bedrock on which Martin and Schinzinger's later argument for informed consent must rest.

Now those who are skeptical about the fruitfulness of introducing informed consent into engineering practice may argue that the foci of medicine and engineering

are so different that this concept will be unable to find any fertile soil in the latter profession. Medicine, it may be said, focuses on maintaining or altering certain physical or psycho-physical states in identifiable individuals; engineering, on the other hand, focuses on the design and production of things or processes. Furthermore, the effects of medical practice, even if they are at times unpredictable, typically are circumscribed, whereas the results of engineering practice, whether predictable or not, typically are widespread and have ill-defined boundaries. A surgical procedure or an hour with a psychiatrist is *for* a specific, known individual, but this is not true of the design and production of an aircraft or an electronic game. The engineers who design and help manufacture aircraft or electronic games are producing commodities to be consumed by an indefinite number of (at least to them) nameless and faceless individuals.

. . . There is, of course, one very limited way in which informed consent obviously does enter into the practice of engineering. Should someone formally contract with an engineer for specified services (for example, the excavation of a chemical dump), then the validity of the contract will depend, in part, on the uncoerced client's competence to sign a contract even when in possession of adequate information. But this is a relatively straightforward contractual matter and certainly is not a major concern of those who are calling for the introduction of informed consent into engineering. Martin and Schinzinger have something far grander, far more sweeping in mind . . .

But if engineering is experimentation, who are the "subjects" who are at risk and whose informed consent should be sought? Posed in this way, the question is unanswerable, just as it is unanswerable when posed of medicine. The issue must be approached by talking about specific engineering projects or medical experiments.

One essential feature of informed consent in medicine is that the potential subject or patient must be presented with certain information prior to any experimentation or therapy and consent must be given *before* anything may be done. Now can such a procedure work for engineering? The question is whether the "affected parties" (that is, those "at risk") of any engineering project can be consulted in such a way that their informed consent can be obtained. . . . Precisely here we see an important *dis*analogy between medical experimentation and engineering. By the very act of refusing to give consent to the medical experiment a person ensures that he or she will be unaffected. Even if all others identified as suitable subjects agree to proceed, they cannot force the lone dissident to accept a risk perceived to be unacceptable. Yet this is exactly what will happen in cases involving engineering projects when one person refuses to consent but is overridden either by the majority or by some combination of special interests. Once the procedure of informed consent enters the *political* arena, then some persons will have risks imposed on them that they deem unacceptable. For these persons, unlike those in the medical setting, the notion of informed consent becomes an empty one.

Suppose an aircraft manufacturer wishes to introduce a radically new, wide-bodied, barely supersonic plane. If the informed consent of all those who will use the aircraft is required *before* production, the manufacturer will be unable to proceed with the design. This is simply because it will not be known in advance who will use the plane. This kind of case is typical in the practice of engineering, for it is one in which the risk that attends the use of the commodity (an aircraft, a bridge, a new antibiotic) is to "the public" and not to individuals specifiable before the process of design and production. For an indefinitely large number of engineering projects it is simply not possible to tell who is at

risk until the products are in the marketplace. Of course, warning labels, safety reports on product performance, and the like may enable the consumer to make an intelligent choice, but if this is informed consent, it is *after* the fact of production.

. . . Genuine consent, that is, uncoerced consent given by competent persons possessing adequate information, simply will not work for the large majority of engineering projects. To take medical experimentation as the model here is to take an activity in which consensual issues are *personalized* before anything is done. It seems clear that except in those few cases in which the situation is very circumscribed, engineering will have to make do with some kind of substitute for informed consent. We shall need to turn to *vicarious* decision-making. Here, again, medicine offers us some models to try.

The most commonly debated models for vicarious decision-making in medicine are the "best interests" standard and the use of "substituted judgment." Both are intended to apply to situations in which consent cannot be given by the patient because of incompetence and so a proxy is sought. Of course, incompetence is not the problem in our example of the proposed wide-bodied aircraft. In this case the problem is an inability to identify those whose consent would be required. . . . A proxy decision based on "best interests" is just that—a decision based on what the proxy believes to be in the best interests of the patient. . . . Now what about proxy consent in an engineering context? Who will be the proxy? If this role is given to management, then the engineers will have no legitimate power to make "best interests" decisions of considerable import for indefinitely many people. To bring proxy consent into the practice of engineering in this way—by giving it to management—will hardly serve to enhance the role of engineering in social experimentation.

Suppose, however, that it is the engineer who is taken as proxy. This would be a radical departure from the medical context, where the therapist and the proxy are never one and the same person. Nevertheless, it is worth exploring such a departure from the medical paradigm.

If the engineer is taken as the proxy, does this mean that each engineer slated to work on a wide-bodied aircraft will be a proxy? If so, then each engineer will have to make a "best interests" decision. Also, the decision will have to be about what is in the best interests of something called "the public welfare." But what is this thing of which the engineer is supposed to know enough to make such a decision? Was Lockheed's decision to build the L1011 Tri-Star in the best interests of the public? Who could have said before its production? In fact, who can say now?

. . . To make *each* engineer on a project a proxy is to defeat the whole purpose of proxy consent. In medicine the very point in seeking a proxy is to *focus* the decision-making process, not to diffuse it. Indeed, in many hospitals there are written regulations that serve to rank-order those persons near to the incompetent patient. . . . Engineers are likely to have different ideas about which engineering projects are in the public interest. This is especially true when the projects are large and involve significant government monies. It is naive to think that every engineer working on a military project even believes (much less knows) that the public interest is best being served. Analogously, disagreement may exist about what should be done to most benefit an incompetent patient. But the use of a proxy, although it may not remove the disagreement, nevertheless allows for therapy to begin. Again, this can come about only because medicine has a recognized procedure for transcending, if not eliminating, discord. Engineering at present has no similar procedure and for the reason given above it is not at all clear that one could be established in a nonarbitrary manner.

There is still the second medical model, namely, "substituted judgment." Could it be successfully introduced into engineering?

In medicine the purpose of "substituted judgment" is to embody the incompetent patient's own desires, likes, and attitudes in the proxy's consent. After inquiry and reflection the proxy is to provide a disposition of the case the incompetent patient *would* provide *if* he or she could. Needless to say, if this type of proxy consent is not to collapse into simply a "best interests" judgment, then considerable information about the patient must be available.

Now how well would this kind of proxy process work in engineering? Again, there is the problem of focusing the judgment. Who would be the proxy? Let us suppose that some reasonable way could be found to settle on one. How would the proxy discover the desires, attitudes, and values of a largely *unknown* public? . . . It might be suggested that the proxy could use methods of discovery somewhat similar to those used in the medical context. In this context the proxy looks for evidence of what the patient *would* say by looking at how the patient lived, what he or she said or wrote in diaries or letters, how those persons close to the situation perceived the patient's life, etc. Could not the engineer-proxy study such things as market research reports, the public's buying habits, and so on?

But what would such a study tell our engineer-proxy? Do the buying habits of the public vis-à-vis automobiles tell us anything about that one factor central to the concerned engineer, namely, *safety*? It is implausible to claim that the average person purchases an automobile only after a careful consideration of the risk factors inherent in the design. In fact, it is very unlikely that most automobile buyers even know anything about these factors and what trade-offs their purchases involve. Also, market research studies, even if very explicit and detailed in their queries, reach only a small percentage of consumers; and if the populations researched are heterogeneous, the results will very probably reveal conflicting attitudes about safety and the willingness to pay for it.

Consent via "substituted judgment" is meaningful in medicine only if it is reasonable to assume that the proxy can come to know, infer, or construct what the patient would say if able. But when the context is engineering and "the patient" is an indefinitely large number of prospective consumers, what is the engineer-proxy to do?

The preceding discussion amply shows the difficulty, if not the impossibility, of introducing informed consent into the practice of engineering. This concept was developed to function as an ethical guide for those professions whose common focus is on identifiable individuals typically encountered in face-to-face situations. It simply will not "travel" well to professions whose practice is very different. Simply to show that engineering practice is in some important sense social experimentation in no way guarantees a meaningful place for informed consent in that practice. And to keep insisting, as Martin and Schinzinger do, that something called "the public" has "the right to make informed decisions about the risks affecting it" is no substitute for a careful analysis that would show just how such talk is to be given meaning across the wide range of engineering practice.

I believe there is value to the suggestion that engineering is social experimentation. Engineering often has a great impact on the well-being and safety of large numbers of people who themselves are not parties to the engineering process. If only for this reason the engineer needs an adequate model for understanding the moral dimensions of the profession. The model of social experimentation serves to emphasize the engineer's responsibility to the ultimate

client, namely, the public. To this extent, but only to this extent, the model is useful.

INFORMED CONSENT IN ENGINEERING AND MEDICINE (Schinzinger and Martin)

. . . Thomas A. Long provocatively contends that the notion of informed consent has little relevance to engineering. The idea's natural habitat is said to lie in professions like medicine, where there are clearly identifiable patients or experimental subjects who have the right to make autonomous decisions about procedures affecting them. While allowing that engineering can fruitfully be modeled as social experimentation, Long urges that there are three insuperable obstacles to recognizing a strong informed consent requirement in engineering. We summarize and christen them as follows.

1. *The Consenter Identification Problem.* Since engineering projects can have unforeseen effects on unforeseen victims, it is sometimes difficult to identify who should give or withhold informed consent.
2. *The Proxy Problem.* Sometimes informed consent in engineering cannot be secured, making it necessary to involve a proxy decision-maker, and there may be difficulties in choosing the appropriate proxy and the relevant criteria for the proxy to use in making decisions.
3. *The Dissident Minority Problem.* Since engineering projects often affect groups of individuals having different viewpoints and values, not all of which can be fully satisfied in every situation, it is unrealistic to always expect personal informed consent from all affected individuals.

The Consenter Identification Problem

If informed consent (or refusal) is to be secured, it must be possible to consult with the morally appropriate individuals who

From Roland Schinzinger and Mike W. Martin, "Informed Consent in Engineering and Medicine," *Business and Professional Ethics Journal*, vol. 3, no. 1 (Fall 1983): 67–77. Reprinted by permission.

have the right to give (or withhold) it. In medicine there would seem to be no problem. We simply look and see whose body or mind will be affected by a given therapeutic or experimental procedure and then inform them of the risks involved. But things are not always so simple.

First, there are conceptual problems about the meaning of informed consent and moral problems about who ought to give it. In order to make an informed decision (consent or refusal), individuals must be presented with the relevant information that a rational person would want, together with any other information they might request; they must understand that information; they must make a voluntary decision based on that understanding; and it is presupposed that they are competent to make such decisions. Who is competent? Children, some developmentally disabled adults, and comatose patients may morally require that proxy decisions be made paternalistically on their behalf. And just how much information would a rational person require in order to make a decision in various circumstances? Such questions have generated a rich literature in medical ethics, and we expect that related concerns will be discussed much more widely in engineering ethics.

A second difficulty lies in identifying the risk of which the subject should be apprised. When pregnant women were prescribed Thalidomide as a tranquilizer, few doctors knew about the hazards to a fetus. Such failures to identify risks tacitly imply failures to identify potential consenters affected by those risks.

A third difficulty is that risks may affect individuals other than those anticipated. Inadequately shielded X-ray machines may unintentionally place medical personnel at risk, as may untested procedures for treating infectious diseases like hepatitis or AIDS.

Yet a further complication is that the risk may not be identified until after the experiment has begun. Drug [and IUD] recalls fall into this category.

The differences between medicine and engineering seem incommensurable when we compare (a) asking a specific patient for consent to a well-tested surgical or psychiatric procedure with (b) developing a new aircraft or electronic game for use by an indefinite number of unidentifiable individuals. But that comparison is not apropos. An appropriate analogy is between (b) as is and (a'), developing a *new* surgical or psychiatric procedure. In both these cases there may be an indefinite number of unidentifiable individuals affected by unforeseen risks—we cannot foresee who in the future will be asked to give informed consent once the procedure or product is made available in the market. . . .

Another appropriate analogy is between (a) as stated originally and (b'), offering a specific consumer the use of a successful airplane service or the chance to purchase an established electronic game. In both (a) and (b') the "subject" should be informed of any reasonably foreseeable risks in language that is easily understood.

The Proxy Problem

In most technologically complex projects one will find engineers representing the sponsors and other engineers representing the clients. Such proxies are readily arranged when there is a clear understanding of the roles of the respective engineers. A different situation is that of the consumer who is interested in a product, the purchase of which does not warrant the paid advice of a consulting engineer. It is reasonable to suggest that consumers who share similar concerns form interest groups, which in turn can engage the services of engineers on their behalf. Consumer advocacy groups are already performing this function. In a more formal setting various regulatory agencies of the government serve the same purpose (the Consumer Products Safety Commission, the National Highway Traffic Safety Administration, the Federal Aviation Administration, and, from the field of medicine the forerunner of them all, the Food and Drug Administration, to name but a few).

If . . . interest groups or government agencies can act as proxies, the engineer's task is facilitated greatly. Vicarious or substituted informed consent can be obtained through interaction with the proxies. If such representation does not exist, it behooves the engineer to encourage the formation of ad hoc committees or task forces for specific experiments. The burden of the smooth workings of such groups is not the engineer's—it is that of the "subjects." Nor is the engineer expected to carry the entire task of securing informed consent alone. It is industry's problem. But the individual engineer must be satisfied that mechanisms are in place within the corporation to handle the task.

The Dissident Minority Problem

Fundamental decisions affecting large numbers of individuals are shaped within the dynamics of competing groups representing different sets of priority preferences. Not every individual's desires can be satisfied.

One patient's desire for a life-saving heart transplant is frustrated by an insurance company's refusal to pay the bill and the government's refusal to fund such transplants. Another person objects to mandatory inoculations for children attending public schools. A number of individuals argue for funding preventative medicine at the cost of support for the terminally ill. Similarly, some people desire to live in a world of mass-transit systems that would put an end to the 50,000 deaths per year on the highways. Many desire an end to nuclear-energy development. In all these cases, personal assent is not given because individual desire is overridden by the preferences of others who win out in the democratic process. Politics within a

democracy is said to be based on the consent of the governed. But where assent is refused isn't it a sham to speak of dissenters as giving informed consent?

Far more needs to be said concerning this problem than space allows here, for it leads directly into wider problems about justifying democratic procedures. When it is said that democracy is founded on "consent of the governed," it is not meant that every individual must agree with every political decision, though informed consent to fundamental decision-making processes does seem implied. It is also implied that every competent individual has a right to a fair degree of participation in the decision-making process, either directly or through proxies representing them. But even when one is acting directly and personally, one's actions must sometimes take effect as part of a wider group with which one may not be in perfect accord. Engineering ethics needs to explore the important concept of informed consent by groups—"informed group consent"—and relate it to the notion of individual informed consent by individuals represented by a group.

Toward this end we wish to offer, in conclusion, a widened notion of informed consent, or what some would call "valid consent." We have said that an individual's consent to be the subject of an experiment is valid if:

1. the consent was given voluntarily;
2. the consent was based on information that a rational person would want, together with any other information requested, presented to them in understandable form; and
3. the consenter was competent to process the information and make rational decisions.

We now suggest two requirements for situations where the subject cannot be readily identified as an individual:

4. information that a rational person would need, stated in understandable form, has been widely disseminated; and

5. the subject's consent was offered in proxy by a group that collectively represents many subjects of like interests, concerns, and exposure to risk.

Respect for the fundamental rights of dissenting minorities and just compensation for harmful effects are matters beyond dispute here.

AUTONOMY AND CONSENT IN EDUCATION

Kenneth Strike

In this selection from his book Liberty and Learning, *Strike examines the dilemmas of authority and consent that arise in education. In educational situations, the student is ignorant of the context and principles of the subject matter; hence there is a significant inequality between the teacher and the student, and the student is not in a position to evaluate fully the competence of the teacher or to agree to the course of study in a fully voluntary way. Nevertheless, Strike argues, teacher and student must be regarded as equal moral agents. This selection particularly strongly emphasizes the relationship between telling the truth, in the form of giving reasons for what is taught to students, and students' consent to being taught.*

The ignorance of the person just beginning the study of a subject has a special character. It is not just that the novice is ignorant of the facts and theories of the subject matter; the student is also ignorant of the principles that govern thought about the subject matter. He does not know what the problems of the field are, he does not know what approaches to take to solve a field's problems, and he does not know how to identify a reasonable solution to the problem.

Consider an example. It has been common to introduce the oxidation theory of combustion by means of an experiment in which students are asked to thrust the smouldering end of a stick of wood into an inverted test tube of oxygen. The stick will normally burst into flames. It is then explained that this is because the test tube contains a higher concentration of oxygen than does the air in the classroom and that this oxygen combines with the material in the wood, yielding carbon dioxide and water plus a residue of ash.

What issue is being addressed by this experiment? Note that the explanation is not focused on burning. No account is given of the flame or the heat. My ten-year-old car, like the stick of wood, has undergone considerable oxidation, producing a noticeable residue of iron oxide. It has not, so far as I have been able to see, burst into flame during the process. Why does the oxidation of the wood produce heat and light in large amounts? This is not explained. The reader might ponder the question of what exactly the explanation explains and how the experiment supports the explanation. One should come to the conclusion that the answer is not very obvious.

With this as background I want to argue two claims that I believe are central in understanding the students' rights and interests in the pedagogical relationships.

1. Students as persons have a right to autonomy. This requires teachers both to give students reasons for what they are asked to

From Kenneth Strike, "Autonomy and Consent in Education," *Liberty and Learning* (New York: St. Martin's Press, 1982), pp. 41–53. Reprinted by permission.

believe, within the students' capacity to grasp them, and to teach so as to expand the students' capacity to comprehend and assess reasons.

2. A variety of processes, which I shall collectively refer to as reason-giving, is essential to the development of the students' capacity to comprehend and assess the claims of any subject matter.

Persons have the right to autonomy. What does this mean? Fundamentally, it means that people have a *prima facie* right to be self-governing. Autonomy is complex; it contains at least three components. The first is psychological freedom: This is the capacity for independent choice, and it requires the capacity for rational judgement and for self-control. The second component is the right of self-determination in those areas of life that are properly left to the individual's discretion: Individuals should have the right to choose their own beliefs and their own lifestyle, and they have a number of other rights that limit a government's or a society's authority over them. Finally, individuals have the right to participate in collective choices.

These rights are rooted in the value of moral agency. *Human beings are ends in themselves and are moral agents who are responsible to choose wisely on their own behalf and act justly with respect to others. They are morally responsible for what they choose and what they do.*

A moral agent who is responsible for his choices must demand both the opportunity and the resources to choose wisely. The opportunity for such choices is autonomy. Autonomy in its several forms specifies both the psychological and political preconditions of responsible choice. A person who is not free in these ways cannot freely choose and act.

The resources to choose responsibly are of essentially two sorts. First, responsible choice depends on information and evidence. One cannot consistently demand that a person make a responsible choice and at the same time withhold information rele-

vant to that choice. Here, indeed, is another kind of argument for rights such as free speech or free press, which serve the function of making information freely available for moral agents who require it to decide responsibly.

Information is not, however, sufficient to allow people to make responsible choices. They must also have the will and ability to do so. The will to choose responsibly, seems to require such virtues as a regard for and commitment to truth, honesty and fairness. These ideals are intellectual virtues in the sense that they are presupposed by the commitment to have one's choices and actions warranted by available evidence. The central point about the ability to choose responsibly is that having information that provides a satisfactory base for a decision is not the same thing as being able to interpret or judge that information in a reasonable way. Two people with the same piece of information can differ vastly in terms of their capacity to draw reasonable conclusions from it. The capacity for responsible choice depends on achieving a degree of intellectual sophistication. Education is a prerequisite of autonomy.

These observations have significant import for the view we must take of the rights of the student in the teacher–student relationship. They imply that *the teacher must see the student as more than a novice who is ignorant of the context and principles of the subject matter. The teacher must also see the student as a responsible moral agent who, because he is responsible for what he will believe and what he will do, must ask for and be given reasons for what he is asked to believe. He must also see the student as one whose capacity for understanding reasons must be expanded.*

Now this may seem paradoxical. I have, it would seem, argued both that the teacher has a moral duty to give reasons to the student and that the student is in no position to grasp these reasons. These claims are not, however, as inconsistent as might first appear to be the case. The argument I have given concerning the student's capacity to appreciate reasons shows that the student is not capable of viewing the subject matter from the perspective of the expert. This is a limit on the kinds of reasons a student can grasp concerning a subject, but it is far from showing that the student is altogether incapable of appreciating any reasons. The expert and the student will both approach any phenomenon with a set of concepts that they will use to assess the phenomenon or arguments concerning it. The concepts of the expert and the student will normally differ in scope and power, but the student does have a set of concepts that he can and will use to judge what he encounters in instruction.

These concepts are the students' court of appeal. They will provide the criteria by means of which the claims of a teacher will be judged and the context in terms of which these claims will be understood. The concepts of a given student may be more or less adequate to the instructional purposes of a teacher. A student, for example, who understands the atomic theory of matter is in a better position to understand the oxygen theory of combustion than one who does not. Students' concepts may also be dysfunctional. A student who sees matter as a continuous substance rather than as consisting of discrete parts cannot understand such phenomena as heat or the compression of gases, and the instructor will need to provide the student with reasons that suggest the inadequacies of this concept and the need for a different one.

We thus know two important things about the "epistemic situation" of the student. We know that the student is not in the same position as the expert to assess the phenomena or the arguments of a discipline. We also know that the student has a position of his own from which the subject matter of a discipline will be assessed. Thus, the teacher cannot appeal to the student's epistemic situation as grounds for not giving the student reasons for what the student is asked to believe, although he may appeal to the student's epistemic sit-uation as grounds for not giving the student the kinds of reasons that would be given to an expert. The teacher continues to have the duty to regard the student as a responsible moral agent, which entails the duty to give reasons within the student's capacity to grasp.

There is a second reason why the teacher has a duty to give the student reasons. The teacher has a duty to expand the capacity of the student for understanding and evaluating reasons. The giving of reasons is a necessary condition of a pedagogy that can expand this capacity. The meaning of the phrase "giving reasons" should be broadly understood. It includes any device whereby a student can be made aware of the evidence for some claim. Verbal accounts of the reasoning for a claim are, no doubt, paradigmatic of giving reasons, but demonstrations, discussions, exercises or assignments that direct the student's attention to evidence are also included.

It is also to be insisted that reason-giving is an interaction between the teacher and the student that requires the student's active participation. Propositions that are objective evidence for some claim must be subjectively seen as evidence by the student. This requires the student to integrate reasons given by an instructor into the student's current concepts in such a way that they are structured as evidence within the student's cognitive structure. We must remember that a proposition or a phenomenon is only evidence for a claim in relation to a set of concepts that interpret it. The burning stick in our experiment is only evidence for the oxygen theory of combustion to the student with a proper set of prior assumptions. The suggestion that evidence is relative to the student's current concepts indicates a need on the part of the teacher to know what the student's current concepts are. There is, I think, no substitute for an active exchange between student and teacher in this regard. The clues to a student's concepts are the questions asked, observations proffered or counter-arguments produced. Reason-giving is thus not simply a process of transmission of ideas from teacher to student. It requires the participation of the student if it is going to succeed.

But reason-giving is far more than the way in which evidence is obtained by students. It is the way in which students come to understand what counts as evidence. It is thus the means whereby students come to internalize the concepts and criteria that are appropriate to thought in a given area. Reason-giving does this in at least two ways: It provides models and exemplars of what counts as a reason in a given area, and it provides practice in the use of relevant criteria and concepts.

To get a handle on the idea of an exemplar we may return to the combustion example and ask what its role in instruction is. One answer is that it is a way of providing the student with evidence for the oxygen theory of combustion. I have already suggested grounds for believing that this is not an altogether acceptable view. While it is the case that the student is being shown a phenomenon that can be interpreted as a piece of evidence for the oxygen theory of combustion, it is also the case that *as evidence* it is a remarkably weak piece, particularly from the student's point of view. The particular phenomena can be given a coherent interpretation within another theory, and the student is not in a position to assess the strength of the interpretation provided.

A more plausible view of the role of such demonstrations is that they are the means whereby students learn how the abstractions contained in the theories, formulae and concepts of a discipline are applied and manipulated. The concepts of a discipline come to have their meaning both in terms of how they are connected with one another and how they are attached to phenomena. A good exemplar exhibits both sorts of meaning. In such a way, the student can begin to get a feel for the criteria that govern the use of such

concepts, not by having the criteria stated, but by seeing them employed. Students learn the syntax of scientific concepts much as they learn the syntax of their own language—by seeing it in use. Exemplars also perform the role of showing how the concepts and abstractions of a field attach to the phenomena with which they are concerned. This "attachment" can involve several things. It can indicate the procedures by which abstract terms are given empirical meaning by showing how quantities are measured or experiments conducted. Simultaneously, an exemplar shows the student how to *see* a phenomenon through the concepts of a theory: The student is taught to see burning as oxidation. An exemplar may be part of the justification for some scientific theory, but its fundamental role in teaching is to allow the student to see the phenomenon in the way in which the expert can see it and in doing so to learn what counts as justification.

An exemplar need not be an empirical demonstration of the application of some scientific theory. What will count as an exemplar will depend on the problem or the field. It may be the analysis of a poem or painting, the diagnosis and treatment of a disease, or a paper that contains a classical treatment of a classical problem. The important thing is to exhibit the application of the concepts and techniques of a field to a representative problem.

The role of the instructor in transmitting the standards of a field is to be a model of competent performance. When a teacher gives the reasons for a given claim, he is giving the student a justification for it. But again, the point of the activity is not so much to justify the claim to the student, but to help the student to see what counts as a justification. The teacher does this by exhibiting the argument forms and criteria extant in a field in the process of giving reasons.

These ways of communicating or exhibiting the concepts and criteria of a field can be successful only when they elicit the active participation of the student. One reason is that the student's participation allows the instructor to see the student's view of the matter and to express a justification in a way appropriate to the student's current concepts. A second reason is that participation is a means of practicing the intellectual skills of a field.

. . . These arguments indicate that the pedagogical relationship should be governed by two fundamental ideas:

1. there is a significant inequality between the student (as novice) and the teacher (as expert) in terms of their current capacity to understand and assess the ideas and arguments of a field;
2. the student and the teacher are equally moral agents and owe one another the rights and respect due moral agents.

The expertise of the teacher conveys certain kinds of authority upon the teacher over the student. The teacher's competence generates the right to govern the intellectually rooted decisions concerning teaching and learning—that is, decisions that require expertise in the concepts of a discipline to make them competently. Included in this category are the selection and organization of the curriculum, the right to direct the process in the classroom in profitable directions, and the right to evaluate the intellectual competence of the student's work. When admission to an intellectual profession is at issue this, too, is the prerogative of experts.

The teacher also owes certain duties to the student. Included are the obligations to represent the field to the student honestly and fairly, to evaluate the student's work on relevant criteria, to give reasons, and to initiate the student into standards of the discipline.

The student likewise has a set of rights and duties. The student has the right freely to inquire, to ask for reasons, to open access to information, and to question and debate the conclusions reached by experts. These "intellectual liberties" secure for the

student the right to participate in the intellectual affairs of the classroom in a way that assists the student in internalizing the standards and procedures of a discipline. And they recognize the student's status as a moral agent who is ultimately responsible for his beliefs and actions.

. . . That the student is a responsible moral agent is grounds for making his participation in an educational situation voluntary. . . . Lest this emphasis on the voluntariness of the student's participation be misunderstood, let me note that this does not entail that there be no required courses, or required standards, or that academic decisions be made either democratically or in response to "consumer demand." There are academic decisions legitimately made by experts. The real issue is that students must accept the legitimacy of the education to which they are asked to submit. Education can take place when students believe that educational institutions are in possession of something worthwhile. Since the values and standards of intellectual enterprises are internal to these enterprises and cannot be fully appreciated by the novice, the student's submission to his education cannot be fully rational. It must be based, in part, on trust.

Education loses its legitimacy when students begin to believe that the values educators or educational institutions pursue are self-serving or perverse. Genuine education ceases when students see themselves as held to their tasks by coercive factors, as, for example, when they see their economic future arbitrarily linked to some level of educational attainment. Students may go through the motions, pass the tests, and gain the certificates. A few may even be seduced into an appreciation of the forms of life intellectual enterprises represent. On the whole, however, when students lack a commitment to the value of what they learn, the consequences of learning on their values and their view of the world—the things that matter—will be minimal.

Demands for democracy or voluntariness in the detail of course selection, curriculum or instructor are signs that education is not seen as legitimate. The "epistemic gap" between novice and expert indicates that yielding to such demands is not the cure for the disease of illegitimacy. Democracy in academic affairs is governance by the incompetent. An institution faced with such demands or with passive resistance to the education it provides needs, rather, to look to the values it pursues and how these values become viable to its students.

Some further caveats concerning the way in which education should be voluntary are required. The first is that a lack of maturity can override the right to voluntariness. General maturity must be distinguished from intellectual competence. The novice in physics lacks competence in the standards of physical argument. Such a person may, however, be mature. Maturity is the general capacity to discover or choose a stable and rational set of goals, needs and interests and make choices that further them. A student who does not know physics may, nevertheless, know himself well enough and know enough about what physics is like to make a competent (if tentative) commitment to study it. A student who lacks maturity cannot do even this. Some form of paternalism toward such a student's education may, therefore, be warranted.

Second, a student's choices may have an impact not only on himself, but on others. A student who fails to learn to read harms not only his own prospects, but those of others. In such cases, the society has some interest in the decision and may act coercively when a significant threat to its legitimate interest exists.

I assume that these restrictions on the voluntariness of student decisions apply primarily to younger children.

This view of the pedagogical relationship can best be summarized by calling it a master–apprentice relationship. Its essential features are that the student is seen as a junior member of a community united by a shared commitment to some intellectual enterprise. Learning is a result of participation in the characteristic activities of the group under the guidance of an expert who sets educational tasks within the student's competence and evaluates performance. The relationship assumes the competence and the honesty of the master. Since the learner is not in a position to evaluate fully the competence of the master, the success of the relationship depends on trust. The learner in turn must willingly submit to the expertise of the master.

When this master–apprentice relationship concerns some intellectual endeavor, I have suggested that the student has intellectual liberties that may appear quite similar to the intellectual liberties that are shared by members of intellectual communities and are exercised in the activity of inquiry. For the student, after all, learning is inquiry. The student thus has the right to relevant information and to question and debate the ideas he encounters.

It is, however, crucial to note that the student's intellectual liberty differs from that of the expert. Intellectual liberty for the expert is justified as an essential component of the institutional arrangements in which inquiry can be conducted and truth pursued. Intellectual liberty is the means whereby new ideas are subjected to the standards of the field and are accepted, rejected or modified. Intellectual liberty for the student, on the other hand, is a condition of the student exercising his responsibility as a moral agent and participating in an intellectual enterprise in a way likely to lead to the internalization of the concepts and standards of that enterprise.

CASE 2.1   *SHOULD THE DOCTOR INSIST ON THE TRUTH?*

As a physician whose specialty is treating cancer, you have seen many kinds of misunderstandings of this disease—often for the worse. Many of your patients believe that cancer always involves extended terminal suffering, and that a diagnosis of cancer is a sentence of death. Few patients understand that more than half of the various kinds of cancer can be permanently arrested or cured.

Fortunately, the patient you are seeing on rounds today, Alex S., is quite different. He is a well-informed young man—a writer at work on his third novel—who understands that "cancer" is a catch-all term for many quite different kinds of diseases, and that for some of them, the cure rate is very good. "That word 'cancer' doesn't scare me," he says; "I know you can get well."

Alex had been brought to the hospital complaining of severe pain in the mid-abdomen, and after a complete workup, a tentative diagnosis of pancreatic mass was made. He underwent surgery, and diagnosis of cancer of the pancreas was confirmed. The surgeons removed most of the visible tumor, but some of the primary malignancy could not be contained, and distant metastases are inevitable. Radiation and chemotherapy are likely to be of little use. Pancreatic cancer is one of the worst of the cancers, with a 2-year survival rate of 1 to 2% at most; this means that after two years, only 1 or 2 percent of patients are still alive. Pancreatic cancer is almost universally fatal.

But Alex, for all his knowledge, does not realize this. You have told him the diagnosis and the survival rate, but he has clearly misunderstood, and like many less knowledgeable patients, he has heard only the most optimistic diagnosis. "Oh," he says, "that's not so bad, if I have a chance of a couple of years. I'll be able to finish my new novel—that's the only thing that really counts for me, anyway. Thanks, doctor, for telling me the truth."

What do you say to Alex now?

CASE 2.2   TELLING YOUR CONGREGATION THE TRUTH

You are the minister of a church in a community that has a large number of elderly persons in its congregation. Over the years you have enjoyed many aspects of your calling, especially preaching and making pastoral visits to the members of your flock. You know that many members of the congregation trust you implicitly, and that the faith that you share with them and preach to them is a source of great strength, especially among those of the elderly who know that death cannot be far away.

Recently, however, a tragic, maliciously arranged "accident" has killed several members of your family and, in the process, has destroyed your faith. It now seems clear to you that the world is not just, that mankind is evil, that there is no divine plan to justify this event, and, in general, that there cannot be a God in a world with such evil. You are quite aware that your change of attitude may be associated with depression as a result of the event, and indeed your denomination has a set of doctrines and teachings concerning the temporary loss of faith. At the moment, however, your loss of faith does not feel temporary; you simply no longer believe the pieties you have been preaching to your congregation, nor do you see any basis for the religious consolation you have been able to offer these people so effectively and reassuringly in pastoral counseling. Yet you cannot forget that you have been an enormous source of strength and hope to many members of your flock.

Tomorrow is Sunday. What should you say in your sermon? Can you answer this question by rereading what the doctrines and teachings of your denomination say about temporary loss of faith? If not, how should you answer this question?

CASE 2.3   GRADING TRUTHFULLY

At the prestigious undergraduate college at which you teach, student suicides have averaged two a year over the last 10 or 15 years. Although the circumstances of these tragedies vary, most of them are attributed to the intensely competitive nature of the school and the anxiety that such an environment evokes for highly motivated students whose grades fall short of their own expectations.

The student now sitting beside your desk seems to fit this description perfectly. He had previously taken another course with you, and he did quite well, but that was a large lecture course in which grading was based largely on familiarity with the reading, and did not give you a real chance to perceive students' differing intellectual skills. During the course he is currently taking with you, the student has clearly revealed that he is a desperate overachiever—driven, you want to say, to a performance well beyond his actual capacities.

The student is singlemindedly intent on entering a specific graduate school. His grades, together with his letters of recommendation, will be a major factor in determining his admission. He has come to ask you to write one of these letters on his behalf, and to tell him the grade he can expect in the course.

If you write a truthful letter, you will have to say that while he is aggressive and highly motivated, his intellectual capacities do not equal those of most of the other students in your class. And if you tell him straightforwardly the grade you will be giving him—rather than offering a noncommittal response like "You'll be getting the grade you've earned," or actually changing his grade to something higher than you think he deserves—you will have to tell him it will be a C+, or maybe, at best, a B−. But you know it would take an A−, at the very least, for him to be admitted to the school on which his heart is set.

You look out the window while you are considering what to do, and you think about the school's average of two suicides a year. Do you tell him the grade? Do you write the letter? You know that failing to get into the graduate school he wants will be a catastrophic blow. What, in this case, should you do?

CASE 2.4   WARNING POSSIBLE PARTNERS

As an experienced psychotherapist, you have counseled many people with sexual problems. Your client today, Rick, a young man whom you have been seeing for a considerable length of time, exhibits a severe version of a behavior pattern that you have seen frequently among patients with sexual identity confusion: Although he insists that he is heterosexual and finds "faggots" disgusting, he has sporadic episodes of aggressive homosexual activity. These episodes take the form of seductions of nonhomosexual men whom Rick knows in everyday contexts, usually by getting them drunk at home when he is not drinking himself. Rick also sometimes frequents gay bathhouses. Both sorts of episodes are followed by extreme self-reproach and then virtually complete suppression; Rick does not and cannot admit that he is gay. Although his therapy sessions with you have helped Rick to make considerable progress in other areas of his life, he still cannot acknowledge, accept, or control his behavior.

Today, Rick has come to you with two bits of disturbing news. First, he has a new roommate, a young man of about the same age. "He's straight as an arrow," insists Rick, "just my kind." (You take this remark as an unwitting piece of self-revelation.) Second, as the result of some blood tests done in connection with a chronic ear infection, Rick has been told that he is seropositive for human immunodeficiency virus (HIV) antibodies. He is completely bewildered. He knows that the condition is a probable precursor to acquired immune deficiency syndrome—AIDS—and that AIDS is transmitted by, among other things, "disgusting" homosexual activity, but he cannot understand how *he* can have it. He finally remembers a bit of minor surgery he had a couple of years ago; they must have surreptitiously given him a blood transfusion, he insists, even though he was not anesthetized.

Now there is Rick's anger to deal with. Based on your past experiences with Rick, you have every reason to believe that it will not be long before his anger erupts into one of his episodic homosexual aggressive behaviors. You also expect that this is likely to take the form of Rick's seducing his new roommate; Rick is attractive and persuasive, and he seems to have a way of manipulating previously inexperienced men into homosexual sex. But while the majority of your homosexual clients are extremely responsible in the use of safer-sex practices to protect themselves and their partners, you are certain that Rick will not be: Since he cannot admit that he is gay, he cannot bring himself even to entertain the idea of taking precautions. "Fags," he says, "they should all get AIDS and die. You'd never catch me with a condom on."

You can think of no way to get Rick to assume responsibility for protecting the roommate, and you expect that the roommate will be in no condition to protect himself if and when the time comes. Rick's seropositivity could convert into full expression of AIDS at any time, and he is already capable of transmitting the AIDS virus to his sexual partners.

You know the roommate's telephone number, of course, since it is the same telephone number as Rick's. Do you warn the roommate, and if so, of what?

CASE 2.5 CONFIDENTIALITY AND THE ARCHITECT

It was clear, even before the FBI arrived, that an unusual sum of money was involved. As a residential architect who had received considerable local recognition in the intermountain West—though you had not yet become nationally known—you had designed homes for a number of distinguished, wealthy clients, and had learned that an essential part of a successful relationship with your clients was sensitivity to their idiosyncratic wishes and peculiarities of taste. In Denver, for instance, you had designed a home for tall people, where everything—the height of the kitchen countertops, the transoms over the doors, even the risers in the stairs—was just a little higher than ordinary. That was an easy beginning. In Salt Lake City, you'd designed a home for a wealthy, music-loving couple who liked to host little chamber concerts, and whose living room was to inconspicuously double as a 150-seat auditorium. That was a little harder, but you liked the challenge of discovering what your clients really wanted and showing them how to achieve it. You began to be known as an architect who could do—with excellent taste—what clients really wanted. You felt that you were on the verge of real national recognition.

Then you designed a house in the canyons outside Las Vegas—the house the FBI has come to talk to you about. There were many remarkable things about this house. For instance, it was to have three equally prominent front doors, each with its own approach and its own stairwell to a suite of bedrooms upstairs. It was to have a kitchen designed for large-scale cooking and sustained storage of food. It had a gun room for what you were told was the owner's large collection of hunting rifles, and it also had an extraordinarily sensitive security system built in throughout the house.

The FBI wants to know what you knew about the purposes for which your clients built the house. They imply that your clients acquired their money in various gambling interests in Las Vegas; you reply that, although you knew that construction costs alone for the house had run several million dollars and that your commission for the design was attractive indeed, you did not inquire into the source of the funds. They tell you more: They suspect that the home is the headquarters of a militant supremacist group, and indeed you can recall consulting with what seemed to be the leaders of three related clans about the architecture of the various entryways and suites of upstairs rooms. They know about the gun room for the hunting rifles.

But they do not seem to know anything about the "annex" that your client also had you design. It is a large underground complex, about three-quarters of a mile from the house and connected to it by a well-concealed tunnel. You remember very well the amount of work you put into it, studying various sophisticated communications systems, special sorts of wiring and control panels, and facilities for a large amount of sophisticated machinery to be installed at a later time. There was even a further tunnel, extending another mile and a half, where whatever was made in the underground installation could be inconspicuously loaded into trucks in an old gravel quarry on the other side of the canyon. You remember obtaining construction permits for the house, but there are no records at all for the annex.

The FBI tells you a complicated tale involving suspicions of guerilla activity, drug manufacture and supply, religiously motivated plans to assassinate state political figures, and so on. But they have no concrete evidence. Neither do you.

Do you tell them what you know about the house?

CASE 2.6 FILING FOR DIVORCE

You represent Brenda Jones in a divorce action in which child custody is in dispute. Brenda had been a battered wife for many years of her marriage. She has previously told you about the serious beatings she received, her fear that her husband might one day turn to physically abusing their four children (now aged 2 to 7), and her ultimate decision to leave her husband because the children were being exposed to the beatings. Brenda's husband Tom has contested custody of their children, arguing that Brenda is too unstable and depressed to care for them.

Brenda has been involved in a battered women's support group and has been seeing a social worker as a private counselor. Her counselor confirms that she is depressed and under much stress, but says that she is fully capable of caring for the children. The court-appointed investigator has recommended that Brenda receive custody because she is fit and has been the children's caretaker all along. Moreover, the investigator has found that Tom had physically abused Brenda, and that his relationship with the children has been negatively affected by their seeing his violent abuse of their mother.

The trial for custody is 1 week away. Brenda comes to your office and tells you that she and Tom talked last night and she wants to give custody to him. She says she doesn't think she can make it through a trial, and she just wants it over. She says her mind is made up and her decision is final.

In your professional opinion, Brenda stands a very good chance—somewhere around 90%, you'd guess—of receiving custody at trial. More likely than not, Tom's attorney will advise him to settle and concede custody to Brenda. Of course, you cannot be sure about either of these things, nor can you be sure of what the impact on Brenda would be of going through a trial and/or losing custody of the children.

As Brenda's attorney, how would you go about obtaining her "informed consent" either to proceeding to trial or to settling the case by giving Tom custody? How important is it that you do so?

Case by Linda F. Smith, University of Utah College of Law.

CASE 2.7 ENLISTING CONSENT

You are one of a group of generals representing the high command controlling the U.S. Army's enlistment facilities. You are to determine what sorts of information will be given to recruits and, in the event that the draft is reinstated, what sorts of information will be given to men (and possibly women) conscripted for service; in general, you are to consider the issue of *informed consent* to military service. In the policy you develop, you will wish to consider what sorts of information are to be given about benefits, including pay, training, education, travel, and so on, and also about risks, including medical, psychological, and social factors as well as the possibility of accident or death. You will also wish to consider what forms of persuasion, if any, are appropriate. News media and other military officials will not have access to your discussions; you may conduct them in complete privacy.

Can you design a policy that will provide for consent to military service that is both *adequately informed* and *voluntary*? Will your policy for persons who enlist be different from the one for those who are drafted? Or is the nature of military service such that informed consent isn't morally required after all?

SUGGESTED READINGS

Models, Paternalism, and Autonomy

BATTIN, MARGARET P. "Non-Patient Decision-Making in Medicine: The Eclipse of Altruism," *The Journal of Medicine and Philosophy* 10 (1985): 19–44.

BEAUCHAMP, TOM, AND LAURENCE MCCULLOUGH. *Medical Ethics: The Moral Responsibilities of Physicians.* Englewood Cliffs, N.J.: Prentice-Hall, 1984, Chapters 2, 4, 5.

BROCK, DAN. "The Nurse–Patient Relation: Some Rights and Duties." In S. Spicker and S. Gadow, eds., *Nursing: Images and Ideals.* New York: Springer, 1980.

CALLAHAN, JOAN. "Academic Paternalism." *International Journal of Applied Philosophy* 3:(1986): 21–31.

DWORKIN, GERALD. "Paternalism." *The Monist* 56(1972): 64–84.

ENGELHARDT, H. TRISTRAM. "Rights and Responsibilities of Patients and Physicians." In M. Bayles and D. High, eds., *Medical Treatment of the Dying: Moral Issues.* Cambridge: Schenkman, 1978, pp. 9–28.

FRIED, CHARLES. "The Lawyer as Friend: The Moral Foundations of the Lawyer–Client Relation." *Yale Law Journal* 85:(1976):1060–89.

GERT, BERNARD, AND CHARLES CULVER. "Paternalistic Behavior" *Philosophy and Public Affairs* 6:(1976):45–57.

FEINBERG, JOEL. "Legal Paternalism." *Canadian Journal of Philosophy* 1:(1971): 105–24.

GOLDMAN, ALAN. *The Moral Foundations of Professional Ethics.* Totowa, N.J.: Rowman & Littlefield, 1980, Chapters 3–4.

MAY, WILLIAM. "Code, Covenant or Philanthropy?" *Hastings Center Report* 5:(1975): 29–38.

MASTERS, ROGER D. "Is Contract an Adequate Basis for Medical Ethics?" *Hastings Center Report* 5:(1975): 24–28.

MILLER, BRUCE. "Autonomy and the Refusal of Lifesaving Treatment." *Hastings Center Report* 11:4(August 1981): 22–28.

PRESIDENT'S COMMISSION FOR THE STUDY OF ETHICAL PROBLEMS IN MEDICINE AND BIOMEDICAL AND BEHAVIORAL RESEARCH. *Making Health Care Decisions,* 3 Volumes. Washington, D.C.: U.S. Government Printing Office, 1982.

RAMSEY, PAUL. *The Patient as Person.* New Haven: Yale University Press, 1970.

SMITH, SHERI. "Three Models of the Nurse–Patient Relationship." In S. Spicker and S. Gadow, eds., *Nursing: Images and Ideals.* New York: Springer, 1980.

VEATCH, ROBERT. "Models for Ethical Medicine in a Revolutionary Age." *The Hastings Center Report* 2:(1972): 5–7.

Truth-Telling

BUCHANAN, ALLEN. "Medical Paternalism." *Philosophy and Public Affairs* 7:(1978): 370–90.

COLLINS, JOSEPH. "Should Doctors Tell the Truth?" *Harper's* 155:(1927): 320–26.

ELLIN, JOSEPH. "Lying and Deception: The Solution to a Dilemma in Medical Ethics." *Westminster Institute Review* 1:(1981):3–6.

KORNFELD, D. S. "Doctor's Dilemma: What Truth for What Patient at What Time?" *CA* 28:4(July-Aug. 1978), 256.

NOVAK, DENNIS H., ROBIN PLUMER, RAYMOND L. SMITH, et al. "Changes in Physicians' Attitudes Toward Telling the Cancer Patient." *Journal of the American Medical Association* 241:(1979): 897–900.

OKEN, DONALD. "What to Tell Cancer Patients: A Study of Medical Attitudes." *Journal of the American Medical Association* 175:(1961): 1120–28.

VANDEVEER, DONALD. "The Contractual Argument for Withholding Medical Information." *Philosophy and Public Affairs* 9:(1980): 198–205.

VEATCH, ROBERT. *Case Studies in Medical Ethics.* Cambridge: Harvard University Press, 1977, Chapter 6.

WEIR, ROBERT. "Truthtelling in Medicine." *Perspectives in Biology and Medicine* 24:1 (Autumn 1980): 95–112.

Confidentiality

BATTIN, MARGARET P. "Telling Confessions: Confidentiality and the Practice of Religion," *Sunstone* 8:6 (Nov.–Dec. 1983): 23–33.

BAYLES, MICHAEL. *Professional Ethics.* Belmont, Calif.: Wadsworth, 1981, Chapter 4.

CURRAN, WILLIAM J. "Confidentiality and the Prediction of Dangerousness in Psychiatry: The Tarasoff Case." *The New England Journal of Medicine* 293:(1975): 285–86.

CURTIS, CHARLES. "The Ethics of Advocacy." *Stanford Law Review* 4:(1951): 3–23.

FREEDMAN, MONROE. "Professional Responsibility of the Criminal Lawyer: The Three Hardest Questions." *Michigan Law Review* 64:(1966): 1469–82.

———. *Lawyers' Ethics in an Adversary System.* Indianapolis: Bobbs-Merrill, 1975.

HAZARD, GEOFFREY. *Ethics in the Practice of Law.* New Haven: Yale University Press, 1978, Chapters 3, 9–10.

KIPNIS, KENNETH. *Legal Ethics.* Englewood Cliffs, N.J.: Prentice-Hall, 1986, Chapters 4–5.

LANDESMAN, BRUCE. "Confidentiality and the Lawyer–Client Relationship." In David Luban, ed., *The Good Lawyer: Lawyer's Roles and Lawyer's Ethics.* Totowa, N.J.: Rowman and Allanheld, 1984, pp. 191–213.

LUBAN, DAVID. "The Adversary System Excuse." In David Luban, ed., *The Good Lawyer: Lawyer's Roles and Lawyer's Ethics.* Totowa, N.J.: Rowman and Allanheld, 1984, pp. 83–122.

SIEGLER, MARK. "Confidentiality in Medicine: A Decrepit Concept." *The New England Journal of Medicine* 307:(1982): 1516–21.

The Repugnant Client

BAYLES, MICHAEL. "A Problem of Clean Hands: Failure to Provide Professional Services." *Social Theory and Practice* 5:(1979): 165–81.

DAVIS, MICHAEL. "The Right to Refuse a Case." In M. Davis and F. Elliston, *Ethics and the Legal Profession.* Buffalo, N.Y.: Prometheus Books, 1986, pp. 441–57.

HAZARD, GEOFFREY. *Ethics in the Practice of Law.* New Haven: Yale University Press, 1978, Chapter 6.

OBERDIEK, HANS. "Clean Hands and Professional Responsibility: A Rejoinder to Bayles." In B. Baumrin and B. Freedman, *Moral Responsibility and the Professions.* New York: Haven, 1983, pp. 141–54.

WOLFRAM, CHARLES. "A Lawyer's Duty to Represent Clients, Repugnant and Otherwise." In David Luban, ed., *The Good Lawyer, op. cit.,* pp. 214–35.

Informed Consent

BATTIN, MARGARET P. "The Least Worst Death: Selective Refusal of Treatment," *The Hastings Center Report,* 13:2 (April 1983) 13–16.

CANTERBURY V. SPENCE. *464 Federal Reporter,* 2d Series, 772.

CAPRON, ALEXANDER. "Informed Consent in Catastrophic Disease Research and Treatment." *University of Pennsylvania Law Review* 123:(1974): 364–76.

DONAGAN, ALAN. "Informed Consent in Therapy and Experimentation." *The Journal of Medicine and Philosophy* 2:(1977): 302–29.

FADEN, RUTH, AND TOM BEAUCHAMP. *A History and Theory of Informed Consent.* New York: Oxford University Press, 1986.

GAYLIN, WILLARD, AND DANIEL CALLAHAN. "The Psychiatrist as Double Agent." *Hastings Center Report* 4:(1974): 11–14.

GOROVITZ, SAMUEL. *Doctor's Dilemmas.* New York: Macmillan, 1982, Chapter 3.

INGELFINGER, FRANZ J. "Informed (but Uneducated) Consent." *The New England Journal of Medicine* 287:(1972): 465–66.

JONAS, HANS. "Philosophical Reflections on Experimenting with Human Subjects." *Philosophical Essays: From Current Creed to Technological Man.* Chicago: University of Chicago Press, 1980, pp. 105–31.

KATZ, JAY. "Informed Consent: A Fairy Tale?" *University of Pittsburgh Law Review* 39:(1977): 137–74.

————. *The Silent World of Doctor and Patient.* New York: Macmillan, 1984.

ROTH, LOREN, ALAN MEISEL, AND CHARLES LIDZ. "Tests of Competency to Consent to Treatment." *American Journal of Psychiatry* 134:(1977): 279–84.

VEATCH, ROBERT. *Case Studies in Medical Ethics.* Cambridge: Harvard University Press, 1977, Chapters 11–12.

THREE

Personal, Professional, and Institutional Obligations

Until recently, the solo practitioner has been the center of attention in most research and teaching on professional ethics. Questions involving the individual physician and her patient, or the independently consulting attorney and his client, have been taken, rightly or not, to be the model issues in the field. Problems arising from group or corporate practice, or from the work of professionals engaged as employees, have been given only secondary consideration. Institutional issues have been addressed all along by specialists in business ethics, and it has always been recognized that a great many professionals, including nurses, academics, military officers, and engineers, pursue careers in large organizational settings. Yet the problems endemic to the corporate employment of professionals have not received the attention one might expect in view of the sheer numbers of people confronting them. And research in applied ethics has concentrated minimally on the special predicaments of practitioners who are employees, administrators, or officers.[1]

It is becoming increasingly clear, however, that professionals working alone as private contractors with individual clients are a vanishing species in the United States, especially in heavily populated areas. Wherever the demand for services is great enough to sustain corporate activity, the facts of modern economic life, the proliferation of narrow specializations, the organizational efficiencies of group practice, and the general need for institutional protection against tort liability all mitigate against the survival of the solo practitioner. Thus, the traditionally individualistic model of the professional–client relationship becomes less and less relevant to ethical inquiry, as ever greater numbers of skilled specialists, including physicians and attorneys, join large group practices, contract their services to organizations, or become participants in various kinds of business enterprises.

The moral importance of this change becomes evident when we think about the heavy emphases placed upon autonomy in decision-making, fidelity to client interests, and peer control of licensure and discipline in the education, training, and socialization of professionals in the United States through most

---

[1] Exceptions to this generalization can be found in some of the essays in Rem B. Edwards, ed., *Psychiatry and Ethics* (Buffalo: Prometheus Books, 1982), and in Malham Wakin's *War, Morality, and the Military Profession* (Boulder: Westview Press, 1986).

of this century. Especially in medicine and law, but in other disciplines as well, apprentice practitioners have been taught to think of themselves as individually responsible for the well-being of their clients, and as answerable primarily to those clients and to colleagues who share their own background and training. Indeed, despite the growing involvement of professionals in institutional employment, some writers have treated the concepts of practitioner autonomy and peer regulation as though they were logically necessary conditions of *bona fide* professional status for occupations.[2] Confidentiality and other individualized values have been given primary status. The involvements of nonprofessionals in decision-making and review processes have been presented as unfortunate, even if inevitable, outside interferences. And novices have gone forth to practice with little understanding of many of the most serious ethical problems they will actually confront.

Imagine, for example, that you are the only physician on duty late at night in the emergency room of a private urban hospital. A young woman in labor arrives at your door in a taxicab. As a physician, your primary professional concern is the well-being of the woman and her baby; yet you must also work within hospital regulations, which prohibit the admission of indigent patients if they are well enough to be moved to publicly funded facilities. Your inclination is to admit the woman to your own maternity ward immediately; but while you are examining her, other staff members determine that she has neither money of her own nor any form of health insurance. Thus, under hospital policy, your only real decision is whether or not she can be transferred safely. Remembering the threats of firings that have occurred recently over allegedly unnecessary admissions of indigents, as well as the weak financial condition of your institution, you reluctantly decide that your patient can manage a move. You call an ambulance and send her off to the county hospital . . . and, on the way, her baby dies.

The situation just described actually occurred at a West Coast hospital in 1986. Unfortunately, conflicts of its kind, many with equally unhappy outcomes, are proliferating in our society as professional practice in nearly every field becomes increasingly bureaucratic and institutional in character. We might disagree for a variety of reasons with the tradition-minded practitioners who remember the decades of professional independence as "the good old days" for both themselves and their clients.[3] But regardless of the evaluation we make of the current scene, the plain facts are that autonomy is decreasing in American professional life as organizational and systematic constraints increase, and that no reversal of this trend is likely to occur in the foreseeable future. Thus, it behooves us to look carefully and realistically at the ethical problems that professionals confront in institutional settings.

As will soon be evident, many of these problems take the form of hard questions about means and ends that arise when professional employees and

[2] See, for example, Michael D. Bayles, *Professional Ethics* (Belmont: Wadsworth, 1981), Chapter 1, and Richard Wasserstrom, "Lawyers as Professionals: Some Moral Issues," in *Human Rights* 5:1 (American Bar Association, 1975), also widely available in texts on professional ethics. Note also the general discussion of specialized role morality and the essentially private models of practitioner–client relationships discussed in Chapters 1 and 2 of this book.

[3] In *The Social Transformation of American Medicine* (New York: Basic Books, 1982), Paul Starr presents a clear and fascinating account of the development of the healthcare industry.

administrators, like our emergency room physician, feel compelled to make decisions that they would not choose to make if they were operating on their own. From the organizational side, these people may feel pressure to cut corners and reduce personal standards of practice in the name of such corporate goals as cost-containment or the protection of market positions. When institutional pressures build, they may find themselves drawn toward drastic responses such as work-stoppages or whistleblowing as strategies for improving conditions that they find intolerable. And in both situations, the central moral question turns out to be whether the end in view justifies the means being considered for its realization.

Ethical theorists have long puzzled over this issue without reaching any widely accepted general conclusions. Some, in the utilitarian or teleological tradition, have argued that the overall desirability of results or outcomes should be the deciding factor. In effect, their claim is that sufficiently valuable ends can justify the employment of otherwise undesirable means. Others, thinking along Kantian or deontological lines, maintain that the rights and wrongs of moral choice must not be worked out in terms of consequences, because a major goal of morality itself is precisely to discourage the employment of bad means for good ends. On this view, certain kinds of actions (or motives for actions) are right, while others are wrong, whether or not they produce desirable results.[4]

It seems clear that we need a compromise between the two theories in order to make sense of our actual moral experience. But the task of developing a mediating third position has proved extremely complicated and difficult. So instead of proposing a general answer, we suggest that each situation be evaluated on its own merits, based on whether the end seems to justify the means. With the utilitarians, we can ask how important the envisaged goal really is, who would benefit from the proposed action, who might be harmed, and what would be the extent of both benefits and harms. With the Kantians, we can ask whether the proposed course of action would involve exploiting or taking advantage of people, and whether we would be willing to have everyone behave in the suggested way in similar circumstances. And finally, appealing to our own senses of justice, we can ask whether the action and its results would be as fair as possible to the legitimate interests of all involved.

PROFESSIONALS AS EMPLOYEES

According to the conventions of modern management practice, the role of an employee is essentially that of a team player. An employee subordinates her own interests to those of the organization and complies with the directives of superiors whether or not she has participated in their formulation. Theoretically, at least, institutional goals are established by boards of directors in the corporate world or by legislators in government. Strategies for achieving these objectives are devised by top management. And lower-echelon employees

---

[4] The classic presentation of the teleological view is John Stuart Mill's *Utilitarianism*. Immanuel Kant defends the deontological side in his *Foundations of the Metaphysics of Morals*. Both books are available in many editions.

carry out the plans set for them, with discretionary authority only within their own departments. As we will soon see, this hierachical arrangement is by no means universal in large organizations.[5] Frequently, there are opportunities, either intended or accidental, for employees to influence decision-making at levels higher than their own. But subordination of judgment and limitations of individual choice are inherent in employees' roles, whether they work in small, relatively democratic companies or in tightly structured institutions such as the armed forces. No matter how much de facto latitude individual employees may enjoy, their activities are in principle subject to review by organizational superiors. Final choices are not ultimately theirs.

For professionals, this invariant feature of the employee–employer relationship often amounts to having responsibility without being able to exercise control. Healthcare providers cannot always simply administer the services they deem best for their patients. Teachers are not always at liberty to make decisions on their own about the educational interests of their students. And field commanders are rarely free to exercise truly independent judgment in matters relating to their military objectives or to the well-being of their troops. As professionals, they may very well know better than anyone else what should be done; but because they are subordinate personnel, their hands are tied by all kinds of institutional constraints. Thus, they may easily find themselves making severely restricted choices in very serious situations. And if the consequences of their decisions are unfortunate, as they were in the medical emergency just discussed, they may rightly feel that they have been assigned significant responsibility and, at the same time, denied the control necessary to carry it out successfully.

Of course it is also true that team play always involves compromise, and that cooperation among participants with varied skills is basic to the success of any corporate enterprise. So it can't be argued plausibly that institutional employment by its very nature diminishes the quality or damages the moral integrity of professional practice. On the contrary, many professional occupations, such as social work, nursing, and engineering, are inherently group-oriented activities, requiring shared responsibility and joint action. There is no professorate without colleges or universities, no military command without organized forces, and no anesthesiology or surgery without hospitals or clinics. Thus, it would be naive to desire that every professional should be a solo practitioner, answering only to clients and peers for her decisions. And it would be worse to think of such radical autonomy as though it were a defining characteristic of professionalism in general. Accordingly, we will treat organizational employment per se as ethically neutral, not rejecting it or wishing it away as inevitably corrupting, but drawing attention to the moral problems it generates for conscientious practitioners.

Organizational Regulation and Individual Competence

In complex institutions such as school systems, governments, and corporations, detailed sets of regulations and hierarchically arranged systems of job descriptions promote order, coherence, and efficiency in group efforts

---

[5] See the essays by John Ladd and Richard Boland in this chapter.

by defining the responsibilities (and rights) of individual participants and by establishing lines (and limits) of accountability for the various activities carried on within the enterprise. But as our contemptuous uses of terms like *bureaucracy* and *red tape* clearly indicate, these same rules and pecking orders are sources of endless frustration to the people who have to deal with them. Anyone who has ever served in the military, negotiated a real estate loan through a bank, or worked on a job that is substantially controlled by a strong union or by the Occupational Safety and Health Administration (OSHA) is painfully aware of the irritations endemic to complicated organizational systems. For professionals, however, these frustrations can be particularly intense, because they often impede the exercise of individual competencies developed in hard years of education and training. Counselors forbidden by school board rules to give information about birth control to sexually active adolescents, engineers denied a voice in decisions about the uses of their own designs, and nurses prohibited from administering needed medication without official approval all may rightly feel hostility toward rules that prevent them from doing what they know how to do, and could do well if given the opportunity.

In these cases and in multitudes like them, the regulations themselves seem to defeat the purposes for which professionals are employed in the first place. Narrow-minded directors can and do set policies that damage the very interests they seek to advance. Chains of command frequently block important flows of information and advice from subordinates to their superiors. And restrictive job descriptions often delay or prevent the delivery of essential services. Furthermore, the politics, social psychology, and economics of rule-setting in large organizations may combine to intensify these unhappy effects. School board members may suspect that the counselors are right about juvenile sexuality, but may defer to the wishes of an ill-informed electorate. Corporate managers may fear the appearance of indecisiveness and the loss of prestige that might result from delegating authority to, or even seeking advice from, engineers employed at levels lower than their own. And the fact that nursing departments in most hospitals are fiscally categorized as consumers rather than producers of revenue helps to perpetuate the traditional gap in authority and power between nurses and physicians.[6]

Yet proponents of corporate law and order are not without answers to these complaints. They can argue that boards of directors are authorized by their own sources of power to establish whatever operating guidelines they deem appropriate. They can point out that clear regulations and delineations of authority are essential to the success of any large organization, since directors, employees, and clients alike must be able to discern where specific responsibilities lie. And they can claim quite plausibly that limits deliberately imposed upon individual discretion are generally beneficial, because they prevent workers from overstepping the boundaries of their own expert knowl-

---

[6] The principle here is that those who pay the piper call the tunes; and physicians, laboratory personnel, and therapists have traditionally been treated as generators rather than consumers of hospital income. But as unionization increases among nurses, and licensing requirements become more specialized and stringent, it appears that this situation will change. More and more U.S. hospitals are now billing their patients separately for nursing services.

edge. They may readily admit that there are many particular situations in which general rules restrict the desirable exercise of professional expertise, sometimes with tragic consequences. But they will also note that uncoordinated decision-making can produce equally drastic results, that armies can not be entirely made up of officers, and that chaos is the inevitable result of too much discretion being granted to individual employees, regardless of their professional backgrounds.

It thus appears that there is a theoretical deadlock between the advocates of practitioner autonomy and the proponents of institutional order. The former discern insults to professional integrity in every bureaucratic regulation, while the latter see anarchy looming behind any deviation from established procedure. Yet it is implausible to suppose either that professional employees have the moral right to accept or reject particular regulations according to their whims, or that rules should always be obeyed. Instead, it must be recognized that both autonomy and order are essential to the success of large enterprises, and that reasonable compromises between the two should be sought when they clash. No easy general formulas are available for resolving these tensions. In the next section, we will explore treating them as conflicts of judgment.

Conflicts of Judgment

In an ideally rational institution, every team member would subscribe without reservation to a clearly defined set of corporate goals, would understand and be prepared to carry out the tasks appropriate to his "station and its duties," and would work smoothly and effectively with his colleagues for the realization of shared aims. Administrators would serve more as coordinators than as supervisors. When divergent opinions arose over policy or tactics, open and honest negotiations would settle issues fairly and in the best interests of all involved. And neither professionals nor other employees would have occasion to wonder about the moral legitimacy of their actions in regard to their own consciences, their employers' interests, or the well-being of the organization's clients. Individual employees would not always agree with the choices made by the group, but they would feel confident about the integrity of the resolutions achieved, and they would be willing to carry out corporate decisions as though they were their own.

Unfortunately, of course, things don't work out this way in the actual world. Like most other people, professionals must usually look for employment where they can find it. They must weigh economic considerations, hopes for career trajectories, family needs and interests, and professional values against one another as they decide among job opportunities. This means that they, like others, are likely to find themselves working in organizations whose goals they support to some degree, but not entirely; whose strategies they approve of more often than not, but by no means always; and whose assignments of duties seem generally appropriate, but do not fully correspond to their own ideals of professional responsibility. This, in turn, means that conflicts of judgment are almost inevitably part of the territory they acquire when they accept corporate or institutional employment.

Accountants, for example, confront problems of this kind when other members of corporate management teams favor actions that are legally or financially dubious. And nurses in hospitals struggle with such dilemmas when they are constrained to follow physicians' orders in conflict with what they perceive to be their patients' interests. In both situations, there may be no cause at all for doubt about the integrity of the opposing views; that is, there may be no basis for designating one side as "good guys" and the other as "bad guys." It might be, for instance, that the accountant senses a violation of the tax code where others honestly perceive only a liberal interpretation of the law, or that the nurse sees a need for gentle handling while the attending physician believes that rigorous therapy is a medical requirement. But the sincerity of the clashing views is unlikely to give much comfort to professionals who feel prepared and obligated to exercise the independent judgment for which they have been trained, but also find themselves under pressure to defer to the opinions of others. Nor is there any real satisfaction in being able to say "I told you so" when things turn out badly. If my group makes a serious mistake, I may very well feel partially responsible for its consequences, even if I saw the trouble coming and warned my colleagues about it in advance.

Some professionals manage to cope with conflicts of this kind by distancing themselves emotionally from the processes and outcomes of group decision-making. They define their own functions in the narrowest possible terms, provide competent advice when called upon to do so, and then shrug off responsibility for the overall results. Engineers, for example, adopt this strategy when they try to convince themselves that their only duties are the specific assignments they are given, and that they have no obligations beyond serving the immediate interests of their employers. Academics use a similar approach when they restrict their involvement as much as they can to their own specialized research and teaching, engage themselves in institutional issues only under pressure, and shun responsibility for policies and practices of which they disapprove.

But while this tactic may relieve some workers of moral burdens that they should not have to carry and may prevent others from becoming busybodies, it can hardly be commended as a satisfactory approach to professional life. Psychologically, it is a destructive form of self-alienation, opening a gap between the practitioner's identity as a professional and her own behavior on the job. Ethically, it amounts to the abdication of precisely those broad commitments to the general good that are often seen as the primary justification for the existence of the professions as privileged occupations. Conditions are bad enough when employees in general distance themselves from the larger concerns involved in their own work. They are worse when professional employees do it, because the adoption of this attitude virtually amounts to the abandonment of a public trust.

An alternative approach is to focus on the organizational decision-making processes themselves, to see whether the incidence of conflicts can be reduced through more effective means of communication and negotiation. Much has been learned in recent decades about styles of management and techniques for resolving conflicts in large organizations. This new knowledge can be a great help to conscientious professionals working in groups.[7] If we recognize that it is not enough just to be right, that our obligations extend beyond stating our own views on a "take-it-or-leave-it" basis, we can begin to see the ethical importance of learning to negotiate effectively with our colleagues, all of whom presumably have as much ego involvement in their own ideas as we have in ours. Dogmatic and confrontational approaches tend to be self-defeating because they generate hostility and defensiveness. More conciliatory strategies, which avoid threats to self-esteem, reduce the risk that conflicts of judgment will deteriorate into struggles for power. And although the acquisition of skills in communication and negotiation can involve hard work and painful self-evaluations, as we learn to perceive ourselves as others do, the payoff may well be a reduction in the number and intensity of the conflicts of judgment that tempt us to "cop out" of organizational commitments.

But it is also important not to hope for too much from improved cooperation. Not all of the ethical issues posed for professionals by organizational employment can be eliminated or even diminished by tactful communication and diplomatic negotiation alone. Many are the results of relatively unalterable features of the employing institution itself, or of the conditions in which it operates, and are thus not readily amenable to any kind of in-house resolution. Among problems of this kind are gatekeeping, burnout, and trade secrets, discussed in the following sections.

Gatekeeping

Intense clashes between individual judgments and institutional policies arise when professionals are required to serve as gatekeepers, controlling the distribution of goods and services according to budgetary or other organizational regulations, rather than client needs. Problems of this type are woefully familiar to social workers and others involved in the administration of entitlement programs, such as welfare, unemployment compensation, and aid to the handicapped, because public funding almost invariably falls short of the needs of the clientele. But they are also growing rapidly in the operation of private institutions, such as health maintenance organizations (HMOs), medical insurance companies, convalescent centers and hospitals, as administrators, physicians, and nurses are compelled to make more and more treatment decisions with the goal of cost-containment centrally in mind.[8] This was the problem of the emergency room physician whose story we told earlier. Such dilemmas are now so common that medical professionals joke defensively about performing "wallet biopsies" on incoming patients in order to determine their eligibility for care.

In some cases, changes in internal policies can at least temporarily alleviate gatekeeping problems through shifts in organizational priorities or modifications of budgets. But in "zero-sum games," when increasing support for one activity necessarily entails cutting the funds available for others of

---

[7] Two useful books on this subject are Robert R. Blake and Jane S. Mouton, *Solving Costly Organizational Conflicts* (San Francisco: Jossey-Bass, 1984), and Roger Fisher and William Ury, *Getting to Yes* (Boston: Houghton Mifflin, 1981).

[8] See Chapter 4 for discussions of ethical issues concerning the general availability and distribution of professional services.

equal importance, or when the organization's general resources are in danger of irreversible depletion, no such compromising solutions may be available. And where cost-containment itself is an important strategy for increasing corporate profits, as it is in many medical insurance companies, HMOs, and private hospitals, gatekeepers are repeatedly called upon to turn away needy clients and to limit service delivery according to budgetary guidelines.

In circumstances such as these, professionals confront very difficult ethical choices. They may be forced to balance their commitments to their employers against their professional standards and their moral values. If they believe that the goals and policies of the organizations they serve are themselves morally appropriate, they may feel justified in playing the gatekeeper's role, no matter how personally distasteful they find it. If rationing must be done, then someone has to do it, and it is no reflection on the integrity of employees who carry out such repugnant duties that they perform them effectively. Indeed, they might well deserve praise for their willingness to undertake tasks that others would strongly prefer to avoid. No one likes to say no to people, especially when they are in need. But when denial is truly inevitable, it may seem that the gatekeeper has no cause for moral qualms, provided that the job is done fairly, consistently, and with as much compassion as the situation permits.

On the other hand, employers' goals and strategies are not always morally appropriate, even when they are both legally permissible and economically sound. If, for example, a university with limited financial resources cuts back admissions to academic programs while continuing to support expensive intercollegiate athletics, or if a training center with restricted enrollment favors less handicapped clients over the more severely impaired, professional staff members have serious reasons for questioning their own participation in gatekeeping operations. If they find that they can't make moral sense of their own situations, they may feel impelled to take actions aimed at institutional change beyond the immediate domains of their own responsibilities. We will say more about activity in this category in the next part of this discussion.

Overwork and Burnout

Most people are familiar with burnout as a problem of public school teachers, who are commonly required to work with far too many students over long stretches of years, in conditions that are thoroughly unfavorable to the realization of significant professional goals. Where classrooms are crowded, facilities dilapidated, supplies inadequate, and support personnel unavailable, teachers become fatigued and discouraged to the point of exhaustion. The quality of their work deteriorates as their hopes for success with their students diminish. If they are not assigned to lighter duties or given some other form of relief, they eventually either abandon their profession or become incompetent. In effect, job-related stress "burns them out." But comparable problems make life difficult for professionals in other fields as well. Engineers struggling under the pressure of contract deadlines, crisis intervention workers who are on call around the clock for enormous caseloads, and medical interns and residents who staff 36-hour shifts on hospital wards and in emergency rooms all experience the debilitating effects of overwork and something akin to burnout.[9]

Burnout sometimes develops as a result of inept planning or poor management and is thus, at least in principle, relatively easy to remedy. More often, however, such difficulties like the problem of gatekeeping, are budget-driven; that is, they result primarily from the inadequate provision of salaries for needed personnel. State psychiatric hospitals, for example, are chronically underfunded by financially beleaguered legislatures; and the psychiatrists, psychologists, and nurses employed in these institutions are left to manage large populations of very ill patients with utterly inadequate resources.[10] For professional employees working under these conditions, the result is overwork, disillusionment, and burnout. For patients, the result is custodial care, rather more like imprisonment than treatment. In effect, budgetary constraints turn mental health specialists into wardens, so burdened by the numbers of their patients that they must concentrate most of their efforts on maintaining order and elementary hygiene, with few personal or institutional resources left for significant therapy.

The obvious solutions to these problems are more staff and better scheduling, with assignments of shifts and responsibilities that impose less heavily on the energy and skills of employees. But where money is not available for the needed help, the professional faces some hard choices: Is it better to offer marginal service than to offer no service at all? Should he continue to work when he is aware that his competence is diminishing? What should he do when he knows that he is making mistakes, but there is no assistance in sight? In short-term emergencies, such as natural disasters or military crises, the best course clearly is to carry on with whatever resources are available. In more normal circumstances, however, this answer loses much of its plausibility. When understaffing and exhausting shifts are the rule, rather than the exception, it may be incumbent upon the professional employee to respond differently in order to preserve his own competence and to increase the quality of the service he performs. Alternatives are discussed in the following section, "Responses to Institutional Pressures."

Research, Trade Secrets, and Espionage

Capitalist economic theory holds that private enterprise and the pursuit of corporate profits contribute substantially (perhaps more than any other economic system could) to the general well-being by encouraging investment in the development of needed products and services and by ensuring the efficient production and distribution of these goods. It draws attention to the enormous costs and financial risks now involved in transforming an idea suggested by an innovator into a commodity or technological process available to the public at large. And it argues that the system can operate successfully only if private interests in inventions, scientific discoveries, and other intel-

---

[9] It is noteworthy that "The New York State health commissioner has proposed new regulations restricting doctors to 16-hour shifts in hospitals and 12-hour shifts in emergency rooms" (*The New Republic*, June 29, 1987, p. 96). The problem of shift assignments for physicians is also discussed in an article and letters in *Time*, August 31 and September 21, 1987.

[10] See Martha Fowlkes' article later in this chapter.

lectual products are legally protected by copyrights and patents, so that valuable creative work can be shielded from plagiarism and theft.

In general, these arrangements seem to operate fairly well in ensuring that the rewards of creative effort go to the people who engage in or provide support for such work.[11] But they also generate ethical problems for professionals employed in corporate enterprises. For example, loyalties to colleagues and employers, as well as commitments to professional standards of conduct, are severely strained when research, development, and production companies attempt to hire key employees away from one another in order to improve their positions in competitive markets. They are also subjected to pressure when an individual member of a research team disagrees with the direction her group decides to take in an investigation or a series of experiments. And they may be stressed to their limits when a promising line of inquiry is closed by management on the basis of its lack of potential profitability for the company.

Many of these problems result directly from tension between the ethical ideals of professional life and the actual workings of marketplace economies. As we noted in Chapter 1, among the defining features of professions are that they should have substantial intellectual content and that their practitioners should contribute to the general fund of knowledge in their own fields. Scientific inquiry is communal by nature, its progress depending upon the publication of new ideas, the unimpeded criticism of theories, and the independent replication of experiments. Thus, we might expect that openness and the widespread sharing of results for the public good would be generally characteristic of professional activity. Yet the market economy provides compelling incentives for privacy in research, secrecy about results, and the legal protection of proprietary interests in intellectual products.[12]

Proponents of the competitive system may argue that this conflict is more apparent than real, since the market eventually makes available most useful discoveries and worthwhile innovations, to the benefit of the public as well as the financial advantage of their developers. But even if this claim is true, it provides little comfort to individual practitioners caught in morally binding situations, because they must decide what to do in the present, not what might be generally best in the long run. Nor does it help to point out that secrecy, cutthroat competition, and sometimes theft and fraud are also characteristic of work carried out in universities and research institutes, even though the monetary stakes are usually not nearly as high as they are in private industry. In these contexts, prominent appointments, career-advancing promotions, and prestigious awards, such as Nobel prizes, offer equally compelling inducements to competition and thereby pose comparable moral problems for conscientious workers.

When the attractions of personal gain override the qualms of individual consciences, we sometimes see scandalous examples of piracy and plagiarism

---

[11] There are, of course, extremely complex problems involved in both the drafting and the enforcement of patent and copyright laws. The controversies over the videotaping of television broadcasts and the duplication of musical recordings show how difficult it can be to protect creative work.

[12] For an informative discussion of some of the complexities involved in this situation, see the essay by Edwin Layton in Chapter 5.

in both the commercial and the academic worlds. Beyond noting that temptations can be very compelling in such cases, however, we need not pay attention to them here, since the more egregious offenses are well covered by relatively uncontroversial laws, enforceable contracts, and widely accepted principles of professional ethics. For our purposes, borderline situations in which professional ideals and corporate loyalties oppose each other are much more important.

Suppose, for example, that you developed a promising formula for the relief of a rare disease while you were employed in the laboratory of a pharmaceutical company, but that management decided to discontinue your project because of its cost and limited market potential. Or imagine that, as a research scientist, you found yourself in the middle of the recent international tug of war over information which slowed research on the AIDS virus. In either case, you might well believe that you had ideas or information that ought to be made available at least to other competent researchers for the public good, but that your efforts were being thwarted for morally unacceptable commercial or bureaucratic reasons. And you might be strongly tempted to seek some way around restrictive regulations and principles in order to get your message out, in an attempt to comply with the letter of the law while evading its spirit. Here, potential benefits to people who are seriously ill could be a much more weighty motivation than the possibility of any personal gain might have been. Your commitments as a professional would pit themselves directly against your obligations as an employee, with a significant common interest in the balance; and the values of the competitive marketplace might well be the loser. In this way, even if you were the sort of person who never felt a strong inclination to cheat for money or prestige, you might find that ethical questions involving trade secrets in research can raise significant challenges to the loyalties of team-playing professional employees.

RESPONSES TO INSTITUTIONAL PRESSURES

Having discussed some of the important ways in which institutional employment can hinder competent professional practice, we now turn to possible responses. Professionals have been no less eager than other workers to assert their own interests against those of their employers, and they have learned a great deal from the successful strategies of political action groups and labor unions. In ethical perspective, however, some of these tactics look very good, while others seem quite dubious because of the special status and moral commitments of professionals in society. Our task is to consider how we can distinguish acceptable responses from unacceptable responses in particular cases.

Negotiation, Lobbying, and Organizational Politics

As we have suggested, many of the ethical problems encountered by professional employees result directly from inadequate funding for their work. In large enterprises, such as urban hospitals, state universities, and corporations with major national markets, overall budgets may be fixed by unalterable limits on revenues in any given period of operation. But it is worth noting that, in many cases, there is significant latitude for the movement of money from one budget category to another within such organizations. Skillful administrators and managers work at maintaining flexibility in their control over departmental resources, and they try to build up contingency funds over which they can exercise discretionary authority. Thus, even in situations of general financial hardship, when institutional income is severely limited, there is often money to be found for needs that are perceived by those who hold the internal purse strings to be both pressing and important. And this in turn means that relief is sometimes available to beleaguered professionals through the mechanisms of negotiation, lobbying, and organizational politics within their own institutions. Presidents and other administrative officers can be induced to consolidate operations for greater efficiency, to transfer funds across division boundaries, or to release contingency funds for the benefit of specific programs.

In situations of this kind, professionals must become effective advocates of their own activities, because they are participants in zero-sum games, in which any victory for one program necessarily entails a corresponding loss for another. They must not only do their jobs well, but also be able to persuade others that their work is urgently needed and in danger of failure if better support is not provided. And they must honestly believe that the problems they confront are of greater relative importance than those of competitors within their own organizations. Otherwise, their efforts to divert funding from other uses to their own programs will constitute nothing more than self-interested empire building.

Competition of this kind is, of course, destructive and ugly, because it pits colleagues against one another in struggles for jobs, perquisites, and institutional power. But if the professionals involved believe that their concerns are surpassingly urgent, they may feel justified in playing the game well, despite its heavy costs in human relationships. Suppose, for instance, that the chair of a university language department had a severe understaffing problem, with an already overworked faculty and many more students needing classes than there were spaces available. And suppose further that she discovered the departments of leisure studies and domestic science to have diminishing enrollments and, in consequence, several unnecessary faculty positions. Under these circumstances, she might lobby for more appointments for her own program, even though she knew that success would mean the loss of jobs in the competing departments. She might well regard the study of language as a more important element of higher education than recreation or home economics, and she would very likely believe that teaching loads should be distributed equitably across departmental boundaries. Thus, she might proceed in the conviction that her actions were ethically appropriate despite their potentially unfortunate consequences for colleagues in the targeted programs.

In more prosperous times, when budgets are not unalterably fixed, professionals can also become effective advocates outside their own organizations. Where public or charitable funding is an important source of revenue, they can help to increase agency income by giving speeches to raise public awareness of their needs, by meeting with legislators and other influential people, and by testifying before appropriations committees. Since they are likely to be more aware than anyone else of the value of their own work, they are natural candidates for roles as public advocates. They can speak with authority about the services they offer, and they are often able to build effective cases for their claims in competition with those of other worthwhile enterprises. In this way, they can reduce the systematic pressures of institutional employment by increasing the financial support available for their own activities.

Within limits, advocacy of this kind can be perceived as a normal part of professional life, since ethical codes commonly enjoin practitioners to "aid the public in developing informed judgments, opinions, and choices"[13] about their work. On the other hand, it can easily become a burdensome distraction, drawing time and energy away from primary responsibilities. Every hour spent in lobbying is, after all, an hour not spent in research or in consultation with clients. It can also generate conflicts with employers who are concerned about maintaining their own budget priorities and other managerial prerogatives and about preventing subordinates from going over their heads to funding agencies, legislators, or the public. And it can fail to achieve the desired results as well. Thus, the professional employee who contemplates becoming an advocate of his own program must deal with a cluster of related ethical and strategic questions: He must decide whether he can simultaneously be both an effective lobbyist and a responsible practitioner, whether he will violate important organizational loyalties if he tries to promote his own particular cause, and whether his efforts at advocacy are likely to succeed under existing political, economic, and social conditions. The answers to these questions will, of course, vary with the particular circumstances in which decisions have to be made.

Protest Resignations

When negotiation and advocacy do not offer promising solutions, professional employees often consider protest resignations as a way of responding to urgent problems. They see that by quitting their jobs, they can force their employers to pay attention to their complaints, demonstrate the seriousness of their concerns, and possibly bring about improvements in working conditions for those who will replace them.

Consider, for example, the situation of a psychiatrist employed as the supervisor of mental health care in a large metropolitan jail. In recent years, the inmate population in her jail has been expanding far more rapidly than the facilities and staff provided for their housing, supervision, and care. One result is that mentally ill prisoners, whose numbers are also increasing dramatically, are frequently held for weeks, or even months, in her overcrowded mental health unit, with little or no treatment other than the tranquilizing drugs routinely administered to control their behavior. Since most are indigent, they must wait for overworked public health personnel to evaluate their cases, and then for similarly overloaded prosecutors and public defenders

---

[13] From the "Ethical Principles of Psychologists," adopted by the American Psychological Association in 1981. For related examples, see Appendix II in this book.

to arrange hearings and dispositions of charges for them. And because they are confined in packed holding cells with others in equally poor health, and with no one available to provide effective individual therapy, their conditions often deteriorate badly while they wait.

Faced with hopelessly inadequate facilities and staff support, as well as a professional practice amounting to little more than the management of custodial care, our psychiatrist might come to regard a protest resignation as her most plausible option. Noting that there is not much public sympathy at present for the problems of prisoners, she might see little hope for success in negotiating or lobbying for a larger share of the municipal budget. She would be aware that the federal courts have ordered the improvement of some U.S. jails and prisons in response to civil suits filed on behalf of inmates. But she would also know that lawsuits can take years to move through the legal system, that final judgments in particular cases are not reliably predictable, and that official responses in the form of constructive action, such as raising money for salaries and building new facilities, can take even longer than the litigation itself. Thus, she might well conclude that her only choices are to stay with a demoralizing job or to resign in protest, hoping to embarrass her employers into action on behalf of her clients.

When they confront decisions of this kind, professionals are obviously entitled to give careful consideration to their own alternatives for employment. Opportunities are scarce in many fields, including some specialty areas in health care, and it would be both imprudent and morally unnecessary in most circumstances to abandon a professionally unsatisfactory job only to take up an equally compromising appointment elsewhere or to give up professional employment altogether.[14] Furthermore, the interests of present clients or patients must also be taken into account. Will their situations improve as a result of a protest resignation, or are they more likely to receive similar or less competent treatment from replacement personnel? If the resigning practitioner is unlikely to find a better opportunity to exercise her skills elsewhere, or if her clients will not benefit more from her departure than they would from her staying, then her resignation might turn out to be a hollow gesture, personally gratifying, but of no real value otherwise. In professional employment, as elsewhere in the real world, the maintenance of pure principles is a rare luxury, and making the utilitarian best of a bad situation may be the most that can be achieved.

On the other hand, some employment situations compromise professional competence and integrity so seriously that they seem to demand protest resignations regardless of the consequences. As F. H. Bradley wrote many years ago, "Where all is rotten it is a man's work to cry stinking fish."[15] When bad working conditions or the mistaken judgments of employers threaten

---

[14] It is worth noting, however, that commendable prudence in these situations can easily turn into rank self-interest. Many of the federal officials who have resigned over issues of policy and principle in recent administrations have done so very quietly, in order to preserve their own employability as consultants, lobbyists, or officers of corporations involved in government business. For a careful discussion of this matter, see Terry L. Cooper's *The Responsible Administrator* (Port Washington: Kennikat Press, 1982).

[15] F. H. Bradley, *Appearance and Reality: A Metaphysical Essay*, first published in 1893 (Oxford: Clarendon Press, 9th impression, 1959), Preface, p. x.

to prevent practitioners from carrying out their professional responsibilities, they may decide, in Kantian style, that all is indeed rotten and that they have no choice but to cry "stinking fish" by resigning and making the reasons for their resignations clear to the people who might do something about the problems. The psychiatrist in our previous example might find herself in that position with regard to working conditions; and the government lawyers involved in the famous "Saturday Night Massacre" during the Watergate investigation clearly reached the same conclusion as they confronted President Nixon's decision to fire the special prosecutor. Protests of this kind may not eliminate the problems to which they draw attention; but at the very least, they help to preserve or restore the integrity of the protesters. And in this, they have much in common with whistle-blowing.

Whistle-Blowing

Whistle-blowers are people who "go public" with complaints about their employers, notifying law enforcement agencies or providing stories to news reporters in order to force the correction of evils that they perceive in their workplaces. The general idea is that public disclosure will bring about the prosecution of criminal behavior, embarrass managerial wrongdoers into reform, or generate support for needed legislative regulation. And because it exposes colleagues and organizations to general scrutiny, and perhaps to legal action, whistle-blowing is usually a more drastic response to institutional pressures than protest resignation. Employees commonly resign in protest quite inconspicuously, informing only a few involved associates of their real reasons for quitting; but whistle-blowing is by definition a public action, opening the behavior of all involved to examination and reaction from the outside. It is therefore plausibly regarded as an act of betrayal by the people whose activities are publicized, and by much popular sentiment as well. Whistle-blowers are often treated as traitors by their colleagues and by others, because they discard organizational loyalties and violate the principles of team play by striking out on their own against their own.

Yet it seems clear that many instances of whistle-blowing are fully justified or even morally mandatory. Where human safety is at stake, or where large amounts of money are being misused, and when less drastic measures have been tried unsuccessfully or are unavailable, appealing to the police or the press may be the only effective recourse for the concerned observer. In 1967, for example, Kermit Vandivier, a data analyst and technical writer at the B. F. Goodrich Company in Troy, Ohio, blew the whistle on his colleagues and employers over the falsification of testing results concerning a newly designed system of brakes for military aircraft.[16]

As he worked at the routine task of writing an official report on the brakes required by the Air Force, Vandivier discovered that the system had failed all of its tests, but that some of the company's engineers and the plant management were prepared to misrepresent the results of their laboratory studies, certifying the mechanism as safe for production and trials in prototype

---

[16] A full account of this episode is presented in Robert Heilbroner, et al., *In the Name of Profit* (Garden City: Doubleday, 1972).

planes. He and an engineer involved in the testing tried to persuade their colleagues to refrain from submitting the fraudulent report and to redesign the faulty mechanism. But parts were already being shipped to Goodrich by suppliers, a contract deadline was approaching, and both the report and the brakes were sent out on schedule. Eventually, Vandivier notified the FBI, and the mechanisms were replaced, but only after several near crashes during test landings, including one plane skidding 1,500 feet on a locked wheel.

In cases of this kind, it seems clear that whistle-blowers deserve praise as heroes, rather than condemnation as snitches. No doubt they are troublemakers and renegades in the eyes of some of their co-workers. But they are also quite often the only sources of information in situations of danger or large-scale fraud urgently requiring public attention. Furthermore, they usually suffer severe penalties for their actions: They often lose their jobs and are shunned within their own professions. Even where it is illegal to fire them outright, angry employers find ways to make their lives at work so uncomfortable that they eventually resign; and when they do, they find that their reputations have been badly damaged and that no one is willing to hire them. Thus, employees who decide to blow the whistle make extremely difficult and serious choices, weighing their own welfare and ambitions, as well as their professional and organizational loyalties, against public interests in safety and honest business practices. And when they choose correctly, not just airing personal grudges but exposing serious problems, they often make valuable contributions to the well-being of society.

Strikes and Job Actions

Finally, we turn to strikes and other job actions as means of reducing or eliminating institutional pressures. Despite the long history of union-like activities on the part of many professional groups, such as the American Medical Association (AMA) and the American Association of University Professors (AAUP), it was long believed by both practitioners and the public that the withholding of services by professionals constituted unethical behavior. To many, it seemed acceptable for laborers or factory workers, and perhaps even some white-collar employees, to join unions and to engage in slowdowns or strikes in order to improve their wages and working conditions. But professionals, like law enforcement officers and firefighters, were seen as having special obligations to the public because of the importance of their work and the general need for their services, particularly in fields such as health care and education. Furthermore, it was widely believed that marching in the streets with picket signs or making other dramatic displays of grievances would be beneath the dignity and social standing enjoyed by the professions.

More recently, however, the picture has changed considerably. Many have come to see the professional associations as having a great deal more in common with trade unions than was previously admitted; and numerous professionals, most notably school teachers and nurses, have adopted the view that public respect is insufficient compensation for skimpy paychecks and exhausting work loads. Like the police and firefighters, they have claimed that if their services are vital to community interests, the public, either as taxpayers or consumers, should be willing to provide sufficient financial support to ensure adequate salaries, functional facilities, and manageable burdens of responsibility. And where that help has not been forthcoming, they have formed strong unions, like the American Federation of Teachers (AFT), and have forced responses to their complaints by means of work slowdowns and stoppages.

There is no doubt that strikes by professionals are often quite successful in achieving the goals of their organizers. They have reduced the problems of overwork and burnout, increased levels of compensation, and generally improved working conditions in many institutional settings. But it is equally clear that there are costs attached to these victories. If there is a moral basis for the prestige enjoyed by professionals in our society, it is most likely to be found not only in the value of the services performed, but also in the dedication, reliability, and public-mindedness of the providers. And this base is easily eroded. When professionals create the impression that they are willing to assert self-interested claims at the expense of the public good, or that their help is available only at exorbitant cost, they invite mistrust and disapproval by associating their own organizations with the least respected labor unions and political pressure groups. For this reason, practitioners who contemplate withholding their services to improve salaries or working conditions ought to think carefully about both the merits of their causes and the reactions likely to be provoked by their behavior. Strikes, slowdowns, and other job actions may well be appropriate responses to intolerable conditions. But for professionals, they require unusually thorough study of the moral relationships between ends and means, because their effectiveness depends entirely upon the threat of depriving people of needed, and sometimes essential, help.[17]

PROFESSIONALS AS ENTREPRENEURS AND ADMINISTRATORS

We will now look briefly at the other side of the organizational coin, to draw attention to some of the ethical issues professionals encounter as they become owners and managers of businesses. Many of these problems are just the flip sides of matters we have already discussed in connection with professionals as employees. Others arise at the point where business and professional ethics meet, drawn (or pushed) toward each other by the economic and political realities of our time. About the former, we will say little more, other than to make the obvious comment that administrators do well to avoid the development of these problems whenever they can. Instead, we will focus on the latter, noting a few of the particular questions that arise when professionals enter the corporate world as profit seekers.

Ethical questions about reasonable profits and fair returns on investments can, of course, arise whenever someone does unusually well in our market economy. But we ordinarily think that businesspeople deserve substantial rewards when they develop needed products or services and make them available at affordable prices. And we appear not to resent the very high

---

[17] The issues raised here are discussed more fully in Mary Gibson's article later in this chapter.

profits that sometimes accrue to ingenuity, talent, or even sheer luck. Thus, the Japanese who first sold relatively inexpensive automobiles with front-wheel drive in areas of heavy snowfall seemed entitled to the money they made in the process, as did the developers of the low-cost polio vaccines that have saved many millions of children from the threat of a debilitating disease. And few object seriously to the profits made by the manufacturers of fad items, to the high earnings of major league athletes and entertainers, or to the enormous prizes awarded to lottery winners. But when profit-making takes on the aspect of gouging, extortion, or monopolistic control of essential commodities or services, our moral sentiments turn rapidly against the entrepreneurs involved, especially when they are professionals.

Professionals as Businesspeople

The reasons for this special animosity toward profiteering professionals are not difficult to find. One is that, by definition, professionals are highly educated people, in possession of specialized knowledge that is for all practical purposes unavailable to most outsiders. They are thus quite well situated to take unfair advantage of the consumer's ignorance if they are disposed to do so. Another is that practitioner–client relationships are essentially fiduciary in character. The public is encouraged to trust professionals and to rely upon their advice, and guileless clients make especially easy prey for unscrupulous practitioners. A third reason is that professionals are respected and accorded high social and economic status in large part because of their commitment to responsible service and to the well-being of their communities; thus, misdeeds in the form of unethical business practices make them look especially bad. In effect, their power and social standing tend to magnify their offenses in the eyes of both their victims and the public.

It is arguable, of course, that professionals should not be held to higher standards of conduct than other people, that practitioners do not achieve sainthood by earning advanced degrees and becoming members of professional associations, any more than they would by taking golf lessons or joining plumbers' unions. But this line of thinking ignores the considerations, discussed in Chapter 1, that support the assignment of special privileges and responsibilities to the professions in the first place. The point is not that professionals should be saints, unaffected by self-interest or the profit motive, but that they should not exploit the public trust which is invited by their credentials. For if they are unable in general to meet this requirement, and to take appropriate action against those who fail, then they are not entitled to the special status they enjoy.[18]

The evident conclusion is that professionals ought to be meticulous about their activities as businesspeople, avoiding the appearance of misconduct as well as wrongdoing itself. Our economic ideology sanctions and encourages their participation in corporate enterprise, and success in their professional lives often requires that they become effective entrepreneurs. But their

---

[18] Many U.S. attorneys are rightly concerned about the widespread public impression that lawyers are merely legal "guns for hire," available to the highest bidder and uninterested in the merits of the cases they advance. See Wasserstrom, "Lawyers as Professionals," note 2 in this chapter.

positions of trust and power require them to be very cautious in choosing the kinds of business they will conduct, in establishing clienteles and price schedules, and in working out consulting relationships with colleagues. Otherwise, they may find themselves peddling unneeded services to vulnerable buyers at exorbitant cost, and inviting professional and public condemnation of their behavior in the process.

On the other hand, there is no denying that the avoidance of wrongdoing in these matters often requires much more than the resolution not to be avaricious or exploitive. The restrictive licensing requirements in fields such as law, which provide quality assurance to consumers, also motivate the sellers of services to make referrals only to practitioners within closed circles of recognized colleagues, and monopolistic business practices emerge from legislation aimed at protecting the public. Efforts by government agencies and insurance companies to hold down the costs of reimbursed services move providers in the direction of price-fixing. And the widespread availability of lucrative consulting contracts offers powerful inducement to cross the thin line between providing needed expert help and taking advantage of an unsophisticated market. In effect, the complex interactions among the social, economic, legal, and political systems in the United States at present make it very difficult to maintain professional integrity and achieve success in business at the same time.

Consider, for example, Robert Reich's statement that "Two-thirds of all basic research in America . . . is funded by the government, the bulk of it by the Pentagon," and that in 1986, "almost two-thirds of the dollar volume of Pentagon contracts was awarded without competitive bidding."[19] Under these circumstances, if you were a research scientist and one of the principals in an engineering company, it is most likely that the success of your business would depend at least in part, and perhaps entirely, on obtaining government contracts, or on serving as a subcontractor to larger firms engaged in government business. Modern scientific research is generally very expensive; and few organizations other than the government can afford to pay for it, with fewer still being willing to finance basic research without direct commercial applications. Thus, if your company specialized in some highly technical field, such as experimental work on lasers or superconductivity, you might well find the government, either directly or indirectly, to be your only reliable source of corporate income.

This financial dependence would not, of course, be inherently or necessarily corrupt. But it would inevitably give key roles in decision-making about your research projects and goals to government or military officials, who presumably would not share your particular professional ideals. It might very well insulate your firm against the kind of economic competition that can keep businesses operating honestly and efficiently. It might invite the development of an exclusive group of specialist colleagues doing business with you and with one another, and with no outsiders. And, in the worst case, it might move your company toward a mess like the Goodrich scandal discussed earlier. Here as elsewhere, when professionals become businesspeople, they may encounter moral challenges that develop in subtle forms,

---

[19] Robert M. Reich, "Bread and Circuits," in *The New Republic*, August 3, 1987, pp. 33–34.

often without malicious intent or discernible negligence on the part of anyone involved, and frequently under the influence of economic and political forces beyond the control of the practitioner-entrepreneurs who must deal with them.

Hiring and Management

Many large organizations are now managed by administrators who were specifically educated for their institutional roles in colleges of business or public administration, and organizational administration is now widely recognized as a profession in its own right. But there remain significant numbers of upper-level administrators and chief executive officers in both public and private enterprises who were initially trained as professionals in other fields and who continue to see themselves as practitioners in those areas. There are many engineers, for example, who head their own corporations. There are physicians who own clinics or direct public health services. And more often than not, the deans and presidents of universities and colleges are specialists in traditional academic disciplines, rather than educational administration. Thus, the practice of wearing two professional hats continues, even though its popularity may be waning. The ethical problems of professionals who engage in such practices deserve our attention, because the interests of efficiency in management quite commonly conflict with accepted standards of professional service.

Apart from the administrative sides of issues discussed earlier, such as gatekeeping, burnout, and job actions, the main focus of interest here is the delegation of responsibility to apprentices, paraprofessionals, and other subordinate personnel. For obvious reasons of economy, it is often attractive to assign work traditionally done by professionals to employees with less education or experience and hence lower rates of pay. Senior partners in large law firms hire fledgling associates to carry out research and write briefs for them. Overworked social service agencies hire intake workers to conduct initial interviews with clients. And physicians employ clinical assistants and nurse practitioners to take case histories and to perform routine diagnostic work.

These practices may benefit both employers and clients by helping to control costs and (because junior staff members are often newly trained) by making the most current knowledge available at the point of service delivery. But anyone who has suffered through a university course badly conducted by an inept teaching assistant will recognize the pitfalls of this kind of arrangement. Novices are by definition short on experience, and may be immature in judgment as well. Semiprofessionals may not feel the same levels of commitment to individual clients as traditional practitioners would, because the clients are not ultimately their own. And it is often not evident that the savings achieved through the employment of paraprofessionals are actually passed along to the clients who pay the bills. On the contrary, patients and clients may well find themselves paying higher and higher fees for services that they perceive, rightly or not, to be decreasing in quality and increasing in impersonality.

These considerations draw attention once again to the fiduciary character of professional relationships, showing the need for a morally suitable balance between the efficiencies of the division of labor and the requirements of conscientious, individualized service. The delegation of routine responsibilities to paraprofessionals and other support personnel is now and will continue to be an essential strategy for cost containment, especially in the healthcare industry, which is presently consuming more than 11 percent of the U.S. gross national product. But administrators who are professionals are not at liberty simply to adopt production line techniques in order to control costs. Nor can they be excused for low-quality work performed by their employees. For they are not simply business managers concerned with organizational economy and productivity. As professionals, they also have obligations, often of surpassing importance, to the individual clients who trust them to provide services that meet or exceed accepted standards of practice.

The practitioner-administrator thus has special responsibility for quality assurance in the hiring, deployment, and supervision of paraprofessionals. If there are ample funds available for salaries and benefits, these responsibilities need not be burdensome, since thoroughly trained and competent paraprofessional help is often readily available. They become onerous, however, when budgets are limited and supervisors are tempted to hire underqualified people and then demand too much of them. But in either case, as long as the authority exercised by paraprofessionals is delegated to them by others, accountability for their performance ultimately rests with the professionals who employ them.

Malpractice Avoidance

In August, 1987, Lee Iacocca, the celebrated chairman of the Chrysler Corporation, warned the ABA at its convention in San Francisco that U.S. industry is losing ground in its competition with foreign producers because of the nationwide fear of liability suits filed by consumers and others.[20] He argued that the United States has become so litigious, with people looking for "deep pockets" and then suing one another at every imaginable opportunity, that industrial production is being made inefficient and innovation is being stifled by managerial efforts to avoid lawsuits. In effect, he claimed, we are diminishing our capacity for successfully carrying on the nation's business by devoting more and more of our effort and energy to protecting ourselves from tort liability.

Some find this grim view of the legal system and the danger of lawsuits to be much exaggerated, since the actual success rates and final awards in our civil court procedures are much lower than the more spectacular news stories might lead us to believe. Nevertheless, it is clear that the fear of lawsuits is intense and widespread in the United States at present, especially among professionals, and that individuals and institutions everywhere are engaging in "conservative practice" and other defensive measures in the hope of staying out of the courts. Physicians now prescribe extra tests and consult

---

[20] Lee Iacocca's speech was reported by United Press International in the *Salt Lake Tribune,* August 11, 1987, p. B8.

specialists to corroborate their diagnoses, teachers exercise new caution in advising and disciplining their students, and social workers take extra measures to guard the confidentiality and other legal interests of their clients, all in order to protect themselves and their organizations against legal attack.

In many cases, of course, these strategies benefit the recipients of professional services, in addition to protecting providers, by safeguarding important rights and diminishing negligence in practice. However, there is also a downside for everyone involved. Beyond the skyrocketing costs of malpractice insurance, which are driving some practitioners out of business and substantially increasing the fees charged by others, "conservative practice" often means the proliferation of expensive and unnecessary services, hesitation where decisive action is required, and the unavailability of help for people with significant needs. Obstetricians, for example, are strongly inclined to order complex fetal monitoring even in apparently normal deliveries, and they almost universally insist upon Caesarean sections when fetuses are in breech position, for fear of the lawsuits that follow the births of damaged infants. The threat of parental retaliation sometimes prevents teachers from exercising firm control over their classes, and frequently from providing realistic advice on such urgent but controversial matters as human sexuality. And social workers often find themselves handicapped in their efforts to assist mentally ill street people by their agencies' unwillingness to assume legal responsibility for their actions.

In this tense atmosphere, professionals who are administrators or entrepreneurs are once again required to strike a delicate moral balance, this time between the avoidance of unnecessary risks and their duties to their clients. Except in the most unusual circumstances, no one has an obligation to jeopardize his own or his organization's financial welfare by violating civil law or deviating from well-established standards of practice. But the offering of professional help by individuals or agencies establishes a reasonable expectation that the proffered services will be performed efficiently and in good faith, with assistance to clients, rather than the evasion of liability, as the principal objective. Even if it is true that every client is a potential legal opponent, professional strategies should not emphasize defense at the expense of effectiveness. Nor should they impose gratuitous expenses on consumers or their insurers for services performed exclusively, or even primarily, for the protection of the providers. Given the realities of our legal and political system, the assumption of some risk is an inevitable element of any situation in which significant help is made available to people with real needs. The trick, obviously, is to exercise the kind of courage that strikes the Aristotelian mean between rashness and timidity in particular cases, to discriminate between unnecessary and inescapable risks in the avoidance of malpractice litigation.

INTERACTIONS AMONG PROFESSIONALS

Finally we turn to ethical issues concerning the relationships among professionals working together in multidisciplinary organizations, or sharing responsibility in joint projects and programs. Here, as elsewhere, we find that ideals of moral cooperation are difficult to realize in practice, and that when groups must make decisions, individual members are often hard pressed to maintain their own professional standards. In theory, it might appear that practitioners of differing specialities should be able to agree with one another about means as well as ends, since all are committed to lofty principles of service to their clients. In fact, however, professionals are no more immune than anyone else to the divisive influences of self-interest, differences in social status, and the desire to protect established territory; and their interactions are often further complicated by deeply divergent opinions about the value and significance of one another's work. Thus, while it may be granted that shared responsibility is sometimes comfortingly diminished responsibility, this thought does little to solve the real problems of professionally conscientious individuals working in group settings.

Consulting

Especially in large and complex operations, the need for interprofessional consultations grows as dependence upon specialists increases. No single person or small group can deal effectively with all the intricacies involved in conducting a naval operation, designing and producing a line of automobiles, or running a major foreign aid program. It is thus imperative that experts be consulted, that specialized needs and concerns be taken seriously into account, and that balanced decisions be reached before action is taken. Otherwise, success becomes a matter of luck, and failure the more likely outcome. Indeed, it seems almost self-evident that the open exchange of professionally qualified ideas and opinions is a *sine qua non* of favorable results for any technologically complicated enterprise.

Yet there is no denying that people who work in large institutional settings have strong motives for guarding their own positions, for promoting the views of like-minded colleagues, for avoiding the exposure of their own mistakes and uncertainties, and thus for limiting open consultation with experts. Particularly in organizations that are structured along rigidly hierarchical lines, as many churches and the armed forces are, senior officials tend to isolate themselves in order not to appear weak or indecisive, and junior employees maintain diplomatic silence as a means of protecting their jobs and careers. Vertical communication through organizational ranks is thus restricted by the insecurities of both those who need sound advice and those who have the knowledge necessary for providing it.

Furthermore, comparable constraints impede horizontal exchanges of information across disciplinary and divisional lines. The destructive rivalries among the several branches of the military services are notorious, as are the hostilities between physicians and lawyers, and between faculty members in the sciences and the humanities in many universities. In all these cases, competition among disciplines and the desire to preserve and expand professional turf and prestige inhibit free and open critical thinking and discussion. And when territorial jealousies limit or prevent consultation in this way, both practitioners and their clients lose the potential benefits of shared expertise.

Finally, it is worth mentioning the problem of the professional consultant as "hired gun." During recent decades, consulting itself has become a significant industry in the United States, with government officials, business executives, military officers, and university scholars retiring from their traditional occupations to become members of think tanks, political lobbies, and consulting firms. Many of these consultants perform valuable and honorable services, using their experience and expertise to help in planning and carrying out worthwhile public and private enterprises. But others become intellectual hacks, selling their skills and professional status to anyone willing to pay their substantial fees. Their kind of consulting constitutes unprofessional conduct, because, like the provision of unnecessary medical services mentioned earlier, it violates the trust accorded to the professions, and because the research upon which it is based tends to be carried out with little regard for the truth.[21]

To avoid these pitfalls, professionals need only to exercise the virtues of courage, honesty, and open-mindedness. But as usual, this advice is much more easily given than acted upon. When we discussed conflicts of judgment, we mentioned that recently developed styles of management and techniques for arriving at consensus are proving to be quite helpful in resolving disagreements within organizations. The same approaches can assist in the encouragement of free and open consultation among professional colleagues of differing backgrounds and ranks. If it is possible to create an atmosphere in which people are not fearful of displaying uncertainty or admitting mistakes, and if respect for alternative approaches is actively promoted as policy, many of the consulting problems we have noted can be prevented. Admittedly, the adoption of such new strategies and attitudes can itself be a difficult task, especially where traditional management styles and pecking orders are firmly established. But professionals do well to participate constructively in making these changes before their integrity as practitioners is threatened.

Authority and Compliance

In many institutional settings, professionals working together in single fields experience problems similar to those involved in consulting over matters relating to rank and authority. Most conspicuously in the military, but in other fields as well, rank has its privilege, and junior team members are routinely expected to defer to seniority. Presumably, the idea is that experience, maturity, and recognized accomplishment deserve respect and the status of leadership, while youth and inexperience need steady and sober direction. Thus, senior members of law firms, surgical services, research teams, and ecclesiastical establishments routinely hold primary responsibility for the assignment of work to their younger colleagues, and for the supervision and evaluation of their efforts. And until the junior practitioners have attained some seniority themselves, even their continuation in employment is likely to depend upon the approval of these superiors.

The obvious difficulty with such arrangements is that senior standing can mask inflexibility and diminished competence. People with long records of success in established patterns of decision and action may find it difficult

---

[21] For a discussion of this development, see "The Washington Intellectual," by Jefferson Morley, in *The New Republic*, August 11 and 18, 1986, pp. 10–15.

to entertain novel ideas, and impossible to adopt new techniques. For young professionals, trained, as we have so often noted, in autonomous judgment and schooled in the most recent developments in their fields, this kind of situation can be both psychologically frustrating and morally problematic. Stupid or inept orders are difficult to obey; and when mistakes can cause real damage, it may be obligatory to raise loud objections or to reject them.

On the other hand, it is also clear that immaturity and misguided zeal can masquerade as youth and enthusiasm. Newcomers are often severely critical of established patterns that they fail to understand completely, and novelty can appeal even when it carries no credible promise of real improvement. History and folklore are full of stories about foolish instructions being carried out at great cost by slavishly obedient subordinates; but there are surely as many horrific tales of immature judgment and enthusiasm leading to disaster.

The appropriate conclusion may be that age and experience create a moral presumption in favor of senior authority, but that these considerations are defeasible by compelling evidence of negligence, incompetence, or malicious intent. Ideally, disagreements about instructions and compliance among professionals should be settled by mutually respectful negotiation. When such resolutions are not possible, however, practitioners may rightly turn to the other measures discussed earlier under the heading of "Responses to Institutional Pressures."

Conflicts Among Professional Goals

Our final concern about the ethics of interactions among professionals has to do with commitments to mutually incompatible objectives. In journalism, for example, the requirements of editorial accuracy and thoroughness frequently clash with the need to publish or broadcast quickly and in ways that attract attention. In battlefield medicine, the goals of patient care can conflict with the strategic imperative to return soldiers to duty as quickly as possible. And in colleges and universities, research and teaching, both very labor-intensive when they are done well, often draw faculty time and energy in opposing directions. All these situations clearly call for compromises, but in specific actual cases, it is difficult to find a middle ground without abandoning professional integrity along the way.

One approach begins by evaluating the general value of the enterprise itself and the moral significance of one's own involvement in it. If the overall goals of the operation are of surpassing importance, compromised practices may be acceptable, however regrettably, in order to achieve those ends. But if there is no overriding value at stake, reductions in standards are much harder to justify. Consider, for example, the difference between sending a wounded soldier back into battle and sending an injured athlete out to play football. In the first case, if the cause of war were just and if fighting personnel were urgently needed, a conscientious physician might patch the soldier up as much as possible and send him out to fight. But if the same physician found herself treating a serious athletic injury during a game, she would more likely refuse to do any patching up, because there would be no life-or-death justification for doing only part of her job and for risking further damage to her patient. If the game were critically important to the player involved, he might not see things her way, and it would clearly be his right to reject treatment. But in the imagined circumstances, she would be under no obligation to lower her standard of care.

Cases like these show that ends can indeed justify means—up to a point. There are situations, however, in which utilitarian calculations about the values of results are defeated by deontological standards of professional integrity. We have talked about some of these before in connection with such problems as gatekeeping, overwork, and burnout. If conflicts among goals become so pressing that the practitioner begins to feel that he is not really doing the work for which he was educated, it is time to look for a way out. When the journalist suspects that she is turning into an entertainer, or the professor senses that his teaching and research are both deteriorating in quality, the compromise may have extended too far. In the end, here as elsewhere, the individual may have to weigh personal, professional, and institutional obligations against one another in order to arrive at a balanced judgment.

CONCLUSION

We noted at the outset that professionals working in groups, rather than in solo practice, seem to be the wave of the future. Thus the familiar values of professional ethics, so commonly worked out in reference to individuals functioning with a high degree of autonomy, must be revised to accommodate the exigencies of group practice and corporate life. If the material in this chapter is considered in the light of the ideas about professionals and role morality developed in Chapter 1, as well as the traditional conceptions of practitioner–client relationships in Chapter 2, it can provide a useful base for the larger questions of social, economic, and political policy which are the concerns of Chapters 4 and 5.

CORPORATE GOALS AND INDIVIDUAL VALUES I

John Ladd

In this well-known discussion, the author argues on conceptual grounds that the rational pursuit of organizational objectives inevitably generates conflict with the moral values of individuals working in corporate settings. By drawing attention to the systematic aspects of this situation, Ladd helps us to understand the general nature of the ethical predicaments encountered by professional employees.

I. Introductory

The purpose of this paper is to explore some of the moral problems that arise out of the interrelationships between individuals and formal organizations (or bureaucracies) in our society. In particular, I shall be concerned with the moral implications of the so-called ideal of rationality of formal organizations with regard to, on the one hand, the obligations of individuals both inside and outside an organization to that organization and, on the other hand, the moral responsibilities of organizations to individuals and to the public at large. I shall argue that certain facets of the organizational ideal are incompatible with the ordinary principles of morality and that the dilemma created by this incompatibility is one source of alienation in our contemporary, industrial society. The very conception of a formal organization or bureaucracy presents us with an ideological challenge that desperately needs to be met in some way or other.

The term "formal organization" will be used in a more or less technical sense to cover all sorts of bureaucracies, private and public. A distinctive mark of such organizations is that they make a clear-cut distinction between the acts and relationships of individuals in their official capacity within the organization and in their private capacity. Decisions of individual decision-makers in an organization are attributed to the organization and not to the individual. In that sense, they are impersonal.

Individual office-holders are in principle replaceable by other individuals without affecting the continuity or identity of the organization. In this sense, it has sometimes been said that an organization is "immortal."

This kind of impersonality, in particular, the substitutability of individuals, is one way in which formal organizations differ from other kinds of social systems, e.g. the family, the community or the nation, which are collectivities that are dependent for their existence on specific individuals or groups of specific individuals and that change when they change.

Under formal organizations I shall include not only all sorts of industrial, military and governmental bureaucracies but also formal organizations like large universities (multiversities), hospitals, labor unions, and political machines. For our purposes, we may even include illegal and undercover organizations like the Mafia, the Communist party, the FBI, and the CIA. One of the distinctive features of formal organizations of the type we are interested in is that they are ordinarily hierarchical in structure; they not only have a "horizontal" division of labor but a "vertical" one as well.

There is good reason for choosing the ethics of formal organizations as a subject for philosophical inquiry, for many of the older and traditional issues of political philosophy, e.g. those relating to authority, obedience, welfare, and justice, have now turned into issues involving the relation-

From John Ladd, "Morality and the Ideal of Rationality in Formal Organizations," *The Monist* 54:4 (Oct. 1970), pp. 488–516. Reprinted by permission.

ship of individuals to formal organizations and of formal organizations to society. Formal organizations of all types have in fact come to dominate our individual and social life in a way that was earlier thought to characterize only the state. The extraordinary growth in power, scope, and complexity of large formal organizations requires us to revamp, e.g. the traditional question of the freedom of the individual. Traditional political theory conceived of authority and responsibility as more or less concentrated in one sovereign power, but now we have a new problem that comes from the fact that through formal organizations, authority and responsibility have become quite diffused. As a result the "point of contact" between the individual and the powers that be can hardly be ascertained, for indeed there is no such point; our contact with formal organizations, their power and authority over us is continuous and blurred.

It is not my purpose here to decry once more the unhappy condition of man occasioned by his submergence as an individual in the vast social, economic and political processes created by formal organizations. Instead, I shall try to show that the kind of alienation that we all feel and complain about is, at least in part, a logical necessity flowing from the concept of formal organizations itself, that is, it is a logical consequence of the particular language-game one is playing in organizational decision-making. My analysis is intended to be a logical analysis, but one that also has important ethical implications.

Here we may find the concept of a language-game, as advanced by Wittgenstein and others, a useful tool of analysis. The point about a language-game is that it emphasizes the way language and action are interwoven. A language-game is thus more than simply an abstract set of propositions constituting, say, a formal system. The game not only determines what should and what should not be done, but also sets forth the goals and the moves by which they are to be attained. More important even than

these, a particular language-game determines how the activities within it are to be conceptualized, prescribed, justified and evaluated. Take as an example what is meant by a "good" move in chess: we have to refer to the rules of chess to determine what a "move" is, how to make one, what its consequences will be, what its objective is and whether or not it is a good move in the light of this objective. Finally, this system of rules performs the logical function of defining the game itself.

One advantage of the language-game model is, therefore, that it enables us to describe a kind of activity by reference to a set of rules that determine not only what should or should not be done, but also how what is done is to be rationally evaluated and defended. And it allows us to describe the activity without reference to moral rules (or norms). In other words, it provides us with a method of analyzing a rational activity without committing ourselves to whether or not it is also moral.

If we pursue the game-analogy one step further, we find that there may be even more striking similarities between the language-game of formal organizations and the language-game of other types of games. For instance, the rules and rationale obtaining in most typical games like chess and baseball tend to make the activity logically autonomous, i.e. the moves, defenses and evaluations are made independently of external considerations. In this sense they are self-contained. Furthermore, while playing a game it is thought to be "unfair" to challenge the rules. Sometimes it is even maintained that any questioning of the rules is unintelligible. In any case, there is a kind of sanctity attached to the rules of a game that renders them immune to criticism on the part of those engaged in playing the game. The resemblance of the autonomy of the activity and the immunity of the rules governing the game to the operations of bureaucracies can hardly be coincidental.

II. The Concept of Social Decision and Social Action

Let us take as our point of departure Herbert Simon's definition of a formal organization as a "decision-making structure."[1] The central concept with which we must deal is that of a decision (or action) that is attributable to the organization rather than to the individuals who are actually involved in the decisional process. The decision is regarded as the organization's decision even though it is made by certain individuals acting as its representatives. The latter make the decision only for and on behalf of the organization. Their role is, i.e. is supposed to be, impersonal. Such nonindividual decisions will be called *social decisions,* choices or actions.

When the official decides for the organization, his aim is (or should be) to implement the objectives of the organization *impersonally,* as it were. The decisions are made for the organization, with a view to its objectives and not on the basis of the personal interests or convictions of the individual official who makes the decision. This is the theory of organizational decision-making.

One might be tempted to call such organizational decisions "collective decisions," but that would be a misnomer if we take a collective decision to be a decision made by a collection of individuals. Social decisions are precisely decisions (or actions) that are to be *attributed* to the organizations themselves and not to collections of individuals. In practice, of course, the organizational decisions made by officials may actually be collective decisions. But in theory the two must be kept separate; for the "logic" of decisions attributed to organizations is critically different from the "logic" of collective decisions, i.e. those attributed to a collection of individuals.

Underlying the concept of social decisions (choices, actions) as outlined here is the notion that a person (or group of persons) can make decisions that are not his, i.e. are not attributable to him. He makes the decisions on behalf of someone else and with a view to the latter's interest, not his own. In such cases, we ordinarily consider the person (or group) that acts to be a representative or agent of the person or thing he is acting for.

A social decision, as intended here, would be an action performed by an official as actor but owned by the organization as author. For all the consequences of the decision so made are imputed to the organization and not to the individual decision-maker. The individual decision-making official is not personally bound by the agreements he makes for the organization, nor is he personally responsible for the results of these decisions.

The theory of social decision-making that we are considering becomes even clearer if we examine the theory of organizational authority with which it is conjoined. Formal organizations are hierarchical in structure, that is, they are organized along the principle that superiors issue commands to those below them. The superior exercises authority over the subordinates.

In terms of the model I suggested earlier, this principle is part of the language-game; it is a logical requirement of the game, regardless of whether or not it actually corresponds to empirical reality. Furthermore, we may extend the notion of abdication of choice even further, to the hierarchy as a whole, for the authority of the superior official is itself based on his "abdication of choice" in favor of the social decisions of the organization. These social decisions are, strictly speaking, not his; they are not "owned" by him.

We now turn to another essential facet of the organizational language-game, namely, that every formal organization must have a goal, or a set of goals. In fact, organizations are differentiated and defined by reference to their aims or goals, e.g. the aim of the Internal Revenue Service is to collect taxes. The goal of most

---

[1] Herbert A. Simon, *Administrative Behavior,* 2nd ed. (New York: Free Press, 1965), p. 9.

business ventures is to maximize profits, etc. We may find it useful to distinguish between the real and stated goals of an organization. Thus, as Galbraith has pointed out, although the stated goal of large industrial organizations is the maximization of profits, that is a pure myth; their actual, operative goals are the securing of their own survival, autonomy and economic growth.[2]

For our present purposes, we may consider the real goal of an organization to be that objective (or set of objectives) that is used as a basis for decision-making, i.e. for prescribing and justifying the actions and decisions of the organization itself, as distinct from the actions and decisions of individual persons within the organization. As such, then, the goal is an essential element in the language-game of a formal organization's activities in somewhat the same way as the goal of checkmating the king is an essential element in the game of chess.

The logical function of the goal in the organizational language-game is to supply the value premises to be used in making decisions, justifying and evaluating them.

It follows that any considerations that are not related to the aims or goals of the organization are automatically excluded as irrelevant to the organizational decision-making process. This principle of the exclusion of the irrelevant is part of the language-game. It is a logical requirement of the process of prescribing, justifying and evaluating social decisions. Consequently, apart from purely legal considerations, decisions and actions of individual officers that are unrelated to the organization's aims or goals are construed, instead, as actions of those individuals rather than of the organization. If an individual official makes a mistake or does something that fails to satisfy this criterion of social decision, he will be said to have "exceeded his authority," and will probably be sacked

or made a vice-president! Again, the point is a logical one, namely, that only those actions that are related to the goal of the organization are to be attributed to the organization; those actions that are inconsistent with it are attributed to the individual officers as individuals. The individual, rather than the organization, is then forced to take the blame for whatever evil results.

Thus, for example, a naval officer who runs his ship aground is court-martialed because what he did was inconsistent with the aims of the naval organization; the action is attributed to him rather than to the Navy. On the other hand, an officer who successfully bombards a village, killing all of its inhabitants, in accordance with the objectives of his organization, is performing a social action, an action that is attributable to the organization and not to him as an individual. Whether or not the organization should take responsibility in a particular case for the mistakes of its officials is a policy decision to be made in the light of the objectives of the organization.

In other words, the concept of a social decision or action is bound up logically with the notion of an organizational aim. The consequence of this co-implication of action and aim is that the notion of an action or decision taken by an organization that is not related to one of its aims makes no sense. It is an unintelligible notion within the language-game of formal organizations. Within that language-game such an action would be as difficult to understand as it would be to understand how a man's knocking over the pieces in a chess game can be part of playing chess.

We finally come to the concept of "rationality." From the preceding observations concerning the organizational language-game, it should be clear that the sole standard for the evaluation of an organization, its activities and its decisions, is its effectiveness in achieving its objectives—within the framework of existing conditions and available means. This kind

[2] See John Kenneth Galbraith, *The New Industrial State* (Boston: Houghton Mifflin, 1967), pp. 171–78.

of effectiveness is called "rationality." Thus, rationality is defined in terms of the category of means and ends.

"Rationality," so construed, is relative, that is, to be rational means to be efficient in pursuing a desired goal, whatever that might be. "Rationality" is an incomplete term that requires reference to a goal before it is completely intelligible. Despite asseverations to the contrary, these analyses are not ethically neutral, much less "value-free."

Let us return to the organizational language-game. It was observed that within that game the sole standard of evaluation of, e.g. a decision, is the "rational" one, namely, that it be effective in achieving the organization's goal. Hence, any considerations that are taken into account in deliberation about these social decisions and in the evaluation of them are relevant only if they are related to the attainment of the organization's objectives. Let us suppose that there are certain factual conditions that must be considered in arriving at a decision, e.g. the available means, costs and conditions of feasibility. The determination of such conditions is presumably a matter of empirical knowledge and a subject for empirical investigation. Among these empirical conditions there is a special class that I shall call *limiting operating conditions*. These are conditions that set the upper limits to an organization's operations, e.g. the scarcity of resources, of equipment, of trained personnel, legal restrictions, factors involving employee morale. Such conditions must be taken into account as *data*, so to speak, in organizational decision-making and planning. In this respect information about them is on a par logically with other information utilized in decision-making, e.g. cost–benefit computations.

Now the only way that moral considerations could be relevant to the operations of a formal organization in the language-game that I have been describing is by becoming limiting operating conditions. Strictly speaking, they could not even be introduced as such, because morality is it-

self not a matter of empirical knowledge. Insofar as morality in the strict sense enters into practical reasoning it must do so as an "ethical" premise, not as an empirical one. Hence morality as such must be excluded as irrelevant in organizational decision-making—by the rules of the language-game. The situation is somewhat parallel to the language-game used in playing chess: moral considerations are not relevant to the decisions about what move to make there either.

Morality enters in only indirectly, namely, as moral opinion, what John Austin calls "positive morality."[3] Obviously the positive morality, laws and customs of the society in which the organization operates must be taken into account in decision-making and planning. The same thing goes for the religious beliefs and practices of the community. A decision-maker cannot ignore them, and it makes no difference whether he shares them or accepts them himself personally. But the determination of whether or not there are such limiting conditions set by positive morality, customs, law, and religion is an empirical matter. Whether there are such limitations is simply a matter of fact and their relevance to the decision-making is entirely dependent upon how they affect the efficiency of the organization's operations.

Social decisions, then, are not and cannot be governed by the principles of morality, or, if one wishes, they are governed by a different set of moral principles from those governing the conduct of individuals as individuals. For, as Simon says: "Decisions in private management, like decisions in public management, must take as their ethical premises the objectives that have

---

[3] "The name *morality*, when standing unqualified or alone, may signify the human laws which I style positive morality, without regard to their goodness or badness. For example, such laws of the class as are peculiar to a given age, or such laws of the class as are peculiar to a given nation, we style the morality of that given age or nation, whether we think them good or bad, etc." John Austin, *Province of Jurisprudence Determined*, H.L.A. Hart, ed. (New York: Noonday Press, 1954), p. 125. The study of positive moralities belongs to what I call "descriptive ethics." See my *Structure of a Moral Code* (Cambridge, Mass: Harvard University Press, 1957).

been set for the organization."[4] By implication, they cannot take their ethical premises from the principles of morality.

Thus, for logical reasons it is improper to expect organizational conduct to conform to the ordinary principles of morality. We cannot and must not expect formal organizations, or their representatives acting in their official capacities, to be honest, courageous, considerate, sympathetic, or to have any kind of moral integrity. Such concepts are not in the vocabulary, so to speak, of the organizational language-game. (We do not find them in the vocabulary of chess either!) Actions that are wrong by ordinary moral standards are not so for organizations; indeed, they may often be required. Secrecy, espionage and deception do not make organizational action wrong; rather they are right, proper and, indeed, *rational,* if they serve the objectives of the organization. They are no more or no less wrong than, say bluffing is in poker. From the point of view of organizational decision-making they are "ethically neutral."

Of course, I do not want to deny that it may be in the best interests of a formal organization to pay lip service to popular morality (and religion). That is a matter of public relations. But public relations operations themselves are evaluated and justified on the same basis as the other operations of the organization. The official function of the public relations officer is to facilitate the operations of the organization, not to promote morality.

Therefore, if one expects social decisions to conform to the principles of morality, he is simply committing a logical mistake, perhaps even what Ryle calls a category mistake. In a sense, as we shall see, organizations are like machines, and it would be a category mistake to expect a machine to comply with the principles of morality. By the same token, an official or agent of a formal organization is simply violating the basic rules of organizational activity if he allows his moral scruples rather than the objectives of the organization to determine his decision. In particular, he is violating the rule of administrative impartiality, that is, the rule that administrative officials "faithfully execute policies of which they personally disapprove."[5]

Once again, it should be observed that the conclusions reached here relate only to the ideal-type, the theory of "how an organization should be constructed and operated in order to accomplish its work efficiently," that is, to what is essentially a normative order consisting of a set of non-moral rules of conduct. It is unnecessary to point out that in actual fact many organizations fail to approximate the ideal outlined here. Nevertheless, it is important to recognize that this ideal makes demands and claims on our conduct if we are involved in the operations of formal organizations. And it is used to justify them.

The upshot of our discussion so far is that actions are subject to two entirely different and, at times, incompatible standards: social decisions are subject to the standard of rational efficiency (utility) whereas the actions of individuals as such are subject to the ordinary standards of morality. An action that is right from the point of view of one of these standards may be wrong from the point of view of the other. Indeed, it is safe to say that our own experience attests to the fact that our actual expectations and social approvals are to a large extent based on a tacit acceptance of a double-standard—one for the individual when he is in his office working for the company and another for him when he is at home among friends and neighbors. Take as an example the matter of lying: nobody would think of condemning Joe X, a movie star, for lying on a TV commercial about what brand of cigarettes he smokes, for it is part of his job. On the other hand, if he were to do the same thing in private among friends, we should consider his ac-

---

[4] Simon, *Administrative Behavior,* p. 52.

[5] Reinhard Bendix, "Bureaucracy and the Problem of Power," in Robert Merton and others, *Reader in Bureaucracy* (New York: Free Press, 1952), p. 132.

tion to be improper and immoral.

The pervasiveness of organizational activity throughout modern society makes the impact of this double-standard on the individual particularly unsettling. It produces a kind of moral schizophrenia which has affected us all. Furthermore, the dilemma in which we find ourselves cannot so easily be conjured away; for it has its logical ground as well as basis in the dynamics of social structure.

III. The Moral Relationship of Individuals to Organizations

It follows from what has already been said that the standard governing an individual's relationship to an organization is likely to be different from the one governing the converse relationship, i.e. of an organization to individuals. The individual, for his part, is supposed to conduct himself in his relationship to an organization according to the same standards that he would employ in his personal relationships, i.e. the standards of ordinary morality. Thus, he is expected to be honest, open, respectful, conscientious, and loyal towards the organization of which he is a member or with which he has dealings. The organization, represented by its officials, can, however, be none of these in return.

The question I now want to explore is whether or not the individual is justified in applying the standard of individual morality to his relations with formal organizations. It will, of course, generally be in the interest of the formal organizations themselves to encourage him to do so, e.g. to be honest, although the organization as such cannot "reciprocate." But we must ask this question from the point of view of the individual or, if you wish, from the moral point of view: What good moral reasons can be given for an individual to assume a moral stance in his conduct and relations with formal organizations, in contradistinction, say, to his conduct and relations with individuals who happen to be employees of such an organization?

The problem, which may be regarded as a question of loyalty and fidelity, puts the age-old problem of authority and obedience in a new light. Authority has become diffused, as I have already pointed out, and the problem of obedience can no longer be treated in terms of the personal relationship of an individual to his sovereign lord. The problem today is not so easily focused on one relationship; for the demands of authority, as represented in modern organizations, are at once more extensive, more pervasive and less personal. The question we face today is, for example, why should I, as an individual, comply with the mass of regulations laid down by an impersonal order, a bureaucratic organization? Why, for example, should I comply with income-tax requirements? with mortgage, credit, licensing, fair-trade regulations or with anti-trust laws?

It might be thought that, before trying to answer such questions, we must be careful to distinguish between individuals within an organization, e.g. officials and employees, and those outside it who have dealings with it, e.g. clients and the general public: what each of these classes ought to do is different. Granting that the specific demands placed on individuals in these various categories may be quite different, they all involve the question of authority in one way or another. Hence, for our purposes, the distinction is unimportant. For example, the authority, or the claims to it, of governmental bureaucracies extends far beyond those who are actually in their employ, e.g. the Internal Revenue Service. For convenience, I shall call those who come under the authority of an organization in some capacity or other, directly or indirectly, the *subjects* of the organization. Thus, we are all subjects of the IRS.

Can any moral reasons be given why individual subjects should comply with the decisions of organizations? Or, what amounts to the same thing, what is the basis of the authority of organizations by virtue of which we have an obligation to accept and obey their directives? And why, if at all, do we owe them loyalty and fidelity?

The most obvious answer, although perhaps not the most satisfactory one ethically, is that it is generally expedient for the individual to go along with what is required by formal organizations. If I want a new automobile, I have to comply with the financing requirements. If I want to avoid being harassed by an internal revenue agent, I make out my income tax form properly.

Still, this sort of answer is just as unsatisfactory from the point of view of moral philosophy as the same kind of answer always has been with regard to political obligation, namely, it fails to meet the challenge of the conscientious objector.

Furthermore, there are many occasions and even whole areas where self-interest is not immediately or obviously involved in which, nevertheless, it makes good sense to ask: Why comply? The traditional Lockian argument that our acceptance of the benefits of part of the social and political order commits us morally to the acceptance and conformity with the rest of it rests on the dubious assumption that the social and political order is all of one piece, a seamless web. But when we apply the argument to formal organizations it becomes especially implausible, because there are so many competing claims and conflicting regulations, not to mention loyalties. Not only logically, but as a matter of practicality, it seems obvious that accepting the benefits of one bureaucratic procedure, e.g. mailing letters, does not, from the moral point of view, *eo ipso* bind us to accept and comply with all the other regulations and procedures laid down by the formal organization and, much less, those laid down by formal organizations in general.

Some of the traditional answers to the problem of political obligation might possibly be relevant to our questions about how we should relate to formal organizations. For example, we could try a contractarian, a utilitarian or a "general will" kind of argument. Although all three of

these have some initial plausibility, on closer inspection we will find, I think, that none of them will do; either they have no application whatsoever to organizations or else they are not specific enough for particular organizations.

Let us begin with the suggestion that our relations with formal organizations are based upon compacts of one sort or another. (I use the term "compact" to indicate that we are talking about a morally binding agreement as distinct from one that is merely legally binding, i.e. a contract.) It seems natural to suppose that we bind ourselves to organizations through agreements, tacit or explicit, of one sort or another. But if we distinguish between a moral agreement, which establishes mutual moral obligations, and a legal agreement, which establishes only legal obligations, it will be evident from what I have said earlier that it is impossible to make a compact with an organization. (Could we make a compact with a machine?) A compact is a bilateral promise and hence a compact can be made only between beings that are capable of making promises. But a formal organization cannot make promises, for it cannot bind itself to a performance that might conflict with the pursuit of its goal. The principle of rationality, as applied to formal organizations, makes no provision for the principle that promises ought to be kept; indeed, if the keeping of promises, or of a particular promise, is inconsistent with the goals of the organization, that principle requires that they be broken.

In sum, we cannot make compacts with organizations because the standard of conduct which requires that promises be honored is that of individual conduct.[6] It does not and cannot apply to formal organizations. This follows from the fact of a double standard.

The utilitarian answer to our question, like its ancestor the utilitarian theory of

---

[6] The fact that promising involves an extremely personal relation between individuals is almost universally overlooked by philosophers who discuss promises.

political obligation, maintains that somehow or other an individual act of compliance with the established order inevitably contributes to the stability of the whole system, whereas an individual act of defiance inevitably contributes to its instability. There is, it appears, no empirical evidence to support the contention that an individual act will strengthen or weaken the system. Nor is there any reason to suppose that the preserving of the status quo is either necessary or sufficient for promoting the public interest. In view of the complexity of the impact of modern social and political organizations on society, it is difficult, if not impossible, to accept a utilitarian argument as the basis of an individual's obligation towards formal organizations.

Finally, we come to those arguments that appeal to some sort of common interest or identity of goals as the basis of the authority of organizations over the individual. On this view, the goals of formal organizations are identified with the goals of its individual members, taken collectively perhaps. Galbraith, in *The New Industrial State,* refers to this as the "principle of consistency": "There must be a consistency in the goals of society, the organization and the individual."[7] He assumes that, in many cases at least, the objectives of all three are basically the same, their goal is the same, e.g. a rising standard of living. To serve the organization is to serve one's own goals and the goals of society.

So construed, the principle of consistency represents a value-judgment. It places a premium on the sharing of goals, no matter what these goals might be. But, as I have already argued at some length, the standards of individual moral conduct and of rational organizational activity are so completely different that a collision between them is inevitable. The only way

that the predicated consistency could be secured is for the individual to give up his own moral principles and adopt the goals of the organization as his own.

In the final analysis perhaps the most plausible basis of the authority of formal organizations, or at least within formal organizations, is the Platonic one, namely, that the commands of officials should be complied with because they have superior knowledge. The superiors, like the guardians in Plato's *Republic,* are experts; they have the expertise that the subordinates do not possess but need in order to act effectively. That much of the authority relationship within military and industrial organizations is founded on expert-know-how or alleged know-how is unquestionable. Many organizations, however, (e.g. the public bureaucracies) make decisions that are not based upon superior knowledge, but involve the same kind of information and knowledge that is available to the general public, and in particular, to many individuals outside the organization.

The breakdown of the argument from superior expertise is due no doubt to advances in technology, mass education and mass communication. More information of a higher quality is available to large numbers of people who are simply subjects and do not have command positions within the bureaucracies to which they are subject. It is too easy to see through the claims to superior knowledge when we also have some knowledge of our own about what is going on.

I have been able to touch only on some very limited aspects of the relationship of individuals to organizations. I hope, however, that it is now abundantly clear that some sort of crisis is taking place in our moral relationships, and in particular in our conceptions of authority, and that this crisis is due not only to complex historical, psychological and sociological factors, but also to an inherent *logical* paradox in the foundations of our social relations.

---

[7] Galbraith, *The New Industrial State,* p. 159.

CORPORATE GOALS AND INDIVIDUAL VALUES II*

Richard J. Boland

Attacking one of the fundamental claims of Ladd's argument, Boland denies that large organizations are in fact governed by coherent sets of objectives and strategies. He then offers some suggestions about the protection of professional standards in corporate employment, presenting a more optimistic picture than the one we found in our first selection.

Those concerned with professional ethics are also interested in the design of organizational control systems. For them, a well-controlled organization would be one in which the ethical concerns of its members were identified, analyzed and acted upon in a rational, coherent way. De George, for instance, has voiced the proposition that organizations should be designed so engineers do not need to be moral heroes.[1] He desires the restructuring of organizations to include control mechanisms for bringing to the surface and resolving significant ethical problems that may be experienced by its engineers.

Westin's recent collection of case studies on whistle-blowers concludes with this same theme.[2] The mechanisms that are proposed include statements of organizational principles and policies; procedures for filing complaints of possible violations; an impartial, thorough method for conducting investigations; use of fair-hearing procedures; and an objective decision-making process. A strong ombudsman program would be a companion measure to these formal procedures. It is possible that these recommendations could provide valuable and needed improvements in the function-ing of a large organization. However, it is important to realize the limitations of these methods of organizational control and the resulting implications for the ethically concerned professional.

The discipline of management has been working on the design of improved systems of organizational control throughout this century. Recent developments in mathematical modeling and computer technology have accelerated this effort in management system design. These attempts to improve organizational control through the design of improved management systems use an underlying image of control similar to that used by De George, Westin and others. It is a cybernetic image in which communication channels feed information about an error condition back to a central decision-maker for an error-correcting response.

In a cybernetic control process, sensors report local conditions to a central source where they are compared to a standard. Deviations from the standard become error signals that are fed back to decision-making and action-taking components for error correction. This is a very powerful, flexible image of control: the components can include automatic devices or human beings in any appropriate mix, and the system allows for learning through trial and error.

[1] Richard T. De George, "Ethical Responsibilities of Engineers in Large Organizations: The Pinto Case," *Business and Professional Ethics Journal*, 1:1 (Fall 1981), pp. 1–14.

[2] Alan F. Westin, *Whistle-Blowing: Loyalty and Dissent in the Corporation* (New York: McGraw-Hill, 1981).

* Some references have been deleted without indication.

From Richard J. Boland, Jr., "Organizational Control, Organizational Power, and Professional Responsibility," in *Business and Professional Ethics Journal* 2:1 (Fall 1982): pp. 15–25.

Yet, as powerful, flexible and appealing as this image is, management system designers have not experienced the successes they had hoped for. While some improvements have been made, many systems are designed and developed but never successfully implemented or used. Others have too infrequently delivered the improved organization control that was promised during their design.

The cybernetic image of control is, in turn, based on an unstated assumption of a coherently rational process that is of central importance to these suggestions for improved organizational control systems. Management system designs and the structural reforms proposed by Westin and others are based on a rational-bureaucratic ideal of organizations. The organization is pictured as purposive, directed from the top by a series of commands to subordinates. It is imagined that functional units are coordinated in an integrated fashion. Standard operating procedures, clearly defined decision-making responsibilities and feedback control systems to handle exceptions are the vehicles for implementing this coherent management process.

The important failing of the rational-bureaucratic image is its assumption that a coherent vision of the organization is used by management to establish priorities and to make key decisions. In short, organizations are assumed to be guided by managers who know what they are doing and where they are going, and reveal it through planning.[3] Planning is seen as a forward

looking, intentional process in which goals are defined, alternatives are examined, and courses of action are chosen based on the highest return to the organization.

There may be some conflict among managers and some decisions may be politically based; but essentially, we assume there is a logical coherence to the organization's activities that emanates from its center of management control. We assume that those higher up on the management ladder see a bigger picture, reconcile competing claims and values, and responsibly choose a direction for the future. The feedback mechanisms of the cybernetic control process are intended to ensure that higher management has all the relevant data in exercising its coherent understanding and making management decisions.

De George, for instance, reviewed the responsibility of the Ford engineers in the Pinto gas tank decision and concluded that their ethical responsibility was met by providing complete and objective data to top management decision-makers. Once the data had been provided, the valuing of alternative courses of action was a management decision, not an engineering decision. The decision made by the Ford executives might have been a good or bad business decision, but the engineer is not morally responsible for it.

A rational-bureaucratic image of Ford is important to De George's conclusion. If no one in Ford's management actually made any decisions relevant to the Pinto gas tank, if managers who claimed to make such decisions instead engaged in aimless, wandering conversations, or if they routinely ignored critical data presented to them, De George could not so easily dismiss the engineer's responsibility. De George and Westin are not isolated instances. Designers of computer-based and other management systems have also relied primarily on an image of the management process as being comprehensive, coherent, intentional and rational. However, the experience of failures and unmet expectations with these

[3] Even Herbert Simon's Neo-Weberian formulation that recognizes the bounded rationality of humans and the procedural rather than substantive rationality of organizations ultimately rests on the assumption of a coherent managerial vision "at the top." For him organizational control becomes the problem of designing a vocabulary and reward system that will shape the premises of the decision-making by organization members. The objective is for each decision-maker to "see the proper thing in the proper light." Still, the manager, as designer of these attention-directing mechanisms for subordinates, is assumed to possess a coherent vision of the whole—a special comprehension denied to others in the organization. For the best summary of his position, see James G. March and Herbert A. Simon, *Organizations* (New York: John Wiley & Sons, Inc., 1958).

management control systems suggests that the use of a rational-bureaucratic image to guide their design is often mistaken.

II

The image of organizations as coherently rational is widely shared in modern society, almost to the point of being modern mythology of organizations. Yet, no matter how firm its ideological foundations, it is more a flattery to managements than a defensible statement of what organizations are like. When we look at more recent developments in the theory of organizations, we see a movement away from the rational-bureaucratic image. Field research that observes management decision-making in action reveals a much more chaotic, much less coherent process than we so often imagine.

Groups have power not because their understanding of the organization is coherent, complete or wise, but because they control a resource seen as critical to its continued functioning. Control over funds, markets, labor, supplies or information can all be sources of power, depending on the nature of the environment. What is seen as critical is primarily socially defined.

We see, for example, that the backgrounds of company presidents change over time as the critical factors in the environment change. In the period from 1940 through 1960, we saw engineering as the predominant background; from 1960 through 1970 it was marketing that provided presidential training; and from 1970 on, the emphasis has been on financial backgrounds for corporate leaders. These changes in both leadership emphasis and in ways of seeing the organization's problems result from the struggle of power groups within the organization, in light of a cultural image of rational management.

Power is not an aberration in organizations, but is a natural consequence of their structure with its specialization and limited communication. Similarly, competing centers of power are not a problem to be corrected. Rather, the responsible exercise of power by various groups within the organization is part of a necessary process of aligning the organization with the appropriate factors, resources, opportunities and constraints of its environment. The need for the responsible development and exercise of power, *in addition* to the establishment of feedback control mechanisms, is the central point of this paper.

III

What can professionals do? First, they can realize that the exception-based feedback control mechanisms so often suggested are nice, but will not solve the problems they experience. Professionals are inspired by a fantasy of rational management that has little relation to real organizations. Second, they can accept the responsibility to develop and exercise power within the organizations so they can affect the quality of dialogue and the ways of defining situations that emerge from power struggles.

To use engineering as an example, it has a wide-spread impact on the critical needs of innovation, productivity and regulatory requirements. Thus, it has control over resources that should be an important base of power. In addition, engineers have many characteristics that tend to enhance power in organizations. They are professionals with their own language, experts with control over secrets useful to others. The work of an engineer is hard to evaluate, especially by the uninitiated. Finally, in one form or another, engineers have control over information that others in the organization need, and they are in a position to create a sense of obligation in others for sharing that information.

Engineers can be the source of their own undoing by failing to take advantage of their potential for developing a power center in the organization. To the extent that they allow their work to be proceduralized and routinized, they lose the basis for developing power. To the extent that they allow themselves to be physically isolated, with limited reporting status, they lose the possibility of developing power. If they allow a narrow definition of their task and responsibilities to be imposed on their work, they further lose power. And if they allow the organization to use outside consultants for nonroutine problems on a regular basis, they will have little left in the way of a power base.

In order to effectively develop and exercise power, engineers in organizations can take several positive steps. First, they must establish themselves as participants in as wide a range of activities within the organization as possible. They should increasingly insist on the use of teams in which engineers can play key liaison roles linking different departments together in a common problem focus. They should insist on having participation in these problem-solving teams from the initial stages of a decision process through its final conclusion.

Engineers should work to develop an effective network of peer communication throughout the organization in order to avoid physical isolation from one another and to create opportunities for meeting on a regular basis to discuss common concerns and develop positions with respect to those concerns. Finally, engineers must learn to use their unique control over the critical resources of information and innovation to establish their agenda and concerns as an integral part of the organization's dialogue on its problems. At times, this might require holding back certain projects or analyses; at other times, it may mean sharing their influence to support another group which will later be in a position to reciprocate.

For engineers who would seek to increase their power within organizations, perhaps the most important lesson to learn is that change in organizations is most frequently and effectively instituted by external pressures, not by internal deliberation. It is here that the engineer is in a very strong position to develop external contacts who will share their definition of the organizations' problems and will work to shape the external environment, and thereby, the forces for change being placed on the organization.

Engineers make a mistake if they agree to the frequently cited claim that an employee must first and foremost recognize the organization's right to privacy and must exhaust appropriate organizational channels before sharing troublesome information with outside parties. Quite the contrary, concerned engineers enhance their ability to control the dialogue of management if they can have their views incorporated into the set of external pressures being put on the organization by legislatures, regulatory agencies, customers, suppliers, and special interest groups.

The idea that a coherent management vision serves as a basis for rational decision-making is undoubtedly tempting for professionals in large organizations. It could provide a plausible basis for restricting one's own managerial inner-sanctum with coherent knowledge, it is but a short step to the belief that the coherent understanding of those "up there" in management is a more valid and reliable basis for decision-making than one's own.

Unfortunately for the weak-hearted, what we imagine to be a coherent management process is a shifting, incoherent dialogue among partial, resource-based centers of power. The erratic quarrels of these competing voices in the struggle for power is as close to a managerial "understanding of the situation" that can be hoped for in an organization of any size and complexity.

Professionals cannot relinquish responsibility for an organization's use of their data in decision-making processes. Unless they are seduced by the fantasy of a coherent, rational management, they must take responsibility not only for the generation of valid data but also for the disjointed process of its use in incremental decisions. They cannot make the management process coherent or reliable. They can only hope to include their interests in its quarreling.

The feedback control systems that have been suggested can help. But, it is necessary that professionals also accept responsibility for full participation in the power struggle that lies behind the facade of coherent management. Failing to do so only means they fall prey to another, even more disturbing fantasy—that of their own innocence.

AN ENGINEERING DISASTER: THE PINTO CASE*

Richard T. De George

Ford Pinto automobiles manufactured between 1971 and 1977 were built with a design flaw that caused a number of the cars to explode in flames in rear-end collisions. This situation resulted in many lawsuits, including one in which the Ford Motor Corporation itself was charged with homicide. De George made a thorough study of the records of these cases and here offers a careful analysis of the ethical positions of the Ford engineers.

The myth that ethics has no place in engineering has been attacked, and at least in some corners of the engineering profession has been put to rest. Another myth, however, is emerging to take its place— the myth of the engineer as moral hero. A litany of engineering saints is slowly taking form. The saints of the field are whistle blowers, especially those who have sacrificed all for their moral convictions. The zeal of some preachers, however, has gone too far, piling moral responsibility upon moral responsibility on the shoulders of the engineer. This emphasis, I believe, is misplaced. Though engineers are members of a profession that holds public safety paramount,† we cannot reasonably expect engineers to be willing to sacrifice their jobs each day for principle and to have a

whistle ever by their sides ready to blow if their firm strays from what they perceive to be the morally right course of action. If this is too much to ask, however, what then is the actual ethical responsibility of engineers in a large organization?

I shall approach this question through a discussion of what has become known as the Pinto case.

In August 1978 near Goshen, Indiana, three girls died of burns in a 1973 Pinto that was rammed in traffic by a van. The rear-end collapsed "like an accordion," and the gas tank erupted in flames. It was not the first such accident with the Pinto. The Pinto was introduced in 1971 and its gas tank housing was not changed until the 1977 model. Between 1971 and 1978 about fifty suits were brought against Ford in connection with rear-end accidents in the Pinto.

What made the Winamac case different from the fifty others was the fact that the

---

* Some references have been deleted without indication.

† For a sample code of ethics for engineers, see Appendix II in this book.

From Richard T. De George, "Ethical Responsibilities of Engineers in Large Organizations: The Pinto Case," *Business and Professional Ethics Journal* 1:1 (Fall 1981): pp. 1–14.

State prosecutor charged Ford with three (originally four, but one was dropped) counts of reckless homicide, a *criminal* offense, under a 1977 Indiana law that made it possible to bring such criminal charges against a corporation. The penalty, if found guilty, was a maximum fine of $10,000 for each count, for a total of $30,000. The case was closely watched, since it was the first time in recent history that a corporation was charged with this criminal offense. Ford spent almost a million dollars in its defense.

With the advantage of hindsight I believe the case raised the right issue at the wrong time.

The prosecution had to show that Ford was reckless in placing the gas tank where and how it did. In order to show this the prosecution had to prove that Ford consciously disregarded harm it might cause and the disregard, according to the statutory definition of "reckless," had to involve "substantial deviation from acceptable standards of conduct."

The prosecution produced seven witnesses who testified that the Pinto was moving at speeds judged to be between 15 and 35 mph when it was hit. Harly Copp, once a high ranking Ford engineer, claimed that the Pinto did not have a balanced design and that for cost reasons the gas tank could withstand only a 20 mph impact without leaking and exploding. The prosecutor, Michael Cosentino, tried to introduce evidence that Ford knew the defects of the gas tank, that its executives knew that a $6.65 part would have made the car considerably safer, and that they decided against the change in order to increase their profits.

Federal safety standards for gas tanks were not introduced until 1977. Once introduced, the National Highway Traffic Safety Administration (NHTSA) claimed a safety defect existed in the gas tanks of Pintos produced from 1971 to 1976. It ordered that Ford recall 1.9 million Pintos. Ford contested the order. Then, without

ever admitting that the fuel tank was unsafe, it "voluntarily" ordered a recall. It claimed the recall was not for safety but for "reputational" reasons. Agreeing to a recall in June, its first proposed modifications failed the safety standards tests, and it added a second protective shield to meet safety standards. It did not send out recall notices until August 22. The accident in question took place on August 10. The prosecutor claimed that Ford knew its fuel tank was dangerous as early as 1971 and that it did not make any changes until the 1977 model. It also knew in June of 1978 that its fuel tank did not meet federal safety standards; yet it did nothing to warn owners of this fact. Hence, the prosecution contended, Ford was guilty of reckless homicide.

The defense produced testimony from two witnesses who were crucial to the case. They were hospital attendants who had spoken with the driver of the Pinto at the hospital before she died. They claimed she had stated that she had just had her car filled with gas. She had been in a hurry and had left the gas station without replacing the cap on her gas tank. It fell off the top of her car as she drove down the highway. She noticed this and stopped to turn around to pick it up. While stopped, her car was hit by the van. The testimony indicated that the car was stopped. If the car was hit by a van going 50 mph, then the rupture of the gas tank was to be expected. If the cap was off the fuel tank, leakage would be more than otherwise. No small vehicle was made to withstand such impact. Hence, Ford claimed, there was no recklessness involved.

The jury deliberated for four days and finally came up with a verdict of not guilty. When the verdict was announced at a meeting of the Ford Board of Directors then taking place, the members broke out in a cheer.

These are the facts of the case. I do not wish to second-guess the jury. Based on my reading of the case, I think they arrived at a proper decision, given the evidence. Nor do I wish to comment adversely on the judge's ruling that prevented the prosecution from introducing about 40% of his case because the evidence referred to 1971 and 1972 models of the Pinto and not the 1973 model.

The issue of Ford's being guilty of acting recklessly can, I think, be made plausible, as I shall indicate shortly. But the successful strategy argued by the defense in this case hinged on the Pinto in question being hit by a van at 50 mph. At that speed, the defense successfully argued, the gas tank of any subcompact would rupture. Hence that accident did not show that the Pinto was less safe than other subcompacts or that Ford acted recklessly. To show that would require an accident that took place at no more than 20 mph.

The contents of the Ford documents that Prosecutor Cosentino was not allowed to present in court were published in the *Chicago Tribune* on October 13, 1979. If they are accurate, they tend to show grounds for the charge of recklessness.

Ford had produced a safe gas tank mounted over the rear axle in its 1969 Capri in Europe. It tested that tank in the Capri. In its over-the-axle position, it withstood impacts of up to 30 mph. Mounted behind the axle, it was punctured by projecting bolts when hit from the rear at 20 mph. A $6.65 part would help make the tank safer. In its 1971 Pinto, Ford chose to place the gas tank behind the rear axle without the extra part. A Ford memo indicates that in this position the Pinto has more trunk space, and that production costs would be less than in the over-the-axle position. These considerations won out.

The Pinto was first tested it seems in 1971, after the 1971 model was produced, for rear-end crash tolerance. It was found that the tank ruptured when hit from the rear at 20 mph. This should have been no surprise, since the Capri tank in that position had ruptured at 20 mph. A memo recommends that rather than making any

changes Ford should wait until 1976 when the government was expected to introduce fuel tank standards. By delaying making any change, Ford could save $20.9 million, since the change would average about $10 per car.

In the Winamac case Ford claimed correctly that there were no federal safety standards in 1973. But it defended itself against recklessness by claiming its car was comparable to other subcompacts at that time. All the defense showed, however, was that all the subcompacts were unsafe when hit at 50 mph. Since the other subcompacts were not forced to recall their cars in 1978, there is *prima facie* evidence that Ford's Pinto gas tank mounting was substandard. The Ford documents tend to show Ford knew the danger it was inflicting on Ford owners; yet it did nothing, for profit reasons. How short-sighted those reasons were is demonstrated by the fact that the Pinto thus far in litigation and recalls alone has cost Ford $50 million. Some forty suits are still to be settled. And these figures do not take into account the loss of sales due to bad publicity.

Given these facts, what are we to say about the Ford engineers? Where were they when all this was going on, and what is their responsibility for the Pinto? The answer, I suggest, is that they were where they were supposed to be, doing what they were supposed to be doing. They were performing tests, designing the Pinto, making reports. But do they have no moral responsibility for the products they design? What after all is the moral responsibility of engineers in a large corporation? By way of reply, let me emphasize that no engineer can morally do what is immoral. If commanded to do what he should not morally do, he must resist and refuse. But in the Ford Pinto situation no engineer was told to produce a gas tank that would explode and kill people. The engineers were not instructed to make an unsafe car. They were morally responsible for knowing the state of the art, including that connected with placing and mounting gas tanks. We can assume that the Ford engineers were cognizant of the state of the art in producing the model they did. When tests were made in 1970 and 1971, and a memo was written stating that a $6.65 modification could make the gas tank safer, that was an engineering assessment. Whichever engineer proposed the modification and initiated the memo acted ethically in doing so. The next step, the administrative decision not to make the modification was, with hindsight, a poor one in almost every way. It ended up costing Ford a great deal more not to put in the part than it would have cost to put it in. Ford still claims today that its gas tank was as safe as the accepted standards of the industry at that time. It must say so, otherwise the suits pending against it will skyrocket. That it was not as safe seems borne out by the fact that only the Pinto of all the subcompacts failed to pass the 30 mph rear impact NHTSA test.

But the question of wrongdoing or of malicious intent or of recklessness is not so easily solved. Suppose the ordinary person were told when buying a Pinto that if he paid an extra $6.65 he could increase the safety of the vehicle so that it could withstand a 30 mph rear-end impact rather than a 20 mph impact, and that the odds of suffering a rear-end impact of between 20 and 30 mph was 1 in 250,000. Would we call him or her reckless if he or she declined to pay the extra $6.65? I am not sure how to answer that question. Was it reckless of Ford to wish to save the $6.65 per car and increase the risk for the consumer? Here I am inclined to be clearer in my own mind. If I choose to take a risk to save $6.65, it is my risk and my $6.65. But if Ford saves the $6.65 and I take the risk, then I clearly lose. Does Ford have the right to do that without informing me, if the going standard of safety of subcompacts is safety in a rear-end collision up to 30 mph? I think not. I admit, however, that the case is not clear-cut, even if we

add that during 1976 and 1977 Pintos suffered 13 fiery fatal rear-end collisions, more than double that of other U.S. comparable cars. The VW Rabbit and Toyota Corolla suffered none.

Yet, if we are to morally fault anyone for the decision not to add the part, we would censure not the Ford engineers but the Ford executives, because it was not an engineering but an executive decision.

My reason for taking this view is that an engineer cannot be expected and cannot have the responsibility to second-guess managerial decisions. He is responsible for bringing the facts to the attention of those who need them to make decisions. But the input of engineers is only one of many factors that go to make up managerial decisions. During the trial, the defense called as a witness Francis Olsen, the assistant chief engineer in charge of design at Ford, who testified that he bought a 1973 Pinto for his eighteen-year-old daughter, kept it a year, and then traded it in for a 1974 Pinto which he kept two years. His testimony and his actions were presented as an indication that the Ford engineers had confidence in the Pinto's safety. At least this one had enough confidence in it to give it to his daughter. Some engineers at Ford may have felt that the car could have been safer. But this is true of almost every automobile. Engineers in large firms have an ethical responsibility to do their jobs as best they can, to report their observations about safety and improvement of safety to management. But they do not have the obligation to insist that their perceptions or their standards be accepted. They are not paid to do that, they are not expected to do that, and they have no moral or ethical obligation to do that.

In addition to doing their jobs, engineers can plausibly be said to have an obligation of loyalty to their employers, and firms have a right to a certain amount of confidentiality concerning their internal operations. At the same time engineers are required by their professional ethical codes to hold the safety of the public paramount. Where these obligations conflict, the need for and justification of whistle blowing arises. If we admit the obligations on both sides, I would suggest as a rule of thumb that engineers and other workers in a large corporation are morally *permitted* to go public with information about the safety of a product if the following conditions are met.

1. If the harm that will be done by the product to the public is serious and considerable;
2. If they make their concerns known to their superiors; and
3. If, getting no satisfaction from their immediate superiors, they exhaust the channels available within the corporation, including going to the board of directors.

If they still get no action, I believe they are morally *permitted* to make public their views; but they are not morally *obliged* to do so. Harly Copp, a former Ford executive and engineer, in fact did criticize the Pinto from the start and testified for the prosecution against Ford at the Winamac trial. He left the company and voiced his criticism. The criticism was taken up by Ralph Nader and others. In the long run it led to the Winamac trial and probably helped in a number of other suits filed against Ford. Though I admire Mr. Copp for his actions, assuming they were done from moral motives, I do not think such action was morally required, nor do I think the other engineers at Ford were morally deficient in not doing likewise.

For an engineer to have a moral *obligation* to bring his case for safety to the public, I think two other conditions have to be fulfilled, in addition to the three mentioned above.

4. He must have documented evidence that would convince a reasonable, impartial observer that his view of the situation is correct and the company policy wrong.

Such evidence is obviously very difficult to obtain and produce. Such evidence, however, takes an engineer's concern out of the realm of the subjective and precludes that concern from being simply one person's opinion based on a limited point of view. Unless such evidence is available, there is little likelihood that the concerned engineer's view will win the day simply by public exposure. If the testimony of Francis Olsen is accurate, then even among the engineers at Ford there was disagreement about the safety of the Pinto.

5. There must be strong evidence that making the information public will in fact prevent the threatened serious harm.

This means both that going public the engineer should know what source (government, newspaper, columnist, TV reporter) will make use of his evidence and how it will be handled. He should also have good reason to believe that it will result in the kind of change or result that he believes is morally appropriate. None of this was the case in the Pinto situation. After much public discussion, five model years, and failure to pass national safety standards tests, Ford plausibly defends its original claim that the gas tank was acceptably safe. If there is little likelihood of his success, there is no moral obligation for the engineer to go public. For the harm he or she personally incurs is not offset by the good such action achieves.

My first substantive conclusion is that Ford engineers had no moral *obligation* to do more than they did in this case.

My second claim is that though engineers in large organizations should have a say in setting safety standards and producing cost–benefit analyses, they need not have the last word. My reasons are two. First, while the degree of risk, e.g., in a car, is an engineering problem, the acceptability of risk is not. Second, an engineering cost–benefit analysis does not include all the factors appropriate in making a policy decision, either on the corporate or the social level. Safety is one factor in an engineering design. Yet clearly it is only one factor. A Mercedes-Benz 280 is presumably safer than a Ford Pinto. But the difference in price is considerable. To make a Pinto as safe as a Mercedes it would probably have to cost a comparable amount. In making cars as in making many other objects some balance has to be reached between safety and cost. The final decision on where to draw the balance is not only an engineering decision. It is also a managerial decision, and probably even more appropriately a social decision.

The difficulty of setting standards raises two pertinent issues. The first concerns federal safety standards. The second concerns cost–benefit analyses. The state of the art of engineering technology determines a floor below which no manufacturer should ethically go. Whether the Pinto fell below that floor, we have already seen, is a controverted question. If the cost of achieving greater safety is considerable— and I do not think $6.65 is considerable— there is a built-in temptation for a producer to skimp more than he should and more than he might like. The best way to remove that temptation is for there to be a national set of standards. Engineers can determine what the state of the art is, what is possible, and what the cost of producing safety is. A panel of informed people, not necessarily engineers, should decide what is acceptable risk and hence what acceptable minimum standards are. Both the minimum standards and the standards attained by a given car should be a matter of record that goes with each car. A safer car may well cost more. But unless a customer knows how much safety he is buying for his money, he may not know which car he wants to buy. This information, I believe, is information a car buyer is entitled to have.

In 1978, after the publicity that Ford received with the Pinto and the controversy surrounding it, the sales of Pintos fell dramatically. This was an indication that consumers preferred a safer car for comparable money, and they went to the competition. The state of Oregon took all

its Pintos out of its fleet and sold them off. To the surprise of one dealer involved in selling turned-in Pintos, they went for between $1,000 and $1,800. The conclusion we correctly draw is that there was a market for a car with a dubious safety record even though the price was much lower than for safer cars and lower than Ford's manufacturing price.

The second issue is the way cost–benefit analyses are produced and used. I have already mentioned one cost–benefit analysis used by Ford, namely, the projection that by not adding a part and by placing the gas tank in the rear the company could save $20.9 million. The projection, I noted, was grossly mistaken for it did not consider litigation, recalls, and bad publicity which have already cost Ford over $50 million. A second type of cost–benefit analysis sometimes estimates the number and costs of suits that will have to be paid, adds to it fines, and deducts that total amount from the total saved by a particular practice. If the figure is positive, it is more profitable not to make a safety change than to make it.

A third type of cost–benefit analysis, which Ford and other auto companies produce, estimates the cost and benefits of specific changes in their automobiles. One study, for instance, deals with the cost–benefit analysis relating to fuel leakage associated with static rollover. The unit cost of the part is $11. If that is included in 12.5 million cars, the total cost is $137 million. That part will prevent 180 burn deaths, 180 serious burn injuries and 2100 burned vehicles. Assigning a cost of $200,000 per death, $67,000 per major injury, and $700 per vehicle, the benefit is $49.5 million. The cost–benefit ratio is slightly over 3–1.

If this analysis is compared with a similar cost–benefit analysis for a rear-end collision, it is possible to see how much safety is achieved per dollar spent. This use is legitimate and helpful. But the procedure is open to very serious criticism if used not in a comparative but in an absolute manner.

The analysis ignores many factors, such as the human suffering of the victim and of his or her family. It equates human life to $200,000, which is based on average lost future wages. Any figure here is questionable, except for comparative purposes, in which case as long as the same figure is used it does not change the information as to relative benefit per dollar. The ratio, however, has no *absolute* meaning, and no decision can properly be based on the fact that the resulting ratio of cost to benefit in the above example is 3 to 1. Even more important, how can this figure or ratio be compared with the cost of styling? Should the $11 per unit to reduce death and injury from roll-over be weighed against a comparable $11 in rear-end collision or $11 in changed styling? Who decides how much more to put into safety and how much more to put into styling? What is the rationale for the decision?

In the past consumers have not been given an opportunity to vote on the matter. The automobile industry has decided what will sell and what will not, and has decided how much to put on safety. American car dealers have not typically put much emphasis on safety features in selling their cars. The assumption that American drivers are more interested in styling than safety is a decision that has been made for them, not by them. Engineers can and do play an important role in making cost–benefit analyses. They are better equipped than anyone else to figure risks and cost. But they are not better equipped to figure the acceptability of risk, or the amount that people should be willing to pay to eliminate such risk. Neither, however, are the managers of automobile corporations. The amount of acceptable risk is a public decision that can and should be made by representatives of the public or by the public itself.

Since cost–benefit analyses of the types I have mentioned are typical of those used in the auto industry, and since they are inadequate ways of judging the safety a car should have, given the state of the art, it is clear that the automobile companies should not have the last word or the exclusive word in how much safety to provide. There must be national standards set and enforced. The National Highway Traffic Administration was established in 1966 to set standards. Thus far only two major standards have been established and implemented: the 1972 side impact standard and the 1977 gasoline tank safety standard. Rather than dictate standards, however, in which process it is subject to lobbying, it can mandate minimum standards and also require auto manufacturers to inform the public about the safety quotient of each car, just as it now requires each car to specify the miles per gallon it is capable of achieving. Such an approach would put the onus for the basic safety on the manufacturers, but it would also make additional safety a feature of consumer interest and competition.

Engineers in large corporations have an important role to play. That role, however, is not usually to set policy or to decide on the acceptability of risk. Their knowledge and expertise are important both to the companies for which they work and to the public. But they are not morally responsible for policies and decisions beyond their competence and control. Does this view, however, let engineers off the moral hook too easily?

To return briefly to the Pinto story once more, Ford wanted a subcompact to fend off the competition of Japanese imports. The order came down to produce a car of 2,000 pounds or less that would cost $2000 or less in time for the 1971 model. This allowed only 25 months instead of the usual 43 months for design and production of a new car. The engineers were squeezed from the start. Perhaps this is why they did not test the gas tank for rear-end collision impact until the car was produced.

Should the engineers have refused the order to produce the car in 25 months? Should they have resigned, or leaked the story to the newspapers? Should they have refused to speed up their usual routine? Should they have complained to their professional society that they were being asked to do the impossible—if it were to be done right? I am not in a position to say what they should have done. But with the advantage of hindsight, I suggest we should ask not only what they should have done. We should especially ask what changes can be made to prevent engineers from being squeezed in this way in the future.

Engineering ethics should not take as its goal the producing of moral heroes. Rather it should consider what forces operate to encourage engineers to act as they feel they should not; what structural or other features of a large corporation squeeze them until their consciences hurt? Those features should then be examined, evaluated, and changes proposed and made. Lobbying by engineering organizations would be appropriate, and legislation should be passed if necessary. In general I tend to favor voluntary means where possible. But where that is utopian, then legislation is a necessary alternative.

The need for whistle blowing in a firm indicates that a change is necessary. How can we preclude the necessity for blowing the whistle?

The Winamac Pinto case suggests some external and internal modifications. It was the first case to be tried under a 1977 Indiana law making it possible to try corporations as well as individuals for the criminal offenses of reckless homicide. In bringing the charges against Ford, Prosecutor Michael Cosentino acted courageously, even if it turned out to have been a poor case for such a precedent-setting trial. But the law concerning reckless homicide, for instance, which was the charge in question, had not been rewritten with the corporation in mind. The penalty, since

corporations cannot go to jail, was the maximum fine of $10,000 per count—hardly a significant amount when contrasted with the 1977 income of Ford International which was $11.1 billion in revenues and $750 million in profits. What Mr. Cosentino did *not* do was file charges against individuals in the Ford Company who were responsible for the decisions he claimed were reckless. Had highly placed officials been charged, the message would have gotten through to management across the country that individuals cannot hide behind corporate shields in their decisions if they are indeed reckless, put too low a price on life and human suffering, and sacrifice it too cheaply for profits.

A bill was recently proposed in Congress requiring managers to disclose the existence of life-threatening defects to the appropriate Federal agency. Failure to do so and attempts to conceal defects could result in fines of $50,000 or imprisonment for a minimum of two years, or both. The fine in corporate terms is negligible. But imprisonment for members of management is not.

Some argue that increased litigation for product liability is the way to get results in safety. Heavy damages yield quicker changes than criminal proceedings. Ford agreed to the Pinto recall shortly after a California jury awarded damages of $127.8 million after a youth was burned over 95 percent of his body. Later the sum was reduced, on appeal, to $6.3 million. But the criminal proceedings make the litigation easier, which is why Ford spent $1,000,000 in its defense to avoid paying $30,000 in fines. The possibility of going to jail for one's actions, however, should have a salutary effect. If someone, the president of a company in default of anyone else, were to be charged in criminal suit, presidents would soon know whom they can and should hold responsible below them. One of the difficulties in a large corporation is knowing who is responsible for particular decisions. If the president were held responsible, outside pressure would build to recognize the corporation so that responsibility was assigned and assumed.

If a corporation wishes to be moral or if society or engineers wish to apply pressure for organizational changes such that the corporation acts morally and responds to the moral conscience of engineers and others within the organization, then changes must be made. Unless those at the top set a moral tone, unless they insist on moral conduct, unless they punish immoral conduct and reward moral conduct, the corporation will function without considering the morality of questions and of corporate actions. It may by accident rather than by intent avoid immoral actions, though in the long run this is unlikely.

Ford's management was interested only in meeting federal standards and having these as low as possible. Individual federal standards should be both developed and enforced. Federal fines for violations should not be token but comparable to damages paid in civil suits and should be paid to all those suffering damage from violations.

Independent engineers or engineering societies—if the latter are not co-opted by auto manufacturers—can play a significant role in supplying information on the state of the art and the level of technical feasibility available. They can also develop the safety index I suggested earlier, which would represent the relative and comparative safety of an automobile. Competition has worked successfully in many areas. Why not in the area of safety? Engineers who work for auto manufacturers will then have to make and report the results of standard tests such as the ability to withstand rear-end impact. If such information is required data for a safety index to be affixed to the windshield of each new car, engineers will not be squeezed by management in the area of safety.

The means by which engineers with ethical concerns can get a fair hearing without endangering their jobs or blowing the whistle must be made part of a corporation's organizational structure. An outside board member with primary responsibility for investigating and responding to such ethical concerns might be legally required. When this is joined with the legislation pending in Congress which I mentioned, the dynamics for ethics in the organization will be significantly improved. Another way of achieving a similar end is by providing an inspector general for all corporations with an annual net income of over $1 billion. An independent committee of an engineering association might be formed to investigate charges made by engineers concerning the safety of a product on which they are working; a company that did not allow an appropriate investigation of employee charges would become subject to cover-up proceedings. Those in the engineering industry can suggest and work to implement other ideas. I have elsewhere outlined a set of ten such charges for the ethical corporation.

In addition to asking how an engineer should respond to moral quandaries and dilemmas, and rather than asking how to educate or train engineers to be moral heroes, those in engineering ethics should ask how large organizations can be changed so that they do not squeeze engineers in moral dilemmas, place them in the position of facing moral quandaries, and make them feel that they must blow the whistle.

The time has come to go beyond sensitizing students to moral issues and solving and resolving the old, standard cases. The next and very important questions to be asked as we discuss each case is how organizational structures can be changed so that no engineer will ever again have to face *that* case.

Many of the issues of engineering ethics within a corporate setting concern the ethics of organizational structure, questions of public policy, and so questions that frequently are amenable to solution only on a scale larger than the individual—on the scale of organization and law. The ethical responsibilities of the engineer in a large organization have as much to do with the organization as with the engineer. They can be most fruitfully approached by considering from a moral point of view not only the individual engineer but the framework within which he or she works. We not only need moral people. Even more importantly we need moral structures and organizations. Only by paying more attention to these can we adequately resolve the questions of the ethical responsibility of engineers in large organizations.

RESPONSIBILITY FOR HARM

Martin Curd and Larry May

These authors oppose De George's effort to limit the responsibility of professional employees for injurious corporate actions. They propose a theory that holds professionals more individually accountable, but they also consider ways to protect the interests of employees as they carry out their duties.

What have we learned . . . about the concept of professional responsibility? Perhaps the most important thing is the difficulty of ascribing responsibility for harm to individual engineers when they are employed by large corporations. It is much easier to assign such responsibility to doctors and lawyers, because these professionals, unlike engineers, are not usually corporate employees as well. Professional engineers in corporations rarely have complete control over decisions about how much risk to take with the safety and well-being of others since they are influenced by supervisory management.

Professional responsibility is easy to recognize and appreciate if one is one's own boss. What could be more reasonable than to be held potentially liable for the harms that one causes as a free and responsible professional? But if one is employed by someone else and if one no longer has complete control over the decisions which fall within the sphere of one's competence then one's professional integrity may be compromised. In such situations, it is tempting to believe that one is not fully responsible or, perhaps, not responsible at all for the harms that one causes either by act or omission. This is especially true when one merely acquiesces in a state of affairs in which one has not taken any personal initiative. This is why so many engineers might readily agree about cases involving other people but still fail to act in what they themselves would regard as a fully responsible manner in their own jobs. We shall now consider the general question: What is the responsibility of professional engineers for harms which result from decisions taken within the corporations of which these engineers are employees?

Frank Camps, who was principal design engineer for the Ford Motor Company in the early 1970's when the first Ford Pinto prototype was being tested, also attests to the important role that the engineer can play in preventing harm because of his or her special knowledge. Camps confesses:

I was instructed to inform the federal government only of our successful test crashes—and not the many failures. . . . I became part of the Ford scheme. I was expected to be loyal to the company's policies and to ignore my own

From Martin Curd and Larry May, "Professional Responsibility for Harmful Actions," in the *CSEP Module Series in Applied Ethics* (Dubuque, IA: Kendall/Hunt, 1984). Reprinted by permission.

uneasiness about the safety of the cars we were approving.[1]

Camps later found out that if he had not gone along with the management cover-up, he could have prevented Ford from making unsafe Pintos. Perhaps Camps's experience is unusual given his part engineering, part supervisory role at Ford. But it illustrates the general rule that the more control an engineer has over management decisions, the more responsible he or she is for the company's actions.

A common way of talking about corporations and companies encourages the mistaken view that these collectivities, not individual human beings, are responsible for the harms caused by corporate decisions. We say, for example, that Ford Motor Company produced an unsafe Pinto and that Ford is responsible for the resulting harmful consequences. But "Ford Motor Company" cannot act harmfully since it cannot, properly speaking, "act" at all. It is merely a fictitious "person," recognized as having a certain status at law, but incapable of performing actions for itself.

The corporation or company only truly acts through its members or employees. This is called *vicarious* acting or agency and should be distinguished from the individual action or agency of the members or employees of such collectivities. In an important sense, the corporation is dependent on its members and employees, for the corporation cannot act without at least one of its employees or members acting *for it.* If none of these human beings chose to act, then the corporation could not act either. Thus the members of the corporation must share individually in the corporation's responsibility.[2]

How should this responsibility be distributed? Surely it is unreasonable to hold any single member or employee solely responsible for consequences which require collective action or endorsement. Even though a single supervisory or line engineer could have prevented a harm, it is generally true that a number of other corporate members or employees could have done so too. One could try to base the degree of individual responsibility on a member's salary relative to that of other corporate members on the grounds that one's responsibility is a cost which should reflect the financial benefits of corporate membership. But this principle has nothing to do with fault, causation or negligence and hence could be applied, if at all, only in a narrowly legalistic way that does not reflect morality.

Alternatively, one could base the degree of individual responsibility on the individual's degree of authority in the organization. This seems to be what Frank Camps and his fellow engineers were doing implicitly. Since most engineers do not have much authority over corporate decisions, their degree of responsibility should be correspondingly small. On such a view engineers would, in practical terms, become mere employees and relinquish all pretensions to professional status. They would, just like other employees, merely be following orders from a higher authority with no responsibility for their subsequent effects. This is something of a paradox for professional engineers. They want to be seen as independent professionals like lawyers and physicians, yet most of them are employees of large corporations. Moreover, unlike corporate lawyers, they are dispersed throughout the whole corporate structure. They do not even have their own corporate niche with authority over their own departments.

What can be done to enable corporate engineers to become independent of management to the extent necessary for their integrity as professionals? First and fore-

---

[1] Alan Westin, ed., *Whistle-Blowing* (New York: McGraw-Hill, 1981), pp. 119, 121.
[2] For an analysis of what it means for a corporation to act, and of the conditions that must be met before the corporation can be held responsible for the harms it causes, see L. May, "Vicarious Agency and Corporate Responsibility," *Philosophical Studies 43* (1983), 69–82.

most, engineers must regard themselves as fully responsible for the results of their actions and omissions. This means that where there are risks of harm, engineers must strive assiduously to minimize negligence, both for themselves and for others within the corporation. When all else fails this might involve blowing the whistle on other members of the corporation. Such action need not be interpreted as disloyalty to the company. After exposing defects in the design of the Pinto windshield, Camps commented:

My attempt to bring the dangers of the Pinto vehicle to the attention of the public was not a disloyal act, but rather one designed to avoid tragedy—an act in the public interest. I did not turn away from Ford but in my own way I rose to its defense. . . . the truly loyal employee is the one who helps keep the company on the right track—producing a good product that is safe for the consumer to use.[3]

Richard De George has recently taken a position opposed to ours. He contends that: "Engineers in large firms have an ethical responsibility to do their jobs as best they can, to report their observations about safety and improvement of safety to management. But they do not have the obligation to insist that their perceptions or their standards be accepted. They are not paid to do that, and they have no ethical or moral obligation to do that."[4]

De George has two arguments for this view. First, he says that it is too much to expect of engineers to demand that they risk their jobs for the public. Second, he argues that since engineers are not paid to make *ultimate* safety decisions, (this being the job of upper management), their contractual obligation does not require them to do anything more than to inform their supervisors about safety problems. Both of these arguments are initially appealing given

our insistence that the demands of morality require only what it is reasonable to expect of engineers.

We acknowledge the force of De George's first argument. It is unreasonable to expect engineers to speak out about safety problems if they are not protected from retaliation by their employers. But as De George concedes, the judgment that engineers are not morally required to jeopardize their jobs to safeguard the public depends on the situation. If the danger is great and if it is probable that nothing will be done unless the engineer speaks out, then clearly the engineer is morally required to inform the public, especially if the project is one in which he or she is personally involved. Certainly, when engineers are protected from retaliation by their employers, they have a strong moral duty to inform the public of dangers to its safety.

We find De George's second argument unsound. Specific contractual obligations constitute only a very small part of our obligations and duties. Teachers, lawyers, nurses and architects are expected and required, as a matter of common morality and as a matter of professional ethics, to do many things in the practice of their profession which they are not specifically enjoined to do by any contract. Why should things be any different for engineers in large corporations? Since the responsibilities of the rest of us, whether or not we are professionals, go far beyond our contractual duties, then it seems reasonable to expect the same to hold true of engineers.

The sociologists Perrucci and Gerstl have found that engineering "lacks the one characteristic traditionally deemed the essence of professionalism—a community of shared values."[5] . . . Perhaps the most important shared value that engineers as a group could easily attain would be to

[3] Westin, *Whistle-Blowing*, p. 129.
[4] Richard De George, "Ethical Responsibilities of Engineers in Large Organizations: The Pinto Case," in *Business and Professional Ethics Journal*, 1:1, p. 5.

[5] Robert Perrucci and Joel Gerstl, *Profession Without Community: Engineers in American Society* (New York: Random House, 1969), p. 176.

hold each engineer personally responsible for harms which result from his or her own actions (or omissions) even if that act or omission was not sufficient to cause the harm by itself. Committing themselves to this value would mean that engineers working in large corporations would no longer be able to pass the buck when it comes to assigning blame in the way that Camps's colleagues did. More importantly, engineers would require protection from management retaliation when they refuse to act negligently themselves or when they refuse to condone negligence in others.

At a recent conference on the professional responsibility of engineers, the most commonly voiced concern was the problem of engineers maintaining their professional integrity in large corporations. A number of people suggested increasing the strength of professional engineering associations or turning them into full-fledged unions which could demand increased independence for their members and fight management attempts to retaliate against whistleblowers. This is an appropriate response, though not itself a complete solution, to a difficult problem. Unless engineers present a united front and show that they are not afraid to take full responsibility for their actions,

corporate managers will continue to coerce them to act negligently. Taking full responsibility for one's actions is the hallmark of the true professional.

In this essay we have given a philosophical analysis of the responsibility of professionals for their harmful actions. The detailed study of two airline disasters, as well as several other cases of negligence and recklessness, illustrate the complex problems faced by today's professionals. We have argued that it is not enough that professionals merely conform to the accepted standards of their professions. They should aspire to a standard of reasonable care whenever this conflicts with the professional norm. We have also argued that professionals should not be held to too strict a standard of responsibility until they are protected from retaliation by their supervisors and employers. Professionals should not be expected to be saints, but neither can they avoid moral responsibility by hiding behind professional codes or the corporate veil. We are all better off when each one of us takes full responsibility for his or her actions. Any changes in social and economic institutions that help bring this about will improve the moral environment for each of us.

DIVIDED LOYALTIES IN INSTITUTIONAL EMPLOYMENT

Ruth Macklin

Professionals in many fields experience conflicts between the interests of their employers and those of the clients they serve. These conflicts are particularly intense for mental health workers employed by large institutions such as school districts and the armed services. Ruth Macklin explores the situation of the psychiatrist as "double agent," suggesting some ways in which these conflicts might be diminished.

A spy who serves two warring states is the classic example of the double agent. He has obligations to two different factions—factions whose interests are starkly opposed. Less portentous than an actor in a drama of international intrigue but nonetheless a significant figure in the lives of those he affects, is the psychiatrist em-

From Ruth Macklin, *Man, Mind, and Morality: The Ethics of Behavior Control* © 1982, pp. 104–10. Reprinted by permission of Prentice-Hall, Inc., Englewood Cliffs, New Jersey.

ployed by an institution. The institution may be a prison, a university, or the military. It may be a mental hospital—public or private. In a broader sense of "institution," psychiatrists may choose or be called on to serve the largest possible organization in society possessing the power to affect people's liberty: the government itself.

Whatever the size or character of the institution, psychiatrists employed in such settings are beset with an ongoing dilemma: Whom do they serve? The institution that employs them? Or the individual who is diagnosed and treated—the patient, in the ordinary medical sense? What are the moral claims on the psychiatrist in such a situation? Whose interests should take precedence when they come into conflict? If the international spy does not confront an insoluble dilemma of double agency, it is because he usually "really" works for one government or the other when he acts as double agent. So might the psychiatrist in fact have clear priorities when interests clash. But this does not solve the moral issue: To whom *ought* psychiatrists be loyal when they face conflicting duties? This set of ethical issues can be classed under the heading "moral problems for the psychiatrist as double agent."

Most double-agency situations are best viewed from the moral point of view as cases of conflict of loyalty or clashes of duty, both of which cannot be performed simultaneously. One psychiatrist describes the situation as follows:

The psychiatrist or any other professional in the double-agent situation always has a dilemma when he is not in concordance with the values of the agency. The typical example conjured up is the psychiatrist in the military who feels a tension with the stated grounds of the military at a particular historical moment, like the Vietnam war.

Consider the alternative situation where the psychiatrist is ideologically in agreement with the military, as were many psychiatrists in World War II. For those people there was no doubt that the psychiatrist had a moral obligation to the society; for them that moral obligation may have had a higher moral value than the obligation to the distressed single individual. For the military psychiatrist it was not a question of being an agent of an immoral or nonmoral situation, it was a dilemma between two moral commitments: loyalty to a set of values threatened in a wartime situation and loyalty to the value of treating individuals who may or may not be in distress. The double-agent problem is qualitatively different, depending upon whether the psychiatrist is committed to a moral situation.[1]

It is not clear to begin with whether there is one right answer to the question: Whom ought military psychiatrists primarily serve—their patients or the military? Some espouse the radical view that military establishments are inherently unjust institutions. Their answer to the question would probably express the underlying moral assumption that when actions defy military authority or sabotage the system, they are justifiable. Others would argue just as forcefully that some wars, such as World War II, not only are justly fought but that they must be fought for reasons of group survival as well as for preservation of a way of life. Their answer to the double-agent question would most likely depend on the particular war and other related circumstances. Still others will assert that the demands of the society always take precedence over those of the individual, so that the psychiatrist's duty is first to the group, then to the patient, whether the war is a just one or not. This utilitarian position need not be limited to the practice of psychiatry in wartime, but has been used to justify activities such as psychological research in support of CIA efforts in time of peace, as well.

Military Psychiatry: A Case Study

To fix ideas, let us focus on a case study of military psychiatry in peacetime. In the case to follow, the psychiatrist was not being

[1] Gerald L. Klerman, "In the Service of the State: The Psychiatrist as Double Agent," *Hastings Center Report* 8 (April 1978), p. 4.

asked as part of his job to diagnose and treat conditions (whether they are called illnesses or not) whose presence is relevant to the very purpose of the military, the conduct of war. Being a homosexual does not hinder a soldier's efforts to do what he is expected to do in the military, and that posed a moral problem in the following case.

A young psychiatrist doing required military service was stationed in a remote Pacific location for one year. The United States military base was fairly far from cities or recreational areas and there was no war or other relevant military activity in progress. With regularity, authorities on the base sent military personnel for a psychiatric evaluation of their sexual orientation, seeking to discover whether they were homosexuals. The psychiatrist initially could not decide how to respond and remained in a quandary, early in his stay, about how to deal with these requests. Eventually he developed a strategy for dealing with what he was being asked to do. He agreed to perform psychiatric evaluations when ordered (since that was, in fact, his job), but refused to comment on the individual's sexual status unless, in his professional judgment, there was psychiatric illness present *and* the illness was functionally related to homosexuality. In addition, he always told the men sent to him exactly what his evaluation to the authorities would be. This psychiatrist's frank admission—after reflecting for some time—was that the task of evaluating soldiers as homosexuals simply was not part of his job as a psychiatrist.[2]

It was hard for this young psychiatrist to think through the problem in a clear way when these requests first began, since nothing in his medical education or psychiatric training had prepared him for the role he was forced to adapt to. Once he formed the value judgment that what the

military authorities were asking him to do was outside the bounds of proper professional practice, he then had to use his ingenuity to develop an appropriate response. The psychiatrist never was fully informed about the reasons why all these requests for homosexual evaluations were forthcoming, yet he was aware that those requesting the sexual status evaluations took a dim view of homosexuals, so his own compliance might result in specifc harms to some soldiers. It is worth noting that this psychiatrist thought his own theoretical position on homosexuality—whether it is a psychiatric disease or not—was quite irrelevant to the moral dilemma into which he was thrust. Other psychiatrists would have come to a different decision about what to do; some probably would not have perceived any ethical conflict at all in the situation.

The psychiatrist in this situation later realized that much of his initial confusion stemmed from trying to distinguish what he knew as an expert from what the military was willing to accept he knew.

They often wanted me, as an authority, to say things beyond my expertise. For example, I had no professional way to identify a homosexual, yet the Marine Corps would have gladly added my opinion to their evidence in such a case. The only way that I, as a psychiatrist, could be helpful would be to use my authority and role as a professional to obtain information. This would involve dishonesty towards the patient and the military. To the patient I would be obtaining information falsely under the guise of being an interested expert, and to the military I would be pawning off personal judgment under the guise of expert opinion. I chose instead to delineate those areas I could not know and address myself to what I could know: the presence or absence of psychopathology.[3]

This case study portrays a scene in military psychiatry where the fear of losing life or limb, often operating in wartime, is absent and thus does not distort the dilemma of double agency.

[2] This story was reported in personal conversation with the author by Howard Fenn, M.D., the psychiatrist who experienced the dilemma.

[3] Howard Fenn, correspondence with the author.

School Psychiatry: A Case Study

It is useful to cite a somewhat different example, a case involving school psychiatry, to illustrate another ethical aspect of double-agent problems.

A young first year medical student was having a severe emotional crisis. Obviously on the verge of a complete breakdown, he went to a private psychiatrist. He was agitated, anxious, didn't know if he could handle his studies. He had a brilliant college record, and clearly outstanding intellectual capacity.

He was in acute distress and seemingly in the process of disintegration. The psychiatrist, trying very hard to avoid hospitalization, started intensive psychotherapy. The student was already at a point where it looked like he was going to have a schizophrenic break: reality testing was impaired, ideas of reference were occurring, and a hypomanic mood with grandiose ideation was forming. To relieve the pressures on him the psychiatrist wrote a letter for him saying that he was treating the student for "emotional problems" and recommended a medical leave of absence.

The next fall the student attempted to return to medical school but was refused readmission, even though the psychiatrist had written a letter, as the physician in charge of the treatment, that he was medically able to continue his studies. They gave no reason for not reinstating him except that he was not considered suitable. He then began to apply to other medical schools at his psychiatrist's suggestion and was refused in every case. Before seeing the private psychiatrist the student had consulted the school psychiatrist who made a diagnosis of latent schizophrenia.

When other medical schools wrote to his former school, the reason for discharge was medical leave with latent schizophrenia. It is known that about half of those with schizophrenia in remission will have another break. In the case of this student there was a real risk to future patients. He was planning to become a surgeon. The combination of a grandiose self-appraisal with the power of a surgeon could cause serious harm.

The private psychiatrist recognized that there may be psychiatric conditions which would interfere with a career in medicine and therefore might be grounds for exclusion from medical school. The problem, as he saw it, was whether the school psychiatrist was seeing the student in his role as psychiatrist or in his role as part of the school administration, and whether these two roles could be separated.[4]

Conflicting Roles of Institutional Psychiatrists

Double-agency problems such as this are almost inevitable features of institutional psychiatry. A straightforward conflict occurs between two different social roles—roles that pose no moral dilemmas when they exist alone. An employee of an institution normally has—or ought to have—some loyalty to the employer. Whether this loyalty takes the form of refusing to impart industrial product information to competitors or defending the institution in public places, there is a reasonable expectation that working for an organization carries some commitment to what it stands for and a willingness to defend it. Often, there are specific obligations that are based on contract. At other times, the duties of an employee derive from a structural hierarchy of authority within an organization. There are, of course, notable and justifiable exceptions. When people face virtual enslavement at the hands of their employers, and there are no alternative opportunities for work, forms of disloyalty designed to better their condition could be defended by sound moral arguments. A general presumption of loyalty is not an absolute one. Like most guides to moral action, general rules have notable exceptions.

Psychiatrists must come to grips with conflicting loyalties, however. Especially since they are educated as physicians and socialized into the medical profession, as well as trained in the specialty of psychiatry, there is an overwhelming moral force behind the dictates of keeping patients'

---

[4] "The Psychiatrist as Double Agent," *Hastings Center Report* 4 (February 1974), p. 12.

confidentiality and respecting their privacy. Problems of double agency are not confined to the psychiatric branch of medicine, however. Doctors who work for institutions such as schools or prisons are likely to face many instances of conflicting loyalties. As physicians are employed more and more by industry and by insurance companies, moral dilemmas of this sort will arise with ever greater frequency. Yet the problem seems more profound in psychiatry, in part because successful therapy often depends on maintaining a relationship of trust between therapist and patient. Another reason is that the psychiatrist in an institution is frequently looked to as an agent of social control, unlike the ordinary doctor in most settings. Psychiatrists in mental hospitals have to confront patient management problems that constantly plague the regular attending staff. Equipped with powerful tools in the form of antipsychotic medication and electroconvulsive therapy, psychiatrists have the capacity to alter radically their patients' behavior as well as their moods. Add to that their medical authority in the hospital setting, and it is easy to see how psychiatrists become—wittingly or unwittingly—agents of social control in institutions. The situation is even more pronounced in prisons, perhaps because there is little or no presumption of sickness (or else the inmate would be in a medical rather than a penal institution).

It is not surprising that psychiatrists achieve legitimate authority in mental hospitals. The power they wield might be considered justifiably exercised. They are, after all, the experts in emotional and behavioral disorders. If there is a valid notion of psychiatric expertise, then psychiatrists—at least good ones—must be the ones to possess it. If, as some have argued, mental illness is a myth and, consequently, there is no subject matter about which to be an expert, then any argument defending psychiatrists' place of authority in mental institutions—based on their alleged expertise—may lose its soundness. But continuing

to accept the premises with which we began, let us assume there is some body of knowledge concerning the cause and cure of human emotional and behavioral disorders. While acknowledging this does not eliminate moral dilemmas arising out of conflict of loyalty to institutional employer and to the patient, there is nonetheless more reason to grant psychiatrists a role of authority and expertise in this type of institution than in settings unrelated to the diagnosis and treatment of psychopathology.

In prisons, the role of psychiatrists may remain systematically ambiguous. Prisoners do not have the normal characteristics of patients. In most cases, prisoners do not think they are mentally ill, nor are they diagnosed as such. One psychiatric viewpoint nonetheless holds that anyone capable of committing the violent, horrible deeds performed by many criminal offenders could not possibly be normal, sane, or healthy. This position is not convincing as it stands, however, especially in the absence of a personality theory or a theory of psychopathology on which to base judgments about violent or antisocial behavior. This view aside, there may still be a legitimate role for psychiatrists in prisons when treatment programs exist. . . . Behavior modification and other attempts at psychological rehabilitation have been introduced in prisons. To the extent that these remain and show some success as therapy, the situation bears some similarity to the doctor–patient relationship in mental hospitals. Yet the psychiatrist is likely to serve as an agent of social control anyway, because of the primary function of penal institutions.

Even though the role of prison psychiatrists is ambiguous in these ways, moral presumptions still govern their behavior. Psychiatrists acting as agents of social control in prison settings are more likely using their authority than using their expertise. There is relatively little agreement on the causes of violence. Strong arguments have been advanced in support of the view that violent behavior has primarily social and environmental causes rather than being a pathological condition within a person that warrants psychiatric management. Whatever the correct explanation for the actions of violent criminal offenders, behavior control in prisons confronts the psychiatrist with problems of conflicting duties: to the prisoners who end up becoming patients, and to the employing institution.

Approaches to Resolving Problems of Double Agency

What solutions are promising for moral problems of double agency in behavior control? In addition to specific strategies like the one the young psychiatrist on the military base worked out for himself, three different approaches cover the basic options in this range of cases.

The first approach—not always possible to adopt—is for a psychiatrist or psychologist to avoid such conflicts by refusing to work in a situation that gives rise to them. The hardest one to avoid is obviously the military, as long as virtually all physicians are required to serve. Mandatory military service aside, practicing psychiatrists voluntarily enter most other institutional settings. With enough foreknowledge and sufficient concern, psychiatrists could deliberately shun this type of employment as a matter of policy. But would this yield the happiest solution? There would almost surely be a genuine loss of quality in therapeutic and counseling services if psychiatrists and psychologists who are most sensitive to ethical issues and conflicts of duty were to make themselves unavailable for such employment. It is often remarked that the quality of institutional psychiatry is considerably lower than the level found among private practitioners in urban settings and psychiatrists in teaching hospitals. If those already sensitive to moral concerns were to shrink from employment in educational and penal institutions, the moral dilemmas

would not go away. They would remain, at worst, unrecognized; at the least, unheeded.

A radically different approach might be taken by psychiatrists who choose to work for an organization or institution, as well as by all who must serve time in the military. In this view, institutional psychiatrists should not really consider the people they treat as patients, in the usual sense implied by the doctor–patient relationship. Instead, psychiatrists in the employ of institutions should think of their seeming patients as impaired creatures sent by a different official for some sort of treatment—much as you might take a broken machine to the repair shop. This may sound crass, but it is an attitude not unheard of in prisons, according to some observers. Like the first approach, this method deals with the double-agent problem by trying to make it go away. To urge that the psychiatrist ought always serve the organization he is employed by, rather than show primary loyalty to the individual sent to him as a patient, is to take an ideological stance with few sound reasons behind it.

The third approach amounts to a form of compromise. A solution suggested by some psychiatrists who came together to grapple with these very issues was for the therapist to issue something akin to a "Miranda warning" in potential double-agent settings. Just as a policeman apprehending a suspect is required to inform the captive of his legal rights—most importantly, warning that anything he says may be held against him—so might a psychiatrist act in institutional settings. Recognizing that there is always a strong presumption favoring a doctor's primary loyalty to his patient, these psychiatrists realistically acknowledged that there are times when the moral presumption may legitimately lie elsewhere. The use of a "psychiatric Miranda warning" succeeds in confronting the potentially conflicting roles some psychiatrists may be forced to embrace as well as or better than any other policy for dealing with clashes of duty. Individual resolutions of particular double-agent dilemmas will differ in their fine points. But telling a patient that what he says may be held against him has at least the virtue of honesty. A large part of what is wrong with the questionable moral practice of breaking patients' confidentiality is ignoring or dashing their legitimate and justified expectations. If expectations become changed, by the use of something like a psychiatric Miranda warning, then the moral presumptions regarding confidentiality and privacy shift slightly from what they would be in the usual therapist–patient relationship. According to some practitioners, however, adopting this procedure might have the unwanted effect of undermining therapeutic prospects. In addition, some psychiatric patients could hardly be expected to assess such "Miranda warnings" correctly. Those who are less than fully competent stand in need of greater protection than the typical adult who is presumed rational and autonomous.

This device could not hope to resolve all duty conflicts or competing loyalties in behavior control any more than other rather simple solutions proposed for knotty moral problems. It may, however, force psychologists and psychiatrists who are employees of an institution to face squarely the matter of their priorities. It is one thing to adhere somewhat vaguely to the dictates of patient privacy and confidentiality while serving as an employee of an organization with its own agenda. It is quite another thing to have to decide, in diagnosing and treating patients, just what warnings or information should be imparted to whom and why. The prison psychiatrist may hope to serve the interests of criminal justice and also try to rehabilitate hardened criminals. The school psychiatrist may take the students' wishes and desires to heart, while continuing to maintain the goals and purposes of the educational institution. It is often hard, in practice—if not impossible, in principle—to do both simultaneously.

DIFFICULT WORKING CONDITIONS: A TEXTBOOK CASE*

Martha R. Fowlkes

Written by a professor and sociologist, Fowlkes' study documents the hardships confronted by professionals (and their patients) in state psychiatric hospitals. These hospitals have diminished in number, but they still operate in many areas, and there is some pressure to open more of them. Their chronic problems provide vivid examples of the kinds of difficulties often encountered by professionals in public employment.

Despite official policy and professional emphasis to the contrary, the custodial mental hospital continues to exist as a major form of state-provided mental health care. In this [selection], one such institution, "New England State Hospital,"[1] is described, and the various features of hos-

pital organization that sustain a system of custodial care are discussed. Although the custodial hospital offers little to its patients, its persistent survival can be explained by the number of non-patient vested interests that are well served by the state hospital, precisely in its existing custodial form. The case study of New England State Hospital suggests that reform of state mental insti-

[1] The name of the hospital is fictitious.

* Some references have been deleted without indication.

From Martha R. Fowlkes, "Business as Usual—At the State Mental Hospital," *Psychiatry* 38:1 (February 1975): pp. 55–65. Reprinted by permission.

tutions depends less on a programmatic formulation of desired changes than on an understanding of the structured resistance to such changes.

It is common knowledge that the custodial state mental hospital is obsolete. From a variety of sources—whether Wiseman's notorious and unsettling film *Titticut Follies*, Kesey's popular novel *One Flew Over the Cuckoo's Nest*, or the sociological studies of Goffman (1961), Dunham and Weinberg (1960), Belknap (1956), and others—comes overwhelming evidence of the failure of such institutions to provide personalized care or active rehabilitative treatment. In a major address in 1963, President Kennedy condemned the "cold mercy of custodial isolation" and urged an end to the practice of confining patients "in an institution to wither away." Congress followed suit by enacting the Mental Retardation and Community Mental Health Centers Act in the same year. Certainly it would be impossible to find any authority in the field of mental health care who would have a kind word for the custodial care of the traditional large-scale state mental hospital. Mental health professionals are everywhere being trained in new multidisciplinary approaches and community rehabilitation. Indeed, a growing number of psychiatrists, following the lead of Szasz (1961), are rejecting the notion of mental illness altogether and are openly critical of the utilization of conventional medical solutions for what they view as a nonmedical problem.

Szasz notwithstanding, the real issue in the past decade has not been the abolition but the reform of the state mental hospital. In this connection custodial forms of care have been conceptually, professionally, and officially rejected. Yet in reality, the custodial institution lives on as a dominant, if not *the* dominant, form of state-provided mental health care. In spite of a noticeable decline in the resident population of the nation's state mental institutions in the last half decade, there nonetheless remain over

half a million residents in state facilities for the mentally disabled. To be sure, a few of these facilities have made the transformation from custodial to therapeutic and community-oriented care, and most recently a series of "right to treatment" lawsuits have attempted to establish minimally acceptable guidelines for patient care and treatment in the state hospitals of a number of regions across the country. There is little doubt, however, that most state facilities continue essentially unaltered, maintaining dismally low standards of care and treatment, oblivious to the brave new world of mental health care. In the following description of a state hospital I will attempt to indicate why changes that seem obviously desirable seldom occur.

New England State Hospital

The enduring custodial character of the state hospital is well exemplified by the case of New England State Hospital. Established well over 100 years ago, the hospital has in years past housed a peak population of up to 2,000 patients. At present there are some 100 patients resident at any given time, one-third of whom are geriatric. Probably two-thirds of all the hospital's patients are "chronic," that is, permanent or long-term residents or regular returnees to the hospital.

New England State Hospital, which serves an area comprising several counties, is situated on hundreds of acres of state land in a sparsely populated part of a small town. The original hospital building, which houses half of all the patients, is a gloomy, fortress-like structure with barred windows. Inside, tiny rooms once intended for single occupancy are now double bedrooms; beds are also lined up in rows against the walls of vast rooms originally meant for use as solariums and infirmaries. Furnishings are sparse, air is close, paint is peeling, and the urine and disinfectant smells of the decades have soaked into walls and floors and mingle to make a permanent stench. Within each major residential unit, patients live in wards, each ward a segment of a hierarchical structure representing degrees of so-called wellness or illness. The traditional locked wards for those the hospital considers the worst of its patients are very much in evidence and contain provisions for restraints and seclusion.

Although occasional happenings of a sensationalist nature are often associated with mental hospitals, the true picture of hospital life is relentlessly passive and inert. For patients on the back or locked wards, life means being locked in, locked up, or tied down. Life on these wards is literally in a perpetual state of suspended animation. Patients elsewhere in the hospital who are less deteriorated, or who are more "manageable" through the heavy use of drugs, have more freedom and are seemingly more active in a physical sense. However, the quality of the activity is aimless and repetitive and is prompted by no particular motivation or encouragement to do anything or go anywhere. People travel incessantly the same route day after day; others stare vacantly at (frequently unfocused) television pictures, or pace the floor, or rock ceaselessly back and forth, or repeat gestures and phrases for hours on end, or sit, or sleep.

Though many patients work regularly at jobs throughout the hospital (it is essential for the maintenance of the hospital that the patients do chores), futility is built into occupations that typically carry with them no pay or promotion or any real appreciation. Occasional movies, dances, a few athletic events, and some sparsely available occupational therapy provide diversions for those who wish to participate. But even those patients who make a relatively busy routine for themselves have no purpose to their busy-ness. They have simply settled into an essentially passive hospital life in a more active way than some others.

Despite the dreariness of the living conditions and the rare instances of brutality, the single most outstanding fact about life in this mental hospital (and the one with the most consequence to patients) is that *nothing ever happens.* The people there as patients have no sense of being there for a purpose, as one would go to a general hospital, say, for an appendectomy and recovery period and then go back to rejoin the outside world. The longer the period of a patient's residence the greater the loss of time perspective. For some the passage of time seems to have become virtually meaningless, marking neither the accomplishment of individually significant tasks or routines in the short run, nor a steady progression toward the achievement of specified ends in the long run. In the mental hospital people just are, that is all, and the hospital is merely custodian of their existence.

The prevailing custodial emphasis of New England State Hospital, however, is not necessarily the product, as is often popularly thought, of patients who are universally so disturbed or helpless as to make the custodial approach inevitable. Rather, the custodial emphasis is sustained by quite specific and predominating features of hospital culture and organization. These same features also operate to make unlikely the introduction of change, or to make unlikely the possibility that change will be successful once introduced.

The Admissions Process

The custodial process is set in motion by hospital admissions policies and procedures. Admission to the hospital occurs primarily as a technical-legal process. Persons are admitted indiscriminately, whether voluntary, physician-referred, or court-referred. The hospital administrators seldom exercise their prerogative to evaluate the qualitative need or reasons for admission, because they believe they might either offend referring parties or prompt a would-be patient to sue the hospital for dereliction of its duties. Either possibility could jeopardize good public relations.

Because the hospital absorbs virtually all comers, outside doctors and agencies often have little sense of what the resources and facilities of the hospital actually are. One local doctor, believing that New England State Hospital performed electric shock treatments, had been referring patients to the hospital for that purpose for some time. The hospital admitted them all, though shock treatments have been discontinued for years.

Lacking a clear sense of treatment goals and what it is trying to accomplish in general for its patients, the hospital does not find it necessary to formulate any meaningful criteria for admission over and above those required by law. In true "chicken and egg fashion," the lack of criteria for admission creates a highly diverse patient population, whose needs and problems are so varied that it becomes nearly impossible for the hospital to formulate overall treatment goals. Within the hospital are to be found alcoholics, drug addicts, persons being examined in connection with court charges, retarded and otherwise organically brain-damaged persons, the elderly and infirm, persons undergoing marital or life adjustment or even post-operative crises, teen-age runaways, and finally persons whose confusion, hallucinations, and disassociated speech obviously indicate a psychotic state. With this kind of admixture of patients, the easiest course for the hospital is to minimize the individuality and variety of patient problems, and to emphasize instead the lowest common denominators of patient needs—food, shelter, and sedation with drugs to ensure cooperative behavior.

Professional Marginality

Although active treatment and rehabilitation programs could be provided for even such a large and diverse patient population, in none of its ranks does the hospital have the professional competency to do so. All but one of the twenty-odd clinical doctors who staffed the various units of the hospital were foreign-born, foreign-trained, and unlicensed, and have little or no psychiatric training. These doctors, by their failure to meet prevailing medical standards and to pass the general medical examinations for foreign doctors, are *legally* unfit and incompetent to enter the mainstream of American medicine and to engage in private medical practice. Yet the state has permitted their indefinite practice in the state mental hospitals. A recent state ruling that would require even these doctors to demonstrate some minimal competence in the basic sciences and English language has been predictably greeted with defensive, self-righteous outrage, by the older doctors especially, who stand to lose their undemanding, relatively well-paid (considering their lack of qualifications), housing-provided niche in the hospital hierarchy.

Aside from their basic medical and psychiatric ineptitude, these doctors generally speak and understand English only poorly and are without the awareness of American culture and social life that would permit understanding of a patient's life situation or background. One doctor, for example, became very confused about why a newly admitted patient was so worried about money, when she had said her husband was a photographer. What the woman had actually said, however, was that her husband was on *welfare*. The doctors often view mentally disturbed behavior with the hostility and contempt that derive from their own unexamined cultural and class biases, and they may be quite patrician in their demeanor with patients.

The professional qualifications of other staff members are comparably weak. Attendants need not even have a high school diploma to qualify for work. Licensed Practical Nurses far outnumber the better trained and educated Registered Nurses. As recently as the spring of 1971, about two-thirds of a social work staff of twenty had only a BA degree. The psychology department numbered more advanced degrees and professional credentials among its members, but the senior psychologist could always be counted on to offer extremely cynical commentary whenever discussion in meetings turned to possibilities for change in the hospital. He once wrote an article in his professional field on the impossibility of doing treatment with mental hospital patients!

The patient, then, is a victim of the limited qualifications of the staff and receives only limited care at their hands. Doctors define their roles very narrowly to include only those functions which they are quite certain they can perform. Therefore, they will interview patients and register diagnoses for legal record-keeping purposes, but the interview is not meant to suggest a doctor–patient relationship, nor does the diagnosis imply a program of treatment. Social workers have traditionally been at the service of both the hospital record room and the doctors, for whom they are expected to gather odds and ends of facts, necessary to complete various patient records but usually socially and psychologically irrelevant.

The nursing role is reduced to its most fundamental and traditional level—that is, simply taking care of people. A "good" patient is one who is easy to care for and have around. Such a patient also becomes a display model of behavior for all other patients. For example, the head nurse on a ward called attention to a pitiful, severely retarded, docile, grinning young man. "He's so good," she said. "We wish all of our patients were like this." (Here, indeed, is proof of the nonfictional nature of Kesey's "Big Nurse," in *One Flew Over the Cuckoo's Nest.*) Of course, a more alert, more capable patient quickly learns to suppress those characteristics which might indicate a greater sense of self-interest and more potential for mental health lest he become a nuisance to the nursing staff. The regression and inertia of the custodial patient becomes the norm.

The Medical Model

Particularly in the context of a staff of poorly qualified physicians, the hierarchical organization of personnel along the lines of the medical model—according to which the doctor not only is in charge but also has unquestioned and unquestionable authority—further fragments and minimizes patient care. Echoing the unimaginative approach of the doctors to whom they are subordinate, personnel in all other departments also function within narrow limits, performing mostly of-the-moment compartmentalized tasks. There is little communication or interrelationship between the various departments. As there is no comprehensive treatment program for an individual patient, there is little incentive for one department to have any interest in or knowledge of what another department might be doing on a patient's behalf. Doctors sometimes discharge patients without informing or consulting any of the other professionals involved.

The doctors are at the top of a status hierarchy that ranks all other jobs as beneath the doctors' in importance and prestige. It is the job of the nonphysician staff simply to complement the "expertise" of the doctors, rather than to make integral contributions of their own to patient care. It is not only lack of money which prevents available job blocs for additional registered nurses from being filled; it is also the lack of encouragement for the well-trained nurse to use her talents in interesting and innovative ways. Similarly, although a new director of social service has been able to hire a number of professionally trained social workers, they can have little impact in a system where their talents are not put to maximum use nor their skills respected. The idea that a social worker might take an active clinical and diagnostic role was greeted with derisive laughter by doctors and psychologists alike in one meeting.

The doctors jealously guard their authority, knowing possibly how little they are respected by other staff members, who frequently make disparaging remarks about them. They also display great resistance to shared professional contributions to patient care, as the following indicates (the reference is to an experimental admissions screening program begun by the social service department and is taken from a letter written by one of the hospital doctors to the local paper):

(Social workers) spend six months or so in an office next to the admissions room eagerly awaiting the proper time to pounce upon the . . . patient with a barrage of prepared social questions, becoming oblivious for an hour or more of his medical and mental needs. And after the patient is thus traumatized . . . the patient is thus released to the doctor.

Schools of social work everywhere will surely be astonished by this news that a patient's mental and medical needs are entirely unrelated to his social self!

Leadership as Public Relations

The hospital administrators themselves do not lead; they simply oversee the *status quo.* Although the superintendent and his two assistants are licensed doctors and trained psychiatrists, they assumed a consultant role, rather than an ongoing active clinical role, in the hospital. All three men are in their sixties and obviously have a vested interest in maintaining their good standing with the state department of mental health until the time of their retirement. They take no issue with the hospital as custodial facility and have no aspirations for it to be otherwise. Nor do they judge it possible to alter the custodial emphasis.

There is great administrative sensitivity to how the hospital appears to the public, and the administrators seem to be primarily concerned with promoting good public relations rather than patient care *per se.* When a group of concerned citizens requested a tour of the hospital, the supervisor ordered all patients normally kept in restraint or seclusion to be released for the period of the visit. Fresh paint on the normally dingy walls of the ward heralded a guided tour for the visiting committee of the state mental health association, who had come to evaluate hospital conditions. Outside donation of clothes is no longer permitted, lest the community think the hospital is not meeting patient needs.

Official statements emphasize the hospital as residential rather than treatment facility and call attention to the improvement of current living conditions over those of the past. When a controversy arose over the numbers of unlicensed physicians in state mental hospitals, the supervisor of New England State Hospital skillfully diverted attention from the real issue of the quality of patient care by threatening that the hospital might have to close and neglect its patients if he lost his staff of doctors through their mere inability to pass exams. Not long afterward the local paper printed a full-page-complete-with-pictures report of progress, comfort, and dedication at New England State Hospital.

The hospital and the semi-rural communities and small urban areas that it serves coexist peacefully. Local people seem to regard the hospital as meeting their needs in a suitably benign and low-keyed manner. They note with appreciation, for example, the recreational use they are permitted of a parcel of hospital land. As volunteers and participants in local mental health organizations, they are gratified to assist the much touted, well-intentioned work of the hospital. During the debate about accreditation of doctors, local public response was supportive of the hospital generally and sympathetic specifically to the doctors, who were clearly seen as underdogs.

From the administrative point of view, the duty of the hospital is to be the waiting receptacle for anyone who comes its way by whatever route. Patients are to be duly admitted, processed, housed, and maintained. Discharge has no specified qualitative meaning. Patients leave when the length of stay required by the admitting paper is up, or a voluntary patient decides to leave, or a family takes a relative home in its custody. The overriding concern of the administrators with regard to any or all parts of this cycle is to comply with all legal requirements and to avoid scandal. Some social workers have attempted to gain placement elsewhere for long-term patients who no longer require hospitalization. Many relatives of such patients, however, have clearly stated their wish that their patient-kin remain where they are. The administration is reluctant to intervene lest the hospital become a target of the families' anger.

Resistance to Change

The administrators have only a passive acceptance of change. Although staff members are not particularly encouraged to try out new ideas or programs, they are usually given indifferent permission to do so on their own motivation. Any changes, of course, require that the formal authority of the doctors and administration is left intact and legal requirements are not interfered with. But attempts to individualize and humanize the system of patient care are outside the scope of the official definition of patient care. While such efforts may be tolerated, therefore, they are not facilitated by any structural changes which would ensure the shared concern and communication necessary for those efforts to be permanently successful.

The experimental admissions program, undertaken in 1971 by the social service department, is a case in point. It was an attempt to replace previous automatic, rubber-stamped procedures with support, advice, and, if possible, referral elsewhere for the person seeking admission. For those finally admitted, the intention was to emphasize helpful involvement with both patient and family from the beginning, and to collect information pertinent to eventual diagnosis and treatment.

It quickly became clear that screening patients had little meaning, when most doctors and hospital administrators had no real interest in formulating specific guidelines for admission and did not wish to hear social service suggestions in that regard. There was also nowhere to go with painstakingly gathered data, when doctors were unresponsive to its use for their understanding or diagnosis of a patient. Significantly, the program was openly welcomed only by the one clinical doctor who happened to be a fully trained psychiatrist.

Like the experimental admissions program, other efforts to broaden the scope of patient care invariably have an idiosyncratic base rather than a structural one and consequently meet with similarly qualified success. The years since 1971 have seen the introduction of a program of behavioral modification on one of the back wards, the provision of in-hospital legal services, and the establishment of an incentive community to aid in the resocialization of 60 chronic patients. In none of these cases, however, was the change suggested or initiated by either the hospital administrators or medical staff, and in two of the three instances, the impetus for change originated outside the hospital altogether, with professionals who wished to establish training opportunities for students. In the face of varying degrees of official indifference, the continued existence of such programs rests mainly on the amount of time and energy that a few individuals are able to give to them.

Even the most dedicated individual efforts, however, are not sufficient to do the job these programs were intended to do, for they exist at arm's length from the ongoing system of patient care; they leave untouched the core structure of custodial care, which tends by its very functioning to weaken the objectives of the new programs. The behavioral modification program, for example, does not involve the ward personnel, who continue to carry out their duties in routine custodial fashion.

Thus, the behavioral modification approach receives none of the reinforcement or follow-through necessary to build its effectiveness. In the case of the legal services program, insofar as patients know of its availability, they find their way to legal advice on their own. Only rarely has a staff member referred a patient to the service, and then only with regard to a purely private matter. While not prohibited from doing so, patients are not encouraged by physicians, social workers, or other staff to use the legal service to seek clarification of the legal terms of their own admission and commitment to and discharge from the hospital.

It is far too soon to make any general statement about the long-range success of the incentive community in preparing patients for, and placing them in, living and work settings outside of the hospital. Undoubtedly the incentive community (which receives its own federal funds) actually benefits in many ways by its almost total isolation from the rest of the patient and staff community. But to some degree the potential of the incentive community depends on the potential of the patients referred for participation from the regular hospital wards. Referrals are supposed to reflect a qualitative evaluation of a patient's readiness and capacity to accept the increased responsibility entailed by the resocialization process. The consulting psychologist for the incentive community mentions the problem of inappropriate referrals—patients who are shuttled off into the incentive community less because of their ability to participate than because it is a convenient way to reduce the census population of a given ward. Once again signs of the familiar pattern of cross-purposes at work!

Expectations of Patient Families

Patients and patient families are hardly in a position to offer any criticism of the hospital as it is. For persons with limited ability to pay, New England State Hospital, costing less than $15 a day, is the only care available. Frequently lacking the knowledge with which to judge the quality of hospital care, families are reassured that the care at New England State Hospital is the only care possible. "Your boy is so sick, you'd better sign this paper so we can keep him here (another few weeks) (indefinitely)." I think here of the mother who mentioned that her daughter had been badly bruised in the hospital and said resignedly, "They told me she was hard to handle."

The rigid medical diagnostic approach used by the hospital no doubt conveys the impression to families that mental illness is a sort of irreversible disease entity and leads to rather low expectations of what can be done for a patient in the first place. Thus if a patient has to make frequent return trips to the hospital, as many do, it is not because the hospital might have done a better job of treatment or aftercare planning. It is rather because mental illness is always there and prone to act up, and when it does, it is the accepted rule of the hospital to take care of the patient until symptoms abate.

Families themselves often seek to relieve a host of family tensions by seeking admission for a family member whose behavior is particularly disturbed or disturbing. When they visit their patient-relative in the hospital, they are relieved to see that he or she is calmer or more "normal," the result usually of heavy doses of chlorpromazine or other drugs. Seldom are they concerned with the means used to bring about the change or with how durable or deep the change is. In any case, it is the patient who is expected to change. Hospitalization encourages a focus on the behavior of the patient alone, and spares other family members the need for consideration of their own interactive behavior with the patient and even possible contributions to his problems. Ex-patients whose behavior at home is not as compliant as a family might wish can be readmitted to the hospital as punishment. One woman came with the necessary papers to admit her ex-patient husband, who had evidently been having an affair with a neighbor. The wife didn't like this at all and decided he "must be getting sick again"!

There is no doubt that a more questioning and assertive group of families and patients could motivate the hospital to better safeguard patient interests. For example, a well-educated, once-affluent woman of professional background was admitted to the hospital by her relatives because it was inexpensive and geographically convenient for them. She challenged furiously everything about the hospital, from cleanliness to diagnosis to her own civil rights. Although her refusal to fit in easily with regular hospital routine made her a "problem" case in the eyes of the staff, the fact is that the level of hospital care rose to meet her needs and expectations. She was soon taken out of her restraints and moved to a more open ward, visited by an outside doctor and lawyer upon her request, and permitted to leave the hospital before her required length of stay was technically over. More important, she escaped being permanently committed, as her relatives had wished her to be, because the doctors in charge frankly admitted that she would raise too many objections, and it was unlikely that they could make the psychotic diagnosis "stick."

Custodial Care—Who Benefits?

Now it is easy enough to postulate the kinds of changes needed if mental health care is actually to accomplish anything on behalf of its patients, in contrast to the custodial process discussed above. Much reform could take place within the existing hospital setting that would personalize patient care and facilitate treatment. Ideally the large-scale state institutions would be closed down altogether and replaced, say, by the less removed, more intimate, active settings of day-care centers, foster homes,

half-way houses, psychiatric wards in general hospitals, and, of course, greatly expanded outpatient services in community mental health centers. Finally, even those persons whose disabilities are apparently permanent and who are consequently in need of ongoing custodial care surely deserve more cheerful, less-stowed-away existences. This utopian state of affairs, of course, presupposes an underpinning of both widespread community concern and generous financial support.

But all that this is really saying is that patient interests ought to be central to mental health care. Indeed, if they were, custodial institutions such as New England State Hospital would long ago have ceased to exist. The explanation for their continued survival, as well as their resistance to change, is to be found in the many vested interests of nonpatient persons and groups, which are well served by the state mental hospital, precisely in its existing custodial form. From a sociological point of view, a New England State Hospital is quite functional—for everyone but its patients. The interests served by each custodial facility as an individual institution are manifest in the very organization of the hospital itself as it has been discussed here:

1. For the community and region, a large state hospital that admits all comers creates the illusion that all local mental health care needs are being met, thus eliminating the need for the tedious and unwelcome business of local planning and spending for mental health care.

2. For the small town especially, a large-scale custodial mental institution offers employment to many people. As a service, the hospital creates no jarring discrepancy between itself and the often traditional character of other community institutions (education, politics, and the like).

3. For hospital administrators, the safest route to status, job security, and pensions lies in the maintenance of the *status quo* and the promotion of good public relations.

4. For poorly qualified, even incompetent professionals, otherwise unavailable jobs exist to which are attached income security, benefits, and at least hospital-defined status and power.
5. For the hospital staff, custodial care is the easiest form of care.
6. For a family, the hospital acts as stabilizer when the behavior of one of its members has become annoying or burdensome.

Furthermore, as part of an entire system of mental health care, the state institution undoubtedly receives continual support and reinforcement for its custodial operation from an even broader and more pervasive set of public and professional self-interests than those enumerated above:

1. For the general hospital and the general public, the state hospital conveniently eliminates the disturbed and disturbing from its midst.
2. For many outside psychiatrists and other clinical professionals, the hospital siphons off the least affluent and least attractive of the mentally disturbed, whom they would prefer not to serve anyway.
3. For a state department of mental health, the choice of hospital administrators is more easily made on a utilitarian basis of, say, seniority than on the more complicated and uncertain basis of suitability for implementing specific formulated goals for patient care.
4. For a state legislature, custodial care often appears to be the cheapest way, on a short-run, annual budget basis, of providing for a population doubly stigmatized by mental illness and lack of financial resources.
5. Finally, for a whole society, the public mental hospital reassuringly clarifies matters by officially separating "them" from "us." Persons on the "outside" thus come to develop a sense of their own comparative well-being and a conviction of the rightness and stability of their own ways of life.

The apparent contradiction of the continuing existence of a New England State Hospital in an era dedicated to mental health reform is, thus, more easily understood. For the successful outcome of any decision to supersede custodial care with genuinely therapeutic help is necessarily dependent on two further decisions: to shape mental health policy around the interests of patients, rather than the claims of nonpatients; to design mental health services that reflect, in their own organization and procedures, the increased humanity and involvement of all concerned, rather than considerations of mere expediency. In a time when many pressing social problems clamor for attention and priority, it is perhaps not surprising that the public—legislators, taxpayers, and professionals alike—often chooses the path of least resistance in allowing the problem of mental health care to remain "out of sight, out of mind"—neatly packaged in the form of the custodial institution.

THE RIGHTS OF PROFESSIONALS IN HEALTH CARE

Robert W. Gibson

This selection was written by a psychiatrist and former president of the American Psychiatric Association (APA). It responds to current public interest in the rights of patients and to problems such as those described in our previous selection by arguing for the rights of staff members in treatment facilities.

From Robert W. Gibson, "The Rights of Staff in the Treatment of the Mentally Ill," *Hospital and Community Psychiatry* 27:12 (December 1976), pp. 855–59. Reprinted by permission.

The rights of the individual in our society are in danger and must be protected. Perhaps this situation is an inevitable consequence of the increased size, complexity, and power of government, business, and all of our institutions. Whatever the cause, the threat is there. And we can be grateful that dedicated individuals and organizations are trying to counteract it.

The loss of basic personal rights is not a new experience for the mentally ill. Probably no other group has been so consistently persecuted and deprived of basic human rights as those who suffer from psychiatric illness. Many of the problems arise from the dehumanization that comes from the increasing size and complexity of our health care system. Whatever difficulties exist generally are magnified by the underfunding of the facilities and programs for the mentally ill. Added to this are the consequences of suspicion and fear of those whose behavior is seen as deviant.

In an effort to protect the interests of patients generally, the American Hospital Association [AHA] set forth a Patient's Bill of Rights in 1973. Many of these rights, such as consideration and respect, the right to adequate information, and the right to know the terms and conditions under which care is given, are not unique to health care. Some of the rights do deal with specific treatment issues as, for example, the right to know the risks and medical alternatives, the right to confidentiality, the right to expect continuity of care, and the right to know if human experimentation is to be considered.

The AHA Bill of Rights has received a varied response. Some states have enacted legislation to guarantee those rights. Some hospitals have adopted those rights as policy. The legal counsel to hospitals have generally cautioned that such a bill of rights could be construed as a legal document and be introduced as evidence in court actions. They express concern about the vagueness and open endedness of statements such as "The patient has the right to expect that within its capacity a hospital must make reasonable response to the request of a patient for services." How can the capacity of a hospital to respond be determined? What is a reasonable response? Is there any limitation to the requests that can be made by a patient?

A different concern was expressed by Willard Gaylin, who asserted, "The objection to this well-intended though timid document is that it perpetuates the very paternalism that precipitated the abuses." And, "The hospital has no power to grant these rights. They were vested in the patient to begin with. If the rights have been violated they have been violated by the hospital and its hirelings."[1]

The AHA Patient's Bill of Rights is directed toward the general hospital, and thus does not address many problem areas for the mentally ill. The heavy emphasis on openness of communication and access to medical records overlooks the sensitive nature of much of the material contained within the psychiatric record. The bill of rights was not designed with an awareness of the various defense mechanisms of denial, resistance, and displacement that are inherent in psychiatric treatment.

A bill of rights modified expressly to meet the needs of hospitalized mental patients appeared recently in *Psychiatric Annals*, but even this bill would cause legal counsel considerable concern. Consider the closing statement: "The above rights have been constructed with calculated ambiguity to permit agency personnel to balance patient medical and legal interests appropriately."[2] Ambiguity is undesirable in what

---

[1] W. Gaylin, "The Patient's Bill of Rights," *Saturday Review of the Sciences*, Vol. 1, March 1973, p. 22.

[2] P. B. Hoffman and R. C. Dunn, "Guaranteeing the Right to Treatment," *Psychiatric Annals*, Vol. 6, June 1976, pp. 258–82.

may turn out to be a legal document introduced in a malpractice suit.

Hospital staff members who enthusiastically supported the move toward a better deal for their patients have been dismayed to discover they may be the targets of civil actions. They find themselves in seemingly insoluble dilemmas. For example, if a medication is forced upon a patient, it would violate the right to refuse treatment, yet failure to give adequate treatment might be the basis of a charge of neglect.

The efforts to protect the rights of patients are based on good intentions and, on balance, are a positive force. The problem is that at times these efforts have been initiated by individuals who are unfamiliar with the needs of the mentally ill and the potential impact their efforts could have on the treatment process. The adversarial climate gives the impression that the rights of patients are in opposition to the rights of staff; a gain for one is perceived as a loss for the other.

Some suggest, philosophically, that the pendulum, having swung in one direction, will surely swing back and will eventually come to a midpoint. I admit that this is begging the question. The rights of patients must be protected and should not be in opposition to the legitimate interests and concerns of staff.

During the 1960s there evolved in this country a national policy that adequate health care is the right of every individual. If we accept that premise, and if we really mean adequate health care is a right, it follows that the provider, as a basic right, must have the opportunity and the conditions necessary to give adequate health care. Starting from this position there is a commonality of interests, not a conflict. Adequate health care for all is the goal of both patient and provider: the patient has the right to receive it; the provider must have those rights needed to give it.

A Set of Staff Rights

In roughing out a set of staff rights, I have concentrated on those rights that bear directly on the treatment process. Each right supports the common goal of adequate health care for all. I have not addressed issues such as working conditions, right to organize, career ladders, and appeal mechanisms. These also are legitimate concerns. My objective, however, is to begin identifying those staff rights essential to providing adequate treatment of the mentally ill.

The right of staff to have sufficient resources to provide adequate health care. During the past decade the cost of health care has consumed an increasingly greater portion of the gross national product. This increase indicates that more resources (money, personnel, facilities, equipment, and supplies) have been made available for health care. Those resources were needed to meet higher expectations and standards of treatment. The volume of services has increased as unmet needs have been identified. Wages and salaries in the health field have been brought up to a reasonable level.

Whether the increased expenditures for mental health have, in the aggregate, kept up with inflation I am not sure. We hear of hospital facilities in many state systems losing their accreditation. Commissions appointed by state governments, citizen advocate groups, and even the consultation and evaluation services board of the American Psychiatric Association report gross inadequacies in the treatment programs for the mentally ill. Our society does not even come close to providing adequate care for the mentally ill. The assertion that adequate health care is a right will remain a hollow promise unless state and national leaders take steps to ensure equal coverage for the treatment of the mentally ill.

Because there is a limit to the number of dollars, it is unrealistic to expect a blank check. Staff will be challenged to demonstrate that they are using existing resources efficiently and effectively. Nevertheless, staff have a right, and indeed an obligation, to press for all that is needed to provide adequate mental health care.

When staff members seek to expand and improve the quality of treatment programs, they are sometimes accused of acting out of self-interest. Limitations in insurance coverage and benefits of government programs are often portrayed as problems for the provider of care when, in fact, they are problems for those in need of treatment—the consumer. The mentally ill have seldom been articulate spokesmen able to advance their interests. Staff members, individually and collectively through their professional organizations, must serve as advocates seeking coverage for treatment of the mentally ill equal to that of general medical care.

The right of staff to participate in the allocation of resources and the setting of priorities. In the foreseeable future there will not be enough resources available to provide all the treatment programs that are necessary and desirable. The mental health delivery system is going to be under heavy financial pressure. Since it is simply not possible to do everything at once, difficult choices about what to do first will have to be made.

Unfortunately the decision-making process is becoming further and further removed from those providing direct patient care. As the administrative structure has expanded, more and more decisions are made by individuals lacking clinical experience and sometimes even lacking sensitivity to the needs of the mentally ill. The planning and decision-making process must include staff members involved in patient care. Only in this way can treatment programs be developed that are responsive to patient needs.

Even though staff members have the right to participate in the allocation of resources and the setting of priorities, they cannot expect to have the final say; this is a prerogative of top management. To be a part of top management one must have an overview of the total situation. This does not mean that to be heard every clinician must understand all the intricacies of budgeting and personnel management. It does mean, however, that top clinician-administrators must acquire such expertise. Clinical directors of programs, for example, must at least understand fiscal, administrative, and political implications.

The right of staff to be accountable for clinical matters to the highest governing authority. The ultimate responsibility for patient care rests with the governing body, not with the clinical staff. It is true that governing bodies generally look to the staff to develop and to maintain standards of care. But they cannot delegate this responsibility and, therefore, must maintain direct communication with the staff.

There was a time when the director of a major clinical program, the superintendent of a psychiatric hospital, or the director of a state mental health program was always a clinician, usually a physician. As such he was accountable to the highest governing authority, whether it was the board of a private institution, a state legislature, or the chief executive of a state government. As systems have become larger and administrative demands have become greater, there has been an increasing reliance on nonclinical administrators. This change has some merit. Administrative pressures are intense; few clinicians are willing to master a second profession.

In dealing with this issue the Joint Commission on Accreditation of Hospitals, in its standards for governing body and management, indicates: "In any psychiatric hospital in which the chief administrative officer is not a psychiatrist, the ultimate responsibility for the diagnosis and treatment of patients shall rest with a psychiatrist, who is accountable therefore to the governing body."[3] This concept should be applied to any organizational structure so a direct line of communication and accountability is always retained between the clinical staff and the authority with ultimate responsibility.

For clinicians this right carries new responsibilities. The demands and expectations for quality assurance have escalated. The traditional method of clinical conferences and individual supervision is seldom adequate to meet these new expectations. We have just begun to scratch the surface in developing new methodologies for systematic review including utilization review, determinations of medical necessity, medical audit, and medical care evaluation. Clinicians must assume a leadership role in quality assurance by developing the techniques to identify inadequacies in the treatment process and by seeking ways to use such findings systematically to improve the treatment program.

The right of staff to the free and complete exercise of clinical judgment and skill under conditions that will not cause the deterioration of the quality of care. It has long been recognized that clinical practice can be influenced adversely by the particular circumstances or conditions under which it is conducted. Indeed, the American Medical Association code of ethics explicitly forbids physicians from practicing under circumstances that could lead to a deterioration in the quality of care. Obvious abuses such as fee-splitting are forbidden. As the health care system becomes more complex, more subtle problems are being identified. Some of the attempts to control and modify the health care delivery system create new ethical questions.

For example, a concerted effort is being made to shift the locus of care from hospitals to outpatient and day treatment programs within the community. The therapeutic advantages of this approach are so well known that they need no elaboration. Unfortunately the concept of deinstitutionalization has, in some instances, become a political slogan used to empty hospitals for the purpose of saving money rather than promoting the best interests of the patients. This is particularly true when the push to get patients out of the hospital is undertaken without provision of adequate treatment facilities in the community. A staff member can easily be caught in an ethical dilemma if he is directed to discharge patients when he knows that adequate treatment resources are not available.

Of course, the reverse of this problem can occur in an institution that is dependent upon revenues derived from patient care. To maintain the flow of dollars from patient services, staff members could feel pressured to prolong the hospital stay. The point is, staff members must be free to carry out their treatment in accord with their best clinical judgment.

Staff must be wary of still another subtle danger. Numerous studies have shown that staff members are more likely to select the attractive, highly verbal patient, presumably because of the greater interest and challenge. Understandably, staff members seek satisfaction from their clinical practice, but in exercising the right to free clinical judgment, they must be scrupulous in keeping the patient's interests in the forefront. The commitment must be to the common goal of staff and patients for adequate health care for all.

The right to have clinical practice reviewed by peers. The clinician, almost as a matter of reflex, perceives the review of treatment practices as an unwarranted intrusion into professional autonomy. Legislation calling for professional standards review organizations evoked violent protest and a spate of lawsuits. At this point, it is no longer a

[3] Joint Commission on Accreditation of Hospitals, *Accreditation Manual for Psychiatric Facilities*, Chicago, 1972, p. 22.

question of whether clinical practice is going to be reviewed, but simply by whom. All federal health programs require such review as a condition of payment, and every national health insurance proposal mandates such review. Private health insurance programs have a less visible but equally potent mechanism in their claims review procedures.

Any attempt to monitor professional services must start with a set of standards and criteria. The American Psychiatric Association has participated vigorously in developing such standards and criteria, and the product of one of these efforts is incorporated into the American Medical Association's *Sample Criteria for Short Stay Hospital Review.* A cursory look at these standards reveals that they are just the beginning; they provide for only the grossest screening to identify those cases that warrant individualized review.[4]

Governmentally mandated systems of PSRO, utilization review, and the like have undoubtedly been stimulated by the desire to contain costs. That causes many professionals to be wary, and with good reason. But cost containment, if properly done, is of considerable merit in that it permits us to use resources with the greatest possible effectiveness. Beyond that, however, the growing attention and support of quality assurance offers clinicians an unparalleled opportunity to get data that will form some rational basis for continuing education, certification and recertification of specialists, and the basic training of mental health professionals.

We must not be turned off by the bureaucratic overtones of federal legislation and regulation. Inherent in all of these systems is the concept of standard-setting, review, and corrective action by professional peers. It is different from what we have known, but it can be used to fulfill traditional responsibilities of professions to maintain standards of practice and the ethical conduct of colleagues.

In my judgment several years of hard work will be required to develop quality assurance systems. Clinicians must provide the leadership in this time-consuming and unfamiliar task. The peer review committees of many APA district branches are demonstrating that it can be done.

The right of staff to practice without excessive and unnecessary regulation. Most of the regulatory efforts are well-intentioned; there have been abuses and less-than-desirable treatment practices. Regulations seem to dig into every aspect of care through utilization review, determinations of medical necessity, standards for medical records, and even control of specific treatment modalities. Still other controls are aimed at protecting patients' rights, ensuring a safe environment, fixing hospital charges, and eliminating discrimination. Like it or not, the day has passed when we can expect to conduct treatment relatively free from external requirements.

Unfortunately the controls overlap, at times are contradictory, and add directly to the cost of care. Preoccupation with these multiple requirements may distract mental health professionals from their main goal: providing high-quality treatment services appropriate to the patient's needs. In exasperation staff protest that it has become more important to document that some arbitrary requirement has been met than it is to do something that will be really helpful to the patient.

The most desirable solution would be to effect changes at the source: the regulatory agencies themselves. It would seem that some kind of streamlining and coordination of controls would be possible, but I'm not optimistic they could be carried out. Short of that, we may just have to accept the fact that meeting the regulatory requirements is part of the cost of doing business. Just as we have a financial office to handle fiscal matters and a personnel department to handle the affairs of em-

[4] American Medical Association, Chicago, 1976.

ployees, it may now be time to establish a department to assist in meeting the regulatory demands. For example, the staff of such a department might be involved in each involuntary admission, seeing that all the precise legal requirements are met within the appropriate time frame. Perhaps this sounds drastic, but it may be the only way to prevent external requirements from disrupting the treatment process.

The privilege of staff members to practice their profession.   Rapid social changes, new patterns of health care, and technological developments have placed new demands on all of the mental health professions. The increased emphasis on accountability strikes at the core of every profession: self-discipline through standards of training, continuing education, and voluntarily adopted codes of ethics enforced by the professional group itself. The proliferation of formalized regulatory requirements challenge the basic concept that the members of a profession are capable of self-discipline. Have we failed to maintain adequate standards of professional responsibility? Do our systems overlap so much that responsibility must be shared? Have professions lost the public trust?

Instead of looking to the professions, the public is now turning to the courts for answers to questions about voluntary and involuntary admissions, periodic review of confinement, the right to treatment, the right to refuse treatment, civil rights, confidentiality, payment for work, restraints, shock therapy, sterilization, psychosurgery, and legal competence. Some of the court decisions on these matters offer the hope of better treatment services for patients.

Some do not. The adversarial climate, the recurrent threat, and the sense of vulnerability push the professional into a defensive position. Forced to direct more attention to the protection of self-interests, the professional is less able to maintain the altruistic goal of service to others.

Many clinicians, particularly physicians, have become so accustomed to society's sanction that they are convinced all aspects of professional practice are prerogatives automatically granted with a degree. This is simply not true. Practice of a profession is not a right. It is a privilege to be earned and repeatedly reaffirmed by responsible actions and behavior.

Thus the rights of patients and the rights of staff are not in conflict; together patients and staff share a common goal—adequate health care for the mentally ill. Staff must have adequate resources and an opportunity to practice their profession under conditions that permit them to use these resources in the best interest of the patients.

The public has a right to expect accountability from the professions. As a consequence, we must strengthen and refine our internal systems of review to keep pace with the advances in mental health care and the increasing complexity of the delivery system. We must press ahead to define more clearly the standards and criteria for quality care. Beyond that we must develop mechanisms to use our findings to improve all elements of professional activity. We must demonstrate that our own voluntary systems of peer review and quality assurance are more effective than the external requirements imposed by government and third-party payers. In short, we must reaffirm our stature as professions worthy of the public trust.

PROTECTING TRADE SECRETS*

Michael S. Baram

This discussion explores the legal, ethical, and managerial aspects of the protection of commercially valuable intellectual property. Baram suggests a series of measures to safeguard corporate interests without sacrificing the rights of professional employees.

In 1963, the Court of Appeals of Ohio heard an appeal of a lower court decision from The B.F. Goodrich Company. The lower court had denied Goodrich's request for an injunction, or court order, to restrain a former employee, Donald Wohlgemuth, from disclosing its trade secrets and from working in the space suit field for any other company.

This case, as it was presented in the Court of Appeals, is a fascinating display of management issues, legal concepts, and ethical dilemmas of concern to research and development organizations and their scientist and engineer employees. The case also represents an employer-employee crisis of increasing incidence in the young and vigorous [Research and Development] R&D sector of U.S. industry. Tales of departing employees and threatened losses of trade secrets or proprietary information are now common.

Such crises are not surprising when one considers the causes of mobility. The highly educated employees of R&D organizations place primary emphasis on their own development, interests, and satisfaction. Graduates of major scientific and technological institutions readily admit that they accept their first jobs primarily for money and for the early and brief experience they feel is a prerequisite for seeking more satisfying futures with smaller companies which are often their own. Employee mobility and high personnel turnover rates

are also due to the placement of new large federal contracts and the termination of others. One need only look to the Sunday newspaper employment advertisements for evidence as to the manner in which such programs are used to attract highly educated R&D personnel.

This phenomenon of the mobile employee seeking fulfillment reflects a sudden change in societal and personal values. It also threatens industrial reliance on trade secrets for the protection of certain forms of intellectual property. There are no union solutions, and the legal framework in which it occurs is an ancient structure representing values of an earlier America. The formulation of management responses—with cognizance of legal, practical, and ethical considerations—is admittedly a difficult task, but one which must be undertaken.

In this article I shall examine the basic question of industrial loyalty regarding trade secrets, using the Goodrich-Wohlgemuth case as the focal point of the challenge to the preservation of certain forms of intellectual property posed by the mobile employee, and then offer some suggestions for the development of sound management policies.

THE APPEALS CASE

Donald Wohlgemuth joined The B.F. Goodrich Company as a chemical engineer in 1954, following his graduation from the

---

* References have been deleted without indication.

From Michael S. Baram, "Trade Secrets: What Price Loyalty?" 46:6 (Nov.–Dec. 1968), pp. 66–74. Reprinted by permission of *Harvard Business Review*.

University of Michigan, and by 1962 he had become manager of the space suit division. As the repository of Goodrich know-how and secret data in space suit technology, he was indeed a key man in a rapidly developing technology of interest to several government agencies. Nevertheless, he was dissatisfied with his salary ($10,644) and the denial of his requests for certain additional facilities for his department.

A Goodrich rival, International Latex, had recently been awarded the major space suit subcontract for the Apollo program. Following up a contact from an employment agency hired by Latex, Wohlgemuth negotiated a position with Latex, at a substantial salary increase. In his new assignment he would be manager of engineering for industrial products, which included space suits. He then notified Goodrich of his resignation, and was met with a reaction he apparently did not expect. Goodrich management raised the moral and ethical aspects of his decision, since the company executives felt his resignation would result in the transfer of Goodrich trade secrets to Latex.

After several heated exchanges, Wohlgemuth stated that "loyalty and ethics have their price and International Latex has paid this price. . . ." Even though Goodrich threatened legal action, Wohlgemuth left Goodrich for Latex. Goodrich thereupon requested a restraining order in the Ohio courts.

At the appeals court level, the Goodrich brief sought an injunction that would prevent Wohlgemuth from working in the space suit field for *any* other company, prevent his disclosure of *any* information on space suit technology to *anyone*, prevent his consulting or conferring with *anyone* on Goodrich trade secrets, and finally, prevent *any* future contact he might seek with Goodrich employees.

These four broad measures were rejected by the Ohio Court of Appeals. All were too wide in scope, and all would have protected much more than Goodrich's le-

gitimate concern of safeguarding its trade secrets. In addition, the measures were speculative, since no clear danger seemed imminent. In sum, they represented a form of "overkill" that would have placed undue restraints on Wohlgemuth.

The court did provide an injunction restraining Wohlgemuth from disclosure of Goodrich trade secrets. In passing, the court noted that in the absence of any Goodrich employment contract restraining his employment with a competitor, Wohlgemuth could commence work with Latex. With ample legal precedent, the court therefore came down on both sides of the fence. Following the decision, Wohlgemuth commenced his career with Latex and is now manager of the company's Research and Engineering Department.

COMMON-LAW CONCEPTS

The two basic issues in crises such as the Goodrich-Wohlgemuth case appear irreconcilable: (1) the right of the corporation to its intellectual property—its proprietary data or trade secrets; and (2) the right of the individual to seek gainful employment and utilize his abilities—to be free from a master–servant relationship.

There are no federal and but a few state statutes dealing with employment restraints and trade secrets. The U.S. courts, when faced with such issues, have sought to apply the various common-law doctrines of trade secrets and unfair competition at hand to attain an equitable solution. Many of these common-law doctrines were born in pre-industrial England and later adopted by English and U.S. courts to meet employment crises of this nature through ensuing centuries of changing industrial and social patterns. In fact, some of the early cases of blacksmiths and barbers seeking to restrain departing apprentices are still cited today.

To the courts, the common legal solution, as in *Goodrich v. Wohlgemuth*, is pleasing because it theoretically preserves the rights of both parties. However, it is sadly lacking in practicality, since neither secrets nor individual liberty are truly preserved.

The trade secrets which companies seek to protect have usually become an integral portion of the departing employee's total capabilities. He cannot divest himself of his intellectual capacity, which is a compound of information acquired from his employer, his co-workers, and his own self-generated experiential information. Nevertheless, all such information, if kept secret by the company from its competition, may legitimately be claimed as corporate property. This is because the employer–employee relationship embodied in the normal employment contract or other terms of employment provides for corporate ownership of all employee-generated data, including inventions. As a result, a departing employee's, intellectual capacity may be, in large measure, corporate property.

Once the new position with a competitor has been taken, the trade secrets embodied in the departing employee may manifest themselves quite clearly and consciously. This is what court injunctions seek to prohibit. But, far more likely, the trade secrets will manifest themselves subconsciously and in various forms—for example, as in the daily decisions by the employee at his new post, or in the many small contributions he makes to a large team effort—often in the form of an intuitive sense of what or what not to do, as he seeks to utilize his overall intellectual capacity. Theoretically, a legal injunction also serves to prohibit such "leakage." However, the former employer faces the practical problem of securing evidence of such leakage, for little will be apparent from the public activities and goods of the new employer. And if the new employer's public activies or goods appear suspicious, there is also the further problem of distinguishing one's trade secrets from what may be legitimately asserted as the self-generated technological skills or state of the art of the new em-

ployer and competitor which were utilized.

This is a major stumbling block in the attempt to protect one's trade secrets, since the possessor has no recourse against others who independently generate the same information. It is therefore unlikely that an injunction against disclosure of trade secrets to future employers prevents any "unintentional" transfer (or even intentional transfer) of information, except for the passage of documents and other physical embodiments of the secrets. In fact, only a lobotomy, as yet not requested nor likely to be sanctioned by the courts, would afford security against the transfer of most trade secrets.

Conversely, the departing employee bears the terrible burden of sensitivity. At his new post, subconscious disclosure and mental and physical utilization of what he feels to be no more than his own intellectual capacity may result in heated exchanges between companies, adverse publicity, and litigation. He is marked, insecure, and unlikely to contribute effectively in his new position. In fact, new co-workers may consider him to be a man with a price, and thus without integrity. Frequently, caution on the part of his new employer will result in transfer to a nonsensitive post where he is unlikely to contribute his full skills, unless he has overall capability and adaptability.

The fact that neither secrets nor individual liberty will be truly preserved rarely influences the course of litigation. Similarly, these practical considerations are usually negligible factors in the out-of-court settlements which frequently terminate such litigation, because the settlements primarily reflect the relative bargaining strengths of disputing parties.

Finally, there is the full cost of litigation to be considered. In addition to the obvious court costs and attorney's fees, there is the potentially great cost to the company's image. Although the drama enacted in court reflects legitimate corporate concerns, the public may easily fail to see more than an unequal struggle between the powerful corporate machine and a lonely individual harassed beyond his employment tenure. Prospective employees, particularly new and recent graduates whose early positions are stepping stones, may be reluctant to accept employment with what appears to be a vindictive and authoritarian organization.

Practical and Legal Aspects

Trade secrets are, of course, a common form of intellectual property. Secrecy is the most natural and the earliest known method of protecting the fruits of one's intellectual labors. Rulers of antiquity frequently had architects and engineers murdered, after completion of their works, to maintain secrecy and security. The medieval guilds and later the craftsmen of preindustrial Europe and America imposed severe restraints on apprentices and their future activities.

Recognition and acceptance of the practice of protecting intellectual property by secrecy is found throughout Anglo-American common or judge-made law, but statutory protection has not been legislated. Perhaps the failure to do so is because of the recognition by the elected officials of industrial societies that secrecy is not in the public interest and that the widest dissemination of new works and advances in technology and culture is necessary for optimal public welfare. . . .

To summarize this common law briefly, virtually all information—ranging from full descriptions of inventions to plant layouts, shop know-how, methods of quality control, customer and source lists, and marketing data—is eligible for protection as trade secrets. No standard of invention or originality are required. If such information is not known to the public or to the trade (or it is known but its utility is not recognized), and if such information is of value to its possessor, it is eligible for protection by the courts.

Further, and of greatest importance in terms of favorably impressing the courts, there must be evidence that the possessor recognized the value of his information and treated it accordingly. In the context of confidential relationships, "treatment" normally means that the possessor provided for limited or no disclosure of trade secrets. This means many things: for example, total prohibition of disclosure except to key company people on a need-to-know basis; provision of the information to licensees, joint ventures, or employees having contractual restraints against their unauthorized disclosure or use; division of employee responsibilities so that no employee is aware of more than a small segment of a particular process; and use in labs of unmarked chemicals and materials.

There must also be evidence that particular efforts were expended for the purpose of preserving secrecy for the specific data claimed as trade secrets. General company policies indiscriminately applied to data and employees or licensees will not suffice in the legal sense to convince the courts of the presence of trade secrets.

When the possessor and his information do fulfill such criteria, court recognition and the award of compensation to damaged parties, or injunctive restraints to protect parties in danger of imminent or further damage, will follow. If there is evidence of (a) breach of confidential relationships (contracts or licenses) which were established to preserve the secrecy of company information, (b) unauthorized copying and sale of secrets, or (c) conspiracy to damage the possessor, the courts will act with greater certitude. But in many cases, such as in the Goodrich-Wohlgemuth litigation, no such evidence is present.

Finally, the courts will not move to protect trade secrets when an action is brought by one party against another who independently generated similar information, or who "reverse-engineered" the publicly sold products of the party petitioning the court, unless there is some contractual, fiduciary, or other relationship based on trust connecting the parties in court.

Other Considerations

In addition to the foregoing practical and legal aspects, basic questions of industrial ethics and the equitable allocation of rights and risks should be examined to provide management with intelligent and humane responses to employer-employee crises that involved intellectual property. The patent and copyright systems for the stimulation and protection of such property are premised on dissemination of information and subsequent public welfare. These systems reflect public concern with the proper use of intellectual property, which the common law of trade secrets lacks.

Will the courts continue to utilize common-law concepts for the protection of trade secrets, when such concepts are based solely on the rights of the possessors of secret information, and when the application of such concepts has a detrimental effect on both the rights of employees and the public welfare? Since current court practice places the burden of industrial loyalty solely on the employee, the skilled individual has to pay the price. In other words, the law restricts the fullest utilization of his abilities. And the detrimental effect on public welfare can be inferred from recent federal studies of technology transfer, which indicate that employee mobility and the promotion of entrepreneurial activities are primary factors in the transfer of technology and the growth of new industries.

The continuation of trade secret concepts for the preservation of property rights in secret information at the expense of certain basic individual freedoms is unlikely. The law eventually reflects changing societal values, and the mobile R&D employee who seeks career fulfillment through a succession of jobs, frequently in sensitive trade secret areas, is now a reality—one

not likely to disappear. Thus it is probable that the courts will eventually adopt the position that those who rely on trade secrets assume the realities or risks in the present context of public concern with technological progress and its relationship to the public good, and with the rights of the individual. Resulting unintentional leakage of secret information through the memory of a departing employee is now generally accepted as a reasonable price to pay for the preservation of these societal values. However, the courts will never condone the theft or other physical appropriation of secret information, nor are the courts likely to condone fraud, conspiracy, and other inequitable practices resulting in some form of unfair competition.

The failings of the statutory systems serve, not as justification for the inequitable application of medieval trade secret concepts, but as the basis for legislative reform. Injunctive restraints against the unintentional leakage of secrets and the harassment of departing employees through litigation should not be part of our legal system. This is especially true when there is a growing body of evidence that management can respond, and has intelligently done so, to such crises without detriment to the individual employee, the public good, or the company itself.

MANAGEMENT RESPONSE

How then shall managers of [R&D] organizations respond to the reality of the mobile employee and his potential for damage to corporate trade secrets?

Contractual Restraints

An initial response is invariably consideration of the use of relevant contractual prohibitions on employees with such potential. For a minority of companies, this means the institution of employment contracts or other agreements concerning terms of employment. For most, a review of existing company contracts, which at a minimum provide for employee disclosure of inventions and company ownership of subsequent patents, will be called for to determine the need for relevant restraints.

Contractual prohibitions vary somewhat, but they are clearly of two general types: (1) restraints against unauthorized disclosure and use of company trade secrets of proprietary information by employees during their employment tenure or at any time thereafter; (2) restraints against certain future activities of employees following their employment tenure.

A restraint against unauthorized disclosure or use is normally upheld in the courts, provided it is limited to a legitimate company concern—trade secrets. But it is usually ineffective, due to the unintentional leakage and subconscious utilization of trade secrets, and the difficulties of "policing" and proving violation, as discussed earlier. In fact, several authorities feel that this type of restraint is ineffective unless coupled with a valid restraint against future employment with competitors. . . .

Courts have been naturally reluctant to extend protection to trade secrets when the freedom of an individual to use his overall capability is at stake. In addition, the former employer faces the practical difficulty of convincing almost any court that a prohibition of future employment is necessary, since the court will look for clear and convincing evidence that the ex-employee has, or inevitably will, exercise more than the ordinary skill a man of his competence possesses. A few states—such as California by statute and others by consistent court action—now prohibit future employment restraints.

It therefore appears that a contractual prohibition of future employment in a broad area, which prevents an ex-employee from using his overall capability. is invalid in most states. . . .

Internal Policies

Another response of R&D management to the mobile employee and his potential for damage to corporate trade secrets is the formulation of internal company policies for the handling of intellectual property of trade secret potential. Such policies may call for the prior review of publications and addresses of key employees, prohibition of consulting and other "moonlighting," dissemination of trade secrets on a strict "need to know" basis to designated employees, and prohibitions on the copying of trade secret data. More "physical" policies may restrict research and other operational areas to access for designated or "badge" employees only and divide up operations to prevent the accumulation of extensive knowledge by any individual—including safety and other general plant personnel. Several companies I know of distribute unmarked materials—particularly chemicals—to employees.

Although internal policies do not necessarily prevent future employment with competitors, they can serve to prevent undue disclosures and lessen the criticality of the departure of key personnel. All must be exercised with a sophisticated regard for employee motivation, however, because the cumulative effect may result in a police state atmosphere that inhibits creativity and repels prospective employees.

Several farsighted R&D organizations are currently experimenting with plans which essentially delegate the responsibility for nondisclosure and nonuse of their trade secrets to the key employees themselves. These plans include pension and consulting programs operative for a specified postemployment period. In one company, for example, the pension plan provides that the corporate monies which are contributed to the employee pension fund in direct ratio to the employee's own contributions will remain in his pension package following his term of employment, providing he does not work for a competing firm for a specified number of years. In another company, the consulting plan provides that certain departing employees are eligible to receive an annual consulting fee for a given number of years following employment if they do not work for a competitor. The consulting fee is a preestablished percentage of the employee's annual salary at the time of his departure.

Obviously, such corporate plans are subject to employee abuse, but if limited to truly key employees, they may succeed without abuse in most cases. They not only have the merit of providing the employee with a choice, an equitable feature likely to incur employee loyalty, but they also have no apparent legal defects.

Another valid internal practice is the debriefing of departing employees. The debriefing session, carried out in a low-key atmosphere, affords management an excellent opportunity to retrieve company materials and information in physical form, to impart to the employee a sense of responsibility regarding trade secrets and sensitive areas, and to discuss mutual anxieties in full.

External Procedures

Several management responses relating to external company policies are worth noting, as they also serve to protect trade secrets in cases involving employee departures. Among several industries, such as in the chemical field, it is common to find gentlemen's agreements which provide mutuality in the nonhiring of competitors' key employees, following notice. Employees who have encountered this practice have not found the experience a pleasant one. This same practice is also found in other areas, such as the industrial machinery industry, that are in need of innovation; and it appears that the presence of such agreements helps to depict these industries in an unappealing fashion to the types of employees they need.

Another external response for management consideration is company reliance on trademarks. Given a good mark and subsequent public identification of the product with the mark, a company may be able to maintain markets despite the fact that its intellectual property is no longer a trade secret. Competitors may be hesitant about utilizing the former trade secrets of any company whose products are strongly identified with trademarks and with the company itself.

CONCLUSION

A major concern of our society is progress through the promotion and utilization of new technology. To sustain and enhance this form of progress, it is necessary to optimize the flow of information and innovation all the way from conception to public use. This effort is now a tripartite affair involving federal agencies, industry, and universities. A unique feature of this tripartite relationship is the mobility of R&D managers, scientists, and engineers who follow contract funding and projects in accordance with their special competence. Neither the federal agencies nor the universities rely on trade secret concepts for the protection of their intellectual property. However, industry still does, despite the fact that trade secret concepts bear the potential ancillary effect of interfering with employee mobility.

It is becoming increasingly clear that new societal values associated with the tripartite approach to new technology are now evolving, and that the common law dispensed by the courts has begun to reflect these values. A victim of sorts is trade secret law, which has not only never been clearly defined, but which has indeed been sustained by court concepts of unfair competition, equity, and confidence derived from other fields of law. The day when courts restrict employee mobility to preserve industrial trade secrets appears to have passed, except—as we noted earlier—in cases involving highly charged factors such as conspiracy, fraud, or theft.

In short, it is now unwise for management to rely on trade secret law and derivative employee contractual restraints to preserve trade secrets. Companies must now carefully weigh the nature and value of their intellectual property, present and potential employees, competition, and applicable laws in order to formulate sound management policies.

Programmed Approach

Regarding the challenge to the preservation of trade secrets posed by the mobile employee, sophisticated management will place its primary reliance on the inculcation of company loyalty in key employees, and on the continual satisfaction of such key employees. For example, management might consider adopting the following five-step basis for developing an overall approach to the challenge:

1. Devise a program for recognition of employee achievement in the trade secret area. At present, this form of recognition is even more neglected than is adequate recognition of employee inventions.

2. Make an appraisal of trade secret activities. This should result in a limitation of (a) personnel with access to trade secrets, (b) the extent of trade secrets available to such personnel, and (c) information which truly deserves the label of trade secret.

3. Review in-house procedures and the use of physical safeguards, such as restrictions on access to certain specified areas and on employee writings for outside publication. Restrictions may tend to stifle creativity by in-hibiting communication and interaction conducive to innovation. Striking the balance between too few and too many safeguards is a delicate process and depends on employee awareness of what is being sought and how it will benefit them.

4. Appraise the legal systems available for the protection of intellectual property. Utility and design patents may be advisable in some cases. The copyright system now offers some protection to certain types of industrial designs and computer software. Trademarks may be adroitly used to maintain markets.

5. Recognize that all efforts may fail to persuade a key employee from leaving. To cope with this contingency, the "gentle persuasion" of a pension or consulting plan in the postemployment period has proved effective and legally sound. A thorough debriefing is a further safeguard. Other cases wherein employee mobility is accompanied by fraud, unfair competition, or theft will be adequately dealt with by the courts.

The problem of the departing employee and the threatened loss of trade secrets is not solved by exhortations that scientists and engineers need courses in professional ethics. Management itself should display the standards of conduct expected of its employees and of other companies.

Finally, let me stress again that success probably lies in the inculcation of company loyalty in key employees, not in the enforcement of company desires or in misplaced reliance on the law to subsidize cursory management. Better employee relations—in fact, a total sensitivity to the needs and aspirations of highly educated employees—requires constant management concern. In the long run, total sensitivity will prove less costly and more effective than litigation and the use of questionable contractual restraints.

WHISTLEBLOWING I*

Sissela Bok

Written by a prominent authority on applied ethics, this selection discusses the moral conflicts involved in employees "going public" with information about misconduct in their own organizations. Bok sees the problem of whistleblowing essentially in terms of clashes between personal and group loyalties and public interests.

"Whistleblowing" is a new label generated by our increased awareness of the ethical conflicts encountered at work. Whistleblowers sound an alarm from within the very organization in which they work, aiming to spotlight neglect or abuses that threaten the public interest.

The stakes in whistleblowing are high. Take the nurse who alleges that physicians enrich themselves in her hospital through unnecessary surgery; the engineer who discloses safety defects in the braking systems of a fleet of new rapid-transit vehicles; the Defense Department official who alerts Congress to military graft and overspending: All know that they pose a threat to those whom they denounce and that their own careers may be at risk.

Moral Conflicts

Moral conflicts on several levels confront anyone who is wondering whether to speak out about abuses or risks or serious neglect. In the first place, he must try to decide whether, other things being equal, speaking out is in fact in the public interest. This choice is often made more complicated by factual uncertainties: Who is responsible for the abuse or neglect? How great is the threat? And how likely is it that speaking out will precipitate changes for the better?

In the second place, a would-be whistleblower must weigh his responsibility to

serve the public interest against the responsibility he owes to his colleagues and the institution in which he works. While the professional ethic requires collegial loyalty, the codes of ethics often stress responsibility to the public over and above duties to colleagues and clients. Thus the United States Code of Ethics for Government Servants asks them to "expose corruption wherever uncovered" and to "put loyalty to the highest moral principles and to country above loyalty to persons, party, or government." Similarly, the largest professional engineering association requires members to speak out against abuses threatening the safety, health, and welfare of the public.†

A third conflict for would-be whistleblowers is personal in nature and cuts across the first two: Even in cases where they have concluded that the facts warrant speaking out, and that their duty to do so overrides loyalties to colleagues and institutions, they often have reason to fear the results of carrying out such a duty. However strong this duty may seem in theory, they know that, in practice, retaliation is likely. As a result, their careers and their ability to support themselves and their families may be unjustly impaired. A government handbook issued during the Nixon era recommends reassigning "undesirables" to places so remote that they would

---

* References have been deleted without indication.

† For the Code of Ethics of the National Society of Professional Engineering, see Appendix II in this book.

From Sissela Bok, "Whistleblowing and Professional Responsibility," in the *New York University Education Quarterly* 11:4 (1980): pp. 2–10. Reprinted by permission.

prefer to resign. Whistleblowers may also be downgraded or given work without responsibility or work for which they are not qualified; or else they may be given many more tasks than they can possibly perform. Another risk is that an outspoken civil servant may be ordered to undergo a psychiatric fitness-for-duty examination, declared unfit for service, and "separated" as well as discredited from the point of view of any allegations he may be making. Outright firing, finally, is the most direct institutional response to whistleblowers.

Add to the conflicts confronting individual whistleblowers the claim to self-policing that many professions make, and professional responsibility is at issue in still another way. For an appeal to the public goes against everything that "self-policing" stands for. The question for the different professions, then, is how to resolve, insofar as it is possible, the conflict between professional loyalty and professional responsibility toward the outside world. The same conflicts arise to some extent in all groups, but professional groups often have special cohesion and claim special dignity and privileges.

The plight of whistleblowers has come to be documented by the press and described in a number of books. Evidence of the hardships imposed on those who chose to act in the public interest has combined with a heightened awareness of professional malfeasance and corruption to produce a shift toward greater public support of whistleblowers. Public service law firms and consumer groups have taken up their cause; institutional reforms and legislation have been proposed to combat illegitimate reprisals.

Given the indispensable services performed by so many whistleblowers, strong support is often merited. But the new climate of acceptance makes it easy to overlook the dangers of whistleblowing: of uses in error or in malice; of work and reputations unjustly lost for those falsely accused; of privacy invaded and trust undermined. There comes a level of internal prying and mutual suspicion at which no institution can function. And it is a fact that the disappointed, the incompetent, the malicious, and the paranoid all too often leap to accusations in public. Worst of all, ideological persecution throughout the world traditionally relies on insiders willing to inform on their colleagues or even on their family members, often through staged public denunciations or press campaigns.

No society can count itself immune from such dangers. But neither can it risk silencing those with a legitimate reason to blow the whistle. How then can we distinguish between different instances of whistleblowing? A society that fails to protect the right to speak out even on the part of those whose warnings turn out to be spurious obviously opens the door to political repression. But from the moral point of view there are important differences between the aims, messages, and methods of dissenters from within.

Nature of Whistleblowing

Three elements, each jarring, and triply jarring when conjoined, lend acts of whistleblowing special urgency and bitterness: dissent, breach of loyalty, and accusation.

Like all dissent, whistleblowing makes public a disagreement with an authority or a majority view. But whereas dissent can concern all forms of disagreement with, for instance, religious dogma or government policy or court decisions, whistleblowing has the narrower aim of shedding light on negligence or abuse, or alerting to a risk, and of assigning responsibility for this risk.

Would-be whistleblowers confront the conflict inherent in all dissent: between conforming and sticking their necks out. The more repressive the authority they challenge, the greater the personal risk they take in speaking out. At exceptional times, as in times of war, even ordinarily tolerant authorities may come to regard dissent as unacceptable and even disloyal.

Furthermore, the whistleblower hopes to stop the game; but since he is neither referee nor coach, and since he blows the whistle on his own team, his act is seen as a violation of loyalty. In holding his position, he has assumed certain obligations to his colleagues and clients. He may even have subscribed to a loyalty oath or a promise of confidentiality. Loyalty to colleagues and to clients comes to be pitted against loyalty to the public interest, to those who may be injured unless the revelation is made.

Not only is loyalty violated in whistleblowing, hierarchy as well is often opposed, since the whistleblower is not only a colleague but a subordinate. Though aware of the risks inherent in such disobedience, he often hopes to keep his job. At times, however, he plans his alarm to coincide with leaving the institution. If he is highly placed, or joined by others, resigning in protest may effectively direct public attention to the wrongdoing at issue. Still another alternative, often chosen by those who wish to be safe from retaliation, is to leave the institution quietly, to secure another post, and then to blow the whistle. In this way, it is possible to speak with the authority and knowledge of an insider without having the vulnerability of that position.

It is the element of accusation, of calling a "foul," that arouses the strongest reactions on the part of the hierarchy. The accusation may be of neglect, of willfully concealed dangers, or of outright abuse on the part of colleagues or superiors. It singles out specific persons or groups as responsible for threats to the public interest. If no one could be held responsible—as in the case of an impending avalanche—the warning would not constitute whistleblowing.

The accusation of the whistleblower, moreover, concerns a present or an imminent threat. Past errors or misdeeds occasion such an alarm only if they still affect current practices. And risks far in the future lack the immediacy needed to make the alarm a compelling one, as well as the close connection to particular individuals that would justify actual accusations. Thus an alarm can be sounded about safety defects in a rapid-transit system that threaten or will shortly threaten passengers, but the revelation of safety defects in a system no longer in use, while of historical interest, would not constitute whistleblowing. Nor would the revelation of potential problems in a system not yet fully designed and far from implemented.

Not only immediacy, but also specificity, is needed for there to be an alarm capable of pinpointing responsibility. A concrete risk must be at issue rather than a vague foreboding or a somber prediction. The act of whistleblowing differs in this respect from the lamentation or the dire prophecy. An immediate and specific threat would normally be acted upon by those at risk. The whistleblower assumes that his message will alert listeners to something they do not know, or whose significance they have not grasped because it has been kept secret.

The desire for openness inheres in the temptation to reveal any secret, sometimes joined to an urge for self-aggrandizement and publicity and the hope for revenge for past slights or injustices. There can be pleasure, too—righteous or malicious—in laying bare the secrets of co-workers and in setting the record straight at last. Colleagues of the whistleblower often suspect his motives: they may regard him as a crank, as publicity-hungry, wrong about the facts, eager for scandal and discord, and driven to indiscretion by his personal biases and shortcomings.

For whistleblowing to be effective, it must arouse its audience. Inarticulate whistleblowers are likely to fail from the outset. When they are greeted by apathy, their message dissipates. When they are greeted by disbelief, they elicit no response at all. And when the audience is not free to receive or to act on the information—when censorship or fear of retribution stifles response—then the message rebounds to injure the whistleblower. Whistleblowing also requires the possibility of concerted public response: The idea of whistleblowing in an anarchy is therefore merely quixotic.

Such characteristics of whistleblowing and strategic considerations for achieving an impact are common to the noblest warnings, the most vicious personal attacks, and the delusions of the paranoid. How can one distinguish the many acts of sounding an alarm that are genuinely in the public interest from all the petty, biased, or lurid revelations that pervade our querulous and gossip-ridden society? Can we draw distinctions between different whistleblowers, different messages, different methods?

We clearly can, in a number of cases. Whistleblowing may be starkly inappropriate when in malice or error, or when it lays bare legitimately private matters having to do, for instance, with political belief or sexual life. It can, just as clearly, be the only way to shed light on an ongoing unjust practice such as drugging political prisoners or subjecting them to electroshock treatment. It can be the last resort for alerting the public to an impending disaster. Taking such clearcut cases as benchmarks, and reflecting on what it is about them that weighs so heavily for or against speaking out, we can work our way toward the admittedly more complex cases in which whistleblowing is not so clearly the right or wrong choice, or where different points of view exist regarding its legitimacy— cases where there are moral reasons both for concealment and for disclosure and where judgments conflict. Consider the following cases:

1. As a construction inspector for a federal agency, John Samuels (not his real name) had personal knowledge of shoddy and deficient construction practices by private contractors. He knew his superiors received free vacations and entertainment, had their homes remodeled and found jobs for their relatives—all courtesy of a private contractor. These superiors later approved a multimillion no-bid contract with the same "generous" firm.

Samuels also had evidence that other firms were hiring nonunion laborers at a low wage while receiving substantially higher payments from the government for labor costs. A former superior, unaware of an office dictaphone, had incautiously instructed Samuels on how to accept bribes for overlooking subpar performance.

As he prepared to volunteer this information to various members of Congress, he became tense and uneasy. His family was scared and the fears were valid. It might cost Samuels thousands of dollars to protect his job. Those who had freely provided Samuels with information would probably recant or withdraw their friendship. A number of people might object to his using a dictaphone to gather information. His agency would start covering up and vent its collective wrath upon him. As for reporters and writers, they would gather for a few days, then move on to the next story. He would be left without a job, with fewer friends, with massive battles looming, and without the financial means of fighting them. Samuels decided to remain silent.

2. Engineers of Company "A" prepared plans and specifications for machinery to be used in a manufacturing process and Company "A" turned them over to Company "B" for production. The engineers of Company "B," in reviewing the plans and specifications, came to the conclusion that they included certain miscalculations and technical deficiencies of a nature that the final product might be unsuitable for the purposes of the ultimate users, and that the equipment, if built according to the original plans and specifications, might endanger the lives of persons in proximity to it. The engineers of Company "B" called the matter to the attention of appropriate officials of their employer who, in turn, advised Company "A." Company "A" replied that its engineers felt that the design and specifications for the equipment were adequate and safe and that Company "B" should proceed to build the equipment as designed and specified. The officials of

Company "B" instructed its engineers to proceed with the work.

3. A recently hired assistant director of admissions in a state university begins to wonder whether transcripts of some applicants accurately reflect their accomplishments. He knows that it matters to many in the university community, including alumni, that the football team continue its winning tradition. He has heard rumors that surrogates may be available to take tests for a fee, signing the names of designated applicants for admission, and that some of the transcripts may have been altered. But he has no hard facts. When he brings the question up with the director of admissions, he is told that the rumors are unfounded and asked not to inquire further into the matter.

Individual Moral Choice

What questions might those who consider sounding an alarm in public ask themselves? How might they articulate the problem they see and weigh its injustice before deciding whether or not to reveal it? How can they best try to make sure their choice is the right one? In thinking about these questions it helps to keep in mind the three elements mentioned earlier: dissent, breach of loyalty, and accusation. They impose certain requirements—of accuracy and judgment in dissent; of exploring alternative ways to cope with improprieties that minimize the breach of loyalty; and of fairness in accusation. For each, careful articulation and testing of arguments are needed to limit error and bias.

Dissent by whistleblowers, first of all, is expressly claimed to be intended to benefit the public. It carries with it, as a result, an obligation to consider the nature of this benefit and to consider also the possible harm that may come from speaking out: harm to persons or institutions and, ultimately, to the public interest itself. Whistleblowers must, therefore, begin by making every effort to consider the effects of speaking out versus those of remaining silent. They must assure themselves of the accuracy of their reports, checking and rechecking the facts before speaking out; specify the degree to which there is genuine impropriety; consider how imminent is the threat they see, how serious, and how closely linked to those accused of neglect and abuse.

If the facts warrant whistleblowing, how can the second element—breach of loyalty—be minimized? The most important question here is whether the existing avenues for change within the organization have been explored. It is a waste of time for the public as well as harmful to the institution to sound the loudest alarm first. Whistleblowing has to remain a last alternative because of its destructive side effects: It must be chosen only when other alternatives have been considered and rejected. They may be rejected if they simply do not apply to the problem at hand, or when there is not time to go through routine channels, or when the institution is so corrupt or coercive that steps will be taken to silence the whistleblower should he try the regular channels first.

What weight should an oath or a promise of silence have in the conflict of loyalties? One sworn to silence is doubtless under a stronger obligation because of the oath he has taken. He has bound himself, assumed specific obligations beyond those assumed in merely taking a new position. But even such promises can be overridden when the public interest at issue is strong enough. They can be overridden if they were obtained under duress or through deceit. They can be overridden, too, if they promise something that is in itself wrong or unlawful. The fact that one has promised silence is no excuse for complicity in covering up a crime or a violation of the public's trust.

The third element in whistleblowing—accusation—raises equally serious ethical concerns. They are concerns of fairness to the persons accused of impropriety. Is the message one to which the public is entitled in the first place? Or does it infringe on personal and private matters that one has no right to invade? Here, the very notion of what is in the public's best "interest" is at issue: "Accusations" regarding an official's unusual sexual or religious experiences may well appeal to the public's interest without being information relevant to "the public interest."

Great conflicts arise here. We have witnessed excessive claims to executive privilege and to secrecy by government officials during the Watergate scandal in order to cover up for abuses the public had every right to discover. Conversely, those hoping to profit from prying into private matters have become adept at invoking "the public's right to know." Some even regard such private matters as threats to the public: they voice their own religious and political prejudices in the language of accusation. Such a danger is never stronger than when the accusation is delivered surreptitiously. The anonymous accusations made during the McCarthy period regarding political beliefs and associations often injured persons who did not even know their accusers or the exact nature of the accusations.

From the public's point of view, accusations that are openly made by identifiable individuals are more likely to be taken seriously. And in fairness to those criticized, openly accepted responsibility for blowing the whistle should be preferred to the denunciation or the leaked rumor. What is openly stated can more easily be checked, its source's motives challenged, and the underlying information examined. Those under attack may otherwise be hard put to defend themselves against nameless adversaries. Often they do not even know that they are threatened until it is too late to respond. The anonymous denunciation, moreover, common to so many regimes, places the burden of investigation on government agencies that may thereby gain the power of a secret police.

From the point of view of the whistleblower, on the other hand, the anonymous message is safer in situations where retal-iation is likely. But it is also often less likely to be taken seriously. Unless the message is accompanied by indications of how the evidence can be checked, its anonymity, however safe for the source, speaks against it.

During this process of weighing the legitimacy of speaking out, the method used, and the degree of fairness needed, whistleblowers must try to compensate for the strong possibility of bias on their part. They should be scrupulously aware of any motive that might skew their message: a desire for self-defense in a difficult bureaucratic situation, perhaps, or the urge to seek revenge, or inflated expectations regarding the effect their message will have on the situation. (Needless to say, bias affects the silent as well as the outspoken. The motive for holding back important information about abuses and injustice ought to give similar cause for soul-searching.)

Likewise, the possibility of personal gain from sounding the alarm ought to give pause. Once again there is then greater risk of a biased message. Even if the whistleblower regards himself as incorruptible, his profiting from revelations of neglect or abuse will lead others to question his motives and to put less credence in his charges. If, for example, a government employee stands to make large profits from a book exposing the iniquities in his agency, there is danger that he will, perhaps even unconsciously, slant his report in order to cause more of a sensation.

A special problem arises when there is a high risk that the civil servant who speaks out will have to go through costly litigation. Might he not justifiably try to make enough money on his public revelations—say, through books or public speaking—to offset his losses? In so doing he will not strictly speaking have *profited* from his revelations: he merely avoids being financially crushed by their sequels. He will nevertheless still be suspected at the time of revelation, and his message will therefore seem more questionable.

Reducing bias and error in moral choice often requires consultation, even open debate: methods that force articulation of the moral arguments at stake and challenge privately held assumptions. But acts of whistleblowing present special problems when it comes to open consultation. On the one hand, once the whistleblower sounds his alarm publicly, his arguments will be subjected to open scrutiny: He will have to articulate his reasons for speaking out and substantiate his charges. On the other hand, it will then be too late to retract the alarm or to combat its harmful effects, should his choice to speak out have been ill-advised.

For this reason, the whistleblower owes it to all involved to make sure of two things:

that he has sought as much and as objective advice regarding his choice as he can *before* going public; and that he is aware of the arguments for and against the practice of whistleblowing in general, so that he can see his own choice against as richly detailed and coherently structured a background as possible. Satisfying these two requirements once again has special problems because of the very nature of whistleblowing: the more corrupt the circumstances, the more dangerous it may be to seek consultation before speaking out. And yet, since the whistleblower himself may have a biased view of the state of affairs, he may choose not to consult others when in fact it would be not only safe but advantageous to do so; he may see corruption and conspiracy where none exists.

WHISTLEBLOWING II*

Ronald Duska

This selection challenges the widely held assumption that whistleblowers violate a prima facie *duty of loyalty to their employers. (See the previous selection.) The author argues that there are no obligations of loyalty to profit-making corporate enterprises.*

The releasing of evidence of the rushed cleanup at Three Mile Island is an example of whistleblowing. Norman Bowie defines whistleblowing as "the act by an employee of informing the public on the immoral or illegal behavior of an employer or supervisor." Is it right to report the shady or suspect practices of the organization one works for? Is one a stool pigeon or a dedicated citizen? Does a person have an obligation to the public which overrides his obligation to his employer or does he simply betray a loyalty and become a traitor if he reports his company?

* References have been deleted without indication.

Discussions of whistleblowing generally revolve around four topics: (1) attempts to define whistleblowing more precisely; (2) debates about whether and when whistleblowing is permissible; (3) debates about whether and when one has an obligation to blow the whistle; and (4) appropriate mechanisms for institutionalizing whistleblowing.

In this [selection] I want to focus on the second problem, because I find it somewhat disconcerting that there is a problem at all. When I first looked into the ethics of whistleblowing it seemed to me that whis-

From Ronald Duska, "Whistleblowing and Employee Loyalty," in Joseph Desjardins and John McCall, eds., *Contemporary Issues in Business Ethics* (Belmont, CA: Wadsworth Publishing Co., 1985), pp. 295–300. Reprinted by permission.

tleblowing was a good thing, and yet I found in the literature claim after claim that it was in need of defense, that there was something wrong with it, namely that it was an act of disloyalty.

If whistleblowing was a disloyal act, it deserved disapproval, and ultimately any action of whistleblowing needed justification. This disturbed me. It was as if the act of a good Samaritan was being condemned as an act of interference, as if the prevention of a suicide needed to be justified. My moral position in favor of whistleblowing was being challenged. The tables were turned and the burden of proof had shifted. My position was the one in question. Suddenly instead of the company being the bad guy and the whistleblower the good guy, which is what I thought, the whistleblower was the bad guy. Why? Because he was disloyal. What I discovered was that in most of the literature it was taken as axiomatic that whistleblowing was an act of disloyalty. My moral intuitions told me that axiom was mistaken. Nevertheless, since it is accepted by a large segment of the ethical community it deserves investigation.

In his book *Business Ethics,* Norman Bowie, who presents what I think is one of the finest presentations of the ethics of whistleblowing, claims that "whistleblowing . . . violate[s] a *prima facie* duty of loyalty to one's employer." According to Bowie, there is a duty of loyalty which prohibits one from reporting his employer or company. Bowie, of course, recognizes that this is only a *prima facie* duty, i.e., one that can be overridden by a higher duty to the public good. Nevertheless, the axiom that whistleblowing is disloyal is Bowie's starting point.

Bowie is not alone. Sissela Bok, another fine ethicist, sees whistleblowing as an instance of disloyalty.

The whistleblower hopes to stop the game; but since he is neither referee nor coach, and since he blows the whistle on his own team, his act

is seen as a *violation of loyalty* [italics mine]. In holding his position, he has assumed certain obligations to his colleagues and clients. He may even have subscribed to a loyalty oath or a promise of confidentiality. . . . Loyalty to colleagues and to clients comes to be pitted against loyalty to the public interest, to those who may be injured unless the revelation is made.

Bowie and Bok end up defending whistleblowing in certain contexts, so I don't necessarily disagree with their conclusions. However, I fail to see how one has an obligation of loyalty to one's company, so I disagree with their perception of the problem, and their starting point. The difference in perception is important because those who think employees have an obligation of loyalty to a company fail to take into account a relevant moral difference between persons and corporations and between corporations and other kinds of groups where loyalty is appropriate. I want to argue that one does not have an obligation of loyalty to a company, even a *prima facie* one, because companies are not the kind of things which are proper objects of loyalty. I then want to show that to make them objects of loyalty gives them a moral status they do not deserve and in raising their status, one lowers the status of the individuals who work for the companies.

But why aren't corporations the kind of things which can be objects of loyalty? . . .

Loyalty is ordinarily construed as a state of being constant and faithful in a relation implying trust or confidence, as a wife to husband, friend to friend, parent to child, lord to vassal, etc. According to John Ladd "it is not founded on just *any* casual relationship, but on a specific kind of relationship or tie. The ties that bind the persons together provide the basis of loyalty." But all sorts of ties bind people together to make groups. I am a member of a group of fans if I go to a ball game. I am a member of a group if I merely walk down the street. I am in a sense tied to them, but don't owe them loyalty. I don't owe loyalty to just anyone I encounter. Rather

I owe loyalty to persons with whom I have special relationships. I owe it to my children, my spouse, my parents, my friends and certain groups, those groups which are formed for the mutual enrichment of the members. It is important to recognize that in any relationship which demands loyalty the relationship works both ways and involves mutual enrichment. Loyalty is incompatible with self-interest, because it is something that necessarily requires we go beyond self-interest. My loyalty to my friend, for example, requires I put aside my interests some of the time. It is because of this reciprocal requirement which demands surrendering self-interest that a corporation is not a proper object of loyalty.

A business or corporation does two things in the free enterprise system. It produces a good or service and makes a profit. The making of a profit, however, is the primary function of a business as a business. For if the production of the good or service was not profitable the business would be out of business. Since non-profitable goods or services are discontinued, the providing of a service or the making of a product is not done for its own sake, but from a business perspective is a means to an end, the making of profit. People bound together in a business are not bound together for mutual fulfillment and support, but to divide labor so the business makes a profit. Since profit is paramount if you do not produce in a company or if there are cheaper laborers around, a company feels justified in firing you for the sake of better production. Throughout history companies in a pinch feel no obligation of loyalty. Compare that to a family. While we can jokingly refer to a family as "somewhere they have to take you in no matter what," you cannot refer to a company in that way. "You can't buy loyalty" is true. Loyalty depends on ties that demand self-sacrifice with no expectation of reward, e.g., the ties of loyalty that bind a family together. Business functions on the basis of enlightened self-interest. I am devoted to a com-

pany not because it is like a parent to me. It is not, and attempts of some companies to create "one big happy family" ought to be looked on with suspicion. I am not "devoted" to it at all, or should not be. I *work* for it because it pays me. I am not in a family to get paid, but I am in a company to get paid.

Since loyalty is a kind of devotion, one can confuse devotion to one's job (or the ends of one's work) with devotion to a company.

I may have a job I find fulfilling, but that is accidental to my relation to the company. For example, I might go to work for a company as a carpenter and love the job and get satisfaction out of doing good work. But if the company can increase profit by cutting back to an adequate but inferior type of material or procedure, it can make it impossible for me to take pride in my work as a carpenter while making it possible for me to make more money. The company does not exist to subsidize my quality work as a carpenter. As a carpenter my goal may be good houses, but as an employee my goal is to contribute to making a profit. "That's just business!"

This fact that profit determines the quality of work allowed leads to a phenomenon called the commercialization of work. The primary end of an act of building is to make something, and to build well is to make it well. A carpenter is defined by the end of his work, but if the quality interferes with profit, the business side of the venture supercedes the artisan side. Thus profit forces a craftsman to suspend his devotion to his work and commercializes his venture. The more professions subject themselves to the forces of the marketplace, the more they get commercialized; e.g., research for the sake of a more profitable product rather than for the sake of knowledge jeopardizes the integrity of academic research facilities.

The cold hard truth is that the goal of profit is what gives birth to a company and forms that particular group. Money is what ties the group together. But in such a commercialized venture, with such a goal there is no loyalty, or at least none need be expected. An employer will release an employee and an employee will walk away from an employer when it is profitable to do so. That's business. It is perfectly permissible. Contrast that with the ties between a lord and his vassal. A lord could not in good conscience wash his hands of his vassal, nor could a vassal in good conscience abandon his lord. What bound them was mutual enrichment, not profit.

Loyalty to a corporation, then, is not required. But even more it is probably misguided. There is nothing as pathetic as the story of the loyal employee who, having given above and beyond the call of duty, is let go in the restructuring of the company. He feels betrayed because he mistakenly viewed the company as an object of his loyalty. To get rid of such foolish romanticism and to come to grips with this hard but accurate assessment should ultimately benefit everyone.

One need hardly be an enemy of business to be suspicious of a demand of loyalty to something whose primary reason for existence is the making of profit. It is simply the case that I have no duty of loyalty to the business or organization. Rather I have a duty to return responsible work for fair wages. The commercialization of work dissolves the type of relationship that requires loyalty. It sets up merely contractual relationships. One sells one's labor but not one's self to a company or an institution.

To think we owe a company or corporation loyalty requires us to think of that company as a person or as a group with a goal of human enrichment. If we think of it in this way we can be loyal. But this is just the wrong way to think. A company is not a person. A company is an instrument, and an instrument with a specific purpose, the making of profit. To treat an instrument as an end in itself, like a person, may not be as bad as treating an end as an instrument, but it does give the instrument a moral status it does not deserve,

and by elevating the instrument we lower the end. All things, instruments and ends, become alike.

To treat a company as a person is analogous to treating a machine as a person or treating a system as a person. The system, company, or instrument get as much respect and care as the persons for whom they were invented. If we remember that the primary purpose of business is to make profit, it can be seen clearly as merely an instrument. If so, it needs to be used and regulated accordingly, and I owe it no more loyalty than I owe a word processor.

Of course if everyone would view business as a commercial instrument, things might become more difficult for the smooth functioning of the organization, since businesses could not count on the "loyalty" of their employees. Business itself is well served, at least in the short run, if it can keep the notion of a duty to loyalty alive. It does this by comparing itself to a paradigm case of an organization one shows loyalty to, the team.

What is perceived as bad about whistleblowing in business from this perspective is that one blows the whistle on one's own team, thereby violating team loyalty. If the company can get its employees to view it as a team they belong to, it is easier to demand loyalty. The rules governing teamwork and team loyalty will apply. One reason the appeal to a team and team loyalty works so well in business is that businesses are in competition with one another. If an executive could get his employees to be loyal, a loyalty without thought to himself or his fellow man, but to the will of the company, the manager would have the ideal kind of corporation from an organizational standpoint.

But businesses differ from teams in very important respects, which makes the analogy between business and a team dangerous. Loyalty to a team is loyalty within the context of sport, a competition. Teamwork and team loyalty require that in the circumscribed activity of the game I cooperate with my fellow players, so that pulling all together, we can win. The object of (most) sports is victory. But the winning in sports is a social convention, divorced from the usual goings on of society. Such a winning is most times a harmless, morally neutral diversion.

But the fact that this victory in sports, within the rules enforced by a referee (whistleblower), is a socially developed convention taking place within a larger social context makes it quite different from competition in business, which, rather than being defined by a context, permeates the whole of society in its influence. Competition leads not only to winners but to losers. One can lose at sport with precious few serious consequences. The consequences of losing at business are much more serious. Further, the losers in sport are there voluntarily, while the losers in business can be those who are not in the game voluntarily (we are all forced to participate) but are still affected by business decisions. People cannot choose to participate in business, since it permeates everyone's life.

The team model fits very well with the model of the free-market system because there competition is said to be the name of the game. Rival companies compete and their object is to win. To call a foul on one's own teammate is to jeopardize one's chances of winning and is viewed as disloyalty.

But isn't it time to stop viewing the corporate machinations as games? These games are not controlled and are not over after a specific time. The activities of business affect the lives of everyone, not just the game players. The analogy of the corporation to a team and the consequent appeal to team loyalty, although understandable, is seriously misleading at least in the moral sphere, where competition is not the prevailing virtue.

If my analysis is correct, the issue of the permissibility of whistleblowing is not a real

issue, since there is no obligation of loyalty to a company. Whistleblowing is not only permissible but expected when a company is harming society. The issue is not one of disloyalty to the company, but the question of whether the whistleblower has an obligation to society if blowing the whistle will bring him retaliation. I will not argue that issue, but merely suggest the lines I would pursue.

I tend to be a minimalist in ethics, and depend heavily on a distinction between obligations and acts of supererogation. We have, it seems to me, an obligation to avoid harming anyone, but not an obligation to do good. Doing good is above the call of duty. In between we may under certain conditions have an obligation to prevent harm. If whistleblowing can prevent harm, then it is required under certain conditions.

Simon, Power, and Gunneman set forth four conditions: need, proximity, capability, and last resort. Applying these, we get the following.

1. There must be a clear harm to society that can be avoided by whistleblowing. We don't blow the whistle over everything.
2. It is the "proximity" to the whistleblower that puts him in the position to report his company in the first place.
3. "Capability" means that he needs to have some chance of success. No one has an obligation to jeopardize himself to perform futile gestures. The whistleblower needs to have access to the press, be believable, etc.
4. "Last resort" means just that. If there are others more capable of reporting and more proximate, and if they will report, then one does not have the responsibility.

My position could be challenged in the case of organizations who are employers in non-profit areas, such as the government, educational institutions, etc. In this case my commercialization argument is irrelevant. However, I would maintain that any activity which merits the blowing of the whistle in the case of non-profit and service organizations is probably counter to the purpose of the institution in the first place. Thus, if there were loyalty required, in that case, whoever justifiably blew the whistle would be blowing it on a colleague who perverted the end or purpose of the organization. The loyalty to the group would remain intact.

THE RIGHT TO STRIKE*

Mary Gibson

This selection defends the claim that public employees have a right to strike under certain circumstances, against traditional arguments to the contrary. The author advances considerations that might also apply to professionals in private employment.

Let us now consider the main arguments advanced against the right of public employees to strike. . . . (I should say that I shall understand arguments against the right to strike as supporting specific legislative prohibition, and arguments for the right as supporting specific legislative recognition.)

Perhaps the oldest argument—if it can be called an argument—is based on the doctrine of sovereignty. . . .

As originally conceived, this doctrine was appealed to as justification for denying public employees not only the right to strike, but the right to bargain as well:

What this position comes down to is that governmental power includes the power, through law, to fix the terms and conditions of government employment, that this power cannot be given or taken away or shared and that any organized effort to interfere with this power through a process such as collective bargaining is irreconcilable with the idea of sovereignty and is hence unlawful.[1]

Even if one accepts the doctrine of sovereign authority, it has been argued, it does not follow that collective bargaining or striking by public employees must be prohibited. Legislatures have often waived sovereign immunity in other areas of law. In most jurisdictions, individuals are now able to sue public bodies for negligence, for example. And since sovereignty refers to the people's will as expressed in legislative action, the concept does not preclude—indeed, it seems to require—that the people may, through their representatives, enact legislation authorizing government to engage in collective bargaining and permitting public employees to strike.

A related objection to the claim that sovereignty precludes strikes by public employees distinguishes between what might be called legal and political sovereignty. Legal sovereignty, according to this view, exists in order to meet the need for a peaceful, final, and enforceable means of settling disputes within society. Political sovereignty, on the other hand, refers to the process by which decisions are made in a political system. The American political process, it is pointed out, provides for no ultimate sovereign authority.

It might be added that the role attributed to government by the idea of legal

---

[1] K.L. Hanslowe, *The Emerging Law of Labor Relations in Public Employment* (Ithaca: Cornell University Press, 1967), pp. 14–15.

* References have been deleted without indication.

From Mary Gibson, *Workers' Rights* (Totowa, NJ: Rowman and Allanheld, 1983), pp. 109–21. Reprinted by permission.

sovereignty—that of a neutral or impartial third party for settling disputes—is clearly inappropriate where government itself is one of the parties to the dispute, e.g., as the employer in a labor-management dispute. This is so whatever one may think, in general, of the depiction of government as a neutral in disputes between private parties.

It has also been pointed out that the sovereignty argument as advanced by governmental units sounds suspiciously like the management prerogatives arguments private employers advanced against the rights of workers in the private sector to organize, bargain, and strike. If those arguments are properly rejected for the private sector, it is not clear why they should be accepted for the public sector. It is worth asking, moreover, what our reaction would be to the sovereignty argument if it were advanced by the government of another country as justification for prohibiting strikes by its citizen-employees.

This sort of appeal to the rights of the public, however, is subject to what seems to me a decisive objection. As Ronald Dworkin has argued, it eliminates the protection which recognition of individual rights is supposed to provide:

It is true that we speak of the "right" of society to do what it wants, but this cannot be a "competing right" of the sort that may justify the invasion of a right against the Government. The existence of rights against the Government would be jeopardized if the Government were able to defeat such a right by appealing to the right of a democratic majority to work its will. A right against the Government must be a right to do something even when the majority thinks it would be wrong to do it, and even when the majority would be worse off for having it done. If we now say that society has a right to do whatever is in the general benefit, or the right to preserve whatever sort of environment the majority wishes to live in, and we mean that these are the sort of rights that provide justification for overruling any rights against the

Government that may conflict, then we have annihilated the latter rights.[2]

Thus, if we take seriously the claim that workers in general have a right to strike, we cannot justify abrogating that right by appeal to a conflicting right of the public to decide what services government will supply.

If we reject the argument from sovereignty, then, there are two further arguments against the right of public employees to strike that pick up different threads from the arguments discussed so far. One appeals to preservation of the normal American political process, and the other to the essentiality of government services.

But what is this normal political process? "Is something abnormal because it does not operate in conjunction with the standard political process and procedures of a particular era? Does the normal political process automatically exclude any methods or goals which will disrupt existing power relations?" And if a group "distorts" the political process by having more power than the average interest group, are public sector unions the only, or even the most salient examples? (Note that, by Dworkin's argument above, the "right of government . . . to ensure the survival" of the normal political process cannot be understood simply as a right to prevent individuals or groups from affecting and influencing the political process through the exercise of their rights.)

Is it true that recognizing the right of public employees to strike would give them such irresistable power that the political process would be seriously enough distorted to justify denying them that right? To argue that it would, it seems to me, one would have to base one's case on one or more independent reasons for thinking such disproportionate power would ensue. One of these—essentiality of government services—we shall examine next. Two oth-

[2] Ronald Dworkin, *Taking Rights Seriously* (Cambridge: Harvard University Press, 1978), p. 194.

ers—absence of a competitive market in the public sector, and the idea that public employees have influence over their wages and working conditions through lobbying and voting—we shall consider briefly below.

The claim that government services are essential may be thought to provide support for prohibition of strikes by public employees in one or more of at least three ways. First, it may be argued that, since these services are essential, it is intolerable that they be interrupted, even temporarily, as they would be by a strike. A second argument is that if essential services are interrupted, the public will put enormous pressure on government to restore them, and government will have little choice but to cave in to union demands, no matter what they are. Thus, if such strikes were permitted, public employee unions would be in an extraordinarily powerful position. Indeed, one opponent of the right to strike in the public sector likens public employee strikes to sieges or mass abductions because, in such a strike, an "indispensible element of the public welfare, be it general safety, health, economic survival, or a vital segment of cultural life such as public education, is made hostage by a numerically superior force and held, in effect, for ransom." A third argument is that, since government services are essential, the individual recipients of those services have a right to receive them. A strike that interrupted such services would, therefore, violate the rights of the would-be recipients, and, since the services are essential, the right to receive them must be an important right. These rights of individual recipients, then, may be said to compete with and outweigh any right of public employees to strike. (This appeal to the rights of individual members of the public does not run afoul of Dworkin's objection, above, which rejects only appeals to the rights of society, or the majority, as a whole.)

Clearly, however, not all government services are essential in the ways required

for these arguments to be sound. In addition, somewhat different kinds and degrees of essentiality may be required by each of the three different arguments.

First, from the fact that a given service, such as public education, for example, is essential to society and its members over the long term, it by no means follows that any temporary interruption of such a service is intolerable. Public education is routinely interrupted for summer vacation, spring and fall breaks, holidays, and snow days. Time lost due to (legal or illegal) strikes by school employees can be, and is, made up by scheduling extra days and/or hours of classes. Are transportation services provided by municipal bus lines essential in ways that those provided by privately owned bus companies are not? If hospital workers in voluntary hospitals have the right to strike, why are public hospital employees different? Are their services any more essential? Upon reflection, it appears that few, if any, public services are essential in the way required to make the first argument sound, i.e., that even temporary interruption of them would be intolerable. Many who reject the first argument as applied to most government services do, nonetheless, accept it for two specific categories of service, those provided by police and firefighters. We shall return to these possibly special cases below.

In response to the second argument, that enormous public pressure to end a strike and restore services would force government to yield even to unreasonable union demands, there are at least three things to be said. First, in the absence of the economic pressure that a strike in the private sector exerts on the employer, public pressure to restore services is the only real leverage public employees can bring to bear on management to come to terms. Striking workers, of course, forfeit wages and place their jobs on the line in the public sector just as in the private sector. So the pressure on workers to arrive at an agreement and end a strike is very strong indeed. In contrast, the public sector employer is likely to have tax revenues continue to accrue during a strike, while saving on the wage bill. Without public pressure for the restoration of services, management could comfortably wait out almost any strike, thus rendering the strike weapon totally ineffectual.

Second, the impact on tax rates of wage and benefit packages provides a strong incentive for public sector employers to bargain hard. "For the public employer, increases in the tax rate might mean political life or death; hence, unions are not likely to find him easy prey."

A third response to the second argument is that it is essential to identify the source of the public pressure. As Ronald Dworkin's argument above establishes, public disapproval or displeasure at being inconvenienced or made somewhat worse off does not justify the abrogation of a right. Certainly, then, the anticipation of public pressure arising from such displeasure cannot justify the abrogation of the right to strike. Thus it seems that prohibition of public sector strikes could be justified only by showing that they constitute a very direct and serious threat to the public safety or well-being, or that exercise by public employees of the right to strike would somehow violate more important rights of other members of society, as the third argument from essentiality of government services maintains. The claim that *any* strike would seriously and directly threaten the public safety or well-being does not seem at all plausible applied across the board to public employees. Again, it appears most plausible in the case of police and firefighters, although even here a blanket prohibition may be far more restrictive than is justifiable. We shall return to this question below.

Now let us consider the third argument, that the individual recipients of government services have rights to those services which would be violated if they were interrupted by a strike. First, from the fact

that an individual has a right to a government service it does not follow that the right is violated if the service is temporarily interrupted. Even a very important right to a given service need not be violated by a temporary interruption, as it would be, let us suppose, by permanent cessation of the service. Moreover, from the fact that individuals have very important rights to certain services it does not follow that the onus is entirely upon government workers to provide those services without interruption under whatever conditions management chooses to impose. The right is against government or society as a whole, whose obligation it is to create and maintain conditions in which qualified workers are willing to work and provide those services.

It is worth noting, too, that in many instances the issues over which government employees are likely to strike are issues on which the interests of the recipients of government services coincide with those of the providers. Welfare workers demanding lighter case loads, teachers insisting on smaller classes, air traffic controllers complaining about obsolete equipment, understaffing, and compulsory overtime are all instances of government workers attempting to secure adequate conditions in which to do their jobs. The rights of the recipients of these services are not protected by prohibiting the providers from using what may be the only effective means of securing such conditions—quite the contrary. Even where this is not the case, there appear to be no grounds for a general claim that strikes by public employees would violate the rights of the recipients of governmental services. If such a case is to be made, it must be made in much more particular terms with respect to specific categories of service. Once again, the chief candidates presumably will be policing and firefighting, to be discussed below.

Let us now briefly consider two additional reasons which have been offered in support of the claim that recognizing the right of public employees to strike would give them such power as to seriously distort the political process: absence of a competitive market in the public sector, and the claim that public employees have the opportunity to influence their wages and working conditions through lobbying and voting. The absence of competitive market forces in the public sector has been said to lend disproportionate power to striking public employees in two ways. First, it is argued that in the private sector market forces such as elasticity of demand for the employer's product and the extent of non-union competition limit the ability of an employer to absorb increased labor costs. Since employees recognize these limits, and have no interest in putting the employer out of business, they have reason to limit their demands accordingly. In the absence of such forces, it is held, public employee unions have little reason to restrict their demands to reasonable levels. This argument seems to ignore the fact that all striking workers have a very direct incentive to reach a settlement—they lose wages each day that they are out. Even with a strike fund, strikers' incomes are drastically reduced, and in a prolonged strike, any existing strike fund is in danger of being exhausted. Moreover, unions in the public sector are not entirely insulated from competitive labor. The threat of permanent job loss through layoffs or even complete elimination of public agencies is very real. Santa Monica, California, for example, ended a strike of city employees by threatening to contract out its sanitation work. In Warren, Michigan, a similar threat was carried out.

The second way in which the absence of market forces is said to result in greatly increased power for potential of actual strikers in the public sector is that public employers, not needing to minimize costs to remain competitive and profitable, will not bargain hard. As we saw above, however, the pressure to keep tax rates down can also provide an effective incentive for hard bargaining. Indeed, in many cases,

the absence of a competitive market can work to strengthen the hand of the employer rather than that of the union, since the economic pressure a private sector strike brings to bear on the employer is absent, or greatly reduced, in the public sector.

Our final candidate for an argument showing that granting public employees the right to strike would seriously distort the political process is the claim that, unlike private sector workers, public employees and their unions have the opportunity to affect their wages and working conditions through the political process, so that if they had the right to strike as well, they would wield undue power. Thus it has been argued that, through collective bargaining, public employee unions can acquire the maximum concessions management will offer at the bargaining table, and then they can apply political pressure, through lobbying efforts and voting strength, to obtain additional concessions. If the right to strike were added, according to this argument, public sector bargaining would be heavily weighted in favor of employees.

But the capacity of public employee unions to influence legislative decision-making is a necessary (and often inadequate) counterweight to the tendency of legislators, responding to public pressure to keep taxes down, to solve difficult and ubiquitous fiscal problems at the expense of public employees. Representatives of each of the different categories of government workers must attempt to bring their concerns to the attention of legislators in an effort to avoid being lost in the budgetary shuffle. Further, although they constitute a growing percentage of the workforce, public employees as a group are unlikely to constitute anything approaching a voting majority in any given jurisdiction. And, although public employees as a group may constitute a potentially significant voting block, those workers directly affected by negotiations over any particular contract will almost certainly be a tiny minority. Thus, whatever truth there may be to this argument, it seems grossly inadequate to the task of showing that if on top of their right as citizens to participate in the political process they had, as workers, the right to strike, the political process would be so seriously distorted as to justify prohibiting the exercise of one of these important rights.

We have been unable to find any justification for a general prohibition of strikes by public employees. I conclude that public employees generally, like workers in the private sector, have the moral right to strike, and the right ought to be recognized and protected by law, as it is for all other workers.

We must turn now to consider whether police and firefighters constitute a special case where prohibition of strikes may be justified, even though it is not justified for other public employees. We shall not be able to give this complex and admittedly difficult question adequate discussion here, but we can try at least to identify some of the relevant considerations.

Of the various arguments discussed above, only those appealing to essentiality of services may apply differently to police and firefighters than to other public employees, so those are the only arguments relevant here. As you may recall, there were three arguments from essentiality of services. First, it may be argued that police and firefighting services are essential in a way that makes it intolerable for them to be interrupted, even temporarily. The second argument claims that, if such services were interrupted by a strike, public pressure to have them restored would be so strong that even outrageous demands would be agreed to. Thus police and firefighters are in a position to "hold hostage" the public safety. And, third, individual members of the public may be said to have very important rights to protection of their lives, safety, and property that police and firefighters provide, rights that would be violated if those protections were suspended by a strike.

Concerning the second argument, the burden of proof must be on those who would deny an important right to show that there is more than a theoretical possibility that the right would be abused in seriously harmful ways. More than that, many of our important rights and freedoms are occasionally abused in ways that result in serious harm to others. In most cases, we reluctantly accept the risks in order to preserve the freedoms. Proponents of prohibition of strikes by police and firefighters must, then, provide convincing evidence that legal recognition of their right to strike would create a serious *practical* threat that is out of proportion to the other risks we endure out of respect for rights. I have so far seen no reason to believe that such evidence can be produced. Note, too, that the fact that the restriction in question applies to a minority of the members of society, in contrast to many other possible restrictions of rights that might be adopted, is a reason to be suspicious of it.

Let us grant, though, that one or more of these arguments may have some force in the case of police and firefighters. Is that force sufficient to justify flatly denying to these individuals an important right? The answer to this question seems to depend on what the available alternatives are. It may be that, with some constraints, the right to strike could be retained by these workers without serious threat to the rights or safety of the public. If so, outright prohibition of such strikes still would not be justified.

For example, provision might be made for partial work stoppages with emergency services continued for life-threatening situations. Police functions include many that could be interrupted with some inconvenience but little serious danger to the public; for example, traffic control, parking violations, paper work not immediately essential to protecting the rights either of victims of crime or of the accused. Firefighters might respond to alarms but limit their firefighting to those measures needed in order to carry out all possible rescue efforts.

Another possibility is to provide for a mandatory "cooling off" period of, say, thirty or sixty days. This could be either automatic or available to be invoked by the appropriate public official if he or she deemed it necessary. During this period, mediation could take place in an effort to help the parties reach voluntary agreement. (A mediator is a third party who attempts to help the disputants find a resolution they can agree upon. A mediator has no power to impose a settlement.) Also, during such a period, public officials would have the opportunity to make contingency plans for protecting the public in the event of a strike. It may be objected with some justification that such a "cooling off" period is, or should be, unnecessary. Mediation efforts could be undertaken before, rather than after, a contract runs out, and contingency plans could be made when officials see that negotiations are not going well and the contract is within a month or two of running out. Nevertheless, supposing that public officials sometimes lack wisdom and foresight, and that the public safety may be at stake as a result, there may be some grounds for such a provision.

I see no reason why some such constraints would not suffice to eliminate any serious special threat to the rights and safety of the public that the prospect of a strike by police or firefighters poses. But since some will no doubt remain unpersuaded, and since the precise nature and degree of constraints justifiable on these grounds will be controversial among those who are persuaded, it may be worthwhile to look briefly at what the alternative is if the right to strike is entirely denied. Some procedure must be provided for arriving at a settlement when contract negotiations are at an impasse.

The principal alternative is compulsory binding arbitration. Arbitration differs from mediation in that an arbitrator investigates a dispute and issues a decision which is binding on both parties. There are two sorts of labor disputes in which arbitration may be used. It is most commonly used as a final step for resolving individual grievances that arise under an existing contract. Frequently, the contract itself provides that grievances that are not resolved by the other measures provided in the grievance procedure will go to arbitration. The second kind of dispute is that in question here, where the parties are unable to reach agreement on a contract. We shall be discussing only arbitration of the latter sort.

In the most usual form of arbitration for settling the terms of a contract, the parties present and argue for their positions on the issues that are in dispute, and then the arbitrator draws up terms that he or she considers most fair. Thus the arbitrator may impose terms that were not proposed by either party. It has been objected against this sort of arbitration that, since arbitrators most often "split the difference" between the two sides, there is little incentive for the parties to bargain in good faith, since the more extreme the position they present to the arbitrator the more they are likely to get in the compromise. To avoid this problem, another form of arbitration has been proposed. It is called final-offer arbitration because the arbitrator is restricted to a choice between the final offers of the two parties on all unresolved issues. The arbitrator may not pick and choose among the offers of the parties on different issues—the choice is between one total package or the other. The purpose of this restriction is to provide a strong incentive for each party to make the most reasonable possible proposals— with the hope that, in so doing, they may even arrive at an agreement without going to arbitration. A serious problem with this procedure is that one or both of the final offers may contain some provisions which are eminently reasonable and others which are not. An employer's final offer, for example, might be very reasonable in terms of wages and benefits, but contain a change in the grievance procedure that would be disastrous for the union. In addition, an arbitrator, who is not familiar with the day-to-day operations and problems, may not be in a position accurately to assess which proposals—especially non-economic proposals—are reasonable.

This latter problem constitutes an objection against compulsory arbitration in any form. The parties themselves know best what the issues mean in terms of what it would be like to live and work under a given provision for the next year, two years, or three years, depending on the duration of the prospective contract. They know which issues are so important to them that they are worth risking a strike over, and which provisions they can live with. No third party can know these things as well as the disputants themselves. Thus, both practical considerations and appeal to the right of self-determination argue in favor of allowing the parties to settle their disputes themselves, even if that means strides will sometimes occur.

Another potential problem with final-offer arbitration is that a different form of "splitting the difference" would tend to arise. Since both parties generally have the right to veto the appointment of an individual arbitrator—and surely they must have this right, since this individual will determine the terms and conditions that will govern their working lives for, typically, one to three years—there will be a strong tendency for arbitrators to decide half of their cases in favor of management and half in favor of unions. An arbitrator with a record of decisions going too often either way would soon be out of work. Now it may be thought that this pressure should be welcomed, since it amounts to a strong incentive for arbitrators to be even-handed, and hence fair. But it must be noted that there is little reason to expect that, over any given period of time, for any particular arbitrator, management will have made the most reasonable offer in just 50 percent of the cases he or she hears,

and the union in the other 50 percent. Yet the pressure is to build a record that appears to reflect just this situation.

Finally, whichever form of arbitration is used, some opponents of compulsory arbitration argue—with a good deal of plausibility, in my view—that arbitrators tend to have backgrounds, educations, life-styles, and social contacts that lead them, consciously or unconsciously, to identify more with supervisors, managers, and public officials than with workers. This identification cannot help but influence their sympathies, their assessment of the arguments put forth by the parties, and hence, ultimately, their decisions. Thus, a system of compulsory arbitration is, probably inevitably, biased in favor of management and against workers. Note that this objection is compatible with the previous one, although it may at first appear not to be. If unions are aware of the pro-management bias of arbitrators then they will risk going to arbitration only when their case is particularly strong. They will settle voluntarily in many cases where they ought to win in arbitration but probably would not. In such a situation, unions would have a better case than management in significantly more than 50 percent of the cases that actually got to arbitration, so a fifty-fifty split of the decisions would reflect a promanagement bias.

For all of these reasons, then, compulsory binding arbitration is unsatisfactory as a substitute for the right to strike. As a matter of political reality, however, it may be that, given the kinds and degrees of constraint likely to be placed on their right to strike by legislators in a given jurisdiction, police and firefighters do better to accept a system of arbitration than to retain a right to strike that would be rendered utterly ineffective.

To conclude this discussion of the right of public employees to strike, it must be emphasized that prohibition of strikes does not prevent strikes. Indeed, it can be argued that it is likely to have the opposite effect. New Jersey's Commissioner of Labor and Industry said in 1965 that "it may be more critical to have the strike weapon available to workers to alert management, government, the customers of the government, and the public that they must do something; they cannot go on ignoring the problem." Prohibition of strikes may thus exacerbate the very problems it is intended to solve.

INDUSTRIAL RESEARCH CONTRACTS
AND THE UNIVERSITY

Judith M. Hill

Many observers have charged that American universities have abandoned their responsibilities as institutions of research and teaching in the public interest in favor of lucrative industrial contracts. Hill regards the problem as a serious one. But she argues that inappropriate commercial influences could be eliminated through the development of an independent agency to supervise the distribution of research contracts.

Increasingly in recent years, industry has turned to the university for assistance in research and development. To mention only a few instances, Hoechst AG, a West German chemical manufacturer, is spending $70 million to start a new Department of Molecular Biology affiliated with Harvard University at Massachusetts General Hospital; Monsanto has a $23.5 million, five-year contract with Washington University for research on peptides and proteins; Exxon has a $7 million, ten-year contract with MIT for research on combustion; Celanese and Yale have a $1.1 million, three-year contract for basic research on enzymes. In 1982, the corporate contribution to university research was $280 million.

With this kind of money being made available, it is not surprising that many universities are eager to enter into research contracts with industry. Nevertheless, I have recently heard the opinion expressed, by academics and by nonacademics, that accepting such contracts is tantamount to prostitution on the part of the university. Apparently this accusation is motivated by a sense that in working for industry, the university in some way forsakes its proper role, betrays its proper function, for the sake of financial gain or for the sake of prestige.

This is a vague sort of claim, to say the least, and I have not heard any serious attempts to defend it. However, it merits consideration in that it indicates the need for a careful examination of the role of the university in relation to industry.

Traditionally, the role of the university had nothing to do with research. In medieval times, empirical science was regarded as having dubious value and scientific research as entirely inappropriate for respectable university fellows. The function of the university, rather, was to preserve and transmit the existing, finite body of human knowledge.

It is only within the last hundred years or so that the role of the university has expanded to include research. With the Industrial Revolution, any nation wishing to compete on the world market could not afford to neglect scientific research and the cultivation of new knowledge. Countries in

From Judith M. Hill, "The University and Industrial Research: Selling Out?" *Business and Professional Ethics Journal* 2:4 (Summer 1983), pp. 27–35. Reprinted by permission.

which the government encouraged and supported scientific research had a great advantage in industrial development. Therefore, with government encouragement, the university began to alter its attitude toward research. In the United States, this trend received additional impetus from the demand for weapons development just prior to World War II and from the influx of highly respected scientists from the European academic community. Since the war, research and development has become an increasingly dominant aspect of the university's function, both in this country and in Europe.

Thus, the function of the university in contemporary society is twofold. On the one hand, the university concerns itself with existing knowledge, preserving it and transmitting it to each new generation. On the other hand, it seeks to increase the body of human knowledge. It could be said that the function of the university is analogous to that of a trustee: The university serves as trustee for the body of human knowledge.

In the performance of this function, the university has three tasks: (1) to teach, (2) to provide a forum for critical analysis and debate, and (3) to conduct research. In providing the facilities for teaching and learning, the university ensures that knowledge acquired by past generations will not be lost through forgetfulness, but will continue to live in the minds of present and future generations. In providing a forum for critical analysis and debate concerning the validity of the thought and writings of great and not so great thinkers, the university assesses (and reassesses in the light of new learning) the truth value of received positions, so as to judge what is worthy of inclusion in, and preservation as part of, the body of knowledge. In conducting research, the university adds to humanity's store of knowledge. The body of human knowledge is kept intact and alive and growing through these efforts on the part of the university.

There is, of course, a solid utilitarian reason for the performance of these tasks. The practical value of knowledge—for individuals, for the country, and for civilization—is enormous. Knowledge has enabled us to find and make use of natural resources, to eliminate many diseases, to improve our communications with one another, and to maintain some control over our environment. Knowledge has provided humankind with the means to live longer, more comfortable, more interesting lives. To be sure, not all knowledge is beneficial: Sometimes knowledge is used to bring about suffering rather than pleasure or relief from suffering. Nevertheless, on balance, knowledge is a great benefit. It would be difficult to exaggerate the importance of preserving and transmitting the knowledge that we have or of seeking new knowledge.

For this reason, the university receives support not only from students who expect to benefit directly in exchange for tuition payments, but from sources with no such personal expectations—for example, alumni contributions; grants from private foundations and bequests from private estates; federal and state appropriations. In the recent past, university students have been conferred draft-exempt status and have been eligible for low-interest loans; universities still have a special tax status. Less concretely, but significantly, society has adopted an attitude of indulgent respect toward the university and the people attached to it—much the attitude one adopts towards a very bright child—which enables it freely to explore whatever seems to be of interest, without fear of censure. Such forms of support, many of which benefit private universities as well as public institutions, suggest an impersonal concern for the project of the university, an endorsement of and a desire to underwrite programs perceived to be of social value.

The university's acceptance of such support implies a commitment made to society at large. This is not necessarily a commitment to provide some particular program, some particular benefit. Much of the support I have been talking about has no strings attached, is not earmarked for specific programs, but is evidently intended simply as a contribution to the university's contribution to society. Consequently, the obligation incurred by the university in accepting such support is simply a general obligation to benefit society, presumably through programs designed to preserve, transmit, and increase the body of human knowledge.

The university's obligation to perform the tasks of a trustee for the body of human knowledge does not necessarily entail that it may not properly engage in any other activity. For example, in the United States today most universities of any size maintain large-scale athletic programs. The propriety of such programs is not entirely uncontroversial; but the reasons fueling the controversy are instructive for our purposes. On the one hand, there is some concern that the academic credibility of an institution is undermined by a widespread practice of awarding academic degrees to student athletes who are not academically qualified. On the other hand, there is concern over the fact that university personnel are spending large amounts of time overseeing programs that primarily benefit professional sports; in effect, the university is serving as a "farm" system for professional football and professional basketball. Because there is some dispute as to how well founded is the first of these accusations, and because university sports programs are not only financially self-sufficient but attract alumni contributions for academic programs as well, the programs are not in any danger of being eliminated. However, these savings factors are crucial to the acceptability of university athletic programs. In general, nonacademic programs of any significant size in order to be acceptable (1) should not in any way interfere with or adversely affect the quality of the academic program, (2) must be self-supporting financially, and (3) should

make some positive contribution to the academic goals of the university.

To summarize my conclusions thus far: The primary role that the university plays in contemporary society is trustee for the body of human knowledge. The university preserves and transmits existing knowledge (to a certain extent, it preserves knowledge by transmitting it to the next generation) and seeks to increase the body of human knowledge wherever possible. The normative claim that this is the primary responsibility of the university can be supported either by an appeal to the utilitarian value of this role or by an appeal to an implicit contract between the university and society. This responsibility does not necessarily preclude the university's participation in all other activities; however, it does entail that any other university program (1) should not interfere with the trustee role, (2) should be financially self-sufficient, and (3) should in some way contribute to the university's ability to perform its trustee role.

The question we must address now is whether research programs requested and funded by industry qualify as part of the university's proper function; or, if not, whether they satisfy the three conditions outlined above for programs considered not inappropriate for the university to sponsor.

To begin with, we may point out that there is no question of such programs not paying their own way. The single most important reason the university is eager to enter into such contracts with industry is that they provide a significant source of revenue. Furthermore, the fact that a university is conducting research for industry enables it to attract top-quality faculty and graduate students—because participation in such programs, aside from its intrinsic interest, opens up certain professional doors. Renowned faculty and graduate programs in turn attract more and better undergraduates, which upgrades the whole school. In short, conducting research for industry cannot be faulted on grounds that such programs are financially draining for the university, nor on grounds that they contribute nothing to the university's academic program.

Of course, this does not establish that conducting research for industry is part of the proper function of the university. Nor does it establish that industrial research does not interfere with the university's performance of its proper function. If industrial research is *not* part of the proper function of the university, and *does* significantly interfere with its proper function, then it may be inappropriate even if it does make certain contributions to the university's academic programs. Obviously, the significance of the contribution and the degree of interference must be weighed against one another in such cases. At this point, therefore, it will be useful to distinguish between several kinds of research contracts.

Much of the funding industry is willing to make available to the university in exchange for the university's agreement to conduct research is contingent upon the university's agreement to keep the results of the research confidential. In some cases, confidentiality is required for reasons of national security, as when industry is subcontracting research for government. (The propriety of the university conducting confidential research for government is another issue, which I will not discuss here.) More commonly, research is confidential because information may be involved that the funding corporation wishes to keep inaccessible to its competitors. Patents do not provide adequate protection if the goal is long-term secrecy or if the information one wishes to safeguard lends itself to being pirated without detection. A corporation may prefer to rely on confidentiality, therefore, rather than on patenting the results of research.

In other words, corporations compete with one another for knowledge. The object of research, from the point of view of

industry, is to acquire knowledge before one's competitors do and perhaps, if possible, to prevent one's competitors from acquiring it at all, in order to be in the best position to market it profitably.

In a free-market economy, the marketing of knowledge is no less appropriate than the marketing of food or medical treatment, for example. However, there must be no illusion that the university is working for the benefit of society when it participates in this competition. When the university sells knowledge to the highest bidder with the expectation that this knowledge will not be made generally available to the public, it is working for private industry.

Consequently, the university is not performing an aspect of its proper function in conducting confidential research for industry. Although it is increasing the body of human knowledge—assuming that its research is successful—it is not discharging the obligation it has incurred by accepting the privileged status society has conferred upon it. Society does not subsidize the university so that it may give Exxon the edge in developing and marketing new products.

This is not to say (yet) that the university ought not to conduct confidential research. I have only argued that confidential research is not an aspect of its proper function. It remains to be asked whether such research actually *interferes* with the university's proper function.

In general, understanding of the world is likely to increase, and explanations of phenomena are likely to be discovered, in proportion to the number of people who are working intelligently at finding explanations and achieving understanding. Since more people are able to bring their intelligence to bear more effectively on any given problem if all known information relevant to the resolution of that problem is generally available, a commitment to the advance of human knowledge entails a commitment to the principle of the sharing of knowledge. Therefore, the university should be committed to the dissemination of information, to publishing the results of any research it undertakes.

In other words, the size of the contribution that the university can expect to make to the body of human knowledge is directly affected by confidentiality. For example, suppose that a university conducting research on recombinant DNA discovers information that would greatly speed the progress of researchers in another program who have been making rapid advances in the same general area. The university's obligation to increase the body of human knowledge as much as possible dictates pooling the information in a cooperative effort. But this is precisely the sort of cooperation that confidentiality clauses are designed to prevent: Industry requires confidentiality when it prefers to wait indefinitely for a solution, rather than arrive swiftly at a conclusion that it is then obliged to share. In other words, confidentiality interferes with the growth of the body of human knowledge. Therefore, the university ought not to accept any research contracts that require confidentiality.

University administrators who are eager and grateful for industrial funding will object that a policy of refusing contracts with confidentiality clauses would be self-defeating. Granted that a cooperative pooling of information by researchers in various programs might result in some discoveries that would not otherwise be made, or made so quickly. And granted, therefore, that if a university has the option of publishing the results of its research, it ought to do so. However, in some cases, this is not an option: If the university insists on its right to publish, the funding corporation will go elsewhere with its contract and the university will have no discoveries to share, no information to pool. In short, the university will not add more to the body of human knowledge by refusing to perform confidential research than it would by agreeing to perform confidential research. For if it refuses to perform confidential

research, it may not be able to afford to perform any research at all.

This argument is not particularly convincing, however. It is probably true that if the university (or a particular university) refuses to conduct confidential research, it will, *itself,* contribute less to the body of human knowledge than it might contribute if it were willing to perform confidential research. Nevertheless, *someone* will conduct the confidential research for which industry is willing to pay: if not the university, then someone in the private sector. Thus, it is not the case that the university's refusal to conduct confidential research will result in fewer additions to the body of human knowledge than there might otherwise have been, for it will not result in less research being done. Meanwhile, it *might* result in a greater degree of cooperation among researchers in various programs and more rapid overall progress in research. Consequently, it is not the case that the university defeats its own purpose in refusing to conduct confidential research.

Thus, conducting confidential research for the benefit of one corporation or another is *not* part of the proper function of the university, which is supported by society with the expectation that it will work for society. Furthermore, confidentiality interferes with the proper role of the university in that it hinders the growth of the body of human knowledge. A university that refuses to share information that could be the key to progress in another research program has about as much credibility in the role of trustee for the body of human knowledge as a university that enrolls and graduates student athletes with no intention of educating them. Consequently, unless a university's academic program is likely to benefit greatly by the university's acceptance of a contract for confidential research—and this is unlikely: The quality of the education available at universities able to attract large industrial contracts (Harvard, Yale, MIT) is not much affected by the presence or absence of any single research program—the university should not agree to perform confidential research for industry.

It remains to inquire whether it is appropriate for the university to conduct research for industry when confidentiality is *not* required.

For the purpose of making significant increases in the body of human knowledge, the university should be doing basic research, should be concerned with discovering basic laws and general principles. Basic research is part of the proper function of the university. If industry is interested in such research and is prepared to subsidize such research by the university, no reasonable objection can be made.

Unfortunately, although industry is not necessarily uninterested in basics, it is ultimately interested in *applying* basic principles with a view to discovering or creating products or processes that can be marketed profitably. However, the development of a marketable product, even an extremely profitable one, does not constitute a significant addition to the body of knowledge. It is *not* the proper function of the university to develop better mousetraps, better software, or new techniques for splicing genes.

Of course, it does not immediately follow that it is inappropriate for the university to perform nonbasic research on contract for industry. Such programs are financially self-sufficient, and they may contribute somewhat to the university's academic program. Nonbasic industrially funded research is only inappropriate, then, if it actually interferes with the university's proper function. Does it interfere?

There is a certain potential for interference.

One problem derives from attractiveness of nonbasic research. It is so much easier for the university to get financial support for such projects than for basic research, and the rewards for the people engaged in conducting nonbasic research are so much greater, in financial terms and in terms of creating opportunities for a future career in industry, that when the university has established a precedent of performing nonbasic research it will be tempted to expend more and more of its resources on nonbasic research, and less and less on basic research. The administrators responsible for locating funds for research will focus their energies on industrial sources. The faculty responsible for conducting research will exert pressure to be assigned to industrial projects. Unless the university succeeds in drawing and maintaining an arbitrary line concerning the extent to which it will take on nonbasic research—and there will be every inducement to step over this line, wherever it is drawn—its basic-research program may suffer seriously from neglect.

A second potential problem arises due to the fact that there are certain areas in which university research would be appropriate, but which industry would prefer to leave unexplored. To the extent that a university is dependent upon industrial money, or is courting industrial money, industry can effectively pressure the university to refrain from such research.

For example, in the early 1970s, MIT received two $500,000 grants, from Exxon and from Ford. Shortly afterward, it was offered an unsolicited $100,000 from another source for the purpose of gasohol research. It is no secret that the oil industry had an interest in preventing research into developing methanol as a substitute for gasoline; and it is reasonable to suppose that the automobile industry did not cherish the thought of retooling their production plants for engines taking an alternative fuel. Not surprisingly, MIT refused the $100,000 grant. It would be naive to suppose that this would not happen with increasing frequency as industry's funding of university research continued to increase. Industry has no obligation to refrain from bringing to bear whatever pressure it can muster against the development of substitutes for its products. And it can muster a great deal of pressure if it is a major source of funding for the university.

It may be at this point that the accusation of prostitution becomes pertinent. If the university is so desirous of industrial money that it is willing to do work that is not part of its proper function, and to neglect projects that are more valuable—either because it cannot do both or because the funding corporation makes this a condition of the funding—then "prostitution" is not too strong a word to describe the university's position. It should be stated very clearly, however, that not every university that undertakes research for industry is in this position. There is nothing reprehensible in the university's contracting to do basic research for industry, nor even in contracting to do a certain limited amount of nonbasic research, so long as it maintains its autonomy and its sense of responsibility to make significant contributions to the body of human knowledge.

Is the danger of cooptation by industry so great as to suggest that the university should refuse any sort of contract with industry, or that it should refuse any contract to perform nonbasic research?

There are less drastic solutions.

One possible solution would be to establish a "middleman" institution whose function it would be to receive and evaluate grant proposals from various universities, and to receive and evaluate requests for specific research projects from various corporations, and to match them with one another, awarding the funding the corporation is willing to make available to whichever university the middleman deems most deserving of it. This arrangement would go a long way toward preventing any corporation from exercising undue influence over any university (e.g., concern-

ing research the corporation would prefer that the university not undertake), since it takes the power of benefiting this or that university away from the funding corporation and gives it to a middleman who would have no interest in influencing the university, no personal stake in promoting or preventing any particular project. We could also resolve the problem of the university's understandable inclination to accept a disproportionate number of contracts for research that is not particularly basic or concerned with fundamentals, since we will be giving the power to refuse such contracts to a middleman who, again, has no personal interest in attracting the maximum amount of funding that corporations are able to offer.

The details of such a middleman institution remain to be worked out. How would it be funded so as best to maintain its disinterested status? What criteria would it use for accepting and rejecting and awarding contracts? How would it distinguish between basic and nonbasic research, and how would it decide what amount of nonbasic research it is acceptable for the university to perform? Some of what I have said concerning the function of the university should suggest the proper approach to these questions. My major concern at this point is simply to point out that some such middleman institution could ensure that a partnership between industry and academe for the purposes of research would not get in the way of the university's responsibility to society. Unless some such step is taken, there is a very real and immediate danger that in its eagerness to expand its base of support by cooperating with industry, the university will put itself into the position of neglecting its responsibility to the larger society.

PUBLIC FUNDING AND PRIVATE PROFIT IN RESEARCH
I*

Amnon Goldworth

This selection explores the relationships between publicly funded scientific research and the profitable private commercial enterprises that develop as a result of that research. Using the examples of gene splicing and the artificial heart, the author argues that scientists who become entrepreneurs on the basis of their discoveries often make large amounts of money to which they are not fully entitled.

Private enterprise has spawned the suddenly wealthy scientist-turned-businessman. Gene splicing has produced Genentech and heart research, the Jarvik-7 and the Symbion Corporation. But without the inpouring of millions of dollars to basic research centers and their subsequent outpourings of knowledge, the practical manifestations of this knowledge in money-making technologies could not have occurred.

The common and sometimes querulous response to those who have had doubts about the justice of a social arrangement that permits this use of public funds for private gain has been that things like recombinant genes and artificial hearts are private property; as such, they can legitimately be used to make a profit. To deny this appears tantamount to denying a right to private property and thereby calls into question our fundamental economic institutions and practices.

However, even though the artificial heart and the recombinant gene are, legally at least, now treated as private property, those who profit from them do not automatically have a moral right to do so. Alternatively, although it is usually permissible to make a profit from private property, perhaps things like the artificial heart should not be profit-making or should have limited

profit-making potential.

Although the concept and institution of private property have existed from ancient times, the acquisition of private property was first given a theoretical explanation in a form congenial to modern man by John Locke in the seventeenth century. His theory will then serve as a convenient way to begin our discussion of profit-making. As Locke observed, an original right to property is acquired by an individual when he expends his labor on what is common-wealth so as to increase its value. A derivative right to property is acquired when what is owned by one individual is voluntarily transferred to another.

Locke and the Jarvik-7

Let us see how Locke's theory might be applied to the Jarvik-7 artificial heart. This pump was developed by Robert Jarvik at the University of Utah, which presently owns its patent and which has granted an exclusive license to Symbion Corporation for its sale. The University of Utah owns shares in Symbion Corporation but Jarvik is its president and major stockholder.

First, consider the two decades of labor expended by researchers (other than Jarvik and his associates) whose knowledge contributed ultimately to the development of the Jarvik-7. Second, consider the labor of

* References have been deleted without indication.

From Amnon Goldworth, "The Moral Limit to Private Profit in Entrepreneurial Science," in *The Hastings Center Report*, 17:3 (June 1987), pp. 8–10. Reproduced by permission. ©The Hastings Center.

the taxpayers who over two decades provided the tax revenues of $200 million needed to carry out the research, of which $10 million were given to the University of Utah.

Unfortunately, Locke is not helpful in identifying these different sorts of labor in relation to his concept of private property. Locke's commonwealth consists of undeveloped land and the animals, vegetation, and minerals found on it. Private property is created by cultivating land, tending animals, and mining ore. Thus, any attempt to identify the labors of the taxpayers whose money supported the labors of Jarvik's research predecessors is likely to be hopelessly complicated. Let us then, for the sake of simplicity, view the contributions of these people as the commonwealth to which Jarvik applied his labor. The commonwealth then consists not only of natural resources but of any other resources that can be exploited for private use.

Locke claims that natural resources have no value until they are "mixed" with human labor. But, under my present interpretation, the exploitable resources that are part of the commonwealth consist of the labor of others. This is a departure from Locke's theory, but one that cannot be avoided given contemporary practices and circumstances.

At this point, a major difficulty arises. The commonwealth as a resource that can be exploited for private use already has value. Why then should the individual who applies his labor to the commonwealth, and by so doing makes it his own, derive not only the benefits of his own labor but also the benefits from its prior value as an exploitable resource?

One objection to this construction might be that although Jarvik benefited from the knowledge furnished by his predecessors, this knowledge is not thereby used up or reduced. Thus, unlike Locke's land, which is made inaccessible by becoming private property, the knowledge on which the Jarvik-7 is based is still accessible to all.

However, although this knowledge may be accessible to all *qua* knowledge, it is not accessible as the basis of what is commercially exploitable. It is likely that more uses can be put to the same piece of knowledge than can be put to the same piece of land or other natural resource. But there are a limited number of ways in which the same piece of knowledge can be used commercially, not because there are fewer potential uses than there are users, but because patents and licenses eliminate public use. Patents are like fences put around cultivated land; although we can see the food growing on the land, we cannot touch either.

Thus, access to knowledge for purposes of commercial use is generally restricted in the same manner as access to privately owned land. How then are we to deal with the question of whether a person justifiably may profit, and by so doing, gain economic and social advantages, not only from the labor he applies to the commonwealth but also from its value as an exploitable resource, considering that those who have created the exploitable resource have not themselves profited from it as private property?

Adjusting for Inequalities

One way of resolving this difficulty is suggested by the use of John Rawls's Difference Principle, which says, in part, that "social and economic inequalities are to be arranged so that they are reasonably expected to be to everyone's advantage." As Rawls explains, "[t]he intuitive idea is that the social order is not to establish and secure the more attractive prospects of those better off unless doing so is to the advantage of those less fortunate."

The notion of advantage can be considered in economic terms or in terms of social benefit, which may or may not include economic considerations. According to the first interpretation, the solution is to give the individual in question a property right over the value of the original resource as well as the additional value that he has produced by his labor on condition that he benefits those who are in the lowest economic strata of society. One way of doing this is by conferring a right on the poor to a given level of economic support, which would be achieved by taxing the property holder.

How should this tax be determined? We cannot expect it to be sufficient to provide for the needs of all those who are in the lowest economic strata because their financial need is likely to be more than the entire return on the private property in question. If it is to be some percentage of the return on the property, how is this percentage to be determined? To establish this on the basis of the ratio between the value of the exploitable resource and the value added to this resource will, in most instances, not be possible since we do not have a way of determining the monetary value of the exploitable resource. For instance, although we can refer to the $200 million invested in research on the artificial heart, we have no way of attaching a meaningful dollar value to the results of all the research done by others besides Jarvik and his associates. Thus, any tax percentages we establish that are based on this ratio of values will be arbitrary.

However, if we think in terms of social benefit rather than in economic terms, we can plausibly ask whether the tax percentage should be high or low. In this context we would need to know whether the availability of the artificial heart has had an adverse effect on access to other goods and services in the health field or whether its availability has displaced access to housing, schools, or food programs. Even if the concept of social benefit is restricted in this context to cardiac disease, we would still have to weigh the benefits of the artificial heart against the benefits of such preventive measures as improving diets and discouraging cigarette smoking.

Let us compare the latter with the artificial heart. At this stage in its develop-ment, there is uncertainty as to its effectiveness. But if we assume that it will win final approval as a clinical device, then the best estimate is that its use will add four years of life expectancy to recipients with end-stage cardiac disease. It is also expected that 17,000 to 35,000 artificial hearts will be implanted annually at a cost of between $2.5 billion and $5 billion (1983 dollars). If these amounts of money were used in the prevention and treatment of tobacco addiction, then a reduction of only 1 percent in the use of tobacco would result in a greater cost effectiveness than that produced by the use of the artificial heart. Given these various considerations we can, in this instance, conclude that the added value of the labor of the property owner will be low or perhaps nonexistent. (The University of Utah, which owns the Jarvik-7 patent, did not labor on development, but obtained this patent mainly through the labors of Jarvik and his assistants. In Locke's terms, this might be viewed as obtaining a derivative property right.)

Having demonstrated that the added value of the property owner is low or nonexistent in at least one instance, we now need to ask whether it can ever be high. It is possible, but not very likely, because of the high value of the exploitable resource as compared to the added value of the property owner. Thus, since the tax percentage is inversely related to the value of the taxed artifact, one can conclude that the tax on the property holder should be high rather than low.

Incentives to Take Risks

There is another, entirely different justification for profit making, which is based on the notion of risk taking. Simply put, this argument asserts that those who have invested their money in risky economic ventures should have the benefits in terms of profits. But this approach cannot, in some instances, be applied *unreservedly*. In the case of the artificial heart, the profit maker did take some risks. But the American taxpayer took most of them. In the language of private enterprise, the American taxpayer, in the aggregate, is the major if not the sole investor. Given these considerations, Jarvik and the other shareholders in Symbion Corporation appear to deserve very little, if any, profits from the artificial heart.

In reply, someone might observe that money making is basic to our economy and that one of the functions of government is to use public revenue to promote the development of new ideas and to facilitate the transformation of these into useful applications by generating money-making incentives. There is no question that the money incentive plays an important role in economic activity. Many societies appear to suffer from low productivity because of its lack.

However, the issue of incentive in the context of scientific research is a complex one, having to do with prevailing social institutions and practices, with what is perceived as sanctioned opportunity, as well as with the desires and goals of particular individuals. Louis Pasteur believed that French scientists would consider it demeaning to attempt to profit from their ideas. But this is not the prevailing attitude of research scientists today. In addition, we do not know precisely what levels of monetary incentives will help to generate the production of useful things since these levels vary from individual to individual.

But although money can and does serve to generate scientific activity, it has not been nor is it likely to be a prime incentive. The length and difficulty of the training required to achieve a career in science are hardly conducive to the goal of money making. And one is not normally involved in scientific research unless one already has a strong interest in dealing with scientific problems. If the pecuniary motive fuels the machinery of science, it does so only in conjunction with the more basic incentive generated by scientific curiosity.

Although we cannot determine exactly what amounts of money the individual scientist requires in order to be spurred to do scientific work, these amounts do not have to be enormous. This distinguishes the incentive of the academic scientist from that of the entrepreneur, for clearly the prime motive for entrepreneurial activities is profit. And given the acceptability of this practice in our market economy, there is no way of predicting how much money will be made. Thus, no one can be blamed if he makes a great deal of it.

Given these considerations, we want to achieve a level of incentive sufficient to encourage the commercial exploitation of beneficial scientific findings. But it would be a mistake to consider the notion of benefit only as it applies to the immediate recipient; as my comparison of the artificial heart and the prevention of smoking suggested, what may be beneficial to the recipient may not be as socially beneficial as some alternative.

We want to encourage the commercial exploitation of only those scientific findings that are of greatest social benefit. In addition, fairness in the distribution of benefits and burdens suggests that we ought to accommodate Rawls's Difference Principle. Thus, we want a level of incentive that is sufficient to encourage only the commercial exploitation of those scientific findings that are of greatest social benefit and that also satisfy the Difference Principle.

We have already seen that a high tax on profits will satisfy the Difference Principle. Will it also determine the proper incentive level so that the commercialization of those things of low social benefit will be discouraged or eliminated and those of high benefit will not? Although it will do so in some circumstances, it is not likely to do so in all. Much depends on whether the level of social benefit provided is widely recognized and acknowledged. It is possible that something that has little social benefit can garner large profits while something of great social benefit will not. And this creates an improper incentive level. In addition, some things have no commercial potential but are of great social benefit, such as the prevention of smoking.

Although a high tax is called for in order to satisfy the need for fairness, it will not provide an adequate screening device by which only the most socially beneficial things survive. Government intervention is called for in the form of education and the dissemination of information based on social benefit data, and through economic support of fragile commercial ventures that promise great social benefits.

My analysis suggests that unregulated acquisition of profits from something that clearly derives from public funds and/or is based on the nonprofit research activities of others is unjustified. Furthermore, the present tax structure is clearly inadequate as a mechanism by which those who acquire property rights through the use of public funds and the labor of others can compensate those less fortunate. It is also inadequate to secure the proper incentive level so that things of great social benefit are brought to public use and those of little benefit are not. Traditional arguments in support of profit making cannot be employed effectively to justify earning large amounts of money under these conditions.

PUBLIC FUNDING AND PRIVATE PROFIT IN RESEARCH II*

Loren E. Lomasky

This selection opposes the conclusions reached in our previous selection. Lomasky argues that our present system of development and marketing works effectively and to maximum public benefit in the distribution of the results of scientific research.

The principle that public investment is not to be appropriated for private gain may appear self-evident. It is also thoroughly inapplicable in contemporary American economic life. Everywhere the private and public are inextricably intertwined.

I am the product of twelve years of primary and secondary education, all in public schools. My university experience was primarily in state institutions. Were it not for that prior investment in my "human capital," I would be unable to earn a living, as I now do, as a teacher of philosophy. I confess that I appropriate these earnings with great gusto. I do not regard myself as thereby raiding the public fisc.

* References have been deleted without indication.

Perhaps this displays a certain lack of moral refinement on my part. If so, I am hardly alone. The vast majority of readers of the *Hastings Center Report* are in similar circumstances. We are, on average, the repositories of much public investment from which we derive our current income.

Two questions should be asked: (1) Should individuals derive private profit from public expenditures? (2) Should the state make large investments from which such profits can be derived? These are separate questions; yet they are clearly interrelated. For if the second is answered, "no," then the first becomes moot.

I am strongly inclined to believe that a negative answer *should* be given to the second. I subscribe to a classically liberal position within which the realm of permissible

From Loren E. Lomasky, "Public Money, Private Gain, Profit for All," in *The Hastings Center Report* 17:3 (June 1987), pp. 5–7. Reproduced by permission. ©The Hastings Center.

state action is severely circumscribed. This is not the place, however, to tilt at those particular windmills. Municipal, state, and federal instrumentalities will not any time soon undertake a weight reduction regimen. Hundreds of billions of tax dollars will be appropriated each year for what are essentially private ends. Are individuals morally obliged to forgo all prospects of gain from these appropriations?

To answer "yes" is to endorse a radically restructured economic system. Farmers are the beneficiaries of crop price supports; truckers and their customers use publicly constructed and maintained highways; broadcasters are granted rights to the electromagnetic spectrum; baseball teams play their games in municipal stadiums for which they pay negligible rent. Every corporation in America employs workers who are trained at public expense. If private gain from public expenditure is illegitimate, none of these can stand. The mixed economy gives way to one in which there is only one economic agent, the state.

I believe this to be a terrible alternative. Thoroughgoing socialism is a prescription for rigidity, irrational allocation of productive resources, and general inefficiency. Through its centralization of economic power it also places political liberties in jeopardy. But this is an old story, not worth retelling here. To uphold vintage socialism is to oppose all private enterprise, not merely that which feeds on overflow from the public trough. The position against which I direct my criticism maintains the general legitimacy, even desirability, of private enterprise, but only when it scrupulously refrains from capitalizing on public expenditure. This position is incoherent. Its qualified endorsement of private profit-making activity is incompatible with the proposed constraint. When the public sphere is so much with us, its embrace cannot be totally avoided.

It should be clear why invocation of classical private property theory, such as that set out by Locke, is thoroughly mis-

leading in this context. The Lockean heuristic applies in the first instance to appropriation of previously unowned items by individuals within the state of nature. The reference to the state of nature is not merely an antiquarian indulgence. It is an essential component of Locke's theory, signifying that individuals are not without prior consent to be implicated in each other's designs, let alone in an overarching social enterprise. And when a state does emerge, it functions almost entirely as the protector of the rights that individuals were alleged to enjoy in the state of nature. Classical political philosophy does not endorse the largesse-dispensing state, and it certainly does not suppose that state activity should be permitted to preempt private appropriation and exploitation of property.

I have argued that there exists no general moral presumption against deriving private income from public activities. That is not inconsistent with condemning particular instances of cashing in. A mayor may not award construction contracts to the bidder who most profusely lines his pocket with cash. I may not open up a boutique in the office that the University of Minnesota provides me. These, however, are impermissible because each involves the violation of a specific trust. Is there a corresponding violation when an individual who enjoyed the use of federal research funds attempts to profit by building an artificial heart or splicing genes? No convincing argument for that conclusion comes to mind. Quite a few specious ones do.

The Profit Motive and Scientific Knowledge

It could be claimed that medical and scientific personnel, because of the special nature of their calling, are obliged to eschew such private enrichment. They have committed themselves to the disinterested pursuit of knowledge. Discovery and application of knowledge are to be for the general welfare. It is an instance of bad faith to make these subsidiary to the end of money making.

This argument is vulnerable at several points. First, this represents a contestable view of the priority of purposes that should characterize professionals. It is, definitionally, the scientist's goal to seek knowledge. Similarly, it is the barber's goal to cut hair, the accountant's to balance books, the rancher's to raise steers. Presumably, no one would require of the latter three that they set aside as a primary motivation the making of profit. The barber cuts hair because he aims thereby to gain. No moral injunction is violated. Setting knowledge above profit is one way in which the scientist can elect to structure his ends. But why should it be supposed that the reverse ordering is illicit?

Second, the argument assumes that the aim of generating knowledge is subverted by the pursuit of profit. That assumption is suspect. Discovery and application of knowledge, let us agree, can pay off in the coin of the realm. If that is the coin that jingles in my dreams, then I have a strong incentive to succeed in my scientific endeavors. This is but a particular instance of the economist's insistence that individuals are predictably and reliably motivated by self-interested concern, and that this circumstance tends to be socially beneficial: "He is . . . led by an invisible hand to promote an end which was no part of his intention. Nor is it always the worse for society that it was not part of it. By pursuing his own interest he frequently promotes that of the society more effectually than when he really intends to promote it." The hand may, on occasion, be palsied and require the assistance of a suitable prosthetic, but no evidence has yet been given that pecuniary motivation is inimical to good science.

Third, in somewhat *ad hominem* fashion, I note that a constraint against money making by scientific and medical personnel is elsewhere conspicuous by its absence. Salary schedules indicate that scientists do well, and physicians do very well indeed. If one considers also nonmonetary returns such as prestige, stimulating challenges, social opportunities, and the like, the payoff is even greater. Nor is there much evidence that this is a windfall that has fallen unbidden into checking accounts. If science-for-profit is truly illegitimate, artificial hearts are a trivial component of the malaise.

Another objection is that these profits are incommensurate with effort. A physician is entitled to income from the exercise of his profession, because he provides value-added services. But the builder of an artificial heart is merely appropriating already existing knowledge while supplying nothing of his own (or at least nothing that was not previously paid for by governmental research grants).

This represents a provincial understanding of what constitutes productive knowledge. The entrepreneur just as surely as the scientist generates useful knowledge. It is the knowledge of how scarce resources can more efficiently be applied to the satisfaction of human wants. Scientific knowledge may be good in itself, but it does not contribute to social well-being until transmuted into goods and services.

The process is not automatic; experiments are as much an aspect of the marketplace as they are of the laboratory. Some succeed while others fail. The much-discussed case of the Jarvik-7 is to the point. It may eventually return a profit to investors, but that is a distant prospect. At present, the artificial heart's ink is as red as the blood it pumps. Among the kinds of socially valuable knowledge is knowledge of which deployments of resources are productive and which are not. If the scientist-turned-entrepreneur succeeds in enriching himself, it is almost certainly because he has contributed such useful knowledge.

No investigator does more than push back ignorance a bit at the margin. Whether scientist or entrepreneur, he is the beneficiary of the entire history of human experience. The labor of previous generations and contemporaries alike provides the foundations on which each of us is able to build. No one can claim that a productive innovation stems entirely from his own effort. That should not, however, be taken as warrant for denying that individuals do generate products that are recognizably *theirs,* from which they are entitled to profit. Sociality and individual enterprise are complements, not contraries. Innovation builds on the contributions of others but in turn renders possible still further advance. The process is one on which civilization is built. It is counterproductive to allow envy or suspect ideology to subvert it.

It can be argued in response that profit from publicly funded research is legitimate, but that it should be public profit. Taxpayers have funded the research that makes the Jarvik-7 possible; therefore it is they rather than Jarvik himself who should reap the profits. The point is one of elemental fairness. People should not unduly reap benefits that derive from the contributions of others.

The argument deserves to be taken seriously. That the taxpayer is a much-abused species is a claim I have no wish to contest! Indeed, my quarrel is with its far too limited application. It is nothing short of scandalous that our political institutions routinely redistribute wealth from the less wealthy to the wealthier. That occurs, for example, when taxpayers subsidize farmers and also have to pay higher food prices. It also occurs, and in particularly blatant form, when taxpayers are required to subsidize attendance in business, law, and medical school. Those destined to be among the highest earning of our citizens are boosted into that enviable status on the backs of those distinctly less well off. Should someone wish to launch a campaign against regressive transfer payments, I would be delighted to enlist in the ranks. But, again, I am not here addressing general issues of political philosophy. Rather, I wish to consider whether there may be any special reasons why the government ought to be in the business of investing in the creation and dissemination of knowledge.

Two reasons come to mind. First, it can be claimed that knowledge is in itself a good thing. We ought to have more of it, indeed, more than individuals in their private capacity will provide. Through subsidizing the knowledge business, government causes there to be more of it.

Second, knowledge is, in the parlance of the economist, a *public good.* A public good has two defining traits: (1) if it is consumed by one person, it is difficult or impossible to prevent others from consuming it; (2) if one person consumes the good, the stock of it available to other persons is not thereby diminished. National defense is a good example. If Jones is defended from foreign aggression, it will be impossible to withhold defense from Smith, Jones's neighbor. And defense for Jones does not entail that there is less defense for Smith. Knowledge is, in the relevant respects, similar to defense. Knowledge is not diminished by being shared, nor can it easily be fenced off from appropriation by others.

Public goods will be undersupplied on the market. That is because individuals will be unable to appropriate the full product of their investment. If the good is supplied by one, all reap the benefit. Therefore, each does better when the good is produced by someone else rather than by himself. This argument may appear to reflect a somewhat jaded view of human beings as egoistic creatures who care only for themselves. That surmise is incorrect. Public goods will be undersupplied by individuals who genuinely value the welfare of others, but who value their own welfare just a little bit more. Indeed, even perfect altruists may underinvest in public goods, allocating their resources instead to bequests privately appropriable by the beneficiaries. Public goods problems are not dissolved by moral education.

The dilemma is obvious. So too is the solution. Public goods will be adequately supplied if contributions can be secured from all prospective beneficiaries. Within small groups this sometimes can be accomplished through moral suasion, but in a large collectivity institutional means for securing compliance are required. The state becomes the primary provider of public goods. All political theorists, except some extreme libertarians, agree that this is a legitimate role for government.

If knowledge is valuable in itself, that may be adequate reason to promote through governmental auspices its *discovery*. But that consideration is neutral with respect to how knowledge is to be *applied*. It is the public goods consideration that is relevant to issues of application. And here the balance is decisively on the side of encouraging the widest possible appropriation of knowledge generated through governmental programs. We cannot know in advance who will be best able to distill from the products of pure research those goods and services that most effectively satisfy the preferences of individuals. Competitive deployment of entrepreneurial energies is the surest means we know of to spread the benefits of knowledge to potential consumers, and it is the profit motive that predictably fuels the competition. It is an excess of diffidence to prohibit scientific researchers from joining the fray.

The alternatives to competitive exploitation of knowledge are either allowing knowledge to lie fallow or restricting the exploitation of publicly subsidized knowledge to public enterprises. The former is obviously self-abnegatory, the latter only slightly less so. Whatever public goods argument supports governmental production of knowledge entirely disappears when we turn to consider its application. Individuals can indeed appropriate the fruits of investment in knowledge application, and they will bend their energies to do so unless barred by edict. The market is not without flaws, but even its harshest critics concede that it is remarkably responsive to opportunities for allocative gains. The same cannot be said for state enterprises, as anyone who has walked into a post office can attest. Public monopolies are no more to be welcomed than private ones. Health care is simply too important to be left to the indifferent attention of some public corporation within the hydra that is the Department of Health and Human Services.

Yes, let us attempt to prevent private interests from illegitimately intercepting dollars that belong in the hands of taxpayers. But at the same time, we should beware of seduction by envy or abstract principles of dubious applicability. State intrusions are ubiquitous within ostensibly private enterprises. I believe that to be unfortunate. It would, though, be making a bad thing worse to use that circumstance as a pretext for diminishing further the realm within which individuals who seek profit for themselves simultaneously enrich the lives of us all.

CASE 3.1   LEGAL AND INSTITUTIONAL OBLIGATIONS OF A SOCIAL WORKER-ADMINISTRATOR

You are a licensed clinical social worker employed by a municipal government to, among other duties, supervise the admission and retention of clients in a long-term shelter for homeless families. The people who come to your facility have usually spent at least 6 weeks moving around among various overnight shelters or even living in the streets. And because low-priced rentals are extremely scarce in your area, when clients are given rooms in your building, their average length of stay is 14 months. Families of up to four persons are assigned to single rooms. Larger families are given two rooms. Two-thirds of your residents are children under the age of 14.

According to local law and federal guidelines, preference for admission to your facility is to be given to single-parent families with young children. And because the demand for shelter is so great, all the 200 families in your building (a large and very decrepit hotel) are nominally headed by single females. But many of the frequent visitors to the facility, all of whom must sign in with a guard at the entrance, are obviously the husbands of women and the fathers of children in residence. Most of these men live in the streets or in overnight shelters, working at unskilled jobs when they can find them, and contributing whatever they can to the support of their children.

What, if anything, should you do about this situation? If you identify these men as legally involved with your clients, many of the women and children will have to leave the shelter, and most will lose other welfare entitlements in amounts much larger than the men would be able to replace. But if you ignore the problem, you will be condoning illegal activity within your area of responsibility and running some risk of losing your job.

CASE 3.2   PROFESSIONAL INTEGRITY AND QUALIFICATION FOR ACADEMIC TENURE

You are an assistant professor in your third year of employment in a college of education at a large state university. Your principal research interest concerns the development of aesthetic sensitivities in children, including how they actually develop tastes and preferences, and how classroom instruction in music and art might be improved.

For two years, you have been involved in a long-term study of these matters in the local schools. You have been tracking the activities and development of 75 children who are now in second grade, with the intention of continuing to observe and test as many of them as you can through their high school years. You have constructed a novel hypothesis about aesthetic development, and if the results of your observations confirm that theory, you believe that you will be able to make a major contribution to the theory of art education.

Your problem arises from the fact that the regulations of your university require a decision to be made regarding tenure for you within the next three years. When that decision is made, you must either be given tenure or fired. You realize that the principal criterion for the award of tenure these days is publication, and that it is very unlikely that your main research activity will yield publishable results before the decision must be made.

What should you do? You know that research grants are available for bureaucratic projects that would lead to quick publications, but you regard most of these studies as wastes of time, effort, and money, producing trivial or useless results. Furthermore, if you undertake such projects, you will have to abandon your time-consuming work with your present subjects, thereby giving up a study to which you are deeply committed. On the other hand, if you have no tangible results to present at tenure-decision time, you are likely to lose your job, because your department is under compelling pressure from the administration to raise its publication rate. You believe that your colleagues might favor your retention, because they seem to respect your work; but it seems likely that their recommendation would be overruled by administrators concerned with quantitative productivity.

CASE 3.3   WHISTLEBLOWING IN MEDICAL PRACTICE

You are a junior staff physician at a small community hospital in rural Nevada. You moved to this town two years ago, after the completion of your medical education and training, because you and your spouse wanted to avoid raising your children in a major urban center, because the family enjoys life in the mountains, and because you thought it would be worthwhile to exercise your skills in an area in which medical professionals with current training are not plentiful.

Unfortunately, your situation at the hospital has become increasingly uncomfortable as time has passed because one of your colleagues is, in your judgment, dangerously incompetent. Now approaching his 63rd birthday, this colleague is a senior member of the staff and a highly regarded practitioner in the large area served by the hospital. He was centrally involved in building the hospital more than 25 years ago; he is a prominent member of the community, quite active in civic affairs; and, as a general practitioner, he seems to have played the role of beloved family doctor to most of the town's population.

On more than 30 occasions, which you have documented in private notes, you have either observed this colleague engaging in substandard practices or seen the consequences of such practices in examining his patients. You are quite certain that you can document at least a dozen cases of serious complications that have arisen as a direct result of his work, including three instances of major birth defects. And you suspect, though you cannot prove, that four elderly patients have died in the last year because of mistaken decisions by this physician. Other members of the staff have noticed these problems, but their reactions have been either to express fear of the consequences of a scandal or to dismiss your concerns as highly exaggerated.

As your distress over this situation has increased, you have tried various remedies. You began by speaking to the physician himself, offering suggestions and help, and then urging greater caution and some retraining in current techniques. These efforts were rebuffed. Next you made informal and then formal complaints to the governing board of the hospital, and then to the regional medical society. But in each case, your colleague's long record of service and his high standing in the community prevailed over your protests. On one occasion, he was sued for malpractice in the case of an infant who suffered severe brain damage from oxygen deprivation at birth. But the litigation ended in a settlement out of court; and at the time, the board of the hospital treated the situation as a "judgment call" and backed your colleague fully, admitting nothing more than the fact that he might have been mistaken.

You have thus exhausted all the available remedies, except to take your story (and your data) to the local newspaper or the television station in the nearest city. Should you do it?

CASE 3.4 PROFESSIONALS AS BUSINESSPEOPLE: A PROBLEM IN VETERINARY PRACTICE

You are a veterinarian whose practice specializes in the care of small animals, mostly cats and dogs that are family companion animals. Much of your work involves negotiating conflicts of interest between your patients (the animals) and your clients (their owners). You have learned to work out reasonable solutions to most of these problems; but there are two kinds of cases that trouble you, both centrally involving your own interests as a businessperson trying to run a financially successful veterinary clinic.

One is the occasional request for surgery or euthanasia when there are no medical indications for such procedures. Your clients ask you to remove cats' claws in order to save curtains and furniture, to remove dogs' larynxes to stop barking, or to kill animals that have become nuisances.

The other, more common, problem involves desperate owners urging you to perform medically pointless surgery on animals that are too ill or too badly injured to be saved. In these cases, the clients are so distressed at the prospect of losing loved animals that they are willing to try anything that might imaginably keep the dog or cat alive. At least for the moment, they are willing to ignore the odds against success, the condition of the patient, and the costs of surgery.

These cases are particularly difficult for you, because both raise conflicts between your concerns as a clinician and your interests as the owner of a business. You can do very well financially if you simply perform whatever services are requested. There is no clear prohibition in the law or the veterinary code to prevent you from following this course. And you are aware that if you refuse to perform contraindicated surgery or euthanasia, other practitioners can be found who will provide these services.

As a conscientious provider of health care, you reject the option of simply doing whatever you are asked to do. But this leaves the problem of developing an alternative general strategy for these cases.

CASE 3.5   *JOB ACTIONS IN THE PRACTICE OF NURSING*

As a registered nurse employed in a county-operated general hospital, you have become increasingly concerned in recent months over deteriorating working conditions and their effects on the quality of care provided to patients. Because of cutbacks in federal, state, and local funding, the administration has substantially reduced the size of the hospital's support staff, assigning many jobs usually performed by practical nurses, technicians, and even custodial personnel to the registered nurses. In addition, many of the nurses formerly employed full time have been reduced to "on-call" status, being asked to come in to work long shifts at irregular intervals and without notice, whenever they are needed. Some of your senior colleagues have resigned in response to these difficult conditions. They have been replaced by less experienced nurses, who are available at lower salaries. And throughout the hospital, great pressure has been exerted to limit admissions, especially of indigent patients, and to release patients as quickly as possible in order to cut the costs further.

Nor is there improvement in sight: The budget for the hospital is not likely to increase in the near future. Thus, the laid-off employees will not soon be returned to work, and the job descriptions of the remaining staff are not likely to change. Nor will there be improvements in salaries to compensate for these increased work loads.

You are concerned about all this because your own job has been made tiresome and unpleasant, but also, and more importantly, because you believe that the quality of the hospital's work has become dangerously poor. Patients who need care are being turned away or sent home in increasing numbers. There have been some close calls with mistakes by inexperienced staff members. Extra help has become hard to find and slow in appearing, even during emergencies. And almost everyone employed in the hospital is showing the effects of fatigue and stress.

Despite a county ordinance prohibiting strikes by public employees, some of your colleagues have been urging you to participate in an institution-wide "sick day," when as many nurses as could be recruited would refuse to come to work. Should you support and participate in this protest?

CASE 3.6   CONSULTING IN JOURNALISM

You are a reporter employed by a metropolitan newspaper to cover events involving your state government. In recent months, public opinion has turned against the governor of the state, primarily because he has found it necessary to advocate major tax increases during a statewide economic recession. Editorials on television and in newspapers (including your own) around the state have called upon the governor not to run for reelection; opposition to his continuation has developed within his own party; and public opinion polls indicate that he is perceived as "lacking leadership qualities."

As you are going through some documents relating to his financial history, you discover that 20 years ago, the governor was involved in a dispute with the Internal Revenue Service (IRS) which ended when he paid nearly $10,000 in taxes the IRS claimed, and almost as much in penalties. The disputed taxes involved profits on some out-of-state transactions in real estate that were represented (unsuccessfully) as being tax-sheltered.

You mention this discovery to your editor, and she urges you to write the story immediately for the front page of the local section of tomorrow's paper. She sees a scoop in the story, and you see the opportunity for professional advancement in being identified as the reporter who uncovered the episode. But you are also aware of the fact that the impact of the story would derive from the suggestion, which need not be stated, that the governor had tried to evade legal responsibilities and cheat the IRS. And you are not at all sure that the facts of the case support such an inference.

Knowing that the information you have gathered is accurate, should you run the story immediately, thereby winning a round against your competition? Or should you delay instead, taking the time necessary to consult one or more tax attorneys in order to find out whether the facts really do constitute a black mark on the governor's record?

SUGGESTED READINGS

BEAUCHAMP, THOMAS, AND NORMAN BOWIE, eds. *Ethical Theory and Business,* 2d ed. Englewood Cliffs, N.J.: Prentice-Hall, 1983.

BUCHANAN, ALLEN. *Ethics, Efficiency and the Market.* Totowa, N.J.: Rowman and Allanheld, 1985.

CAHN, STEVEN M. *Saints and Scamps: Ethics in Academia.* Totowa, N.J.: Rowman and Allanheld, 1986.

COOPER, TERRY L. *The Responsible Administrator.* Port Washington, N.Y.: Kennikat Press, 1982.

DONALDSON, THOMAS, AND PATRICIA WERHANE. *Ethical Issues in Business: A Philosophical Approach.* Englewood Cliffs, N.J.: Prentice-Hall, 1979.

EDWARDS, REM B., ed. *Psychiatry and Ethics.* Buffalo, N.Y.: Prometheus Books, 1982.

EZORSKY, GERTRUDE, ed. *Moral Rights in the Workplace.* Albany: State University of New York Press, 1987.

SNOEYENBOS, ALMEDER AND HUMBER, eds. *Business Ethics.* Buffalo, N.Y.: Prometheus Books, 1983.

STARR, PAUL. *The Social Transformation of American Medicine.* New York: Basic Books, 1982.

WAKIN, MALHAM, ed. *War, Morality and the Military Profession.* Boulder: Westview Press, 1986.

FOUR

Access to Professional Services

The subject of this chapter is the distribution of access to professional services. Professionals provide services, such as health care or legal representation, that people want and need. These social "goods" are important to people's lives. In some societies, however, some people may be able to procure high-quality professional services at prices they can easily afford; while others may have a difficult time securing even low-quality services at prices that are very high for them; and still others may be unable to procure such services at all. In such cases, access to these services is not equally distributed. To many, such a distribution is troubling, a matter of injustice.

The concepts of justice and injustice are used to evaluate the distribution of important social and economic goods among the members of a society. This is *distributive, economic,* or *social* justice. (Contrast this with views about punishment that deal with "retributive" or "corrective" justice, and views about compensation, or "compensatory" justice.) When the distribution, whether equal or unequal, seems right and appropriate to us, that society is thought of as being just; when it seems wrong or inappropriate, we register that evaluation by saying that it is unjust. Since professional services are a type of good, questions about the justice of the distribution of access to such goods naturally arise.

Questions of justice also arise when we focus on *who* provides professional services. Professionals engage in interesting and challenging occupations that are often highly rewarded with income and status. Many people would like to be professionals. Access to the occupation is an important social good. But if some people or groups of people—blacks or women, for example—are unable or less able to become professionals than others, there is again a distribution of access which many find unjust. In recent years, policies of "affirmative action" (or "preferential treatment" or "reverse discrimination") have been used as remedies for this alleged injustice. The evaluation of such policies will be another important issue in this chapter.

Since the notion of justice is so central in evaluating questions about the allocation of professional services, this part of the chapter provides a framework for the selections which follow by explaining the most important views about justice and revealing their strengths and weaknesses. It begins with four single-valued, or "unmixed," theories of justice. Next we will consider a framework for combining the values emphasized by the unmixed theories. We will then take up some of the problems posed by economic scarcity for the application of theories of justice. We will conclude with a discussion of issues regarding preferential treatment.

PROFESSIONAL SERVICES AS SOCIAL GOODS

Theories of justice deal with the distribution in a society (and among societies) of important social goods. These goods may be subjective, like well-being, happiness, pleasure, or satisfaction; or they might be "objective," like income, freedom, rights, status, and power. The items in the latter category have been referred to as primary goods—things "a rational man wants whatever else he wants."[1] There are also negative things, burdens, that also must be distributed if benefits are to be produced; burdens include taxation, legal restrictions on behavior, obedience to the law, and military service. The subject of social justice is the distribution of these benefits and burdens.

Professional services are a kind of good. But many professional services seem no different in kind from other consumer goods, such as the services of an architect to make plans for a house addition, an accountant's help with one's tax return, or a continuing-education course in water-color painting. Some people can afford these things and others cannot. This may or may not be just, but it does not seem different from the fact that some can afford fancy cars and expensive trips, others cheap cars and local vacations, and others only bus tokens and staying home. The professional services just mentioned do not seem to be importantly different in the problems about justice raised by their access, for they seem to be just another consumer good. Unlike food or shelter, they are nonessential and, in important ways, optional.

Other professional services do raise special problems, however; such services include health care, legal assistance, and education. These are necessities, not optional goods that we can do without. Without health care, people will die or suffer severe ill health. Adequate legal representation is essential to promoting one's plans and avoiding serious liabilities. Further, as other chapters of this book have made clear, the adversary system of justice can be expected to work as it should only if everyone who needs it has access to decent legal representation. And education is the foundation on which most people's prospects in life are based. Thus, these services have an importance that takes them out of the category of mere optional consumer goods. Moreover, they have two important additional features. First, they can be very expensive, unlike other necessities such as food and clothing. Second, in the case of medical care and legal services, the need for them is unpredictable. During a given period of time, one may end up needing little or much health care, and one usually cannot know in advance. This unpredictability combined with the importance of these goods and their high expense makes insurance, which involves the sharing of risks, a reasonable

[1] See John Rawls, *A Theory of Justice* (Cambridge, Mass.: Harvard University Press, 1971), p. 92.

way to provide access to them. But insurance can also be very expensive, beyond the reach of the normal pocketbook. This, then, brings to the fore the question of subsidy for, or direct provision of, these services by the government. That is why these professional goods, unlike architect's drawings, raise special problems that single them out from other "mere" consumer goods. And that is why the readings in this chapter tend to focus on the provision of medical and legal services and education and omit discussion of other professional goods.

There are four theories of justice that emphasize a single value and that have seemed plausible both to ordinary people and to those who have theorized about these matters. The four include desert theories, egalitarianism, utilitarianism, and libertarianism; they emphasize, respectively, desert, equality, the general welfare, and liberty. Each of these will be explained in turn. Omitted as not in need of discussion are theories that hold that people should receive in accord with their wealth, social position, race, or sex. These plutocratic, aristocratic, racist, and sexist theories are implausible and are almost universally rejected in the modern context.

DESERT

A desert theorist holds that people should receive in accord with their deserts. Those who deserve more should receive more; those who deserve less should receive less. Since most desert theorists believe that people are unequally deserving, desert theories justify an unequal distribution of social goods. An important popular application of desert theory is to the economic market. The market, it is said, gives more to those who are more deserving and less to those who are less deserving. So market-generated inequality is often justified on grounds of desert.

Someone deserves something if it is fitting or appropriate for him to have the thing on the basis of some characteristics of that person. As Feinberg has noted, claims about desert can always be stated in the following form:

S deserves X on the basis of F,

where S is the deserving person, X the deserved treatment, and F the desert basis.[2] For positive desert, the characteristics that form the desert basis must be meritorious, as when an actor deserves praise for his stirring performance. For negative desert, the characteristics must be blameworthy, as when a criminal is said to deserve punishment for a crime. The desert basis is always some kind of worthiness or unworthiness.

Deserving something is different from having a legal or conventional claim to it. Any native-born U.S. citizen over 35 years of age is entitled to run for president but does not necessarily deserve to do so. Further, deserving something is different from the desirability of having it because of the good consequences of having it. A child who produces a drawing typical for children

---

[2] See Joel Feinberg's "Justice and Personal Desert," in his book *Doing and Deserving* (Princeton, N.J.: Princeton University Press, 1974), p. 61.

of that age might be praised for it, as a way of encouraging the child to keep learning. The praise acts as an incentive and thus has good consequences, but it may not be deserved. Desert "looks back" to past accomplishments, as opposed to incentives or consequences, which are "forward looking."

Desert theorists usually refer to people's social contribution or effort as relevant desert bases for the distribution of social goods. Those who have contributed more or have worked harder deserve higher incomes, more status, and so on than those who have contributed or worked less. Thus, distributive justice is reward in accord with contribution or effort.

One of the major drawbacks of such theories, if we focus on contributions, is that such contributions result from one's talents and abilities. But suppose that one person develops such a talent and another person does not. It may be that the second person simply chose not to do so. In such a case, we may have no trouble saying that the first person is more deserving than the second. But it may be that the second person did not develop the talent because, though she had the potential to develop the talent, she had a deprived childhood and was not given the chance to develop the talent. Or it may be that the second person simply lacked the innate capacity to develop that talent. In such a case, it is not so clear that the first person is more deserving. (Or if we still want to say that the first person is deserving, it is not so clear that it is fair that he receive more than the first.) Our intuitions here are based on the following claim:

> A is more deserving than B on the basis of F only if A and B had an equal chance to develop F.

Because of unequal social circumstances and genetic endowments, it is rare that people have the same chance to develop rewarded talents.

A similar problem results when we realize that it is part of our notion of desert that people deserve things only because they have earned that desert by doing something they can claim responsibility or credit for. We might formulate this idea as follows:

> A deserves X on the basis of F only if and to the extent that A is responsible for having or being F.

But, as Rawls has argued, it is unclear how much of our developed talents we can claim full responsibility for, for much of those talents are the result of social circumstances and natural assets that we did nothing to achieve.[3]

This suggests that desert should be based on effort—rather than achievement—on the ground that we are fully responsible for our efforts. But even this is debatable. The willingness and capacity to put forth effort is deeply affected by our upbringing, and those innately more talented will find it easier to put forth efforts to develop their talents, since the exercise of the talents that enable their development will be more enjoyable and more rewarding for them. So there are basic questions of the fairness of rewarding people, as a matter of desert, on the basis of either their talents or their efforts.

---

[3] Rawls, *A Theory of Justice*, pp. 74, 103.

Similar problems affect the application of desert theory to the market. The basic problem is the obvious ways in which the market diverges from rewarding either effort or contribution. Those born to affluent parents and inherited wealth may neither work hard nor make contributions. Luck plays an important role in whether one can pursue the occupation one desires. Apparently "irrelevant" characteristics such as having an amiable personality or "knowing the right people" can also make a difference. Further, it is arguable whether the most highly rewarded occupations make the greatest contributions, as we see when we compare an effective elementary school teacher with a high-salaried entertainer or the vice president of a company that makes frivolous consumer goods. There is no necessary connection between market demand and genuine contribution. Last, if we take seriously the conclusion that the main thing deserving of reward is one's freely chosen effort, it is obvious that the market does not reward this. Well-paid executives and poorly paid teachers and supermarket checkers may work equally hard, and the checker may have had to overcome more obstacles to get where she is. But the market does not and cannot be based on such effort.

Despite these criticisms, it cannot be denied that desert remains an important moral notion. That we can be deserving of various rewards and penalties may be part of our notion of humans as free agents. Great abilities and strenuous efforts elicit admiration that can hardly be said to be undeserved. It seems that there must be a place for desert in a general theory of social justice. But it seems unlikely that desert can be the whole story.

It should also be noted that deserving admiration, recognition, praise, and prizes is one thing; getting money, power, and status is another. The latter affect one's basic well-being in a way that the former do not. Deserving admiration and recognition for talents does not automatically translate into deserving a high income.

Let us apply this briefly to professional goods. The special ones we have singled out—medical care, legal services, and education—seem to be inappropriately based on desert. Everyone needs education to have any chance of developing their innate talents, and a fair rewarding of desert depends on enough people having these chances. That all have an access to legal services, whether deserving or not, is a basic requirement of the adversary system and its capacity to produce justice. And health care seems most reasonably based on need, since poor health and sickness is rarely something for which we can be held responsible. For some, poor health is due at least in part to an unhealthy life-style, including, for example, smoking, excessive drinking, poor diet, and lack of exercise. Perhaps the undeserving ill merit no social support. This is a controversial issue, about which much can be said. But it has little application to most health problems, which are not the result of imprudence alone.

EQUALITY

For egalitarians, justice requires that people fare equally well. The notion of equality is used in different ways, however, and there are ways of being committed to equality that fall short of egalitarianism proper. At least three meanings of equality are weaker than full-scale egalitarianism.

Formal Equality

Some believe that it is a necessary truth that people should be treated equally unless there is something dissimilar about them that justifies unequal treatment. This is often called the *formal principle of equality*. The principle is analytic if it is formulated as follows:

> People who are similar in relevant ways ought to be treated the same with regard to that similarity, and people who are relevantly different ought to be treated differently with regard to that difference.

Although this may be a necessary truth, it is not a significantly egalitarian principle, for it permits justified inequalities and places no restrictions on the factors that justify inequality. A racist, for example, could accept the principle and claim that race is a relevant ground for unequal treatment. Nevertheless, insofar as the principle requires consistency of treatment of similar people, it can be a force against prejudiced treatment, which often involves treating similars unequally on grounds that appear arbitrary when made explicit. And it underlies the important idea of *legal justice*—the equal application of the law to all parties.

Equal Intrinsic Worth

One important reason that the formal principle is not seriously egalitarian is that it does not say that there is any special reason for preferring equality over inequality. Rather, it is symmetrical between the two, requiring equality when there is similarity and inequality when there is dissimilarity. A stronger principle would hold that there is a special reason for equal treatment that justified inequalities must override. This principle can be formulated as follows:

> People ought, *prima facie*, to be treated equally, unless there is overriding reason for treating them unequally.

This puts the burden of proof on the nonegalitarian. But the principle is a substantive moral claim, not a tautology.

The view that people are similar in a way that makes equality the norm is often expressed by the idea that people are equal in their "intrinsic worth."[4] We differ in our abilities, merits, achievements, and so on, but "beneath" that, it is often said, everyone is on equal footing with everyone else. The poorest laborer is "as good as" the richest corporate executive and is equally entitled to respect for his humanity. Commitment to such an idea of equality is inherent in the modern liberal-democratic tradition, with its rejection of caste societies and racial, sexual, and other forms of discrimination and its positive advocacy of the idea that people are "born equal" and are all possessed of basic, "inalienable" rights. This commitment to equal worth, however, is

---

[4] For an important discussion of this idea, see Gregory Vlastos, "Justice and Equality," in Richard Brandt, ed., *Social Justice* (Englewood Cliffs, N.J.: Prentice-Hall, 1962), pp. 31–72.

compatible with various inequalities, so long as they are justified and do not diminish the equal respect owed to all persons.

Equal Opportunity

A different type of equality is *equal opportunity*—that everyone has an equal chance of achieving desirable positions. Rawls has distinguished two varieties of equal opportunity.[5] *Formal* equality of opportunity requires that positions be allocated to people in accord with their merits; that is, positions are given to those who are most qualified. This rules out discrimination and other forms of favoritism. It also forbids the sort of social immobility that fated people from different "ranks" to the same occupations that their parents had held. Formal equality of opportunity requires that those who possess similar developed abilities be equally able to advance, regardless of their social background.

But formal equal opportunity is compatible with people of different backgrounds having an unequal chance to *develop* their talents. Positions may be allocated entirely on the basis of qualifications, even though some have little chance to develop qualifications because of social deprivation and poor education. *Fair* equality of opportunity, then, requires not only that positions be allocated on the basis of merit, but also that all have a chance, regardless of their social backgrounds, to develop the most highly rewarded talents.

Egalitarianism

Equality of opportunity, in either the formal or fair sense, is compatible with inequality of outcome and falls short of the ideals of the thoroughgoing egalitarian. The ideal of the egalitarian is equal well-being for all, at the highest possible level of well-being.[6] The major argument for this view is that people are alike in such fundamental ways that there is no good reason that some should end up being better off than others. People are alike in being rational creatures, and are equally subject to pleasure and pain, satisfaction and frustration, joy and suffering, happiness and discontent. Each has a plan of life that he pursues. Egalitarians believe that beings who are alike in such basic ways ought to be able to do well and to do equally well.

Critics respond that although people are alike in these ways, they are also different. Some develop greater talents and make more important contributions. For the critics, these differences justify inequality. For the egalitarian, these differences are superficial, due to matters of luck and chance. The similarities between people are much more important, morally, than the differences.

Egalitarians must decide on how *equal well-being* is to be defined. Should it be understood in subjective terms, as, say, equality of happiness or satisfaction? If so, it seems impossible to attain, since happiness has much to do with human temperament, which is not amenable to social action. Further, if it takes a great deal to make one person happy and little to make a second

---

[5] Rawls, *A Theory of Justice*, p. 73.

[6] For a fuller explication of this ideal, see Bruce Landesman, "Egalitarianism" in the *Canadian Journal of Philosophy* 13 (1983): 27–56.

person happy, the view would require a very unequal distribution of goods, which will not seem fair to many. The alternative is to call for an equality of basic goods, such as income and liberty. But the problem here is that some—for example, the handicapped and those who are ill—need more than others in order to do as well. So neither specification seems sufficient by itself. How egalitarians—or anyone who considers greater strides toward economic equality an important component of justice—might understand equal well-being is an open and much-discussed question.[7]

It is often said about egalitarianism that it implies uniformity and sterility, "that everything and everybody should be as similar as possible to everything and everybody else."[8] But this is an attack on a straw man. Egalitarianism requires that people be well off, but they can all do well in quite different ways, given their different desires and preferences. Moreover, an egalitarian wants people to experience the good things in life to a high and equal degree. Among such goods, for most egalitarians in liberal-democratic societies, will be material well-being; the various civil and political liberties, such as freedom of speech, freedom of "tastes and pursuits,"[9] and freedom to participate in political affairs; significant control over one's life; and self-respect. The egalitarian wants, not to do away with these goods, but to enable more people to attain them. Utter similarity is hardly likely to produce that end.

This explanation of the egalitarian ideal, however, raises the question as to whether such an outcome is desirable. Egalitarianism has typically been criticized on the following grounds: that it is simply impossible; that its achievement could only come at a low level of well-being; that it is incompatible with liberty; and that it overlooks legitimate claims of desert. The first three of these criticisms have been succinctly expressed by Hume:

> Render possessions ever so equal, men's different degrees of art, care, and industry will immediately break that equality. Or if you check these virtues, you reduce society to the most extreme indigence and, instead of preventing want and beggary in a few, render it unavoidable to the whole community. The most rigorous inquisition, too, is requisite to watch every inequality on its first appearance; and the most severe jurisdiction to punish and redress it. But besides that so much authority must soon degenerate into tyranny and be exerted with great partialities.[10]

It is arguable that approximate equality is possible and is neither inimical to liberty nor incompatible with a limited role for desert—but a discussion of these replies is beyond our scope here. Perhaps the most plausible objection to egalitarianism is the claim that inequality is necessary so that people will have an incentive to undergo the training needed to undertake highly productive positions and, having achieved them, to keep working hard; and, further, that this inequality renders everyone better off than they would be

[7] See Thomas Scanlon's "Preference and Urgency." *Journal of Philosophy* 72 (1975): 655–69; and Ronald Dworkin's "What is Equality?" *Philosophy and Public Affairs* 10 (1981): 185–246, 283–345.
[8] Isaiah Berlin, "Equality." *Proceedings of the Aristotelian Society* 56 (1955–56): 311.
[9] John Stuart Mill's formulation, in *On Liberty* (Indianapolis: Hackett, 1978), p. 12.
[10] David Hume, *An Inquiry Concerning the Principles of Morals* (Indianapolis: Bobbs-Merrill, 1957), p. 25.

under strict equality. Rawls's theory of justice emphasizes this, and we will return to the *incentive principle* in the discussion of Rawls's theory which follows.

Egalitarians will obviously support steps in the direction of equal access to professional services, especially with regard to the most urgent professional goods such as health care, legal representation, and education. As such, egalitarians are likely to be skeptical of market allocation of these goods and will instead be inclined to favor public subsidies or public provision of these goods to all. The pros and cons of these measures are carefully probed with regard to medical care in the first set of readings which follow this essay.

UTILITARIANISM

The third unmixed theory of justice is utilitarianism. Utilitarians hold that the morally right act, rule, or policy is the one that, of the available alternatives, produces the greatest total or aggregative amount of happiness or satisfaction or well-being—"utility," in short—in a society. The utilitarian's slogan is to maximize utility. It does not matter how the utility (or happiness, or satisfaction) is distributed so long as the greatest total amount is produced. If one distribution would render one person rather poorly off but others so well off that the total amount is greater than it would be in a more equal distribution, utilitarians would favor it. Given this, utilitarians do not, as a matter of basic principle, favor a particular distribution, as desert theorists and egalitarians do. Any distribution is acceptable to them if it maximizes utility.

In practice, however, there are grounds both for and against equality from the utilitarian perspective. In favor of an equal distribution of important social goods is the fact that many such goods are characterized by decreasing marginal utility. Thus, additional units of such goods to those who already have a great deal are worth less to them than they would be to those worse off. For example, an additional $1,000 means much less and is less productive of happiness to a millionaire than it would be to a welfare recipient. Given this, utility is more likely to be maximized by moves in the direction of equality rather than inequality. On the other hand, many utilitarians have accepted the idea that inequalities provide incentives that make everyone better off and therefore increase utility. Thus there are tendencies toward both equality and inequality in utilitarian theories, and different utilitarians will understand these matters differently depending on their views about the facts.

Utilitarianism raises a special problem about whether justice can be separated from the rest of morality. Suppose one holds that distributive justice requires a particular distribution—say, for the sake of argument, an equal one. But suppose one accepts the view that some other distribution renders everyone so much better off that it seems, all things considered, more desirable. To clarify, suppose we must choose between the following distributions of money between five groups of equal numbers in a society:

A.	5	5	5	5	5
B.	7	8	9	10	12

Suppose that B is the right choice. Some will say that A is the just distribution but that B is better, all things considered. In this case, general human welfare overrides justice. Others, however, will decide to include considerations of welfare in the notion of justice and conclude that B is not only more desirable but more just as well. The issue is whether the notion of justice should be understood very narrowly, so that it requires a specific distribution but might be overridable, or more broadly, so that it comes close to being an ideal of the good society.

If one holds the narrow view, whether or not one agrees with utilitarians, one will be inclined to say that they do not care about justice (narrowly understood) but want to replace it with something else—considerations of the general welfare. In this case the utilitarians have no particular theories about justice. However, the tendency in modern discussion has been to construe justice more broadly, as a more comprehensive social ideal. In that case, utilitarians do have a theory of justice—the just is whatever maximizes utility—though not a specific one. The current tendency has the advantage of focusing attention on the most important, "bottom line" question of how important goods should be distributed, all things considered. A broadly construed theory of justice is an answer to this question. And utilitarianism gives us such a theory of justice.

The problems with utilitarianism are well known. It requires that we give no special weight to obligations if violating them would produce more happiness than unhappiness. The attempt to maximize utility can also justify acting unfairly and violating rights. Moreover, it may require too much of us: Always trying to maximize utility may leave no room for personal projects and concerns. And it is not easy to measure utility and figure out which acts produce the greatest utility.

Utilitarians offer a variety of responses to these objections. The most notable response denies that the theory should be applied to particular acts. Instead, people should follow rules that would produce well-being if generally followed. This *rule utilitarianism*—as contrasted with *act utilitarianism*—is said to make utilitarianism compatible with our intuitive moral duties, for breaking useful rules in order to maximize utility would eliminate those rules and render us all worse off. But evaluating the utility of rules is a complicated task.[11] Moreover, according to this theory, it will sometimes be right to carry out a particular act when its alternative produces more happiness. It is difficult, however, to see how one can hold that view and still be a utilitarian.[12] Utilitarianism is thus the subject of continuous debate, and the appeal of its application to justice depends on how well it can resolve its difficulties. The problems that afflict general utilitarian theory will also affect the plausibility of its account of justice.

[11] The classic modern discussion of utilitarianism and rules is David Lyons's *Forms and Limits of Utilitarianism* (Oxford: Oxford University Press, 1965), especially Chapter 4.
[12] For a sophisticated response to this problem, see Derek Parfit's *Reasons and Persons* (Oxford: Oxford University Press, 1984), Chapters 1–3.

Utilitarians favor whatever distribution of access to professional goods maximizes aggregate utility. Just what this means for particular utilitarians depends on their reading of the empirical facts. Their particular views will depend largely on views about the efficiency of the market and government subsidies, and on their views about the diminishing marginal utility of professional goods and the importance of inequalities in providing incentives.

LIBERTARIANISM

The last unmixed theory of justice is libertarianism. Nozick's very strong version of the theory has been the subject of much debate.[13] Nozick's basic premise is that people have certain fundamental and near-absolute rights to liberty, including an almost unlimited right to acquire and use private property. Justice is a matter of respecting people's liberty; injustice is violation of liberty. For a libertarian, then, justice requires no specific distribution; rather, the just distribution is whatever distribution results when free people exercise their liberty.

This point is best brought out by considering a poker game that goes on over the course of an evening. At the beginning of the evening, all players have an equal amount of money. Suppose they play a fair game for 3 hours. What is the right distribution at the end of the evening? Clearly, it is whatever distribution happens to result.[14] There is no pattern that must reached if justice is to prevail. The libertarian feels the same way about society as a whole. Justice requires no particular distribution, such as equality or reward in accord with desert. The just distribution is whatever happens to result from the activities of free people. The libertarian is like the utilitarian here in that he requires no specific pattern. But he differs from the utilitarian in viewing the just distribution not as one that produces a certain overall goal (maximizing utility), but as one *generated* in a certain way.

For a libertarian, liberty means being free to do whatever one chooses so long one does not injure, coerce, defraud, or steal from others. The only valid restrictions on people's freedom to act are restrictions that prevent such interference. Given this, the libertarian supports the minimal or "night watchman" state—a state limited to enforcing rules against injury, force, theft, and fraud. Beyond this it may not legitimately go. It may not tax people to produce public goods unless all consent; nor may it raise taxes to provide welfare for those who are unfortunate, for in so doing, it prevents people from using their earnings as they choose and thus interferes in their lives in ways that have nothing to do with the prevention of coercion, theft, injury, and fraud. It violates their liberty and produces not justice, but injustice. Injustice, then, is any interference not based on such grounds. Given this, libertarians adamantly support an unregulated free market, a laissez-faire state. Any interference with market transactions is a violation of liberty.

An important feature of libertarianism is the strong connection it draws between liberty and property. Writers on the subject of liberty typically dwell

---

[13] Robert Nozick, *Anarchy, State and Utopia* (New York: Basic Books, 1974).
[14] This example comes from Rawls, *A Theory of Justice*, p. 86.

on civil and political liberties such as freedom of thought, speech, and belief, including moral, political, and religious belief; freedom to determine one's own activities; freedom of association; and freedom to vote and participate in political affairs. Economic liberty—the right to acquire and use property— is another form of freedom. The connection between civil and economic liberty is controversial. Some believe that civil liberty would be fragile without a large amount of economic liberty; others hold that they are separable. The libertarian, however, sees the two as intrinsically connected. Economic liberty is a crucial aspect of the freedom of self-determination. We acquire property either by finding unowned things, by exchange, or by receiving gifts. In each case, the receipt and transfer of property is a voluntary act, expressive of liberty. Having gained property, we lead and control our lives by using it, and thus exercise our liberty through it. Having property restricted, confiscated, or taxed prevents us from doing as we choose and is thus a restriction of our right to self-determination. In other words, liberty requires a very strong right to property—a right to acquire as much as we can through voluntary efforts and, having acquired it, to use our property as we please, so long as we don't use it to coerce, injure, steal, or defraud. Restrictions on the acquisition or use of property for the public good or to support a welfare system are viewed as unjust limitations on liberty.

Suppose that a society in which people freely express their liberty, as recommended by libertarians, ends up with significant inequality and a large class of citizens who are in dire circumstances. Some libertarians, such as von Hayek and Friedman, would be troubled by this.[15] They defend the minimal state not only on grounds of a right to liberty, but also because they believe that such a state promotes everyone's welfare. They accept Smith's contention that if people are left alone to promote their own individual ends, then their individual strivings will be coordinated by the market, "as if by an invisible hand," to promote the common good.[16] They would then, in consistency, favor state intervention if the common good did not result. In this sense, however, their theory involves utilitarian as well as libertarian elements and is not the sort of unmixed theory we have been considering. Nozick's theory, on the other hand, is not adulterated by concern for the general welfare. If some end up miserable, Nozick would accept this. If a well-off individual has some obligation to help the needy, it is for him a matter of voluntary, private philanthropy. The state has no business enforcing such obligations.

This raises the major criticism of Nozick's pure libertarianism: Libertarians not only emphasize the importance of liberty, but come to see it as the *only* important social value. But other values are important as well, especially general human well-being. If the unregulated exercise of libertarian liberty leads to poverty, misery, and extreme inequality, most of us would

---

[15] For Hayek, see *The Constitution of Liberty* (Chicago: Henry Regenry, 1960), especially Part I; for Friedman, see *Capitalism and Freedom* (Chicago: University of Chicago Press, 1962), Chapters 1–2.

[16] Adam Smith, *The Wealth of Nations* (Indianapolis: Liberty Classics, 1981), Book 4, Chapter 2, p. 456.

think it reasonable to restrict liberty in order to promote these other values. And in so doing, we would not feel that liberty had been destroyed. Against the egalitarian, it has been said that complete equality means universal "beggary." But the same kind of charge can be made against libertarianism if its practice would produce a lot of misery.

An even deeper criticism of the libertarian's conception of liberty is possible, however. To explain this, let's say that when laws prohibit people from doing something, there is a *restriction* on their liberty; and let's say, further, that when this restriction is unjustified, there is a *violation* of liberty. Not all restriction are violations. In most countries, for example, driving on the left side of the road is not permitted. This is a restriction that few would see as a violation. Even libertarians agree that some restrictions on liberty are not violations; such restrictions include prohibitions of force, fraud, and theft. Whether a restriction is a violation depends on whether the restriction is sensible and justifiable. The libertarian believes that only restrictions of force, fraud, and theft are justifiable. But this contention requires argument. It must be based on some theory about what is and what is not a legitimate restriction on liberty. Appealing to a basic right to liberty, even if such a right is well grounded, does not provide such a theory. It does not draw the line between the proper domain of liberty and legitimate restrictions. The libertarians fail to provide such a theory.

We can understand support for this criticism by considering ordinary liberty. Freedom of speech does not include the right to say anything at any time or place. We are quite willing to permit time and place restrictions on speech in order to prevent public nuisances and to allow the orderly expression of speech. And we restrict speech when we rule out libel, false advertising, certain violations of confidentiality, disclosure of national security secrets, and speech that incites panic (such as yelling "fire" in a crowded theater). We shape the right, ruling out expressions of it that have very negative consequences, when doing so does not prohibit an essential and deeply desired exercise of the activity. In sum, particular liberties are shaped by a variety of considerations. The same can be true for property. It may be good that people have a right to acquire and make effective use of their property. But restrictions on the amount and use, and taxation for a variety of public purposes may be justifiable parts of shaping the liberty of property so as to enable it both to fulfill its purposes and to be a force for public good. Libertarians, however, tend to interpret liberty too simply and abstractly, as a right to do whatever one wants without coercion. This view requires defense and overlooks the complex structure of actual liberties.

Libertarians would support the unregulated free market in the provision of professional services and access to those services through ability to pay. They would oppose state intervention not only with respect to subsidy or provision, but even with regard to licensing and regulation. (Opposition to licensing is argued for in Friedman's essay, included in Chapter 5.) Although they may regret that some will be unable to use professional services because they have fared ill in the market, they will not see this as matter of injustice or social obligation. Those who need help must rely on private charity. A particular instance of this issue is discussed in this chapter in the selections that consider whether lawyers should be obligated to provide a certain amount of unpaid service to the needy.

A SCHEMA FOR A MIXED THEORY OF JUSTICE

We have considered four unmixed theories, each of which has its strengths and weaknesses. The weaknesses are the result of the tendency of each to overlook the values emphasized by the other theories. This suggests the possibility of a mixed, comprehensive theory of justice that gives due emphasis to each of the relevant values. The nature of such a theory can be conveyed by means of a schema that can be variously interpreted to produce different particular mixed theories. The schema has two parts. The first asserts a basic equality among individuals and underlies a number of particular measures, such as equality before the law and the prohibition of discrimination. The second justifies inequalities on a number of grounds and under certain conditions. The schema goes as follows:

1. People are equal in their intrinsic worth.
   a. Treatment of all people with equal respect and concern;
   b. Equality before the law and the rule of law;
   c. Rejection of the arbitrary inequalities of race, sex, ethnic and national status, and so on; rejection of prejudice and discrimination;
   d. Equal right to civil liberties;
   e. Equal citizenship and equal right to vote and participate in political affairs (political liberty).
2. Social and economic inequalities are justified on grounds of
   a. desert,
   b. efficiency (providing incentives),
   c. liberty, or
   d. necessity,
   provided that
      i.   No one falls below a minimum "floor" of well-being;
      ii. The inequalities are not "too great"; and
      iii. everyone has an equal opportunity to achieve the advantaged positions.

A mixed theory like this is inherent in the political perspective of modern liberal democracies and would thus be likely to have an immediate intuitive appeal to their citizens. Nevertheless, the theory, especially the second principle, will be interpreted in different ways. Some will be willing to allow only certain grounds for inequality; some will set the floor very high, while others will place it rather low; people will have different views as to when there is too much inequality; and they will differ on their understanding of equality of opportunity. Nevertheless, this schema provides the framework within which many of our disputes about justice take place.

The most famous and controversial such mixed theory is the view of justice developed and defended by Rawls in *A Theory of Justice*. Rawls puts forward two principles of justice, as follows:

1. Each person is to have an equal right to the most extensive basic liberty compatible with a similar liberty for others.[17]
2. Social and economic inequalities are to be arranged so that they are both (a) to the greatest benefit of the least advantaged and (b) attached to offices and positions open to all under conditions of fair equality of opportunity.[18]

The first principle requires equal civil and political liberty. The second has two parts: the difference principle and the equal-opportunity principle. The difference principle requires that departures from an equal distribution are justified only if they render everyone—literally everyone—better off; further, they must improve the position of the worst-off persons to the greatest extent possible, so that any attempt to raise it higher would fail. In other words, inequalities are acceptable only if they maximize the minimum position.

Rawls is an egalitarian "at heart." But he believes that equality would be inefficient. Inequalities act as incentives and motivate productivity, which improves the lot of all. Rawls believes that it would be irrational for an egalitarian-minded person not to accept inequality when it benefits everyone. Such inequalities can be made to benefit everyone in two ways. First, they lead, through the market, to higher productivity, which ultimately improves the standard of living of all, including those on the bottom. Second, the earnings of those who are well off can be taxed to provide both public goods and transfer payments. Such redistributive taxation is inappropriate at the point at which a further increase in taxes would affect productivity so adversely that those at the bottom would be harmed. The second part of the second principle requires equal opportunity in the strong sense—that everyone must have a chance to develop and be rewarded for whatever talents they have, regardless of their social circumstances.

Rawls's acceptance of a mixed theory is special in several respects. He allows inequalities on the grounds of efficiency, but he rejects desert as a criterion. His floor is very high. He would find "too much inequality" very quickly. In addition, he endorses a strong notion of equal opportunity. Other combinations are possible, and others would interpret these matters differently. For example, during his presidential term, Ronald Reagan spoke of a "safety net," rather than a floor, and clearly accepted much more inequality and subscribed to a weaker sense of equal opportunity than Rawls would have. And there are many positions in the middle.

Many people in liberal-democratic societies accept this abstract mixed theory. But views about particular questions of justice require that the ranked values allowed by the schema be carefully chosen. Many of our disputes about justice are disagreements about the weight to be given to different values vis-à-vis one another. In this regard, it is likely that many find themselves deeply drawn to one of the unmixed theories just described but find it difficult to accept the theory as the *sole* and entire truth about justice. One's initial attraction to a theory is likely to influence one's decisions about the relevant tradeoffs. For example, one who is deeply drawn toward equality is more

[17] Rawls, *A Theory of Justice*, p. 60.
[18] *Ibid.*, p. 83.

likely to choose equality over desert when the two conflict. Conversely, one whose basic intuitions are desert-oriented will make the opposite choice. Thus, as we explore particular issues about the allocation of professional services, it is helpful to keep in mind both the unmixed theories and the more complex mixed theories.

ACCESS TO PROFESSIONAL SERVICES

We now turn from general theories of justice to some current controversies about the distribution of professional services. Most of our discussion will deal with health care, legal representation, and entry into the professions in general.

Issues about the allocation of health care tend to arise in liberal-democratic societies with market economies. Until recently, health care was obtained primarily by direct purchase. Allocation was a function of ability to pay. After World War II, the cost of health care rose dramatically. Hospital and physician fees increased, and new but expensive technologies were discovered and put to use. At this point it became common for people to purchase health care indirectly, through insurance. Union contracts typically included medical benefits. But such benefits are unaffordable for many and are thus obtainable for most only as an employment benefit. The failure of the market to provide affordable health care has led to government-subsidized insurance schemes such as Medicare, Medicaid, and, in Britain, the government-administered National Health Service. Current controversies focus on the appropriate role for government in regulating, subsidizing, and providing health care.

An important feature of the current health care environment in the United States is the widely shared view that health care costs have gotten out of control. Prevailing insurance systems have been organized in such a way that no one—not patients, physicians, hospitals, or insurers—has had a strong motivation to keep costs down. Patients have had a large part of their fees paid by insurers and thus have not had the usual consumer incentives to shop around for the most economical care. Physicians and hospitals have received from insurance companies whatever they have asked and have thus had no motivation to keep fees down (but rather have been motivated to increase them). And insurers have paid their bills by raising premiums, with the resulting increases spread around enough so that they did not, until recently, evoke significant complaints. Efforts are now being made to introduce greater cost-consciousness and more competition into health care with the development of new institutions such as HMOs. Concern about putting a lid on rising health care costs is now a basic political fact.

There are now three fundamental but connected health care controversies. The first concerns greater access to care by those unable to afford it—the poor, the unemployed, the elderly, the disabled, and so on. Medicare and Medicaid leave large gaps both in the allocation of coverage and in the percentage of medical bills covered. For example, in a given year, 16 percent of the U.S. population is without insurance coverage.[19] Many believe that justice requires more significant moves toward equal access or at least the guarantee of an adequate level of health care for all. Such moves would be supported by egalitarians, by some utilitarians, and by followers of a Rawlsian mixed theory. They are resisted by libertarians and by those who believe that the market will do the job most efficiently if health care is made fully competitive. These issues are examined in the selections by Fried, Gutmann, and Will.

The concern about making health care more available to the poor raises questions about scarcity. Are we able to do it? Are we affluent enough to afford good health care for all? In trying to answer this question, we must confront the issue of spending on health care as opposed to spending on other goods, such as defense, advertising, and the production of trivial consumer products. Perhaps we would have more than enough for health care if we cut back on some of these other expenditures. But is this so? And would such cuts be justifiable or politically feasible?

An interesting issue about equal access is whether we should have the same health care for all or a "two-tier" system in which all receive a minimum level of care but those who can afford it are able to buy additional care. Egalitarians would find the two-tier system objectionable. But, as Gutmann points out in her article in this chapter, there is something odd in allowing people to use their extra income to buy frivolous items like expensive cars and electronic "toys," but forbidding them to buy life-saving therapies. And last, there is the knotty question of how to define a minimum or adequate level of care.[20]

The second issue concerns tradeoffs within health care. Could we provide more people with better and more essential care if we cut back on care that is less urgent, perhaps even unnecessary? Some think that a good deal of health care supplied in this country is unnecessary—extra diagnostic tests, unneeded medication, overlong hospital stays, and so on. But even if there is waste that could be eradicated, choices will still have to be made. We spend great amounts of money to prolong the lives of the terminally ill elderly and to save severely handicapped newborns. We also spend a great deal of money on acute care, and much less on illness prevention. Perhaps if we were to spend less on some of this kind of care, we could provide more adequate basic care to greater numbers and more cost-effective acute care to others. But should we make this choice, and, if so, how? This is a question of health care rationing, which, until now, citizens of the United States have been able to avoid. But the time for some difficult decisions seems to have come. These issues are fully canvassed in the selections by Aaron and Schwartz, Daniels, and Engelhardt.

A third issue, which is also a rationing issue, is the question of very expensive technology, such as heart transplants and artificial organs. Should

---

[19] President's Commission for the Study of Ethical Problems in Medicine and Biomedical and Behavioral Research, *Securing Access to Health Care* (Washington, D.C.: U.S. Government Printing Office, 1983), I, 93.

[20] For discussion of this question, see Norman Daniels, *Just Health Care* (Cambridge, England: Cambridge University Press, 1985), Chapters 1–3; and Allen Buchanan, "The Right to a Decent Minimum of Health Care." *Philosophy and Public Affairs* 13 (1984): 55–78.

we continue to provide such treatment? If so, how do we decide who gets what? Or can we no longer afford such expensive technologies when more basic needs are still to be met? Engelhardt discusses these questions as part of the political conflicts within democratic societies.

In comparison with the controversy about access to health care, the debate about legal services has taken a different turn. Legal insurance is not nearly as commonplace as health insurance. Instead, legal care for the poor has been provided through legal aid societies, public defenders' offices, and, for a while, government-supported legal assistance groups. It is a widespread perception, however, that in the United States, those who are well off are able to purchase the services of high-quality lawyers, while those who are less well-off do with poor services, inadequately financed services, or no services. Thus, issues about the justice of access come to the fore. Many lawyers who are concerned about this problem do their part by providing a certain amount of free legal representation each year for those unable to pay for it. This is called *pro bono* service. The lawyers' *Code of Professional Responsibility* calls upon lawyers to provide such service. However, this is put forth not as an enforceable requirement, but as an aspiration that the ideal lawyer will fulfill.

Proposals have been advanced in recent years to turn this aspiration into a lawyer's duty. It has been argued that the inequity in access to legal services could be significantly lessened if all lawyers had an obligation to render a certain amount of *pro bono* aid each year. The mandate would be enforced by local bar associations. This proposal has generated much controversy. Those who favor it believe that the lawyers' monopoly over who gets to practice law, and their corresponding ability to set fees due to their freedom from serious competition, places a duty upon the law profession in general and upon individual lawyers to see that adequate legal services are available to all. This position is supported in Christensen's selection. Others respond, however, that mandating such service interferes inappropriately with the lawyer's own liberty to choose his clients, reduces the moral worth of representing the poor by making it mandatory, will be ineffective, and raises the possibility of increasing state interference. These arguments are set forth in Shapiro's selection.

The background for this issue, as it applies not just to the law but to other professions as well, is explored in the essays by Kipnis in this chapter and Friedman in Chapter 5. Kipnis explains the establishment by professions of a monopoly on service and fees and, on this basis, supports a strong view of professional obligations to society. Friedman goes the other way. He believes that professional self-regulation, even licensing, should be eliminated. Thus he supports the libertarian view that the free market alone should regulate access to professional services. (This issue is discussed further in Chapter 5.)

OPPORTUNITY IN THE PROFESSIONS

Professional occupations are considered desirable, and questions of justice can be raised about access to professional positions. Most professionals in the United States are white males. It is difficult to deny that, in the past, racial and sexual discrimination played a large role in keeping women, blacks, and members of other minority groups out of the professions. Members of such groups have been denied the equal opportunity to achieve these highly advantageous positions. But what, if anything, should be done to change this situation?

For those eager to remedy this unequal access, the goal is both formal and fair equality of opportunity. People should be able to achieve positions for which they are qualified and should not be discriminated against because of their race or sex. Further, all people, regardless of their gender, social position, or racial and ethnic background should have a reasonable chance to develop the talents that would enable them to succeed as professionals, if they so desire. The small number of blacks and women in the professions is evidence of past and present discrimination, and constitutes a continuing barrier to access. When few members of a group have attained such positions, others are unlikely to try. They lack the "role models" needed to enable them to believe that they have a chance for success in those positions. Further, the only black or woman in a professional enterprise may correctly fear that she will be judged by different and more stringent standards than members of other groups would be. If blacks and women could achieve professional positions in closer proportion to their percentages in the population, then race and sex would lose their importance and barriers to access would weaken.

The issue of preferential treatment arises because many believe that formal equality of opportunity—no formal discrimination—will be insufficient to prevent continuing informal discrimination and to remove the barriers to access. This is so mainly because the past discrimination against women and the continuing discrimination against blacks makes it difficult for them, as compared with white males, to develop the qualifications needed for entry into the professions. The policy of preferential treatment is a temporary policy of favoring a certain number of qualified blacks and women for positions and admissions over more qualified white males. Note that the claim is not that unqualified blacks and women should be given jobs and positions. Rather, qualifications are measured by various factors and candidates are ranked. Of the group who are qualified to succeed in law school, for example, some will score higher on the admission tests and thus will be considered more qualified. The policy of preferential treatment requires that some of the less qualified (but still qualified) minority candidates be taken over more qualified white males. Moreover, the policy is put forth as a temporary one—until enough progress has been made toward the development of both formal and fair equality of opportunity. The ideal of both proponents and opponents of preferential treatment is color- and gender-blindness in the long run.

Two different types of arguments are put forth in favor of preferential treatment. One is an appeal to compensatory justice. Blacks and women were discriminated against in the past. Preferential treatment is a morally required policy that compensates for the past wrong. This argument is open to several objections. First, compensation is due to one who is injured at the expense of the perpetrator of the injury—but the white males who might lose positions due to preferential treatment are not those who caused the discrimination. They are—at least most of them—innocent of any wrongdoing and are thus not justifiably held responsible for righting the wrong. Second, some blacks and women were in fact not discriminated against or unjustly deprived of opportunities and thus do not deserve compensation. Third, even if most blacks and women deserve compensation, it is unclear that preferential treatment is the justifiable method by which to provide such compensation. Perhaps enhanced educational opportunities and job training—this kind of favoritism—is more appropriate.

The second justification for preferential treatment is perhaps more plausible. This view maintains that preferential treatment has two kinds of positive consequences. First, it will promote a more just society by promoting more genuine equality of opportunity. And second, it will increase general utility by raising the well-being of minority members, both by making it more possible for them to enter well-rewarded professions and by affording them greater access to professional services. Critics often respond by rejecting these empirical claims. They doubt that preferential treatment, even if useful, will have much impact. It may also lead to less-competent professionals and can damage the self-esteem of blacks and women who suspect that they received their jobs because of their gender or race, and not because of their abilities. And last, they hold that once in place, the policy will be difficult to dislodge. Constituencies who have a stake in the policy will attempt to continue it, thus defeating its temporary nature and destroying the long-run ideal of a color-blind and gender-blind society.

Beyond these empirical matters, critics mount an even deeper objection: that even if preferential treatment has positive consequences, it would still be wrong, for it is unjust, a form of discrimination, which cannot be justified by its long run consequences. Those who make this charge accept something like the following as a basic requirement of justice: Jobs and positions should be allocated to people in accord with their qualifications; those with the highest qualifications should get the jobs. Call this the meritocratic criterion. It is the ideal of the color- and gender-blind society. All that matter are qualifications.

Supporters of preferential treatment ask what underlies this meritocratic criterion. What are the grounds for it? If it rests on considerations of efficiency—that social welfare is most likely to be produced if the criterion is followed—then they can respond that temporary policies of preferential treatment are more likely to produce long-run welfare.[21] But suppose that the principle is based on more deontological arguments—that people have a right to be treated this way. If the ground of the right is that people have come to expect they will be treated in accord with their qualifications, then there is a legitimate expectation that is denied by the policies of preferential treatment. But if such legitimate expectations are unjust expectations, then it might be justifiable, all things considered, to override them. The critic must justify those expectations. The basic defense of the claim is that any departure from it is a form of discrimination—treating people differently on irrelevant grounds—and this is one of the paradigms of injustice. The meritocratic-criterion principle is the only alternative to unjust discrimination.

---

[21] For a discussion of this defense of meritocracy, see Norman Daniels, "Merit and Meritocracy" in *Philosophy and Public Affairs* 7 (1978): 206–23.

Against this, proponents of preferential treatment point out that the meritocratic criterion is not always followed. Universities take geographical spread and athletic prowess into account in admissions decisions. Private employers remain free to hire friends and relatives. More significantly, it is argued that such preferential treatment is not a matter of bias. The old form of racial discrimination was a matter of prejudice—treating people unequally on arbitrary grounds. That form of discrimination expressed disrespect and contempt for the deprived group. Preferential treatment, on the other hand, has a clear and reasonable purpose and is intended to show no disrespect for white males. It is not an arbitrary inequality.

This argument is also bolstered by the uncertainty and arbitrariness of many tests of qualifications. Further, it is arguable that the meritocratic criterion is fully fair only if all have an equal chance to develop the appropriate qualifications—that is, jobs and admissions should go to the most qualified only when all have had an equal or fair chance to develop their qualifications. If this is the right way to understand the principle, then it is not clear that pure meritocratic treatment is required, since differences between people with respect to actual qualifications continue to result from past discrimination. Thus proponents do not believe that the meritocratic criterion is so fundamentally founded that it cannot be overridden by the kinds of consequentialist considerations to which they appeal. Both sides of this controversy are strongly expressed in the selections by Gross and Wasserstrom in this chapter.

HEALTH CARE, COST CONTAINMENT, LIBERTY

Charles Fried

Fried says that health care costs have gotten out of control only because we believe that whatever is available to anybody should be available to everybody. He argues against such equal access and holds that health care is an optional consumer good, best allocated by the market. For the unemployed, aged, and dependent unable to afford health care, he recommends government-subsidized vouchers with which they can purchase care or insurance.

There is a widespread view that health costs are out of control, that we already spend too much on health care and that we are in great danger of spending even more. Although many people feel that the same is true in respect to beer or cigarettes, these expenditures are not thought to present the same kind of problem presented by health care costs. When people suggest that as a nation we spend too much money on beer (or comic books or pantyhose) a particular kind of judgment is being emitted: That judgment is that though people have a right to spend this much money on beer, it says something about our values, our level of education and so on that this is so. Certainly very few people (though there are some and we will have to deal with them later in this analysis) would say that therefore the government should step in and place a ceiling on expenditures (per capita or total or whatever) on beer or any other consumer goods. Yet this is precisely what is being proposed in a wide variety of places in respect to health care costs.

HEALTH CARE COSTS ARE OPTIONAL

The concern about health care cost escalation is thoroughly justified. The spectre which haunts us is the spectre of a kind of nightmarish hypertrophy of the health care professions, of health technology and of health facilities. To be sure, we are also concerned that those in the professions and those who own or supply the facilities will contribute to the excess costs by charging ever higher prices per unit, even as the number of units also escalates beyond all bounds. Now why are we so panicked by this possibility—why, for instance, are we not panicked by the possibility that an ever larger proportion of personal and national income will go to pay for beer or coffee? There is one obvious answer: If coffee becomes too expensive, we can all cut down on coffee consumption (as recent buying patterns demonstrated), but somehow the amount of medical services we consume is not within our control. Medical services are seen to be somehow nonoptional, and therefore a rise in prices is seen to be particularly threatening, because we are powerless to respond by trimming consumption—and incidentally thereby taking the steam out of the inflationary pressures. But the disanalogy between coffee and health care is deeper and subtler. We are frightened of health care because of its potential to get better! There is literally no limit to our capacity to do more for people if we spend more money. I once read that if the kind of dental care which is consumed as a matter of course by health-conscious, middle-income professional people were made available to the whole nation, the total cost would rise to something like $25 billion. And I suspect that sum is too small, since such a quantum leap in demand would in all probability require a total reordering of that particular sector of the economy. But this doesn't make the potential of health care costs really palpable enough. The fact of the matter is that in that potential must be counted not only the extension to *everybody* of whatever may be useful and available to *somebody*, but also the potential expenditures on research to develop cures and preventatives to all the ailments and conditions which are now beyond our reach. And it is, after all, only a difference of degree, not one of kind, which separates the decision to make dialysis available to all who suffer from kidney disease from the decision to devote whatever research funds promise any chance at all of shedding light on presently unsolved health problems. It is this potentially omnivorous quality of the health care sector which so terrifies us.

Now it is not just the fact that there is no limit to what we might do in medicine which creates the problem. After all, there is also no limit to how much we might spend on housing, developing space travel, or what have you. The problem arises from the convergence of the two features I have described: virtually limitless potential for expenditures and the sense that those expenditures are nonoptional. So the first thing we must do in any analysis of the problem is consider this aspect of it: that health expenditures are nonoptional.

Well, of course, health expenditures are *not* nonoptional. One may forego marginal increments in consumption of health care (even on the assumption that some corresponding increment in health or life expectancy is necessarily associated with such increased consumption) in favor of other types of expenditures. There is nothing *logically* implausible about that. Then why is it that the expenditure is thought to be nonoptional? Surely there is some notion that though people might forego productive expenditures on health care in favor of other goods, it is irrational of them to do so. That is an intuitive sense. It is both

logically and factually false. Even if expenditures on health care correlated not just with better functioning or comfort but even with life expectancy itself, there is nothing at all irrational about decisions preferring a particular style of life, though a shorter one, or perhaps longer life for one's children as against a shorter one for oneself. Far from being irrational, the claim that such trade-offs may not be made is wholly implausible and should be dismissed out of hand.

Why, then, does the nonoptionality claim have such a hold? I think the hold comes from an overemphasis on one kind of case: the case where the expenditure will offer some chance of prolonging life, when that life is under an immediate threat. The picture is that of paying ransom to a kidnapper in deadly earnest. This is the case which Calabresi and Bobbitt have recently identified as "desperation bidding," and it is a large part of the haunting spectre which moves us. I am perfectly willing to concede that where one is being held to ransom, the only competing considerations are the well-being of other persons who are not similarly endangered. It is indeed the case that it makes no sense to keep back any amount of money from such a kidnapper, when the victim would not be alive to enjoy the results of his parsimony in the event that the ransom were not paid.

And it is certainly true that *some* decisions regarding health care have this quality. This, however, is not usually the case. We are not often confronted with sudden medical crises in which certain death is the imminent alternative to a choice of some kind of therapy. Usually the terrible result is away in the future, so that immediately it makes sense to weigh the diminished enjoyment in that intervening period against the possibility of putting off the evil day somewhat longer. And so in those cases it is simply not true that health costs are nonoptional. . . .

. . . Indeed, it may be argued that it is of the utmost importance that such costs—

costs which have to do with the choice and shaping of our life plans and our lifestyles—should above all remain optional, if we are to be free. Those who would decide this issue for us would decide the most crucial issues about the shape of our lives, taking those decisions out of our hands. Thus, it seems to me plain that those who would impose on their fellow citizens some particular level of spending for health care—whether setting those levels far higher or far lower than the individual would choose—arrogate to themselves control over the most intimate decision by which the individual shapes his own life. . . .

The Principle of Equality

. . . In a society which (rightly to my mind) believes that some degree of inequality of material circumstances (of income and wealth) is consistent with distributive justice, it should follow that inequality in respect to the enjoyment of one particular form of material consumption (that is, the consumption of medical resources) would also be acceptable. But the fact is that to some it is not acceptable. There is a sense abroad that whatever inequalities we might be ready to live with, in other respects, in respect to health, inequality is intolerable. It is worth drawing attention to how extraordinary an idea this is. For this is an idea which goes beyond the argument for equality as such, and argues that not only should each person have an equal claim on the society's scarce resources, but that each person *must* dispose of his share of resources in the same way: that is, to insure the contingency of future health needs at precisely the same level as everyone else and at a cost of precisely the same amount from his disposable income. So the question is not really just one of equality but of a particularly intrusive form of paternalism.

Perhaps the claim for equal access to health care is really a surrogate for the claim for equality in general, that claim being made in respect to a particularly dramatic and visible good. If indeed we had a distribution of income which the society felt confident about (whether it be an equal distribution or some other pattern of distribution), perhaps the question of access to health care would not loom so large—unless the paternalistic and statist views were to gain an independent foothold. But as matters presently stand we are in a situation of confusion, and the slogan of equal access of health care is being made to bear the brunt of that confusion.

The Interplay of Equality and Cost Containment

Now let me return to our principal subject, which is containment of health costs. It is only when we stand bemused by the shibboleth of equal access that keeping down the costs of health care seems an urgent goal of public policy. After all, if the costs of health care are true costs— that is, they accurately represent the value of the resources expended on health care relative to their next-best uses—then it really does not even make sense to say that health care costs too much. Everything just costs whatever it costs. It is only when we feel under some special imperative to purchase health care at any particular level that the cost becomes a problem. And it seems to me that that imperative arises out of the concept of equality. As soon as any particular expenditure is available to anybody, that very fact in a regime of equal access already represents a new claim on the part of every other citizen to that same thing. And then cost does become a problem, because we have created an artificial level of demand. We have created a regime whereby as soon as anybody successfully demands a particular good (or a particular level of enjoyment of a good), we are obliged to provide the same level of enjoyment of that good to everyone.

Obviously this is an unstable and unsatisfactory situation. The costs of health care must spiral, and the proportion of *everyone's* disposable income sucked up by health care must constantly increase. But this is only because we have adopted a principle which quite irrationally denies us the power to recognize that not everybody wants to consume health care at the same level, and which denies us at the same time the one sure way to determine what the proper level of health care consumption is by consumer choice. What, for instance, is the proper level of consumption for clothing, or beer? There is no single proper ration of these things. And imagine the absurdity of believing that whatever ration the most fortunate person (most fortunate in respect to beer—perhaps quite unfortunate in respect to other things) enjoys must *ipso facto* then be accorded to everybody else. There is no problem about determining what the "correct" level of consumption of beer is; it is whatever it is. And so also there is no problem about containing the cost of beer. When we are cut adrift from the one sure determinant of the proper level of consumption—that is, whatever level people choose—we are forced to recur to bureaucratic or political determination of consumption levels. But such determination must be arbitrary, because divorced from the pull of actual choices and demand of actual consumers the decisionmakers have no criterion for the levels they set—unless it is their own sense of what is right, or necessary. . . .

The Medical Profession as a Barrier to Free Choice

Now it is altogether clear that today the forces of the market are also not working to give consumers a full range of cost alternatives nor yet to keep down costs nor yet to allocate medical personnel in a reasonable way. This is in large part not because the market and consumer sovereignty cannot operate in this domain, but because the free market has never been allowed to operate. The medical profession has historically operated as a tight monopoly whose conspiracy in restraint of trade has been justified by moralizing slogans virtually identical to those used by other self-protective cartels, such as funeral directors, optometrists, and retail liquor merchants. The governmental response has been to overlay the medical cartel's restrictive practices with a system of irrational, politically motivated, inept controls and compensation schemes.

There is in principle no reason why, just as the market should determine in terms of consumer preferences what the level of health care expenditures will be, it should not also determine the prices to be received by those supplying the services. But plainly it has not. The most obvious reason is the organization of the market, which has insulated itself in every conceivable way from competitive pressures, which has managed to create mechanisms by which almost any price increases will be met and which has severely restricted entry. . . .

The Shape of the Solution

What is needed first is government action to spur the widest array of competing structures of health care delivery. Obviously health maintenance organizations offer the greatest potential for providing good care at reasonable cost, but also they offer the best chance of viable competitive structures. HMOs can compete against each other for both group and individual subscriber dollars. Group and individual subscribers should be able to develop experience not only with price differentials between competing HMOs but also differentials in range and quality of benefits. Finally, a vigorous system of HMOs should put pressure on the fee-for-service sector to control costs, if it is to survive as anything but a quaint and luxurious anachronism.

Going along with such action should be an effort to meet what is valid in the equal access rhetoric; i.e., reasonable access by everybody to a decent level of health care. But it is not necessary to restructure the whole medical care sector in order to provide for the minority which cannot provide for itself—and it must be a minority, for if a majority could not provide for its own health care where exactly are the resources to come from? With a competitive, efficient structure in place caring for the needs of most of the population at the levels and prices which the population desires (*not* at the level the profession or the government desires) benchmarks would naturally develop as to what is a reasonable, decent level of care. The unemployed, the aged, the dependent could then be provided with health care vouchers (medical green stamps) enabling them to purchase services in the market along with everyone else.

EQUAL ACCESS TO CARE*

Amy Gutmann

Gutmann considers three grounds for equal access to care: that it is necessary for equality of opportunity, that it is necessary for equality of respect, and that people with the same medical need ought to receive the same treatment. However, equal access requires a one-tier system in which the well-off are not permitted to purchase additional care. She considers the pros and cons of this kind of system.

. . . A principle of equal access to health care demands that every person who shares the same type and degree of health need must be given an equally effective chance of receiving appropriate treatment of equal quality so long as that treatment is available to anyone. Stated in this way, the equal access principle does not establish whether a society must provide any particular medical treatment or health care benefit to its needy members. . . . The principle requires that if anyone within a society has an opportunity to receive a service or good that satisfies a health need, then everyone who shares the same type and degree of health need must be given an equally effective chance of receiving that service or good.

Since this is a principle of equal *access*, it does not guarantee equal *results*, although it probably would move our society in that direction. Discriminations in health care are permitted if they are based upon type or degree of health need, willingness of informed adults to be treated, and choices of lifestyle among the population. The equal access principle constrains the distribution of opportunities to receive health care to an egalitarian standard, but it does not determine the total level of health care available or the effects of that care (provided the care is of equal quality) upon the health of the population. . . .

Practical Implications

Since the equal access principle requires equality of effective opportunity to receive care, not merely equality of formal legal access, it does not permit discriminations

* References have been deleted without indication.

From Amy Gutmann, "For and Against Equal Access to Health Care," *Milbank Memorial Fund Quarterly*, 59:4 (1981): 542–60. Reprinted by permission.

based upon those characteristics of people that we can reasonably assume they did not freely choose. Such characteristics include sex, race, genetic endowment, wealth, and, often, place of residence. Even in an ideal society, equally needy persons will not use the same amount or quality of health care. Their preferences and their knowledge will differ as will the skills of the providers who treat them.

A One-Class System

The most striking result of applying the equal access principle in the United States would be the creation of a one-class system of health care. Services and goods that meet health care needs would be equally available to everyone who was equally needy. As a disincentive to overuse, only small fees for service could be charged for health care, provided that charges did not prove a barrier to entry to the poorest people who were needy. A one-class system need not, of course, be a uniform system. Diversity among medical and health care services would be permissible, indeed even desirable, so long as the diversity did not create differential access along nonconsensual lines such as wealth, race, sex, or geographical location.

Equal access also places limits upon the market freedoms of some individuals, especially, but not exclusively, the richest members of society. The principle does not permit the purchase of health care to which other similarly needy people do not have effective access. The extent to which freedom of the rich must be restricted will depend upon the level of public provision for health care and the degree of income inequality. As the level of health care guaranteed to the poor decreases and the degree of income inequality increases, the equal access standard demands greater restrictions upon the market freedom of the rich. Where income and wealth are very unevenly distributed, and where the level of publicly guaranteed access is very low,

the rich can use the market to buy access to health care goods unavailable to the poor, thereby undermining the effective equality of opportunity required by an equal access principle.

The restriction upon market freedoms to purchase health care under these circumstances creates a certain discomforting irony: The equal access principle permits (or is at least agnostic with respect to) the free market satisfaction of preferences for nonessential consumer goods. Thus, the rigorous implementation of equal access to health care would prevent rich people from spending their extra income for preferred medical services, if those services were not equally accessible to the poor. It would not prevent their using those same resources to purchase satisfactions in other areas— a Porsche or any other luxurious consumer good. . . .

Hard Cases

As with all principles, hard cases exist for the equal access principle. Without dwelling upon these cases, it is worth considering how the principle might deal with two hard but fairly common cases: therapeutic experimentation in medicine, and alternative treatments of different quality.

Each year in the United States, many potentially successful therapies are tested. Since their value has not been proved, there may be good reason to limit their use to an appropriate sample of sick experimental subjects. The equal access principle would insist that experimenters choose these subjects at random from a population of relevantly sick consenting adults. A randomized clinical trial could be advertised by public notice, and individuals who are interested might be registered and enrolled on a lottery basis. The only requirement for enrollment would be the health conditions and personal characteristics necessary for proper scientific testing.

How does one apply the principle of equal access when alternative treatments are each functionally adequate but aesthetically or socially quite disparate? Take the hypothetical case of a societal commitment to adequate dentition among adults. Replacement of carious or mobile teeth with dentures may preserve dental function at relatively minor cost. On the other hand, full mouth reconstruction, involving periodontal and endodontal treatment and capping of affected teeth, may be only marginally more effective but substantially more satisfying. The added costs for the preferred treatment are not inconsiderable. The principle would seem to demand that at equal states of dental need there be equal access to the preferred treatment. It is unclear, however, whether the satisfaction of subjective desire is equivalent to fulfillment of objective need.

In cases of alternative treatments, proponents of equal access could turn to another argument for providing access to the same treatments for all. A society that publicly provides the minimal acceptable treatment freely to all, and also permits a private market in more expensive treatments, may result in a two-class system of care. The best providers will service the richest clientele, at the risk of inadequate treatment for the poorest. Approval of a private market in alternative treatments would rest upon the empirical hypothesis that, if the publicly funded level of adequate treatment were high enough, few people would choose to short-circuit the public (i.e., equal access) sector; the small additional free market sector would not threaten to lower the quality of services universally available.

Most cases, like the one of dentistry, are difficult to decide merely on principle. Proponents of equal access must take into account the consequences of alternative policies. But empirical knowledge alone will not decide these issues, and arguments for or against a particular policy can be entertained in a more systematic way once one exposes the values that underlie support for an equal access principle. One can

then judge to what extent alternative policies satisfy these values.

Supporting Values

Advocates of equal access to health care must demonstrate why health care is different from other consumer goods, unless they are willing to support the more radical principle of equal distribution of all goods. Norman Daniels[1] provides one foundation for distinguishing between health care and other goods. He establishes a category of health care needs whose satisfaction provides an important condition for future opportunity. Like police protection and education, some kinds of health care goods are necessary for pursuing most other goods in life. Any theory of justice committed to equalizing opportunity ought to treat health care as a good deserving of special distributive treatment. Equal access to health care provides a necessary, although certainly not a sufficient, condition for equal opportunity in general.

A precept of egalitarian justice that physical pains of a sufficient degree be treated similarly, regardless of who experiences them, establishes another reason for singling out certain kinds of health care as special goods. Some health conditions cause great pain but are not linked to a serious curtailment of opportunity. The two values are, however, mutually compatible.

A theory of justice that gives priority to the value of equal respect among people might also be used to support a principle of equal access to health care. . . .

Conditions of Self-Respect

It is not easy to determine what social conditions support or undermine self-respect. One might plausibly assume that equalizing opportunity and treating similar pains similarly would be the most essential supports for equal respect within a health

[1] Norman Daniels, "Health Care Needs and Distributive Justice," *Philosophy and Public Affairs* 10, no.2 (1981), 146–79.

care system. And so, in most cases, the value of equal respect provides additional support for equal access to the same health care goods that are warranted by the values of equal opportunity and relief from pain. But at least some kinds of health care treatment not essential to equalizing opportunity or bringing equal relief from pain may be necessary to equalize respect within a society. It is conceivable that much longer waiting time, in physicians' offices or for admission to hospitals, may not affect the long-term health prospects of the poor or of blacks. But such discriminations in waiting times for an essential good probably do adversely affect the self-respect of those who systematically stand at the end of the queue.

Some of the conditions necessary for equal respect are socially relative; we must arrive at a standard of equal respect appropriate to our particular society. Universal suffrage has long been a condition for equal respect; the case for it is independent of the anticipated results of equalizing political power by granting every person one vote. More recently, equal access to health care has similarly become a condition for equal respect in our society. Most of us do not base our self-respect on the way we are treated on airplanes, even though the flight attendants regularly give preferential treatment to those traveling first class. This contrast with suffrage and health care treatment (and education and police protection) no doubt is related to the fact that these goods are much more essential to our security and opportunities in life than is airplane travel. But it is still worth considering that unequal treatment in health care, as in education, may be understood as a sign of unequal respect even where there are no discernible adverse effects on the health or education of those receiving less favored treatment. Even where a dual health care system will not produce inferior medical results for the less privileged, the value of equal respect militates against the perpetuation of such a system in our society. . . .

Equality of opportunity, equal efforts to relieve pain, and equal respect are the three central values providing the foundation of support for a principle of equal access to health care. Any theory of justice that gives primacy to these values (as do many liberal and egalitarian theories) will lend prima facie support to a health care system structured along equal access lines. . . .

RATIONING HOSPITAL CARE: LESSONS FROM BRITAIN*

Henry J. Aaron and William B. Schwartz

In this summary of their book The Painful Prescription, *the authors hold that reducing health care costs requires rationing—saying no to patients who could potentially benefit from treatment. Rationing is part of the British National Health Service, where less money is spent and where some patients are not treated who would be treated in the United States. They note, however, that in Britain, physicians are forced to act as budgetary officials and tend to rationalize nontreatment as medically unnecessary.*

* References have been deleted without indication.

From Henry Aaron and William B. Schwartz, "Rationing Hospital Care: Lessons from Britain." Excerpted with permission from *The New England Journal of Medicine*, 310:1 (1984), 52–56.

Resistance to the decades-long rise in the cost of hospital care in the United States is growing rapidly. In consequence, all physicians and patients soon may have to live with, and within, a system that limits expenditures. The process has, in fact, already begun. Fixed per diem reimbursement, reimbursements according to specific diagnosis, and overall revenue limits are currently being implemented by several states or by the federal government under Medicare. In addition, many businesses are pursuing cost containment through so-called preferred-provider organizations.

It is unclear how far our efforts to control hospital costs will go, but one thing is clear: If we go far enough some medical benefits will have to be withheld from at least some patients. Under such circumstances, key questions will arise. Who will decide whether a particular patient is entitled to treatment? What criteria will be used to make the choice? And how will we learn to live with the answers?

An indication—probably a good one—comes from Britain, which has had long experience with medical rationing and now spends half the amount per capita on hospital care that we do. Although there are differences between our two countries, our shared language and the common elements in our political and medical cultures make the British experience relevant to the United States. To be sure, the British experience cannot be taken as a literal forecast for the coming years in the United States. For example, it seems unlikely that Americans would accept rationing as willingly as have the British, who have had a special affection for the National Health Service since its creation just after World War II. Nevertheless, the British experiment has yielded the best data we are likely to find in advance of embarking on an intensive program to curb medical expenditures. . . .

Three kinds of treatment are provided at essentially the same level in Britain as in the United States: All patients with hemophilia obtain high-quality treatment, including adequate supplies of the required clotting factors; megavoltage radiotherapy appears to be readily available in England to virtually all cancer patients who can benefit from it; and bone-marrow transplantation is performed at the same relative frequency as in the United States.

The other treatment methods are rationed. The British perform only half as many x-ray examinations per capita as do Americans, and they use only half as much film per examination. Furthermore, the overall rate of treatment of chronic renal failure in Britain is less than half that in the United States. Kidneys are transplanted at a comparable rate, but dialysis is carried out in Britain at a rate less than one third that in the United States. In addition, total parenteral nutrition is undertaken only about one fourth as often as in the United States, and Great Britain has only one sixth the CT [computerized tomography]-scanning capability of the United States. The British hospital system has only one fifth to one tenth the number of intensive-care beds, relative to population, that the United States has. Finally, the rate of coronary-artery surgery in Britain is only 10 percent that in the United States.

Chemotherapy for cancer has, perhaps, an intermediate position between unrationed and rationed treatment methods. Chemotherapy for potentially curable tumors is administered at approximately the same rate as in the United States. On the other hand, tumors that are not highly responsive to chemotherapy are treated far less often.

To sustain acceptance of a health system that systematically denies many patients useful, even lifesaving, care is no easy task. Physicians, who are the principal gatekeepers of the system, must find ways to reconcile the economic limitations with their personal and professional values. Patients must either adjust to the restrictions of which they are aware or circumvent them;

they may often, of course, be unaware of the medical possibilities.

The Physician as Gatekeeper

Explicit limitation of medical resources puts physicians in a position that many of them find awkward. Neither the training nor the ethics of medicine prepare most physicians to make the required decisions in economic terms. Therefore, whenever possible, British doctors recast a problem of resource scarcity into medical terms. They have developed standards of care that incorporate economic reality into medical judgments.

Rationalization

Physicians and other health-care personnel seek ways to make the denial of potentially beneficial care seem either routine or, for the particular patient, optimal. For example, an internist confronted with a patient beyond the prevailing, if unofficial, age at which one's chances of receiving dialysis become slight is likely to tell the patient and family that nothing of medical benefit can be done and that he or she will simply make the patient as comfortable as possible. A nephrologist with a patient for whom dialysis would be technically or socially difficult to manage may well say that dialysis would be painful and burdensome. A resident alien from a poor country may be told that he or she should return home—where, as it happens, modern care is likely to be unavailable.

Likewise, relatively restrictive criteria for coronary-artery surgery are employed. By focusing on the class of cases in which coronary-artery surgery demonstrably increases survival rates or relieves anginal pain that is altogether disabling, surgeons can discount the benefit of the procedure for those whose pain is less severe. . . .

It is clear that not all British doctors believe that they are providing all potentially beneficial care to their patients. Many realize that they are acting as society's agent in the rationing process. One consultant spoke of the process as follows:

The sense that I have is that there are many situations where resources are sufficiently short so that there must be decisions made as to who is treated. Given that circumstance, the physician, in order to live with himself and to sleep well at night, has to look at the arguments for not treating a patient. And there are always some—social, medical, whatever. In many instances he heightens, sharpens, or brings into focus the negative component in order to make himself and the patient comfortable about not going forward.

Although most British doctors would like to deploy more resources than are now available, they seem to recognize that their country is not rich enough to provide all the possible benefits of medical care. . . .

Clinical Freedom and Resource Constraints

The British profess that all doctors in consultation with their patients should be entirely free to determine diagnoses and treatments and that their decisions should not be subjected to second guessing except in egregious situations, and then only by medical colleagues or the courts. This principle reflects the need for doctors to make dozens of choices a day quickly and decisively.

Under the rubric of clinical freedom, physicians can sometimes divert scarce resources to patients in whom they are interested, but by doing so they lower the quality or quantity of care available to others. Other doctors may intervene when they recognize that such a situation exists. The British system is almost optimally constructed to deal with the threats to budget limits posed by the abuse of clinical freedom because day-to-day budgetary decisions fall mainly to tenured physicians who are employed on salary. Because the participants have no direct financial interest in the allocation of the hospital's resources, debates about the budget are not shadowed by personal financial consequences. Budget negotiations are said to be marked by compromise and by trade-offs born of the recognition that the participants must spend all or most of their professional lives in each other's company.

For the most part, these debates concern questions of capacity and maintenance—what equipment to buy, what rehabilitations to seek, what staff to hire, what vacancies to leave unfilled—but normally not the medical practice of individual physicians. Problems in that area do occur, however. For example, the aggressive use of chemotherapeutic agents in one leading hospital and the introduction of total parenteral nutrition in another created serious budgetary problems. In each case, actions were taken by the senior staff that led to voluntary curbs by the physicians responsible for the excessive expenditures.

Short-Circuiting Delays

A major consequence of limited resources in British hospital care is that familiar British phenomenon, the queue. Except in emergencies, care may be considerably delayed. For example, of the 566,000 patients awaiting surgery of all kinds in 1979, 31 percent had waited for more than one year. Cases classified as urgent represented 7 percent of those on the waiting list, and nearly three fourths of those cases had been on the lists for more than one month. The concerned physician can exploit several mechanisms to short-circuit the waiting period. The general practitioner who thinks that a patient should be seen by a consultant without a long delay knows that by telephoning the consultant he or she is more likely to get the patient seen than by writing a letter. If the physician wants even faster action, he or she can declare, perhaps with some exaggeration, that the patient is too sick to travel and must be seen at home. Domiciliary visits—house calls—are made promptly. The number of domiciliary visits

increased about one third during the 1970s. Although these short-circuiting mechanisms are useful in a few cases, British clinicians think they do little to break through the constraints of the system.

The Problem of Saying No

Physicians often must refuse treatment to certain patients; the older patient who is a candidate for long-term dialysis is the prime example. Saying no to such a patient will always be difficult. Often in such a case the local internist either does not raise the possibility of dialysis or simply states that the treatment does not seem to be indicated. Because of the respect that most patients have for physicians, the doctor's recommendations are usually followed with little complaint. We were repeatedly told by physicians who have worked in both the United States and Britain that the readiness of the British patient to defer to the doctor's authority largely explains a willingness to forgo the various kinds of care that are in short supply.

The local physician's role as gatekeeper explains why dialysis centers rarely have to turn away patients. Older patients are not usually referred because the local physician is well aware that they could not be accommodated. The general practitioner or internist thus spares the nephrologist from having to say no, spares the patient and family a painful rejection, and avoids having to face the patient and relatives after rejection. . . .

In summary, it seems clear that the acceptance of scarcity as a general feature of British society and affection for the National Health Service have all contributed to a widespread acceptance of the rationing process. Moreover, various safety valves have provided outlets for the most disaffected. It appears doubtful that citizens of the United States would accept such limits—or even less severe ones—as readily. If limits are set, however, we believe that they will stimulate responses in physicians and patients that will be similar in many respects to those we observed in Britain.

WHY SAYING NO TO PATIENTS IN THE UNITED STATES IS SO HARD*

Norman Daniels

The British health care system provides high-quality basic care for all and makes rationing decisions in terms of a centralized budget. Thus, Daniels argues, when care is denied, physicians are assured that the funds will be used to meet more urgent medical needs. He argues that saying no is less justifiable in the United States because neither of these assurances is available in our decentralized, market-oriented system.

. . . If cost-containment measures, such as the use of Medicare's diagnosis-related groups (DRGs), involved trimming only unnecessary health care services from public budgets, they would pose no moral problems. Instead, such measures lead physicians and hospitals to deny some possibly beneficial care, such as longer hospitalization or more diagnostic tests, to their own patients—that is, at the "micro" level. Similarly, if the "macro" decision not to disseminate a new medical procedure, such as liver transplantation, resulted only in the avoidance of waste, then it would pose no moral problem. When is it morally justifiable to say no to beneficial care or useful procedures? And why is it especially difficult to justify saying no in the United States?

Justice and Rationing

Because of scarcity and the inevitable limitation of resources even in a wealthy society, justice—however we elucidate it—will require some no-saying at both the macro and micro levels of allocation. No plausible principles of justice will entitle an individual patient to every potentially beneficial treatment. Providing such treatment might consume resources to which another patient has a greater claim. Similarly, no class of patients is entitled to whatever new procedure offers them some

* References have been deleted without indication.

benefit. New procedures have opportunity costs, consuming resources that could be used to produce other benefits, and other classes of patients may have a superior claim that would require resources to be invested in alternative ways. . . .

Saying No in the British National Health Service

Aaron and Schwartz have documented how beneficial services and procedures have had to be rationed within the British National Health Service, since its austerity budget allows only half the level of expenditures of the United States [see previous selection.] The British, for example, use less x-ray film, provide little treatment for metastatic solid tumors, and generally do not offer renal dialysis to the elderly. Saying no takes place at both macro and micro levels.

Rationing in Great Britain takes place under two constraints that do not operate at all in the United States. First, although the British say no to some beneficial care, they nevertheless provide universal access to high-quality health care. In contrast, over 10 percent of the population in the United States lacks insurance, and racial differences in access and health status persist. Second, saying no takes place within a regionally centralized budget. Decisions

From Norman Daniels, "Why Saying No to Patients Is Hard in The U.S." Excerpted with permission from *The New England Journal of Medicine*, 314:21 (1986), 380–83.

about introducing new procedures involve weighing the net benefits of alternatives within a closed system. When a procedure is rationed, it is clear which resources are available for alternative uses. When a procedure is widely used, it is clear which resources are unavailable for other uses. No such closed system constrains American decisions about the dissemination of technological advances except, on a small scale and in a derivative way, within some health maintenance organizations (HMOs).

These two constraints are crucial to justifying British rationing. The British practitioner who follows standard practice within the system does not order the more elaborate x-ray diagnosis that might be typical in the United States, possibly even despite the knowledge that additional information would be useful. Denying care can be justified as follows: Though the patient might benefit from the extra service, ordering it would be unfair to other patients in the system. The system provides equitable access to a full array of services that are fairly allocated according to professional judgments about which needs are most important. The salve of this rationale may not be what the practitioner uses to ease his or her qualms about denying beneficial treatment, but it is available.

A similar rationale is available at the macro level. If British planners believe alternative uses of resources will produce a better set of health outcomes than introducing coronary bypass surgery on a large scale, they will say no to a beneficial procedure. But they have available the following rationale: Though they would help one group of patients by introducing this procedure, its opportunity cost would be too high. They would have to deny other patients services that are more necessary. Saying yes instead of no would be unjust.

These justifications for saying no at both levels have a bearing on physician autonomy and on moral obligations to patients. Within the standards of practice deter-

mined by budget ceilings in the system, British practitioners remain autonomous in their clinical decision making. They are obliged to provide the best possible care for their patients within those limits. Their clinical judgments are not made "impure" by institutional profit incentives to deny care.

The claim made here is not that the British National Health Service is just, but that considerations of justice are explicit in its design and in decisions about the allocation of resources. Because justice has this role, British rationing can be defended on grounds of fairness.

Saying No in the United States

American physicians face a problem even when the only incentive for denying beneficial care is the hospital's, not theirs personally. For example, how can they justify sending a Medicare patient home earlier than advisable? Can they, like their British peers, claim that justice requires them to say no and that therefore they do no wrong to their patients?

American physicians cannot make this appeal to the justice of saying no. They have no assurance that the resources they save will be put to better use elsewhere in the health care system. Reducing a Medicare expenditure may mean only that there is less pressure on public budgets in general, and thus more opportunity to invest the savings in weapons. Even if the savings will be freed for use by other Medicare patients, American physicians have no assurance that the resources will be used to meet the greater needs of other patients. The American health care system, unlike the British one, establishes no explicit priorities for the use of resources. In fact, the savings from saying no may be used to invest in a procedure that may never provide care of comparable importance to that the physician is denying the patient. In a for-profit hospital, the profit made by denying beneficial treatment may be returned to investors. In many cases, the physician can be quite sure that saying no to beneficial care will lead to greater harm than providing the care.

Saying no at the macro level in the United States involves similar difficulties. A hospital deciding whether or not to introduce a transplantation program competes with other medical centers. To remain competitive, its directors will want to introduce the new service. Moreover, they can point to the dramatic benefit the service offers. How can opponents of transplantation respond? They may (correctly) argue that it will divert resources from other projects—projects that are perhaps less glamorous, visible, and profitable but that nevertheless offer comparable medical benefits to an even larger class of patients. They insist that the opportunity costs of the new procedure are too great.

This argument about opportunity costs, so powerful in the British National Health Service, loses its force in the United States. The alternatives to the transplantation program may not constitute real options, at least in the climate of incentives that exists in America. Imagine someone advising the Humana Hospital Corporation, "Do not invest in artificial hearts, because you could do far more good if you established a prenatal maternal care program in the catchment area of your chain." Even if correct, this appeal to opportunity costs is unlikely to be persuasive, because Humana responds to the incentives society offers. Artificial hearts, not prenatal maternal-care programs, will keep its hospitals on the leading technological edge, and if they become popular, will bring far more lucrative reimbursements than the prevention of low-birth-weight morbidity and mortality. The for-profit Humana, like many nonprofit

organizations, merely responded to existing incentives when it introduced a transplantation program during the early 1980s, at the same time prenatal care programs lost their federal funding. Similarly, cost-containment measures in some states led to the cutting of social and psychological services but left high-technology services untouched. Unlike their British colleagues, American planners cannot say, "Justice requires that we forgo this procedure because the resources it requires will be better spent elsewhere in the system. It is fair to say no to this procedure because we can thereby provide more important treatments to other patients."

The failure of this justification at both the micro and macro levels in the United States has the same root cause. In our system, saying no to beneficial treatments or procedures carries no assurance that we are saying yes to even more beneficial ones. Our system is not closed; the opportunity costs of a treatment or procedure are not kept internal to it. Just as important, the system as a whole is not governed by a principle of distributive justice, appeal to which is made in decisions about disseminating technological advances. It is not closed under constraints of justice. . . .

. . . Economic incentives such as those embedded in current cost-containment measures are not a substitute for social decisions about health care priorities and the just design of health care institutions. These incentives to providers, even if they do eliminate some unnecessary medical services, will not ensure that we will meet the needs of our aging population over the next several decades in a morally acceptable fashion or that we will make effective—and just—use of new procedures. These hard choices must be faced publicly and explicitly.

ALLOCATING SCARCE MEDICAL RESOURCES
AND ORGAN TRANSPLANTS*

H. Tristram Engelhardt

Engelhardt argues that secular, pluralist societies lack a public consensus about the good sufficient to settle questions about the rationing of medical care. Such settlements must thus be created and discovered through the democratic political process. The attempt is complicated by the tension between respecting freedom and pursuing the good, when a desirable allocation of care conflicts with liberty.

Some controversies have a staying power because they spring from unavoidable moral and conceptual puzzles. The debates concerning transplantation are a good example. To begin with, they are not a single controversy. Rather, they are examples of the scientific debates with heavy political and ethical overlays that characterize a large area of public-policy discussions. The determination of whether or not heart or liver transplantation is an experimental or nonexperimental procedure for which it is reasonable and necessary to provide reimbursement is not simply a determination on the basis of facts regarding survival rates or the frequency with which the procedure is employed. Nor is it a purely moral issue.

It is an issue similar to that raised regarding the amount of pollutants that ought to be considered safe in the work place. The question cannot be answered simply in terms of scientific data, unless one presumes that there will be a sudden inflection in the curve expressing the relationship of decreasing parts per billion of the pollutant and the incidence of disease or death, after which very low concentrations do not contribute at all to an excess incidence of disability or death. If one assumes that there is always some increase in death and disability due to the pollutant, one is not looking for an absolutely safe level but rather a level at which the costs in lives

and health do not outbalance the costs in jobs and societal vexation that most more stringent criteria would involve. Such is not a purely factual judgment but requires a balancing of values. Determination of whether a pollutant is safe at a particular level, of whether a procedure is reasonable and necessary, of whether a drug is safe, of whether heart and liver transplantations should be regarded as nonexperimental procedures are not simply factual determinations. In the background of those determinations is a set of moral judgments regarding equity, decency, and fairness, cost–benefit trade-offs, individual rights, and the limits of state authority.

Since such debates are structured by the intertwining of scientific, ethical, and political issues, participants appeal to different sets of data and rules of inference, which leads to a number of opportunities for confusion. The questions that cluster around the issue of providing for the transplantation of organs have this distracting heterogeneity. There are a number of questions with heavy factual components, such as, "Is the provision of liver transplants an efficient use of health-care resources?" and "Will the cost of care in the absence of a transplant approximate the costs involved in the transplant?" To answer such questions, one will need to continue to acquire data concerning the long-

* References have been deleted without indication.

From H. Tristram Engelhardt, "Allocating Scarce Medical Resources and Organ Transplants." Excerpted with permission from *The New England Journal of Medicine* 311:1 (1984), 66–71.

term survival rates of those receiving transplants. There are, as well, questions with major moral and political components, which give public-policy direction to the factual issues. "Does liver or heart transplantation offer a proper way of using our resources, given other available areas of investment?" "Is there moral authority to use state force to redistribute financial resources so as to provide transplantations for all who would benefit from the procedure?" "How ought one fairly to resolve controversies in this area when there is important moral disagreement?" . . .

Why Debates About Allocating Resources Go On and On

The debates concerning the allocation of resources to the provision of expensive, life-saving treatment such as transplantations have recurred repeatedly over the past two decades and show no promise of abating. To understand why that is the case, one must recall the nature of the social and moral context within which such debates are carried on. Peaceable, secular, pluralist societies are by definition ones that renounce the use of force to impose a particular ideology or view of the good life, though they include numerous communities with particular, often divergent, views of the ways in which men and women should live and use their resources. Such peaceable, secular societies require at a minimum a commitment to the resolution of disputes in ways that are not fundamentally based on force. There will thus be greater clarity regarding how peaceably to discuss the allocation of resources for transplantation than there will be regarding the importance of the allocation of resources itself. The latter requires a more concrete view of what is important to pursue through the use of our resources than can be decisively established in general secular terms. As a consequence, it is clearer that the public has a right to determine particular expenditures of common re-

sources than that any particular use of resources, as for the provision of transplantation, should be embraced.

This is a recurring situation in large-scale, secular, pluralist states. The state as such provides a relatively neutral bureaucracy that transcends the particular ideological and religious commitments of the communities it embraces, so that its state-funded health-care service (or its postal service) should not be a Catholic, Jewish, or even Judeo-Christian service. This ideal of a neutral bureaucracy is obviously never reached. However, the aspiration to this goal defines peaceable, secular, pluralist societies and distinguishes them from the political vision that we inherited from Aristotle and which has guided us and misguided us over the past two millennia. Aristotle took as his ethical and political ideal the city-state with no more than 100,000 citizens, who could then know each other, know well whom they should elect, and create a public consensus. It is ironic that Aristotle fashioned this image as he participated in the fashioning of the first large-scale Greek state.

We do not approach the problems of the proper allocations of scarce resources within the context of a city-state, with a relatively clear consensus of the ways in which scarce resources ought to be used. Since the Reformation and the Renaissance, the hope for a common consensus has dwindled, and with good cause. In addition, the Enlightenment failed to provide a fully satisfactory secular surrogate. It failed to offer clearly convincing moral arguments that would have established a particular view of the good life and of the ways in which resources ought to be invested. One is left only with a general commitment to peaceable negotiation as the cardinal moral canon of large-scale peaceable, secular, pluralist states.

As a result, understandings about the proper use of scarce resources tend to occur on two levels in such societies. They occur within particular religious bodies, political and ideological communities, and interest groups, including insurance groups. They take place as well within the more procedurally oriented vehicles and structures that hold particular communities within a state. The more one addresses issues such as the allocation of scarce resources in the context of a general secular, pluralist society, the more one will be pressed to create an answer in some procedurally fair fashion, rather than hope to discover a proper pattern for the distribution of resources to meet medical needs. However, our past has left us with the haunting and misguided hope that the answer can be discovered.

There are difficulties as well that stem from a tension within morality itself: a conflict between respecting freedom and pursuing the good. Morality as an alternative to force as the basis for the resolution of disputes focuses on the mutual respect of persons. This element of morality, which is autonomy-directed, can be summarized in the maxim, Do not do unto others what they would not have done unto themselves. In the context of secular pluralist ethics, this element has priority, in that it can more clearly be specified and justified. As a result, it sets limits to the moral authority of others to act and thus conflicts with that dimension of morality that focuses on beneficence, on achieving the good for others. This second element of morality may be summarized in the maxim, Do to others their good. The difficulty is that the achievement of the good will require the cooperation of others who may claim a right to be respected in their nonparticipation. It will require as well deciding what goods are to be achieved and how they are to be ranked. One might think here of the conflict between investing communal resources in liver and heart transplantations and providing adequate general medical care to the indigent and near indigent. The more one respects freedom, the more difficult it will be for a society to pursue a common view of the

good. Members will protest that societal programs restrict their freedom of choice, either through restricting access to programs or through taxing away their disposable income.

The problem of determining whether and to what extent resources should be invested in transplantation is thus considerable. The debate must be carried on in a context in which the moral guidelines are more procedural than supplied with content. Moreover, the debate will be characterized by conflicting views of what is proper to do, as well as by difficulties in showing that there is state authority to force the participation of unwilling citizens. Within these vexing constraints societies approach the problem of allocating scarce medical resources and in particular of determining the amount of resources to be diverted to transplantation. This can be seen as a choice among possible societal insurance mechanisms. As with the difficulty of determining a safe level of pollutants, the answer with respect to the correct level of insurance will be as much created as discovered.

Insurance Against the Natural and Social Lotteries

Individuals are at a disadvantage or an advantage as a result of the outcomes of two major sets of forces that can be termed the natural and social lotteries. By the natural lottery I mean those forces of nature that lead some persons to be healthy and others to be ill and disabled through no intention or design of their own or of others. Those who win the natural lottery do not need transplantations. They live long and healthy lives and die peacefully. By the social lottery I mean the various interventions, compacts, and activities of persons that, with luck, lead to making some rich and others poor. The natural lottery surely influences the social lottery. However, the natural lottery need not conclusively determine one's social and economic power, prestige, and advantage. Thus, those who lose at the natural lottery and who are in need of heart and liver transplatation may still have won at the social lottery by having either inherited or earned sufficient funds to pay for a transplantation. Or they may have such a social advantage because their case receives sufficient publicity so that others contribute to help shoulder the costs of care.

An interest in social insurance mechanisms directed against losses at the natural and social lotteries is usually understood as an element of beneficence-directed justice. The goal is to provide the amount of coverage that is due to all persons. The problem in such societal insurance programs is to determine what coverage is due. Insofar as societies provide all citizens with a minimal protection against losses at the natural and the social lotteries, they give a concrete understanding of what is due through public funds. At issue here is whether coverage must include transplantation for those who cannot pay.

However, there are moral as well as financial limits to a society's protection of its members against such losses. First and foremost, those limits derive from the duty to respect individual choices and to recognize the limits of plausible state authority in a secular, pluralist society. If claims by society to the ownership of the resources and services of persons have limits, then there will always be private property that individuals will have at their disposal to trade for the services of others, which will create a second tier of health care for the affluent. Which is to say, the more it appears reasonable that property is owned neither totally societally nor only privately, and insofar as one recognizes limits on society's right to constrain its members, two tiers of health-care services will by right exist: those provided as a part of the minimal social guarantee to all and those provided in addition through the funds of those with an advantage in the social lottery who are interested in investing those resources in health care.

In providing a particular set of protections against losses at the social and natural lotteries, societies draw one of the most important societal distinctions—namely, between outcomes that will be socially recognized as unfortunate and unfair and those that will not be socially recognized as unfair, no matter how unfortunate they may be. The Department of Health and Human Services, for instance, in not recognizing heart transplantation as a nonexperimental procedure, removed the provision of such treatment from the social insurance policy. The plight of persons without private funds for heart transplantation, should they need heart transplantation, would be recognized as unfortunate but not unfair. Similarly, proposals to recognize liver transplantation for children and adults as nonexperimental are proposals to alter the socially recognized boundary between losses at the natural and social lotteries that will be understood to be unfortunate and unfair and those that will simply be lamented as unfortunate but not seen as entitling the suffering person to a claim against societal resources.

The need to draw this painful line between unfortunate and unfair outcomes exists in great measure because the concerns for beneficence do not exhaust ethics. Ethics is concerned as well with respecting the freedom of individuals. Rendering to each his or her due also involves allowing individuals the freedom to determine the use of their private energies and resources. In addition, since secular pluralist arguments for the authority of peaceable states most clearly establish those societies as means for individuals peaceably to negotiate the disposition of their communally owned resources, difficulties may arise in the allocation of scarce resources to health care in general and to transplantation in particular. Societies may decide to allocate the communal resources that would have been available for liver and heart transplantation to national defense or the building of art museums and the expansion of the national park system. The general moral requirement to respect individual choice and procedurally fair societal decisions will mean that there will be a general secular, moral right for individuals to dispose of private resources, and for societies to dispose of communal resources, in ways that will be wrong from a number of moral perspectives. As a result, the line between outcomes that will count as unfortunate and those that will count as unfair will often be at variance with the moral beliefs and aspirations of particular ideological and moral communities encompassed by any large-scale secular society.

Just as one must create a standard of safety for pollutants in the work place by negotiations between management and labor and through discussions in public forums one will also need to create a particular policy for social insurance to cover losses at the natural and social lotteries. This will mean that one will not be able to discover that any particular investment in providing health care for those who cannot pay is morally obligatory. One will not be able to show that societies such as that of the United Kingdom, which do not provide America's level of access to renal dialysis for end-stage renal disease, have made a moral mistake. Moral criticism will succeed best in examining the openness of such decisions to public discussion and control.

It is difficulties such as these that led the President's Commission for the Study of Ethical Problems in Medicine and Biomedical and Behavioral Research to construe equity in health care neither as equality in health care nor as access to whatever would benefit patients or meet their needs. The goal of equality in health care runs aground on both conceptual and moral difficulties. There is the difficulty of understanding whether equality would embrace equal amounts of health care or equal amounts of funds for health care. Since individual health needs differ widely, such interpretations of equality are fruitless. Attempting to understand equality as providing health care only from a predetermined list of services to which all would have access conflicts with the personal liberty to use private resources in the acquisition of additional care not on the list. Construing equity as providing all with any health care that would benefit them would threaten inordinately to divert resources to health care. It would conflict as well with choices to invest resources in alternative areas. Substituting "need" for "benefit" leads to similar difficulties unless one can discover, among other things, a notion of need that would not include the need to have one's life extended, albeit at considerable cost.

The commission, as a result, construed equity in health care as the provision of an "adequate level of health care."[1] The commission defined adequate care as "enough care to achieve sufficient welfare, opportunity, information, and evidence of interpersonal concern to facilitate a reasonably full and satisfying life." However, this definition runs aground on the case of children needing liver transplants and other such expensive health-care interventions required to secure any chance of achieving "a reasonably full and satisfying life." There is a tension in the commission's report between an acknowledgement that a great proportion of one's meaning of "adequate health care" must be created and a view that the lineaments of that meaning can be discovered. Thus, the commission states that "[i]n a democracy, the appropriate values to be assigned to the consequences of policies must ultimately be determined by people expressing their values through social and political processes as well as in the marketplace." On the other hand, the commission states that "adequacy does require that everyone receive care that meets standards of sound

---

[1] President's Commission for the Study of Ethical Problems in Medicine and Biomedical and Behavioral Research, *Securing Access to Health Care*, Vol. I (Washington, D.C.: Government Printing Office, 1983), 20.

medical practice." The latter statement may suggest that one could discover what would constitute sound medical practice. In addition, an appeal to a notion of "excessive burdens" will not straightforwardly determine the amount of care due to individuals, since a notion of "excessiveness" requires choosing a particular hierarchy of costs and benefits. Neither will an appeal to excessive burdens determine the amount of the tax burden that others should bear, since there will be morally determined upper limits to taxation set by that element of property that is not communal. People, insofar as they have private property in that sense, have the secular moral right, no matter how unfeeling and uncharitable such actions may appear to others, not to aid those with excessive burdens, even if the financial burdens of those who could be taxed would not be excessive.

Rather, it would appear, following other suggestions from the commission, that "adequate care" will need to be defined by considering, among other things, professional judgments of physicians, average current use, lists of services that health-maintenance organizations and others take to be a part of decent care, as well as more general perceptions of fairness. Such factors influence what is accepted generally in a society as a decent minimal or adequate level of health care. . . .

Is Transplantation Special?

All investments in expensive life-saving treatment raise a question of prudence: Could the funds have been better applied elsewhere? Will the investment in expensive life-saving treatment secure an equal if not greater decrease in morbidity and mortality than an investment in improving the health care of the millions who lack health-care insurance or have only marginal coverage? If the same funds were invested in prenatal health care or the treatment of hypertension, would they secure a greater extension of life and dim-

inution of morbidity for more people? When planning for the rational use of communal funds, it is sensible to seek to maximize access and contribution to the greatest number of people as a reasonable test of what it means to use communal resources for the common good. However, not everything done out of the common purse need be cost effective. It is unclear how one could determine the cost effectiveness of symphony orchestras or art museums. Societies have a proclivity to save the lives of identifiable individuals while failing to come to the aid of unidentified, statistical lives that could have been saved with the same or fewer resources. Any decision to provide expensive life-saving treatment out of communal funds must at least frankly acknowledge when it is not a cost-effective choice but instead a choice made because of special sympathies for those who are suffering or because of special fears that are engendered by particular diseases.

The moral framework of secular, pluralist societies in which rights to health care are more created than discovered will allow such choices as morally acceptable, even if they are less than prudent uses of resources. It will also be morally acceptable for a society, if it pursues expensive life-saving treatment, to exclude persons who through their own choices increase the cost of care. One might think here of the question whether active alcoholics should be provided with liver transplants. There is no invidious discrimination against persons in setting a limit to coverage or in precluding coverage if the costs are increased through free choice. However, societies may decide to provide care even when the costs are incurred by free decision. . . .

Living with the Unfortunate, Which Is Not Unfair

Proposals for the general support of transplantation are thus restricted by various elements of the human condition.

There is not simply a limitation due to finite resources, making it impossible to do all that is conceivably possible for all who might marginally benefit. There are restrictions as well that are due to the free decisions of both individuals and societies. Individuals will often decide in ways unsympathetic to transplantation programs that would involve the use of their private resources, including their organs. Insofar as one takes seriously respect for persons, one must live with the restrictions that result from numerous free choices. One may endeavor to educate, entice, and persuade people to participate. However, free societies are characterized by the commitment to live with the tragedies that result from the decisions of free individuals not to participate in the beneficent endeavors of others. There are then also the restrictions due to the inability to give a plausible account of state authority that would allow the imposition of a concrete view of the good life. Secular, pluralist societies are more neutral moral frameworks for negotiation and creation of ways to use their common resources than modes for discovering the proper purpose for those resources. If societies freely decide to give a low priority to transplantation and invest instead in generally improving health care for the indigent in the hope of doing greater good, there will be an important sense in which they have acted within their right, even if from particular moral perspectives that may seem wrongheaded.

These reflections on the human condition suggest that we will need in the future to learn to live with the fact that some may receive expensive life-saving treatment while others do not, because some have the luck of access to the media, the attention of a political leader, or sufficient funds to purchase care in their own right. The differences in need, both medical and financial, must be recognized as unfortunate. They are properly the objects of charitable response. However, it must be understood that though unfortunate circumstances are always grounds for praiseworthy charity, they do not always provide grounds, by that fact, for redrawing the line between the circumstances we will count as unfortunate but not unfair and those we will count as unfortunate and unfair. To live with circumstances we must acknowledge as unfortunate but not unfair is the destiny of finite men and women who have neither the financial nor moral resources of gods and goddesses. We must also recognize the role of these important conceptual and moral issues in the fashioning of what will count as reasonable and necessary care, safe and efficacious procedures, nonexperimental treatment, or standard medical care. Though we are not gods and goddesses, we do participate in creating the fabric of these "facts."

FOR THE HANDICAPPED: RIGHTS BUT NO WELCOME

George F. Will

Will asserts that it may be self-defeating to attempt to secure aid for the handicapped or any needy group by appeal to rights, for claims of rights are contentious, evoke hostility, and lead to the neglect of needy people once formal rights are granted. The needy will receive better treatment, Will claims, if their advocates appeal to the community's sense of benevolence and achieve benefits for them through the legislative process rather than through rights-enforcing litigation.

From George F. Will, "For the Handicapped: Rights But No Welcome," *The Hastings Center Report* 16:3 (1986), 5–8. Reproduced by permission. © The Hastings Center.

My belief is that the multiplication of rights can carry us only so far. Rights—by which I mean legally enforceable claims on the attention, actions, and resources of others—are not the full answer to the achievement of a properly gentle and humane society.

Obviously, a structure of rights is necessary to protect us all, and not least the handicapped. A structure of rights is especially necessary for those (to use the language of the Supreme Court) "discrete and insular" minorities, such as the mentally or physically handicapped, who have suffered from society's hardness of heart—from indifference or hostility—and who are handicapped in their use of political processes for the amelioration of their conditions. But when you are manufacturing, distributing and handling rights, as when you are handling any other sharp cutting instrument useful in aggression, prudence is in order.

All of us, but especially the handicapped, depend for a humane life on goods that cannot be reduced to rights or guaranteed through the multiplication of fundamental or "constitutional" rights. They depend, inevitably, on community benevolence. Such benevolence cannot be *elicited* by any structure of rights. Indeed, class action litigation and other assertions of group rights can impede the emergence in the community of the virtue of benevolence. . . .

We who are not physically handicapped are the "temporarily able-bodied." . . . [A]ffliction and decline are coming to us all; they are incidental to our humanity. To be human is always to be more or less needy; it is to be increasingly needy the longer we live.

This sense of common vulnerability should give rise in "the temporarily able-bodied" to a sense of how unmerited is their fortunate condition. A sense of our shared susceptibility to the sharp edges of life and a sense of our unearned exemption from affliction, should stir a sense of identification with the handicapped, a sense

that gives rise to generosity. This should be particularly so with regard to the mentally retarded. [Leon] Kass makes the point that neediness, isolation, and impairment of the retarded are, in their human meaning, not different from the diminishment of mental capacity that afflicts many of the elderly and awaits most of us. . . .

Kass, the moral philosopher, believes something that I, an observer of politics, believe. It is that improvements for the handicapped depend primarily on improving the thoughts and practices of the non-handicapped majority. Such improvement depends primarily on appeals to conscience and good will. These appeals, in turn, depend for their effectiveness on a moral insight by the majority. That depends on the nonhandicapped—"the not-yet-handicapped?"—understanding the continuum of neediness that is common to humanity. Equity to the handicapped rests not on recognition of special rights but rather on appreciation of our common dependency on a community of good will—on benevolence understood as the inclination to do good.

The obvious dependence of the handicapped on a social habit of benevolence can teach everyone something that is true but not obviously so. It can teach the universal truth that none of us is as independent as all of us tend to think. Living in full community with handicapped persons is sensitizing because their dependence is a chastening reminder of how unearned are our natural capacities. Therefore the access of the handicapped to a truly open society can shape a more civilized, wiser consensus.

There are times when law must move in advance of opinion, blazing a path rather than being pulled along in the van of an evolving consensus. Laws can be, and should be, and frequently are, teaching instruments. Statecraft frequently is soulcraft. Government must use laws to shape the values of the governed. Am I saying, contrary to the conventional wisdom, that morality can be legislated? Yes, indeed, I am. Morality cannot always be shaped by law, but sometimes it can be.

We did that with the landmark civil rights legislation of the mid-1960s. That legislation was, of course, designed to improve conditions for the descendants of slaves. But it had an ancillary purpose. It was supposed to improve the conditions for blacks by altering the operations of the minds of many white Americans. The theory was that if you compelled people to change their behavior in certain ways, certain desirable changes in their values would follow. Compel white people to eat and work and study and play with the black people that the white people had hitherto kept away, and the white people would become more tolerant, open, accepting— in a word, better. And that is what happened.

Laws are helping something similar happen for the benefit of the handicapped. Before the handicapped, by example of their courage and capacities, can exert a wholesome pull on the moral imagination of the community, the handicapped must be one thing: they must be *visible*. They must not be warehoused; they must not be shunted aside into excessively "sheltered" environments; they must not be prevented by physical or, more importantly, attitudinal barriers from being noticeable in the mainstream of the nation's life.

Opening the doors sometimes requires more than a polite knock. Some doors must be pounded open, aggressively. And if that gets some people's backs up, so be it. But be warned. A community of people who constantly have their backs up about one another is not a true community.

The assertion of rights is not just the assertion of "rights *for*" particular classes of people. It also is an assertion of "rights *against*" other people. The assertion of rights usually is, to some extent, a prickly business. It is an adversarial, indeed confrontational, process. As such, it carries two sorts of dangers for handicapped people.

One danger is that the nonhandicapped community will lose whatever spontaneous sympathy it has for the handicapped. The second, and more serious danger, is that the rhetoric and procedures the handicapped use in asserting rights will turn on them and injure them.

One problem with an aggressive rights-based strategy for improving the lot of the handicapped is that the handicapped can easily be perceived as trying to have things both ways. On the one hand, they want equal rights. On the other hand, they insist, reasonably, they have special needs that make them deserving of special consideration. They claim, correctly, that their handicap is irrelevant to their moral worth. Yet, they use the fact of a handicap as a justification for special rights—special entitlements, special enforceable claims against others. Kass correctly argues that a fact, such as a physical handicap, that is ethically irrelevant cannot be the basis of a social entitlement. This following is, as Kass says, a philosophic truth: "The mere fact that an individual has been unfortunate does not invest that individual with special 'natural' or 'constitutional' rights—special claims against other citizens." The fact that life has been unfair to an individual does not invest that individual with a claim that must be made good by others. One person's misfortune does not translate into another person's legal duty.

What is true of the nonhandicapped is true of the handicapped: The fact that we desire or need something does not entitle us to it. Neither a need nor a desire in and of itself generates an enforceable claim against the community. We desire, and often need, training, medical care, rehabilitation, a job, even a "meaningful" job, and other help to develop to our maximum potential. But we do not have standing to insist on these things as a "right" inherently owed us by other individuals whose duty it is to supply the desired goods to us.

There is a style of public discourse that is becoming a plague. It is a form of moral exhibitionism. It confuses attitudinizing with ethical behavior. It confuses right-mindedness with right action. It consists of rhetorical extravagance in the assertion of rights.

The language of rights springs naturally—at times, it seems, unbidden—to the lips of citizens in a society like ours. A society constituted as ours is, along liberal democratic lines, is organized for the enhancement, enlargement and protection of individual liberty. Such a society speaks not only naturally, but increasingly, and eventually, almost exclusively the language of severe individualism. The language of rights predominates over the language of responsibilities and duties, including the duty to look after the unfortunate.

The language of rights is the language of pride, of autonomy, of the sovereign individual asserting his or her imperatives. It is language suited to individual declarations of social independence, even of a desire to be left alone. We have quite enough of that language of rights in our society. Such language numbs us all to the fact that no one of us, handicapped or not, is independent of the community on which we depend for our moral fulfillment.

Rights are part of justice. But the experience of justice can never be reduced to an array of rights. Justice is getting what one deserves. The handicapped deserve *more* than rights—they deserve acceptance that cannot be derived from enforceable claims on the community. This nation, at this moment, is less in need of new rights than it is in need of the quickened capacity for social sympathy, a capacity that comes from a lively sense of common neediness.

. . .

America's reformers have usually thought of themselves as liberals. Many of the political forces generally clustered under the umbrella label of "liberalism" are suffering anemia at the moment. That is in part the result of ill-gotten successes.

The anemia is the price paid for surrendering to a debilitating temptation. It is the result of a strategy of evading the central responsibility of politics in a democracy, the responsibility to persuade. Too much social *change*—too much social improvement, even—has been achieved outside of and even against the popular branches of our governments—the legislative branches. There has grown up an essentially lazy preference for litigation rather than legislation as the instrument of social change. Courts, you see, are quicker than legislatures, and so much tidier. It is simpler to find a sympathetic judge than it is to persuade law makers and their constituents.

So nowadays if you favor abortion or oppose capital punishment; or favor racial or sexual hiring quotas or oppose nuclear power; or favor forced busing or oppose construction of a highway (such as Westway in New York City); or favor overturning labor unions' seniority systems or oppose financing public schools with property taxes; or oppose a moment of silence in public schools or favor better treatment of handicapped persons—well, do not legislate, litigate. Legislation involves persuasion and compromise. It demands the peculiar patience—and at times the strenuous nature—of politics. Legislation, therefore, suggests that you are seeking to receive the community's favor rather than to coerce acknowledgment of some preexisting right.

Consider, for example, something that is dear to me as it is to all other parents of handicapped children—Public Law 94-142, the Education of All Handicapped Children Act. This established for handicapped children a right to a free, appropriate public education in the least restricted environment suitable. This law established an entitlement. But it does not rest on an assertion of a natural or constitutional right. The benefits it secures did not come about because the handicapped or their spokesmen managed to wring them from the community by litigation asserting the existence of the rights owed to the handicapped by virtue of their misfortunes. Rather, Public Law 94-142 was passed because the community wanted to—was persuaded to—act decently. It was passed not because the handicapped had a preexisting right to such treatment, but because the community decided that such treatment is right. It was, as Kass says, an act of community good will—or, if you will, of benevolence. . . .

When the language of benevolence is stigmatized as condescending; when acts of benevolence are dismissed as insultingly paternalistic and inconsistent with the dignity of the benefited group—when this occurs, we are left with a cold polity. . . .

Let me conclude by underlining what I have not said. I have not questioned the value of the work done in establishing many protections and entitlements for the hand-

icapped. I have questioned neither the purity of motive nor the nobility of spirit of the people who have worked on behalf of the handicapped. And I am not arguing that such work is finished—that nothing remains to be done.

Indeed, I am arguing that the hardest work remains to be done. Most of what remains is hard work because it is not lawyer's work. It is political work in the grandest sense. Politics is the conversation of the community, a conversation about the assignment of values. The next stage in the full acceptance of the handicapped into civic life must involve less recourse to juridical subtlety and more appeals to the community's sense of moral fitness. Progress based on anything other than a broad and stable sense of moral duty is progress resting on sand.

PROFESSIONAL RESPONSIBILITY AND THE DISTRIBUTION OF LEGAL SERVICES*

Kenneth Kipnis

Kipnis argues that a morally justified legal system must make information about the law and the ability to exercise one's legal rights available to all. He contends that lawyers' monopoly over legal services carries with it a duty to ensure that these conditions of "information and exercise" are fulfilled. The provision of free legal services to those who cannot pay for them is thus not a matter of charity but a basic requirement of professional responsibility.

When goods or services of any type are distributed in society (henceforth, the term "goods" will refer to both), a choice must be made whether these will enter the market to be bought and sold there, or whether they will be distributed or rationed wholly or in part in accordance with some principle other than the ability and willingness

to pay the market price. Few would question that with respect to some goods—after shave lotion, for example—market mechanisms are a reasonable and appropriate means of distribution. In efforts to maximize their profits designers, manufacturers, and distributors compete with one another to produce the highest-quality goods at the

---

* References have been deleted without indication.

From Kenneth Kipnis and Diana T. Meyers, eds., *Economic Justice: Private Rights and Public Responsibilities* (Totowa, N.J.: Rowman & Allanheld, 1985), 130–142. Reprinted by permission.

lowest cost. Purchasers in turn make independent judgments about whether the goods offered for sale are worth their price. For some other goods, however—childhood vaccinations, secondary education, firefighting services—distributions are not nearly so dependent upon transactions made between the end-users of the goods and their suppliers. We can distinguish therefore between market systems of distribution and rationing systems, understanding by that latter term all systems in which ability and willingness to pay for the goods are not the sole preconditions for receipt.

In some cases, the justification for a rationing system involves an appeal to goals that are shared, more or less, by the community as a whole. We may all be more secure if fires in our community are contained as quickly as possible. The public interest in speed and efficiency here is not served if purchasers of fire protection services must negotiate with sellers while homes, businesses, and factories go up in flames. In a second category, the justification of rationing systems involves an appeal to some right. The arguments can be made that police protection services, legal services in serious criminal proceedings and elementary education must be provided where the need arises, not merely because it is in the public interest that this be done, but, rather, because the beneficiary of the good has some type of right, some entitlement to it. The victim who is being beaten up has a right to the assistance of a law enforcement officer. Those accused of criminal wrongs have a right to legal assistance in proceedings that would be unfairly imposed in the absence of such help. And children arguably have a right to be taught skills that are essential to a decent life in the society that we will leave for them.

In a third category of case—and it will be one of these that will interest us here—nonmarket mechanisms may be justified, not by an appeal to a right enjoyed by the beneficiary of the good, but, rather, by

appeal to a duty or special responsibility assumed by those designated to provide the good. We may wish to say, for example, that where it is vital to their well-being, children should receive medical care, not because they have some kind of inherent right to health care (we may believe that no one does), but, rather, because in becoming parents, mothers and fathers have assumed a responsibility to provide that care. The child is what lawyers would call a "third-party beneficiary."

In the United States, legal services in civil proceedings are for the most part made available through market distribution systems. To be sure, many attorneys and firms provide services at reduced fees or for no fees at all to people who might otherwise have to go without needed legal advice or representation. Additionally, private organizations (the American Civil Liberties Union or the National Association for the Advancement of Colored People) and government-funded organizations like the Legal Services Corporation also make available legal services without reliance upon market pricing systems in distribution. In its state and national bar associations, the organized bar has played a role in the provision of legal services to those who cannot obtain them because of an inability to pay. While it is clear that legal services in civil matters have been made available outside of market distribution systems, it is less clear that these services have been adequate to meet the general needs for them. But it will not be our purpose here to explore the dimensions of such shortcomings. Rather, our central concern will be to identify who it is that has central responsibility for the provision of such services, the form that such responsibility takes, and the grounds for that obligation. . . .

The Conditions of Information and Exercise

It would seem that for any legal system worthy of respect, the protection and support that the community provides for some should be made available to all whose claims are similar. To the extent that the community fails to make this protection so available, it fails to provide equal protection: It fails to be just. Two conditions must be met if the protection afforded by legal rights is to be available to all with sound claims to it. First, it should be possible for citizens to obtain, at least generally, *information* about what the law requires or permits. There may be some cases, as when the law is unsettled, when only educated guesses are possible: Adequate authoritative information is not available because it does not exist. To be sure, even when rights are problematic, a commitment to adjudication secures for members of the community a right to an authoritative clarifying judgment in the event of a dispute. But when information does exist, it should be possible for a member of the community to find out what the legal standards are. Legal rights have little value (and legal obligations can be unfairly perilous) to those who cannot find out which ones they have.

Second, when members of the community have a legal right to something that has been denied to them, it should be possible for them to obtain whatever protection and support the community guarantees to them as a matter of law. In other words, it should be possible for them to *exercise* what rights they have. Thus if Potter has the legal right that Watson not build the tall orange fence on the boundary separating their two lots, it should be possible for her to commence some community-constituted process that will have as its effect the rectification of Watson's wrong. Potter might be able to invoke some legal requirement that Watson remove, relocate, or repaint his fence or that he compensate her for a continuing encroachment upon her interests. If the community is serious in its commitment to adjudication as a means of clarifying and securing legal rights for its citizenry, it must begin by securing generally for all citizens a right to information about what the law permits

and requires, and a right as well to appeal to the law to secure that which the law guarantees to them.

Adversarial systems seem to have the serious disadvantage that complaints may not be made and cases may be wrongly decided if the party in the right doesn't bring the case or loses it because of an inability to present intelligibly and persuasively what is, in fact, a solid case. Some citizens—let us call them nonparticipants—may be effectively excluded from the courts because of inadequate resources of one kind or another. Since the judge in an adversarial proceeding depends upon the parties to do the investigative work and to present the results to the court in a useful way, serious injustices may be tolerated when they shouldn't be or cases may be wrongly decided if one of the parties is unable to meet the requirements of adversarial adjudication. Where this happens, the judicial system may serve generally to protect some perpetrators of injustice; may serve, in other words, to further injustice. Certain sectors of the community may be forced to put up with wrongs that the rest of us would not tolerate for an instant. Being unable to participate in the mechanism that the community provides for the settling of disputes, these persons will be exposed to wrongs without the prospect of legal recourse. . . .

At the broadest level, adversarial legal systems can meet the conditions of information and exercise in several ways. Because each of these approaches ameliorates some difficulties while exacerbating others, they may be thought of as representing different agendas: With what kinds of problem do we wish to be occupied? The first solution is that of the "convivial" legal system.[1] In such a system care is taken so that people can generally be expected to understand their legal positions with respect to most matters and to be able to

---

[1] I have taken the term "convivial" from the chapter entitled "Institutional Spectrum" in Ivan Illich's *Deschooling Society.*

function within the legal system without assistance. This is brought about by (1) employing programs of mass legal education to ensure that virtually everyone has the knowledge and skill that are needed, and (2) opting for a simple legal system so that only minimal instruction is required.

The system can be kept simple using a number of methods. Judges can be limited in the degree to which they are able to become specialists. They might receive only a small amount of specialized training, perhaps only after they are selected. And they could be rotated in and out of short single terms in office. Because in terms of training and experience judges would not be all that different from the litigants, courtroom discourse would not differ strikingly from the language of everyday life. Indeed, experience in the courtroom, as litigant and as judge, might be fairly commonplace among members of such a community. A convivial arrangement has the advantage that each person would know just about everything anyone would need to know about the legal system: both what the law was on most matters and how to function in the courts. . . .

On the other hand, the community could choose to make no effort whatever to educate the general public to the point at which it has an adequate understanding of the provisions of the law and the niceties of legal procedure. The legal system itself could be permitted to become as complicated as it may, with only highly educated and experienced specialists sitting on the bench. In such a "sophisticated" system, the ordinary person cannot be expected to understand his or her legal position with respect to many matters, and neither can the layman be expected to secure, all alone, what the law guarantees. In a legal system like this, justice requires that there exist some mechanism for making available both information about the requirements of the law and skilled legal assistance. Without such a mechanism, a sophisticated legal system cannot be justified. Justice can thus require that a sophisticated adversarial system of adjudication be a "professionalized" system.

Sophisticated Adversarial Systems

Unlike the convivial arrangement, sophisticated legal systems do not provide for mass legal education, nor do they incorporate structural features that serve to limit the complexity of the system. Accordingly, in order to meet the conditions of information and exercise, they must provide for some sort of intermediary between laypersons and what will generally be a mysterious and intimidating legal system. There are three main approaches to the provision of such an intermediary: the free market, the liberal profession, and the public agency.

The Free Market. In the absence of mass legal education, judicial specialists create the need for lawyers. Just as—historically—shoemakers and repairers of appliances can materialize without invitation, so pettifoggers will appear about the courts to make specialized services available to those who have business there. In exchange for a fee, these self-designated attorneys will give legal advice, draft legal documents, and, with the court's permission, represent clients before the judge. It is important to note that these "proto-professionals" differ greatly from what we now know as attorneys. For example, they will not have standardized educational experiences, nor will they be certified in familiar ways. Though some may have been to "law school," completion of such a course of study will not be a prerequisite to the practice of law. Just as anyone can hold himself out as a gardener or as an automobile front-end specialist—and let the buyer beware!—so pettifoggers will fall all along the spectra of competence and integrity. There will be virtually no formal restrictions on entry into the field. Of course, some may not be able to earn a living in the legal services business and will turn to other callings. Consumer services may alleviate some of the problems created by variations in quality, selling information to potential clients about the relative merits of attorneys. Still, the purchaser of legal services will generally have no assurance (except for the word of the attorney) that the goods received are of their putative quality. . . .

Sectors of the community that are without adequate legal services will almost naturally generate their own specialists as legal tradesmen seek out untapped markets. On the other hand, where poverty is significant in sectors of the community or where legal services are for other reasons not made available by market forces, the problems may be more difficult. Still, the proto-professional lawyer may nobly offer legal services "pro bono publico" (for the good of the public). A sufficient level of such charity may serve adequately to address the community's concern to meet the conditions of information and exercise. . . .

The Liberal Profession.   The development of a trade into a profession is a lengthy process, and occupations can be located at virtually any point along the continuum. In American legal history, the process of professionalization can perhaps be said to have begun in 1870 with the organization of the Association of the Bar of the City of New York. . . . The transition from something close to what we have described as a "free market" to the modern legal profession took many decades, but the three critical steps in the process are roughly as follows.

First, organized practitioners within the trade begin to make a *claim to maximal competence.* Through representatives, one begins to hear that a certain discrete class of lawyers, in virtue of superior training, education, and experience, exceeds in skill all others in legal knowledge and skill. Two conditions must be satisfied before such a claim can be made: (1) there must be some organization of practitioners within the fa-

vored class; not necessarily all, but enough to warrant a claim to speak for the whole class. And (2) there must be some criterion for deciding who belongs to the class of favored practitioners and who does not. (In the end, this evolves into an elaborate gatekeeping procedure involving education, accreditation of schools, and certification of new members.) The esoteric nature of the legal knowledge and skill possessed by this select class of practitioners implies that those outside the favored class simply lack the standing to make sound judgments about the competence of these specialists. As the claim to maximal competence becomes generally accepted, it becomes more and more reasonable to let the select class of practitioners certify and evaluate itself, excluding from practice those of dubious expertise. The organization of favored practitioners stands ready to assume this responsibility.

Second, since in a society that is committed to a sophisticated adversarial system special legal knowledge and skill are vital to the achievement of justice, the process of professionalization requires that the profession make a *public commitment* to use its distinctive abilities in the realization of that significant social value. The profession pledges to give due attention to the special responsibilities it will assume in ensuring that the system of adversarial adjudication succeeds in its task of justly addressing conflicts emerging within the community. Typically these commitments are expressed in the codes of ethics that have become virtually the hallmark of professionalism itself. . . .

Third and most important, the process of professionalization requires that the community recognize the favored members of the profession as the sole means by which legal skill and knowledge are to be applied. This exclusive *social reliance* upon licensed attorneys is based upon the preceding two stages. For if there is confidence that the favored members of the class of practitioners possess maximal competence in matters legal, and if there is trust that these same lawyers are reliably committed to the responsible application of their distinctive skills, then there will seem to be neither the ability nor the need to designate nonprofessionals as overseers of professional practice. No one is competent to do the job, and we don't need to have it done in the first place. As the profession secures trust and confidence, it takes control over the selection and training of candidates, the accreditation of professional schools and programs, the certification of new members, and the promulgation and enforcement of standards of professional conduct. It becomes, in essence, an unregulated legal monopoly with respect to legal services, unauthorized practice being a criminal offense. In the end, of course, it is the citizenry who, through representatives, delegate responsibility to professions or relieve them of it. Though permission to practice in the courts—admission to the bar—is initially granted by the judiciary, the privileges that lawyers enjoy can be ratified, extended, and revoked by legislatures.

It is helpful to compare the monopoly status of public utilities with the standing of the professionalized bar. Corporations that operate as public utilities receive from the community an exclusive legal right to distribute some good or service within a defined geographical area. It is a great advantage to the corporation to have the assurance that it will not face competition and, because of this, it may be able to keep its costs low and achieve economies of scale. From the point of view of the citizenry however, the deal makes sense only if the corporation assumes the responsibility of providing reasonable service to all those within its area. As the United States Supreme Court put it in 1918:

Corporations which devote their property to a public use may not pick and choose, serving only the portions of the territory covered by their franchises which it is presently profitable for them to serve, and restricting the development of the remaining portions by leaving their inhabitants in discomfort without the service which they alone can render.[2]

Without the commitment to provide service, the granting of the exclusive right to the corporation—the barring of all others from entering the market—does not make sense.

Likewise, in the absence of a commitment from the legal profession to provide service to all who need it, the granting of an exclusive right to the bar becomes a decision to exclude some sectors of the community from participation in the system of adjudication. Where only attorneys are permitted to advise and represent members of the community, but where no attorneys will agree to serve some community members with need for legal assistance, the community does not meet the conditions of information and exercise and is to that extent unjust. One mechanism for meeting the two conditions is a responsible legal profession. Those in it would possess the knowledge and skill that the ordinary members of the community would lack. They would have an exclusive right to counsel and represent clients in legal matters. And finally, the profession as a whole would acknowledge its obligation to serve adequately as the necessary intermediary between the public and an otherwise inaccessible judiciary. Understood in this way, the liberal legal profession serves as an integral part of the legal system: Though they retain their autonomy, lawyers are *officers* of the court. Thus a serious failure of the legal profession is a serious failure of the legal system. The standards of practice that the profession as a whole imposes upon its members must ensure that the counseling and representational services that must be made available if the legal system is to make sense are made available to the public in an adequate way.

[2] *New York and Queens Gas Co. v. McCall*, 245 U.S. 345, 351.

Speaking through professional associations in codes of ethics, lawyers have acknowledged the bar's duty to serve all members of the community. Thus the first Ethical Consideration of the American Bar Association's Code of Professional Responsibility begins:

A basic tenet of the professional responsibility of lawyers is that *every person* in our society should have ready access to the independent professional services of a lawyer of integrity and competence.

The legal profession, the collectivity of licensed attorneys, thus does provide a guarantee to the community as a whole that competent and responsible attorneys will be available to those with need for it. . . .

In granting the legal profession monopoly status, the community relies to its detriment upon the profession's collective representation that it will meet the conditions of information and exercise. The community loses something universally acknowledged to be of inestimable value if the legal profession fails to meet the responsibilities it has assumed in the process of professionalization. Of course, if we assume that the granting of monopoly status to the bar is the "consideration" that the bar receives in return for having agreed to meet the conditions of information and exercise, then the contract is a much more ordinary one. In either event, unlike the free-market pettifogger, professional attorneys have a clear duty to address the legal needs of nonparticipants; indeed, a duty to see to it that there are no nonparticipants. It is not a matter of gratuitous charity "pro bono publico." It is a "basic tenet" of the bar's professional responsibility. . . .

The Public Agency. The community takes the third approach to providing the intermediary between the lay public and the sophisticated adversarial system when it decides to employ attorneys directly, much as it does with fire fighters, judges, and police officers. If the interests that citizens

have are important enough (it is difficult to think of a more important interest than civil justice), and if neither the free market nor the liberal profession can be relied upon to do the job, the principal remaining option is directly to employ attorneys in organizations set up to provide legal services to the general public. Though lawyers will *work for* their clients (just as teachers work for their students), they will be *paid by* and will have some of their working conditions set by their employers—in this case, civil government. Where gratuitous charity and professional responsibility have failed, "conditions of employment" that are set by the community can perhaps succeed.

The most serious problem that can emerge within the public agency approach is the compromising of professional autonomy, the damaging erosion of the bar's independence. Even though agency attorneys are nominally employed to provide legal services to the public, government officials may try to discourage these lawyers from bringing certain types of complaint—especially complaints against the government—even when the cases are legitimate. Government, the employer of attorneys, may be able to limit the degree to which citizens can challenge the state for having exceeded its proper authority. As the legal profession's "boss," it will do this by setting conditions of employment that restrict the types of case that can be brought to court. In controlling the legal profession—and thus access to the judiciary—the state can circumvent all legal limits to its authority. Though in some sense or other citizens may still "enjoy" legal rights against the community, they will not be able to appeal to the courts to obtain that which the law guarantees to them. Their rights will not have been secured.

Autonomy problems within legal-services agencies can be addressed by carefully attending to the structure of the organization. In universities, for example, the problem of unwarranted encroachment upon professional autonomy has been extensively addressed under the general heading of "academic freedom." In practice, this entails a separation of administrative and professional functions within the institution so as to guarantee that academicians have the latitude that is required if they are to do their work. It is a secured limitation on the employer's right to determine the conditions and content of the professional's work. Substantial control is in the hands of members of the affected profession. By far the most important factor in securing professional autonomy within an employing organization is the type of association created by the professionals themselves.

Trade associations and professional associations are the characteristic organizations with respect to the two approaches discussed earlier. The social organization that can be expected to emerge among publicly employed attorneys is the public sector labor union. Labor unions exist primarily to negotiate with the employer (in this case, the community) the terms and conditions of employment. The distinction drawn earlier between trade associations and professional associations parallels the two distinct sets of interests that can be furthered by a public-sector legal-services labor union. Employed attorneys may identify themselves as employees. They may feel that the work they are doing is not really their work but, rather, the agency's work. If the quality of service provided is low, that is not the employee's responsibility. Think of an assembly-line worker,

building a badly engineered product. "I am just doing a job, earning a living." To the extent that attorneys think of themselves in this way, the collective bargaining process will focus upon "bread and butter" issues: wages, hours, and general working conditions. The employee's posture will in essence be "more money for less work," mirroring the employer's posture of "more work for less money."

On the other hand, attorneys may identify themselves as professionals; not being paid for their work, *but in order that they may do their work.* Employed professionals may focus not upon their interests as employees, but upon their interests as professionals with final responsibility for the quality of their work. Decent salaries and appropriate working conditions may be important, not because it is nice to earn more in better circumstances, but because adequate attention must be given to these matters if the agency and its professional staff are to serve their public purpose. Likewise, if professional autonomy is under attack by administrators (or even by fellow professionals), the membership of a public sector labor union has the option of placing those values high upon its agenda in negotiations. Of course, where the community as a whole adequately appreciates the argument for an independent bar, it is unlikely that employer and employee will be at odds on this issue. Still, provided that lawyers have not lost their sense of responsibility in their roles as employees, labor unions can serve to further professionalism and buttress autonomy should the need arise to protect these critical values.

THE LAWYER'S DUTY TO SERVE*

David L. Shapiro

Shapiro considers the recent history of attempts to mandate that lawyers provide a certain level of pro bono publico *service. He argues against such a requirement, on the grounds that it is not needed to improve the image of lawyers, runs into constitutional difficulties, and, by making service mandatory, deprives lawyers of opportunities to engage in morally worthy behavior on the basis of their voluntary choice.*

For centuries, lawyers have given their services without charge to causes they thought worthwhile, and to clients who could not afford to pay. During this period, and especially in recent decades, the question whether and to what extent they could, as lawyers, be required to serve without compensation has frequently been raised. And if the vehemence with which the discussion has been carried on is any indication, the issue is far from being resolved.

Paralleling the existence of service without compensation has been the articulation of ethical standards that, to some degree, make such service an "obligation"—at least in the sense of the aspirations of the profession. And relying in part on their understanding of the tradition, and on these very standards, courts have often required lawyers to represent indigents or other litigants for little or no pay.

Recently, these matters have been raised to a new level of visibility by efforts within the bar itself to make the professional standards of service mandatory and subject to disciplinary sanctions. Starting with Canon 4 of the former Canons of Professional Ethics, which limited its application to lawyers assigned to represent indigent criminal defendants,[1] the American Bar Association moved in 1969, in its Code of Professional Responsibility, to "Ethical Considerations" that spoke of the duty of individual lawyers to render services to those unable to pay.[2] There followed in 1975 a resolution, approved by the ABA House of Delegates, calling it a "basic professional responsibility" of every lawyer to provide "public interest legal service" without fee, or at a substantially reduced fee, and instructing the Association to develop implementing proposals.[3]

Carried along by this momentum, the Kutak Commission of the ABA, which has drafted and proposed a wholly new set of "Rules of Professional Conduct," first recommended a requirement of service "pro bono publico" of "forty hours per year . . . or the [financial] equivalent thereof."[4] In January 1980 the Commission issued a revised draft that broadened the definition of public service, dropped the specification of hours, made the requirement one of service alone (eliminating the financial alternative), and imposed a new obligation to "make an annual report of such service to appropriate regulatory authority."[5] The

---

* References have been deleted without indication.

[1] ABA Canons of Professional Ethics No. 4.

[2] ABA Code of Professional Responsibility, Ethical Consideration [hereinafter EC] 2–25; accord, EC 2–16, EC 8–3.

[3] ABA House of Delegates Resolution on Public Interest Legal Services, August 1975.

[4] This recommendation appeared as Rule 9.1 in a draft prepared by the Commission in 1979 and was given limited circulation.

[5] ABA Commission on Evaluation of Professional Stand-

From David L. Shapiro, "The Enigma of the Lawyer's Duty to Serve," 55 N.Y.U. L. Rev. 735, 735–38, 785–91 (1980).

next step, after considerable discussion and criticism, was to eliminate the reporting requirement but to endorse the idea of including suggested means of enforcement by those states that were prepared to adopt and implement the proposal. Then in November 1980, the Commission returned almost full circle to the approach of the 1969 Code. A new working draft of the entire set of proposed rules—prepared for further discussion prior to submission of a final draft to the ABA House of Delegates for consideration in 1982—no longer said that a lawyer "shall" but rather that he "should" render unpaid public interest service and added in commentary that "[t]he responsibility for pro bono publico service is that of each lawyer individually. This Rule does not specify the contribution to be made or make a lawyer answerable to disciplinary authority for fulfillment of this responsibility."[6]

Thus for the moment at least, the drive for a nationwide system of mandatory service, backed by disciplinary sanctions, has abated, though the controversy is likely to continue at both national and local levels. Criticism of such a service requirement, and of the present practice in some jurisdictions of assigning lawyers to represent indigents without adequate compensation, has been based on many arguments: the asserted unconstitutionality of the state's coercion of legal services, the attendant economic burdens, the impracticability of enforcement, the erosion of personal choice, and the undesirability of forced charity. Arguments in favor have centered on the tradition of service, the ethical obligations of the profession, the need for wider availability of legal services, and the dangers of government regulation and control as an alternative if this approach is not successful. . . .

The Significance of Membership in a Profession

Advocates of a public service requirement have on occasion looked for support to such definitions of a "profession" as "the pursuit of a learned art in the spirit of a public service"[7]—a pursuit in which earning a living is incidental and subordinate to this worthier goal. Some, like George Bernard Shaw, have taken a more cynical view of what membership in a profession is all about. All professions, he said, are "conspiracies against the laity."[8]

My own perspective lies somewhere in between the emphasis on public service and the apprehension of a cabal. The essence of professional standing, I believe, is the acquisition of specialized knowledge and skill through intensive training. There is also, at least in some of the older, established professions, a concept of an organized group with standards of conduct to be lived up to. Some of these ethical standards may exist because the imperfections of the market make it impossible to rely solely on free competition among suppliers. Other standards may reinforce those imperfections. And still others may be rooted in concerns transcending the functioning of the market. But whatever their reason for being, they cover a wide range of subjects, from basic rules of fair dealing to the broadest admonitions of responsibility to society. In the case of lawyers, the Code of Professional Responsibility adopted in 1969 made a conscientious effort to separate out those obligations so basic that violations should be grounds of discipline from those considerations "aspirational in character . . . toward which every member should strive." The idea of a duty of service was quite explicitly placed in the latter category.

---

ards, Model Rules of Professional Conduct, Rule 8.1 (Discussion Draft, Jan. 30, 1980) [hereinafter Kutak Commission Draft Rule (Jan. 1980)].

[6] Kutak Commission Draft, Rule 8.1 (Nov. 1980).

[7] R. Pound, The Lawyer from Antiquity to Modern Times 5 (1953).

[8] The phrase appears in the Preface to "The Doctor's Dilemma."

Though the distinction between enforceable obligation and aspiration has been overlooked by some eminent people, I believe it is an important one that should not evaporate. The progression from one to the other is neither natural nor inevitable. Indeed . . . it finds little support in history and runs into formidable constitutional and practical barriers. Moreover, the idea of an enforceable obligation of this character may be inconsistent with the notion of professional *responsibility*. Responsibility implies an element of choice, of freedom not only to choose membership in the profession but to chart one's course after membership is attained. To turn an aspiration of public service into an enforceable obligation, then, would be to deprive the professional of an element of choice that may be an important part of self-fulfillment. Compelled altruism is not much of a virtue. . . .

The Lawyer's Image

From Shakespeare to Sandburg and beyond, poets have eloquently expressed popular dissatisfaction with lawyers and with their trade. When a lawyer is seen to respond to the need for assistance by donating his services, this attitude may be softened. As one report put it in 1958, in discussing the virtues and defects of the adversary system: "Popular misconceptions of the advocate's function disappear when the lawyer pleads without a fee, and the true value of his service to society is immediately perceived."[9]

This observation has force, especially in a controversy that attracts wide public interest. But for several reasons, I do not believe the argument can be used to justify compulsory service. First, in those matters receiving sufficient notoriety to attract public attention and, it is hoped, to increase public awareness of the contributions the

bar can make, courts or other instrumentalities will have little difficulty enlisting the services of competent lawyers without any necessity of coercion. Second, the unwilling lawyer, dragooned into service in the name of duty, is surely less likely than the volunteer to turn in the kind of performance that will enhance the general reputation of the bar. Finally, and most important, the causes of popular dissatisfaction with law and lawyers run too deep to be profoundly affected by such gestures. To some extent, public unhappiness is endemic for a profession that usually enters people's lives at a time of serious crisis and is often without the capacity to resolve it. And to some extent, the unhappiness results from a system in which law and lawyers are seen to be responsible for complexity, cost, and delay that ought not to exist. Lawyers, like dentists, can perhaps do most to reduce the general level of dissatisfaction by working for those changes that will reduce the demand for their services.

In one way, the point is similar to that made in the discussion of the concept of a "profession." When a lawyer comes forward to perform a service because of a sense of responsibility to the profession and to society, something is surely gained in the measure of public respect for the calling. When unwilling lawyers are drafted into service, with all the quarrels over the nature and extent of their duty that are bound to occur, public esteem may well decline.

Yet I think it unlikely that the bar in this country will ever find itself as heavily dependent on the state for its subsistence as the English bar is becoming. American lawyers tend to be involved in many more areas of private activity, both in and out of the courtroom, than are their English counterparts. The separation in England of the roles of barristers and solicitors, the dependence of solicitors on income from conveyancing, and the traditional acceptance by English lawyers and courts of a

9 Joint Conference on Professional Responsibility, Report, 44 A.B.A.J. 1159, 1216 (1958).

narrower social and political role may all help to account for the difference. But whatever the origins of that difference, it plainly exists, and its existence points to the significance of the private sector in the careers of American lawyers. Whatever the future of state-supported legal services programs may be, the importance of the private sector to American lawyers will endure.

The Fear of State Control

A persistent theme in the call for increased public service is the perceived danger of state control, and even of the "socialization" of the practice of law, if the need is not met by lawyers acting on their own. Indeed, one cannot help thinking that, for many lawyers, this perception lies at the heart of the proposals made.

The possibility is very real that if lawyers do not come forward, and the burden is assumed by the state, more and more lawyers will find their income heavily dependent on state funds. This has occurred in England, especially for barristers, and doubtless also holds in other Western European countries. With state funds, of course, comes at least the threat of state control; the experience of federally funded legal services lawyers, in suffering limitations on the matters they can pursue, is an example of the threat fulfilled. Certainly it is hard to object in principle to the authority of the source of funds to determine how those funds will be used.

As to the question of government control of those lawyers who are paid by the state, there are several appropriate responses. One is for lawyers themselves, acting voluntarily, to join and foster organizations that provide alternatives to state-funded legal services. Another is to attempt to shape legal service programs in a way that leaves enough room to accommodate representation by lawyers who are not government employees and whose choice of clients and causes is subject to the fewest possible limitations.

There are some people who appear to favor, or who at least do not oppose, a vastly expanded role for government in the allocation of legal resources and in the control of the legal profession. That is not my view, nor is it the view of many who have sought to impose on the bar an enforceable public service obligation. It is incongruous, I think, for these people to call for mandatory service, supported by the threat of government-backed professional discipline, disbarment, and even criminal penalties, as a means of avoiding state control. The theory seems to be that we should burn down the house to reduce the risk of fire.

The expressed or implicit fear that the alternative to mandatory service may be reduction of the lawyer's "monopoly" stands on a different footing. As I have already suggested, the scope of American lawyers' special preserve is rapidly shrinking, and in my opinion that is a desirable turn of events. If the rejection of mandatory service means an acceleration of this process, I believe there will be a net gain for society from that result alone.

THE LAWYER'S *PRO BONO PUBLICO* RESPONSIBILITY*

Barlow F. Christensen

Christensen argues that the lawyers' monopoly on the provision of legal services carries with it a duty to enable people to meet their legal needs. Because lawyers have failed to develop programs to provide inexpensive legal services, however, pro bono *service is now in order. There is no call for* pro bono *service in medicine because of government programs that subsidize health care for the needy. Without mandatory* pro bono *assistance, the same may be required for law.*

. . . One authority has dismissed as "absurd" the notion that the lawyer's exclusive right to perform his essential role in the justice system and to render to the public those services defined as "legal" creates any pro bono publico obligation.[1] The argument supporting this opinion is not fully articulated, but apparently it is based on the premise that because admission to law practice is to some extent open and because competition among lawyers results in a substantial amount of no-fee and low-fee work, no monopoly exists and hence no pro bono obligation. The premise is of questionable validity.

The practice of law is a monopoly. And neither the relative openness of admission to the bar nor competition among lawyers relieves it of its monopolistic character. The public may gain access to the justice system and may obtain those services defined by the bar as "legal" only from lawyers. The restraints thus imposed on the public's ability to obtain what lawyers provide is very real.

To begin with, admission to law practice is not nearly so free and easy as has been suggested. The economic and academic barriers are formidable, and the road to a

law license is long, arduous, and expensive. As a consequence, only a comparatively few embark upon it, and fewer still complete it. Despite law school affirmative action admissions programs and despite availability to students of substantial amounts of financial aid, those who surmount the economic and academic barriers nevertheless do constitute a genuine elite, if only in the sense that a relatively small part of the public are thus able finally to become lawyers. By way of contrast, we might ask how many people would be engaging in law practice and how much more free would be public access to legal services if the license were to be had for the asking. To repeat, the practice of law is a monopoly because it is limited to a select few and because that limitation results in restraints upon the public's use of legal services.

Moreover, the process of becoming lawyers socializes those who undergo it to an inherently expensive problem-solving mode, including an elitist attitude toward the monetary rewards of practice; whatever their motivations for entering law, most lawyers want, and expect, to make money, and they accept the fee structure that will help them to realize their expectations. As a result, not only are members of the public limited to a relatively small and select group of lawyers as the source of legal service, but they are also offered generally expen-

* References have been deleted without indication.

[1] Geoffrey C. Hazard," The Lawyer's Pro Bono Obligation 2," discussion paper for the American Bar Association's Second National Conference on Legal Services and the Public, Dec. 7–8, 1979.

From Barlow F. Christensen, "The Lawyer's Pro Bono Publico Responsibility," *The American Bar Foundation Research Journal* (1981), 1–21. Reprinted by permission.

sive solutions to their problems. This is probably not the place to discuss the efficacy and cost of alternative problem-solving methods, but lawyers and law suits are a very costly—although perhaps often necessary—way of getting things done, and the lawyer's monopoly leaves the public with no other way of getting done those things labeled "legal," even though less costly ways might be possible. The end result is that many people are excluded from the justice system and precluded from obtaining help with legal matters at least partly because of the lawyers' monopoly.

Does competition within the bar cure the profession of its monopolistic character? Clearly not. Perhaps it would do so if competition for business resulted in the provision of no-fee and low-fee service to all who needed it or even to all who might otherwise have gotten it were the practice of law not reserved to an elite few. But that is not the result. Consequently, so long as people need service—and they do—and so long as they are precluded from getting it at least partly because only a chosen few may provide it—and they are—and so long as competition among lawyers does not compensate fully for this restraint—and it does not—then the practice of law should be regarded as a monopoly, and those who reap its benefits should be charged with a duty to eliminate the injury that the monopoly may cause to the public.

The real issue, then, is not the monopolistic character of law practice but the nature and extent of the obligation arising therefrom. And there is an obligation.

Rights and privileges, by definition, carry with them duties and responsibilities. So with the exclusive privilege of law practice. It carries with it the responsibilities of competence and honesty, for example. And, unlike the same responsibilities that arise out of the traditional professional ethic, those that stem from the lawyer's exclusive status are imperative duties. The duty of competence is enforced by academic qualifications for admission to law practice, by

bar examinations, and by civil liability for negligence. The duty of honesty is enforced by disciplinary action for malfeasance and in some instances by criminal sanctions.

I submit that the exclusive privilege of law practice also carries with it a similarly imperative duty to see to it that any injury to the public caused by the monopoly is eliminated. This duty does not depend upon the happenstance of people with needs coming to lawyers. Nor does it depend upon the vagaries of individual conscience. It has nothing to do with charity or largesse or benevolence. It is an imperative duty that flows from the exclusive privilege of law practice to every lawyer who claims the privilege. It comes with the territory. But the question remains. Just what is the obligation arising from the lawyer's monopoly?

One of the most telling arguments against mandatory pro bono is the contention that unmet legal needs are but a part of the larger social problem of poverty and that it is unfair to expect lawyers to shoulder a burden that properly belongs to the whole of society. On the surface, at least, this position might seem to have some merit. But does the fact that a problem attributable partly to the profession's privileged status is also part of a larger social problem relieve the profession of any responsibility at all? The so-called energy crisis is a problem of the entire society, but does that fact absolve automobile manufacturers of responsibility for the part of the problem that they helped to create and over which they have control—the designing and building of more fuel-efficient automobiles? Surely not.

I submit, then, that to the extent that monopolistic restraints upon the public's use of legal services add to the larger social problem, the legal profession does retain an obligation. Not the whole burden, perhaps, but responsibility for that part of it that exists because of the bar's privileged status. Obviously, to separate that part of unmet legal need attributable to the lawyer's monopoly from the larger social problem of poverty would be impossible. But some other measure of the obligation may be appropriate. Perhaps it could be started in terms of the bar's capacity. Inasmuch as the lawyer's exclusive privilege contributes to the problem of unmet legal need, the profession perhaps should be held to an obligation to take reasonable measures—those measures within its capacity—to alleviate it.

As thus defined, the profession's public service obligation does not necessarily require mandatory pro bono service. Indeed, the legal profession might have been able, at some time in the past, to discharge the obligation arising out of its monopoly without resort to mandatory pro bono service. Over the past three-quarters of a century, as the bar has expended effort and resources to enforce the monopoly, a corresponding opportunity has existed for the profession to develop remedial measures that would have made the monopoly tolerable. Had the profession seized on this opportunity and exercised its claimed "spirit of public service" to develop and implement effective methods of making legal services readily available to the public, the pro bono issue would probably never have arisen. . . .

Present efforts to encourage voluntary pro bono service and to improve and extend legal service programs are premised on the hope that even now an adequate response to the obligation arising from the lawyer's monopoly might be possible without resort to mandatory pro bono service. But the hope seems a forlorn one. Nothing in the profession's past history or in its apparent present mood gives any cause for optimism.

If the thesis offered above is correct, the obligation stemming from the lawyer's monopoly is an imperative duty of *all* lawyers who share in the privileges of the monopoly. The extent of the obligation is defined not in terms of the extent of public legal needs to be met but in terms of the bar's reasonable capacity. The essence of the concept of "reasonable capacity" must be the involvement of *all* lawyers—not just the public spirited and not just those impelled by economic considerations to provide no-fee and low-fee service—in whatever measures are developed to alleviate the injury to the public by reason of the lawyer's monopoly. Nothing that has thus far been done or proposed, short of mandatory pro bono service, offers even slight promise of involving all lawyers. It would appear that a large number of lawyers will not shoulder their part of the professional burden unless they are compelled to it.

So, we are led, reluctantly and sadly, to the conclusion that mandatory pro bono must be accepted. Even though one consequence may be the loss, by some lawyers, of professional self-image and professional satisfaction, only a mandatory system of public interest service offers any reasonable prospect of meeting adequately the professional obligation arising out of both the lawyer's monopoly and the legal profession's tradition of public service.

As a concluding thought, another perspective might be suggested by the question, Why has the lawyer's "magnificent obsession" with the "spirit of public service" been so persistent, while other professions—most notably the medical profession—have lost any comparable sense of public duty? A service-before-gain ethic that once motivated individual physicians to give substantial amounts of unpaid medical service has, over the past half-century or so, largely dissipated. Today, individual doctors do virtually no unpaid work—except, perhaps, for supposedly paying patients from whom they cannot collect their bills, even through the most rigorous commercial collection procedures, no different from the bad debts accounts of any business. Moreover, modern doctors appear to have no sense of obligation to do unpaid work in the public interest and thus no nagging consciences.

A number of explanations might be found for the change, but surely one major reason has been the development, over the same 50 years, of a fairly complete alternative system for providing medical service to those who need it but cannot pay for it. The development of free legal clinics, a welfare system that provides for medical care, medical insurance, and, more recently, federally funded medical care programs has generally relieved the individual medical practitioner of an apparent need to render unpaid service. Attention could then be devoted fully to paying patients and patients for whom one of the medical care systems would pay the bill, without any qualms of conscience about needy patients or about unmet medical need in the abstract. And so, the medical profession's service-before-gain ethic died.

The legal profession may now be going through much the same kind of transition, although it would appear to be 20 or 30 years behind the medical profession in the evolutionary process. As alternative methods of handling unmet legal needs develop—prepaid legal service systems, group legal services, public defender programs, the federal legal services program, and other governmentally funded legal service efforts—the individual lawyer, like the medical counterpart, may come to have ever decreasing concern for "the cause of the defenseless or oppressed," secure in the belief that those needs are being taken care of adequately. Indeed, the denial by many lawyers of the existence of any public service obligation, as well as the notion that the burden belongs to the whole of society rather than to lawyers, may be reflections of this transition. If so, then we might expect substantial erosion of the legal profession's "spirit of public service" in the years ahead and, ultimately, its total loss.

This suggests that the adoption of a mandatory pro bono program might operate as a truly conservative measure. By causing *all* lawyers to be involved, on an individual basis, in directly serving "the cause of the defenseless or oppressed," mandatory pro bono might help the individual lawyer, and thus the bar as a whole, to retain some sense of the traditional service-before-gain ethic. Could it be that mandatory pro bono is the legal profession's last chance to preserve its "spirit of public service"?

REVERSE DISCRIMINATION AS UNJUSTIFIED

Lisa H. Newton

Newton contends that reverse discrimination favoring blacks and women is unjust because it violates the basic equality of citizenship, understood as the rule of law applied equally to all and prohibiting unjustified and unnecessary inequalities. Further, such policies single out certain minorities when others are just as deserving and will not be temporary, as proponents may argue. Reverse-discrimination policies replace the quest for justice with power struggles.

I have heard it argued that "simple justice" requires that we favor women and blacks in employment and educational opportunities, since women and blacks were "unjustly" excluded from such opportunities for so many years in the not so distant past. It is a strange argument, an example of a possible implication of a true propo-

From Lisa H. Newton, "Reverse Discrimination as Unjustified," *Ethics* 83:4 (1973), 308–12. Reprinted by permission of the University of Chicago.

sition advanced to dispute the proposition itself, like an octopus absent-mindedly slicing off his head with a stray tentacle. A fatal confusion underlies this argument, a confusion fundamentally relevant to our understanding of the notion of the rule of law.

Two senses of justice and equality are involved in this confusion. The root notion of justice, progenitor of the other, is the one that Aristotle (*Nich. Ethics* 5.6; *Politics* 1.2; 3.1) assumes to be the foundation and proper virtue of the political association. It is the condition which free men establish among themselves when they "share a common life in order that their association bring them self-sufficiency"—the regulation of their relationship by law, and the establishment, by law, of equality before the law. Rule of law is the name and pattern of this justice; its equality stands against the inequalities—of wealth, talent, and so forth, otherwise obtaining among its participants, who by virtue of that equality are called "citizens." It is an achievement—complete, or, more frequently, partial—of certain people in certain concrete situations. It is fragile and easily disrupted by powerful individuals who discover that the blind equality of rule of law is inconvenient for their interests. Despite its obvious instability, Aristotle assumes that the establishment of justice in this sense, the creation of citizenship, was a permanent possibility for men and that the resultant association of citizens was the natural home of the species. At levels below the political association, this rule-governed equality is easily found; it is exemplified by any group of children agreeing together to play a game. At the level of the political association, the attainment of this justice is more difficult, simply because the stakes are so much higher for each participant. The equality of citizenship is not something that happens of its own accord, and without the expenditure of a fair amount of effort it will collapse into the rule of a powerful few over an apathetic many. But at least

it has been achieved, at some times in some places; it is always worth trying to achieve, and eminently worth trying to maintain, wherever and to whatever degree it has been brought into being.

Aristotle's parochialism is notorious; he really did not imagine that persons other than Greeks could associate freely in justice, and the only form of association he had in mind was the Greek *polis*. With the decline of the *polis* and the shift in the center of political thought, his notion of justice underwent a sea change. To be exact, it ceased to represent a political type and became a moral ideal: the ideal of equality as we know it. This ideal demands that all men be included in citizenship— that one Law govern all equally, that all men regard all other men as fellow citizens, with the same guarantees, rights, and protections. Briefly, it demands that the circle of citizenship achieved by any group be extended to include the entire human race. Properly understood, its effect on our associations can be excellent: It congratulates us on our achievements of the rule of law as a process of government but refuses to let us remain complacent until we have expanded the associations to include others within the ambit of the rules, as often and as far as possible. While one man is a slave, none of us may feel truly free. We are constantly prodded by this ideal to look for possible unjustifiable discrimination, for inequalities not absolutely required for the functioning of the society and advantageous to all. And after twenty centuries of pressure, not at all constant, from this ideal, it might be said that some progress has been made. To take the cases in point for this problem, we are now prepared to assert, as Aristotle would never have been, the equality of sexes and of persons of different colors. The ambit of American citizenship, once restricted to white males of property, has been extended to include all adult free men, then all adult males including ex-slaves, then all women. The process of acquisition of full citizenship was for these groups a sporadic trial of half-measures, even now not complete; the steps on the road to full equality are marked by legislation and judicial decisions which are only recently concluded and still often not enforced. But the fact that we can now discuss the possibility of favoring such groups in hiring shows that over the area that concerns us, at least, full equality is presupposed as a basis for discussion. To that extent, they are full citizens, fully protected by the law of the land.

It is important for my argument that the moral ideal of equality be recognized as logically distinct from that condition (or virtue) of justice in the political sense. Justice in this sense exists *among* a citizenry, irrespective of the number of the populace included in that citizenry. Further, the moral ideal is parasitic upon the political virtue, for "equality" is unspecified—it means nothing until we are told in what respect that equality is to be realized. In a political context, *equality* is specified as "equal rights"—equal access to the public realm, public goods and offices, equal treatment under the law—in brief, the equality of citizenship. If citizenship is not a possibility, political equality is unintelligible. The ideal emerges as a generalization of the real condition and refers back to that condition for its content.

Now, if justice (Aristotle's justice in the political sense) is equal treatment under law for all citizens, what is injustice? Clearly, injustice is the violation of that equality, discriminating for or against a group of citizens, favoring them with special immunities and privileges or depriving them of those guaranteed to the others. When the southern employer refuses to hire blacks in white-collar jobs, when Wall Street will hire women only as secretaries with new titles, when Mississippi high schools routinely flunk all black boys above ninth grade, we have examples of injustice, and we work to restore the equality of the public realm by ensuring that equal opportunity will be provided in such cases in the future. But of course, when the employers and the schools *favor* women and blacks, the same injustice is done. Just as the previous discrimination did, this reverse discrimination violates the public equality which defines citizenship and destroys the rule of law for the areas in which these favors are granted. To the extent that we adopt a program of discrimination, reverse or otherwise, justice in the political sense is destroyed, and none of us, specifically affected or not, is a citizen, a bearer of rights—we are all petitioners for favors. And to the same extent, the ideal of equality is undermined, for it has content only where justice obtains, and by destroying justice we render the ideal meaningless. It is, then, an ironic paradox, if not a contradiction in terms, to assert that the ideal of equality justifies the violation of justice; it is as if one should argue, with William Buckley, that an ideal of humanity can justify the destruction of the human race.

Logically, the conclusion is simple enough: All discrimination is wrong prima facie because it violates justice, and that goes for reverse discrimination too. No violation of justice among the citizens may be justified (may overcome the prima facie objection) by appeal to the ideal of equality, for that ideal is logically dependent upon the notion of justice. Reverse discrimination, then, which attempts no other justification than an appeal to equality, is wrong. But let us try to make the conclusion more plausible by suggesting some of the implications of the suggested practice of reverse discrimination in employment and education. My argument will be that the problems raised there are insoluble, not only in practice but in principle.

We may argue, if we like, about what "discrimination" consists of. Do I discriminate against blacks if I admit none to my school when none of the black applicants are qualified by the tests I always give? How far must I go to root our cultural bias from my application forms and tests before I can say that I have not discriminated against those of different cultures? Can I assume that women are not strong enough to be roughnecks on my oil rigs, or must I test them individually? But this controversy, the most popular and well-argued aspect of the issue, is not as fatal as two others which cannot be avoided: If we are regarding the blacks as a "minority" victimized by discrimination, what is a "minority"? And for any group—blacks, women, whatever—that has been discriminated against, what amount of reverse discrimination wipes out the initial discrimination? Let us grant as true that women and blacks were discriminated against, even where laws forbade such discrimination, and grant for the sake of argument that a history of discrimination must be wiped out by reverse discrimination. What follows?

First, are there other groups which have been discriminated against? For they should have the same right of restitution. What about American Indians, Chicanos, Appalachian whites, Puerto Ricans, Jews, Cajuns, and Orientals? And if these are to be included, the principle according to which we specify a "minority" is simply the criterion of "ethnic (sub) group," and we're stuck with every hyphenated American in the lower-middle class clamoring for special privileges for *his* group—and with equal justification. For be it noted, when we run down the Harvard roster, we find not only a scarcity of blacks (in comparison with the proportion in the population) but an even more striking scarcity of those second-, third-, and fourth-generation ethnics who make up the loudest voice of Middle America. Shouldn't they demand *their* share? And eventually, the WASPs will have to form their own lobby, for they too are a minority. The point is simply this: There is no "majority" in America who will not mind giving up just a bit of their rights to make room for a favored minority. There are only other minorities, each of which is discriminated against by the favoring. The initial injustice is then repeated dozens

of times, and if each minority is granted the same right of restitution as the others, an entire area of rule governance is dissolved into a pushing and shoving match between self-interested groups. Each works to catch the public eye and political popularity by whatever means of advertising and power politics lend themselves to the effort, to capitalize as much as possible on temporary popularity until the restless mob picks another group to feel sorry for. Hardly an edifying spectacle, and in the long run no one can benefit: The pie is no larger—it's just that instead of setting up and enforcing rules for getting a piece, we've turned the contest into a free-for-all, requiring much more effort for no larger a reward. It would be in the interests of all the participants to reestablish an objective rule to govern the process, carefully enforced and the same for all.

Second, supposing that we do manage to agree in general that women and blacks (and all the others) have some right of restitution, some right to a privileged place in the structure of opportunities for a while, how will we know when that while is up? How much privilege is enough? When will the guilt be gone, the price paid, the balance restored? What recompense is right for centuries of exclusion? What criterion tells us when we are done? Our experience with the civil-rights movement shows us that agreement on these terms cannot be presupposed: A process that appears to some to be going at a mad gallop into a black takeover appears to the rest of us to be at a standstill. Should a practice of reverse discrimination be adopted, we may safely predict that just as some of us begin to see "a satisfactory start toward righting the balance," others of us will see that we "have already gone too far in the other direction" and will suggest that the discrimination ought to be reversed again. And such disagreement is inevitable, for the point is that we could not *possibly* have any criteria for evaluating the kind of recompense we have in mind. The context presumed by any discussion of restitution is the context of rule of law. Law sets the rights of men and simultaneously sets the method for remedying the violation of those rights. You may exact suffering from others and/or damage payments for yourself if and only if the others have violated your rights; the suffering you have endured is not sufficient reason for them to suffer. And remedial rights exist only where there is law: Primary human rights are useful guides to legislation but cannot stand as reasons for awarding remedies for injuries sustained. But then, the context presupposed by a discussion of restitution is the context of preexistent full citizenship. No remedial rights could exist for the excluded; neither in law nor in logic does there exist a right to *sue* for a standing to sue.

From these two considerations, then, the difficulties with reverse discrimination became evident. Restitution for a disadvantaged group whose rights under the law have been violated is possible by legal means, but restitution for a disadvantaged group whose grievance is that there was no law to protect them simply is not. First, outside of the area of justice defined by the law, no sense can be made of "the group's rights," for no law recognizes that group or the individuals in it, qua members, as bearers of rights (hence *any* group can constitute itself as a disadvantaged minority in some sense and demand similar restitution). Second, outside of the area of protection of law, no sense can be made of the violation of rights (hence the amount of the recompense cannot be decided by any objective criterion). For both reasons, the practice of reverse discrimination undermines the foundation of the very ideal in whose name it is advocated; it destroys justice, law, equality, and citizenship itself, and replaces them with power struggles and popularity contests.

PREFERENTIAL TREATMENT*

Richard Wasserstrom

Wasserstrom argues in favor of programs of preferential treatment on the ground that they will alter the social reality in a way that makes our society more just. Critics say that such programs are unjust, even if they have positive consequences, because those who are most qualified deserve to receive the relevant positions. Wasserstrom, noting that our society is not in fact a meritocracy, is skeptical of standard tests of qualifications. Most important, the most qualified may not deserve high positions because their abilities are significantly caused by factors for which they are not responsible.

I

There are few issues of contemporary institutional morality which have engendered more controversy than that of whether programs variously called programs of "affirmative action," "preferential treatment" or "reverse discrimination"

* References have been deleted without indication.

From Richard Wasserstrom, "Preferential Treatment," *Philosophy and Social Issues* (Notre Dame: University of Notre Dame Press, 1980). Reprinted by permission.

are justifiable. Some are convinced that such programs in virtually all of their forms are indefensible—often on the ground that they are racist and sexist in the same way in which earlier, discriminatory practices were. The programs are causally explicable, perhaps, but morally reprehensible. Other persons—perhaps a majority—are sorely troubled by these programs. They are convinced that some features of some programs, e.g., quotas, are indefensible and wrong. Other features and programs are tolerated, but not with fervor or enthusiasm. They are seen as a kind of moral compromise, as, perhaps, a lesser evil among a set of unappealing options. They are perceived and reluctantly implemented as a covert, euphemistic way to do what would clearly be wrong—even racist or sexist— to do overtly and with candor. And still a third group has a very different view. They think these programs are important and justifiable. They do not see these programs, quotas included, as racist, sexist, or otherwise wrong; they see much about the dominant societal institutions that is objectionable, and they think the programs appropriate and important.

I agree with the persons in the last group, and in this essay I present a defense of such programs. More specifically, I articulate and defend a set of arguments for the view that it is both right and good to have programs that take a particular characteristic of individuals—their race or sex— into account in order to increase the number of nonwhites or females in institutions such as the university, the legal system, various occupations and corporate structures. I argue for the appropriateness even of quotas of the sort that were involved in the *Bakke* case[1] and declared by the majority opinion in that case to be unconstitutional. . . .

As is the case in respect to the justifiability of many social policies and programs, the relevant considerations and arguments can to some degree be divided into two major groups. There are, first, those that are more or less consequentialist in nature. These look primarily to the effects of these programs in terms of the goal or ideal that is sought to be attained. And there are, in addition, those that are essentially nonconsequentialist in nature and which focus largely upon what can be called considerations and arguments of justice. The latter concern such things as the rights of individuals, the fairness of institutional arrangements, distributions in accordance with what individuals deserve, and the consistent application of relevant general principles. It is a complicated, complex, and disputed issue within philosophy to what degree considerations of justice (in this general sense) properly function as a constraint upon consequentialist justifications (in this general sense), i.e., to what degree and under what conditions the fact that a given procedure, practice, or program treats persons unjustly requires the conclusion that the procedure, practice or program is unjustifiable—no matter how good or beneficial in other respects the consequences of such procedures, practices, or programs may be for others affected by them. This issue does not, however, have to be confronted directly in thinking about preferential treatment programs. For, despite what many persons believe, the arguments that programs of preferential treatment are unjust to white males are much weaker, and hence less decisive, than is commonly thought to be the case. Much of the burden of my analysis is, in fact, devoted to trying to make explicit the confusions which lead persons erroneously to conclude that these programs are ultimately unjustifiable because they are in some important sense unjust in any of the relevant respects. . . .

[1] Regents of the University of California v. Bakke, 98 S. Ct. 2733 (1978).

One primary argument for preferential treatment programs is that these programs can and do function so as directly to alter the social realities in ways that are both important and desirable. There is, at present, a maldistribution of power and authority along racial and sexual lines that is a part of the social structure. Within the major political and social institutions, such as the university, the bench and the bar, the state and federal executive and legislative branches, and the corporate world, the great majority of positions are held by those who are white and male. One thing to be said for programs of preferential treatment is that by their operation they directly alter the composition of these institutions by increasing the number of nonwhites and women who in fact fill these positions of power and authority. This is desirable in itself because it is a redistribution of positions in a way that creates a new social reality—one which more nearly resembles the one captured by the conception of the good society. For, if what is sought is a society in which the places of significance will be held to a substantially greater degree than they are at present by persons who are nonwhite and female, then these programs quite directly and necessarily make alterations in this direction. They produce a social reality in which these individuals are present in a way in which they previously were not. To be sure, the ideal invoked contains within it the expectation that these positions will eventually be distributed without regard to either race or sex as relevant characteristics. But the argument is not inconsistent with that expectation; its claim is that such an ideal can be plausibly brought more fully into being only if there is first a redistribution of the place holders within the existing institutional arrangements.

Although the argument has the air of paradox to it, it is rather plausible. For

one thing, such a reallocation of status puts members of these groups into positions where they can provide services which directly enrich and benefit the lives of other members of these groups in a way which is not done by the institutions as presently constituted. To the degree to which the present distribution of services and goods is unfair to members of these groups, the distributional change is justifiable simply because it is now a more just distribution. Furthermore, to the degree to which this occurs the social reality is altered so as to make it more likely that all members of these groups will be in a position to participate more fully in the important social institutions. This is something that the existing social reality now makes difficult; the programs help to break the systemic, exclusionary character of the present arrangement and in this way make additional, desirable change easier and more probable.

Concomitantly, the ideological component of the social reality is altered. The presence of nonwhites and women in positions from which they have historically been excluded or in which they have been vastly underrepresented aids in altering the conception of the kinds of individuals who are seen as appropriately the holders of such positions of prestige and influence. Members of the excluded or underrepresented groups are more inclined to see themselves as potential holders of such positions. They are, by the operation of these programs, provided with role models which make becoming a lawyer, doctor, corporate executive, university professor, and the like, now a more plausible aspiration. And the prevailing conception, held implicitly to some degree or other by most members of the society, that these positions are appropriately held in large numbers by white males is also to some degree transformed. Once again, the claim is that in these ways the programs serve as a mechanism which by its presence alters the self-perpetuating character of the existing social reality. . . .

Sometimes opponents of programs of preferential treatment do oppose them on the ground that they will have bad consequences and that they do not or will not work very efficiently or well, although, as will be seen, that is seldom the core of their objection. For example, near the conclusion of his opinion for the majority of the California Supreme Court in the *Bakke* case, Justice Mosk asserted that there were forceful policy reasons against preferential treatment programs based on race. "The divisive effect of such preferences," he said, "needs no explication and raises serious doubts whether the advantages obtained by the few preferred are worth the inevitable cost to social harmony. The overemphasis upon race as a criterion will undoubtedly be counterproductive. . . . Pragmatic problems are certain to arise in identifying groups which should be preferred or in specifying their numbers, and preferences once established will be difficult to alter or abolish. . . ."[2] And Mr. Justice Powell in his opinion in the *Bakke* case pointed to similar matters when he observed both that ". . . preferential programs may only reinforce common stereotypes holding that certain groups are unable to achieve success without special protection based on a factor having no relationship to individual worth," and that "[d]isparate constitutional tolerance of such classifications well may seem to exacerbate racial and ethnic antagonisms rather than alleviate them."[3]

While I do not believe that most opponents of these programs base their opposition primarily on the ground that such programs cannot or will not bring about or create the kinds of desirable changes described above, it must, however, certainly be conceded, that if it were to turn

out, as the Justices and others have predicted, that programs of this sort will in fact exacerbate prejudice and hostility, thereby making it harder rather than easier to alter the social reality so as to achieve something like an assimilationist society, that would be a reason which would count quite directly against the instrumental desirability of these programs. This would still not settle the matter, of course, for these undesirable features would still have to be balanced against all of the respects in which preferential treatment programs would advance the occurrence of the assimilationist society. They are relevant aspects of what is a complicated empirical inquiry of sorts.

But there is reason to think that at least most critics of these programs do not believe these programs to be ineffective in the ways in which I have suggested they might be effective. The reason is simply that most of their arguments are concerned to make one of two rather different points. Sometimes, what looks to be an argument of this sort is in reality an argument about the undesirability of such programs within the good society. Such an objection misses the mark. For as I have indicated, the programs are not offered as constituents of the good society. Indeed, they would make no sense whatsoever within a good society of the assimilationist sort. The objection is miscast and the appropriate question is whether, viewed in the ways I have suggested, such programs could be plausibly regarded as on balance effective in helping to create or bring that society about. Judgment on this matter must, therefore, be restricted to the good and bad changes included within the scope of that question.

Far more often, the core of the objection to programs of preferential treatment is that a consideration of issues of this type is not enough. The essence of the argument in opposition is instead something like this: What these programs are trying to do makes sense; it would be good if we

---

[2] Bakke v. Regents of the University of California, 18 Cal. 3d 34, 61–62 (1976).

[3] Regents of the University of California v. Bakke, 98 S. Ct. 2733, 2753 (1978).

could have the kinds of results, the kinds of alterations in the social reality, these programs do help to bring into being. It would, for example, be a good thing if somehow blacks and women were more substantially present throughout the dominant institutions; it is even a good thing that they are more present today than they have been in the past. In this sense, the changes that have occurred and that are occurring in the social reality are also a good thing. The problem, though, is that such programs go about doing so in an impermissible way. It is not that these programs are not in this sense effective or their results desirable; rather it is that efficacy or effectiveness is just not all there is to it. And when we look to these other considerations—considerations of justice—we see what is fundamentally wrong with programs of preferential treatment. They are unjust; they violate person's rights.

It is these arguments against programs of preferential treatment which must be examined in some detail.

III

One very common criticism of preferential treatment programs goes something like this: There are more questions to be asked about these programs than whether they will work reasonably well to bring about a certain result. There is also the question of the way they will work to bring about that end. And once one sees this then one also has to face the fact that it is simply wrong in principle ever to take a person's race into account. Or, to put what may be the same point differently, persons have a right never to have race taken into account. These programs, by definition, do just that, and that is what makes them impermissible.

A version of this position was taken by Justice Mosk in the *Bakke* case. What is impermissible, said Justice Mosk, is taking race into account where that has the effect of depriving nonminority group members

of benefits they would otherwise have enjoyed.

"We cannot agree with the proposition that deprivation *based* upon race is subject to a less demanding standard of review under the 14th Amendment if the race discriminated against is the majority rather than the minority. We have found no case so holding, and we do not hesitate to reject the notion that racial discrimination may be more easily justified against one race than another. . . ."[4]

One difficulty with statements such as these, whether they occur in a moral or a legal context, is that without more they are incomplete as arguments. What are missing are the reasons for regarding the claim as a sound one. If persons have a right, for example, never to have race taken into account, it is important to be presented with an argument for why they ought to be viewed as having such a right. What is to be said in support of thinking about them and acting toward them in that way? If no reasons are given, it is extremely difficult to decide whether the claim that they have that right is correct. It is certainly not obvious that one just knows that persons have this particular right. When trying to think about the issue of preferential treatment it is difficult simply to "see" or to intuit the existence of this right. Claims about rights in unproblematic contexts are sometimes like descriptions of the world based upon what we directly perceive to be true; in less clear cases, however, they are more properly the conclusions of arguments. Intuitions about rights may be useful points from which to begin or even to test moral arguments, but unsupported by reasoning and analysis they run the great risk of being both ad hoc and inconclusive. In the case of preferential treatment I find it difficult to understand how an unsupported appeal to the right in

---

[4] Bakke v. Regents of the University of California, 18 Cal. 3d 34, 50 (1976).

question can be an intellectually satisfying determination of the issue.

There are, however, reasons and arguments that can be offered in support of this claim about this right. An opponent of programs of preferential treatment might argue that any proponent of these programs is guilty of intellectual inconsistency, if not racism or sexism itself. For, at times past, it might be pointed out, employers, universities, and many other social institutions did have racial and sexual quotas (when they did not practice overt racial or sexual exclusion), and it was clear that these quotas were pernicious. What is more, the argument might continue, many of those who were concerned to bring about the eradication of those racial quotas now seem untroubled by the new programs which reinstitute them. And this is just a terrible sort of intellectual inconsistency which at worst panders to the fashion of the present moment and at best replaces intellectual honesty and integrity with understandable but misguided sympathy. More to the point, even, if it was wrong to take race into account when blacks were the objects of racial policies and practices of exclusion, then it is wrong to take race into account when the objects of the policies have their race reversed. Simple considerations of intellectual consistency—of what it means to have had a good reason for condemning these social policies and practices—require that what was a good reason then is still a good reason now.

An argument such as this one is, I think, both common and closer to the core of the cluster of objections that many persons have to programs of preferential treatment. I think that it is a mistaken one and that recourse to the general mode of analysis I have proposed can show how it is mistaken.

It is certainly correct that the racial quotas and the practices of racial exclusion that were an integral part of the fabric of a culture, and which are still to some degree part of it, were pernicious. They were

and are a grievous wrong and it was and is important that all individuals concerned to be moral work for their eradication from our social universe. Yet, one can grant all of this and still believe that the kinds of racial and sexual quotas that are a part of contemporary preferential treatment programs are commendable and right. There is no inconsistency involved in holding both views. For even if contemporary schemes that take race and sex into account are wrong, they must, I believe, be wrong for reasons different in kind from those that made quotas and the like against blacks and women wrong. The reason why depends, once again, upon an analysis of the social realities.

A fundamental feature of programs that discriminated against blacks and women was that these programs were a part of a larger social universe which systematically maintained a network of institutions which concentrated power, authority, and goods in the hands of white male individuals. This same social universe contained a complex ideology which buttressed this network of institutions and at the same time received support from it. Practices which excluded or limited the access of blacks or women into the desirable institutions were, therefore, wrong both because of the direct consequences of these practices on the individuals most affected by them and because the system of racial and sexual superiority of which they were constituents was an immoral one in that it severely and without any adequate justification restricted the capacities, autonomy, and happiness of those who were members of the less favored categories.

Whatever may be wrong with today's program of preferential treatment, even those with quotas, it should be clear that the evil, if any, is simply not the same. Neither women nor blacks constitute the dominant social group. Nor is the conception of who is a fully developed member of the moral and social community one of an individual who is either black or female.

Quotas which prefer blacks or women do not add to an already overabundant supply of resources and opportunities at the disposal of members of these groups in the way in which exclusionary practices of the past added to an already overabundant supply of resources and opportunities at the disposal of white males. If preferential treatment programs are to be condemned or abandoned, it cannot, therefore, be because they seek either to perpetuate an unjust society in which all the desirable options for living are husbanded by and for those who already have the most, or to realize a corrupt ideal of distinct classes and grades of political, social, and moral superiority and inferiority. When viewed and offered as instrumentalities for social change they do neither.

The same point can be made in a somewhat different way. Sometimes people say that what was wrong with the system of racial discrimination in the South was that it took an irrelevant characteristic, namely race, and used it systematically to allocate social benefits and burdens of various sorts. The defect was the irrelevance of the characteristic used, i.e., race, for that meant that individuals ended up being treated in a manner that was arbitrary. On this view, the chief defect of the system of racial segregation was its systemic capriciousness.

That does not seem to me to have been the central flaw at all. Consider, for instance, the most hideous of the practices, human slavery. The primary thing that was wrong with that institution was not that the particular individuals who were assigned the place of slaves were assigned that place arbitrarily because the assignment was made in virtue of an irrelevant characteristic, i.e., their race. Rather, the fundamental thing that was and is wrong with slavery is the practice itself—the fact that some human beings were able to own other human beings and all that goes with that practice and that conception of permissible interpersonal relationships. If one wants a clear case of the violation of the

Kantian Categorical Imperative, if one wants a clear case of what it is to treat a person wholly as a means rather than an end in itself, human slavery is the historically real paradigm. It would not matter by what criterion persons were assigned within that institution, human slavery would still be wrong. And a comparable criticism can be made of most if not all of the other discrete practices and institutions which comprised the system of racial discrimination even after human slavery was abolished. The practices were unjustifiable— they were oppressive—and they would have been so no matter how the assignment of the victims had been made. In particular, very few of the institutions were involved in allocating either social positions or other resources in a way such that a concern for the arbitrariness of the method of selection was even an issue. As I have tried to indicate, what made it worse, still, was that the institutions and ideology were a part of a comprehensive system. The parts interlocked and that is what made it a *system* of human oppression whose effects on those living under it were as devastating as they were unjustifiable. For women and for blacks the system is less firm than at times past, but it still exists and its presence is still a central reality. . . .

The discussion so far may appear to have avoided what is to many a central defect of all preferential treatment programs: that these programs are wrong because they take race or sex into account rather than the only thing that does matter, namely, an individual's qualifications. What all such programs have in common and what makes them all objectionable, so the argument goes, is that they necessarily do give a preference to those who are less qualified in virtue of their being black or female over those who are more qualified.

There are, I think, a number of features of this objection based on qualifications that require careful examination, and the first thing that merits notice is the implicit background assumption that our society is one in which persons occupy positions of substantial power and authority in virtue of their being the most qualified for the positions. They do not. Nor, more significantly is it even a part of the social ideology that in many cases they should be the most qualified. For example, there is no general expectation that the persons who comprise the judiciary are either the most qualified lawyers or the most qualified persons to be judges. The expectation here, typically, is only that they be qualified. Similarly, it would be difficult for anyone to claim that a person such as Henry Ford II is the head of the Ford Motor Company because among all the persons interested in the job he is the most qualified for the job. Or that the 100 persons who are Senators of the United States are the most qualified persons to be Senators. Part of what is wrong with the context in which discussion about qualifications and merit usually occurs is that the argument against programs of preferential treatment derives some of its force from the erroneous notion that we would have a meritocracy were it only not for programs such as these. In reality, the higher the position in terms of prestige, power, and the like, the less being the most qualified seems ever to be a central concern. Rather, it is only for certain classes of jobs and places that qualifications are used to do more than establish the possession of certain minimum competencies. And, of course, all of the preferential treatment programs which have been proposed or implemented also contain minimum competency requirements that must be satisfied by all.

But this contextual difficulty to one side, there are also theoretical difficulties which cut much more deeply than is often recognized into the argument about qualifications. To begin with, it is important to establish what the ground of the argument is for making selections based solely upon who is the most qualified. One such argument for the exclusive relevance of qualifications—although it is seldom stated ex-

plicitly—is that the most qualified persons should be selected to perform the relevant social tasks because those tasks will then be done in the most economical and efficient manner. Now, there is nothing wrong in principle with an argument based upon the good results that will be produced by maintaining a social practice of selection based solely upon qualifications. Certainly such an argument cannot be ruled out *a priori* on the ground that it is an argument about the consequences or results. But there is a serious problem that many opponents of preferential treatment programs must confront. It may be impermissible for them to attach too much weight to an exclusive preoccupation with qualifications *on this ground,* if it was an analogous appeal to the good consequences of programs of preferential treatment that the opponent of preferential treatment thought was wrong in the first place with viewing these programs in instrumentalist terms. That is to say, as was indicated, one plausible argument offered for these programs was that they would have desirable consequences. They were in this sense potentially effective means by which to bring about a society more consonant with the appropriate conception of the good society. A central objection to that way of thinking about things was that it was concerned with consequences or effects rather than with other things that really mattered, such as considerations of justice. If, therefore, the chief thing to be said in favor of always preferring the most qualified is that this is the most efficient way of getting things done, then the inquiry has returned to an instrumental assessment of the different consequences that will flow from different programs. . . .

Nor is that all there is to be said about the argument for selection based only upon qualifications. It is important to note that qualifications, at least in the educational context, are often not even connected very closely with any plausible conception of social effectiveness. To admit the most qualified students to law school, for instance—given the way qualifications are now determined—is primarily to admit those who have the greatest chance of achieving the highest grades in law school. This says nothing directly about efficiency except perhaps that these students are the easiest for the faculty to teach. Since so little is known about what constitutes being a good, or even a successful, lawyer, and since even less is known about the correlation between being a good law student and being a good lawyer, it can hardly be claimed with the degree of confidence often exhibited by opponents of preferential treatment that the legal system will operate most effectively if those deemed the most qualified, in virtue of their test scores and the like, are alone admitted to law school.

What is more, the university situation is not even representative in its use of what might be termed "objective qualifications," such as test scores or grade point averages. When it comes to the alleged qualifications for many desirable social positions—in particular, jobs—the qualifications claimed to be required are not capable of anything resembling systematic or statistical measurement or assessment. Yet, a number of programs of preferential treatment are directed at increasing directly the number of minorities in careers such as the police force, the building trades, and the corporate structures. Traditionally, they were excluded from these desirable vocations by exclusionary policies. Today, many minority applicants are as qualified for the positions as the whites who obtained them in the past and obtain them still. The difficulty is that there are often no agreed upon, or objectively defensible, measures of relative qualification for these positions. The accepted and prevailing method of entry into these vocations can and does depend instead to some degree upon such factors as whom one knows, how one presents oneself, and the subjective, ill-defined evaluations of qualification made by those already engaged in the management and

control of the activity. When conditions such as these obtain, programs of preferential treatment can be defended both because they break the chain of interlocking factors which trade upon the favored place of white males in the society and because the white males who make the subjective evaluations concerning whom to hire are not likely to do so in a wholly fair and impartial manner. Once again, this may not be because these individuals are in any deliberate or intentional fashion seeking to implement exclusionary policies, but because in a variety of subtle and unsuspected ways the lives they have lived and the ways they have been socialized will lead them to view as more qualified those who are and who act most like themselves. Both objective and subjective determinations of who is the most qualified are, therefore, often properly subject to the charge that what will count as evidence of superior qualification will have embedded within it an appreciable degree of preference for the perpetuation within institutions of those persons whose attitudes, attributes, and ways of behaving are most like those of the persons doing the selection and which have nothing much at all to do with any set of genuinely definable qualifications for the job. When this phenomenon occurs, programs of preferential treatment can be defended on the quite conventional grounds that they make it more likely than would otherwise have been the case that positions will be filled with equally or more qualified persons than would have been so in their absence. When this state of affairs exists, programs of preferential treatment are not even subject to the charge that they necessarily impair rather than promote efficiency.

The analysis cannot, however, rest upon considerations such as these. For it may surely be the case that for some social places and in some important respects there are neutral, objective, and defensible notions of qualification and of being the most qualified that are connected to the role, job, or place in question. Where such is the case, the considerations just discussed do not apply. What still remains unspecified, however, is the reason why, apart from matters of overall efficiency, selection in terms of the most qualified should be thought the fundamental, if not decisive, issue.

The argument, perhaps, is this: Selection should be made in terms of who is the most qualified because those who are the most qualified *deserve* to receive the benefits (the job, the place in law school, etc.) because they are the most qualified. The introduction of the concept of desert does make the argument a thoroughly nonconsequentialist one of the sort promised by the original objection to the programs. But now the question is whether there are grounds for thinking that the most qualified deserve anything in virtue of their being the most qualified. The grounds are more elusive than may be thought.

Consider, for example, the case of preferential treatment in respect to admission to college or graduate school. There is a gap in the inference from the claim that a person is most qualified to perform a task, e.g., be a good student, to the conclusion that he or she deserves to be admitted as a student. Even if it be conceded that those who deserve to be admitted should be admitted, it is far from clear why the most qualified students thereby deserve to be admitted.

They might deserve it if there were a discoverable general and necessary connection between the idea of being the most qualified and the idea of deserving something. But such a connection is neither as general nor as obvious as might be thought.

Suppose, for instance, that there is only one resource of a certain sort in a community and that some people are more qualified to use it than are others. That means, it seems, that they are better at using it than are others, or that they will use it better than will others. Suppose it is a tennis court. Is it clear that the two

best tennis players ought to be the ones permitted to use it? Why not those who were there first? Or those who will enjoy playing the most? Or those who are the worst and therefore need the greatest opportunity to practice? Or those who have the chance to play least frequently? Each of these criteria appears to be as plausible a candidate for allocation as this idea of being the most qualified.

There might, of course, be a rule that provides that the best tennis players get to use the court before the others. If there were, it could then be said that under such a rule the best players deserve the court rather than the poorer ones. But that is primarily just to push the inquiry back one stage. There should then be a reason to think that there ought to be a rule giving good tennis players such a preference. The arguments that might be advanced for or against such a rule are many and varied, and surprisingly few of the arguments that might be offered as a justification for this rule would depend upon a connection between competence as a tennis player and deserving to use the court.

Perhaps, however, the claim is that at least in many of the relevant contexts the most able do deserve the benefits and opportunities because they are the most qualified. Apart from matters of efficiency, so the argument might go, a system based upon merit is clearly desirable. And for substantial segments of the social system the merit to be rewarded is that which manifests itself in superior ability. That, it might be concluded, is certainly the way the university is—or would be—operating were it not for these programs.

The difficulty with this argument is that it is in part tautological and in part incomplete. The tautology occurs because of the meaning of "merit." The concept of merit almost surely implies the idea of what is deserved. It is, therefore, analytic that merit is at least an appropriate condition (and perhaps the sole appropriate condition) for deserving something positive or good. If so, then it is also analytic that a system based upon merit is desirable.

This, though, says nothing so far about the connection between merit and the idea of being the most qualified in terms of ability. What is there about ability that permits an identification with the idea of merit? There is a sense in which there is tension rather than compatibility between the two concepts. For part of the idea of merit (or, to put it somewhat differently, one idea of merit) is the idea that the only kinds of things which can lead appropriately to persons meriting goods, or to the idea of personal merit, are those things which persons can claim responsibility for having brought into being, created, developed, brought to fruition, and the like. This may not be all there is to the idea of merit but it is a familiar and substantial, if not essential, component.

If this feature is given prominence, then the argument has doubtful applicability to the university and to many other institutions. Many of what are regarded as the most important characteristics for higher education have a great deal to do with things over which the individual has neither control nor responsibility: natural talent, home environment, socioeconomic class of parents, race, and the quality of the primary and secondary schools attended. Since individuals do not, therefore, merit having had any of these things vis-à-vis other individuals, they do not, for the most part, merit their qualifications. And since they do not merit their qualifications they do not in either a strong or direct sense deserve to be admitted because of their qualifications. . . .

It is possible, to be sure, that some of the most qualified students can claim that they do deserve to be admitted to school because their qualifications are merited in virtue of the extra effort they expended in comparison with the others who also seek admission. Effort is clearly a more plausible condition for merit within this view than is, say, I.Q. or race, although

there are problems with the idea of effort, too. But even if effort is appropriately linked with merit and, hence, with desert, there is no general congruence between, for instance, being the most qualified applicant to the university and having been the applicant who expended the greatest amount of effort. In our society, surely, it is seldom thought relevant, and almost never decisive, to the determination of who are the most qualified that the effort expended by the applicants be first ascertained.

Effort might, however, be thought indirectly to be present and taken into account in the following way. If persons have developed reasonable expectations concerning the connection between their qualifications and their selection by an institution, and if they have relied upon these expectations, they have an additional claim of desert, deriving from the effort manifested in their reliance, to be selected on this ground as well. This claim can, however, only be made by those who reasonably developed these expectations and relied upon them. In the case of higher education, it is rather unconvincing for many applicants to maintain that the grades, test scores, and the like that they present as the qualifications in virtue of which they deserve admission over others are causally connected with their earlier reliance upon the announced criteria for admission. This is so because in the past colleges and universities almost always had announced criteria which disclosed that things other than qualifications (in this sense) would be taken into account, e.g., athletic ability, relationships with alumni, even geographical location of the applicant. As a result, it could not have been reasonable in respect to most colleges and universities for persons to have expected selection to have been made *solely* on the basis of qualifications. In addition, the appearance of preferential treatment programs itself makes a difference. After these programs have a public existence there must come a time at which continued reliance on the existence of some other selection process is no longer reasonable. The claim of mere *de facto* reliance, and of the additional effort thereby engendered, is both implausibly derived from the educational system of the past and wholly unavailable to those whose expectations were formed after the announced implementation of preferential treatment programs of admission.

The general point is that if the only thing that is known of an individual is that he or she is the most qualified in the sense of the most able, nothing necessarily follows about what that individual deserves except, perhaps, the description of being the most qualified or the most able. More must be known about the context or the situation before determinations of desert can appropriately be made. . . . In some . . . cases it will surely be very important that great weight be attached to the determination of who in fact is the most qualified, and it will be both reasonable and important to allocate the places within these activities very largely, if not exclusively, on the basis of the qualifications of the individuals seeking the positions. As among the applicants who desire to be neurosurgeons or commercial airline pilots, it seems defensible to make the process of selection depend heavily, if not solely, on their respective abilities. But the argument for doing so is not that they *deserve* to be selected because they are the most qualified. Instead, the argument for doing so is that, all things considered, it is good to make the selection on that basis. The severity of the risks to others, as well as considerations of efficiency, are what justify attaching so much importance to the selection of those who are the most qualified in terms of ability or competence.

Yet, even in cases such as these, it is in principle still an open and contingent question whether qualifications determined solely by ability ought to be the only relevant criteria. Where the differences in ability are very slight so that, for instance,

the differences in levels of performance are correspondingly small, there is no reason in principle why other criteria, such as the race or sex of the individuals could not justifiably be taken into account in order to achieve a better result overall.

What is significant for any well-founded appraisal of programs of preferential treatment is how dissimilar are most of the social activities with which those programs are typically concerned from the sorts of cases just described. To be a member of a student body, even to be a member of a faculty, to say nothing of being a banker, lawyer, policeman, or corporate executive, is not in the usual case very much like being a violinist in the Philadelphia Orchestra, a neurosurgeon, or the pilot of a commercial 747. What the former do have in common is the need for certain, identifiable competencies. What differentiates them from the latter cases is that many persons may be fully competent to perform the task or assume the role and not be the most able of applicants.

Preferential treatment programs typically, if not invariably, do regard qualifications, specified in terms of competency or ability, as decidedly relevant, and it is inaccurate to suppose that they do not. They do so for several reasons. In the first place, given the existing structure of any institution, there is almost always some minimal set of qualifications without which one cannot participate meaningfully within the institution. In addition, there is no question but that the degree of competence of those involved in the enterprise or institution will affect the way the institution works and the way it affects others in the society. The consequences will vary depending upon the particular institution. Considerations such as these are always, therefore, an appropriate part of the calculus. But all of this only establishes that qualifications are relevant, not that they are decisive. Thus, this concern for qualifications is wholly consistent with the claim that race or sex is today also properly relevant when it comes to matters such as admission to college or law school, or entry into the more favored segments of the job market. And that is all that any preferential treatment program—even one with the kind of quota involved in the *Bakke* case— has ever sought to establish. The general case against such programs has, in short, yet to be made, while the case for them remains persuasive.

CASE 4.1   MEDICAL PRIORITIES WITHIN A CLOSED SYSTEM

The Veterans Administration (VA) Medical Center at which you are medical director is allocated a fixed amount of money every year to be spent on patient care, and you and your staff must determine how these funds are to be apportioned to what sorts of care. As you recognize, the VA system is a "closed" one—that is, it has a fixed pool of resources which will neither grow nor shrink. Thus, money that you spend on one sort of patient care cannot be spent on another, and savings made in one area can be used in a different one.

In this budget year, there is not enough money to go around, and there is no hope of getting the overall allocation to your medical center increased. Consequently, you must decide which kinds of patient care are to be funded, and which not. At the moment, you are considering three kinds of care—heart transplants, alcohol detoxification, and primary care in rural areas—which, given the frequency of their usage, involve approximately equal costs. You could fund two of the three in full, but not all three; or you could fund each partially but have to exclude some patients in each category.

The heart transplant program is a high-profile program for your medical center; it has a superior survival rate and is sufficiently respected to attract able surgeons to the program. Each transplant case costs about $75,000 for the testing, surgery, and hospitalization; costs for immunosuppressive therapy are about $20,000 per patient for the first posttransplant year, and about $10,000 per patient for each year after that. Immunosuppressive therapy must be continued for the remainder of the patient's life. Approximately 10 cases can be done each year within the $1 million available, though supplying continuing immunosuppressive therapy to previous patients brings the figure to over $1 million. Two-year survival is 90%; this means that after 2 years after their transplants, 9 of the 10 patients will still be alive, when without a transplant they would have died within a few months.

The acute alcohol detoxification program, on the other hand, makes no headlines, although it prevents a major cause of suffering when it is successful. The usual course of therapy involves 2 weeks in the hospital at a cost to you of about $150 a day; together with ancillary costs, this amounts to about $3,000 per episode. You have a 13-bed detoxification ward which, if adequately funded, would be filled year-round. This adds up to just a little over $1 million a year. Detoxification therapy has about a 20% long-term success rate, which means that of the 338 alcoholics you could treat every year, 68 would be cured.

The third of the programs that you are considering eliminating involves a series of primary-care clinics in rural areas of your state. Some 80% of the patients who use such clinics have chronic disease such as diabetes, hypertension, or chronic bronchitis. If care were not available in the rural clinics, the 20% with more severe disease would require more frequent hospitalization, and the 80% whose disease is less severe would go without treatment until their condition progresses to severe disease and hospitalization is also required. Each clinic serves about 600 patients a year, averaging 5 visits each, and there are enough clinics so that the total just happens to approximately equal the costs of either your heart transplant or detoxification programs. It is the cost of the *clinics* that happens to equal the costs of your other programs, but of course the cost of eventual hospitalization of patients who are not treated would be much, much higher.

You can fund two of the three—heart transplant, alcohol detoxification, or primary care clinics—but not all three, or you can fund some portion of each one. What is the best thing to do, and on what basis should you decide?

CASE 4.2   FUNDING JOYCE'S FERTILITY

As you sort through the piles of correspondence on your desk at the fertility clinic of a major medical center one afternoon, you come upon a note from someone named Joyce C. The note is handwritten, in awkward, poorly spelled script; it is obviously the work of someone without much education. It reads:

> Dear Mr. Director:
>
> Please help me. I been to the clinic a couple of times, and they tol me to go away, they couldn't do nuthin for me. I cant have a baby, my tubes is stuck or sumthin. They said they could try to unstick them if I had the money, but I dont, I dont even have a job or a husband or anything. But I want a baby, real bad. Please help me.
>
> Joyce C.

You ask for Joyce's file, and discover that the facts are pretty much as she's claimed—at least as far as they go. She has made use of the free clinic at your hospital on three occasions, each about a year apart, to discover why she has not become pregnant, for although she is not married, she is sexually active and uses no contraceptive measures. Notes in the record indicate that she is suspected of having tubal occlusions, though she has not been given—nor offered—the salpingogram that would establish such a diagnosis.

Joyce is now 28 years old. She is unemployed and without education or training; she survives on welfare and on various odd jobs, and lives in what you know to be abominable city housing. You wonder why on earth she would want a child, given the troubles she already has.

You turn the note over in your hands a few times, reflecting on the differences between Joyce and the patients you usually see in your fertility practice. Although most of them are Joyce's age—late 20s, early 30s—and have the same complaints and the same anxieties, your patients are largely white, middle- and upper-class, educated women, married to husbands in reasonably prominent positions. They've all already had extensive infertility workups before being referred to your clinic, and they all seem to know, even before you confirm the diagnosis and tell them that salpingoplasty or in vitro fertilization is the only possible way in which they will be able to have a child, that few medical insurance policies will cover the surgery, and that since your in vitro program is still experimental in several aspects, none will cover the entire cost. The costs for salpingoplasty, without complications, run about $7,500, including hospitalization. For the in vitro program, you require an advance payment of $5,000, which is nonrefundable. This payment includes testing and the first attempt at in vitro fertilization and implantation; however, the first attempt is not likely to be successful, and each additional attempt involves a further $3,000 fee. This too is nonrefundable, even if no pregnancy or full-term neonate results.

You turn the note over again in your hands and think about Joyce, whom you have never even seen. You imagine how a conversation with her might go:

DIRECTOR: But Joyce, you're not married, you have no job, you've got nothing. How could you possibly manage a child?

JOYCE: Lots of women have babies out of wedlock. I'll still love the baby, and it'll still love me. I've always gotten along; I'll still be able to do so.

DIRECTOR: But is there any reason that we should make it possible for you to have a child? Aren't you on welfare? Wouldn't the child be on welfare too?

JOYCE: Probably so. But it's not my fault if I'm on welfare, and it wouldn't be right to say that the child shouldn't be born just because it would be on welfare too. Whether I'm on welfare shouldn't have anything to do with whether I can have a baby or not.

DIRECTOR: But you just don't qualify for this program—financially, I mean, not medically. You haven't any way of covering the diagnostic testing, let alone the in vitro fee.

JOYCE: It's just not fair if all those rich white women can have children through this program, but I can't because I'm poor and black. That they have money may be a reason for helping someone get a new house or a fancy car, but not a *baby*—there's only one reason for helping someone have a baby, and that's because she wants one, because it means something to her, because she wants to give it life, give it love. It's a natural thing for a woman to want. Well, I'm a woman just as much as they are and I want a baby just as much as they do, and I think it's only fair to try to help me have one, too.

As the imaginary conversation ends, you stare at the note once more. You could put it in the wastebasket right now. You could remind Joyce of the center's policy affirming that only married women with cooperating husbands are considered as candidates, though you know that exceptions are sometimes made. Or you could summon Joyce for further testing and enroll her in the in vitro program, if the tests indicate that she would stand some chance of conceiving. You could try to influence insurance and Medicaid policies governing the charges for infertility treatment. You could increase the charges for women who can pay to, say, $8,000 for the first attempt and testing, and fund Joyce and other poor women that way. Or you could let the note lie around on your desk until it is buried under a pile of other papers, hoping that enough time will pass until Joyce changes her mind.

What should you do?

Based on a case by Christine Wessel Kapsa.

CASE 4.3　THE LAW AND THE TAX COLLECTOR

Part of your job as a director at Legal Services, which provides legal assistance to low-income clients who cannot afford to pay ordinary attorney's fees, is to decide which cases should be pursued and which not. You are currently considering the request of a young man named Ramon G., whose problem has to do with income tax.

Two years ago, Ramon, who had been working part time as a waiter, had filed a return that showed only the extremely modest hourly wages he was paid, but no income in tips. The IRS had replied that his income in tips must have been underreported, that his total income must have therefore been much higher, and demanded an additional $700. Ramon insists that he did not underreport, and that as a matter of principle he refused tips, or when they were left on the table or included in a bill he turned them over anonymously to a charitable soup kitchen associated with the restaurant. Because he did so anonymously, he says, there are no receipts or records of these donations. He says that his income was not higher than the tiny hourly wages, that he lived extremely frugally during this period, and that he does not owe the $700.

In listening to Ramon's account, you realize that you have no idea of whether he is telling the truth. You are also aware that Ramon's chances of prevailing against the IRS will be fairly good if you take the case, even without concrete evidence, but not otherwise. You are also aware that many other people in this poor community would be willing to tell tales like Ramon's.

Should you take Ramon's case, or not? In general, what should your policy be about the support of legal services for the poor?

CASE 4.4   PRO BONO: *THE LAWYER AND THE STOCKBROKER*

A lawyer and a stockbroker are arguing over the obligations of professionals to perform *pro bono* work.

STOCKBROKER: Of course lawyers ought to do *pro bono* work, probably for as much as 10 percent of their total working time. After all, they're paid an enormous amount for their billed work, and they supply services that are very important even for people who can't afford them. In this society, everybody ought to be able to get legal help and protection of their rights.

LAWYER: But this is a very heavy expectation to impose only on lawyers. If lawyers should have to do *pro bono* work, shouldn't stockbrokers have to do it too? After all, what poor people need most is someone who could help them turn whatever little resources they have into something bigger, and this way help them out of poverty. Being saved from poverty is just as important as getting legal services.

STOCKBROKER: Stockbrokers do *pro bono* work? Impossible. Why, there'd be nothing to work with, no investment to start. You can't make money without money to begin with.

LAWYER: That's just the point. As things are now, the poor have nowhere to begin. But a stockbroker working on a *pro bono* basis—no commissions fees, no charges, no minimum investment—could eventually make the difference between poverty and modest comfort for a lot of people. You could develop ways of pooling resources for clients who began with virtually nothing at all. You could also provide all sorts of sensible financial advice and keep people from being victimized by loan sharks and high-interest credit agencies. Why, if you stockbrokers did this sort of *pro bono* work for, say, 10 percent of your working time, you'd make at least as big a difference as we lawyers do. Every argument that supports *pro bono* work by lawyers supports it just as strongly for stockbrokers.

STOCKBROKER: Nonsense. The mere idea of *pro bono* work for stockbrokers is ridiculous; you lawyers should do it, but not us. You obviously don't understand the nature of money in this society, or what it's supposed to do.

Whose case is stronger, the lawyer's or the stockbroker's?

CASE 4.5   UNIVERSITY ADMISSIONS RESTRICTIONS

You are director of admissions at a large state university. Your university is the flagship of the state system, which also includes three other four-year institutions, and three two-year community colleges. Recently, the state board of regents has directed your university to begin cutting back on the number of undergraduates you admit. The regents' request is due in part to a prolonged economic recession in your state. It is also due to the regents' realization that it is more expensive to educate an undergraduate at your institution than at other institutions in the state. They have developed a master plan for the state system which will increasingly shift undergraduate education to other institutions in the state.

You firmly believe that your university offers the best undergraduate education in your state. It is the only institution that offers undergraduates the opportunity to be in advanced classes with graduate students in many fields. It has library resources and laboratory facilities that are unparalleled elsewhere in the state. Programs in many popular fields such as pharmacy and journalism are not available at the other colleges.

Up until now, your university has followed an open admissions plan: All students who have graduated from an accredited high school in your state are admitted. Over the next three years, however, you will have to reduce the size of the entering freshman class from about 5,000 to about 4,000. You know that many of the 1,000 will be able to enter other colleges in the state, but some will not. Some will find a higher education more inconvenient or impractical, because your university is the only four-year school in the state's largest urban area.

You are charged with developing a plan for achieving the reductions. The easiest method for you would be to develop an index of predicted success, based on high school grades and scores on standardized tests, but this method will disadvantage students who did not do well in high school and students who do not perform well on standardized tests. The data suggest that adopting the index will decrease the percentage of minority students in your entering class, an already small percentage. The index will also decrease the numbers of several other groups of students: students with poor high school grades who entered the military and later decided to go to college; and students, particularly women, who married early and have spent most of their young adulthood raising children. You are also concerned that the index will decrease the numbers of students from rural areas who are admitted to the university. Do you recommend adoption of the index? Should there be any exceptions to the index? If so, how should an exceptions policy be designed?

SUGGESTED READINGS

Justice in Allocation and Access

AARON, HENRY J., AND WILLIAM B. SCHWARTZ. *The Painful Prescription: Rationing Hospital Care.* Washington: The Brookings Institutions, 1984.

ARRAS, JOHN D. "Health Care Vouchers and the Rhetoric of Equity." *Hastings Center Report* 11:(1981): 29–39.

ARROW, KENNETH. "Uncertainty and the Welfare Economics of Medical Care." *The American Economic Review* LIII:(1963): 941–70.

BAILY, MARY ANN. " 'Rationing' and American Health Policy." *Journal of Health Politics, Policy and Law* 9:(1984): 489–501.

BATTIN, MARGARET, "Age Rationing and the Just Distribution of Health Care: Is There a Duty to Die?," *Ethics* 97:(1987): 317–40.

BAYLES, MICHAEL. *Professional Ethics.* Belmont, Calif.: Wadsworth, 1981, Chapter 3.

BROCK, DAN W., AND ALLEN BUCHANAN. "Ethical Issues in For-Profit Health Care." In Bradford Gray, ed., *For-Profit Enterprise in Health Care.* Washington, D.C.: National Academy Press, 1986, pp. 224–49.

BUCHANAN, ALLEN. "The Right to a Decent Minimum of Health Care." *Philosophy and Public Affairs* 13:(1984): 55–78.

CAPLAN, ARTHUR. "Organ Transplants: The Costs of Success." *Hastings Center Report* 13:(1983): 23–32.

CHILDRESS, JAMES F. "Who Shall Live When Not All Can Live?" *Soundings* 53:(1970): 339–55.

———. "Priorities in the Allocation of Health Care Resources." *Soundings* 62:(1979): 258–69.

DANIELS, NORMAN. "Health Care Needs and Distributive Justice." *Philosophy and Public Affairs* 10:(1981): 146–79.

———. *Just Health Care.* Cambridge: Cambridge University Press, 1985.

———. *Am I My Parent's Keeper?* Oxford: Oxford University Press, 1987.

DYER, ALLEN R. "Should Doctors Cut Costs at the Bedside?" *Hastings Center Report* 16:(1986): 5–7.

ENTHOVEN, ALAIN. *Health Plan.* Reading, Mass: Addison-Wesley, 1980.

EVANS, ROBERT G. "Universal Access: the Trojan Horse." In Philip Slayton and Michael J. Trebelcock, eds., *The Professions and Public Policy.* Toronto: Toronto University Press, 1978, pp. 191–208.

EVANS, ROGER W. "Health Care Technology and the Inevitability of Resource Allocation and Rationing Decisions." *Journal of the American Medical Association* 249:(1983): 2047–53, 2208–19.

FRIED, CHARLES. "Equality and Rights in Medical Care." *Hastings Center Report* 6:(1976): 29–34.

GINZBERG, ELI. "The Monetarization of Medical Care." *The New England Journal of Medicine* 310:(1984): 1162–65.

GOROVITZ, SAMUEL. "Equity, Efficiency and the Distribution of Health Care." *Philosophic Exchange* 2:(1979): 3–12.

JONSEN, ALBERT, AND ANDREW JAMETON. "Social and Political Responsibilities of Physicians." *The Journal of Medicine and Philosophy* 2:(1977): 376–400.

LOMASKY, LOREN. "The Small but Crucial Role of Health Care Vouchers." *Hastings Center Report* 11:(1981): 40–42.

McCULLOUGH, LAURENCE B. "The Right to Health Care." *Ethics in Science and Medicine* 6:(1979).

MECHANIC, DAVID. "Cost Containment and the Quality of Medical Care: Rationing Strategies in an Era of Constrained Resources." *Milbank Memorial Fund Quarterly* 63:(1985): 453–75.

MILLER, FRANCIS, AND GRAHAM MILLER. "*The Painful Prescription:* A Procrustean Perspective?" *The New England Journal of Medicine* 314:(1986): 1383–85.

NICKEL, JAMES. "Should Undocumented Aliens Be Entitled to Health Care?" *Hastings Center Report* 16:(1986): 19–23.

OPPENHEIMER, GERALD M. and ROBERT A. PADGUG. "AIDS: The Risks to Insurers, the Threat to Equity." *Hastings Center Report* 16, no.5:(1986): 18–22.

OSBORNE, DAVID. "Rich Doctors, Poor Nurses." *Harper's* 265:(September 1982): 8–18.

OUTKA, GENE. "Social Justice and Equal Access to Health Care." *Journal of Religious Ethics* 2:(1974): 11–29.

PIERCE, CHRISTINE, AND DONALD VANDEVEER. *Aids: Ethics and Public Policy.* Belmont, Calif.: Wadsworth, 1988.

President's Commission on Ethical Problems in Medicine and Biomedical and Behavioral Research. *Securing Access to Health Care,* 3 Volumes. Washington, D.C.: U.S. Government Printing Office, 1983.

RELMAN, ARNOLD, AND UWE REINHARDT. "An Exchange on For-Profit Health Care." In Bradford Gray, ed., *For-Profit Enterprise in Health Care.* Washington, D.C.: National Academy Press, 1986, pp. 209–23.

RESCHER, NICHOLAS. "The Allocation of Exotic Medical Lifesaving Therapy." *Ethics* 79:(1969): 173–86.

RHODE, DEBORAH L. "Policing Lay Practice." *California Lawyer* (1983): 19–22.

RHODES, ROBERT P. "Optimizing Health: Why Equality of Access to Health Care Based on Need Leads to Injustice." In D. H. Smith, *Respect and Care in Medical Ethics.* Lanham, Md.: University Press of America, 1984, pp. 187–213.

ROSENFELD, STEPHEN P. "Mandatory *Pro Bono.*" *Cardozo Law Review* 2:(1981): 255–97.

SADE, ROBERT. "Is Health Care a Right?" *Image* (1974): 11–18.

SHELP, EARL E. *Justice and Health Care.* Dordrecht, The Netherlands: Reidel, 1981.

SMEEDING, TIMOTHY, MARGARET BATTIN, LESLIE FRANCIS, AND BRUCE LANDESMAN, eds., *Should Health Care Be Rationed By Age?* (Totowa, N.J.: Rowman and Littlefield, 1987).

SMITH, CHESTERFIELD H. "A Mandatory *Pro Bono* Standard: Its Time Has Come." *University of Miami Law Review* 35:(1981): 727–37.

VEATCH, ROBERT M. "Voluntary Risks to Health: The Ethical Issues." *Journal of the American Medical Association* 243:(1980): 50–55.

———. "What is a 'Just' Health Care Delivery?" In R. Veatch and R. Branson, eds., *Ethics and Health Policy.* Cambridge: Ballinger, 1976, pp. 131–42.

———. *Case Studies in Medical Ethics.* Cambridge: Harvard University Press, 1977, Chapter 4.

WIKLER, DANIEL. "Persuasion and Coercion for Health: Ethical Issues in Government Efforts to Change Lifestyles." *Milbank Memorial Fund Quarterly* 56:(1978): 223–41.

Preferential Treatment

BLACKSTONE, WILLIAM, AND ROBERT HESLEP. *Social Justice and Preferential Treatment.* Athens, Ga.: University of Georgia Press, 1977.

BOXILL, BERNARD. "The Morality of Preferential Hiring." *Philosophy and Public Affairs* 7:(1978): 246–68.

COHEN, MARSHALL, THOMAS NAGEL, AND THOMAS SCANLON. *Equality and Preferential Treatment.* Princeton, N.J.: Princeton University Press, 1977.

DANIELS, NORMAN. "Merit and Meritocracy." *Philosophy and Public Affairs* 7:(1978): 206–23.

DWORKIN, RONALD. "The DeFunis Case: The Right to go to Law School." *New York Review of Books* 23:(1976): 29–33.

———. "Why Bakke Has No Case." *New York Review of Books* 10:(1977): 11–15.

FULLINWIDER, ROBERT K. *The Reverse Discrimination Controversy: A Moral and Legal Analysis.* Totowa, N.J.: Rowman & Littlefield, 1980.

———. "Preferential Hiring." In Vetterling-Braggin, Mary, Frederick A. Elliston, and Jane English, eds., *Feminism and Philosophy.* Totowa, N.J.: Littlefield, Adams and Co., 1981, pp. 210–24.

GROSS, BARRY. "Is Turn-About Fair Play?" *Journal of Critical Analysis* 5:(1975): 126–34.

———, ed. *Reverse Discrimination.* Buffalo, N.Y.: Prometheus, 1977.

NAGEL, THOMAS. "Equal Treatment and Compensatory Justice." *Philosophy and Public Affairs* 2:(1973): 348–63.

NEWTON, LISA. "Reverse Discrimination as Unjustified." *Ethics* 83:(1973): 308–12.

NICKEL, JAMES. "Preferential Policies in Hiring and Admissions: A Jurisprudential Approach." *Columbia Law Review* 75:(1975): 534–58.

Regents of the University of California v. Allan Bakke, 438 U.S. 265, 98 S.Ct. 2733, 46 L.W. 4896 (1978).

SHER, GEORGE. "Justifying Reverse Discrimination in Employment." *Philosophy and Public Affairs* 4:(1975): 159–70.

THOMSON, JUDITH JARVIS. "Preferential Hiring." *Philosophy and Public Affairs* 2:(1973): 364–84.

WASSERSTROM, RICHARD. "The University and the Case for Preferential Treatment." *American Philosophical Quarterly* 13:(1976): 165–70.

FIVE

Regulation of the Professions

The Hyatt Regency Hotel collapses and scores of people die. An engineer smokes marijuana and a train derails. An obstetrician is drunk and a baby is born brain-damaged. A lawyer forgets to file a complaint on time and an injured accident victim can no longer sue on her claim. In each of these cases, substandard conduct by a professional may have gravely damaged the lives and happiness of others. Professionals are not perfect; mistakes are inevitable. Yet how should we respond? Should we regulate and discipline professionals? How can we reduce the likelihood of professional misconduct and improve the chances that professionals will live up to the high standards often expressed in the preambles to codes of professional ethics?

Government regulation has been a popular answer to some social ills, but in the late 1970s, government regulation came under increasing challenge. In the United States, trucking, airlines, and natural gas, to name a few, became "deregulated industries." The professions, in contrast to such industries, have traditionally enjoyed relative freedom from government regulation. Nonetheless, the argument to let market competition proceed more freely has been applied in ways that can have important effects on professions, such as in the testing of new drugs or in the repeal of certificate-of-need legislation as a limit on construction of new hospital facilities.

It is difficult to discuss the moral issues raised by regulation of professionals without some understanding of how professionals are governed today, if indeed they are governed at all. To provide important background, this chapter begins with a discussion of the various ways in which the professions today are or are not regulated. It then discusses the major arguments for and against regulation of professionals, the advantages and disadvantages of professional self-regulation, and some of the conflicts of conscience that regulation may raise for the individual professional.

THE CONTEMPORARY CONTEXT OF PROFESSIONAL REGULATION

Introduction

If regulation of one or more aspects of professional behavior is thought to be justifiable, who should regulate? And by what processes? In contemporary

U.S. professional life, three regulatory answers have been paramount: federal regulation; state regulation; and "self-regulation"—regulation of professionals by their own professional organizations.

Self-regulation, and the privileges and respect for expertise that it brings, has been regarded as one of the hallmarks of professionalism. Yet the professions vary greatly in the extent to which they have and exercise the powers of self-regulation. Some professions regulate themselves, to the full extent of having the power to set professional standards, award licenses, and prohibit practice. Self-regulation is largely the norm for lawyers, judges, physicians, nurses, actuaries, accountants, and architects, among others. Other professions, such as education, the military, and public administration, are regulated by state or federal law or by the public employment contexts in which they are practiced. Still other professions, such as journalism and the ministry, are largely left alone, at least in part for constitutional reasons.

In even the most thoroughly self-regulating professions, however, external and economic factors are growing in importance in influencing professional behavior. The costs of malpractice and other liability awards and professional insurance have become as much an issue in fields such as accounting, architecture, and engineering as they are in health care, where they are most publicized. Third-party payers for services in health care particularly are attempting to influence the quality of professional practice by such means as second opinions and utilization reviews. Emerging theories of liability are affecting professionals in new ways. For example, as we saw in the discussion in Chapter 2 of the *Tarasoff* case, some courts have held that psychiatrists have a duty to warn about clearly dangerous patients; and some states have recognized causes of action for clergy malpractice.

Government Regulation

For the most part, regulation of the professions is carried out by individual states under the exercise of their police powers. Several aspects of federal constitutional and statutory law have important effects on professional self-regulation, however.

State regulation—and professional self-regulation as it exercises delegated state powers—is subject to federal constitutional standards. The First Amendment, together with most other Bill of Rights guarantees, has been applied to states through the Fourteenth Amendment's prohibition on state action that deprives citizens of life, liberty, or property without due process of law. State regulatory activities may not, therefore, impermissibly burden free speech, freedom of the press, or the free exercise of religion.

A major area of constitutional dispute for a number of professions has been advertising. Professional advertising was commonly banned—because of concern that it violated professional dignity—until the U.S. Supreme Court decided *Bates v. Arizona State Bar* in 1977. Although commercial speech, such as advertising, is not granted the full constitutional protection afforded political speech, the law has nonetheless become increasingly protective of professional advertising since the *Bates* decision. The yellow pages, classified ads, and even radio and television carry increasingly eye-catching offers of professional services. State interests, such as preventing the public from being misled and protecting the vulnerable from overbearing pressure, are regarded as substantial enough to warrant regulation, but professional image and dignity are not.

Professional regulation has been used to further self-protection by professionals; indeed, cynics would say that this is its major unstated purpose. The Sherman Antitrust Act prohibits price-fixing and other forms of anticompetitive activity. State governments are exempt from the Sherman Act, but professional organizations are not. Professional organizations do have the benefit of the state's Sherman Act exemption when they act with authority from state government to further state purposes. However, self-regulating professional organizations are prohibited by the Sherman Act from acting on their own, beyond state authorization, to limit competition. The 1978 decision of *Goldfarb v. State Bar,* in which action by the Virginia Bar Association to set minimum price floors was held to violate the Sherman Act, has set the stage for antitrust scrutiny of the activities of other professional organizations. Professional limits on price competition, on competition for employment, and on numbers entering the profession are likely violations of the Sherman Act. Thus a state could set licensing standards with an eye to limiting numbers in a particular profession, but professional organizations may not do so without state authorization.

Since the passage of the Sherman Act at the beginning of this century, federal regulation has grown monumentally in many ways that affect the professions. As with the Sherman Act, the bulk of this regulation has occurred under the congressional power to regulate interstate commerce. In some cases, therefore, federal statutory schemes may be designed specifically to apply only in the interstate realm; Food and Drug Administration (FDA) regulations, for example, are targeted to the introduction of products into interstate commerce. However, interstate and intrastate commerce are so intrinsically linked that apparently local matters may have far-reaching effects; therefore, some federal regulatory schemes clearly reach into limited arenas, and it is constitutionally permissible for them to do so. For example, Title VII of the Civil Rights Act, which prohibits employment discrimination, applies to private employers with more than 15 employees.

To the extent that constitutionally permissible regulations apply to commerce within states, they supersede contradictory state regulation. Complementary state and federal regulation remains a possibility, however, as does state regulation that extends beyond federal regulation, so long as the state regulation does not interfere with the federal scheme. For example, federal regulations protect human subjects in federally funded projects or in research on new drugs or medical devices intended for marketing; some states impose more stringent protections on a wider range of research with human subjects. These regulations are consistent extensions of the federal scheme and so may stand constitutionally. This kind of federal-state regulatory partnership allows both national uniformity about minimum standards and state innovation about additional requirements.

Of particular interest to the professions are federal regulations about the environment, workplace safety, employment practices, product safety, fair trade practices, and consumer protection. Environmental protection includes standards for emission of hazardous air pollutants under the Clean Air Act, restrictions on water pollution under the Clean Water Act, and especially stringent standards for hazardous waste disposal—all of which impose limits on professionals but which, ironically, have also become an entirely new source of professional specialties. Under the Occupational Safety and Health Act, employees must be protected from workplace health hazards ranging from excessive noise to exposure to toxic chemicals. Under the Fair Labor Standards Act, employers may not pay below minimum wage or discriminate in pay based on sex. Title VII of the Civil Rights Act prohibits discrimination in the terms or conditions of employment based on race, sex, or religion, and allows such affirmative action as the court may judge appropriate as a remedy. New drugs or medical devices cannot be marketed without FDA scrutiny of research on their safety and efficacy. Unsafe products are subject to recall by the Consumer Products Safety Commission (CPSC), and unfair trade practices such as deceptive advertising are investigated by the Federal Trade Commission (FTC). And this is only a fraction of the list. Moreover, the list does not touch the ways in which federal funding policies affect professional practices. The introduction of prospective payment for Medicare—under which hospitals make a profit if their treatment of a patient costs less than the standard payment for the patient's diagnosis, but lose money if their treatment costs more—is only one illustration of how federal funding can change the shape of professional practice.

Self-Regulating Professions

Law   Of all the professions in the United States, law is perhaps the fullest example of professional self-regulation. Regulation of the conduct of lawyers includes setting standards for qualification and licensure, stipulating rules of conduct, and disciplining lawyers for violations of the rules. All of this is a matter of state law, within federal constitutional limits, such as the protection of commercial speech, and statutory limits, such as the antitrust laws. Typically, because lawyers are officers of courts, ultimate supervision of their behavior rests with the highest state court, which is itself composed of lawyers. The normal practice is for the state supreme court to delegate the bulk of responsibility for licensure and for drafting and enforcing codes of ethics to state bar associations, exercising only the power to enact rules and to review orders imposing discipline on lawyers.

In their efforts to formulate codes and engage in lawyer discipline, state bar associations are largely guided by the American Bar Association (ABA). While membership in a state bar is usually a condition of professional licensure, the ABA is a voluntary association, joined largely by the more prosperous members of the profession. The ABA, founded in 1878, has taken the lead in studying and drafting codes of ethics for lawyers. In this century, it has recommended three: the Canons (1908), the Model Code of Professional Responsibility (1969), and the Model Rules of Professional Conduct (1982). Each was discussed and passed by the ABA House of Delegates, a body comprising representatives from each state. The ABA also publishes formal and informal opinions interpreting provisions of recommended ethical codes. Although ABA recommendations are not binding as a matter of state law, they tend to be highly influential on states' interpretations of their rules of lawyer conduct. The recent adoption of the Model Rules by the ABA House of Delegates, for example, has stimulated state bar reexamination of ethical rules, and a number of state bar associations have now recommended adoption of the Rules. ABA representatives also investigate and offer recommendations on state bar disciplinary proceedings.

Some state legislatures have intervened in lawyer regulation. For example, state statutes may stipulate that conviction of a felony is automatic grounds for disbarment. A number of states have recently enacted statutes limiting lawyers' contingent fees in medical malpractice suits (under a contingent fee, a lawyer receives a percentage of a successful plaintiff's damage recovery). These statutes have been hotly contested between lawyers and physicians. Although challenges to such statutes have never been fully tested, the statutes are constitutionally suspect in states with strong constitutional provisions regarding separation of powers, because they involve legislative intervention into the courts' supervision of their own officers.

Health Care Medicine, too, has been largely self-regulated, although recent efforts to curb costs have been more intrusive on the healthcare professions than on the legal profession. Licensure, conduct, and discipline are usually lodged by statute in state boards of medicine, nursing, chiropractic, and psychology, among other health fields. There has recently been a movement for lay representation on these boards, although in no state has lay representation reached beyond a minimum. Board certification of specialists is under the control of various professional societies. In medicine, 23 approved medical specialty boards certify specialists on the basis of training programs and examinations; the newest of these, family practice, was established in 1969. Accreditation of medical schools is under the joint authority of the AMA and the Association of American Medical Colleges, and accreditation of postgraduate physician training programs is handled by the AMA and the American Hospital Association (AHA). In nursing, the American Nursing Association (ANA) certifies clinical proficiency in some 15 specialties, and nursing specialty associations also certify specialists in such fields as midwifery.

Historically, the growth of self-regulation of training and licensure in the healthcare professions involved controversy and struggle. In the nineteenth century—when, it must be emphasized, being treated by a physician may have been riskier than not being treated by one—many different schools of medical practice flourished essentially unregulated. It was not until the early twentieth century that some standardization was introduced into medical education and that medical education became largely the province of four-year, nonprofit universities such as Johns Hopkins. Specialization and board certification are exclusively twentieth-century phenomena. Nursing is still embroiled in disputes over training and certification of credentials. The ANA has sought to require bachelors-level training of nurses but has thus far been unsuccessful and has lost membership in the battle. A number of associations issue credentials for nurse specialists, despite ANA efforts to standardize the process.

More recently, new regulatory forces have been introduced into health care, largely as a result of concerns about costs. The Joint Commission on Accreditation of Hospitals (JCAH) sets quality-assurance standards such as record keeping, regular staff meetings, and organized clinical evaluations of the quality of care. Although JCAH accreditation is voluntary, it plays an increasingly important role in certification of hospitals for reimbursement by both public and private insurance. Medicare's recent shift to prospective payment has prompted concerns about inroads on the quality of care. As a result, the shift was accompanied by a revamped federal quality-assurance program. This program of Professional Review Organizations (PROs) reviews the frequency and necessity of hospital admissions and the medical justification for performing procedures. Other third-party payers, such as Blue Cross and other large employee insurance benefit plans, are increasingly concerned about ensuring cost-effective care, care that does not waste resources, care that is necessary, and care that reduces risks and the need for further treatment. Mandatory second opinions and utilization reviews are illustrations of interventions by such third-party payers.

The perceived crisis in malpractice has introduced another method of affecting physician conduct and the quality of care. In response to higher rates of malpractice suits and vastly greater jury verdicts for plaintiffs, physicians may increasingly be practicing "defensive" medicine—for example, ordering diagnostic testing in cases in which there is minimal need for it. Whether this is better medicine is a different question. Some insurers are now refusing to renew coverage for physicians sued for malpractice who fail to meet predetermined standards of patient care. Because of the possibility that they themselves might be held liable for patient injuries, hospitals are more closely scrutinizing the qualifications of their employees and the levels of mortality and morbidity resulting from treatment by particular staff members. Finally, most states have passed legislation reforming the system of malpractice lawsuits; such legislation typically includes limits on damage awards to patients for "pain and suffering" and procedures to screen out frivolous lawsuits, in addition to the previously mentioned limits on contingent fees. Some states have coupled these changes with requirements for licensing review of physicians who have been found liable for malpractice. In other states, state medical associations have voluntarily tightened review of incompetence in the profession.

Finally, as more physicians practice in institutional settings, such institutions can be expected, for cost-based reasons, to set standards for practice. In order to avoid losses under prospective payment, hospitals are reportedly encouraging, more or less gently, cost-cutting practices such as shorter lengths of stays for patients. HMOs, paid a set amount for treating each patient per year, often impose stiff cost limits on care. To the extent that cost cutting eliminates unnecessary or substandard treatment, it improves the quality of medical care. Concerns persist, however, that cost-cutting will result in poorer overall patient care and will deprive some patients of access to care altogether.

Business-Related Professions Several business-related professions, such as accounting, have also been allowed by state law to self-regulate to a large extent. Most states restrict the preparation of opinions on financial statements to certified public accountants (CPAs). In order to be licensed by state boards of accountancy, CPAs must have passed an examination prepared by the American Institute of CPAs (AICPA), and in many states must meet educational and experience criteria as well. The AICPA promulgates a code of ethics, which includes technical auditing standards and rules of conduct, such as a prohibition on involvement in conflicts of interest. (See Appendix II.) Discipline of accountants for violations of these standards is in a somewhat confused state, however. The AICPA can expel members for ethics code violations—and over 80 percent of accountants are AICPA members—but lacks the power to subpoena evidence. State licensing boards set their own standards and in some cases allow expelled accountants to continue to practice. Moreover, the federal government has played a growing role in the regulation of accountants. The Securities and Exchange Commission (SEC) has the power to regulate financial information submitted with securities offerings, in order to protect the public against securities fraud. The SEC will discipline accountants responsible for the submission of inadequate financial statements. SEC discipline can involve reprimands, exclusion from practice before the SEC, or even criminal investigation and prosecution for violation of the federal securities laws. Recently, another weapon has been added to the federal arsenal: the Racketeer-Influenced and Corrupt Organizations Act (RICO). The Act allows suits in federal court, by private individuals, to recover *triple* damages for losses caused by "patterns of racketeering activity." This phrase has been broadly construed to cover two or more fraudulent violations of the securities acts or fraudulent uses of the U.S. mail, a reading that at least one dissenting justice regards as "revolutionizing" business fraud litigation.[1]

Architecture   Unlike the self-regulating professions discussed thus far, architects do not have a monopoly on delivery of services, although they do control use of their professional name. Licensed contractors and engineers can perform many of the services performed by architects. Architects' licensing is regulated by state licensing boards, which are largely controlled by state associations of architects and which set their own educational and examination requirements. Uniformity is encouraged by a national group, the National Council of Architectural Registration Boards, but it has by no means been achieved, and architects moving from one state to another may find themselves facing new registration requirements. As is the case in law, complaints recur that architectural licensing serves the interests of the profession in limiting competition, beyond legitimate concerns about competence and public safety.

Moreover, licensing procedures in architecture devote little, if any, overt attention to aesthetic or environmental values.[2] Perhaps this is as it should be, if these values are to be left up to the judgment of architects or of clients when they select architects. On the other hand, the architect–client relationship affects the public more directly than do relationships in other client-centered professions such as medicine or law. Although building design may be selected by client and architect, it also affects the public, by changing the skyline of a city, for example, or increasing the likelihood of traffic congestion.

The American Institute of Architects (AIA), founded in 1857, is the national association of architects; membership in it is voluntary. Until 1981,

[1] *Sedima, S.P.R.L. v. Imrex*, 473 U.S. 479, 501 (1985) (Marshall, J., dissenting).
[2] Groves, John Russell, Jr., "Architectural Education: Teaching Professional Practice—Heroics, Hypocrisy, or Hyperbole?" *Architectural Record*, Vol. 174, July 1986, pp. 49–51.

the AIA's Standards of Ethical Practice set mandatory standards for members, who could be disciplined for noncompliance. In 1981, AIA efforts to discipline an architect for violating the Standards' prohibition on "supplanting"—taking over a job begun by one architect before his contractual relationship with the client had ended—was held to violate the Sherman Antitrust Act. The AIA has since replaced the Standards with a set of voluntary Ethical Principles, which counsel members in very general terms to uphold professional dignity, conform to law, compete fairly, be competent, be truthful and respect confidences, and thoughtfully consider the social and environmental impact of their work.[3] (For the Principles, see Appendix II.)

Malpractice is a serious issue in architecture, perhaps even more serious than in medicine, although it is less publicized. A tragedy such as the collapse of the Hyatt Regency Hotel in Kansas City involves not only the loss of a building but also the potential loss of many lives. Architectural disasters—unlike medical malpractice, but like engineering debacles—can kill many people at once.

Engineering Engineering is another illustration of a profession that is relatively strongly organized but lacks control over the exclusive delivery of professional services. Although states do have licensing procedures for engineers, it is possible to work as an engineer without a license; Baum estimates that less than half of the approximately 1 million engineers practicing in the United States today are licensed.[4] Moreover, formal engineering education is not required for licensure, so the educational element of professional control is lacking as well. Because many engineers ultimately assume managerial responsibilities, the definition of what it is to work as an engineer is itself fluid. However, although organizations of professional engineers do not control licensing, there is a possibility that their standards may be used as a basis for judgments of liability, as setting the standard for professional care. Indeed, in one controversial case, the American Society of Mechanical Engineers (ASME) was itself held liable for the use of its standards for boilers. Two ASME volunteers had interpreted the ASME standards so that their companies'—but not their competitors'—boilers met the standards. ASME itself was subject to damages for violation of the antitrust laws.[5]

Engineering grew rapidly with industrialization and became defined as a profession during the nineteenth century. As described in Chapter 3, engineers have typically worked in large business or government organizations with the capacity to support research. Engineering professional societies have been shaped in a wide variety of ways by their symbiotic relationships with industry. The engineering profession today boasts some 150 professional organizations, most grouped by specialty. National specialty societies have the largest membership. Five of these—the American Society of Civil Engineers, which, as the earliest, dates from 1852; the American Institute of Mining, Metallurgical, and Petroleum Engineers; the American Society of Mechanical

---

[3] Greenstreet, Bob, and Karen Greenstreet. *The Architect's Guide to Law and Practice.* New York: Van Nostrand Reinhold, 1984.

[4] Baum, Robert J., *Ethics and Engineering Curricula.* New York: The Hastings Center, 1980.

[5] *American Society of Mechanical Engineers v. Hydrolevel Corp.*, 456 U.S. 556 (1982).

Engineers; the American Institute of Electrical Engineers; and the American Institute of Chemical Engineers—are known as "founder" societies and play perhaps the largest role in professional activities. These larger organizations publish codes of ethics and expel members for violations. From the outset, these organizations have struggled with the question of business influence; some, such as the American Society of Civil Engineers (whose members, it should be noted, are more likely to be employed by government than by industry) have set high technical standards for membership and have played lead roles in formulating technical and ethical standards. Others, such as the American Institute of Mining, Metallurgical, and Petroleum Engineers, have remained largely industry-oriented.

The first ethical code for engineers was promulgated by the American Institute of Electrical Engineers in 1912; it emphasized the engineer's duty to protect the interests of his client or employer and treated the public interest only tangentially through concern for educating the public about engineering matters. To this day, the Institute of Electrical Engineers' code, reprinted in Appendix II, says only that engineers have responsibilities for protecting the public health and safety; it does not confront the hard issue of whether these responsibilities take precedence over responsibilities to employers and clients. Other engineering societies have now modified their codes to place greater emphasis on the public interest. In this they have been encouraged by the efforts of several umbrella organizations linking professional engineering societies: The Canons of Ethics for Engineers of the Engineers' Council for Professional Development, used as a model by many of the specialty societies and reprinted in Appendix II, provide that "Engineers shall hold paramount the safety, health, and welfare of the public in the performance of their professional duties."[6] Like other professional codes, however, engineering codes deal only with the engineers' responsibilities and ignore questions of engineers' rights, such as the right to protection in cases of legitimate whistle-blowing.[7]

Engineers are unlike other professions in that the major regulatory structures that they encounter focus on what they *produce*. An engineer's principal function is the design and production of physical objects, from toasters to nuclear power plants to pollution control systems, rather than the provision of a service.[8] Much regulation of the behavior of engineers is thus accomplished by regulation of what they produce, as in pollution control or product safety regulation. Engineers who work for large, usually corporate, employers may also be subject to ethical standards set by their employers. Corporate employers have also exerted significant influence on engineering professional societies, even to the point of dictating what is published in professional journals.

Professions Without Extensive Traditions of Self-Regulation

The drive for professional self-regulation was a movement of the late nineteenth and early twentieth centuries. For a variety of reasons, however, a number of professions did not organize or develop strong self-regulatory

[6] Baum, *op. cit.*, p. 9.
[7] *Ibid.*
[8] *Ibid.*, p. ix.

bodies. The contemporary interest in professional ethics has touched some of these professions, and there is renewed interest in the development of professional codes in such areas as public administration. As discussed in Chapter 1, part of the interest in such codes of ethics stems from the view that it will enhance the perception of these occupations as genuinely "professional."

Public Service   Public administrators, teachers, the police, and the military usually work in the public sector and have, in the main, been governmentally regulated. The constraints of the public interest are apparent in these professions. Not surprisingly, the military is the most rigidly regulated of the public professions. For those in training, living on base or on shipboard, or for those on active duty, there may be no easy separation between private life and life as a soldier. Military discipline extends to what would be considered "private" conduct for other professions; for example, a number of court decisions have upheld discharges of members of the military for being homosexual. The military also has its own system of justice, not only for infractions of military obligations but also for criminal offenses committed on base—on military territory, as it were.

In the other public professions, however, legal restraints are likely to represent only minimum conduct requirements—prohibiting conflicts of interest and other forms of corruption, for example. The American Society for Public Administration has recently adopted an aspirational ethical code which urges such behavior as serving the public interest. Elementary and secondary school teachers are organized in the National Education Association, which functions more as an education lobby than as a regulatory professional organization. Because of concerns about setting examples for school children, elementary and secondary school teachers have sometimes been dismissed for what is viewed as unacceptable off-duty sexual behavior. Dismissals of public school teachers must comport with the requirements of due process of law, however; roughly, this means that they must be based on education-related reasons rather than on stereotypes, and the days of automatic termination of employment because of pregnancy, for instance, are a thing of the past. The AAUP is the only nationwide organization of university faculty; its chief concern is the protection of academic freedom and scholarship rather than the establishment of common ethical standards for university faculty. Indeed, college faculty work in such a wide variety of settings—from small religious institutions to huge state universities—that standards are set on an institutional, rather than a more universal, level. What unity there is tends to be introduced by groups based on academic specialty, such as the Modern Languages Association (English, foreign languages) or the American Psychological Association.

Journalism   In other professions, self-regulation may not have emerged because of traditions of independence protected by the First Amendment. The press is one example of a profession given First Amendment protection. What it means to have a "free" press, and how the value of press freedom is to be reconciled with such other values as honesty and adequate public information, is the chief issue in journalism ethics. Libertarians take the view that this requires a laissez-faire approach to the media, with limits on force and fraud enforced by such means as libel suits. On the other side, concerns about the responsibilities of the press were given voice in the 1947 report of the Commission of Freedom of the Press, led by Robert M. Hutchins. The Hutchins Report, "A Free and Responsible Press," broadly advocated the press's obligations to be truthful, to provide full access to the news, and to give a representative picture of different groups and points of view within society. However, concerns that the Report provides little useful guidance in real conflict settings, together with recent scandals involving the reliability of the press, have led to calls to reconsider ethics for journalists.[9] Individual media employers have also taken steps to bolster credibility by tightening codes of ethics for journalists whom they employ. For example, in 1984, the *Wall Street Journal* publicized the case of its columnist, R. Foster Winans, who had made advance disclosures of market-sensitive information that was to appear in his "Heard on the Street" column. The *Journal* also responded with a stiffer code of ethics for its writers, emphasizing duties to the public in addition to such employer–employee matters as expense accounts.

The Ministry   In the ministry, which is also afforded First Amendment protection, regulation is a denominational affair. In some Protestant churches, regulation is performed by organized synods; in others, control of ministers is left to individual congregations. The Catholic Church places regulation in the hands of a clergical hierarchy, who may extract discipline for heretical views. However, the persistent scandals about television preachers and dissident synods suggest that regulation of religious leaders varies widely.

ISSUES IN JUSTIFYING REGULATION

Costs and Benefits

Regulation has serious disadvantages. Any case for it must overcome these concerns. In the first place, it is costly. Resources are consumed in formulating, implementing, and enforcing regulations, even in the most efficient regulatory system. Just to take one example, FDA regulations designed to ensure the safety and efficacy of new pharmaceuticals are estimated to delay the introduction of new drugs in the United States by approximately 3 years. Perhaps the delay can be shortened, but it cannot be eliminated: Testing, submitting, and evaluating results takes time and costs money. The delays can also be beneficial, however: Because of the stringent regulatory process, thalidomide—a tranquilizer that, when taken by pregnant women, caused serious birth defects such as the absence of limbs—had not been widely introduced in the United States by the time its tragic side effects became apparent. Nevertheless, the costs of regulation should not be ignored in discussions of its justifiability.

Another argument against regulation is that it may be poorly directed. In his famous essay *On Liberty*, as we saw in Chapter 2, Mill pointed out that

[9] Lambeth, Edmund, *Committed Journalism*. Bloomington: Indiana University Press, 1986.

those who would impose paternalistic restraints on the behavior of others risk interfering in the wrong way at the wrong time. Mill's concern applies to regulation generally. At the very least, regulation may have unanticipated consequences. Efforts under the Clean Air Act to improve local ambient air quality, for example, have apparently contributed to acid rain as tall smoke-stacks deliver pollutants higher into the atmosphere. Professional groups often charge that government regulators lack the expertise necessary to understand the issues and possible solutions. Professional self-regulation—governance of professionals by professionals—is offered as an alternative, although it raises problems of its own, such as protectionism.

Among the most important consequences of regulation are the incentives it creates. If one part of an industry is regulated and thus faces costs that an unregulated part does not, for-profit economic activity is likely to increase in the unregulated sector. Thus, for example, when prospective payment was introduced to control costs in hospital sectors of the healthcare industry but was not introduced into other sectors such as outpatient surgery centers, predictable growth in the latter occurred. These shifts in incentives, some economists contend, may represent losses in overall social utility. The technical issues here are complex and controversial. If we assume that unregulated market transactions yield preferred distributions, however, then shifts away from these distributions caused by regulation represent overall social losses.

Supporters of regulation point out that there are many ways in which the real world differs from a theoretical market. One important disanalogy is the difficulty of entry and exit. Pure free-market models assume complete freedom of entry and exit into the market in response to consumer demand. Without this assumption, market outcomes will not be efficient because consumers' most preferred products will not appear in the market despite demand. In the real world, however, there are economic and natural barriers to entry into the market. Examples of economic and natural barriers range from the time and money needed to acquire professional skills to the capital investment required for new medical technologies. Perhaps the best example of a natural monopoly affecting the professions is the limited availability of broadcast frequencies, but there are others, such as scarce supplies of transplantable body parts; limited sites for the location of buildings, bridges, or schools; or the difficulty of having more than one army officially responsible for defending a given territory.

Another way in which the real world differs from an ideal market involves what economists call *transaction costs*. A pure free-market model assumes that willing buyers and willing sellers can locate each other with complete ease. In the real world, however, it takes time, knowledge, skills, and money for consumers to search out the product or service they prefer. Women, for example, may prefer obstetricians who favor natural childbirth but may not be able to obtain information about who these practitioners are. Lawyers may not advertise "success" rates, principally because of concerns that cases differ so much that such statistics are inherently misleading, and clients have little way of assessing the significance of differences among cases. Consumers may require a great deal of sophistication to understand the differences among types of therapists, or to assess the competence of structural engineers.

Another problem with the market is described by economists as *market failure*, the failure of the market to generate preferred alternatives. For example, the free market may not produce goods that economists call "public goods." These are goods whose enjoyment cannot be limited to those who pay for their production, such as clean air. The air is more or less polluted for everyone; it cannot be cleaned up for some but not for others. Gas masks or roads, by contrast, can be made available only to those who pay for them. Everyone is better off if public goods are produced, even if they have to pay for them; but because the enjoyment of public goods cannot be limited, everyone is still better off if they let others pay the costs of the production of these goods. Without a mechanism for ensuring that the burdens of producing public goods are coordinated and shared, therefore, public goods will not be produced at all. Hence, the case for legal intervention in the market: Coercion or taxation is required to ensure that public goods are produced at all.

Some professionals are involved directly in the production of public goods: Public administrators design health reporting regulations in the public interest; educators produce literate citizens for a democracy; and the military and the police promote public safety. These professional services are traditionally supported by taxation.

A related issue is posed by what economists term *externalities*. Externalities are costs or benefits not reflected in the price paid by consumers for products or services. Professionals, as described in Chapter 3, have traditionally produced services in response to payment by individuals and can refuse to perform if they are not paid. Nevertheless, what occurs in relationships between individual professionals and their clients may produce externalities to the professional–client relationship. For example, architects design buildings that affect the aesthetic environment for better or worse; physicians treat patients for communicable diseases; journalists write stories for newspapers and thereby shape public perceptions and public events; and engineers design emissions control devices for automobile manufacturers. Transactions between individual professionals and clients may not reflect these costs or benefits; regulation may be necessary to ensure that individual transactions do not impose unjustifiable costs on others.

Beyond the problems of public goods and externalities, there are other goods that, for one reason or another, the market fails to produce. Orphan drugs, for example, are drugs that are medically beneficial but not profitable because production costs are high and the numbers of potential consumers are low; the U.S. government currently sets aside a small sum to underwrite production costs of some of these pharmaceuticals. To be sure, the failure to produce orphan drugs is not a pure efficiency concern. It is, however, an example of how the market fails to respond to suffering or injustice.

A final important criticism of the market model is the potential confusion between willingness to pay and ability to pay. This criticism raises issues of distributive justice discussed in Chapter 4. The conclusion that market choices maximize utility rests on the assumption that consumers' willingness to purchase goods reflects their preferences. However, if people are unable because of lack of resources to purchase what they very much want, then their actual choices will not maximize their preferences. For example, suppose that a high percentage of minorities fail to seek prenatal care. This may be taken as evidence that prenatal care is unwanted or unneeded. The literature on access to care suggests, however, that it more likely shows lack of resources.

Depending on one's underlying moral view, the inefficiencies of regulation are not conclusive reasons for rejecting it. Nonetheless, they must be weighed in the balance. If the benefits of a particular regulatory scheme are outweighed by its costs, then the scheme is unjustified, unless other moral reasons tip the balance. Moreover, costs should be mitigated, if possible, in the design of the regulatory scheme.

Liberty, Rights, and Justice

Costs are not the only important objection to regulation. Regulation interferes with liberty, sometimes in ways that are very serious and inhibiting. FDA regulations prevent willing, even desperate, purchasers from obtaining laetrile in interstate commerce. State statutes prohibiting the unauthorized practice of medicine prevent herbalists from earning their livings as they choose and potential clients from patronizing them. Statutes barring the unauthorized practice of law forbid energetic marriage counselors from working out the terms of divorce decrees and accountants from giving legal advice to their clients. Judges may not practice law, and public administrators are not allowed to profit from dealing with the government.

The significance of interferences with liberty is philosophically controversial, however. There is a familiar distinction in political philosophy between having a right to do something in the sense of being at moral liberty to do it, and having a right to do something in the sense of having a claim to be spared interference in doing it. Individuals affect one anothers' choices all the time, in the sense of affecting what they can actually do, by making it difficult to pursue options that they might otherwise have preferred. When I arrive at the airport 2 minutes before you do and purchase the last ticket on a flight to New York, your options are thereby curtailed. But the interference is not morally problematic in itself, unless other features of the situation make it so. If my getting there first was arguably unfair because, for example, I had cheated you in getting a parking space or had had access to a limousine reserved for whites only, then my subsequent interference with your options is morally questionable. My interference would also be questioned if my ticket purchase interfered with your rights, say, under an earlier ticket purchase contract with the airline or under a program of preference in standby ticket sales to members of the armed forces.

Critical to the justification of regulation, therefore, is whether the regulation interferes with liberty in ways that are morally suspect because they are unfair, unjust, or in violation of rights. To state the point differently, justifications of regulation depend on a political theory about the nature and scope of individuals' claims to being left alone.

Some—libertarians particularly—take a very strong, rights-based stand against regulation, including regulation of professional practice. Libertarians believe that both professionals and their clients should be left at liberty to do as they wish, so long as they do not interfere with others' rights. Others' rights are very limited: to protection from force or fraud, and to the fruits of voluntary transactions, including labor and contract. Government regulation, libertarians believe, is appropriate to protect these rights. But further regulation is unjustifiable because it interferes with individuals' liberties. The plausibility of the libertarian position depends on its underlying claims about rights, however. If individuals have claims on each other that extend beyond protection from force, fraud, or interference with voluntary transactions, then the libertarian position against regulation cannot stand.

More limited theories about rights to noninterference have also been used to restrict government regulation. For example, the postulated right to use talents and skills as one chooses, so long as others are not thereby intentionally harmed, has been used as an objection to mandatory *pro bono* service or to licensing requirements. The supposed right to acquire the fruits of one's talents and skills as property has been used to defend profit-making in the professions. The assumed right to contract freely has been used in opposition to limits on lawyers' fees or to restrictions on permissible services. The plausibility of each of these arguments rests on the underlying right claimed. This is not to say that the positions are untenable, but it is to say that the really difficult issues lie in examination of fundamental claims made about individual rights.

Rights theories may ultimately prove less of a bar to regulation of professionals than is initially apparent. Even libertarians admit that regulation intended to protect consumers against fraud is appropriate. More generally, misleading or inadequate information may interfere with individual autonomy, because of the importance of accurate and complete information to rational choice. Autonomy thus can be used to defend regulation that protects consumers against defective information. Many current instances of professional regulation—from restrictions on misleading advertising to requirements that costs of services be posted—serve consumers' interests in access to adequate information.

Advertising and credentialing are useful examples here. The position of a libertarian such as Milton Friedman permits regulation of advertising or credentialing to protect the public against fraudulent information; for instance, it would permit prohibition of misleading advertising. It would also permit requiring standardized ways of designating credentials, such as those found in specialization programs, since this would serve to provide the public with uniform and accurate information about professional qualifications. Libertarians will not support credentialing regulations that reach beyond informational interests, however, as many regulations surely do. For example, a regulation that health professionals clearly list degrees and qualifications could serve informational interests acceptable to the libertarian. By contrast, a prohibition on practice by those without degrees, in the interests of public health, would not fit within libertarian limits. Informational arguments could be offered for the latter position, such as that the public cannot be expected to appreciate the significance of having a degree qualification. But these arguments are disingenuous, the libertarian would say, to the extent that they rely on blanket critiques of public capacities.

Those with more complex moral theories than the libertarian's—some rights-based, others not—may defend the use of professional regulation in light of other moral concerns. One frequent example is respect for persons, which can furthered by, for example, requirements of professional confidentiality of the sort described in Chapter 2. Another example is loyalty, which is given as a reason for regulations such as prohibition of conflict of interest, and which may or may not be given deeper support by a theory of respect for persons. Professional regulation can also be used to promote distributive justice, as discussed in Chapter 4. Examples of such regulation are infrequent in professions that are privately practiced, such as law or medicine—witness the resistance of lawyers to mandatory low- or no-cost service—but may be built into the very job description of the public school teacher or the public administrator.

Professional Roles

As we saw in Chapter 1, it is important to distinguish moral problems of professionals as professionals from moral problems of individuals who happen to be professionals. Whether professionals have special ethical status depends both on the values we accept and on the factual context of the particular profession. If a profession does have special ethical status, this may have implications for regulation of that profession.

One possibility is that the presence of special professional obligations itself enhances the case for enforcement. The case for transforming ordinary moral obligations into legal enforcement depends on the importance of the obligations, the likelihood that others would be harmed if they are not honored, and possibly other factors. With professional role obligations as well, importance and potential harm are arguably relevant to the issue of enforcement. For example, the potential for harm to clients supports enforcement of at least minimal standards of professional competence. Again, as with ordinary moral obligations, one of the chief concerns about enforcement of professional obligations is interference with liberty. There may also be cases in which an important professional role obligation should not be enforced, because of the desire to allow flexibility despite general commitment to the obligation. The liberal view about matters of conscience, for example, is to allow individual professionals as much scope as possible to act on their own moral beliefs by leaving room in physicians' ethics to refuse to perform abortions and in lawyers' ethics to turn down clients regarded as morally reprehensible. Yet this view may ultimately clash with other obligations of the profession, such as if access to services is threatened because all the professionals in a given area refuse a particular client. Regulations may be necessary in such cases, but they may pose conflicts with individual conscience and may thus raise the issues of disobedience discussed later in this chapter.

On the other side, it is also possible that the role-based obligations or liberties of professionals might conflict with proposed regulations. For example, suppose that policymakers attempt to construct a just system of allocating transplantable organs. This system might include potential graft success as a factor to take into account in selecting transplant recipients. According to some views of the physician–patient relationship, individual physicians have the duty to try to obtain all desired, medically beneficial care for their patients. This duty might require physicians to do whatever they can to obtain organs for their patients, including representing their patients' medical status in the best possible light. Representing patients in the best light might conflict with the organ allocation scheme, however.

The possibility of such conflicts between role-based professional obligations and regulation of the profession is certainly a concern for regulation. If proponents of the role-based view of professional obligations are correct, then the existence of role-based obligations is an additional objection to regulation that impinges upon them, as well as an additional argument for regulation that facilitates their performance.

ISSUES IN THE DEBATE OVER PROFESSIONAL SELF-REGULATION

One of the most controversial issues facing the professions today is professional self-regulation. Professional groups such as the AMA have struggled to achieve—and lobbied to preserve—self-regulation. The power of self-regulation has long been regarded as a hallmark, if not a defining characteristic, of professionalism, as Chapter 1 discusses. Yet newer members of the professions increasingly hold non-traditional values and are entering practice contexts shaped by governmental regulation. If only because of changes in the institutional context and in the funding of professional practice, professional self-regulation seems likely, at the least, to become a less independent function. But should it?

The case for professional self-regulation rests, in the first place, on professional expertise. Particularly in the technological professions, professional skills and practice quality are difficult to understand and assess. The need to have skill in order to judge skill is certainly an argument for significant participation by professionals in the regulatory process. It supports professional representation on whatever body is responsible for judging professional training. It supports professional representation on committees that review substandard practice, impose discipline, or revoke licenses. It is an argument for requiring expert-witness testimony about standards of practice in malpractice cases.

Indeed, the need for professional skill supports involving professionals, in rule-making whenever there is need for knowledge of the nature of professional practice. This need for knowledge is far-reaching and arguably extends to all professional regulation. Lawyers' participation in discussions of contingent fees, for example, can illuminate the extent to which these fees improve access to legal services by cross-subsidizing clients who would otherwise be unable to obtain a lawyer. Lawyers' impressions about the impact of confidentiality on the right to counsel for criminal defendants are surely helpful in debates over confidentiality. But as these examples illustrate, professional skill is not the only expertise relevant to rule-making for the professions. Sociological and economic analyses of malpractice cases and settlement rates are important to judging whether access to legal services remains problematic in many cases of malpractice despite contingent fees, and whether contingent fees encourage unwarranted lawsuits in other cases. Moreover, other solutions might be considered to problems of access to legal services, such as low-cost or *pro bono* programs. These alternatives, however, are less likely to be preferred by lawyers; recent efforts to reform lawyers' rules to require *pro bono* service proved a resounding failure.

Examples of the need to draw on expertise outside the profession at issue to evaluate professional performance are not confined to the law. Knowledge of epidemiology can be important to decisions about standards for patient care, in such matters as whether to immunize or whether to screen routinely for health conditions. Knowledge of risk assessment may be critical to expert engineering judgments about the design of nuclear power plants or to expert architectural judgments about the location of buildings in areas prone to earthquakes.

Moreover, assessment of many policy questions does not depend solely on technical expertise. Members of the public can understand such issues as the conflict between protecting a journalist's source and the need for evidence at a trial, or the tradeoff between economic development and protection of landmarks. The policy-making process today is increasingly involved in making judgments about the allocation of health care. Thus, although the need for professional expertise is an argument for significant participation by professionals in the regulatory process, it is not an argument for exclusive professional self-regulation.

A second major argument for professional self-regulation is that members of a given profession are more likely to be interested in what happens to their profession. *Interest* in this argument has a double meaning: Professionals have a great stake in what happens to their working lives, and are therefore highly likely to become active, interested participants in the regulatory process. Like knowledge, however, interest is an argument for significant, but not exclusive, professional participation. Because their jobs are commonly an extremely important part of professionals' lives—more so than nonprofessionals, professionals identify with their work, enjoy it, work augmented hours, and continue their training—professionals surely have a stake in their work contexts. The way in which physicians have found increased vulnerability to malpractice suits extremely disturbing on a personal level is illustrative of the profound impact on professionals of changes in the context of professional work.

But professionals are not the only ones with substantial stake in the effects of professional regulation. Consumers of professional services, third parties, and even the public are also deeply and directly affected by professional conduct. The person who cannot gain access to professional services because she cannot pay, or the person who is injured by substandard professional care, surely is as severely affected by regulation of these matters as is the regulated professional. Moreover, although it is likely that professionals will remain involved in regulation—if longstanding activities of professional organizations are indicative—others with sustained interests in professional practice are also likely to remain involved on a continuing basis. The emerging role of consumer groups in medicine is a case in point.

The very stake that professionals have in regulation is, indeed, the basis of an argument against exclusive self-regulation. The concerns of professionals, no matter how intense, are likely to be only a part of the picture. Professional interest is all too likely to be manifest as professional self-interest.

Claims that lawyers' self-regulation has served the interests of more prosperous segments of the profession, in such areas as advertising, competition, and fees, reflect this concern. The ABA Model Rules of Professional Conduct, for example, protect client confidentiality to the utmost—except when human life is at stake—but permit the lawyer to violate confidentiality in order to establish a defense against the client or to collect a fee.

Another argument for professional self-regulation is that it will foster professional community. Professional community is important in several ways. Through education by other professionals and by participation in professional activities, new members of the profession come to understand professional aspirations. Practice with other professionals may foster development of the habits and character traits of the good professional. In addition, regulatory organizations have been a major way of stimulating professional interchange and of improving the quality of professional service.

Despite the importance of professional community, it, too, is troubling as an argument for exclusive professional self-regulation. The unattractive side of community is clannishness. Plaintiffs in malpractice suits against physicians argued for years that a "conspiracy of silence" made it difficult for them to get expert witnesses to testify against other physicians, especially when testimony of an expert from the same locale was required. In the past, allegations were frequent that instances of poor professional care, rather than being fully investigated and appropriately monitored or disciplined, were hushed up within professional communities. Charges of a conspiracy of silence have been mitigated more recently in medicine—where they were strongest— by tougher institutional stances, such as reviews of adverse patient outcomes, or legal changes, such as the shift away from reliance on testimony from local experts in malpractice cases. However, many of these changes have been motivated by external concerns, rather than initiated by the profession itself.

A final argument for professional self-regulation relies upon an important benefit of professional silence: the need for trust and confidentiality in professional practice and thus in certain aspects of professional regulation. Professional disciplinary proceedings, for example, sometimes raise sensitive and private questions about both professional and client. Privacy values are not implicated in every type of professional regulation, however; this argument highlights the issue that requires emphasis throughout the discussion of professional self-regulation: the importance of distinguishing various aspects of the regulatory process. Formulating professional rules is minimally, if at all, dependent on confidential information; data on quality assurance, lawyer–client relationships, or professional disciplinary processes—to name three areas in which confidential information might seem necessary—can be reported without revealing private information about individual practitioners or clients. Moreover, if there is a public stake in rules governing professional conduct, then perhaps the formulation of these rules should be part of the public policy-making process and subject to public debate and critique.

It is in discussions of individual cases—reviews of the quality of particular professional services, disciplinary proceedings against individual practitioners, investigation of individual impairments, and the like—that information about individuals must be presented. It is also here that the case for confidentiality is strongest. Challenges to the quality of professional services could be deterred if clients must themselves suffer unfavorable or damaging publicity. Professional reputations should not be harmed by charges or investigations that turn out to be unfounded—but reputations are inevitably affected by publicity.

There are arguments to be made for publicity even here; the most important is the public's interest in the efficacy of the disciplinary process. The confidentiality of professional investigatory proceedings is currently offered legal protection, however; in many states, records of hospital conferences on quality of care are not admissible in medical malpractice cases, and disciplinary proceedings against lawyers for minor infractions can result in private discipline. To be sure, if information about the conduct of individual professionals is presented only to other professionals, then existing professional obligations will protect confidentiality. Strictures of confidentiality can be extended to nonprofessionals included in the review process, however. Indeed, in many states, disciplinary panels in law, medicine, nursing, and other professions now include at least one lay member. A number of states have set up systems to identify nonmeritorious medical malpractice suits; these mechanisms typically include lay persons in confidential proceedings. Citizen representatives are now commonly included on a wide variety of public panels with confidential functions, from state water boards to boards reviewing the manner in which research is conducted on human subjects.

Bias, self-interest, and narrowness of perspective are the most common arguments against professional self-regulation. Two other arguments are made less frequently but are equally worthy of emphasis: social interests in the practice of the professions, and the need for interconnection among professions.

Professionals play an important role in social life and deliver many of our most critical social services. Beyond the "public service" professions such as public administration and teaching, lawyers are officers of the court, architects shape our public spaces, and healthcare professionals deal with issues affecting both public and private health. Thus the public has interests in how these professions are practiced—interests that tend to be ignored in the absence of public representation in the rule-making process.

At times, these public interests involve interrelationships among various professions. Consider, for example, the public interest in the availability of medical treatment. It is fair to say that perceptions of a malpractice crisis are affecting access to health care, particularly in rural areas where access was already minimal and in specialities such as obstetrics in which insurance coverage has become very expensive. It is also fair to say at a minimum—regardless of one's views of whether there is a malpractice crisis and of what the crisis is—that conflicts between physicians and lawyers have not helped the situation. Yet regulatory structures in which physicians govern physicians and lawyers govern lawyers entrench these conflicts.

Lack of coordination among professions also affects the types of services available. Lawyers, for example, zealously guarding against the unauthorized practice of law, prohibit practice structures in which lawyers form partnerships with nonlawyers. The justifications for the rule include protecting clients from incompetence, diluted loyalty, or weakened professional obligations, such as the obligation to maintain confidentiality. The cynical view of this rule is that it protects the economic interests of lawyers. The practical effect of the rule, however, is to prohibit coordinated forms of service delivery that might prove extremely useful to certain types of clients. Lawyers and accountants may not form partnerships to provide contract and financial advice to professional athletes. Divorce lawyers may not work in tandem with family counselors; counselors may not provide low-cost legal advice. To be sure, lawyers are the most isolationist of the professions; physicians and nurses, for example, may legally practice together. Nonetheless, there are persistent conflicts among the various health professions, too. Perhaps the most long-standing of these are conflicts between physicians and nurses over such issues as the exercise of independent judgment. Regulation along individual professional lines balkanizes the professions in ways that render these conflicts institutionally more difficult to resolve.

RESPONSES OF PROFESSIONALS TO REGULATION

A final set of problems arises when professionals respond to regulation. The problems here are layered and complex, especially on the view that professionals have separate, role-generated obligations. The professional's moral landscape may include at least the following factors: her own conscientious beliefs, requirements of her professional role, orders from her work context, and the requirements of law. All or any of these may conflict. Even the most traditional professional—the independent provider of services, such as the physician in solo practice—may encounter questionable demands from clients, third-party payers, the law, or other regulatory bodies.

One approach to such conflicts is prudence. Job security is an obvious immediate concern for employed professionals. Within an organization, disobedience may result in unpleasant working relationships, mistrust, retaliation, or discharge; whistle-blowers, as we saw in Chapter 3, are notoriously no one's friend. Longer-range concerns include licensure, civil liability, criminal punishment, and self-respect. For example, nurses are subject to independent civil liability for malpractice, even when they act under the direction of a physician. Associates in law firms can be disciplined for obeying orders that violate professional ethical standards; although inexperience may be mitigation, subordinate lawyers have been disbarred for following their superiors' orders. Engineers, nurses, business executives—indeed, any professional, but these are likely to participate in risk-imposing behavior—can be held criminally liable for taking reckless risks with human life, even when they act under orders from their superiors. Army officers may be court-martialed or tried for violations of international law, despite their obedience to orders from superiors. Thus, although short-term self-interest may appear to counsel following orders, disobedience may be the more prudent choice in the longer run.

Rawls's distinction between conscientious refusal and civil disobedience is helpful in analyzing the moral landscape here. *Conscientious refusal*, according to Rawls, is deliberate noncompliance, for reasons of conscience, with an applicable legal order. It may be overt or covert; in the latter case, Rawls suggests, it is more appropriately described as "conscientious evasion."[10] Conscientious refusal is not aimed to appeal to the sense of justice of the majority or to bring about legal change. Rather, it is a statement by the actor that, on grounds of conscience, he must refuse to do what the law requires. Classic examples are Thoreau's refusal to pay his taxes because to do so would make him an agent of injustice to others, or the pacifist's refusal to participate in war. Reasons of conscience may include reasons of justice, such as the view that it is wrong to deny healthcare resources to someone who does not meet eligibility requirements for care. They may be religious reasons, such as opposition to abortion on theological grounds. They may include other moral reasons, such as protection of clients or others to whom one has professional obligations; examples include the journalist's protection of the confidentiality of her sources despite a court order; the research physician's decision to try an experimental medical device that she believes has some hope of therapeutic efficacy, despite FDA disapproval; or the lawyer's refusal to reveal the whereabouts of a client.

The conscientious refuser, as described by Rawls, has no claim on society to mitigate punishment, since he makes no more general appeal to social justice. A tolerant society, we might hope, would attempt to avoid conflicts and arrange for alternatives, such as the option to declare oneself a conscientious objector to the military draft. Statutes permitting termination of medical treatment, for example, typically provide that a physician who disagrees with a nontreatment directive, such as a living will, should make other arrangements for patient care. Deliberate failure to comply with a nontreatment directive constitutes professional misconduct in many states, however, and alternative care may not be easy to arrange. In the final analysis, the conscientious refuser must weigh the strength of his reasons of conscience against the likely consequences of disobedience. For the professional, these consequences may include loss of funding, loss of professional privileges, or loss of a license, in addition to legal sanctions.

Civil disobedience, in contrast to conscientious refusal, is not a private judgment that following the law would be immoral. It is aimed to bring about legal change. In Rawls's words, civil disobedience is

> a public, nonviolent, conscientious yet political act contrary to law usually done with the aim of bringing about a change in the law or policies of the government. By acting in this way one addresses the sense of justice of the majority of the community and declares that in one's considered opinion the principles of social cooperation among free and equal men are not being respected.[11]

Because it may undermine support for otherwise just institutions and ignore reciprocity to fellow citizens, civil disobedience, according to Rawls's view, can only be justified under limited circumstances. It must be aimed to correct substantial injustice, especially structural injustice that blocks removal of other injustices. Normal appeals to the political process must have been tried without success, and further attempts must reasonably seem fruitless; in this, Rawls's

---

[10]Rawls, John, *A Theory of Justice.* Cambridge: Harvard University Press, 1971, p. 369.
[11]*Ibid.*, p. 364.

account of civil disobedience parallels the account of whistle-blowing in Chapter 3. Finally, it must be unlikely that the disobedience will raise the level of disorder to an extent that risks breakdown of just institutions overall. When disobedience meets these conditions, the disobedient arguably ought not to suffer penalties, for he is the moral hero correcting grave injustice.

Professional role requirements are a complicating factor here. The issue is whether the problem of disobedience must be viewed differently *because one is a professional.* Lawyers and judges, for example, are sworn to obey the law. A record of civil disobedience may raise questions about fidelity to law and has been a reason for delay at least in admission to the bar. Military officers contend that obedience is necessary for effective fighting and that disobedience can be grounds for court-martial and discharge. A plausible view is that role obligations provide an additional, but not conclusive, argument against disobedience. On the other side, professionals may be led to disobedience by their views about the requirements of their role. Their professional knowledge and interests may also be part of their decision to take a stance in favor of disobedience. Many of the civil rights demonstrators were lawyers or law students; many who protested the war in Vietnam and who continue to object to the development of nuclear weapons are healthcare professionals. A full resolution of the issue of the relevance of role obligations to disobedience may require understanding of the purposes of the professional role.

CONCLUSION

As we saw in Chapter 1, the question of whether professionals have special ethical status depends on our moral values and on the nature of the profession. In this chapter, we have seen that regulation of the professions takes many forms and can be defended in many ways. From this rich variety, is it possible to draw any general conclusions about regulation of the professions? We hazard four suggestions.

First, as we saw in Chapter 1, there are special professional obligations, based on the values we accept and the context of professional practice. These special obligations may support regulation. Second, whether professional role obligations should be regulated depends on the importance of the obligations and the likely harm to others if they are violated; on the costs and likely success of regulation; on the rights and liberties protected or impaired by regulation; and perhaps on other moral values as well. Third, the arguments for regulation by professionals themselves are strongest when the role obligation in question is best understood, inculcated, and fostered in professional communities; they are weakest when professional self-interest blinds professionals to the needs of others. Finally, as professionals are subject to regulation, they are increasingly likely to face conflicts among their own conscientious convictions, norms of professional practice, and legal obligations. It is not easy or morally comfortable to be a professional today.

OCCUPATIONAL LICENSURE

Milton Friedman

Friedman argues against licensure—the restriction of professional activity to those approved for practice by other members of the profession. He claims that licensing physicians is not necessary to prevent the public from incompetent practice. Rather, he argues that medical licensure itself has reduced the quantity and quality of health care and raised its costs.

The overthrow of the medieval guild system was an indispensable early step in the rise of freedom in the Western world. It was a sign of the triumph of liberal ideas, and widely recognized as such, that by the mid-nineteenth century, in Britain, the United States, and to a lesser extent on the continent of Europe, men could pursue whatever trade or occupation they wished without the by-your-leave of any governmental or quasi-governmental authority. In more recent decades, there has been a retrogression, an increasing tendency for particular occupations to be restricted to individuals licensed to practice them by the state. . . .

Licensure is a special case of a much more general and exceedingly widespread phenomenon, namely, edicts that individuals may not engage in particular economic activities except under conditions laid down by a constituted authority of the state. Medieval guilds were a particular example of an explicit system for specifying which individuals should be permitted to follow particular pursuits. . . .

Policy Issues Raised by Licensure

It is important to distinguish three different levels of control: first, registration; second, certification; third, licensing.

By registration, I mean an arrangement under which individuals are required to list their names in some official register if they engage in certain kinds of activities. There

is no provision for denying the right to engage in the activity to anyone who is willing to list his name. He may be charged a fee, either as a registration fee or as a scheme of taxation.

The second level is certification. The governmental agency may certify that an individual has certain skills but may not prevent, in any way, the practice of any occupation using these skills by people who do not have such a certificate. One example is accountancy. In most states, anybody can be an accountant, whether he is a certified public accountant or not, but only those people who have passed a particular test can put the title CPA after their names or can put a sign in their offices saying they are certified public accountants. Certification is frequently only an intermediate stage. . . .

The third stage is licensing proper. This is an arrangement under which one must obtain a license from a recognized authority in order to engage in the occupation. The license is more than a formality. It requires some demonstration of competence or the meeting of some tests ostensibly designed to insure competence, and anyone who does not have a license is not authorized to practice and is subject to a fine or a jail sentence if he does engage in practice.

The question I want to consider is this: Under what circumstances, if any, can we justify the one or the other of these steps? There are three different grounds on which

From Milton Friedman, *Capitalism and Freedom* (Chicago: University of Chicago Press, 1962), Chap. 9, 137–60. Reprinted by permission. © University of Chicago Press.

it seems to me registration can be justified consistently with liberal principles.

First, it may assist in the pursuit of other aims. Let me illustrate. The police are often concerned with acts of violence. After the event, it is desirable to find out who had access to firearms. Before the event, it is desirable to prevent firearms from getting into the hands of people who are likely to use them for criminal purposes. It may assist in the pursuit of this aim to register stores selling firearms. . . .

Second, registration is sometimes a device to facilitate taxation and nothing more. The questions at issue then become whether the particular tax is an appropriate method to raise revenue for financing government services regarded as necessary, and whether registration facilitates the collection of taxes. It may do so either because a tax is imposed on the person who registers, or because the person who registers is used as a tax collector. For example, in collecting a sales tax imposed on various items of consumption, it is necessary to have a register or list of all the places selling goods subject to the tax.

Third, and this is the one possible justification for registration which is close to our main interest, registration may be a means to protect consumers against fraud. In general, liberal principles assign to the state the power to enforce contracts, and fraud involves the violation of a contract. It is, of course, dubious that one should go very far to protect in advance against fraud because of the interference with voluntary contracts involved in doing so. But I do not think that one can rule out on grounds of principle the possibility that there may be certain activities that are so likely to give rise to fraud as to render it desirable to have in advance a list of people known to be pursuing this activity. Perhaps one example along these lines is the registration of taxicab drivers. A taxicab driver picking up a person at night may be in a particularly good position to steal from him. To inhibit such practices, it may be

desirable to have a list of names of people who are engaged in the taxicab business, to give each a number, and to require that this number be put in the cab so that anyone molested need only remember the number of the cab. This involves simply the use of the police power to protect individuals against violence on the part of other individuals and may be the most convenient method of doing so.

Certification is much more difficult to justify. The reason is that this is something the private market generally can do for itself. This problem is the same for products as for people's services. There are private certification agencies in many areas that certify the competence of a person or the quality of a particular product. The *Good Housekeeping* seal is a private certification arrangement. For industrial products there are private testing laboratories that will certify to the quality of a particular product. For consumer products, there are consumer testing agencies . . .

Licensure seems to me still more difficult to justify. It goes still farther in the direction of trenching upon the rights of individuals to enter into voluntary contracts. Nonetheless, there are some justifications given for licensure that the liberal will have to recognize as within his own conception of appropriate government action, though, as always, the advantages have to be weighed against the disadvantages. The main argument that is relevant to a liberal is the existence of neighborhood effects. The simplest and most obvious example is the "incompetent" physician who produces an epidemic. Insofar as he harms only his patient, that is simply a question of voluntary contract and exchange between the patient and his physician. On this score, there is no ground for intervention. However, it can be argued that if the physician treats his patient badly, he may unleash an epidemic that will cause harm to third parties who are not involved in the immediate transaction. In such a case, it is conceivable that everybody, including even the potential patient and physician, would be willing to submit to the restriction of the practice of medicine to "competent" people in order to prevent such epidemics from occurring.

In practice, the major argument given for licensure by its proponents is not this one, which has some appeal to a liberal, but rather a strictly paternalistic argument that has little or no appeal. Individuals, it is said, are incapable of choosing their own servants adequately, their own physician or plumber or barber. In order for a man to choose a physician intelligently, he would have to be a physician himself. Most of us, it is said, are therefore incompetent and we must be protected against our own ignorance. This amounts to saying that we in our capacity as voters must protect ourselves in our capacity as consumers against our own ignorance, by seeing to it that people are not served by incompetent physicians or plumbers or barbers.

So far, I have been listing the arguments for registration, certification, and licensing. In all three cases, it is clear that there are also strong social costs to be set against any of these advantages. . . .

The most obvious social cost is that any one of these measures, whether it be registration, certification, or licensure, almost inevitably becomes a tool in the hands of a special producer group to obtain a monopoly position at the expense of the rest of the public. There is no way to avoid this result. One can devise one or another set of procedural controls designed to avert this outcome, but none is likely to overcome the problem that arises out of the greater concentration of producer than of consumer interest. The people who are most concerned with any such arrangement, who will press most for its enforcement and be most concerned with its administration, will be the people in the particular occupation or trade involved. . . .

Certification is much less harmful in this respect. If the certified "abuse" their special certificates—if, in certifying newcomers, members of the trade impose unnecessarily stringent requirements and reduce the number of practitioners too much—the price differential between certified and non-certified will become sufficiently large to induce the public to use non-certified practitioners. . . .

In consequence, certification without licensure is a half-way house that maintains a good deal of protection against monopolization. It also has its disadvantages, but it is worth noting that the usual arguments for licensure, and in particular the paternalistic arguments, are satisfied almost entirely by certification alone. If the argument is that we are too ignorant to judge good practitioners, all that is needed is to make the relevant information available. If, in full knowledge, we still want to go to someone who is not certified, that is our business; we cannot complain that we did not have the information. Since arguments for licensure made by people who are not members of the occupation can be satisfied so fully by certification, I personally find it difficult to see any case for which licensure rather than certification can be justified.

Even registration has significant social costs. It is an important first step in the direction of a system in which every individual has to carry an identity card, every individual has to inform authorities what he plans to do before he does it. Moreover, as already noted, registration tends to be the first step toward certification and licensure.

Medical Licensure

The medical profession is one in which practice of the profession has for a long time been restricted to people with licenses. Offhand, the question, "Ought we to let incompetent physicians practice?" seems to admit of only a negative answer. But I want to urge that second thought may give pause.

In the first place, licensure is the key to the control that the medical profession can exercise over the number of physicians. To understand why this is so requires some discussion of the structure of the medical profession. The American Medical Association is perhaps the strongest trade union in the United States. The essence of the power of a trade union is its power to restrict the number who may engage in a particular occupation. . . .

The American Medical Association is in this position. It is a trade union that can limit the number of people who can enter. How can it do this? The essential control is at the stage of admission to medical school. The Council on Medical Education and Hospitals of the American Medical Association approves medical schools. In order for a medical school to get and stay on its list of approved schools it has to meet the standards of the Council. The power of the Council has been demonstrated at various times when there has been pressure to reduce numbers. For example, in the 1930s during the depression, the Council on Medical Education and Hospitals wrote a letter to the various medical schools saying the medical schools were admitting more students than could be given the proper kind of training. In the next year or two, every school reduced the number it was admitting, giving very strong presumptive evidence that the recommendation had some effect. . . .

Control over admission to medical school and later licensure enables the profession to limit entry in two ways. The obvious one is simply by turning down many applicants. The less obvious, but probably far more important one, is by establishing standards for admission and licensure that make entry so difficult as to discourage young people from ever trying to get admission. Though most state laws require only two years of college prior to medical school, nearly 100 percent of the entrants have had four years of college. Similarly, medical training proper has been length-

ened, particularly through more stringent internship arrangements. . . .

The rationalization for restriction is . . . that the members of the medical profession want to raise what they regard as the standards of "quality" of the profession. The defect in this rationalization is a common one, and one that is destructive of a proper understanding of the operation of an economic system, namely, the failure to distinguish between technical efficiency and economic efficiency.

A story about lawyers will perhaps illustrate the point. At a meeting of lawyers at which problems of admission were being discussed, a colleague of mine, arguing against restrictive admission standards, used an analogy from the automobile industry. Would it not, he said, be absurd if the automobile industry were to argue that no one should drive a low quality car and therefore that no automobile manufacturer should be permitted to produce a car that did not come up to the Cadillac standard. One member of the audience rose and approved the analogy, saying that, of course, the country cannot afford anything but Cadillac lawyers! This tends to be the professional attitude. The members look solely at technical standards of performance, and argue in effect that we must have only first-rate physicians even if this means that some people get no medical service—though of course they never put it that way. Nonetheless, the view that people should get only the "optimum" medical service always lead to a restrictive policy, a policy that keeps down the number of physicians. . . .

. . . Let me now ask the question: Does licensure have the good effects that it is said to have?

In the first place, does it really raise standards of competence? It is by no means clear that it does raise the standards of competence in the actual practice of the profession for several reasons. In the first place, whenever you establish a block to entry into any field, you establish an incentive to find ways of getting around it, and of course medicine is no exception. The rise of the professions of osteopathy and of chiropractic is not unrelated to the restriction of entry into medicine. On the contrary, each of these represented, to some extent, an attempt to find a way around restriction of entry. Each of these, in turn, is proceeding to get itself licensed, and to impose restrictions. The effect is to create different levels and kinds of practice, to distinguish between what is called medical practice and substitutes such as osteopathy, chiropractic, faith healing and so on. These alternatives may well be of lower quality than medical practice would have been without the restrictions on entry into medicine.

More generally, if the number of physicians is less than it otherwise would be, and if they are all fully occupied, as they generally are, this means that there is a smaller total of medical practice by trained physicians—fewer medical man-hours of practice, as it were. The alternative is untrained practice by somebody; it may and in part must be by people who have no professional qualifications at all. Moreover, the situation is much more extreme. If "medical practice" is to be limited to licensed practitioners, it is necessary to define what medical practice is, and featherbedding is not something that is restricted to the railroads. Under the interpretation of the statutes forbidding unauthorized practice of medicine, many things are restricted to licensed physicians that could perfectly well be done by technicians, and other skilled people who do not have a Cadillac medical training. I am not enough of a technician to list the examples at all fully. I only know that those who have looked into the question say that the tendency is to include in "medical practice" a wider and wider range of activities that could perfectly well be performed by technicians. Trained physicians devote a considerable part of their time to things that might well be done by others. The result

is to reduce drastically the amount of medical care. The relevant average quality of medical care, if one can at all conceive of the concept, cannot be obtained by simply averaging the quality of care that is given; that would be like judging the effectiveness of a medical treatment by considering only the survivors; one must also allow for the fact that the restrictions reduce the amount of care. The result may well be that the average level of competence in a meaningful sense has been reduced by the restrictions.

Even these comments do not go far enough, because they consider the situation at a point in time and do not allow for changes over time. Advances in any science of field often result from the work of one out of a large number of crackpots and quacks and people who have no standing in the profession. In the medical profession, under present circumstances, it is very difficult to engage in research or experimentation unless you are a member of the profession. If you are a member of the profession and want to stay in good standing in the profession, you are seriously limited in the kind of experimentation you can do. A "faith healer" may be just a quack who is imposing himself on credulous patients, but maybe one in a thousand or in many thousands will produce an important improvement in medicine. . . .

When these effects are taken into account, I am myself persuaded that licensure has reduced both the quantity and quality of medical practice; that it has reduced the opportunities available to people who would like to be physicians, forcing them to pursue occupations they regard as less attractive; that it has forced the public to pay more for less satisfactory medical service, and that it has retarded technological development both in medicine itself and in the organization of medical practice. I conclude that licensure should be eliminated as a requirement for the practice of medicine.

When all this is said, many a reader . . . will say, "But still, how else would I get any evidence on the quality of a physician. Granted all that you say about costs, is not licensure the only way of providing the public with some assurance of at least minimum quality?" The answer is partly that people do not now choose physicians by picking names at random from a list of licensed physicians; partly, that a man's ability to pass an examination twenty or thirty years earlier is hardly assurance of quality now: hence, licensure is not now the main or even a major source of assurance of at least minimum quality. But the major answer is very different. It is that the question itself reveals the tyranny of the status quo and the poverty of our imagination in fields in which we are laymen, and even in those in which we have some competence, by comparison with the fertility of the market. Let me illustrate by speculating on how medicine might have developed and what assurances of quality would have emerged, if the profession had not exerted monopoly power.

Suppose that anyone had been free to practice medicine without restriction except for legal and financial responsibility for any harm done to others through fraud and negligence. I conjecture that the whole development of medicine would have been different. The present market for medical care, hampered as it has been, gives some hints of what the difference would have been. Group practice in conjunction with hospitals would have grown enormously. Instead of individual practice plus large institutional hospitals conducted by governments or eleemosynary institutions, there might have developed medical partnerships or corporations—medical teams. These would have provided central diagnostic and treatment facilities, including hospital facilities. Some presumably would have been prepaid, combining in one package present hospital insurance, health insurance, and group medical practice. Others would have charged separate fees for

separate services. And of course, most might have used both methods of payment.

These medical teams—department stores of medicine, if you will—would be intermediaries between the patients and the physician. Being long-lived and immobile, they would have a great interest in establishing a reputation for reliability and quality. For the same reason, consumers would get to know their reputation. They would have the specialized skill to judge the quality of physicians; indeed, they would be the agent of the consumer in doing so, as the department store is now for many a product. In addition, they could organize medical care efficiently, combining medical men of different degrees of skill and training, using technicians with limited training for tasks for which they were suited, and reserving highly skilled and competent specialists for the tasks they alone could perform. The reader can add further flourishes for himself, drawing in part, as I have done, on what now goes on at the leading medical clinics.

Of course, not all medical practice would be done through such teams. Individual private practice would continue, just as the small store with a limited clientele exists alongside the department store, the individual lawyer alongside the great many-partnered firm. Men would establish individual reputations and some patients would prefer the privacy and intimacy of the individual practitioner. Some areas would be too small to be served by medical teams. And so on.

I would not even want to maintain that the medical teams would dominate the field. My aim is only to show by example that there are many alternatives to the present organization of practice. The impossibility of any individual or small group conceiving of all the possibilities, let alone evaluating their merits, is the great argument against central governmental planning and against arrangements such as professional monopolies that limit the possibilities of experimentation. On the other side, the great argument for the market is its tolerance of diversity; its ability to utilize a wide range of special knowledge and capacity.

It renders special groups impotent to prevent experimentation and permits the customers and not the producers to decide what will serve the customers best.

WHY THE ABA BOTHERS: A FUNCTIONAL PERSPECTIVE ON PROFESSIONAL CODES*

Deborah Rhode

The most recent revision of the lawyers' code of ethics is the Model Rules of Professional Conduct, drafted by the Kutak Commission and adopted by the ABA in 1982. Consideration of the Model Rules spawned debate over particular proposals, such as stringent protection of client confidences, and over the desirability of relying on lawyers to regulate lawyers. This selection was part of the larger debate over self-regulation. Rhode argues that interests of the profession—for example, income and image—do not correspond fully to public interests in competence, access to legal services, and the administration of justice.

From the profession's standpoint, codes of ethics are a primary instrument for attaining what Talcott Parsons posited as the dominant goals for any occupation: objective achievement and recognition. Codified standards can generate monetary and psychic benefits by enhancing occupational status and self-image; constraining competition; preserving autonomy; and reconciling client, colleague, and institutional interests. From a societal perspective, however, professional codes are desirable only insofar as they serve common goals to a greater extent than other forms of control, namely market forces or government regulation. For the legal profession, such goals presumably would include promoting the impartial and efficient administration of justice and ensuring competent legal assistance at the lowest possible price.

As the Kutak Commission acknowledges, the regulatory interests of the public and the profession are not always coextensive. Rather, difficult ethical problems arise from conflict between a lawyer's responsibilities to clients, to the legal system and to the lawyer's own interest in remaining an upright person while earning a satisfactory living.[1] Given this concession, it is striking that so little effort is made to justify the bar's arrogation of exclusive authority to resolve such conflicts. In marked contrast to the recently appointed British Royal Commission on Legal Services, which has a majority of laymen, only one of the Kutak Commission's thirteen members is not an attorney. This imbalance between professional and public representation in the drafting phase is exacerbated by a ratification process in which only the views of professionals are systematically solicited, and in which they alone cast the decisive vote. . . .

---

* References deleted and edited without indication.

[1] American Bar Association, *Model Rules of Professional Conduct*, Preamble, p. 2.

Published originally in 59 *Texas Law Review* 689–721 (1981). Copyright 1981 by the *Texas Law Review*. Reprinted by permission.

. . . Neither the Code nor the Model Rules indicate why the bar should proceed as if it were exempt from the natural human tendency to prefer private over public ends. Confronted with conflict between their self-interest and their perception of societal interests, many individuals will attempt to discount or reconstrue the less immediate concern so as to reduce internal tension. Simply through normal processes of dissonance—reduction and acculturation—professionals may lose sensitivity to interests at odds with their own. Nothing in the bar's extended history of self-governance suggests it to be an exception. . . . [B]oth the Code of Professional Responsibility and the Canons of Ethics it replaced consistently resolved conflicts between professional and societal objectives in favor of those doing the resolving. So too, given the political constraints under which the Kutak Commission is operating, one would expect the Model Rules to serve first and foremost the interests of the bar.

Of course, this observation, without more, is neither startling nor especially damning. By choice or inertia, we often delegate responsibility for monitoring professional conduct to private organizations or member-dominated licensing boards. Whether such delegations are prudent depends in large measure on the degree to which public and professional objectives converge. Thus, this [selection] attempts, through a functional overview of the bar's objectives, to lodge them in the context of broader social concerns. . . .

Enhancing Status and Self-Image

A principal function of all professional organizations is to protect their members' economic and psychological stake in public esteem. Codes of ethics are useful insofar as they define a satisfactory self-image and help persuade the general public that practitioners are especially deserving of confidence, respect, and substantial remuneration. Never the best beloved of professionals, lawyers have been particularly preoccupied with enhancing their status.

The profession's preoccupation with status is not confined to rules of etiquette for acquiring clients. It also figures prominently in a variety of other Code prescriptions, such as those governing courtroom decorum, commingling of funds, conflicts of interest, and public service. In general, the Kutak draft either replicates unobjectionable provisions of its antecedents or effects significant improvements. There are, however, two exceptions worth noting.

The first is the Commission's treatment of a problem frequently discussed in the literature on public interest representation: A nominal client's interests may not fully coincide with his attorney's ideological aspirations. Few would contest the Model Rules' general admonition that a lawyer should not accept employment if his personal concerns or responsibilities to third parties might "adversely affect the best interest of the client."[2] Yet this maxim presupposes a monolithic client, whose "best interest" can be readily ascertained and made controlling throughout the course of representation. Such a paradigm is out of step with much public interest advocacy, in which the client is a diffuse class with shifting or divergent preferences that the lawyer must intuit or impute rather than systematically solicit. The reality of test case litigation is that "the client" often enables the attorney to express his views, not the converse. Having failed to confront this fact of life, the Rules may prove unilluminating to those most in need of guidance.

Equally dissatisfying is the Commission's attempt to come to terms with lawyers' pro bono responsibilities. No code of ethics would, of course, be complete without some recognition of its disciples' commitment to good works. Although few members of the public are likely to be aware of, let alone

[2] *Ibid*, Rule 1.7.

impressed by, such testimonials, code rhetoric nonetheless serves a significant expressive function. By codifying their role . . . professionals reinforce their sense of self-importance and entitlement to special status. An ostensibly altruistic involvement in pro bono activity is one of the traditional "signs and symbols" used to distinguish professionals from the laity. Yet it is not necessarily in any individual practitioner's interest that the public service obligation have teeth, particularly if an impression of commitment can be engineered without financial sacrifice. It is to that end that both the Code and the Model Rules evidently aspire.

The current Code offers much admonition but no disciplinary rule regarding pro bono work; Canon 2 contains the relevant void. Initially, the Kutak Commission proposed to replace this reticence with a mandatory requirement. In their original form, the Model Rules required a minimum of forty hours work per annum for no, or reduced, compensation, or the financial equivalent. Considering the modest number of hours proposed and the liberal definition of public interest activities, the contribution envisioned was unlikely to effect major changes in the allocation of legal services. The definition of pro bono services would, for example, have encompassed assistance to relatives in temporarily straitened circumstances or service on bar committees. Indeed, data on lawyers' current pro bono activities suggest that most of the profession could have used their public service contribution to generate remunerative work. Nonetheless, vehement protest quickly convinced the Commission to delete the mandatory minimum and to substitute an annual reporting requirement. When this compromise proved unacceptable, the Commission retreated to a purely hortatory formulation similar to that presently in effect.

. . . Finally, codes of ethics enhance status in two additional ways that deserve at least passing reference. . . . Specifying minimum standards permits the bar to oust individuals whose conduct jeopardizes the standing of the profession as a whole. And, in a more subtle but equally significant sense, codification fosters self-esteem by rationalizing a convenient definition of the professional's moral role. On the whole, the Kutak draft perpetuates a vision of attorneys as technicians, whose assistance "does not constitute an endorsement of the client's political, economic, social or moral views or activities."[3] This codification of "role-differentiated morality" affords an expedient escape from contexts of ethical complexity.[4] For the attorney unsettled by involvement in activities of dubious social value, the Model Rules offer reassurance; legal representation should not be denied to those whose "cause is controversial or the subject of popular disapproval."[5]

Yet, lest this disclaimer of responsibility either grate unduly on those practitioners who do exercise moral choice, or contribute to the lawyer's already tarnished image, the Kutak draft temporizes somewhat. If a client "insists upon pursuing an objective that the lawyer considers repugnant or imprudent, the lawyer may withdraw if doing so can be accomplished without material adverse effect on the interests of the client. . . ."[6] Of course, it may well be that such equivocation also serves a useful social function by reinforcing individuals willing to defend social pariahs, as well as those desiring some congruence between their own and their clients' objectives. Still, from the profession's point of view, a more congenial compromise is difficult to envision. In general, a lawyer asked to espouse a morally distasteful cause is neither damned if he does, nor damned if he doesn't.

[3] *Ibid.*, Rule 1.2(b), reprinted in Appendix II.
[4] Wasserstrom, "Lawyers as Professionals."
[5] Model Rules, *op. cit.*, Rule 1.2, Comment [3], (see Appendix II).
[6] American Bar Association, *Model Rules of Professional Conduct*, Proposed Final Rule, 1.2(c). Rule 1.2(c), as it was finally adopted, is reprinted in Appendix II.

Constraining Competition

A principal force animating any occupation's efforts at self-regulation is a desire to minimize competition from both internal and outside sources. . . . Although the last decade has witnessed some infusion of a capitalist ethos into bar policies on advertising, solicitation, minimum fees, and group legal services, the profession's response has been generally grudging. Neither the Commission nor local bar associations have supported innovations that would significantly facilitate comparison shopping by consumers, such as directories with standardized information concerning attorney's fees, qualifications, and previous client complaints.

To be sure, the Model Rules . . . are less rabidly protectionist than their precursors. Not only has the Commission loosened restrictions on advertising and solicitation, it has dropped entirely the limitations on group legal services. However, ABA members responsible for these revisions disproportionately represent the elite of the profession, which is least threatened by the rivalry that such reforms could encourage. And, as previously noted, the Rules can be amended by individual states, and will be construed by local enforcement committees, many of whose members have displayed little support for Commission proposals. It strains credulity to believe that these committees, with all the features of trade associations, will behave otherwise when confronted with issues involving competition. Thus, the Commission's unwillingness to address the structural defects of a regulatory system controlled by the regulated makes significant liberalization unlikely. So long as the bar's self-governance structure remains unchanged, the best one can reasonably expect is a policy somewhat tempered by the fear of outside intrusion if protectionist sentiment becomes too overt. . . .

Reconciling Client, Colleague, and Institutional Interests

In any system of justice, particularly one whose central premise is combative, participants must share a common understanding of the ground rules that constrain their partisanship. Some restraints on advocates' ability to delay, distort, or circumvent basic objectives of the legal system are essential to maintaining its efficacy and legitimacy. Yet, by definition, an adversarial structure also limits the extent to which partisans can be made responsible for the consequences of their advocacy. Such a system depends on clients' continued willingness to repose trust and confidence in attorneys whom they employ for assistance rather than censure.

In large measure, lawyers' status and autonomy are tied to client, colleague, and public perceptions about the quality of justice they help generate. Accordingly, a primary function of ethical codes is to reconcile the sometimes competing interests of these three constituencies. A good deal of discussion has focused on the merits of various accommodations proposed by the Kutak draft concerning attorneys' obligations of candor, confidentiality, and zealous representation. That debate need not be recounted here. Rather, the following discussion seeks only to highlight one point that has been somewhat obscured throughout the controversy. Although the disputants generally frame their arguments in terms of client or societal interests, lawyers' own status and security are very much at issue in rules governing relationships within the adversary system. Even if the bar does not enforce such rules through disciplinary proceedings, attorneys nonetheless have a tangible stake in their content.

To take an obvious example, compliance with prohibitions on misrepresentation in negotiations, unfounded pleadings, and subordination of perjury can facilitate collegial relationships. These rules may also promote the appearance and reality of justice, both of which ultimately redound to the benefit of the profession. The difficulty, of course, is that it may not always be advantageous for any particular member to abide by such constrains. "Cheap rider" problems make ethical codes particularly vulnerable to erosion. There are insufficient rewards not only for adhering to code provisions, but also for reporting violations. How many individuals wish to incur the stigma and possible retaliation that attend informing on their colleagues, when any ensuing advantages will accrue only to the profession as a whole? Given this incentive structure, it is not surprising that attorneys have proved highly reluctant to report misconduct in litigation or negotiations.

. . . Yet . . . it does not follow from the absence of formal enforcement that code precepts lack "instrumental" significance. . . . [T]here has been little empirical investigation regarding compliance with professional standards, particularly among elite lawyers. . . . [O]ne need not conclude that the subsequent promulgation of the Code of Professional Responsibility and its inclusion in law school curricula and bar examinations have played no role in professional socialization.

Rather, even those ethical requirements unlikely to give rise to formal disciplinary proceedings could prove significant in several respects. By clarifying standards and sensitizing individuals to the full ethical dimensions of their conduct, codes of conduct may induce greater peer pressure and self-restraint. To the extent that such rules express shared values, compliance can occur through internalization of common norms. More rigorous standards, such as the Model Rules' prohibition of pleadings without good grounds (as compared with the Code's injunction against claims intended merely to harass), thus may have some salutary effect, simply by narrowing

attorneys' capacity for self-delusion about the propriety of a given action.

In addition, codes can help lawyers resist overreaching by third parties. An attorney reluctant to invoke only his own moral intuitions in challenging a client's or supervising lawyer's directives might find that code provisions afford more politic means of registering objections. Prohibitions on dilatory pleadings, subornation of perjury, or misrepresentations in negotiation can function as defense mechanisms for attorneys who want neither to exude arrogance before clients and superiors, nor to jeopardize their self-esteem or standing in the eyes of judges and other colleagues.

Finally, code formulations may assume instrumental importance through judicial decree. Notwithstanding its express disclaimer, the Code of Professional Responsibility has been employed to set standards of conduct in both civil and criminal contexts. As the organized bar is acutely aware, the Kutak draft could well suffer a similar fate, despite its protestations to the contrary. Provisions governing frivolous pleadings might, for example, be incorporated in state court rules whose violation would trigger sanctions against the responsible attorney. Or . . . the Model Rules' restrictions on suborning client perjury could prove persuasive to trial and appellate courts. And there is always the possibility that some tribunal will deem certain violations of the Model Rules a sufficient predicate for imposing civil liability.

Maintaining Autonomy

From a sociological vantage, one distinguishing feature of a profession is its autonomy. Correspondingly, one significant function of a professional code is to perpetuate that status. As the Kutak draft pointedly notes, "[t]o the extent that lawyers meet the obligations of their professional calling, the occasion for governmental regulation is obviated."[7] Codes of ethics can preempt such regulation in two ways: by persuading the public that the profession has itself adopted appropriate standards of conduct, and by generating sufficient enforcement activity to convey at least an impression of adequate self-governance.

Undoubtedly, the uncongenial prospect of external interference has figured prominently in the drafting of many of the Model Rules discussed earlier, particularly those concerning advertising, disclosure of client fraud, and public service obligations. The spectre of intrusion looms still larger in areas more directly affecting public satisfaction with lawyers' services. Since most consumer complaints concern competence, neglect, and fees, those issues require special attention if professional autonomy is to be maintained. The challenge for code draftsmen is to frame standards sufficient to stave off public protest without, as one bar committee suggests, simultaneously "invit[ing] a disciplinary proceeding or a malpractice suit."[8] In both respects, the Kutak Commission has achieved modest success.

On their face, the Model Rules governing competence, delay, and billing practices seem well calculated to defuse consumer criticism. Lawyers must charge "reasonable" fees,[9] keep a client "reasonably informed,"[10] act with "reasonable promptness and diligence,"[11] and provide the "legal knowledge, skill, thoroughness, preparation, and efficiency reasonably necessary"[12] in representing particular clients. Of course, formulations at this level of generality are always open to charges. . . . But it is instructive to note how rarely such criticisms are coupled with more precise alternatives. Considering the highly variegated contexts

in which the Model Rules will apply, recourse to some "weasel words" is surely defensible. What is problematic about the current draft is less its level of abstraction than its occasional descent into qualifying particulars and its failure to address deficiencies in the structure through which standards are (or more accurately, are not) enforced.

Perhaps in an effort to allay professional anxieties, the Commission's Commentary adds several caveats that significantly relax requirements that the Model Rules purport to prescribe. For example, obligations to inform a client depend on the extent to which the lawyer believes his client is able "to participate intelligently in decisions concerning the objectives of the representation."[13] And even an inexperienced lawyer may provide "adequate representation in a wholly novel field through intensive study," presumably at the client's expense.[14] Of course, some allowance must be made for start-up costs among the uninitiated. Less obvious is whether clients should bear those costs absent informed consent, a consideration on which the Model Rules are notably silent. Moreover, the presence of qualifying commentary has done little to reassure certain vocal segments of the bar. Since it is lawyers, not clients, who cast the determinative votes, the final format of the Kutak draft may well replicate a pattern frequently encountered in the current Code: What the Rules giveth, the Commentary taketh away.

Even more unsettling is the Kutak draft's disinclination to confront the difficulties of implementing quality controls under current market and disciplinary structures. . . . [T]here are substantial imperfections in the market for legal services. Few buyers can accurately evaluate lawyers' performance either before or after purchase, and channels of communication between consumers remain rudimentary. These information

---

[7] Model Rules, *op. cit.*, Preamble, p. 2.
[8] Report of the Special Committee of the New Jersey State Bar Association to Review the [ABA] Rules of Professional Conduct, April 7, 1980, p. 3.
[9] Model Rules, *op. cit.*, Rule 1.5(a) (see Appendix II).
[10] *Ibid.*, Rule 1.4(a) (see Appendix II).
[11] *Ibid.*, Rule 1.3.
[12] *Ibid.*, Rule 1.1 (see Appendix II).
[13] *Ibid.*, Rule 1.4, Comment [1] (see Appendix II).
[14] *Ibid.*, Rule 1.1, Comment [2] (see Appendix II).

barriers, coupled with high transaction costs and stringent proof requirements, also render malpractice litigation an unsuitable vehicle for redressing most client grievances. As a result, professional self-governance constitutes the primary means of enforcing cost and quality standards. Both the bar's sorry performance in this regard, and the Commission's failure to acknowledge it, are deeply troubling.

Notwithstanding its avowed commitment, the bar's membership has displayed little enthusiasm for the practical aspects of implementing professional standards. Attorneys are understandably reluctant to invest the time necessary to convince themselves that a colleague's competence, diligence, or fees warrant official scrutiny. Even those with ready access to inculpatory evidence appear disinclined to cast the first stone; only a small fraction of bar disciplinary actions arise from lawyers' complaints.

Perhaps in recognition of these constraints, the Model Rules relax the Code's unqualified requirement that attorneys report any misconduct. The current Kutak draft imposes such obligations only where an ethical violation raises a "substantial question as to that lawyer's honesty, trustworthiness, or fitness as a lawyer in other respects. . . ."[15] As to what constitutes a "substantial question," the Commentary is not particularly forthcoming. Lawyers are to use "a measure of judgment . . . in complying with the provisions of this Rule. The term 'substantial' refers to the seriousness of the possible offense and not to the quantum of evidence of which the lawyer is aware."[16] The draftsmen provide no clues to the meaning of "seriousness," beyond the implication that it is synonymous with "substantial."

Objections to the laxity of this standard are understandable but probably pointless. A more stringent alternative would, like its analogue in the current Code, remain unenforced and unenforceable. Those who find the current formulation inexacting could as easily denounce a more rigorous requirement as unrealistic and hence hypocritical. A different, and potentially more fruitful, approach would call for institutionalized self-monitoring, such as arbitration and systematic peer review procedures. Yet these possibilities receive only the most tepid support from the Commission. The Rules advise simply that "*if* a system of peer review has been established, a lawyer should *consider* making use of it in appropriate circumstances."[17] Similarly, "*if* a procedure has been established for resolution of fee disputes . . . the lawyer should *conscientiously consider* submitting to it."[18]

Still less enthusiasm is displayed for modifying the bar's current disciplinary structure despite its obvious deficiencies. Protecting the inept, a tradition common to most professions, has always enjoyed a devoted following in bar disciplinary committees. Even when misconduct is reported, all but the most egregious code violations remain uninvestigated or unpunished. In 1978 there were 30,836 "complaints or other information brought to the attention of a disciplinary agency in which a file was opened," but only 626 incidents of "public discipline" (2%) and 124 disbarments (0.4%). A survey of disciplinary screening procedures in California, Illinois, Michigan, and New York City revealed that between ninety-one and ninety-seven percent of complaints were dismissed with no investigation. In short, every major study of bar disciplinary agencies has found them grossly unresponsive both to serious misfeasance and to garden-variety consumer complaints about the cost and quality of services. Yet the Commission contents itself with citing the studies, rather than confronting their conclusions. So long as dis-

---

15 *Ibid.*, Rule 8.3.
16 *Ibid.*, Rule 8.3, Comment.

17 *Ibid.*, Rule 1.1, Comment [6].
18 *Ibid.*, Rule 1.5, Comment [5].

ciplinary proceedings remain firmly under professional control, substantial improvement is unlikely. However, the Commission evidently conceives its mission as preempting rather than inviting lay involvement in the regulatory enterprise. As a result, the Kutak draft provides no meaningful approach to the problem of implementing its own standards. . . .

Conclusion

In a celebrated history of the profession prepared under ABA auspices, Roscoe Pound reassured his sponsor that it was not, after all, "the same sort of thing as a retail grocers' association."[19] If he was right, it was almost certainly for the wrong reasons. Lawyers no less than grocers are animated by parochial concerns. What distinguishes professionals is their relative success in packaging occupational interests as societal imperatives. In that regard, codes of ethics have proved highly useful. Seldom, of course, are such documents baldly self-serving; it is not to a profession's long-term advantage that it appear insensitive to the common good. But neither are any profession's own encyclicals likely to incorporate public policies that might significantly compromise members' status, monopoly, working relationships, or autonomy.

In part, the problem is one of tunnel vision. Without doubt, most lawyers—including those on the Kutak Commission—are committed to improving the legal system in which they work. What *is* open to doubt is whether a body of rules drafted, approved, and administered solely by at-

torneys is the most effective way of realizing that commitment. No matter how well-intentioned and well-informed, lawyers regulating lawyers cannot escape the economic, psychological, and political constraints of their position. If, as one Commission member readily acknowledges, the bar's past regulatory endeavors have foundered on self-interest and self-deception, what justifies attorneys' continued resistance to any external oversight? By abjuring outside interference, professionals can readily become victims of their own insularity, losing perspective on the points at which fraternal and societal objectives diverge. No ethical code formulated under such hermetic constraints can be expected to make an enduring social contribution. The Model Rules are no exception.

To effect significant improvements in the quality, cost, and delivery of legal services, the bar must accept fundamental changes in its regulatory structure. Anointing a few laymen to serve on drafting commissions or disciplinary committees will not suffice. As experience with token representation in other contexts makes clear, such cosmetic gestures serve more to legitimate than to affect the decisions of professionally controlled regulatory systems. Rather, structural deficiencies in the bar's present governance system mandate reforms offering nonprofessionals more than a supporting role. Lacking a constituency intent on such reforms, the Kutak Commission has proposed none. This is not, of course, to suggest that the recodification enterprise was meaningless from the profession's point of view. Quite the contrary, it is obvious why the ABA bothers. What remains is to convince the public to do likewise.

[19] Roscoe Pound, "The Causes of Popular Dissatisfaction with the Legal Profession," *ABA Reporter*, Vol. 29 (1906), p. 395.

AN OVERVIEW OF STATE MEDICAL DISCIPLINE

Richard P. Kusserow, Elizabeth A. Handley, and Mark R. Yessian

Can the traditional self-regulatory organizations in the health professions take the tough disciplinary stances that seem likely to reduce malpractice rates or to address the concerns of consumer groups? This selection discusses the limits of self-regulation in the medical profession. Boards charged with disciplining healthcare professionals are overworked, have limited investigatory resources and powers, and face reluctance on the part of professionals to report misconduct by their peers. The authors argue that the resources of regulatory boards must be increased and that practitioners must be required to report misconduct and must be protected from liability if they do. The authors are from the U.S. Department of Health and Human Services, and they urge federal and interstate cooperation in cases of misconduct by healthcare professionals.

In the two decades following the advent of the Medicare program, we have observed state medical boards undergoing great change. Their responsibilities have expanded tremendously from the licensure and discipline of physicians to include a growing number of other health care professionals such as nurses, podiatrists, physician assistants, physical therapists, and emergency medical technicians. Additionally, consumer awareness has grown with a concomitant rise in consumer reporting to state boards. These factors have resulted in an increasing work load.

Boards are increasingly strained to handle the growing disciplinary work load before them. It is not uncommon for them to have backlogs of hundreds of cases pending assignment while investigators are weighted down with active caseloads of 60 to 70 or more cases. Board officials offered a number of factors that have contributed to this. Not only must they regulate more professions, they must also deal with a rising number of cases due to an increase in consumer complaints, more active law enforcement involving physicians, and mandated reporting of malpractice cases in some states.

LITTLE RISE IN BOARD RESOURCES

In response to their expanded responsibilities and work loads, nearly all states have been raising their fees in recent years. In most states, medical board revenues derive entirely from fees imposed on physicians. Two thirds of this fee income comes from renewal fees paid by licensed physicians. The remainder is from fees charged to those seeking licensure on the basis of a license held in another state or endorsement of a certificate received from the National Board of Medical Examiners. Boards are typically part of the state budget process and subject to the same budgetary and personnel controls as other state agencies.

Renewal fees, usually good for two to three years, have increased from an average annual level of about $31 in 1979 to $51 in 1985. (These data were obtained from annual reviews done by the American Medical Association and from a state-by-state survey conducted by the Office of Inspector General.) However, they have barely kept pace with inflation. Moreover, many state boards are not necessarily allowed to spend all the money they collect from fees. Instead, this money goes into

From Richard P. Kusserow, et al., "An Overview of State Medical Discipline," *Journal of the American Medical Association*, 257:6 (Feb. 13, 1987), 820–24.

the state's general revenue funds.

Severe budgetary constraints are precluding boards from enhancing the number or quality of investigators and from taking better advantage of computer technology that could improve their productivity. Laborious and costly procedures geared to quieter times, long since past, contribute to the time and complexity of internal review and due process hearings.

Combined, these factors leave boards in an extremely vulnerable position, with investigatory and administrative resources well below the level necessary to handle the job before them effectively. Thus, although medical licensure and discipline is about a $50 million a year enterprise, many board officials feel as though they can make only limited progress in improving their licensing and disciplining performance. (This estimate is based on a 50-state survey done by the Office of Inspector General.)

INSPECTOR GENERAL'S ROLE

In the last few years, the involvement of the Office of Inspector General of the US Department of Health and Human Services (DHHS) in a number of activities made it increasingly aware of the limitations within which state medical boards were operating. The Inspector General is charged by law with the responsibility of policing the Medicare and Medicaid programs for fraud and abuse.

From the scandals involving fraudulent medical credentials from two Caribbean medical schools, it became apparent that the credentials verification capabilities of most states might be seriously flawed. Because of the Office of Inspector General's role in prosecuting criminal cases and imposing exclusions on hundreds of health care providers, it was also clear that communication between those in a position to witness unprofessional practice and those with the authority to do something about it was inadequate. In many cases, information about practitioners with recurrent cases of misbehavior or malpractice never reached medical boards.

The Office of Inspector General became aware of loopholes through which poor health care providers could slip. Many physicians under investigation would voluntarily surrender their licenses in one state and then would continue practicing medicine by moving to another state where they also had a license. Under current law, the Office of Inspector General found that it had no authority to exclude these physicians from Medicare and Medicaid participation except in the state in which the license had been initially revoked or suspended. . . .

OTHER FORCES INFLUENCING BOARDS

Boards have had to contend with increased work loads and responsibilities without a concomitant real increase in resources. There are several other significant factors that have played a role in states' abilities to license and discipline physicians. . . .

CHANGED PUBLIC PERCEPTION AND MALPRACTICE

In recent years, public perception about the adequacy of board disciplinary actions has shifted. Newspaper exposés have berated boards for not better protecting the public. Headlines scream "Doctor Sued 14 Times, But No State Hearing," (*Chicago Tribune*, May 10, 1982, p. 1) and "Doctors Practice While Wheels Turn" (*Detroit Free Press'* examination was a particularly extensive one. It led to a seven-part report published between April 1 and 8, 1984.) This has placed a lot of pressure on boards to examine their practices.

The editor of the *New England Journal of medicine*, Arnold S. Relman, M.D., expressed this view in a March 1985 editorial: "All the evidence suggests that most if not all the States have been too lax—not too strict—in their enforcement of medical professional standards."

The public is also frustrated with the length of time that due process takes, and blames boards for "dragging their feet" on cases. As one high-level official noted, "The public perceives that bad doctors shouldn't be practicing medicine, but we must give these doctors due process. Not everyone understands this."

Physicians' status in society has also been eroding, partially as a result of the liability crisis as it relates to malpractice claims. Many Americans' view of physicians has shifted from reverence to questioning. Indeed, a large number of patients who feel they have been wronged by physicians have been willing to litigate in increasing numbers, with higher dollar awards made by courts and the skyrocketing cost of liability insurance. All of this has put renewed pressure on state medical boards to "weed out" bad doctors. . . .

STATE BOARDS' RESPONSE

State boards have reacted to burgeoning work loads and pressures. Recently, states have strengthened the investigatory powers of boards (for instance, the granting of subpoena powers); expanded their disciplinary authorities (most notably, the authorization to immediately suspend physicians posing a "clear and present danger" to the public); widened their access to disciplinary actions taken in other places (through mandatory reporting laws); and broadened the grounds on which they can take disciplinary action.

Incidence of Disciplinary Actions

Over the past few years, the number of disciplinary actions taken against physicians has been increasing. National tabulations made by the FSMB [Federation of State Medical Boards] reveal an increase of 62%

in actions (excluding simple administrative actions), from 953 in 1982 to 1540 in 1984. . . .

However . . . the most serious actions such as revocations, suspensions, and probations, have not grown nearly as much as the other actions, increasing only slightly from 600 in 1982 to 788 in 1984. This has occurred despite the fact that approximately 15,000 to 20,000 new physicians enter practice each year. . . . Unfortunately, it has also masked many serious cases and has permitted many physicians to continue practicing who would otherwise have lost their licenses.

Types of Violations

The inappropriate writing of prescriptions is by far the most common violation on which disciplinary actions are based, accounting for about one half of all actions taken by state boards. These are serious matters involving not only excessive or unnecessary prescribing of drugs to patients, but also unlawful distribution to drug addicts. They are also the easiest kinds of cases for investigators to develop, especially in states with triplicate prescription laws.

The second major type of violation is the self-abuse of drugs and/or alcohol. In most states, this category is expanding, both in absolute and proportionate terms. Together with overprescribing, it accounts for three fourths or more of all disciplinary actions.

Throughout the nation, programs designed to help impaired physicians have been expanding and receiving increased attention. Typically these programs are run by medical societies or other private organizations. While the exact approaches vary, they generally involve group sessions, signed agreements stipulating the terms of participation, and periodic monitoring to ensure that participating physicians are adhering to the agreements. Some programs, such as the one in Oregon, stress inpatient care, while others focus on outpatient treatment.

While these programs have been generally well received, they have met with some criticism and skepticism. Some interested parties are concerned about physicians being treated too sympathetically for behavior that can be harmful to their patients. The result in some states has been a tightening of monitoring practices and a closer examination of the responsibilities these programs have to report violations to the boards. Since a substantial number of physicians have enrolled in these programs voluntarily (without any board involvement), the issue of reporting violations to the boards has become an especially sensitive one because physicians signed up with the understanding that their participation would be confidential.

The minimal response in the area of physician incompetency is placing boards in an increasingly untenable position as the incidence of malpractice cases and public concern about the implications of these cases increase. As noted before, it is increasingly believed that boards can and should do something about this situation.

Why, then, the minimal response to date? At least three factors seem to be involved: (1) the complexity, length, and cost of cases concerning alleged incompetence, even where a malpractice judgment has been rendered; (2) the substantial burden of proof that tends to call for "clear and convincing" evidence rather than the "preponderance of evidence"; and (3) the considerable variations among physicians themselves about what constitutes acceptable practice in many facets of medicine.

Yet in the course of addressing rising malpractice costs, some states are taking initiatives that could prove to be consequential. Particularly noteworthy are two amendments Wisconsin made in 1985 to its medical practice act. One allows for a court finding of physician negligence in patient care to serve as conclusive evidence that a physician is guilty of negligence of

treatment. This frees the board from the need to hold a probable cause hearing in such cases. Another more significant amendment provides the board with a lesser burden of proof in disciplinary proceedings, one that calls for a "preponderance of evidence" rather than "clear and convincing evidence."

Also of note are laws in California and Oregon that authorize boards to compel a physician to take a clinical competency examination if there is reasonable cause to believe that his or her skill level is inadequate. The California effort allows a physician two chances to pass an oral examination conducted by a panel of two physicians. The Oregon effort, under way for a number of years, may involve oral or written examinations, but generally employs the latter because they offer a firmer legal basis for subsequently denying a license or imposing discipline.

Source of Disciplinary Actions

Earlier we mentioned that during the past few years, the number of consumer complaints received by boards has been rising, often quite substantially. The greater visibility of boards and the establishment of toll-free complaint lines in some states have contributed to this development.

These consumer complaints, together with information provided by government agencies (mainly law enforcement agencies), account for most of the disciplinary actions eventually taken by boards. Strikingly few such actions first come to a board's attention as a result of referrals from those who would most naturally make referrals and who are the most qualified to make referrals—medical societies, PROs, health care institutions, and individual health care professionals. The reason for this seems mostly to stem from a lack of an affirmative legal duty to report individuals and from the fear of being sued for reporting someone. . . .

CONCLUSION AND RECOMMENDATIONS

We have shown how boards have been confronted with increased work loads, inadequate financial support, and many conflicting pressures. Yet, their ability to act as necessary is predicated on their resource level. Accordingly, we believe physician license renewal fees should be set at a level sufficient to support expansion and improvement of the enforcement activities of the boards. . . . These fees should be dedicated to board activities and not be diverted to general revenue funds. At the end of 1985, the average annual renewal fee rose to $51, a level that barely kept pace with inflation in the 1980s.

Of the issues previously addressed, the boards' inability to help abate the flood of malpractice cases is the most troublesome. In recent years, the small increases in funding made available to boards have often been made with the expectation that boards would help stem the tidal wave of cases. Some of the recent initiatives have been noted; however, without doubt, the public's expectations have been rising much faster than boards have been able to respond.

Medical malpractice that is not rectified is a twofold problem for American society. Clearly, the safety and well-being of patients seeking medical care is threatened when incompetent physicians remain in practice—however large or small their numbers. (We believe that the current level of litigation overrepresents the number of physicians who perform negligently. Not all physicians who are sued for malpractice are guilty of negligence or misconduct, in our opinion. However, it is important to eliminate poor practitioners through disciplinary action, whenever possible.) Additionally, all patients pay higher prices due to the escalating cost of premiums and awards and the defensive medicine practiced to minimize the likelihood of successful malpractice suits. Many observers also believe that incompetent physicians also unnecessarily add billions of dollars annually to the nation's health expenditures. . . .

For boards to play an important part in addressing this problem, it is clear that there must be substantial changes in the legal ground rules governing their handling of malpractice cases. The fear of being sued has had a chilling effect on reporting of incompetence. Perhaps states should consider ways to limit the liability of those making good-faith referrals at the same time that they create affirmative legal duties to report professional misconduct or incompetency. No less clear than the chilling effect of potential litigation is the fact that the resources available to boards must be increased. At present, most boards lack sufficient resources to devote serious attention to such cases without jeopardizing their other disciplinary and licensing responsibilities. We are hopeful that an increase in renewal fees, which boards are allowed to keep, could help eliminate this problem.

We in the federal government can provide some help in improving medical discipline efforts without undermining the central state role in this arena. One form of assistance we can provide is to assure more affirmative action within our own domain. That is, we can help ensure that PROs and Medicare carriers provide more extensive and timely reporting to state medical boards of cases involving physician misconduct or incompetence.

THE ENGINEER AND BUSINESS*

Edwin T. Layton, Jr.

Engineers apply science to the development of products and technologies, and work for organizations large enough to support their research. The growth of industrialization and large-scale corporations has been the chief factor shaping the engineering profession. Major engineering societies have been heavily influenced by business. Engineering codes of ethics emphasize obligations to employers and have been slow to incorporate concerns of social responsibility or rights of employed engineers, such as protection for whistle-blowers. This selection is from Layton's classic historical study of the engineering profession, which depicts efforts by engineers to come to terms with professionalism and to escape business domination.

The engineer is both a scientist and a businessman. Engineering is a scientific profession, yet the test of the engineer's work lies not in the laboratory, but in the marketplace. The claims of science and business have pulled the engineer, at times, in opposing directions. Indeed, one outside observer, Thorstein Veblen, assumed that an irrepressible conflict between science and business would thrust the engineer into the role of social revolutionary.

While nothing like a soviet of engineers has appeared, the tensions between science and business have been among the most important forces shaping the engineer's role on the job, in his professional relations, and in the community at large. Veblen assumed that science and business made mutually exclusive demands on the engineer; in fact, however, they often complement one another. Both, for example, may benefit from technological progress. Nor is the existence of tensions necessarily detrimental to engineering work: Attempting to resolve them may account for some of the engineer's drive and creativity.

Despite his mordant irony, Veblen was, in one sense, an optimist; he assumed that the tensions between business and science were resolvable, if only through a cata-

* Footnotes have been deleted without indication.

clysmic destruction of the former by the latter. In this he missed the essence of the engineer's dilemma which is, at base, bureaucracy, not capitalism. The engineer's problem has centered on a conflict between professional independence and bureaucratic loyalty, rather than between workmanlike and predatory instincts. Engineers are unlikely to become revolutionaries because such a role would violate the elitist premises of professionalism and because revolution would not eliminate the underlying source of difficulty. The engineer would still be a bureaucrat. Tensions with business have been dominant because in the American context economic development has been carried out principally through the agencies of private capitalism. But engineers in government have experienced quite analogous conflicts, if anything more severe than those of privately employed engineers; and it can be argued that the market system, in providing a final test acceptable to both the engineer and his employer, has served to buffer discord between the two. Perhaps the engineer's problem ultimately is marginality: He is expected to be both a scientist and a businessman, but he is neither. A social revolution would merely alter the terms of his marginality without ending it.

From Edwin T. Layton, Jr. *The Revolt of the Engineers*, 2d ed. (Baltimore: Johns Hopkins University Press, 1986), pp. 1–9. Reprinted by permission.

The engineer's relation to bureaucracy is not new; he is the original organization man. The scientifically trained, professional engineer has characteristically appeared on the technical scene at the point of transition from small to large organizations. Economically, it makes little sense for small enterprises to employ engineers; the gains are not worth the costs. Large corporations, on the other hand, can more readily support engineers and research establishments, since they represent a small percentage of their total costs. Large corporations can get substantial net returns from rather small percentage gains in efficiency. Where large investments are at stake, the engineer can serve a useful function in eliminating guesswork and minimizing risks. Technically, large works are more likely to involve complexities than are small ones; and the larger the project, the more likely it is that such difficulties will transcend the capabilities of artisans and businessmen.

In the eighteenth and through much of the nineteenth century, America developed quite diverse and advanced technologies without requiring a corps of scientifically trained experts. The Mississippi River steamboat, for example, was developed in an era of relatively small, highly competitive enterprise by the cut-and-try methods of the practical mechanic, rather than by the rational analysis of scientists. It was large-scale organizations, such as the navy and private corporations, that supported experts who could approach the steam engine through the laws of thermodynamics. Similarly, it was not the small ironmasters who first called on the aid of science, but the corporate giants of the post–Civil War era. From the start, engineers have been associated with large-scale enterprises.

There were two stages in the emergence of the engineering profession in America in the nineteenth century. The first demand for engineers came from the construction of large public works, such as canals and railroads, particularly in the period 1816 to 1850. The organizations that undertook these works were pioneers in technology and were also among the largest enterprises in America, representing aggregations of capital that were huge for their day. The civil engineering profession was called into being to meet the technical needs of these organizations.

In 1816, the engineering profession scarcely existed in America. It has been estimated that there were only about thirty engineers or quasi-engineers then available; but by 1850, when the census first took note of this new profession, there were 2,000 civil engineers. Canal and railroad construction generated not only the demand for engineers but, in large measure, the supply as well. From an early stage, organizations employing engineers found it convenient to group their technical staffs into a hierarchy of chief engineer, resident engineers, assistant engineers, and the like. Within this bureaucratic context, regular patterns of recruitment and training emerged on the job, and early engineering projects like the Erie Canal and the Baltimore and Ohio Railroad became famous as training schools for engineers.

The rising demand for engineers by industry began the second stage in the emergence of the engineering profession. The golden age for the application of science to American industry came from 1880 to 1920, a period which also witnessed the rise of large industrial corporations. In these forty years, the engineering profession increased by almost 2,000 percent, from 7,000 to 136,000 members. The civil engineer was overshadowed by the new technical specialists who emerged to meet the needs of industry: by the mining, metallurgical, mechanical, electrical, and chemical engineers. The astonishing growth of engineering continued, though at a less rapid rate, after 1920. In 1930, there were 226,000 engineers when the depression put a brake on expansion; by 1940, the number was but little higher—260,000. Postwar prosperity increased the size of the profession past the half-million mark in 1950, and to over 800,000 by 1960. Engineering is by far the largest of the new professions called forth by the industrial revolution.

The rise of the engineering profession was accompanied by a scientific revolution in technology. The change was not a sudden one; in most cases engineering built upon and extended traditional techniques. But professionalism was associated with a slow incorporation of scientific methods and theory into technology and the accumulation of an esoteric body of technical knowledge. Professionalism was a means of preserving, transmitting, and increasing this knowledge. The transition from traditional rule-of-thumb methods to scientific rationality constitutes a change as momentous in its long-term implications as the industrial revolution itself.

The development of engineering education constitutes a sensitive indicator of the shift from art to science in technology. The early civil engineers were educated by self-study and on-the-job training. Only a minority received a college degree. By 1870, there were twenty-one engineering colleges, but only 866 degrees had been conferred. College education became increasingly common after 1870. By 1896, there were 110 engineering colleges. The number of students increased rapidly, from 1,000 in 1890 to 10,000 in 1900. Only with the twentieth century, however, did the college diploma become the normal means of admission to engineering practice.

College training was a sign of a greater emphasis on science. But even here the change was evolutionary. The engineering curriculum of the latter nineteenth century placed as much or more emphasis on craft skills as upon scientific training. . . . Despite an increasing emphasis on science, engineering educators down to 1920 seriously debated whether engineering students ought to learn the calculus. Some of them thought such courses were "cultural"

embellishments to the curriculum. Only since the end of the Second World War has the balance in engineering education shifted unequivocally toward science.

The origin of engineers carries with it built-in tensions between the bureaucratic loyalty demanded by employers and the independence implicit in professionalism. It is important to note, however, that these tensions are not, as Veblen thought, the outgrowth of a clash between the rationality of science and the irrationality of capitalism. The scientific knowledge possessed by the engineer is highly rational, but his professionalism derives from the mere possession of esoteric knowledge, not its specific content. Incomprehensibility to laymen, rather than rationality, is the foundation of professionalism. In essence, the professional values adopted by American engineers are the same as those of other professions. They may be summarized under the headings of autonomy, collegial control of professional work, and social responsibility.

Perhaps the most invariant demand by all professions is for autonomy. The classic argument is that outsiders are unable to judge or control professional work, since it involves esoteric knowledge they do not understand. Autonomy operates on at least two distinct levels: It applies to engineers in their corporate sense as an organized profession and to the individual engineer in relation to his employer. In both cases, conflicts have appeared between business demands and the ideal of professional independence. Businessmen usually concede that engineering societies should be free of external control, but in practice business domination is not uncommon. Employers have been unwilling to grant autonomy to their employees, even in principle. They have assumed that the engineer, like any other employee, should take orders. Some engineers, however, have maintained that the engineer, like the doctor, should prescribe the course to be followed and that the very essence of professionalism lies in not taking orders from an employer. The employer, of course, has the power to reward and punish. But the value of the engineer generally hinges on his being a professional in the sense of being both a master of an ever-growing body of knowledge and a creative contributor to that knowledge. Such men are the ones most likely to be inspired by professional ideals. As a result, the role of the engineer represents a patchwork of compromises between professional ideals and business demands.

The argument for collegial control of professional work is closely related to that for autonomy. Since professional work cannot be understood fully by outsiders, the person in charge of such work should be a member of the profession. In this manner, doctors have insisted that the heads of hospitals and medical schools should be members of the medical profession. In the same vein, engineers have mantained that engineers should be in charge of engineering work. In practice, engineering departments are usually headed by engineers. But in the case of engineering, this principle can be extended much further. Engineering is intimately related to fundamental choices of policy made by the organizations employing engineers. This can lead to the assertion that engineers ought to be placed in command of the large organizations, public and private, which direct engineering. This is tantamount to saying that society should be ruled by engineers. A more representative manifestation of the ideal of collegial control has been the repeated demand by the profession for reform of governmental public-works policy. Engineers have advocated the creation of a cabinet-level department of engineering to be headed by a civilian engineer.

Although the arguments for autonomy and collegial control are fundamentally similar, one of the basic dilemmas of modern engineers has been that these two goals are not completely compatible. Organizations like the federal government or a modern corporation have other ends in view than the best and most efficient engineering. Doctors are in a more fortunate position, since it may be assumed that the professional aim—health—is identical to the ends of the large organizations employing doctors, such as hospitals and medical schools. But unlike medicine, engineering serves purposes ulterior to itself. Collegial control of engineering implies, in the extreme, a change in basic social values, to make those of engineering supreme. Such aspirations open up the possibility that outside organizations might reciprocally seek to control engineering, as something potentially dangerous to their purposes.

Professional freedom implies social responsibility. The professional man has a special responsibility to see that his knowledge is used for the benefit of the community. Social responsibility points in two directions: inwardly, at self-policing to prevent abuses by colleagues, and outwardly, to the making of public policy. In either case, it is with social responsibility that professionalism comes most clearly into conflict with bureaucracy. This may be seen in two possible meanings of the term "responsibility." On the one hand, there is the bureaucratic sense implied in the phrase "responsible public official." This denotes responsibility in executing policies, but not necessarily in formulating them. On the other hand, the term "professional responsibility" entails an independent determination of policy by the professional man, based on esoteric knowledge and guided by a sense of public duty. An assertion of professional responsibility, therefore, may signify a rejection of bureaucratic authority. In this manner, the scientists' crusade against the May-Johnson Bill for postwar control of atomic energy was both an assertion of a professional responsibility and a rebellion against General Groves and the formal hierarchy of the Manhattan Project.

For engineers, the most overt element of professionalism has been an obsessive concern for social status. Although the income and the power of engineers would of course be enhanced by professionalism, these ends have been given second place, at least verbally. Professionalism has induced engineers to seek greater deference, in particular, to gain the same social recognition accorded to the traditional learned professions, law and medicine. Spokesmen for the engineering profession have, in fact, frequently made status the fundamental aim, and other professional values means to this end. Thus, engineers have argued that in order to gain more status their profession should show a greater sense of social responsibility.

Although engineers emphasize the importance of status, it is not clear that this distinguishes their goals from those of other interest groups. Engineers differ from nonprofessional groups chiefly in that they are more likely to rationalize their ambitions in terms of protecting the public. Following the cue of the older professions, engineers have secured the enactment of licensing laws, and they have endeavored to raise standards in education and practice. Such measures enable professions to limit competition and alter supply-and-demand relationships in their favor. Engineers have hoped to achieve in this way many of the same goals sought by labor unions through such devices as the closed shop and strike. Professional autonomy and control of the profession's work by colleagues, if fully realized, would lead to control of the conditions of work, an end pursued equally, if by other means, by labor unions. As an interest-group strategy, professionalism offers several advantages. It is "dignified," since the professional abjures "selfish" behavior, at least verbally, and gains group advantage on the pretext of protecting the public. Professionals emphasize the intimacy of the personal relationship with clients, rather than the cash nexus between buyer and seller, employer and employee.

Professionalism for engineers is not exclusively a matter of esoteric knowledge.

Engineers do not seek autonomy simply because they are professionals; to some extent they have adopted professionalism as a way of gaining autonomy. Professionalism was, in part, a reaction against organization and bureaucracy. It was a way to prevent engineers from becoming mere cogs in a vast industrial machine. . . .

Professionalism carries overtones of elitism that grate against the egalitarian assumptions of American democracy. Professionalism stresses hierarchy and the importance of the expert; its emphasis is on the creative few, rather than on the many. But professionalism, not itself democratic, may serve democratic ends. It is one means of preserving the ideal of the autonomous individual, without which democracy could scarcely exist. Democracy requires not only freedom, but an informed public opinion. One of the problems of the modern age is that many issues of public policy involve technical matters. Independent and informed judgments of these questions are badly needed by the public. Professionalism, because of its stress on social responsibility, offers one way of meeting this need by establishing a legitimate role for private judgment by engineers, protected and encouraged by an organized profession.

Whether the emphasis be on esoteric knowledge, public service, or selfish interest, professionalism requires that engineers identify themselves with their profession. Engineers must think of themselves as engineers before they can constitute a profession. There are several factors that link engineers together as a group and encourage self-consciousness. As with all professions, the fundamental tie is a common body of knowledge. Self-interest is another powerful cohesive force. Both find a natural focus in the professional society, which brings engineers together and gives them a sense of corporate identity. These factors have helped to produce a steady push toward professionalism among engineers.

Professionalism, however, has met powerful resistance from business. Business has been reluctant to grant independence to employees. The claims of professionals rest fundamentally on esoteric knowledge; to reduce the importance of this knowledge is to weaken the engineers' aspirations for autonomy. To some extent this may take the form of a depreciation of "theory" and an emphasis on practicality. But if businessmen tend to depreciate esoteric knowledge, they cannot wish it away. Experts have been of increasing, not diminishing importance. A more pervasive and effective argument is the priority of business needs over technical considerations. This contention is not without force. The transition from art to science in engineering has been slow and partial. Even where technical knowledge has achieved a high state of perfection, its importance is limited by the exigencies of business. Engineers work in complex organizations. Engineering is only one factor among many that contribute to their success.

In the long run, the most effective check on professionalism by business has been a career line that carries most engineers eventually into management. The promise of a lucrative career in business does much to ensure the loyalty of the engineering staff. Conversely, it undermines engineers' identification with their profession. Social mobility carries with it an alternative set of values associated with the businessman's ideology of individualism. These values compete with, and to some degree conflict with, those of professionalism. Thus, professionals stress the importance of expert knowledge, but businessmen stress the role of personal characteristics, such as loyalty, drive, initiative, and hard work. Professions value lifetime dedication. But business makes engineering a phase in a successful career rather than a career in itself. . . .

The selectivity in recruitment of engineering students from middle-class, small-town, and old-stock families goes far to account for the profession's strong commitment to traditional individualism. . . . A frequent theme in discussions of success in engineering is the importance of an "inner drive," or an "inner urge," or more simply of initiative. It is perhaps no accident that the term "rugged individualism" was given currency by an engineer, Herbert Hoover. But predisposition to individualism also provides the foundations for the development of a commitment to business.

Engineering education is susceptible to business influence in a number of ways. Businessmen serve as trustees of colleges, on alumni boards, and on committees of technical societies concerned with technical education. Engineering educators suffer from the same divided loyalties as other engineers, and some of them have been important spokesmen for a business point of view. Many businessmen, and some engineering educators, have assumed that the buyer, business, has the right to determine both the technical skills to be taught and the ideas to be implanted in students' minds.
. . .

Most engineers work in industrial bureaucracies, which are capable of exerting a considerable amount of pressure on the individual. The effectiveness of this influence is heightened when the individual seeks not only to keep his job, but to rise in the hierarchy. The price of success, in at least some cases, is total and undivided loyalty. . . .

Conformist pressures on the job are not limited to company loyalty; they extend to all sorts of social and political norms. . . . Pressure appears to be especially great against heterodox ideas. . . .

Employers have occasionally urged engineers to show more social responsibility. But by this they generally have in mind the defense of business, rather than independent action by the profession. Engineering support for business is often taken for granted. . . .

The final phase of the engineer's development, not achieved by all, is the transition from professional engineering to business management. . . . It is not uncommon for engineers who have risen into managerial positions to think of themselves as businessmen. John Mills, a discerning observer of his profession, noted that as engineers climb into supervisory positions, they tend to be blinded by visions of future promotions and to lose sight of colleagues lower down. Although many such men no longer think of themselves as engineers, they may retain professional-society membership for business reasons. But professional commitment is clearly diminished. Others sever their ties with engineering completely. The 1960 census, which relied on the self-identifications of respondents for occupations, counted 541,000 engineers and scientists in manufacturing, the bulk of whom were engineers. A follow-up survey by the National Science Foundation discovered an additional 73,000 technically qualified persons who had been missed because they had identified themselves with nontechnical occupations, presumably managerial.

A number of engineers have looked to the major professional associations to offset the power of business. . . .

[However] engineers who have risen into top management present a dilemma for engineering societies. Although it has been generally conceded that engineers engaged in technical management are still engineers, this is far from clear in the case of those who have gone up the corporate hierarchy to positions involving general management and administration. Some engineers have argued that such men are no more practicing their profession than a lawyer in a similar position is practicing his. This argument implies that such men should be excluded from the higher grades of membership of engineering societies and, hence, from effective control of their profession. Other engineers have taken a contrary position. They have maintained

that the engineer in top management has fulfilled the engineer's cherished ideal of success and that even those who have lost any active interest in technical matters should be encouraged to join engineering societies and participate in their government. . . .

Censorship is made more effective by the codes of ethics adopted by some societies. These codes may prohibit criticism of fellow engineers and the discussion of engineering subjects in the general press. These codes of ethics are seldom enforced, so the sanction is perhaps limited. But it is not trivial, either. In order to circumvent the restriction on publication outside the society, Frederick W. Taylor had one of his works privately printed and gave a free copy to each member of the American Society of Mechanical Engineers prior to general circulation. This expedient, however, was available only to those with considerable means. . . .

In many matters, such as censorship, engineers who hold managerial positions have been the principal agents of business influence in engineering societies. But they are by no means the only source of business power within the profession. Even if such men were excluded from the higher grades of membership—a favorite remedy for some reformers—business influence would remain substantial. Virtually all American engineering societies are financially dependent on business. This is clearest in those smaller societies that have company members; here the subsidy is direct. Other engineering societies are nominally supported solely by the dues of members. But in fact, they receive indirect financial support from business. A substantial number of members have their dues paid by their employers. A survey in 1947 revealed that, in the sample studied, some 30 percent of the employers regularly paid the dues of some of their employees in certain societies. In 1940, a spokesman for the membership committee of the American Institute of Mining Engineers complained that qualified men were not joining the institute because they were waiting for their employers to pay their dues; he found it necessary to remind them that membership in the institute was a personal matter.

To some extent business influence is checked by the power of majority rule. But engineering societies are not perfectly functioning democracies, and there are serious limitations to the control that rank-and-file members can exercise. Some societies long denied younger members the right to vote; even without formal restrictions on voting, the idea of a hierarchy of professional excellence implicit in membership grades tends to give power to the senior full members and to deny significant influence to junior members. In certain specific instances, employers have canvassed their technical staffs to line-up votes on particular issues. But more commonly, widespread ignorance and apathy give inordinate power to comparatively small minorities. Most members live in remote parts of the country and are little interested in society affairs. Nominations are controlled by committees whose actions are usually shrouded in secrecy; the election presents a mere formality.

It is considered bad form to publicize the inner workings of engineering societies. Even in those rare cases where elections have been contested, both parties have usually taken precautions to keep the real issues secret. In 1914, Morris L. Cooke led a revolt against excessive dominance of the American Society of Mechanical Engineers by the utilities. His election to the society's governing board was opposed by a rival candidate put up by the utility interests. Not only did no mention of this appear in the ASME's official publications, but it was deliberately obscured in the informal circulars distributed by both sides. . . .

Perhaps the most influential committees of engineering societies are those concerned with publications. Such committees can control the publication of technical papers, censor heretical opinions, or silence proposals that might embarrass particular business interests. The electric utilities have been especially active and successful in this respect. Their power in the American Institute of Electrical Engineers led to a prohibition of papers dealing with costs and rate making. According to Governor Pinchot of Pennsylvania, this practice seriously hampered the efforts of public agencies to regulate utilities.

A second form of indirect business subsidy is that of employers paying traveling expenses and allowing time off for employees to attend engineering-society meetings, especially when presenting a paper, serving on a committee, or participating in a discussion.

Business subsidies pose a delicate problem for engineers. Some societies have openly admitted the practice and defended it. *Mechanical Engineering* urged employers to look on engineering-society activities of an employee as an "assignment" . . . A further problem here is that "pure" professional organizations, such as the NSPE, do not publish technical papers. It would be financially impossible for them to do so, even if employers would permit publication of papers by their employees by an organization outside their influence.

Although there are significant areas of conflict between business and professionalism, the dimensions of the clash should not be exaggerated. Neither could exist under present circumstances without the other. Modern business needs highly esoteric technical knowledge, and only professionals can supply it. Technologists need organizations in order to apply their knowledge; unlike science, technology cannot exist for its own sake. The problem has been to find suitable mechanisms of balance and accommodation. One of the basic problems of American engineers is that the balance has tended to shift too far in the direction of business, and accommodation has taken place largely on terms laid down by employers. The professional independence of engineers has been drastically curtailed. The losers are not just engineers. The public would benefit greatly from the unbiased evaluations of technical matters that

an independent profession could provide. American business too might profit in the long run from the presence of a loyal opposition.

A CODE OF ETHICS FOR PUBLIC ADMINISTRATION?*

Ralph Chandler

Public administration is not a self-regulating profession. Instead, public administrators are governed by statute or government regulation. In this selection, Chandler analyzes the case for and against an ethics code for public administrators. Chandler's discussion raises issues common to the professions, such as the desirability of moralizing, and issues more particular to public administration, such as involvement in the policy process. The National Council of the American Society for Public Administration approved a code of ethics in March 1985; it appears in Appendix II.

The ethics debate in American public administration has centered in recent months on a proposed code of ethics for the American Society for Public Administration (ASPA). Is a code desirable? Can the language of a code possibly comprehend the diversity of the field and the complexity of the problems of moral reasoning? The National Council of ASPA has said no and adopted a statement of principles in lieu of a code of ethics in late 1981, doing so on recommendation of its Professional Standards and Ethics Committee. Thus, ASPA remains one of the "few" professional associations without a code of ethics. It continues to operate on the margins of a professional development continuum which includes systematic theory, clientele-recognized authority, community sanction, professional culture, and a code regulating the relations of professionals with clients and colleagues. Without joining the debate within ASPA's infrastructure about why a particular code was rejected, we might offer some analysis of

* Footnotes have been deleted without indication.

why codes of ethics are in disrepute among many, but why others believe a code is highly appropriate at this juncture of American administrative history.

Arguments Against a Code of Ethics

The first argument against a code of ethics is that we should resist moralizing as a practical matter. We live in the residue of the implicit but clearly understood American tradition that liberty is the first principle of the republic, with prosperity close behind. If the framers had allowed the Presbyterians to take us too far into a discussion of the public good, the result would probably have been the kind of regimentation, ordering, and indoctrination that might have worked in Geneva and the Massachusetts Bay Colony, but was not preferred in New York and Virginia. Theocracy was out, not because the framers were immoral, but because a self-consciously moral society would have to put duties first and relegate rights and every-

From Ralph Chandler, "A Code of Ethics for Public Administration?" *Public Administration Review* 43-1 (Jan./Feb. 1983), 32-38. Reprinted by permission.

thing else that is private to a subordinate place in the life of the republic. It was clear to Publius in *The Federalist* as well as in the debates of the Constitutional Convention, that political liberty and economic energy unavoidably engender some immorality, but that government can control it without the institutional consequences of preaching and being preached to. The tradition of American public administration came to be that we ought to live with a moderate degree of immorality and condemn the occasional self-righteous moralist who forgets that men and women are not angels. The tradition has served us well.

Another reason some of us are less than enthusiastic about a code of ethics is that our pathfinders periodically celebrate the unique virtues of consensus building and proceduralism in American society. By this line of reasoning, the lack of stated public purpose is one of the nation's fundamental strengths, because throughout our national history continuing redefinitions of purpose and compromise of principle have allowed us to make the incremental changes necessary for political stability. They have also permitted us to flourish at once as a republic and as an empire, as a constitutionally limited federal state governed by law and as an unlimited unitary state with expanded economic and territorial ambitions. Proceduralism is necessary because in a pluralist pressure system an article of faith must be that from the clash of opposites, contraries, extremes, and poles will come not the victory of any one, but the mediation and accommodation of all. Truth, unity, and especially morality can never be forged from one ideal form. They must be hammered out on the anvil of debate. Thus necessity has become a virtue in public administration, and consensus is built around the agreement to agree on nothing substantive. Assent is given not to value, but to value default. The irony of the proceduralist position, of course, is that as the need for shared values in an increasingly factionalized and anomic society

grows, adversaries who no longer find in their disagreements a basis for common norms are transformed from adversaries into enemies.

A third reason which helps to explain our discomfort with a code of ethics is the lingering influence of both Woodrow Wilson and Max Weber. Wilson maintained that administration stands apart. . . . It follows that where there is no discretion there is no moral responsibility. Weber also spoke of "the bureaucratic machine" in which the honor of the civil servant is vested in his or her ability to execute conscientiously the order of superior authorities. Thus Weber's administrator considers it moral to avoid morality, with the result that the organization in which he or she serves becomes incapable of determining how its power should be used. The organization schools itself in moral illiteracy and the administrator becomes the victim of his or her own success. . . .

There are many other arguments against a code of ethics. Although some of us would be uncomfortable with the comparison, a large number of American public administrators agree with the prophet Jeremiah that the laws of right behavior are written on one's heart, not on paper. Others think that professional organizations such as ASPA are too diverse for a code to apply to all parts of it, and that, since an ethics code is largely unenforceable anyway, we should not have one. Still others resist what they call the overly moralistic and preachy language of ethics codes in general, which raises for these critics the specter of the profession caving in to the moral majority.

Arguments for a Code of Ethics

The first argument *for* a code might be called the argument from objectivism. To take objectivism seriously, however, or indeed to take seriously any of the affirmative arguments, one probably must agree . . . that administrative discourse at any level of sophistication frequently resolves itself into problems of political theory. This is a difficult saying for pluralists and proceduralists, because they tend to take as an article of faith that the process of arriving at consensus is ultimately more important than both theory and the substance of any words agreed upon. Nevertheless, as long as the letterhead of the American Society for Public Administration says it exists to advance the science and art, as well as the processes, of public administration, the analysis of thought and language becomes more than a frivolous exercise.

Objectivism refers to the ancient debate in philosophy about transcendent values. It posits a center of value external to human collectivities. . . . In a code of ethics it typically is reflected in such phrases as "public morality," "the sovereignty of the people," and in references to the law. Objectivism is best understood in comparison to its opposite, subjectivism, which holds that the center of value is somewhere in the human condition. Subjectivism is represented in such concepts as humanism, happiness, and "the dignity of man." . . . Subjectivists tend to reject "public morality," for example, as a self-contradictory term. They translate "the sovereignty of the people" into "the best interests of the public," and they change *the* law, which has no objective existence, into *laws*, which are culturally determined. Thus morally transcendent ideas become ethically relative ones.

Objectivists maintain that ontological ethics invite the administrator to be ethical, because they encourage him or her to make choices and judgments and to pursue actions. Actions are the predicates of being. Unless one assumes the risks attendant on them, he or she vacates the ethical arena. Objectivist codes therefore frequently employ active transitive verbs rather than intransitive verbs of being. Note the verbs "fight," "revere," "obey," "incite," "strive," "quicken," and "transmit" in one of the best-known of the objectivist codes.

The Athenian Oath

We will never bring disgrace to this our city
by any act of dishonesty or cowardice,
nor ever desert our suffering comrades in
the ranks;

We will fight for the ideals and the sacred
things of the city,
both alone and with many;

We will revere and obey the city's laws and
do our best to incite to a like respect and
reverence
those who are prone to annul or set them
at naught;

We will strive unceasingly to quicken
the public sense of public duty;

That thus, in all these ways, we will transmit
this city
not only not less, but greater, better and
more beautiful
than it was transmitted to us.

The Athenian Oath also illustrates the second argument for a code of ethics. It is the argument from community. In this view, moral behavior in public administration is not just a matter of private preferences and personal integrity. The determination of what is a gift and what is a bribe rests with the giver as well as the receiver. Judgments about right and wrong are community decisions as well as private ones. The community is the arbiter of what is ethical. The communal "we," with its varied implications of personalized ownership, is strikingly apparent in the Athenian Oath and in other codes. . . . Proponents of a code argue that the self-interestedness of relativism represents a loss of paradigm, and with it a loss of a sense of community. There cannot be a paradigm without a community.

A third argument advanced for a code of ethics is the argument from courage. . . . Courage holds up idealism in a field where the practice of *realpolitik* reflects our true learnings that human life is characterized by a little more or a little less justice, and a little more or a little less equity. Theologian Reinhold Neibuhr has told us why impossible ideals are nevertheless relevant: They function prophetically. They demand the best, while they expose "the impotence and corruption of human nature." Sin-talk is admittedly old-fashioned, restrictive, and somewhat embarrassing, but if this is the only reason that the parlance of idealism is rejected, we also put ourselves out of touch with a rich classical tradition which sought for moral unity and a higher law in conversation that has little to do with sin. . . .

PROFESSIONAL-ETHICS INSTRUCTION IN TEACHER EDUCATION

John Martin Rich

Like public administration, the teaching profession does not self-regulate. Teachers are subject to the laws of their jurisdictions and to rules set by their employers. These standards may impose significant limits even on personal behavior, particularly for public school teachers. As a whole, however, the teaching profession has constructed little common ethical ground. Regulation of university faculty, preschool teachers, and private-school teachers is largely left up to individual employers. In this selection, Rich argues for the addition of training in ethics to teacher education programs.

In sharp contrast to increased courses in medical, legal, and business ethics, few teacher education programs provide a systematic study of professional ethics, although teachers will be held fully accountable for observing ethical behavior. Most professions show an ethical violation rate of 10 to 20 percent of their membership a year, and educators are no exception.

But why should teacher education assume more responsibility for professional ethics? It may be claimed that professional ethics are not primarily the responsibility of teacher education. Classroom teachers are largely regulated by local school boards, although the National Education Association (NEA) has, since 1929, promulgated its code of ethics. But if professional ethics are lax, the teaching profession is ultimately damaged, students are hurt, and the public interest is ill-served. If teacher education had a greater role in professional ethics, initial ethical problems could be observed in preservice programs rather than expecting local administrators and/or the NEA to deal with most infractions.

Since teacher educators assume responsibility for developing teacher competence, one necessary condition is to observe ethical principles. Without high standards of professional ethics, it is doubtful that teaching could ever be regarded as a full-fledged profession or that parents would want to entrust their children to teachers.

It might also be claimed that professional ethics are already being handled satisfactorily in teacher education. While it is true that the [NEA] has disseminated its code of ethics widely, that alone is insufficient to assure ethical behavior, which is more complex than following the rules of a code, also involving learning to think, act, and acquire the attitudes of a professional teacher and to be guided by one's own philosophy of education. It is necessary for the prospective teacher to adopt relevant ethical principles, understand the grounds for holding them, and practice

From John Martin Rich, "Professional Ethics Instruction in Teacher Education," *The Education Digest* 51 (1986): 44–46. Reprinted by permission.

applying them in daily situations. It is rare that a systematic understanding of ethics can be gained with the press of daily classroom problems. There is little evidence, in contrast to business ethics, that such a systematic study is currently being provided in teacher education programs; and, in contrast to medical ethics, the ethics-in-education literature is slight.

Overloaded Programs?

Finally, it might be argued that teacher education programs are already overloaded, and no place is available for professional ethics. There is no denying that many programs require students to carry a full load each semester, and the number of electives and options is usually not large. But as programs solidify over time, vested interests arise and faculty members react adversely to any changes that might endanger those interests. Thus, after all faculty viewpoints are presented in open discussion, needed changes may have to be left in the hands of administrators or any faculty members who can view the program as a whole more dispassionately.

What forms of knowledge and types of experiences should preservice teachers have in professional ethics? Beginning teachers need to know the nature of a profession, the extent to which education is a profession, what it means to be a professional educator, and the roles that professional ethics serve in professions generally and in education in particular. They should thoroughly familiarize themselves with the NEA code of ethics and with other pertinent codes. Students' questions should be elicited about the application of rules and

standards of the various codes before examining the principles that underlie the codes. Since the principles are usually tacit, it would be the instructor's task to uncover and fully develop their meaning and application.

Also to be considered are problems of developing, disseminating, interpreting, implementing, and enforcing ethical codes. Explored here would be the areas of self-regulation and autonomy, the role of institutions, professional organizations, and lay bodies in enforcement.

Ethical problems that arise out of classroom situations should be a focal point of study. These problems include academic freedom, the ethical use of tests and testing, student dishonesty, the student's freedom to learn, and the student's right to privacy.

Professional Relations

Beginning teachers should also investigate relations with colleagues and education officials. Studied are ethical issues raised by such topics as the recruitment of teachers, their evaluation, tenure practices, nepotism rules, retirement policies, and ethical issues involving faculty dissent, strikes, and disobedience to institutional policies.

The beginning teacher should also understand community expectations and teacher rights. This area concerns the teacher's rights and responsibilities as a citizen, community misconduct and the grounds for dismissal, teachers' relations with parents, the holding of public office, and conflicts over employment and outside income.

IN BUSINESS TO TREAT CANCER

Robin Marantz Henig

One of the most extensively regulated areas of research in the world today is research involving human subjects. In the United States, new pharmaceuticals and medical devices cannot be marketed without data from controlled clinical trials. These trials must meet stringent standards protecting the human subjects involved in them: For example, the benefits of the research must outweigh the risks, subjects must give fully informed consent, and selection of subjects must be equitable. Although recent amendments in FDA regulations now permit manufacturers to charge patients for experimental drugs, manufacturers must base charges on costs and may not profit from the experimentation. Biotherapeutics Inc., a private, for-profit cancer research center, is not covered by the current federal regulations, unless it wishes to obtain permission to market any of the substances it develops.

Sitting in her Jefferson, La., home, Dale Armand mused on the cancer that had plagued her for seven years. Diagnosed as having breast cancer in 1979, she had undergone a single mastectomy and two years of chemotherapy at the M.D. Anderson Hospital and Tumor Institute of the University of Texas, in Houston, a leading institution for cancer research and therapy.

"We thought the cancer was all gone," recalled Ms. Armand, a 40-year-old mother of three children. "But two years ago, I got sick again. I thought it was the flu—that's what it felt like." She returned to Houston, where doctors discovered that the cancer had spread. "They didn't give me any hope whatsoever," she said.

Instead of yielding to the dire prognosis, Ms. Armand went home and—on the advice of her sister, who is a physician, and a local oncologist—eventually found her way to Franklin, Tenn. There, in September 1985, doctors removed one of her cancerous ovaries, and with the tumor cells from it began to develop a new treatment for her. The experimental therapy utilizes monoclonal antibodies, biological agents drawn from the patient's own immune system and created by genetic engineering.

. . . The monoclonals, it is hoped, will attack Ms. Armand's cancerous cells without harming healthy cells, as chemotherapeutic drugs do.

But perhaps more dramatic than the substance being used on Dale Armand's cancer is the way she is obtaining it. Most patients receive experimental therapies, such as monoclonal antibodies, by signing up to be research subjects at the National Institutes of Health (NIH), a federal research institution in Bethesda, Md., or at facilities around the country financed by the NIH. Others are treated with experimental drugs, often donated by pharmaceutical manufacturers, at academic medical centers, such as the Memorial Sloan-Kettering Cancer Center in New York City. Regardless of their circumstances, the patients receive the treatment free; in return, they assume risks associated with blind studies, in which some patients receive placebos, others compounds of which the side effects, complications—even efficacy—are unknown.

Dale Armand looked into the possibility of receiving monoclonal therapy through the traditional route. But she was told, she says, that the National Cancer Institute (NCI), one of the NIH's 12 institutes, "would not be doing breast cancer for 10 years."

So Ms. Armand went another route, to a research facility whose patrons are not the federal government or major research institutions, but the patients themselves.

She sought out treatment at Biotherapeutics Inc., a small, private, for-profit cancer research center that opened early last year and is the only such enterprise within the continental United States. Her family is paying for her experimental therapy. The monoclonal antibody treatment is expected to cost $35,000—not counting the expense of several weeks of hospitalization to receive it.

After a year of laboratory development, Dale Armand's treatment began Sept. 8. "I'm determined not to die," she said, "and my family's not ready to have me go."

Because of the unusual way Dale Armand and more than 150 other cancer patients are underwriting their own cancer treatment and research at Biotherapeutics, the company is currently the topic of heated debate in medical circles. Biotherapeutics' mere existence has raised the question of whether it is ethical for human subjects to pay for the often-risky research on them. Another issue is whether it is fair to limit certain state-of-the-art treatment only to those who can afford the enormous out-of-pocket expense. As Dr. Bruce Chabner, director of the division of cancer treatment of the NCI, puts it: "You can't buy high-quality research. You get high-quality research by coming to high-quality research institutions. It's not something you can purchase."

In addition, biological cancer therapies are so highly experimental that evidence of their efficacy is still spotty, at best. And Biotherapeutics is so new that it has no track record in treating patients and, of course, no claims to success in curing cancer. The company keeps monthly tabs on the amount spent for research on each patient, and its declared policy is to repay the unused portion if the patient dies or is removed from treatment before all the money is spent. Most patients pay the entire amount up front, although installment-payment options exist. Approximately 40 to 50 patients are awaiting treatment at any given time; about one-third of those whom Biotherapeutics prepares to treat die before therapy can begin—because of the advanced state of their disease.

Then there are issues relating to the quality of the research and the therapy. Quality-control mechanisms, such as peer evaluation of research-grant proposals and publication in juried medical journals, may be missing in fee-for-service research. In addition, traditional research requires that potential subjects meet strict criteria regarding type of cancer, prior treatment, age and other health and life-style variables that could affect the outcome of a study. If the primary criterion for a patient's admission to a study is the ability to pay, the results might be considered scientifically suspect.

The most significant question being asked by medical researchers is whether the free flow of scientific information will be interrupted if research becomes a profit-making enterprise. Will the scientists conducting this research be willing to publicize their failures, or even their successes, through the traditional mechanisms of scientific meetings and professional journals?

Despite the controversy surrounding Biotherapeutics, investors, among others, seem to believe in the organization. The company went public on the over-the-counter market last June 17, opening at $11 a share, doubling in price by the close of trading that day. In early November, its stock was trading at around $20. With budget cutbacks forcing the government to limit the scope and number of its research grants, for-profit companies like Biotherapeutics may be one example of what the future holds for medical research.

Biotherapeutics operates out of a low brick building just off the highway that connects Franklin to Nashville, half an hour

away. Prominently displayed in the hall-
ways are architects' plans for two new facilities that are to house laboratories, offices and a clinic for the Biological Therapy
Institute, a clinical research organization
associated with Biotherapeutics.

"Cancer research was like a pie, with
everyone trying to get their own piece,"
says Dr. Robert K. Oldham, the boyish-
looking 45-year-old founder and scientific
director of Biotherapeutics. "What we did
was create a new pie. As a small for-profit
research organization, we have access to
capital, an ability to expand, and a chance
to respond to market needs that are unique
in the research enterprise."

A 1968 graduate of the University of
Missouri medical school, Dr. Oldham
worked as a research scientist at the [NCI]
in Maryland. In 1975, he was hired by
Vanderbilt University in Nashville to establish a division of oncology at its medical
school; he directed the program for five
years while living in nearby Franklin, a
quaint town of about 15,000 residents.

In 1980, Dr. Oldham returned to the
NCI to start the biological response mod-
ifiers program, to conduct research into
emerging biological alternatives to highly
toxic chemotherapeutic drugs.

Shortly after his second NCI stint, Dr.
Oldham began to develop a plan for a
private company. "I had worked in the
government, I had worked in a university,
and I could see that the patients weren't
being served as well as they could be by
either system," Dr. Oldham recalls. "Neither delivers the technology that is available."

Dr. Eugene Nakfoor, a retired physician
from Lansing, Mich., was one cancer sufferer who felt ill-served by the conventional
system. Dr. Nakfoor, 63, has had lymphoma—cancer of the lymphatic system—
since 1983. For a year, he received radiation treatment in Lansing and chemotherapy at the University of Wisconsin at Madison, one of numerous cancer centers across

the country that are considered on the
cutting edge of cancer research and therapy, and which receive NCI support.

By the spring of 1985, Dr. Nakfoor's
condition was worsening. He wanted to try
a new method—monoclonal antibodies. He
talked to several centers doing government
research on the use of monoclonals in
treating lymphoma, "but their grants were
to treat localized lymphoma, and mine was
diffused," he recalls. Dr. Nakfoor had run
smack into a dilemma often met by people
suffering from cancers not easily susceptible to traditional treatments. "You have
to have exactly what they're studying," he
says, "or they cannot help you."

One of the physicians Dr. Nakfoor called
suggested he talk to Dr. Oldham. "My first
impression of Oldham was extremely favorable," says Dr. Nakfoor. "But the idea
of paying for my own research bothered
me." He says he felt guilty about buying
a chance at recovery that others could not
afford.

Nevertheless, Dr. Nakfoor took out a
loan, sold off some real estate to pay it
back, and signed on with Biotherapeutics
in June 1985. He paid the company a fee
of $35,000 to treat him with monoclonal
antibodies.

"Even though I'm not in the terminal
stages, I've got an incurable illness that will
get worse month by month," says Dr. Nakfoor, who spent his career as a family doctor and emergency-room physician. "It suits
me much better to go for the experimental
therapy, to go for something that just might
beat it, than to do nothing." Dr. Nakfoor
began his monoclonal antibody treatment
in mid-September.

Not every patient finds it as easy to sign
on with Biotherapeutics as Eugene Nakfoor
did. It's not enough simply to be able to
pay up front; the patient must have a cancer that has not responded to conventional
therapy, or one for which conventional
therapy is known not to be effective. And
there are other criteria for patient admis-

sion, although they may differ from those guiding NIH-sponsored research institutions. Especially in the monoclonal program—one of several experimental treatments now being offered by Biotherapeutics—a patient must have a reasonably good prognosis, because it takes about 12 months to develop the antibody. This means a patient must be, on the one hand, healthy enough to wait for the treatment to be ready, yet on the other hand sick enough to have exhausted all other medical options—a problem that exists with government-sponsored monoclonal-antibody research as well.

"Of 100 calls that come in because of referrals or publicity, only about 25 are medically and financially qualified," says April Brasher, a former director of patient services at Biotherapeutics (she has since left to attend medical school). "And for every 25 who would be brought down here for evaluation," only about five or six actually sign on with Biotherapeutics as contract patients.

Biotherapeutics offers four contract packages. The first is a basic, six-month tumor acquisition, processing and preservation (TAPP) program. The $2,750 TAPP contract pays for Biotherapeutics to harvest a patient's tumor cells, grow them in culture to increase their number, and freeze them. The cells can later be utilized to create a "custom-made" biological therapy with monoclonal antibodies.

The second option, called the specific immunization program, was offered for the first time in September, and comes in two parts. For about $9,500, a patient can be injected with his own tumor cells (which stimulate the immune response) mixed with a commercially developed biological substance called Detox, a chemically detoxified modification of endotoxin, which is also thought to stimulate the immune system. For an additional $19,500, the self-immunized patient can also order antibodies developed in the laboratory to respond to

his tumor, and attached to a chemotherapeutic drug.

Another option is the $19,400 lymphokine-activated "killer" cell, or LAK cell, program, in which about 60 patients have enrolled. This program is similar to the three-step "adoptive immunotherapy" procedure developed by Dr. Steven A. Rosenberg, chief of surgery at the NCI. First, some of the patient's white blood cells, or lymphocytes, are removed. These cells are incubated with interleukin-2 (IL-2), a natural substance that can be synthesized in quantity through genetic-engineering technology. IL-2 converts the white blood cells into LAK cells, which seem to have a specific anticancer effect. The patient is reinfused with these LAK cells, along with enough additional IL-2 to keep the LAK cells proliferating. Biotherapeutics says about a third of its IL-2 patients have responded to treament—results similar, the organization claims, to those at the NCI.

LAK-cell therapy can be risky, and patients must be scrupulously monitored. Side effects can include fever, chills and changes in liver function. At Biotherapeutics, about 20 percent of the patients have had to be taken off LAK-cell therapy because of adverse side effects.

The fourth and most dramatic program offered by Biotherapeutics is the concoction of a monoclonal antibody "cocktail" tailor-made to a patient's individual cancer. It is also the most expensive: patients are charged $35,000 for the laboratory work involved in developing a monoclonal against that patient's particular cancer cells. "When I worked in the government, it cost $50,000 to $75,000 to develop a monoclonal," says Dr. Oldham, explaining the pricing. "I figured private industry could do it for about half that amount."

So far, about 100 patients have been treated with experimental therapies at Biotherapeutics, most of them with IL-2; it is too early to assess whether the treatments have been effective. There are currently about 30 monoclonal antibody cocktails brewing in the Biotherapeutics lab. Dale Armand was the first patient to receive her tailor-made monoclonal, which was linked to the anticancer drug doxorubicin. Two months after her treatment began, Ms. Armand seemed to feel better, but her tumor apparently had not shrunk. Dr. Nakfoor, too, felt better after his initial monoclonal treatment, but there was no clinical evidence that his condition had improved, either.

"When you look in this petri dish, remember: this is me," a cancer patient once told researchers at Biotherapeutics during a tour of the lab—part of Biotherapeutics' standard process of introducing patients to its operations. Indeed, the chance to have a direct impact on peoples' lives is what seems to have drawn scientists to Biotherapeutics.

"I like the philosophy here," says Dr. Mong Tan, who came to Biotherapeutics from the Roswell Park Memorial Institute in Buffalo and who has been with the company for about a year and a half. "I had reservations at first, having our 'clients' come into the laboratory and interrupt our work, but now I find that this kind of visit boosts our morale."

Dr. Gary Thurman, the company's associate scientific director, spent three years as a researcher at the [NCI] before leaving for Biotherapeutics. "In other labs, the major objective of a research project is to write a paper and get it accepted for publication," he says. "After a while, the research becomes more important than the application of the research."

Biotherapeutics' staff—some 35 scientists and 85 support personnel previously affiliated with major medical centers—are paid on a scale much closer to that of a university than to the high salaries of other biotechnology companies. Salaries at Biotherapeutics average in the high-$20,000 range for new PhD's to no more than about $50,000 for the most experienced scientists. More than half the employees receive stock options and other forms of compensation, but, says Dr. Oldham, "what really brings them here is not the money, but the chance to do something directly for patients."

Being able to conduct research unencumbered by bureaucratic constraints is another factor that has attracted scientists to Biotherapeutics. At the NCI, says Dr. Thurman: "I constantly felt like we were fighting with an unseen system. Here, there's a tremendous opportunity to do science, without all that paperwork and scavenging for research funds. It's never a problem here of not having enough money; it's always a problem of not having enough time."

Biotherapeutics has stirred skepticism, even animosity, among some academic and government scientists.

"Is this simply another attempt to separate dying patients from their money?" asked Dr. Stuart E. Lind of the Massachusetts General Hospital in an opinion piece in *The New England Journal of Medicine.* Adds Dr. Frank J. Rauscher Jr., senior vice president for research of the American Cancer Society: "Making profit on other people's misery makes me uncomfortable."

Dr. Oldham bristles at this. "People act as though having cancer takes away an individual's ability to reason," he says. "But if they're not smart enough to write a check," he asks, "are they smart enough to sign an informed consent" for experimental therapy in a government-sponsored research project?

Biotherapeutics has also been criticized as a medical haven for the rich. Dr. Thomas H. Murray, a bioethicist at the University of Texas Medical Branch in Galveston, even suggested in *Genetic Engineering News*, a biotechnology-industry newsletter, that it might be morally preferable for the therapies to fail than to work. If Dr. Oldham's techniques are successful, he wrote, "we will have a situation where . . . the wealthy live, and the poor die."

But people are denied experimental therapy all the time, counters Dr. Oldham. When Dr. Steven Rosenberg's interleukin-2 research at the National Cancer Institute was first publicized early this year, says Dr. Oldham, the institute got "a thousand calls a day from people who wanted to receive it," but only a few patients a week were put on the medication. "Is one set of exclusionary criteria godly and the other one wrong?" asks Dr. Oldham.

Scientists generally agree that, depending on the disease, new treatments can best be studied in a program in which an experimental group is given the new treatment and a control group is provided either conventional treatment or no treatment at all. Comparisons between the two groups help to determine an experimental therapy's efficacy.

But when an individual pays for his own research, says Dr. Paul Carbone, director of the Clinical Cancer Center at the University of Wisconsin at Madison, "I can tell you what would happen—no one would want to be the control."

Dr. Oldham maintains that he is investigating IL-2 and Detox in compliance with [FDA] regulations. Although the FDA regulates the use of some monoclonal antibodies, according to Dr. Oldham, the development and use of *custom-designed* monoclonal antibodies for specific individuals are considered a medical service, not a drug, and hence need not come under government scrutiny. The FDA, however, says that it is "looking into" whether Dr. Oldham is operating in accordance with government regulations.

But, Biotherapeutics has stirred controversy for more than ethical and procedural issues. Dr. Bruce Chabner, director of the division of cancer treatment of the NCI, and other researchers have been strongly critical of Biotherapeutics' science.

The scientific rationale for the programs Biotherapeutics offers is that cancer is an individualized, idiosyncratic, heterogeneous disease—so heterogeneous that it varies not only from person to person but even within the same individual, at different tumor sites or in different stages of the disease. This, according to Dr. Oldham, requires that cancer be approached with custom-made treatments that are just as heterogeneous.

"Cancer comes from our own cells, which are totally different in any two people except identical twins," says Dr. Oldham. "If both you and I get cancer," he asks rhetorically, "are we suddenly going to be exactly alike?"

Yes, says Dr. Chabner, who concedes he has never talked to Dr. Oldham directly about the program—or at least alike enough to benefit from the same therapy. The argument about the uniqueness of cancer cells "is a lot of baloney," he says. "There's no need to make an antibody specific for a patient's tumor."

Yet Dr. Oldham's scientific viewpoint appears to have been given some empirical support in 1984 by a research team at Stanford University under the leadership of Drs. Jeffrey Sklar and Ronald Levy. The Sklar-Levy group found that the kind of cancer they studied, B-cell lymphoma, can be so heterogeneous that more than one tumor-cell type can sometimes be found in the same patient. Ten percent of the patients in the Stanford study had two cell types in their tumors.

Beyond the strictly scientific questions, one of the most prevalent concerns expressed about Biotherapeutics is whether Dr. Oldham and his co-workers will treat research results as trade secrets. "Free access to scientific information must be maintained if others are to reproduce and refine medical and scientific research," wrote Dr. Stuart Lind in his article in *The New England Journal of Medicine.* "Conceivably, a proprietary interest in a particular treatment might keep a company from fulfilling this obligation in order to remain one step ahead of the competition."

Dr. Oldham counters that he has already submitted for publication in *The New Eng-*

land Journal of Medicine a paper describing his experiences with the first group of LAK-cell patients. In March, he will present a paper at an international meeting on immunoconjugates—the term for monoclonal antibodies hooked onto drugs or other agents—describing his first 15 or 20 patients to be treated with monoclonals. He says he will continue to publish his Biotherapeutics findings as quickly as he did his research results when he was at the NCI.

The criticism of Dr. Oldham and his entrepreneurial approach to cancer research, at first muted, has grown in intensity. He claims he has suddenly become a pariah and is not invited to some oncological conferences because his hands have been sullied with profit.

Dr. Rauscher of the American Cancer Society, even though he is uncomfortable with Biotherapeutics' for-profit status, says that if Dr. Oldham really is being shunned by his peers, "that would be unfortunate, and I'd be on his side on that one. The guy's got a different mechanism, but he doesn't have different science."

The criticisms of Biotherapeutics have not deterred the patients, people who think it is worth up to $35,000 to gamble on a new kind of cancer treatment.

"I'm extremely excited about this program," says Dale Armand, who is back at home in Louisiana after the first phase of her monoclonal antibody treatment in Tennessee. "I still get a little afraid when I think about it, but in my mind there's no question that this is the way to go. Without this, I have no chance whatsoever."

DESIGNER GENES THAT DON'T FIT: A TORT FOR COMMERCIAL RELEASE OF GENETIC ENGINEERING PRODUCTS*

A persistent difficulty with regulation is lack of expertise on the part of the regulators about the area being regulated. In scientific areas in which research is widely diffused and rapidly developing, such as genetic engineering, enforcement is also a problem. This selection, published as a law review note, outlines some of the difficulties encountered in regulating genetic engineering research. It then proposes complementary development of the tort system to create incentives for safety in genetic engineering research. Tort law—the law of private damages—shifts losses from one individual to another. A successful medical malpractice suit, for example, shifts the loss from the injured patient to the physician rendering substandard care, who most likely will in turn be insured in a manner in which losses are widely pooled.

Proving injuries caused by risky genetic experimentation is likely to be frustrating for many plaintiffs. The tort system proposed is therefore modified to deal with some of the difficulties of proof. The system proposed is one of "strict liability"—liability based not on fault, but on the inherent riskiness of the activity. Moreover, firms engaged in genetic engineering would be required to carry insurance, lest they be unable to pay the judgments awarded to injured consumers—just as many states require insurance of all motorists. Finally, when injuries are caused by environmental damage from genetic developments, it may be impossible to delineate the individual contributions of various producers. Therefore, the suggestion is made that experimenters

---

* References deleted without indication.

From "Designer Genes that Don't Fit," 100 *Harvard Law Review* 1086 (1987). Copyright © 1987 by the Harvard Law Review Association.

should be held jointly and severally liable—liable together and individually—for damage resulting from genetic engineering.

Genetic engineering, the deliberate alteration of an organism's genetic material, has revolutionized applied biology and created a vigorous biotechnology industry that has recently taken tremendous strides toward developing a vast array of commercially feasible products. These new products promise a variety of benefits, including cleaning up toxic waste and oil spills, protecting crops from frost, and providing society with new chemicals, drugs, and foods. Genetic engineering, however, also poses a substantial risk of serious ecological disruption. Commercial tests and applications may cause new and untreatable diseases, alter radically the balance of nature within ecosystems, or develop into new strains of crop-ravaging "superpests." Although the probability of these events appears slight, the catastrophic consequences that would follow should any of them actually occur are cause for deep concern. As a result, several federal agencies have taken steps to impose regulations on the emerging biotechnology industry.

This selection argues that, by itself, direct government regulation cannot adequately protect the public from the hazards of genetic engineering. The answer lies in a reformed tort system. Only such a system, by relying on the market to generate information and allocate risk, is able to capture the advantages of decentralized decisionmaking by individual biotechnology firms. Part I of this selection describes and assesses current regulatory efforts, concluding that existing regulatory regimes are too diffuse and too lenient to police the biotechnology field effectively. Part II identifies the flaws in the current tort regime and proposes substantial modifications, including a system of presumptions to ease difficulties in proving causation; financial responsibility requirements such as mandatory insurance; and the imposition of joint and several strict liability.

REGULATORY EFFORTS TO DATE

Government agencies and commentators have emphasized an administrative solution to the risks posed by commercial genetic engineering. From the beginning, this approach has taken the form of a case-by-case, adjudicative style of decisionmaking, a costly and inefficient method of regulation that requires the government to obtain sufficient information and expertise to evaluate individual experiments on their own merits.

In 1973, scientists first announced that they had developed the capability of modifying genetic material. Soon afterwards, the National Institutes of Health (NIH), the coordinating federal medical research organization, assumed responsibility for promulgating standards for laboratory work involving recombinant DNA (rDNA). The NIH Guidelines for Research Involving Recombinant DNA Molecules (the Guidelines), initially published in 1976, establish various levels of physical and biological containment procedures to which NIH-funded research scientists must adhere in handling genetic material. The first version of the Guidelines primarily concerned laboratory research and prohibited altogether the deliberate release of rDNA matter into the environment. Because the Guidelines govern only rDNA research "conducted at or sponsored by" the NIH, they leave unrestricted private research conducted by commercial entities wholly unconnected with NIH.

In 1978, the NIH revised the Guidelines to reflect the commercial promise of the emerging biotechnology industry and to incorporate new evidence indicating that the initial doomsday prophecies of rDNA critics had been overblown. For example, the revised Guidelines allow the director of NIH to permit "exceptions" to the original blanket prohibition on deliberate release experiments.

As research increasingly moves out of government-supported laboratories and into commercial markets, the ability of the NIH—both legally and practically—to regulate genetic engineering will diminish. Despite their limited scope, the NIH Guidelines, by adopting at the outset a case-by-case process that balanced the possible risks and payoffs of individual experiments, set the pattern for future regulatory strategies. The combination of a new technology, with which even the NIH was initially unfamiliar, and sporadic applications for a wide variety of experiments necessitates a focus on individual firms and proposals to the exclusion of a more generalized system of administrative rulemaking. This adjudicatory mode of decisionmaking, however, requires a high degree of government expertise and will likely prove quite expensive and time-consuming as the number of experiments increases.

Even a more comprehensive regulatory scheme for commercial biotechnology, the Coordinated Framework for Regulation of Biotechnology (the Framework), has fallen into the case-by-case trap first established by the NIH Guidelines. Formulated over the last three years by the White House's Office of Science and Technology Policy, the Framework ratifies the existing hodgepodge arrangement whereby each of several agencies—the NIH, the Environmental Protection Agency (EPA), the Department of Agriculture (USDA), the Food and Drug Administration (FDA), and the Occupational Safety and Health Administration (OSHA)—possesses regulatory authority over certain aspects of biotechnology by virtue of existing statues. Two coordinating groups, the Domestic Policy Council Working Group on Biotechnology (DPCWGB) and the Biotechnology Science Coordinating Committee (BSCC), attempt to smooth out differences among the agencies. The Framework calls for the EPA to employ the Toxic Sub-

stances Control Act (TSCA) to regulate all commercial releases not covered by narrower statues. Because many technologies fall within the EPA "catch-all" provision, the TSCA constitutes the principal federal biotechnology regulatory regime.

Although the goal of the Office of Science and Technology is that "responsibility for a product use . . . lie with a single agency," in practice this is not the case. Private industry often has been unable to predict which federal agency will have regulatory jurisdiction over new discoveries, especially when biotechnologies blur the line between conventional product categories. In addition, regulatory requirements—or at least terminology—vary among the agencies, and there is no standard definition of the phrase "genetic engineering." Overlapping jurisdictions will likely produce confusion and delay commercialization of genetic engineering.

In addition, the EPA's intended statutory authority for its biotechnology regulation, the Toxic Substances Control Act, was originally crafted as a measure to regulate toxic chemicals and is ill-suited to the genetic engineering field. First, it is unclear whether the statute, which by its terms covers only "chemical substances," can be extended to include genetic engineering. Even if a court could be convinced that it can be so stretched, litigating that issue will precipitate a new round of regulatory delay and uncertainty. In addition, the act places the burden on the EPA to demonstrate the existence of a hazard before it can take regulatory action. Yet a new technology like genetic engineering with largely unstudied risks should not enjoy a de facto presumption of safety. Moreover, a firm has no incentive to supply the EPA with the information necessary to demonstrate "unreasonable risk," the prerequisite finding required by the TSCA, because such information might result in a ban of the firm's own product. The Toxic Substances Control Act presupposes the need for an improvement of our assessment of the hazards posed by toxic substances, but it creates no incentive for industry to increase governmental knowledge of existing risks. Although the act establishes reporting requirements, industry can comply by halfheartedly completing the appropriate forms, and such a pattern of perfunctory compliance will not generate a deep understanding on the part of the EPA.

More generally, lack of knowledge and expertise within administrative agencies represents a major obstacle to the Framework's success. Government scientists are forced to operate with "a very skimpy data base" and "no generally accepted procedures for testing biotechnology products." In January 1986, for example, the EPA's Science Advisory Board released a report detailing a wide range of areas in which the agency's research was inadequate or nonexistent. The scientific issues about which there is scant information include the possibility of the survival and growth of recombinant organisms in the environment, the likelihood of genetic transfer between altered and indigenous organisms, the dispersal of altered organisms throughout the ecosystem by insects and wind, the health effects of new organisms on humans, and possible remedial strategies to contain and destroy engineered organisms. The sketchy information on such critical subjects generated by the supposedly "comprehensive" Framework amply dramatizes that the Framework alone cannot adequately regulate the risks posed by genetic engineering.

PROPOSED SOLUTION: A STRENGTHENED TORT REGIME

Although many commentators have proposed and analyzed potential regulatory programs as a means of combating the risks created by biotechnology, relatively little thought has been given to possible tort law reforms toward the same end. On its face, the tort system promises better protection of public health and the environment, and at a lower cost, then does direct government regulation. Currently, however, the classical "private law" model of the tort system imposes limits on that system's ability to mitigate the risks of genetic engineering. Reforms introducing a more "public" character are needed to make the tort system responsive to the challenges posed by genetic engineering cases.

The Promise of the Tort System

Tort law is essentially a market-based system that employs the expertise and information already accumulated by private firms in the ordinary course of their business. Even if Congress enacted a statute to address the shortcomings of current biotechnology regulation, the knowledge of any administrative agency would inevitably prove inferior to that of private actors.

Biotechnology firms have easy access to enormous amounts of scientific expertise, as well as intricate knowledge of the risks and promises of particular genetic engineering techniques, especially those that they themselves have developed. Case-by-case reviews by the EPA or other agencies are inefficient to the extent that they require the government to duplicate this information or develop the expertise and authority to acquire and digest it. Indeed, because biotechnology firms can afford to remunerate the field's most talented scientists according to the market value of their services, the overall level of scientific expertise in government will likely lag behind that in private industry. The tort system should therefore complement direct regulation in the public management of rDNA releases.

Despite the promise of the tort system, plaintiffs currently face many hurdles in their efforts to recover from culpable biotechnology firms. These barriers prevent the system from fully capturing the advantages of decentralized decisionmaking. The first problem is victim ignorance. Many potential plaintiffs may not even be aware of the fact that their injuries are rDNA-related. Failed crops, a severe rainstorm, a nagging cold—these commonplace occurrences may in some cases result from an unknown genetic engineering experiment. Second, many plaintiffs who do suspect that their ailments are rDNA-related may nonetheless choose not to bring suit because their claims are of such low value that the transaction costs of participating in the legal system are prohibitive. Third, those plaintiffs who do litigate may face insuperable barriers in proving causation. Current law generally requires that they isolate the microbe that triggered their injury, eliminate the possibility of alternate natural causes, and pinpoint the source of the genetically engineered material. Where many firms conduct identical experiments with similar microbes, this task may well prove impossible. Fourth, the problem of bankrupt, elusive, or otherwise judgment-proof firms may thwart recovery. The biotechnology industry, like all emerging growth sectors of the economy, is rife with "fly-by-night," undercapitalized operations.

Finally, today's tort system cannot serve as an efficient regulatory regime because biotechnology firms do not uniformly face a strict standard of liability. If, as some commentators contend, genetic engineering is "abnormally dangerous," then courts could apply a standard of strict liability. Others, however, predict that courts will instead employ a standard of negligence, because as experience with rDNA and associated technologies grows, they will no longer be considered "abnormally dangerous." On the other hand, some courts may impose strict liability. . . Uncertainty over the legal standard of liability alone need not produce inefficient results, because under both strict liability and negligence, defendants are in theory led to take optimal care in safety precautions. However, some firms may anticipate, and some may actually face, a standard of negligence, which

is in practice ill-suited to regulation of genetic engineering. The ever-changing nature of biotechnology means, for example, that courts will have difficulty in defining the socially optimal level of due care and in assessing a party's true level of care.

To the extent that courts adopt a standard of strict liability, they will be relieved of the burden of duplicating the knowledge and expertise of biotechnology firms. Strict liability renders the determination of optimal care unnecessary—courts, for example, would not need to define in detail the appropriate safety precautions that should be taken in commercial rDNA releases—and thus imposes less cost on the judicial system. In addition, strict liability eliminates two other dangers: that defendant firms may systematically underspend on safety because they expect that courts will set the legal standard of due care below the socially optimal level; and that they may overspend on safety because they expect courts to set the level of care too high. Strict liability is also preferable because it regulates firms' levels of activity. Unless deliberate release experiments are held to be negligent per se, only strict liability can moderate participation in activities that create high risks despite the exercise of reasonable care. In addition, strict liability, by forcing firms to bear the costs of nonnegligent accidents, creates an incentive for them to research and develop technologies to control the risks of genetic engineering.

The Solution: A Modified Tort System

The solution lies not in abandoning the tort system, but rather in modifying it in cases dealing with genetic engineering. Specifically, the tort system should be reformed to: (1) create a system of rebuttable presumptions in order to ease plaintiffs' burdens in proving causation; (2) impose financial responsibility requirements, such as mandatory insurance, on firms that engage in the release of genetic engineering products into the environment; and (3) create a standard of joint and several strict liability for defendant firms. These changes could be implemented at the federal level, perhaps by including them in any of several pending congressional bills aimed at streamlining the existing regulatory process. The reforms could also be enacted by states and localities, which retain authority over biotechnology activities by virtue of their police powers. In the area of genetic engineering, replete with so many unknowns, it may be wiser to allow individual states to experiment with diverse approaches. On the other hand, uniform federal standards may be preferable in order to avoid conflicting, complex standards and "cut-throat" competition among states to attract biotechnology firms by creating lax regulatory systems.

Even in the absence of such legislative action, answers to the shortcomings of the tort system may develop within the common law. Judicial independence, the multiplicity of jurisdictions, and the parties' adversary posture all stimulate the development of rules to deal with social problems on a flexible, albeit ad hoc, basis. Some observers have pointed to the opportunity for courts themselves to adopt a "public law" vision of the tort system by focusing on the incentives created by that system for the social regulation of risk rather than on the traditional individualized process of private law. Others have advanced the view that the common law progresses systematically toward economically efficient results. Measures that hold the potential for correcting the tort system's shortfalls are currently available, even if they are not yet extensively employed. The class action, for example, represents a solution to otherwise prohibitive transaction costs. Joint and several liability can overcome problems of proof. Statutory action may be required for some tort reforms, but many can evolve independently within the common law.

A System of Presumptions. A system of presumptions should be established in order to assist plaintiffs in proving causation in genetic engineering tort suits. A government regulatory agency should be charged with drawing up a list of types of illnesses and other phenomena that are known to be associated, with specified probability, with the results of genetic engineering experiments. The presumptions could be structured around a "more likely than not" standard, but a better solution would abandon the "preponderance of the evidence" rule and instead impose liability in proportion to the probability of causation. A schedule of probabilities could be constructed for each type of release. For example, suppose crops failed from nitrogen impairment in an area downwind from where a nitrogen fixation experiment occurred several weeks earlier. The court would compute the probability that the crops failed because of the genetic engineering activity, according to tables that took into account the type of experiment, the amount of material released, the particular atmospheric conditions and distance involved, and so on. If the calculated probability was thirty percent, then the crops' owners would be entitled to recover thirty percent of the crops' value. . . .

Given the myriad uncertainties regarding the environmental effects of commercial releases, the presumptions would be based necessarily upon rough estimates. A phenomenon such as the common cold may have so many alternate causes that its causation could never be demonstrated by means of a presumption. But "generalized estimates of the probability of environmental damage" of various kinds of experiments appear feasible, and with the passage of time the presumptions would become more sophisticated. In addition, incorporating other "public law" solutions, such as class actions and fixed schedules of damages, would ensure that the results are accurate in the aggregate, even if individual plaintiffs are sometimes under- or overcompensated by the scheme.

The task of formulating presumptions, moreover, would consume far fewer administrative resources and demand far less government expertise than would the burden of quantifying precisely the risks and benefits associated with each individual experiment. A defendant could rebut scientifically erroneous presumptions by showing that it did not cause a plaintiff's injury. The fact that a firm would reduce its expected liability by producing favorable evidence could provide industry an incentive to conduct research on the environmental risks of biotechnology and to develop new safety technologies, such as a means of "tagging" engineered microbes, making the task of identifying man-made environmental effects much easier. A system of presumptions would place the burden of proof on the defendant, the party with the easiest access to information.

Financial Responsibility Requirements. A financial responsibility requirement such as mandatory insurance should be imposed to deal with the problem of judgment-proof firms. Although individual entrepreneurs may not expect to remain solvent for as long as it takes latent effects of genetic engineering experiments to manifest themselves, insurance companies on the whole *will* remain solvent and therefore have a strong incentive to impose safety standards on their insureds. If insurance companies have access to sufficient information, they can risk-rate the premiums of biotechnology firms and create safety incentives directly. In the early stages of the industry, such information might be rare, but as the number of experiments increases, actuarial data should become more reliable and cheaper to obtain.

Indeed, each firm would have an incentive to educate its insurance carrier, in order to reduce its own costs. If a carrier were unable to monitor the behavior of its insured, the carrier would charge a very high or prohibitive price for its premiums, or it might cancel the policy altogether. Biotechnology firms seeking cheaper insurance would have an incentive to permit, indeed to aid, monitoring by insurance companies. This stands in stark contrast to the situation created by the Toxic Substances Control Act, under which firms profit by hindering government monitoring.

This scheme presupposes the availability of private insurance. Currently, liability coverage for rDNA releases is quite expensive, and imposing an insurance requirement may be tantamount to setting a ceiling on the number of firms in the industry. The present high price of insurance, however, likely reflects the myriad uncertainties associated with genetic engineering. As these uncertainties are reduced, the price of insurance should also decline. If commercial carriers overestimate biotechnology risks and set premiums unrealistically high, firms can turn to self-insurance either by themselves or through mutual pools. Mutual self-insurance pools, which enjoy economies of scale over single-firm self-insurance, are now being formed in many sectors of the economy, from chemical producers to municipal corporations. In the near term, it would be wiser to limit participation in the biotechnology industry to financially responsible firms, because those are the only actors that can be encouraged to adopt the optimal level of safety precautions.

Joint and Several Liability. Joint and several liability constitutes a final necessary component of tort reform. Some commentators have criticized joint and several liability as unfair and inefficient, on the ground that it often forces some firms— usually the wealthy, well-established, or best-known—to bear the costs of the activities of other tortfeasors. In fact, however, joint and several liability should produce a system in which potentially co-liable firms meet *ex ante,* before any accidents or lawsuits have occurred, and allocate risk privately through contract. The firms, for example, might agree to adopt certain specified safety practices. If, as some maintain, causation in genetic engineering accidents cannot be precisely determined because many companies conduct very similar experiments, then many firms would have an incentive to join in such contractual arrangements because an injured plaintiff would be entitled to recover from any firm in the group. Joint and several liability would produce a system of industry self-regulation that could serve as a valuable supplement to direct government regulation.

The transaction costs of private risk allocation through contract would not be prohibitive. Much of the bargaining over the allocation of potential liability would occur between supplier and customer in the normal course of negotiations for the basic product contract. In addition, many biotechnology firms are engaged in joint ventures, under which liability apportionment is customarily specified by a negotiated term of the venture agreement. The transaction costs even among firms that have no other dealings with each other would be reduced by the existence of the Association of Biotechnology Companies (ABC), an industry trade association and a potential forum for negotiations. These costs of private bargaining, because they occur through normal market mechanisms, would probably be less than the administrative costs of after-the-fact adjudication by either a court or governmental agency.

Small firms that expect to escape lawsuits altogether may appear to have little incentive to participate in such a scheme, but a variety of market pressures would encourage them to take precautions. Users of rDNA products, such as large agricultural concerns, would likely require that smaller genetic engineering firms abide by specified safety standards, both to protect themselves from liability and in order to attract the business of larger biotechnology firms

that may otherwise refuse to sell to a buyer that purchases from risky genetics companies. Given the prevalence of joint ventures in the biotechnology industry, many safety standards would be imposed on small firms as negotiated contract provisions. Another risk management strategy for large firms would be simply to acquire possible renegades.

These reforms would enable the tort system to play an important role in the social regulation of genetic engineering risks. Plaintiff attorneys would have the incentive to hire biotechnology experts, perhaps even entire research firms, in order to obtain assistance in exploiting the market of potential claims against biotechnology companies. The ability of private attorneys to educate the public regarding the risks of biotechnology may help overcome the problem of victim ignorance as well.

An Objection: Cost

It might be argued that stringent tort regulation will stifle the infant biotechnology industry. At present, the United States is the world leader in this field, and a federal policy goal is to preserve the international competitiveness of American firms. Any liability system that increases the production costs of domestic companies runs counter to this objective. In addition, the mere announcement of a more onerous tort regime may cause public investors to lose confidence in genetic engineering companies.

This objection is misguided, however, for a number of reasons. Protecting an infant industry through loose standards of liability is an inefficient strategy. It reduces the production costs of all firms in the industry, including those that are already reaping substantial profits and require no governmental assistance at all, by forcing plaintiffs rather than companies to bear the costs of injuries. If particular biotechnology producers require subsidies, then they should be supplied directly, in the form of targeted grants or low-interest loans, not by creating an inefficient regulatory system that subsidizes all genetic engineering firms, regardless of their financial position. A tort-based regulatory regime coupled with a program of direct subsidies would minimize overall cost.

Stringent tort liability, furthermore, need not discourage investment in biotechnology. Some investors seem fascinated by the novelty and sophistication of the technology and are willing to participate in the market at almost any cost, regardless of the liability system. Others appear wary of the scientific unknowns and skeptical of the unconventional managerial styles of many of the genetic engineering entrepreneurs. Tort reform, by creating a more predictable and stable industry, may reassure timid investors, while not decreasing the enthusiasm of those bullish on biotechnology, and thus expand overall investment. Presumptions and damage schedules would give firms an estimate, and perhaps a ceiling, on their expected liabilities, and a system of industry self-regulation stimulated by joint and several liability would produce a pattern of risks allocated through contract that rationalizes an otherwise unfriendly business environment.

Conclusion

A remaining issue is the degree to which the tort system should replace government regulation in this field, rather than merely act as a supplement to it. Given the unique and potentially catastrophic dangers posed by genetic engineering, overlapping regulatory regimes make sense. Although some of the cost savings of the tort system would be lost if government agencies attempted to duplicate the expertise of private firms, the tort system can work in tandem with government regulation. The fact that the proposed tort presumptions would be rebuttable, for example, would create an incentive for private firms to release safety data to the public. The tort reform proposal would likely enhance the ability of the NIH to influence the safety practices of biotechnology firms. In addition, a model code of safety standards developed by an industry trade association could serve as a useful example for government regulatory agencies, although over-reliance on these sources of information by regulatory agencies would alter industry's incentives to disclose them truthfully.

For the foreseeable future, there is no prospect that any conceivable purely administrative scheme can adequately protect public safety and the environment. Hence, tort reform is required, including a system of rebuttable presumptions designed to ease plaintiffs' burden in proving causation, financial responsibility requirements such as mandatory insurance, and a standard of joint and several strict liability. This proposal for regulating rDNA releases could serve as an important model for future regulation of emerging technologies by harnessing the knowledge and expertise of entrepreneurs to serve the public interest.

CONSCIENTIOUS OBJECTIONS BY NURSES

Rebecca Dresser

In this selection, Dresser asks whether nurses should disobey orders. After examining the interests of all concerned—patient, nurse, physician, and hospital—she concludes that disobedience is warranted. It should be noted, however, that this case of contemplated disobedience is an easy one, in the sense that no conflicts of interest emerge. In other cases of medical decision making, however, conflicts may be clear—for example, between the patient's interest in receiving treatment and hospital or social policies for allocating resources, or between the patient's interest in receiving treatment and the family's interest in not having to continue care. An interest analysis will not provide direction in such cases of conflict unless the analysis includes a method for assessing relative strengths of the interests. Classical utilitarians would compare the relative intensity of the various interests. Nonconsequentialists would suggest that other moral considerations must come into play, such as patient autonomy, the nurse's right to monitor the quality of the care given, or the constraints of the nurse's role.

An 18-year-old asthmatic with an acute exacerbation of her condition arrives in the emergency department. The examining physician asks the nurse to give the patient 0.3 cc of epinephrine, 1:10,000 dilution. (The normal dose is 0.3 cc of epinephrine, 1:1,000 dilution.) The nurse questions the order, but the physician is adamant. The nurse is aware that in this case the drug will not cause any ill effect to the patient. However, delay of correct treatment may be detrimental. She has several options: (a) she could give the standard drug dose, (b) she could question the physician again, (c) she could contact another physician (a phone call to his home), or (d) she could follow the emergency physician's orders. She has to work with the ordering physician about every other day. What should she do? Would it make any difference if the physician in this case is a resident? What if he is the patient's outside, private attending physician?

A consensus has emerged in recent years that nurses bear some responsibility for ensuring that physicians' orders are appropriate. Professional, ethical, and legal guidelines, however, are somewhat imprecise regarding the standards and procedures governing the nurse challenging a physician's orders. As a consequence, each specific case must be analyzed to ascertain whether a nurse should object to a physician's instructions and, if so, how she should implement the objection.

SHOULD THE NURSE OBJECT?

In this case, four primary entities will be affected by the nurse's actions: the patient, the nurse, the physician, and the hospital. The nature and magnitude of each entity's interest will be examined to determine how this nurse ought to proceed.

Patient's Interests

The patient has an interest in receiving appropriate medical treatment for her condition. Her goal is to obtain from the emergency department the dose of epinephrine that will bring her relief as soon as possible. If she receives the lower dose prescribed by the physician, her distress will be prolonged and her risk of suffering harm from the episode will increase. This patient's interest in appropriate treatment supports the nurse acting to provide such treatment. This interest, however, is less weighty than

From Rebecca Dresser, "Conscientious Objections (Bad Orders)," in *Ethics in Emergency Medicine,* Kenneth V. Iserson, et. al., eds. (Baltimore: Williams & Wilkins, 1986), pp. 217–220. Reprinted by permission.

it would be if the physician's orders presented a more serious and imminent health threat.

Nurse's Interests

The nurse confronts a complex set of interests in this case, for risks are inherent in any course of conduct she chooses to pursue. If she follows the incorrect order and the patient suffers harm from the delay of proper medication, she could be held liable in a subsequent malpractice action. Further, she could face disciplinary action by the hospital administration and state nursing board for her contribution to the patient's inappropriate treatment. Blind obedience to physicians is no longer an ethically or legally defensible approach for nurses. Modern ethical codes, as well as legal standards, require nurses to question the authority of physicians who issue inappropriate orders that could result in harm to patients.

Yet the nurse will encounter hazards if she challenges the physician. Because of the broader social context in which nurses and physicians work, the nurse who overtly disagrees with a doctor is especially vulnerable. The nurse's refusal to carry out the emergency physician's order will jeopardize her relationship with him. Further, she could be subjected to informal harassment and retaliation by the emergency physician and others who might take his side. The physician could file a complaint with the hospital or with the state nursing board, claiming that the nurse exceeded the legal scope of nursing practice. Some state nursing practice acts permit nurses to engage in certain forms of diagnosis and treatment, while many statutes are imprecise on this matter. Imposition of formal legal sanctions, however, would be unlikely in this case. As long as the nurse carefully orchestrates her objection, the persuasive arguments in favor of her conduct should protect her from official action. But the solid basis of her refusal to follow the physician's order might not protect her

from unofficial punishment. Unfortunately, the nurse cannot avoid exposure to a common fate of "whistle blowers": informal persecution and ostracism. This threat can be minimized, however, by the method in which she challenges the order. Thus, although the nurse will incur some risk in opposing the order, the balance of considerations indicates that it is most advisable for her to ensure that the patient is properly treated.

Physician's Interests

A third set of interests relevant to this conflict is that of the physician. To practice medicine, he needs the cooperation and assistance of other members of the emergency department staff, including the nurse. Yet he will also gain if the nurse acts to ensure that the patient receives the correct dose of medication, for by doing so she deflects a potential malpractice claim against him. Although his pride may be damaged by her challenge, this consideration has little merit and ought not influence the nurse's decision.

Hospital's Interest

The hospital is the fourth entity that will be significantly affected by the nurse's conduct. A smoothly operating institution is one in which members of a health care team work together without serious conflict. More important to the hospital, however, is a system in which individuals on a health care team act as checks against the errors of others. Avoiding harm to patients from improper care, then, is the hospital's overriding concern in this case. As a result, the overall goals of the hospital are best advanced if nurses attempt to rectify physicians' errors.

STATUS OF PHYSICIAN IRRELEVANT

This characterization of the interests at stake remains essentially unchanged if the physician involved is a resident or a private attending. If the physician is a resident, the nurse has even greater reason to challenge the order. Residents are physicians-in-training who must be monitored by more experienced health care personnel, to protect hospital patients. If the physician is a private attending, rather than a staff physician, the nurse probably incurs a lower risk in refusing to carry out the order, for she is likely to have less contact with a private physician and the danger of unpleasant future encounters is correspondingly reduced.

In sum, an analysis of the interests of the parties involved in this case indicates that the nurse should act to protect the patient by objecting to the physician's order. How, then, should she proceed? This question can be answered by once again investigating various interests affected by the nurse's behavior.

HOW SHOULD THE NURSE IMPLEMENT HER OBJECTIONS?

The patient's interest is in receiving prompt relief. This is not a case in which lengthy discussion and negotiation between nurse and physician will benefit the patient. Thus, for the patient's sake, the nurse needs to act quickly. The nurse's interest in maintaining a good relationship with the physician suggests that she should approach him one more time, explaining her doubts about the order and perhaps presenting to him evidence that the standard dose is much higher than the one he has requested.

If the physician refuses to change his order, the nurse should seek assistance from another person with authority over emergency department patient care. To protect herself, she ought not administer the appropriate dose on her own. Accordingly, she should first telephone the other physician and describe the situation. The nurse should present her case professionally, without extreme anger or hostility. Her

aim is to enlist institutional support for her position, rather than to encourage her listener to condemn the emergency physician's acts.

Unfortunately, physicians at times are reluctant to override another physician's decision, especially in support of a nurse's conflicting view. If the second physician refuses to issue the appropriate order or to visit the emergency department to examine the patient, the nurse should notify her supervisor of the problem. In the face of an error as obvious as this one, the supervisor is likely to recognize the mistake and arrange for a physician to order the appropriate dose. Again, by calling the case to the attention of the hospital authorities, the nurse safeguards her professional interests to a greater extent than she would by acting alone. In addition, she should keep detailed notes of her actions in the patient's records, to ensure that an accurate account of the incident is documented in the event of further inquiry into the matter.

The nurse's responsibilities in this case could extend beyond the immediate situation. If the emergency physician refuses to change his order after having ample opportunity to do so, his professional competence is in question. For the good of future emergency department patients, the nurse should raise this issue with her supervisor. Many hospitals and all state medical boards have procedures for reporting and investigating incidents like this one. By reporting the incident, the nurse once more risks informal sanction. Her vulnerability, however, will decrease if others in the hospital support her willingness to challenge the physician. Further, the hospital administrators, as well as other physicians, have ethical and legal grounds for concern about the competence of this physician. Thus, the nurse should, at minimum, consult her supervisor on whether to report this incident to hospital or state medical authorities.

OFFICIAL DISOBEDIENCE

Mortimer R. Kadish and Sanford H. Kadish

In Discretion to Disobey, *Kadish and Kadish argue that there are legally justifiable departures from legal rules—that apparent civil disobedience is in some cases legally permissible. The focus of their argument is disobedience by those who play institutional roles in the legal system, such as prosecutors, judges, and juries. For example, juries sometimes refuse to convict sympathetic defendants despite the prosecution's having proved all the elements of its case. Similarly, prosecutors sometimes do not bring charges despite an apparent offense. Sympathetic examples of suicide assistance that were not prosecuted would appear to fit this pattern.*

A justification for lawful disobedience, Kadish and Kadish contend, must offer a defense of both the action—an argument of merit—and its performance by the agent in question—an argument of appropriateness. Arguments of merit call on general moral theory. Arguments of appropriateness must call on an institutional theory about the allocation of decision-making authority. Kadish and Kadish write as follows about when judgments of appropriateness are required.

DISCRETION TO DISOBEY

Let us put the matter generally, then, to apply to any domain—political, legal, economic, familial, and so on—in which justification for undertaking an action is relevant: For any such domain, the argument to appropriateness demands as a necessary condition an institutional program for the allocation of authority to make decisions along with whatever arguments are needed to sustain such an institutional program. The argument to the merits, however, does not require an institutional program. To show that the war in Vietnam is wrong, it would suffice to point up the attendant toll in life, physical destruction of the country, disruption in the internal affairs of the United States, and so on. There is no need to show the inconsistency of the war in Vietnam with an institutional program, though the war's disruptive consequences for a justifiable institutional program would of course be part of the argument to the merits.

WHEN UNDERTAKING AN ACTION MUST BE JUSTIFIED

As matters stand so far, anyone who wanted to consider decisions to abide by or depart from mandatory rules as, simply, decisions to be made on the merits might easily concede that if such decisions were justified as one justified undertaking an action, then absorbing the proposition of appropriateness into one of merit would be a mistake. But then he could simply deny that departures from mandatory rules were of the kind that required justification for undertaking an action. What conditions pertinent to the plight of citizens and officials call for that special kind of justification? Fortunately, political and moral philosophy have long since explored the circumstances under which it is expected that people will not merely justify their action but justify themselves before the rules.

People recognize that they must justify undertaking an action when they see the action as affecting the interests and preferences of other persons, but not usually when they see it as affecting only themselves. Thus there was no need for Robinson Crusoe to justify undertaking any action until his man Friday appeared. Of course, Crusoe could have continued taking all his actions on himself, merely expanding the range of those actions to include Friday. But to have done so would have denied Friday's existence as a person. If Friday was to be his own man, and not merely Crusoe's, Crusoe became obliged to justify undertaking his actions, and hence to begin the search for propositions of appropriateness. So it is with citizens and officials. To act in their roles preeminently entails affecting the interests and preferences of other persons, since the rules of a legal system characteristically represent settled norms of conduct that adjust the different interests and preferences of persons in the legal community.

Of course, the principle that people must justify undertaking an action when others are affected is based on a system of values, and not on logical necessity. It flows from an underlying commitment that other people are entitled to be treated as autonomous and free beings rather than as manipulable things—a commitment that has informed not only the Rechtsphilosophie of Kant and Hegel, but the entire Western liberal tradition.

Another consideration commonly advanced to induce people to relinquish their claims to act according to their perceptions of the merits of the case is that they might be mistaken even when they feel sure of their grounds. Therefore, the argument runs, a person must not presume to judge unless he has the right to risk being mistaken—and society allocates rights to risk mistakes in a certain domain partly according to an agent's competence in that domain. So it may be argued that a person's private life is his own business, not the government's, for who would know better where the shoe pinched and how to handle his private life? So also it has been argued that the government's power over the economic life of a society ought to be severely limited, since a government cannot adequately make judgments about the multifarious aspects of an economy.

There is much to this more or less classic argument, especially when the risk of being mistaken is seen to include both the probability of making a mistake and the seriousness of the mistake in question. In any domain, as the seriousness of the mistake risked in action increases, the acceptable probability of being mistaken decreases. Regardless of how the seriousness of a mistake is measured, then, the introduction and observance of propositions of appropriateness asserting that a given risk may be assumed by X but not by Y becomes an essential part of a society's structure. By establishing conditions under which an agent may act according to his own judgment and conditions under which he cannot, society minimizes the probability that we will afflict one another with our certitudes. In the domain governed by the law, the consequences of a possible mistake are always too serious to leave to chance, and it becomes the better policy for all members of the community to follow a general strategy for the assumption of risks.

One last set of considerations is essentially Hobbesian. When predictability and peace are considered desirable, rational people are driven to demand a justification for undertaking actions. And predictability and peace are prime ends of the law.

Why would a rational person prefer a society in which decisions are made within a system of licenses and constraints? Why, in effect, would he opt for the social contract, the classic way of insisting that a judgment of an action's merits alone is insufficient as a justification for undertaking the action? Because, to make the predictability point first, if he knows that there exist institutional limits on people's right to undertake actions according to their judgment of the merits, then to that degree he need not know the details of the circumstances surrounding other people's lives when he plans behavior dependent on the behavior of others. If others fail him, he can make a case showing why they ought not to fail him; and to the extent that the institutional framework makes sanctions available, whether the overt sanctions of the law or the covert ones of guilt, he can hope for a measure of control. If another person promises him something, he can exert a pressure to keep that person to his promise even though circumstances arise that make the promiser rue the promise. When a man signs a contract he can be reasonably sure that the other person will either comply with the conditions of the contract or pay for the failure. Business, in the broadest sense, becomes possible; the state of nature has been overcome. And every rational person must desire that end as a condition for reaching his goals, regardless of whether or not the particular arguments of appropriateness generated by his society's institutions are justifiable.

The point about peace follows. In a society where decisions were not made according to a system of rights and obligations for undertaking action but according to what each thought best at the moment, no one could anticipate what anyone else would do next. Peaceable though he might otherwise be, each person would therefore be compelled to wage the war of each against all in order to protect his interests. To use a more modern phrase, he would be compelled by the logic of the preemptive strike; and as Hobbes in effect says, it is that logic, not just a propensity to force or fraud, that precipitates the state of war.

Why, then, must decisions about compliance with mandatory rules be justified as one justifies undertaking an action? The reason is at least in part that legal systems serve in varying measure to protect persons and define the limits to their actions, to assign rights for the assumption of risks, and to increase predictability and secure peace. . . .

Kadish and Kadish then turn to a discussion of arguments of appropriateness. Their account rests on a complex view of the role morality of professionals and citizens. To play a social role is to play an established or continuing part in a social enterprise or institution. Roles have purposes, defined by the institution. Role activities are sustained by the actions of others playing complementary roles. Role activities take place in a context of evaluation, which includes constraints on the means that can be employed by someone acting in the role and an account of the ends proper to the role. Constraints on means encompass both limits to acceptable reasons for action (for example, a judge may not give as a reason for a decision that he wants his neighbor to win) and limits on actions themselves (for example, under the Eighth Amendment, a judge may not sentence someone to be tortured). Constraints on ends are defined by the purpose of the role.

Prescribed Ends.   All roles exist to achieve some end or ends, as we have seen. And the prescribed means just discussed are those constraints on role-agent conduct that have been fashioned to serve those ends. But sometimes a role's context of evaluation will extend to the ends of the role as well, so that the role agent may (or must) consider the mesh between the prescribed means and the role's ends in judging the appropriateness of undertaking some action. The familiar case in which the end of a role becomes part of its context of evaluation, though by no means the only one, as will be subsequently shown, occurs when a role agent is required or permitted to act at his own discretion to achieve the end of his role. It is instructive to consider now the various types of ends that sometimes enter a role's context of evaluation.

The most immediate and least abstract type of end to which a role agent may have recourse in determining appropriate action is the specific task his role is designed to accomplish. For example, the mailman's role could conceivably authorize him to choose his delivery route, to decide his hours of delivery, to give preference to pieces of mail that deserved priority, and the like, so long as he acted in accordance with the end of delivering the mail. Normally, of course, the mailman's role does not allow recourse to ends, even the end of delivering the mail. But it could be structured so that the mailman would determine his actions in accordance with his conception of his task. The same could be said, in fact, for any official role—that action will be appropriate to the degree it is in the interest of accomplishing the task and inappropriate to the degree to which it is not.

Another type of end that may become part of a context of evaluation is a role's function within a larger institution, which may itself be embedded in an entire network of institutions. To the extent that a role is so structured, judging the appropriateness of undertaking action extends to the evaluation of the role's task in the light of the larger institutional ends that the task ends are designed to serve. When this happens both the role's prescribed means and its task ends become subject to modification and interpretation by the role agent as conflicts appear. The institutional organization of society then itself becomes a factor in making judgments in a role. Obviously officials and political leaders, at least those at high levels of government, must constantly reassess the relationship of their role activity to the larger institutional framework within which their roles function. But citizens also have institutional ends they may properly take into account in certain situations. Broadly speaking, those ends are part of the general end of ensuring that the society's system of rules and competences functions successfully. Contributing to that general end will then become a relevant consideration in differentiating appropriate from inappropriate action.

The third type of end that may become part of a context of evaluation derives from commitments to norms that transcend any institutionalized role. There can be no a priori objection to incorporating in the contexts of evaluation of at least some roles, including some of those in the legal and political systems, what we shall call "background ends." Whereas task ends and institutional ends may be invoked to justify actions that serve more or less established task requirements and institutions, background ends enable an individual role agent to conceive of what is proper in his role in a more liberal or open way—or, it must be conceded, in a narrower and more wrongheaded way—and so to alter the institutional pattern in which he finds himself. He may thus invoke ends that are recognized by his society but only incompletely realized by its structure, or even ends his society has completely ignored. He may even look further afield and invoke ends that perhaps no system of roles has ever achieved or could be expected to achieve in full measure: ends such as a finer justice, kindliness, respect for other people, or human creativity. In sum, background ends may serve as a basis for criticizing the humanizing institutional ends. Later we shall argue that background ends do in fact function in the structure of some legally defined roles as points of resistance against the prescribed means for achieving role ends.

Such, roughly, are the elements that may appear in the context of evaluation proper to a role: constraints on reasons for undertaking actions; constraints on actions themselves, and on what will count as role actions; and a variety of different types of role ends of increasing generality that a person may properly take into account under certain circumstances. Our case for the justifiability of departures from mandatory rules by citizens and officials will ultimately depend on the appeal to ends. . . .

A role's context of evaluation may thus allow judgment at many junctures. Constraints on means may be open-ended enough to permit discretionary activity. Where there are questions about constraints on means, such as conflicts between constraints, recourse to the purpose of the role may be requisite. Most relevant to the legal justification of disobedience, however, is the case in which constraints on means apparently conflict with the purpose of the role. In such cases, the role itself may mandate recourse to ends as a critique of means.

RULE DEPARTURES IN ROLES

We must now develop further the premise on which this inquiry into justified rule departures hinges: that in some roles a departure from a mandatory rule can at times be justified in terms of a proposition of appropriateness that leaves it up to the role agent to make judgments on discrepancies between prescribed means and ends and on conflicts among ends. To develop that premise further we must now show how such roles function, how they differ from other roles, and how they originate in a society. Just as the previous section considered the roles of citizen and official primarily in terms of the general properties they share with other roles, now we shall consider the potentialities of roles for justified departures from rules in general, whether they be social or moral conventions, the orders of a superior in a private organization, or the mandatory rules of the law. So doing will exhibit rule departures in legal systems as exemplifications of the possibilities of social organization in general, and not as mere quirks of the law.

Individuals and Roles

As a first step in understanding the rationality of roles that permit rule departures, let us consider the relationship of individuals to their roles not as abstract role agents, but as real people who must convince themselves that they ought to undertake a specific action required by their role. In his role a person may be a doctor, a judge, a senator, a mail carrier, but he is also a person with his own aspirations and ethics. Thus not one but two sets of considerations, broadly speaking, guide his conduct. The first consists of what we call

"role reasons"—reasons based on the constraints of his role tempered by whatever discretion recourse to role ends may afford him. The second consists of reasons that he may recognize as an individual but that in his role he cannot take into account, or what we call "excluded reasons." Frequently a person committed to a role finds himself in situations where the role reasons for undertaking an action and the excluded reasons conflict. In such a case he does not simply weigh the role reasons equally against the excluded reasons, and then act according to whichever set of reasons is greater. Instead he acknowledges his obligation to his role by imposing an extra burden . . . on the excluded reasons, so that they must have significantly greater weight than the role reasons, rather than merely greater weight, in order to sway him. This is a familiar way of dealing with one's role commitments. Nearly everyone has had the experience of acknowledging that he would take a certain course of action if only he were not in a certain position. Usually this means that though the acknowledged merits of the case carry, in one's objective judgment, in favor of the action required, they are insufficient to overcome the demands of one's role. Very rarely, perhaps, it may mean that the excluded reasons never could carry against the role reasons, no matter what their weight.

In effect, in dealing with obligations of role, the surcharge imposed on excluded reasons is either finite, as in the first case, or infinite, as in the second. Imposing a finite surcharge is the practical result of being a person who at once accepts his obligation to a role and continues to think of himself as an individual with other commitments as well; imposing an infinite surcharge is the practical result of being a person who puts his obligation to a role unqualifiedly first. It is difficult to see how an absolutely unqualified commitment to any role can be defended. But a qualified commitment to a role, based on a finite surcharge, might be defended by seeking agreement on the whole institutional program in which that role exists, along with the implications of role deviation of the given sort for a large variety of wider interests. So the student who interrupts a class defends himself by condemning the university's structure and involvement with the military-industrial complex. He counters the accusation that he has taken his role obligations as a student too lightly by urging the overwhelming value of an alternative institutional program. In sum, in defending his judgment of the appropriate surcharge against his action, he engages in social philosophy.

That, very roughly, is how people manage their role commitments, quite apart from all consideration of whether the role somehow permits rule departures. We can now turn to the questions of how rule departures in roles become possible and why a rational society might want to make them possible.

How Rule Departures in Roles Become Possible

Roles, including those of citizen and official, may be structured to take account of the fact that individuals acting in roles nevertheless place for the most part only a finite surcharge on excluded reasons before departing from some role requirement. That fact is taken into account for some roles by incorporating into their contexts of evaluation a principle for acting in the role that, in effect, guides the agent in applying and sometimes extending the context itself. Though such a role may still require a role agent to act in a certain way, it may also permit him to conclude that complying with the role's prescribed means would obstruct the role activity or defeat the role's task or institutional ends. Or it may permit him even to conclude that the required action would defeat certain background ends, which by their nature could never be clearly delineated in the role's context of evaluation. In effect, the role agent is permitted to incorporate into his decision what would ordinarily be excluded reasons, or to put the matter differently, to convert excluded reasons for an action into role reasons. He is at liberty to act on his own judgment in certain circumstances, and he can expect his decision to be supported by others in related roles. This is the finesse that introduces flexibility into role behavior and reduces the instances in which people simply step out of their roles in order to do what must be done.

There is nothing unfamiliar in the extension of a liberty to depart from the rules. It is simply not true that every conception of a soldier's role requires the soldier to obey his superior officer no matter what he may be commanded to do. The soldiers who obeyed Lieutenant Calley's command to fire on civilians might have been expected, as soldiers, to assume the risks of disobedience instead. Central to the physician's role is the requirement that he preserve the life of his patient, but he may, when the costs in pain are great enough, and long before meeting the problem of euthanasia, act to reduce pain in a way that in some measure increases the danger to his patient's life. Few would say in such circumstances that he had failed to act as a physician. In the earlier example of the employee who lost a sale because he refused to act outside his competence, the employer's response was not to commend his dutifulness but to reprimand him for failing to depart from the rules to further the institutional end of his role—to profit the employer's business. Our point is not merely that persons acting in roles sometimes depart from the rules, but that rule departures may on occasion be necessary if one is to be a good soldier, a good doctor, a good employee, and so on.

Two requirements must be met if such rule departures are to be justified. First, extra weight must be given to achieving the role's ends through its prescribed means, including any discretion that the role may provide for; by the same token, an extra burden must be imposed on any reasons there may be for departing from the role's requirements. In effect, the procedure used when conscientious individuals depart from roles that do not provide for justifiable rule departures must be incorporated as a feature of roles that do provide for justifiable departures.

The second requirement is that there be a constraint on the reasons for undertaking the action. A person's reason for departing from a role's prescribed means or for failing to achieve its prescribed end must meet some standard of relevance; otherwise the valuable distinction would be lost between the flexibility afforded by roles providing for justifiable rule departures and the exploitation and misuse of such roles. That standard of relevance is provided by the same set of ends normally taken to guide discretionary action within the role: the task ends, institutional ends, and background ends. Those ends establish the terms on which the role agent considering a departure from a rule, or what is a species of the same thing, an unauthorized extension of his discretion, may hope to reach agreement with those who depend on him and those on whom he depends in the ecology of roles. If he can show that he departed from a rule in order to achieve such an end, he will have begun to make a case. Clearly, as the range of ends a role agent may invoke to justify departing from a rule widens (to institutional ends or, at the extreme, to background ends), the possibility of justifying rule departures in a role widens also. And the wider the possibility for justifying rule departures, the greater the opportunity for role agents both to exercise their intelligence and to commit

egregious and uncontrollable violations.

Rule departures in role are made possible, then, by incorporating into the role a liberty, often of a sort that the role agent takes advantage of at his peril, to undertake actions outside the role's prescribed means to achieve the role's ends. The actions are of a sort that were the liberty not granted, they could not be justified by the role agent through any appeal to his authorized discretion, leaving him in the position of one who broke with his role. The discovery of such rule departures is not new. . . . Our point is merely that the nature of rule departures in role has not always been squarely faced. "Deviance," which, if it means anything, means a departure from some rule or expectation, has often been hidden under the more common notion of indeterminacy, as though to deviate from a rule or requirement were the same as to assume responsibility for acting in ways "not minutely prescribed."

Rule departures in role may seem less anomalous, however, if we can suggest at least in a general way why they occur and what purpose they serve in a rational society.

Why Justified Rule Departures Occur

When a role achieves its prescribed ends through its prescribed means, we shall speak of the role as adequately developed, or simply as adequate. A role is inadequately developed or inadequate, we shall say, when two or more of its prescribed means for achieving the same end are incompatible; or when its prescribed means in a given case fail to achieve the end sought; or when, the end being multiple, the achievement of one end inhibits the achievement of another. The adequacy of a role, therefore, refers not to the value people place on it or even to its effectiveness as such in the world, but to the adequacy of its context of evaluation, from which, finally, propositions of appropriateness stem.

Moreover, since roles do not usually impose requirements that are inconsistent as such (although a role with logically inconsistent requirements would indeed be inadequate), roles are not adequate or inadequate in themselves but with respect to their occasions. It is circumstances that render roles inadequate.

Clearly, then, roles basic to a society cannot be invented that will be adequate for all conceivable occasions. Even roles that grant discretion may be strained, warped, and ultimately shattered by time and circumstances. Hence roles that admit departure from rules are to be expected in any society that manages to respond successfully to radical changes. When unforeseeable circumstances develop, new interests or claims emerge, and perceptions of the balance between competing values change, a natural strategy is to place the responsibility on the role agents themselves to modify their roles as necessary while avoiding gratuitous deviation from role demands.

From another point of view, the inadequacy of roles under the pressure of unforeseeable circumstances is the pivotal consideration in any argument to appropriateness seeking to justify a rule departure in role. "Look," one says, "I have no choice, if I am not to make a mess of things." The other parts of the argument include justifying the degree of surcharge placed on the excluded reasons in question and showing that the role ecology affords agents in the role a liberty to depart from the rule.

The purpose of permitting justifiable rule departures in role is now surely obvious: They offer, suitably hedged, fair gambles for answering social needs that might otherwise go unanswered, where those needs are measured by the ends for which the role was initially instituted. They offer the chance of avoiding the consequences of inadequacy. Thus the soldier commanded to fire at a designated target is obliged by his role to obey, since that is

the way to defeat the enemy. But suppose he believes the troops are friendly and withholds fire. If he is wrong, he may be punished. But if he is right, must he necessarily still be punished? Might he not, on a perfectly rational construction of the military role, be applauded for initiative? Similarly, the sentencing judge, whose role obliges him to serve justice by applying the criminal statutes, finds himself mandated to impose a heavy, and as he has reason to believe, destructive sentence on a youth convicted on a marijuana charge. If he breaches the sentencing restraints imposed by law, should he necessarily be impeached or even criticized? In that breach might lie society's peace. In the facilitation, toleration, or flat prohibition of rule departures, the issue is social utility. It is by no means obvious that prohibition is always the best choice, or even the inevitable choice.

Thus far we have emphasized the positive aspects of rule departures in order to make sense of them as options in legal systems. But there are also major disutilities and risks in establishing roles allowing for rule departures, and these negative aspects often will overbalance the positive. . . .

Types of Roles

We shall now offer a summary view of different types of roles in an effort to show concretely that the notion of justified rule departures is not necessarily anomalous. To be sure, justifying in a role an action that contravenes a mandatory rule of the role seems highly illogical. But while justified rule departures are indeed anomalous for some roles, and with excellent reason, they are not so for others.

The notion of a justified departure in role by a clerk is indeed anomalous. A clerk's role denies him recourse to any of its ends to justify actions outside its prescribed routine. To determine the appropriateness of an action the clerk consults "the book"—a set of rules and procedures established to eliminate any need for him to consider independently what ought to be done. If a case cannot be decided in this manner he must refer it to a higher authority, using formalized procedures ("forms") for submitting questions and receiving answers. The clerk's context of evaluation consists simply of prescribed means. Deviation from those means is his cardinal sin.

The notion of a justifiable rule departure in role is out of place even for roles that, unlike the clerk's, make use of the agent's judgment to achieve role ends. Agents authorized to make decisions in the light of role ends face no problem of justifying rule departures, since the rule in effect obliges them to act on their own judgment. In sentencing within the statutory range of penalties, a judge is simply following the rule. Even when he is authorized to decide whether or not to apply certain rules (as some proponents of the realist school of jurisprudence regard a judge's authority with respect to precedents), no question of rule departures arises. For rules are then in no way mandatory but simply tools that he may use at will to achieve the ends of his role.

Similar conclusions follow even when there are no prescribed means at all to guide a role agent in achieving his role end. There, least of all, despite the absolute reliance on the agent's judgment, are departures from rules possible, for the agent is constrained by only one rule: "Accomplish your mission!" The only problem he faces is the technological one of finding a way to achieve the role end. Thus the only role requirement for the spy is to accomplish his mission, and for the philosopher-king, to succeed in governing. But for the complete freedom to do as they think best in accomplishing their ends, the spy and the philosopher-king must pay the price of absolute responsibility in the event of failure. They may not know failure. Their roles forbid it.

At this point it may seem that to talk about justified rule departures must be to confuse departing from rules with some kind of discretionary action, a major component in the roles of officials and perhaps of citizens. But the ordinary typology of roles omits the possibility of what we shall call "recourse roles"—roles that enable their agents to take action in situations where the role's prescribed ends conflict with its prescribed means, including grants of discretion, broad or narrow. Recourse roles provide for such situations by establishing conditions under which agents may be justified in undertaking actions that depart from role requirements. In short, they extend a liberty in handling obligations.

The problem of conflicting obligations must be handled one way or another in any case. One way, of course, is to organize obligations so that they will not conflict; but as we have seen, this solution is not always feasible. Another is to convert obligations into instrumentalities and authorize the choice of whichever serves a specified purpose. But still another way parallels the process of moral decision, in which the decision among conflicting obligations is left to the agent as his responsibility. Whether any role indeed incorporates this last means of handling conflicting obligations must of course rest on an investigation of that role.

CASE 5.1   THE PLAGIARIZING JOURNALIST

You are the drama critic for the principal newspaper in a midsized city in the midwest. You recently wrote a review of a play that opened at the local theatre. Because the play was one of your favorites, you had kept a file of other reviews it had received over the years, and you studied the file extensively while writing your own review. Today, in the morning mail, you received the following letter:

> I read with interest your review of the play at our theatre. It is one of my favorite plays, too, and I have kept the review of it published in the *New York Times* five years ago. I was greatly distressed to see that your review borrowed heavily from the *Times*. I won't ever tell that you plagiarized, but I think you owe it to your readers to set the record straight.

With a sinking heart, you go to your file of reviews and find that your review is copied in large part from the *Times*. You remember that while writing the review you had taken notes extensively from the *Times* review, but you are otherwise unable to reconstruct how you managed to quote so heavily from the *Times* without acknowledgement.

What will you do? What should you do? Would the presence (or absence) of employer or professional codes of ethics make any difference in your decision?

CASE 5.2   *PROFESSORIAL QUALITY*

The job of a university professor can be an easy life. Scheduled time demands are few: 8 or 10 hours of classes a week, an office hour, and perhaps a committee meeting. Some professors take advantage of this time flexibility. Every student has probably had the misfortune to encounter one of them. Lectures, repeated from year to year, grow ever more out of date. The professor is difficult to find outside of class. Papers are returned late, with few comments except a grade. And this is only what the student sees. The professor's colleagues are all too aware that he has virtually ceased to keep up in his field, that he does little or no research, and that he is rarely willing to help out with university business and is barely competent when he does.

Professional organizations for university faculty are organized by discipline. Professors need not be members, and membership is open not only to professors but to anyone holding an advanced degree or teaching position in the subject. These professional organizations make no attempt to state quality standards or to otherwise regulate the quality of professional services. The American Association of University Professors is a general organization for professors. The AAUP's Statement on Professional Ethics appears in Appendix II. The AAUP also issues guidelines that it recommends universities use in dismissing faculty. The AAUP's chief concern is to protect the academic freedom of both faculty and students—their freedom to voice controversial opinions and study controversial subjects, despite the political pressures of the day. Academic freedom is protected by "tenure"—the right of a faculty member to continued employment. According to the AAUP guidelines, tenured faculty members can be dismissed only for cause, for medical reasons, or when the institution undergoes major financial crises or shifts in program direction. In order to fire a professor for cause, AAUP guidelines require demonstrated incompetence in the performance of professional duties. To protect academic freedom, the AAUP stipulates that controversy is not cause.

The majority of colleges and universities in the United States follow the AAUP guidelines. Under these guidelines, a professor who "just slides by," doing the minimum, could probably not be fired. Universities frequently have programs for reviewing tenured faculty, and these reviews may result in recommendations for improvement. Marginally competent faculty may receive limited or no salary raises. Finally, student course evaluations can sometimes be a way of communicating student opinion to other students and faculty.

Can anything be done about the professor who just gets by? Should anything be done about the quality of services provided by professors? What forms of regulation are available? What forms are desirable? Compare university faculty with other professionals. Should the quality of service be more or less stringently regulated for professors than for doctors or lawyers?

CASE 5.3 CLERGY MALPRACTICE

Max and his family are members of a very close-knit fundamentalist church. Max is 16 years old and deeply troubled about his life. He has experimented with drugs, has stopped going to school, and from time to time has expressed thoughts of suicide to his friends. His parents, who are deeply concerned about him, consult their minister for advice. Their minister is a seminary graduate, ordained in their faith. From time to time, he has taken courses in pastoral counseling offered for ministers of their faith. He is not trained as a psychologist, however.

The minister tells Max's parents that religion can help Max. He offers to pray with them for Max, and to counsel Max to help him bring faith into his life. He does not recommend other counseling or consultation, however. With some effort, Max's parents persuade him to go to see the minister. The minister and Max have several counseling sessions, during which the minister tells Max that his life will be better if he prays to avoid sin. Max makes the effort, but it rings hollow to him and he feels even more sinful as a result. Even more depressed because of the suggestion that he is to blame for his current situation, Max attempts suicide by driving the family car into a tree. Fortunately, Max does not die, but he is left permanently scarred.

Did the minister violate his professional obligations to Max's parents or to Max? What guidance is provided by the Code of Ethics of the American Association of Pastoral Counselors, reprinted in Appendix II? Is this guidance adequate? Should either Max or his parents have a legal cause of action for "clergy malpractice" against the minister? Should any formal steps be taken about such ministerial counseling, either by Max's church or by the state?

CASE 5.4 SCIENTIFIC EXPERIMENTATION AGAINST THE LAW

Dutch elm disease has destroyed nearly all of the beautiful, shady elm trees in the eastern United States, and it is gradually moving west. You have a colleague who has genetically engineered a bacterium that appears to provide immunity against the disease. The bacterium contains only rearranged genetic material from an organism commonly found in the environment. Without legally-required approval from your university's biosafety committee or from the Environmental Protection Agency (the federal agency that regulates field tests of genetically engineered organisms), your colleague has injected 14 trees with the bacterium. He did so because, by his account, the process for approval would have taken too long for him to be able to save the trees during the upcoming winter.

Should your colleague's research be regulated? If so, by whom: the sponsoring institution? the state? the federal government? What regulatory techniques should be employed? Should we rely on tort law (suits for damages after they occur) to deter risky release of the new organisms? Should your colleague have injected the trees with the bacterium? Should he be penalized and, if so, how?

CASE 5.5 "IT'S OVER, DEBBIE"

The call came in the middle of the night. As a gynecology resident rotating through a large, private hospital, I had come to detest telephone calls, because invariably I would be up for several hours and would not feel good the next day. However, duty called, so I answered the phone. A nurse informed me that a patient was having difficulty getting rest, could I please see her. She was on 3 North. That was the gynecologic-oncology unit, not my usual duty station. As I trudged along, bumping sleepily against walls and corners and not believing I was up again, I tried to imagine what I might find at the end of my walk. Maybe an elderly woman with an anxiety reaction, or perhaps something particularly horrible.

I grabbed the chart from the nurses station on my way to the patient's room, and the nurse gave me some hurried details: a 20-year-old girl named Debbie was dying of ovarian cancer. She was having unrelenting vomiting apparently as the result of an alcohol drip administered for sedation. Hmmm, I thought. Very sad. As I approached the room I could hear loud, labored breathing. I entered and saw an emaciated, dark-haired woman who appeared much older than 20. She was receiving nasal oxygen, had an IV, and was sitting in bed suffering from what was obviously severe air hunger. The chart noted her weight at 80 pounds. A second woman, also dark-haired but of middle age, stood at her right, holding her hand. Both looked up as I entered. The room seemed filled with the patient's desperate effort to survive. Her eyes were hollow, and she had suprasternal and intercostal retractions with her rapid inspirations. She had not eaten or slept in two days. She had not responded to chemotherapy and was being given supportive care only. It was a gallows scene, a cruel mockery of her youth and unfulfilled potential. Her only words to me were, "Let's get this over with."

I retreated with my thoughts to the nurses' station. The patient was tired and needed rest. I could not give her health, but I could give her rest. I asked the nurse to draw 20 mg of morphine sulfate into a syringe. Enough, I thought, to do the job. I took the syringe into the room and told the two women I was going to give Debbie something that would let her rest and to say good-bye. Debbie looked at the syringe, then laid her head on the pillow with her eyes open, watching what was left of the world. I injected the morphine intravenously and watched to see if my calculations on its effects would be correct. Within seconds her breathing slowed to a normal rate, her eyes closed, and her features softened as she seemed restful at last. The older woman stroked the hair of the now-sleeping patient. I waited for the inevitable next effect of depressing the respiratory drive. With clocklike certainty, within four minutes the breathing rate slowed even more, then became irregular, then ceased. The dark-haired woman stood erect and seemed relieved.

It's over, Debbie.*

*From the *Journal of the American Medical Association* (January 8, 1988). Copyright 1988, American Medical Association.

This piece appeared in early 1988, as a reader's submission to the *Journal of the American Medical Association.* The author wished his or her name to be withheld, and the *Journal* decided that the piece was important enough to publish anyway. Prosecutors in Chicago, where the *Journal* is published, went to court to get the author's name in order to investigate the possibility of criminal prosecution. The *Journal* resisted successfully.

Should the *Journal* have published the piece? Was this a case of professional disobedience? What rules were violated? Rules of the hospital? Rules of ethics of the medical profession? State law? Were the actions of the unnamed author justified? Should any action be taken against him or her for what was done?

SUGGESTED READINGS

ASHLEY, JO ANN. *Hospitals, Paternalism, and the Role of the Nurse.* New York: Teachers College Press, 1976.

BAUM, ROBERT J. *Ethics and Engineering Curricula.* New York: The Hastings Center, 1980.

CAUSEY, DENZIL Y. *Duties and Liabilities of Public Accountants,* 3d ed. Mississippi State, Miss.: Accountant's Press, 1986.

GOODWIN, H. EUGENE. *Groping for Ethics in Journalism,* 2d ed. Ames: Iowa State University Press, 1987.

GREENSTREET, BOB, AND KAREN GREENSTREET. *The Architect's Guide to Law and Practice.* New York: Van Nostrand Reinhold, 1984.

GROVES, JOHN RUSSELL, JR. "Architectural Education: Teaching Professional Practice—Heroics, Hypocrisy, or Hyperbole?" *Architectural Record,* July 1986, pp. 49–51.

JAMETON, ANDREW. *Nursing Practice: The Ethical Issues.* Englewood Cliffs, N.J.: Prentice Hall, 1984.

KLAIDMAN, STEPHEN, AND TOM L. BEAUCHAMP. *The Virtuous Journalist.* New York: Oxford University Press, 1987.

LAMBETH, EDMUND. *Committed Journalism.* Bloomington: Indiana University Press, 1986.

LAYTON, EDWIN T., JR. *The Revolt of the Engineers: Social Responsibility and the American Engineering Profession,* 2d ed. Baltimore, Md.: Johns Hopkins University Press, 1986.

LUBAN, DAVID, ed. *The Good Lawyer: Lawyers' Roles and Lawyers' Ethics.* Totowa, N.J.: Rowman & Allanheld, 1983.

MALONY, H. NEWTON, THOMAS L. NEEDHAM, AND SAMUEL SOUTHARD. *Clergy Malpractice.* Philadelphia: Westminster Press, 1986.

MARTIN, MIKE W., AND ROLAND SCHINZINGER. *Ethics in Engineering.* New York: McGraw-Hill, 1983.

MILLER, RICHARD L., AND GERALD P. BRADY. *CPA Liability: Meeting the Challenge.* New York: John. Wiley, 1986.

President's Commission for the Study of Ethical Problems in Medicine and Biomedical and Behavioral Research. *Summing Up: Final Report on Studies of the Ethical and Legal Problems in Medicine and Biomedical and Behavioral Research.* Washington, D.C.: U.S. Government Printing Office, 1983.

RAWLS, JOHN. *A Theory of Justice.* Cambridge: Harvard University Press, 1971.

REVERBY, SUSAN. *Ordered to Care: The Dilemma of American Nursing, 1850–1945.* New York: Cambridge University Press, 1987.

SCHAUB, JAMES H., AND KARL PAVLOVIC. *Engineering Professionalism and Ethics.* New York: John Wiley, 1983.

STARR, PAUL. *The Social Transformation of American Medicine.* New York: Basic Books, 1982.

APPENDIX I

INTRODUCTION TO ETHICAL REASONING

Thomas Donaldson and Patricia H. Werhane

This essay is a compact introduction to the three major approaches to ethical theory described in Chapter 1—consequentialism, deontology, and virtue ethics (which the authors here call human nature ethics). The fundamentals of each approach are presented, possible variations are discussed, and the reader is given an account of some of the challenges presented by each theoretical approach.

What is the basis for making ethical decisions? Should Joan challenge Fred the next time he cracks a chauvinist joke? Should John refrain from lying on his job application despite his temptation to do so? What, if anything, should make Hillary decide that eating meat is corrupting whereas vegetarianism is uplifting? It is obvious that the kind of evidence required for an ethical decision is different from that needed to make a nonethical one; but what is the nature of the difference? These questions give rise to a search for a *method* of ethical justification and decision making, a method that will specify the conditions which any good ethical decision should meet. . . .

There have been three classical types of ethical theory in the history of philosophy. Each has been championed by a well-known traditional philosopher, and most ethical theories can be categorized under one of the three headings. The first may be called "consequentialism," the second, "deontology," and the third, "human nature ethics."

CONSEQUENTIALISM

As its name implies, a consequentialist theory of ethical reasoning concentrates on the consequences of human actions, and all actions are evaluated in terms of the extent to which they achieve desirable results. Such theories are also frequently labeled "teleological," a term derived from the Greek word "telos," which refers to an end or purpose. According to consequentialist theories, the concepts of right, wrong, and duty are subordinated to the concept of the end or purpose of an action.

There are at least two types of consequentialist theory. the first—advocated by only a few consequentialists—is a version of what philosophers call "ethical egoism." It construes right action as action whose consequences, considered among all the alternatives, maximizes *my* good, that is, which benefits *me* the most or harms *me* the least. . . . The second type—advocated by most consequentialists—denies that right action concerns only *me*, rather right action must maximize *overall* good; that is, it must maximize good (or minimize bad) from the standpoint of the entire human community. The best accepted label for this type of consequentialism is "utilitarianism." This term was coined by the eighteenth-century philosopher Jeremy Bentham, although its best known proponent was the nineteenth-century English philosopher, John Stuart Mill. As Bentham formulated it, the principle of utility states

From Thomas Donaldson and Patricia H. Werhane, *Ethical Issues in Business: A Philosophical Approach*, 2/ed., © 1983, pp. 7–17. Reprinted by permission of Prentice-Hall, Inc., Englewood Cliffs, N.J.

that an action is right if it produces the greatest balance of pleasure or happiness over pain or unhappiness. The Principle of Utility thus evaluates the rightness or wrongness of actions by measuring this balance of happiness and unhappiness in light of alternative actions. Mill supported a similar principle using what he called the "proof" of the principle of utility, namely, the recognition that the only proof for something's being desirable is that someone actually desires it. Since everybody desires pleasure or happiness it follows, according to Mill, that happiness is the most desirable thing. The purpose of moral action is to achieve greatest overall happiness, and actions are evaluated in terms of the extent to which they contribute to this end. The most desirable state of affairs, the greatest good and the goal of morality, said Mill, is the "greatest happiness for the greatest number."

While later utilitarians accept the general framework of Mill's argument, not all utilitarians are hedonists, that is, not all utilitarians equate "the good" with pleasure or happiness. Some utilitarians have argued that in maximizing the "good," one must be concerned not only with maximizing pleasure, but with maximizing other things such as knowledge, moral maturity, and friendship. Although it could be claimed that such goods *also* bring pleasure and happiness to their possessor, it is arguable whether their goodness is ultimately *reducible* to whatever pleasure they bring. These philosophers are sometimes called "pluralistic" utilitarians. Still other philosophers have adapted utilitarianism to modern methods of economic theory by championing what is known as "preference utilitarianism." Instead of referring to the maximization of specific goods, such as pleasure or knowledge, preference utilitarians understand the ultimate foundation of goodness to be the set of preferences people actually possess. One person prefers oysters to strawberries, another prefers rock music to Mozart. Each person has a *set* of

preferences, and so long as the set is internally consistent it makes no sense to label one set morally superior to another. Preference utilitarianism thus interprets right action as that which is "optimal" among alternatives in terms of everyone's preferences. Disputes, however, rage among preference utilitarians and their critics over how to specify the meaning of "optimal."

Bentham and Mill thought that utilitarianism was a revolutionary theory both because it reflected accurately human motivation and because it had clear application to the political and social problems of their day. If one could measure the benefit or harm of any action, rule or law, they believed, one could sort out good and bad social and political legislation as well as good and bad individual actions.

But how, specifically, *does* one apply the traditional principle of utility? To begin with, one's race, religion, intelligence, or condition of birth is acknowledged to be irrelevant in calculating one's ultimate worth. Each person counts for "one," and no more than "one." Second, in evaluating happiness one must take into account not only present generations but ones in the future. In calculating the effects of, say, pollution, one must measure the possible effects pollution might have on health, genetics, and the supply of natural resources for future generations. Third, pleasure or happiness is measured *en toto* so that the thesis does not reduce to the idea that "one ought to do what makes the most persons happy." Utilitarianism does not reduce to a dictatorship of majority interests. One person's considerable unhappiness might outweigh the minor pleasures of many other persons added together. Utilitarians also consider the long-term consequences for single individuals. For instance, it might be pleasurable to drink a full bottle of wine every evening, but the long-term drawbacks of such a habit might well outweigh its temporary pleasures.

Finally, according to many utilitarians (such as Mill), some pleasures are *qualita-*

tively better than others. Intellectual pleasure, for example, is said to be higher than physical pleasure. "Better to be Socrates unsatisfied," writes Mill, "than a pig satisfied." The reasons that drove Mill to formulate this qualitative distinction among pleasures are worth noting. Since Mill believed that the optimal situation was one of "greatest happiness for the greatest number," then what was he to say about a world of people living at the zenith of merely *physical* happiness? If science could invent a wonder drug, like the "soma" in Aldous Huxley's *Brave New World*, that provided a permanent state of drugged happiness (without even a hangover), would the consequence be a perfect world? Mill believed not, and to remedy this difficulty in his theory, he introduced *qualitative levels* of happiness: e.g., he said that the happiness of understanding Plato is "higher" than that of drinking three martinis. But how was Mill to say *which* pleasures were higher? Here he retreated to an ingenious proposal: When deciding which of two pleasures is higher, one should poll the group of persons who are experienced, that is, who know *both* pleasures. Their decision will indicate which is the higher pleasure. Ah, but might the majority decision not be wrong? Here Mill provides no clear answer.

Modern day utilitarians divide themselves roughly into two groups, *act utilitarians* and *rule utilitarians.* An *act* utilitarian believes that the Principle of Utility should be applied to individual acts. Thus one measures the consequences of each *individual action* according to whether it maximizes good. For example, suppose a certain community were offered the opportunity to receive a great deal of wealth in the form of a gift. The only stipulation was that the community force some of its citizens with ugly, deteriorated houses, to repair and beautify them. Next, suppose the community held an election to decide whether to accept the gift. Now an act utilitarian would analyze the problem of whether to vote for or against the proposal from the standpoint of the *individual voter.* Would an individual's vote to accept the gift be more likely to maximize the community's overall good than would a vote to the contrary?

A *rule* utilitarian, on the other hand, believes that instead of considering the results of specific action, one must weigh the consequences of adopting a *general rule* exemplified by that action. According to the rule utilitarian, one should act according to a general rule which, if adopted, would maximize good. For example, in the hypothetical case of the community deciding whether to accept a gift, a rule utilitarian might adopt the rule, "Never vote in a way which lowers the self-respect of a given class of citizens." She might accept this rule because of the general unhappiness that would ensue if society systematically treated some persons as second-class citizens. Here the focus is on the general rule and not on the individual act.

Critics raise objections to utilitarianism. Perhaps the most serious is that it is unable to account for justice. Because the utilitarian concentrates on the consequences of an action for a majority, the employment of the Principle of Utility can be argued to allow injustice for a small minority. For example, if overall goodness were maximized in the long run by making slaves of 2 percent of the population, utilitarianism seemingly is forced to condone slavery. But clearly this is unjust. Utilitarianism's obvious response is that such slavery will not, as a matter of empirical fact, maximize goodness. Rule utilitarians, as we have seen, can argue that society should embrace the rule, "never enslave others," because following such a principle, in the long run, will maximize goodness. Even so, the battle continues between utilitarians and their critics. Can utilitarianism account for the widely held moral conviction that injustice to a minority is wrong *regardless* of the consequences? The answer is hotly contested.

Another criticism concerns the determination of the good to be maximized. Any consequentialist has the problem of identifying and ranking whatever is to be maximized. For a utilitarian such as Mill, as we have seen, the problem involves distinguishing between higher and lower pleasures. But for "pluralistic" utilitarians a similar problem exists: What is the basis for selecting, for example, friendship and happiness as goods to be maximized and not, say, aesthetic sensitivity? And even granted that this problem can be solved, there is the further problem of arbitrating trade-offs between goods such as happiness and friendship when they *conflict*. When one is forced to choose between enhancing happiness and enhancing friendship, which gets priority? And under what conditions?

An interesting fact about consequentialist reasoning is that most of us employ it to some degree in ordinary decisions. We weigh the consequences of alternatives in choosing colleges, in deciding on a career, in hiring and promoting others, and in many other judgments. We frequently weigh good consequences over bad ones and predict the long- and short-term effects of our choices. We often even cite consequentialist style principles: for example, "No one should choose a college where he or she will be unhappy." Or, "No one should pollute the environment when his or her action harms others."

However, for a variety of reasons including the objections to utilitarianism mentioned earlier, some philosophers refuse to acknowledge counsequentialism as an adequate theory of ethics. They argue that the proper focus for ethical judgments should not be consequences, but moral *precepts*, that is, the rules, norms, and principles we use to guide our actions. Such philosophers are known as "deontologists," and the next section will examine their views.

DEONTOLOGY

The term "deontological" comes from the Greek word for duty, and what is crucial according to the deontologist are the rules and principles that guide actions. We shall discuss here two approaches to deontological ethical reasoning that have profoundly influenced ethics. The first is that of the eighteenth-century philosopher Immanuel Kant and his followers. This approach focuses on duty and universal rules to determine right actions. The second—actually a subspecies of deontological reasoning—is known as the "social contract" approach. It focuses not on individual decision-making, but on the general social principles that rational persons in certain ideal situations would agree upon and adopt.

Kantian Deontology

Kant believed that ethical reasoning should concern activities that are rationally motivated and should utilize precepts that apply universally to all human actions. To this end he opens his treatise on ethics by declaring,

It is impossible to conceive anything at all in the world, . . . which can be taken as good without qualification except a *good* will.[1]

This statement sums up much of what Kant wants to say about ethics—and is worth unraveling. What Kant means is that the only thing which can be good or worthwhile without any provisos or stipulations is an action of the will freely motivated for the right reasons. Other goods such as wealth, beauty, and intelligence are certainly valuable, but they are not good *without qualification* because they have the potential to create both good and bad effects. Wealth, beauty, and intelligence can be bad

[1] Immanuel Kant, *Groundwork of the Metaphysic of Morals*, trans. H. J. Paton (New York: Harper & Row, 1948; rpt. 1956), p. 61.

when they are used for purely selfish ends. Even human happiness—which Mill held as the highest good—can, according to Kant, create complacency, disinterest, and excessive self-assurance under certain conditions.

According to Kant, reason is the faculty that can aid in the discovery of correct moral principles; thus it is *reason, not inclination,* that should guide the will. When reason guides the will, Kant calls the resulting actions ones done from "duty." Kant's use of the term "duty" turns out to be less formidable than it first appears. Kant is simply saying that a purely good and free act of the will is one done not merely because you have an *inclination* to do it, but because you have the right reasons for doing it. For example, suppose you discover a wallet belonging to a stranger. Kant would say that despite one's inclination to keep the money (which the stranger may not even need), one should return it. This is an act you know is right despite your inclinations. Kant also believes you should return the wallet even when you believe the *consequences* of not returning it are better. Here his views are at sharp odds with consequentialism. Suppose the stranger is known for her stinginess, and that you plan to donate the money to a childrens' hospital. No matter. For Kant, you must return the wallet. Thus the moral worth lies in the act itself and not in either your happiness or the consequences brought about by the act. Acts are good because they are done for the sake of what is right and not because of the consequences they might produce.

But how do I know what my duty is? While it may be clear that one should return a wallet, there are other circumstances where one's duty is less evident. Suppose you are in a six-person lifeboat at sea with five others and a seventh person swims up? What is one's duty here? And how does one even know that what one *thinks* is right *is* right? To settle such prob-

lems Kant claims that duty is more than doing merely what you "feel" is right. Duty is acting with *respect for other rational beings.* It almost goes without saying, then, that "acting from duty" is not to be interpreted as action done in obedience to local, state, or national laws, since these can be good or bad. Rather "duty" is linked to the idea of universal principles that should govern all our actions.

But is there any principle that can govern *all* human beings? Kant believes the answer is yes, and he calls the highest such principle the "Categorical Imperative." He formulates the Categorical Imperative in three ways (although we shall only consider two formulations here). The first formulation, roughly translated, is:

One ought only to act such that the principle of one's act could become a universal law of human action in a world in which one would hope to live.

For example, one would want to live in a world where people followed the principle, "return property that belongs to others." Therefore one should return the stranger's wallet. We do not, however, want to live in a world where everyone lies. Therefore one should not adopt the principle "lie whenever it seems helpful."

The second formulation of the categorical imperative is:

One ought to treat others as having intrinsic value in themselves, and *not* merely as means to achieve one's ends.

In other words, one should respect every person as a rational and free being. Hitler treated one group of persons as nonpersons in order to achieve his own ends, and thus acted contrary to the categorical imperative. Another instance of treating persons as means would occur if a teacher looked up the grade records of new students to determine how to assign grades in her own class. She would be treating students as if they had no control over their destinies.

Such actions are immoral according to Kant because they fail to respect the inherent dignity of rational beings.

Ethical reasoning for Kant implies adopting principles of action and evaluating one's actions in terms of those principles. Even Kant grants that the evaluation is sometimes difficult. For example, there is the problem of striking the proper level of generality in choosing a principle. A principle which read, "If one is named John Doe and attends Big State University and has two sisters, then he should borrow fifty dollars without intending to repay it," is far too specific. On the other hand the principle "you should always pay your debts," might be too general since it would require that a starving man repay the only money he possesses to buy a loaf of bread. Because of the problem of striking the proper degree of generality, many modern deontologists have reformulated Kant's basic question to read: "Could I wish that everyone in the world would follow this principle *under relevantly similar conditions?*"

As with utilitarianism, critics challenge deontological reasoning. Some assert that fanatics such as Hitler could at least *believe* that the rule "Persecute Jews whenever possible," is one that the world should live by. Similarly a thief might universalize the principle, "Steal whenever you have a good opportunity." Moreover a strict interpretation of dentological ethical reasoning is said to allow no exceptions to a universal principle. Such strict adherence to universal principles might encourage moral rigidity and might fail to reflect the diversity of responses required by complex moral situations. Finally, critics argue that in a given case two principles may conflict without there being a clear way to decide which principle or rule should take precedence. Jean-Paul Sartre tells of his dilemma during World War II when he was forced to choose between staying to comfort his ill and aging mother, and fighting for the freedom of France. Two principles seemed valid: "Give aid to your father and mother," and "Contribute to the cause of freedom." But with

conflicting principles, how is one to choose? Nevertheless, deontological ethical reasoning represents a well-respected and fundamentally distinctive mode of ethical reasoning, one which, like consequentialism, appears in the deliberations of ordinary persons as well as philosophers. We have all heard actions condemned by the comment, "what would it be like if everyone did that?"

The Contractarian Alternative

Kant assumes that the Categorical Imperative is something all rational individuals can discover and agree upon. A different version of deontology is offered by many philosophers who focus less on the actions of individuals, and more on the principles that govern society at large. [Among these philosophers are] the seventeenth-century political philosopher John Locke and the twentieth-century American philosopher John Rawls. They and others try to establish universal principles of a just society through what might be called "social contract thought experiments." They ask us to imagine what it would be like to live in a situation where there are no laws, no social conventions and no political state. In this so-called "state of nature" we imagine that rational persons gather to formulate principles or rules to govern political and social communities. Such rules would resemble principles derived through the categorical imperative in that they are presumably principles to which every rational person would agree and which would hold universally.

Locke and Rawls differ in their approach for establishing rules or principles of justice, and the difference illustrates two distinct forms of contractarian reasoning. Locke argues from what is called a "natural rights" position, while Rawls argues from what is called a "reasonable person" position. Locke claims that every person is born with, and possesses, certain basic rights that are "natural." These rights are inherent to a person's nature, and they are possessed by every one equally. Like other inherent traits they cannot be taken away. They are, in the words of the Declaration of Independence, "inalienable." When rational persons meet to formulate principles to govern the formation of social and political communities they construct a social contract that is the basis for an agreement between themselves and their government, and whose rules protect natural rights. Rights, then, become deontological precepts by which one forms and evaluates rules, constitutions, governments, and socio-economic systems. While many philosophers disagree with Locke's view that each of us has inherent or *natural* rights, many do utilize a theory of human rights as the basis for justifying and evaluating political institutions. . . .

Rawls adopts a different perspective. He does not begin from a natural rights position. Rather he asks which principles of justice would rational persons formulate if they were behind a "veil of ignorance," i.e., if each person knew nothing about who he or she was. That is, one would not know whether one were old or young, male or female, rich or poor, highly motivated or lazy, or anything about one's personal status in society. Unable to predict which principles, if picked, will favor them personally, Rawls argues, persons will be forced to choose principles that are fair to all.

Rawls and Locke are not in perfect agreement about which principles would be adopted in such hypothetical situations, and more will be said about their views later in the book. For now it is important to remember that the social contract approach maintains a deontological character. It is used to formulate principles of justice which apply universally. Some philosophers note, however, that from an original position in a "state of nature" or behind a "veil of ignorance," rational persons, logically speaking, *could* adopt consequentialist principles as rules for a just society. Thus, while the social contract approach is deontological in style, the principles it generates are not necessarily ones which

are incompatible with consequentialism. . . .

In the moral evaluations of business, all deontologists, contractarians included, would ask questions such as:

a. Are the rules fair to everyone?
b. Do they hold universally even with the passage of time?
c. Is every person treated with equal respect?

What may be missing from a deontological approach to ethical reasoning is a satisfactory means of coping with valid exceptions to general rules. Under what circumstances, if any, are exceptions allowed? Deontologists believe that they can answer this question, but their solutions vary. Suffice it to say that deontologists, just as utilitarians, have not convinced everyone.

HUMAN NATURE ETHICS

According to some contemporary philosophers, the preceding two modes of ethical reasoning exhaust all possible modes: That is to say, all theories can be classified as either "teleological" or "deontological." Whether this is true cannot be settled here, but it will be helpful to introduce briefly what some philosophers consider to be a third category, namely the "human nature" approach.

A "human nature" approach assumes that all humans have inherent capacities that constitute the ultimate basis for all ethical claims. Actions are evaluated in terms of whether they promote or hinder, coincide with, or conflict with, these capacities. One of the most famous proponents of this theory was the Greek philosopher, Aristotle. In Aristotle's opinion, human beings have inherent *potentialities* and thus human development turns out to be the struggle for self-actualization, or in other words, the perfection of inherent human nature. Consider the acorn. It has the natural potential to become a sturdy oak tree. Its natural drive is not to become an elm or a cedar, or even a stunted oak, but to become the most robust oak tree possible. Diseased or stunted oak trees are simply deficient; they are instances of things in nature whose potential has not been fully developed. Similarly persons, according to Aristotle, are born with inherent potentialities. Persons, like acorns, naturally are oriented to actualize their potentialities, and for them this means more than merely developing their *physical* potential. It also means developing their mental, moral, and social potential. Thus human beings on this view are seen as basically good; evil is understood as a deficiency that occurs when one is unable to fulfill one's natural capacities.

Here it is important to understand that the concept of human nature need not be an individualistic one. According to Aristotle, persons are "social" by nature, and cannot be understood apart from the larger community in which they participate. "Man," Aristotle writes, is a "social animal." For Aristotle, then, fulfilling one's natural constitution implies developing wisdom, generosity, and self-restraint, all of which help to make one a good member of the community.

The criterion for judging the goodness of any action is whether or not the action is compatible with one's inherent human capacities. Actions which enhance human capacities are good; those that deter them are bad unless they are the best among generally negative alternatives. For example, eating nothing but starches is unhealthy, but it is clearly preferable to starving.

This theory puts great emphasis on the nature of persons, and obviously how one understands that "nature" will be the key to determining both what counts as a right action and how one defines the proper end of human action in general. Aristotle argued that intelligence and wisdom are uniquely human potentialities and consequently that intellectual virtue is the highest virtue. The life of contemplation, he believed, is the best sort of life, in part because it represents the highest fulfillment of human nature. Moral virtue, also crucial in Aristotle's theory, involves the rational control of one's desires. In action where a choice is possible, one exercises moral virtue by restraining harmful desires and cultivating beneficial ones. The development of virtue requires the cultivation of good habits, and this in turn leads Aristotle to emphasize the importance of good upbringing and education.

One problem said to affect human nature theories is that they have difficulty justifying the supposition that human beings *do* have specific inherent capacities and that these capacities are the same for all humans. Further, critics claim that it is difficult to warrant the assumption that humans are basically good. Perhaps the famous psychoanalyst Sigmund Freud is correct in his assertion that at bottom we are all naturally aggressive and selfish. Third, critics complain that it is difficult to employ this theory in ethical reasoning, since it appears to lack clear-cut rules and principles for use in moral decision making. Obviously, any well-argued human nature ethic will take pains to spell out the aspects of human nature which, when actualized, constitute the ultimate ground for moral judgments.

CONCLUSION

The three approaches to ethical reasoning we have discussed, consequentialism, deontology, and human nature ethics, all present theories of ethical reasoning distinguished in terms of their basic methodological elements. Each represents a type or "model" of moral reasoning that is applicable to practical decisions in concrete situation. . . . The question of which method, if any, is superior to the others must be left for another time. The intention of this essay is not to substitute for a thorough study of traditional ethical theories—something for which there is no substitute—but to introduce the reader to basic modes of ethical reasoning.

APPENDIX II

Selected Codes of Professional Ethics

This appendix is comprised of selections from a wide variety of codes of ethics of different professions. They are edited to serve as a resource for discussion of the ethical issues discussed in earlier chapters. As described in Chapter 1, the formulation of a code is sometimes eagerly undertaken as a mark of professionalization. Beyond the examples here, many other professional groups also have codes. Many employers also promulgate codes for their employees, although these often focus on etiquette or loyalty. It should be emphasized as well that professional codes tend to set minimum consensus standards or avoid the serious ethical issues entirely, rather than defining what it is ultimately right for professionals to do. Some of these codes are enforceable under state law; others are hortatory only. Regardless of their limitations, they all represent efforts by professional groups to identify and come to terms with some of the more important issues facing members of their professions.

CODE OF PROFESSIONAL CONDUCT

American Institute of Certified Public Accountants

Composition, Applicability, and Compliance

The Code of Professional Conduct of the American Institute of Certified Public Accountants consists of two sections—(1) the Principles and (2) the Rules. The Principles provide the framework for the Rules, which govern the performance of professional services by members. The Council of the American Institute of Certified Public Accountants is authorized to designate bodies to promulgate technical standards under the Rules, and the bylaws require adherence to those Rules and standards.

The Code of Professional Conduct was adopted by the membership to provide guidance and rules to all members—those in public practice, in industry, in government, and in education—in the performance of their professional responsibilities.

Compliance with the Code of Professional Conduct, as with all standards in an open society, depends primarily on members' understanding and voluntary actions, secondarily on reinforcement by peers and public opinion, and ultimately on disciplinary proceedings, when necessary, against members who fail to comply with the Rules.

SECTION I—PRINCIPLES

Preamble

Membership in the American Institute of Certified Public Accountants is voluntary. By accepting membership, a certified public accountant assumes an obligation of self-discipline above and beyond the requirements of laws and regulations.

These Principles of the Code of Professional Conduct of the American Institute of Certified Public Accountants express the profession's recognition of its responsibilities to the public, to clients, and to colleagues. They guide members in the performance of their professional responsibilities and express the basic tenets of ethical and professional conduct. The Principles call for an unswerving commitment to honorable behavior, even at the sacrifice of personal advantage.

Article I   Responsibilities

In carrying out their responsibilities as professionals, members should exercise sensitive professional and moral judgments in all their activities.

As professionals, certified public accountants perform an essential role in society. Consistent with that role, members of the American Institute of Certified Public Accountants have responsibilities to all those who use their professional services. Members also have a continuing responsibility to cooperate with each other to improve the art of accounting, maintain the public's confidence, and carry out the profession's special responsibilities for self-governance. The collective efforts of all members are required to maintain and enhance the traditions of the professions.

Article II   The Public Interest

Members should accept the obligation to act in a way that will serve the public interest, honor the public trust, and demonstrate commitment to professionalism.

A distinguishing mark of a profession is acceptance of its responsibility to the public. The accounting profession's public consists of clients, credit grantors, governments, employers, investors, the business and financial community, and others who rely on the objectivity and integrity of certified public accountants to maintain the orderly functioning of commerce. This reliance imposes a public interest responsibility on certified public accountants. The

public interest is defined as the collective well-being of the community of people and institutions the profession serves.

In discharging their professional responsibilities, members may encounter conflicting pressures from among each of those groups. In resolving those conflicts, members should act with integrity, guided by the precept that when members fulfill their responsibility to the public, clients' and employers' interests are best served. . . .

Article III   Integrity

To maintain and broaden public confidence, members should perform all professional responsibilities with the highest sense of integrity.

Integrity is an element of character fundamental to professional recognition. It is the quality from which the public trust derives and the benchmark against which a member must ultimately test all decisions. Integrity requires a member to be, among other things, honest and candid within the constraints of client confidentiality. Service and the public trust should not be subordinated to personal gain and advantage. Integrity can accommodate the inadvertent error and the honest difference of opinion; it cannot accommodate deceit or subordination of principle. . . .

Article IV   Objectivity and Independence

A member should maintain objectivity and be free of conflicts of interest in discharging professional responsibilities. A member in public practice should be independent in fact and appearance when providing auditing and other attestation services.

Objectivity is a state of mind, a quality that lends value to a member's services. It is a distinguishing feature of the profession. The principle of objectivity imposes the obligation to be impartial, intellectually honest, and free of conflicts of interest. Independence precludes relationships that may appear to impair a member's objectivity in rendering attestation services.

Members often serve multiple interests in many different capacities and must demonstrate their objectivity in varying circumstances. Members in public practice render attest, tax, and management advisory services. Other members prepare financial statements in the employment of others, perform internal auditing services, and serve in financial and management capacities in industry, education, and government. They also educate and train those who aspire to admission into the profession. Regardless of service or capacity, members should protect the integrity of their work, maintain objectivity, and avoid any subordination of their judgment. . . .

Article V   Due Care

A member should observe the profession's technical and ethical standards, strive continually to improve competence and the quality of services, and discharge professional responsibility to the best of the member's ability. . . .

Article VI   Scope and Nature of Services

A member in public practice should observe the Principles of the Code of Professional Conduct in determining the scope and nature of services to be provided. . . .

SECTION II—RULES

Applicability

The bylaws of the American Institute of Certified Public Accountants require that members adhere to the Rules of the Code of Professional Conduct. Members must be prepared to justify departures from these Rules.

Definitions

[Adoption of the revised Code of Professional Conduct will require modification of some of the definitions of terms used in the Principles and Rules. The Professional Ethics Executive Committee has this project under way. Until new definitions are adopted, the definitions of terms as they appeared prior to adoption of the new Rules on January 12, 1988, are presented for reference.]

Client. The person(s) or entity which retains a member or his firm, engaged in the practice of public accounting, for the performance of professional services.

Council. The Council of the American Institute of Certified Public Accountants.

Enterprise. Any person(s) or entity, whether organized for profit or not, for which a CPA provides services.

Financial statements. Statements and footnotes related thereto that purport to show financial position which relates to a point in time or changes in financial position which relate to a period of time, and statements which use a cash or other incomplete basis of accounting. Balance sheets, statements of income, statements of retained earnings, statements of changes in financial position, and statements of changes in owners' equity are financial statements.

Incidental financial data included in management advisory services reports to support recommendations to a client and tax returns and supporting schedules do not, for this purpose, constitute financial statements; and the statement, affidavit, or signature of preparers required on tax returns neither constitutes an opinion on financial statements nor requires a disclaimer of such opinion.

Firm. A proprietorship, partnership, or professional corporation or association engaged in the practice of public accounting, including individual partners or shareholders thereof.

Institute. The American Institute of Certified Public Accountants.

Interpretations of rules of conduct. Pronouncements issued by the division of professional ethics to provide guidelines concerning the scope and application of the rules of conduct.

Member. A member, associate member, or international associate of the American Institute of Certified Public Accountants.

Practice of public accounting. Holding out to be a CPA or public accountant and at the same time performing for a client one or more types of services rendered by public accountants. The term shall not be limited by a more restrictive definition which might be found in the accountancy law under which a member practices.

Professional services. One or more types of services performed in the practice of public accounting.

Rules

Rule 101   Independence

A member in public practice shall be independent in the performance of professional services as required by standards promulgated by bodies designated by Council.

Interpretation of Rule 101

Interpretation 101-1. Independence shall be considered to be impaired if, for example, a member had any of the following transactions, interests, or relationships:

A. During the period of a professional engagement or at the time of expressing an opinion, a member or a member's firm
  1. Had or was committed to acquire any direct or material indirect financial interest in the enterprise.
  2. Was a trustee of any trust or executor or administrator of any estate if such trust or estate had or was committed to acquire any direct or material indirect financial interest in the enterprise.
  3. Had any joint, closely held business investment with the enterprise or with any officer, director, or principal stockholders thereof that was material in relation to the member's net worth or to the net worth of the member's firm.
  4. Had any loan to or from the enterprise or any officer, director, or principal stockholder of the enterprise. This proscription does not apply to the following loans from a financial institution when made under normal lending procedures, terms, and requirements:
    a. Loans obtained by a member or a member's firm that are not material

in relation to the net worth of such borrower.
    b. Home mortgages.
    c. Other secured loans, except loans guaranteed by a member's firm which are otherwise unsecured.
B. During the period covered by the financial statements, during the period of the professional engagement, or at the time of expressing an opinion, a member or a member's firm
  1. Was connected with the enterprise as a promoter, underwriter or voting trustee, as a director or officer, or in any capacity equivalent to that of a member of management or of an employee.
  2. Was a trustee for any pension or profit-sharing trust of the enterprise.

The above examples are not intended to be all-inclusive.

Rule 102   Integrity and Objectivity

In the performance of any professional service, a member shall maintain objectivity and integrity, shall be free of conflicts of interest, and shall not knowingly misrepresent facts or subordinate his or her judgment to others.

Rule 201   General Standards

A member shall comply with the following standards and with any interpretations thereof by bodies designated by Council.

A. *Professional Competence.* Undertake only those professional services that the member or the member's firm can reasonably expect to be completed with professional competence.
B. *Due Professional Care.* Exercise due professional care in the performance of professional services.
C. *Planning and Supervision.* Adequately plan and supervise the performance of professional services.
D. *Sufficient Relevant Data.* Obtain sufficient relevant data to afford a reasonable basis for conclusions or recommendations in relation to any professional services performed.

Rule 202   Compliance With Standards

A member who performs auditing, review, compilation, management advisory, tax, or other professional services shall comply with standards promulgated by bodies designated by Council.

Rule 203   Accounting Principles

A member shall not (1) express an opinion or state affirmatively that the financial statements or other financial data of any entity are presented in conformity with generally accepted accounting principles or (2) state that he or she is not aware of any material modifications that should be made to such statements or data in order for them to be in conformity with generally accepted accounting principles, if such statements or data contain any departure from an accounting principle promulgated by bodies designated by Council to establish such principles that has a material effect on the statements or data taken as a whole. If, however, the statements or data contain such a departure and the member can demonstrate that due to unusual circumstances the financial statements or data would otherwise have been misleading, the member can comply with the rule by describing the departure, its approximate effects, if practicable, and the reasons why compliance with the principle would result in a misleading statement.

Rule 301   Confidential Client Information

A member in public practice shall not disclose any confidential client information without the specific consent of the client.

This rule shall not be construed (1) to relieve a member of his or her professional obligations under rules 202 and 203, (2) to affect in any way the member's obligation to comply with a validly issued and enforceable subpoena or summons, (3) to prohibit review of a member's professional practice under AICPA or state CPA society authorization, or (4) to preclude a member from initiating a complaint with or responding to any inquiry made by a recognized investigative or disciplinary body.

Members of a recognized investigative or disciplinary body and professional practice reviewers shall not use to their own advantage or disclose any member's confidential client information that comes to their attention in carrying out their official responsibilities. However, this prohibition shall not restrict the exchange of information with a recognized investigative or disciplinary body or affect, in any way, compliance with a validly issued and enforceable subpoena or summons.

Rule 302   Contingent Fees

Professional services shall not be offered or rendered under an arrangement whereby no fee will be charged unless a specified finding or result is attained, or where the fee is otherwise contingent upon the finding or results of such services. However, a member's fees may vary depending, for example, on the complexity of services rendered.

Fees are not regarded as being contingent if fixed by courts or other public authorities, or, in tax matters, if determined based on the results of judicial proceedings or the findings of governmental agencies. . . .

Rule 501   Acts Discreditable

A member shall not commit an act discreditable to the profession.

Rule 502   Advertising and Other Forms of Solicitation

A member in public practice shall not seek to obtain clients by advertising or other forms of solicitation in a manner that is false, misleading, or deceptive. Solicitation by the use of coercion, over-reaching, or harassing conduct is prohibited.

Rule 503   Commissions

The acceptance by a member in public practice of a payment for the referral of products or services of others to a client is prohibited. Such action is considered to create a conflict of interest that results in a loss of objectivity and independence.

A member shall not make a payment to obtain a client. This rule shall not prohibit payments for the purchase of an accounting practice or retirement payments to individuals formerly engaged in the practice of public accounting or payments to their heirs or estates. . . .

STANDARDS OF PRACTICE

American Association of Advertising Agencies

We hold that a responsibility of advertising agencies is to be a constructive force in business.

We further hold that, to discharge this responsibility, advertising agencies must recognize an obligation, not only to their clients, but to the public, the media they employ, and to each other.

We finally hold that the responsibility will best be discharged if all agencies observe a common set of standards of practice.[1]

To this end, the American Association of Advertising Agencies has adopted the following Standards of Practice as being in the best interests of the public, the advertisers, the media owners, and the agencies themselves.

These standards are voluntary. They are intended to serve as a guide to the kind of agency conduct which experience has shown to be wise, foresighted, and constructive.

It is recognized that advertising is a business and as such must operate within the framework of competition. It is further recognized that keen and vigorous competition, honestly conducted, is necessary to the growth and health of American business generally, of which advertising is a part.

However, *unfair* competitive practices in the advertising agency business lead to financial waste, dilution of service, diversion of manpower, and loss of prestige. Unfair practices tend to weaken public confidence both in advertisements and in the institution of advertising.

1. Creative Code

We the members of the American Association of Advertising Agencies, in addition to supporting and obeying the laws and legal regulations pertaining to advertising, undertake to extend and broaden the application of high ethical standards. Specifically, we will not knowingly produce advertising which contains:

a. False or misleading statements or exaggerations, visual or verbal.

b. Testimonials which do not reflect the real choice of a competent witness.

c. Price claims which are misleading.

d. Comparisons which unfairly disparage a competitive product or service.

e. Claims insufficiently supported, or which distort the true meaning or practicable application of statements made by professional or scientific authority.

f. Statements, suggestions or pictures offensive to public decency.

[1] These Standards of Practice of the American Association of Advertising Agencies come from the belief that sound practice is good business. Confidence and respect are indispensable to success in a business embracing the many intangibles of agency service and involving relationships so dependent upon good faith. These standards are based on a broad experience of what has been found to be the best advertising practice.

From American Association of Advertising Agencies, *Standards of Practice* (1962). Reprinted by permission.

We recognize that there are areas which are subject to honestly different interpretations and judgment. Taste is subjective and may even vary from time to time as well as from individual to individual. Frequency of seeing or hearing advertising messages will necessarily vary greatly from person to person.

However, we agree not to recommend to an advertiser and to discourage the use of advertising which is in poor or questionable taste or which is deliberately irritating through content, presentation or excessive repetition.

Clear and willful violations of this Code shall be referred to the Board of Directors of the American Association of Advertising Agencies for appropriate action, including possible annulment of membership as provided by Article IV, Section 5, of the Constitution and By-Laws.

2. Contracts

a. The advertising agency should where feasible enter into written contracts with media in placing advertising. When entered into, the agency should conform to its agreements with media. Failure to do so may result in loss of standing or litigation, either on the contract or for violations of the Clayton or Federal Trade Commission Acts.

b. The advertising agency should not knowingly fail to fulfill all lawful contractual commitments with media.

3. Offering Credit Extension

It is unsound and uneconomic to offer extension of credit or banking service as an inducement in solicitation.

4. Unfair Tactics

The advertising agency should compete on merit and not by depreciating a competitor or his work directly or inferentially, or by circulating harmful rumors about him, or by making unwarranted claims of scientific skill in judging or prejudging advertising copy, or by seeking to obtain an account by hiring a key employee away from the agency in charge in violation of the agency's employment agreements.

CODE OF ETHICS AND PROFESSIONAL CONDUCT

American Institute of Architects

Preamble

Members of The American Institute of Architects are dedicated to the highest standards of professionalism, integrity and competence. The following principles are guidelines for the conduct of members in fulfilling those obligations. They apply to all professional activities, wherever they occur. They address responsibilities to the public, which the profession serves and enriches; to the clients and users of architecture, and in the building industries, who help to shape the built environment; and to the art and science of architecture, that continuum of knowledge and creation which is the heritage and legacy of the profession.

This Code is arranged in three tiers of statements: Canons, Ethical Standards and Rules of Conduct. The Canons are broad principles of conduct. The Ethical Standards are more specific goals towards which members should aspire in professional performance and behavior. The Rules of Conduct are mandatory, the violation of which is grounds for disciplinary action by the Institute. The Rules of Conduct in some instances implement more than one Canon or Ethical Standard.

Canon I: General Obligations

Members should maintain and advance their knowledge of the art and science of architecture, respect the body of architectural accomplishment and contribute to its growth; learned and uncompromised professional judgment should take precedence over any other motive in the pursuit of the art and science of architecture.

E.S. 1.1 Knowledge and Skill: Members should strive to improve their professional knowledge and skill.

R. 1.101 In practicing architecture, members shall demonstrate a consistent pattern of reasonable care and competence, and shall apply the technical knowledge and skill which is ordinarily applied by architects of good standing practicing in the same locality. . . .
R. 1.102 Members shall not undertake to provide professional services if their competence is substantially impaired by physical or mental disabilities.

E.S. 1.2 Standards of Excellence: Members should continually seek to raise the standards of aesthetic excellence, architectural education, research, training and practice.

E.S. 1.3 Public Understanding: Members should strive to improve public appreciation and understanding of architecture and the functions and responsibilities of architects.

E.S. 1.4 Allied Arts & Industries: Members should promote allied arts and contribute to the knowledge and capability of the building industries as a whole.

Canon II: Obligations to the Public

Members should embrace the spirit and letter of the law governing their professional affairs and should thoughtfully con-sider the social and environmental impact of their professional activities.

E.S. 2.1 Conduct: Members should uphold the law in the conduct of their professional activities.

R. 2.101 Members shall not, in the conduct of their professional practice, knowingly violate the law. . . .
R. 2.102 Members shall neither offer nor make any payment or gift to a local, state or federal official with the intent of influencing the official's judgment in connection with an existing or prospective project in which the members are interested. . . .
R. 2.103 Members serving in a public capacity shall not accept payments or gifts which are intended to influence their judgment.
R. 2.104 Members shall not engage in conduct involving fraud or wanton disregard of the rights of others. . . .
R. 2.105 If, in the course of their work on a project, the members become aware of a decision taken by their employer or client, against the members' advice, which violates any law or regulation and which will in the members' judgment, materially affect adversely the safety to the public of the finished project, the members shall:
(a) refuse to consent to the decision, and
(b) report the decision to the local building inspector or other public official charged with the enforcement of the applicable laws and regulations, unless the members are able to cause the matter to be satisfactorily resolved by other means. . . .
R. 2.106 Members shall not counsel or assist a client in conduct that the architect knows, or reasonably should know, is fraudulent or illegal. . . .

E.S. 2.2 Natural and Cultural Heritage: Members should respect and help conserve their natural and cultural heritage while striving to improve the environment and the quality of life within it.

E.S. 2.3 Civic Responsibility: Members should be involved in civic activities as citizens and professionals, and promote public awareness of architectural issues.

R. 2.301 Members making public statements on architectural issues shall disclose when they are being compensated for making such statements or when they have an economic interest in the issue.

E.S. 2.4 Public Interest Services: Members should render public interest professional services and encourage their employees to render such services.

E.S. 2.5 Human Rights: Members should uphold human rights in all their professional endeavors.

R. 2.501 Members shall not discriminate in their professional activities on the basis of race, religion, gender, national origin, age or nondisqualifying handicap. . . .

Canon III: Obligations to the Client

Members should serve their clients competently and in a professional manner, and should exercise unprejudiced and unbiased judgment on their behalf.

E.S. 3.1 Competence: Members should serve their clients in a timely and competent manner.

R. 3.101 In performing professional services, members shall take into account applicable laws and regulations. Members may rely on the advice of other qualified persons as to the intent and meaning of such regulations.

R. 3.102 Members shall undertake to perform professional services only when they, together with those whom they may engage as consultants, are qualified by education, training, or experience in the specific technical areas involved. . . .

R. 3.103 Members shall not materially alter the scope or objectives of a project without the client's consent.

R. 3.104 When acting by agreement of the parties as the independent interpreter of building contract documents and the judge of contract performance, members shall render decisions impartially, favoring neither party to the contract. . . .

E.S. 3.2 Conflict of Interest: Members should disclose to clients or owners significant circumstances that could be construed as conflicts of interest and should ensure that such conflicts do not compromise those interests.

R. 3.201 Members shall not accept compensation for their services from more than one party on a project unless the circumstances are fully disclosed and agreed to by all interested parties.

R. 3.202 If members have any business association, direct or indirect financial interest, or other interest which could be substantial enough to influence their judgment in connection with their performance of professional services, the members shall fully disclose to their clients or employers the nature of the business association, financial interest, or other interest, and if the clients or employers object to such association, financial interest, or other interest, the members will either terminate such association or interest or give up the commission or employment. . . .

E.S. 3.3 Candor and Truthfulness: Members should be candid and truthful in their professional communications.

R. 3.301 Members shall not intentionally or recklessly mislead existing or prospective clients about the results that can be achieved through the use of the members' services, nor shall the members state that they can achieve results by means that violate applicable law or this Code. . . .

E.S. 3.4 Confidentiality: Members should respect the confidentiality of sensitive information obtained in the course of their professional activities.

R. 3.401 Members shall not reveal information obtained in the course of their professional activities which they have been asked to maintain in confidence, or which the reasonably prudent architect would recognize as likely, if disclosed, to affect the interests of another adversely. However, under the following exceptional circumstances members may reveal such information to the extent the members reasonably believe necessary:

(a) To stop an act which creates an appreciable risk of significant harm to the public health or safety or property of others and which the members are unable to prevent in any other manner; or

(b) To establish claims or defenses on behalf of the members; or

(c) To comply with applicable law or with this Code. . . .

Canon IV: Obligations to the Profession

Members should uphold the integrity and dignity of the profession.

E.S. 4.1 Honesty and Fairness: Members should pursue their professional activities with honesty and fairness.

R. 4.101 Members shall comply with the registration laws and regulations governing their professional practice.

R. 4.102 Members shall not knowingly make false statements or knowingly fail to disclose a material fact requested in connection with their application for registration or their application for AIA membership.

R. 4.103 Members shall not assist the application for registration or AIA membership of a person known by the members to be unqualified with respect to education, training, experience, or character.

R. 4.104 Members having substantial information which leads to a reasonable belief that another member has committed a violation of this Code which raises a serious question as to that member's honesty, trustworthiness or fitness as a member shall report such information to the body charged with enforcing this Code. . . .

R. 4.105 Members shall not sign or seal drawings, specifications, reports or other professional work for which they do not have direct professional knowledge or direct supervisory control; however, in the case of those portions of such professional work prepared by the members' registered consultants, the members may sign or seal said portions of the professional work if the members have reviewed such portions, have coordinated their preparation, or intend to be responsible for their adequacy. . . .

R. 4.106 Members speaking in their capacity as architects shall not knowingly make false statements of material fact.

R. 4.107 Members shall accurately represent their qualifications and the scope and nature of their responsibilities in connection with work for which they are claiming credit. . . .

E.S. 4.2 Dignity and Integrity: Members should strive, through their actions, to promote the dignity and integrity of the profession, and to ensure that their representatives and employees conform their conduct to this Code.

R. 4.201 Members shall not make misleading, deceptive or false statements or claims about their professional qualifications, experience or performance.

R. 4.202 Members shall make reasonable efforts to ensure that those over whom they have supervisory authority conform their conduct to this Code. . . .

Canon V: Obligations to Colleagues

Members should respect the rights and acknowledge the professional aspirations and contributions of their colleagues.

E.S. 5.1 Professional Environment: Members should provide their associates and employees with a suitable working environment, compensate them fairly, and facilitate their professional development.

E.S. 5.2 Professional Recognition: Members should build their professional reputation on the merits of their own service and performance and should recognize and give credit to others for the professional work they have performed.

R. 5.201 Members shall recognize and respect the professional contributions of their employees, employers and business associates.

R. 5.202 Members leaving an employer's service shall not without the permission of the employer take designs, drawings, data, reports, notes, or other materials relating to work performed in the employer's service by the members.

R. 5.203 Members shall not unreasonably withhold permission from departing employees to take copies of designs, drawings, data, reports, notes, or other materials relating to work performed by the employees in the members' service which are not confidential. . . .

PRINCIPLES OF ETHICS AND CODE OF PROFESSIONAL CONDUCT

American Dental Association

The maintenance and enrichment of professional status place on everyone who practices dentistry an obligation which should be willingly accepted and willingly fulfilled. While the basic obligation is constant, its fulfillment may vary with the changing needs of a society composed of the human beings that a profession is dedicated to serve. The spirit of the obligation, therefore, must be the guide of conduct for professionals. This obligation has been summarized for all time in the golden rule which asks only that "whatsoever ye would that men should do to you, do ye even so to them."

The practice of dentistry first achieved the stature of a profession in the United States when, through the heritage bestowed by the efforts of many generations of dentists, it acquired the three unfailing characteristics of a profession: the primary duty of service to the public, education beyond the usual level, and the responsibility for self-government.

Principle—Section 1

Service to the Public and Quality of Care. The dentist's primary obligation of service to the public shall include the delivery of quality care, competently and timely, within the bounds of the clinical circumstances presented by the patient. Quality of care shall be a primary consideration of the dental practitioner.

Code of Professional Conduct

1-A Patient Selection

While dentists, in serving the public, may exercise reasonable discretion in selecting patients for their practices, dentists shall not refuse to accept patients into their practice or deny dental service to patients because of the patient's race, creed, color, sex or national origin.

1-B Patient Records

Dentists are obliged to safeguard the confidentiality of patient records. Dentists shall maintain patient records in a manner consistent with the protection of the welfare of the patient. Upon request of a patient or another dental practitioner, dentists shall provide any information that will be beneficial for the future treatment of that patient.

1-C Community Service

Since dentists have an obligation to use their skills, knowledge and experience for the improvement of the dental health of the public and are encouraged to be leaders in their community, dentists in such service shall conduct themselves in such a manner as to maintain or elevate the esteem of the profession.

1-D Emergency Service

Dentists shall be obliged to make reasonable arrangements for the emergency care of their patients of record.

From American Dental Association, *Principles of Ethics and Code of Professional Conduct.* With official advisory opinions revised to July 1988. Reprinted by permission.

Dentists shall be obliged when consulted in an emergency by patients not of record to make reasonable arrangements for emergency care. If treatment is provided, the dentist, upon completion of such treatment, is obliged to return the patient to his or her regular dentist unless the patient expressly reveals a different preference.

1-E   Consultation and Referral

Dentists shall be obliged to seek consultation, if possible, whenever the welfare of patients will be safeguarded or advanced by utilizing those who have special skills, knowledge and experience.

When patients visit or are referred to specialists or consulting dentists for consultation:

1. The specialists or consulting dentists upon completion of their care shall return the patient, unless the patient expressly reveals a different preference, to the referring dentist, or if none, to the dentist of record for future care.
2. The specialists shall be obliged when there is no referring dentist and upon a completion of their treatment to inform patients when there is a need for further dental care.

1-F   Use of Auxiliary Personnel

Dentists shall be obliged to protect the health of their patient by only assigning to qualified auxiliaries those duties which can be legally delegated. Dentists shall be further obliged to prescribe and supervise the work of all auxiliary personnel working under their direction and control.

1-G   Justifiable Criticism

Dentists shall be obliged to report to the appropriate reviewing agency as determined by the local component or constituent society instances of gross and continual faulty treatment by other dentists. Patients should be informed of their present oral health status without disparaging comment about prior services.

1-H   Expert Testimony

Dentists may provide expert testimony when that testimony is essential to a just and fair disposition of a judicial or administrative action.

1-I   Rebate and Split Fees

Dentists shall not accept or tender "rebates" or "split fees."

1-J   Representation of Care and Fees

Dentists shall not represent the care being rendered to their patients or the fees being charged for providing such care in a false or misleading manner.

Principle—Section 2

Education. The privilege of dentists to be accorded professional status rests primarily in the knowledge, skill and experience with which they serve their patients and society. All dentists, therefore, have the obligation of keeping their knowledge and skill current.

Principle—Section 3

Government of a Profession. Every profession owes society the responsibility to regulate itself. Such regulation is achieved largely through the influence of the professional societies. All dentists, therefore, have the dual obligation of making themselves a part of a professional society and of observing its rules of ethics.

Principle—Section 4

Research and Development. Dentists have the obligation of making the results and benefits of their investigative efforts available to all when they are useful in safeguarding or promoting the health of the public.

Code of Professional Conduct

4-A   Devices and Therapeutic Methods

Except for formal investigative studies, dentists shall be obliged to prescribe, dispense or promote only those devices, drugs and other agents whose complete formulae are available to the dental profession. Dentists shall have the further obligation of not holding out as exclusive any device, agent, method or technique.

4-B Patents and Copyrights

Patents and copyrights may be secured by dentists provided that such patents and copyrights shall not be used to restrict research or practice.

Principle—Section 5

Professional Announcement. In order to properly serve the public, dentists should represent themselves in a manner that contributes to the esteem of the profession. Dentists should not misrepresent their training and competence in any way that would be false or misleading in any material respect. . . .

CODE OF ETHICS FOR ENGINEERS

National Society of Professional Engineers

Preamble

Engineering is an important and learned profession. The members of the profession recognize that their work has a direct and vital impact on the quality of life for all people. Accordingly, the services provided by engineers require honesty, impartiality, fairness and equity, and must be dedicated to the protection of the public health, safety and welfare. In the practice of their profession, engineers must perform under a standard of professional behavior which requires adherence to the highest principles of ethical conduct on behalf of the public, clients, employers and the profession.

I. Fundamental Canons
   Engineers, in the fulfillment of their professional duties, shall:
   1. Hold paramount the safety, health and welfare of the public in the performance of their professional duties.
   2. Perform services only in areas of their competence.
   3. Issue public statements only in an objective and truthful manner.
   4. Act in professional matters for each employer or client as faithful agents or trustees.
   5. Avoid deceptive acts in the solicitation of professional employment.

II. Rules of Practice
   1. Engineers shall hold paramount the safety, health and welfare of the public in the performance of their professional duties.
      a. Engineers shall at all times recognize that their primary obligation is to protect the safety, health, property and welfare of the public. If their professional judgment is overruled under circumstances where the safety, health, property or welfare of the public are endangered, they shall notify their employer or client and such other authority as may be appropriate.
      b. Engineers shall approve only those engineering documents which are safe for public health, property and welfare in conformity with accepted standards.
      c. Engineers shall not reveal facts, data or information obtained in a professional capacity without the prior consent of the client or employer except as authorized or required by law or this Code.
      d. Engineers shall not permit the use of their name or firm name nor

From National Society of Professional Engineers Publ. no. 1102, *Code of Ethics for Engineers* (1987). Reprinted by permission.

associate in business ventures with any person or firm which they have reason to believe is engaging in fraudulent or dishonest business or professional practices.

e. Engineers having knowledge of any alleged violation of this Code shall cooperate with the proper authorities in furnishing such information or assistance as may be required.

2. Engineers shall perform services only in the areas of their competence:

a. Engineers shall undertake assignments only when qualified by education or experience in the specific technical fields involved.

b. Engineers shall not affix their signatures to any plans or documents dealing with subject matter in which they lack competence, nor to any plan or document not prepared under their direction and control.

c. Engineers may accept assignments and assume responsibility for coordination of an entire project and sign and seal the engineering documents for the entire project, provided that each technical segment is signed and sealed only by the qualified engineers who prepared the segment.

3. Engineers shall issue public statements only in an objective and truthful manner.

a. Engineers shall be objective and truthful in professional reports, statements or testimony. They shall include all relevant and pertinent information in such reports, statements or testimony.

b. Engineers may express publicly a professional opinion on technical subjects only when that opinion is founded upon adequate knowledge of the facts and competence in the subject matter.

c. Engineers shall issue no statements, criticisms or arguments on technical matters which are inspired or paid for by interested parties, unless they have prefaced their comments by explicitly identifying the interested parties on whose behalf they are speaking, and by revealing the existence of any interest the engineers may have in the matters.

4. Engineers shall act in professional matters for each employer or client as faithful agents or trustees.

a. Engineers shall disclose all known or potential conflicts of interest to their employers or clients by promptly informing them of any business association, interest, or other circumstances which could influence or appear to influence their judgment or the quality of their services.

b. Engineers shall not accept compensation, financial or otherwise, from more than one party for services on the same project, or for services pertaining to the same project, unless the circumstances are fully disclosed to, and agreed to by, all interested parties.

c. Engineers shall not solicit or accept financial or other valuable consideration, directly or indirectly, from contractors, their agents, or other parties in connection with work for employers or clients for which they are responsible.

d. Engineers in public service as members, advisors or employees of a governmental body or department shall not participate in decisions with respect to professional services solicited or provided by them or their organizations in private or public engineering practice.

e. Engineers shall not solicit or accept a professional contract from a governmental body on which a principal or officer of their organization serves as a member.

5. Engineers shall avoid deceptive acts in the solicitation of professional employment.

a. Engineers shall not falsify or permit misrepresentation of their, or their associates', academic or professional qualifications. They shall not misrepresent or exaggerate their degree of responsibility in or for the subject matter of prior assignments. Brochures or other presentations incident to the solicitation of employment shall not misrepresent pertinent facts concerning employers, employees, associates, joint venturers or past accomplishments with the intent and purpose of enhancing their qualifications and their work.

b. Engineers shall not offer, give, solicit or receive, either directly or indirectly, any political contribution in an amount intended to influence the award of a contract by public authority, or which may be reasonably construed by the public of having the effect or intent to influence the award of a contract. They shall not offer any gift, or other valuable consideration in order to secure work. They shall not pay a commission, percentage or brokerage fee in order to secure work except to a bona fide employee or bona fide established commercial or marketing agencies retained by them.

III. Professional Obligations

1. Engineers shall be guided in all their professional relations by the highest standards of integrity.

   a. Engineers shall admit and accept their own errors when proven wrong and refrain from distorting or altering the facts in an attempt to justify their decisions.

   b. Engineers shall advise their clients or employers when they believe a project will not be successful.

   c. Engineers shall not accept outside employment to the detriment of their regular work or interest. Before accepting any outside employment, they will notify their employers.

   d. Engineers shall not attempt to attract an engineer from another employer by false or misleading pretenses.

   e. Engineers shall not actively participate in strikes, picket lines, or other collective coercive action.

   f. Engineers shall avoid any act tending to promote their own interest at the expense of the dignity and integrity of the profession.

2. Engineers shall at all times strive to serve the public interest.

   a. Engineers shall seek opportunities to be of constructive service in civic affairs and work for the advancement of the safety, health and well-being of their community.

   b. Engineers shall not complete, sign, or seal plans and/or specifications that are not of a design safe to the public health and welfare and in conformity with accepted engineering standards. If the client or employer insists on such unprofessional conduct, they shall notify the proper authorities and withdraw from further service on the project.

   c. Engineers shall endeavor to extend public knowledge and appreciation of engineering and its achievements and to protect the engineering profession from misrepresentation and misunderstanding.

3. Engineers shall avoid all conduct or practice which is likely to discredit the profession or deceive the public.

   a. Engineers shall avoid the use of statements containing a material misrepresentation of fact or omitting a material fact necessary to keep statements from being misleading or intended or likely to create an unjustified expectation; statements containing prediction of future success; statements containing an opinion as to the quality of the Engineers' services; or statements intended or likely to attract clients by the use of showmanship, puffery, or self-laudation, including the use of slogans, jingles, or sensational language or format.

   b. Consistent with the foregoing, Engineers may advertise for recruitment of personnel.

   c. Consistent with the foregoing, Engineers may prepare articles for the lay or technical press, but such articles shall not imply credit to the author for work performed by others.

4. Engineers shall not disclose confidential information concerning the business affairs or technical processes of any present or former client or employer without his consent.

   a. Engineers in the employ of others shall not without the consent of all interested parties enter promotional efforts or negotiations for work or make arrangements for other employment as a principal or to practice in connection with a specific project for which the Engineer has gained particular and specialized knowledge.

   b. Engineers shall not, without the consent of all interested parties, participate in or represent an adversary interest in connection with a specific project or proceeding in which the Engineer has gained particular specialized knowledge on behalf of a former client or employer.

5. Engineers shall not be influenced in their professional duties by conflicting interests.

   a. Engineers shall not accept financial or other considerations, including free engineering designs, from material or equipment suppliers for specifying their product.

   b. Engineers shall not accept commissions or allowances, directly or indirectly, from contractors or other parties dealing with clients or employers of the Engineer in connection with work for which the Engineer is responsible.

6. Engineers shall uphold the principle of appropriate and adequate compensation for those engaged in engineering work.

   a. Engineers shall not accept remuneration from either an employee or employment agency for giving employment.

   b. Engineers, when employing other engineers, shall offer a salary according to professional qualifications.

7. Engineers shall not attempt to obtain employment or advancement or professional engagements by untruthfully criticizing other engineers, or by other improper or questionable methods.

   a. Engineers shall not request, propose, or accept a professional commission on a contingent basis under circumstances in which their professional judgment may be compromised.

   b. Engineers in salaried positions shall accept part-time engineering work only to the extent consistent with policies of the employer and in accordance with ethical consideration.

   c. Engineers shall not use equipment, supplies, laboratory, or office facilities of an employer to carry on outside private practice without consent.

8. Engineers shall not attempt to injure, maliciously or falsely, directly or indirectly, the professional reputation, prospects, practice or employment of other engineers, nor untruthfully criticize other engineers' work. Engineers who believe others are guilty of unethical or illegal practice shall present such information to the proper authority for action.

   a. Engineers in private practice shall not review the work of another engineer for the same client, except with the knowledge of such engineer, or unless the connection of such engineer with the work has been terminated.

   b. Engineers in governmental, industrial or educational employ are entitled to review and evaluate the work of other engineers when so required by their employment duties.

   c. Engineers in sales or industrial employ are entitled to make engineering comparisons of represented products with products of other suppliers.

9. Engineers shall accept responsibility for their professional activities; provided, however, that Engineers may seek in-

demnification for professional services arising out of their practice for other than gross negligence, where the Engineer's interests cannot otherwise be protected.

    a. Engineers shall conform with state registration laws in the practice of engineering.

    b. Engineers shall not use association with a nonengineer, a corporation, or partnership, as a "cloak" for unethical acts, but must accept personal responsibility for all professional acts.

10. Engineers shall give credit for engineering work to those to whom credit is due, and will recognize the proprietary interests of others.

    a. Engineers shall, whenever possible, name the person or persons who may be individually responsible for designs, inventions, writings, or other accomplishments.

    b. Engineers using designs supplied by a client recognize that the designs remain the property of the client and may not be duplicated by the Engineer for others without express permission.

    c. Engineers, before undertaking work for others in connection with which the Engineer may make improvements, plans, designs, inventions, or other records which may justify copyrights or patents, should enter into a positive agreement regarding ownership.

    d. Engineers' designs, data, records, and notes referring exclusively to an employer's work are the employer's property.

11. Engineers shall cooperate in extending the effectiveness of the profession by interchanging information and experience with other engineers and students, and will endeavor to provide opportunity for the professional development and advancement of engineers under their supervision.

    a. Engineers shall encourage engineering employees' efforts to improve their education.

    b. Engineers shall encourage engineering employees to attend and present papers at professional and technical society meetings.

    c. Engineers shall urge engineering employees to become registered at the earliest possible date.

    d. Engineers shall assign a professional engineer duties of a nature to utilize full training and experience, insofar as possible, and delegate lesser functions to subprofessionals or to technicians.

    e. Engineers shall provide a prospective engineering employee with complete information on working conditions and proposed status of employment, and after employment will keep employees informed of any changes.

"By order of the United States District Court for the District of Columbia, former Section 11(c) of the NSPE Code of Ethics prohibiting competitive bidding, and all policy statements, opinions, rulings or other guidelines interpreting its scope, have been rescinded as unlawfully interfering with the legal right of engineers, protected under the antitrust laws, to provide price information to prospective clients; accordingly, nothing contained in the NSPE Code of Ethics, policy statements, opinions, rulings or other guidelines prohibits the submission of price quotations or competitive bids for engineering services at any time or in any amount."

Statement by NSPE Executive Committee

In order to correct misunderstandings which have been indicated in some instances since the issuance of the Supreme Court decision and the entry of the Final Judgment, it is noted that in its decision of April 25, 1978, the Supreme Court of the United States declared: "The Sherman Act does not require competitive bidding."

It is further noted that as made clear in the Supreme Court decision:

1. Engineers and firms may individually refuse to bid for engineering services.
2. Clients are not required to seek bids for engineering services.
3. Federal, state, and local laws governing procedures to procure engineering services are not affected, and remain in full force and effect.
4. State societies and local chapters are free to actively and aggressively seek legislation for professional selection and negotiation procedures by public agencies.
5. State registration board rules of professional conduct, including rules prohibiting competitive bidding for engineering services, are not affected and remain in full force and effect. State registration boards with authority to adopt rules of professional conduct may adopt rules governing procedures to obtain engineering services.
6. As noted by the Supreme Court, "nothing in the judgment prevents NSPE and its members from attempting to influence governmental action. . . ."

CODE OF ETHICS FOR ENGINEERS

Institute of Electrical and Electronics Engineers

Preamble

Engineers affect the quality of life for all people in our complex technological society. In the pursuit of their profession, therefore, it is vital that engineers conduct their work in an ethical manner so that they merit the confidence of colleagues, employers, clients and the public. This IEEE Code of Ethics is a standard of professional conduct for engineers.

Article I

Engineers shall maintain high standards of diligence, creativity and productivity, and shall:

1. Accept responsibility for their actions;
2. Be honest and realistic in stating claims or estimates from available data;
3. Undertake engineering tasks and accept responsibility only if qualified by training or experience, or after full disclosure to their employers or clients of pertinent qualifications;
4. Maintain their professional skills at the level of the state of the art, and recognize the importance of current events in their work;
5. Advance the integrity and prestige of the engineering profession by practicing in a dignified manner and for adequate compensation.

Article II

Engineers shall, in their work:

1. Treat fairly all colleagues and co-workers, regardless of race, religion, sex, age or national origin;
2. Report, publish and disseminate freely information to others, subject to legal and proprietary restraints;
3. Encourage colleagues and co-workers to act in accord with this Code and support them when they do so;
4. Seek, accept and offer honest criticism of work, and properly credit the contributions of others;
5. Support and participate in the activities of their professional societies;
6. Assist colleagues and co-workers in their professional development.

Article III

Engineers shall, in their relations with employers and clients:

1. Act as faithful agents or trustees for their employers or clients in professional and business matters, provided such actions conform with other parts of this Code;

2. Keep information on the business affairs or technical processes of an employer or client in confidence while employed, and later, until such information is properly released, provided such actions conform with other parts of this Code;

3. Inform their employers, clients, professional societies or public agencies or private agencies of which they are members or to which they may make presentations, of any circumstance that could lead to a conflict of interest;

4. Neither give nor accept, directly or indirectly, any gift, payment or service of more than nominal value to or from those having business relationships with their employers or clients;

5. Assist and advise their employers or clients in anticipating the possible consequences, direct and indirect, immediate or remote, of the projects, work or plans of which they have knowledge.

Article IV

Engineers shall, in fulfilling their responsibilities to the community:

1. Protect the safety, health and welfare of the public and speak out against abuses in these areas affecting the public interest;

2. Contribute professional advice, as appropriate, to civic, charitable or other non-profit organizations;

3. Seek to extend public knowledge and appreciation of the engineering profession and its achievements.

CODE OF ETHICS

The Society of Professional Journalists, Sigma Delta Chi

The Society of Professional Journalists, Sigma Delta Chi, believes the duty of journalists is to serve the truth.

We believe the agencies of mass communication are carriers of public discussion and information, acting on their Constitutional mandate and freedom to learn and report the facts.

We believe in public enlightenment as the forerunner of justice, and in our Constitutional role to seek the truth as part of the public's right to know the truth.

We believe those responsibilities carry obligations that require journalists to perform with intelligence, objectivity, accuracy, and fairness.

To these ends, we declare acceptance of the standards of practice here set forth:

I. RESPONSIBILITY

The public's right to know of events of public importance and interest is the overriding mission of the mass media. The purpose of distributing news and enlightened opinion is to serve the general welfare. Journalists who use their professional status as representatives of the public for selfish or other unworthy motives violate a high trust.

II. FREEDOM OF THE PRESS

Freedom of the press is to be guarded as an inalienable right of people in a free society. It carries with it the freedom and the responsibility to discuss, question, and challenge actions and utterances of our government and of our public and private institutions. Journalists uphold the right to speak unpopular opinions and the privilege to agree with the majority.

III. ETHICS

Journalists must be free of obligation to any interest other than the public's right to know the truth.

1. Gifts, favors, free travel, special treatment or privileges can compromise the integrity of journalists and their employers. Nothing of value should be accepted.

2. Secondary employment, political involvement, holding public office, and service in community organizations should be avoided if it compromises the integrity of journalists and their employers. Journalists and their employers should conduct their personal lives in a manner that protects them from conflict of interest, real or apparent. Their responsibilities to the public are paramount. That is the nature of their profession.

3. So-called news communications from private sources should not be published or broadcast without substantiation of their claims to news value.

4. Journalists will seek news that serves the public interest, despite the obstacles. They will make constant efforts to assure that the public's business is conducted in public and that public records are open to public inspection.

5. Journalists acknowledge the newsman's ethic of protecting confidential sources of information.

6. Plagiarism is dishonest and unacceptable.

IV. ACCURACY AND OBJECTIVITY

Good faith with the public is the foundation of all worthy journalism.

1. Truth is our ultimate goal.

2. Objectivity in reporting the news is another goal that serves as the mark of an experienced professional. It is a standard of performance toward which we strive. We honor those who achieve it.

3. There is no excuse for inaccuracies or lack of thoroughness.

4. Newspaper headlines should be fully warranted by the contents of the articles they accompany. Photographs and telecasts should give an accurate picture of an event and not highlight an incident out of context.

5. Sound practice makes clear distinction between news reports and expressions of opinion. News reports should be free of opinion or bias and represent all sides of an issue.

6. Partisanship in editorial comment that knowingly departs from the truth violates the spirit of American journalism.

7. Journalists recognize their responsibility for offering informed analysis, comment, and editorial opinion on public events and issues. They accept the obligation to present such material by individuals whose competence, experience, and judgment qualify them for it.

8. Special articles or presentations devoted to advocacy or the writer's own conclusions and interpretations should be labeled as such.

V. FAIR PLAY

Journalists at all times will show respect for the dignity, privacy, rights, and well-being of people encountered in the course of gathering and presenting the news.

1. The news media should not communicate unofficial charges affecting reputation or moral character without giving the accused a chance to reply.

2. The news media must guard against invading a person's right to privacy.

3. The media should not pander to morbid curiosity about details of vice and crime.

4. It is the duty of news media to make prompt and complete correction of their errors.

5. Journalists should be accountable to the public for their reports and the public should be encouraged to voice its griev-

ances against the media. Open dialogue with our readers, viewers, and listeners should be fostered.

VI. PLEDGE

Adherence to this code is intended to preserve and strengthen the bond of mutual trust and respect between American journalists and the American people.

The Society shall—by programs of education and other means—encourage individual journalists to adhere to these tenets, and shall encourage journalistic publications and broadcasters to recognize their responsibility to frame codes of ethics in concert with their employees to serve as guidelines in furthering these goals.

MODEL RULES OF PROFESSIONAL CONDUCT
CLIENT–LAWYER RELATIONSHIP

American Bar Association

Rule 1.1 Competence

A lawyer shall provide competent representation to a client. Competent representation requires the legal knowledge, skill, thoroughness and preparation reasonably necessary for the representation.

Comment:

Legal Knowledge and Skill

1. In determining whether a lawyer employs the requisite knowledge and skill in a particular matter, relevant factors include the relative complexity and specialized nature of the matter, the lawyer's general experience, the lawyer's training and experience in the field in question, the preparation and study the lawyer is able to give the matter and whether it is feasible to refer the matter to, or associate or consult with, a lawyer of established competence in the field in question. In many instances, the required proficiency is that of a general practitioner. Expertise in a particular field of law may be required in some circumstances.

2. A lawyer need not necessarily have special training or prior experience to han-dle legal problems of a type with which the lawyer is unfamiliar. A newly admitted lawyer can be as competent as a practitioner with long experience. Some important legal skills, such as the analysis of precedent, the evaluation of evidence and legal drafting, are required in all legal problems. Perhaps the most fundamental legal skill consists of determining what kind of legal problems a situation may involve, a skill that necessarily transcends any particular specialized knowledge. A lawyer can provide adequate representation in a wholly novel field through necessary study. Competent representation can also be provided through the association of a lawyer of established competence in the field in question. . . .

Rule 1.2 Scope of Representation

(a) A lawyer shall abide by a client's decisions concerning the objectives of representation, subject to paragraphs (c), (d) and (e), and shall consult with the client as to the means by which they are to be pursued. A lawyer shall abide by a client's decision whether to accept an offer of settlement of a matter. In a criminal case, the lawyer shall abide by the client's decision, after consultation with the lawyer, as to a plea to be entered, whether to waive jury trial and whether the client will testify.

(b) A lawyer's representation of a client, including representation by appointment, does not constitute an endorsement of the client's political, economic, social or moral views or activities.

(c) A lawyer may limit the objectives of the representation if the client consents after consultation.

(d) A lawyer shall not counsel a client to engage, or assist a client, in conduct that the lawyer knows is criminal or fraudulent, but a lawyer may discuss the legal consequences of any proposed course of conduct with a client and may counsel or assist a client to make a good faith effort to determine the validity, scope, meaning or application of the law.

(e) When a lawyer knows that a client expects assistance not permitted by the Rules of Professional Conduct or other law, the lawyer shall consult with the client regarding the relevant limitations on the lawyer's conduct.

Comment:

Scope of Representation

1. Both lawyer and client have authority and responsibility in the objectives and means of representation. The client has ultimate authority to determine the purposes to be served by legal representation, within the limits imposed by law and the lawyer's professional obligations. Within those limits, a client also has a right to consult with the lawyer about the means to be used in pursuing those objectives. At the same time, a lawyer is not required to pursue objectives or employ means simply because a client may wish that the lawyer do so. A clear distinction between objectives and means sometimes cannot be drawn, and in many cases the client–lawyer relationship partakes of a joint undertaking. In questions of means, the lawyer should assume responsibility for technical and legal tactical issues, but should defer to the client regarding such questions as the expense to be incurred and concern for third persons who might be adversely affected. Law defining the lawyer's scope of authority in litigation varies among jurisdictions. . . .

Independence from Client's Views or Activities

3. Legal representation should not be denied to people who are unable to afford legal services, or whose cause is controversial or the subject of popular disapproval. By the same token, representing a client does not constitute approval of the client's views or activities.

Services Limited in Objectives or Means

4. The objectives or scope of services provided by a lawyer may be limited by agreement with the client or by the terms under which the lawyer's services are made available to the client. For example, a retainer may be for a specifically defined purpose. Representation provided through a legal aid agency may be subject to limitations on the types of cases the agency handles. When a lawyer has been retained by an insurer to represent an insured, the representation may be limited to matters related to the insurance coverage. The terms upon which representation is undertaken may exclude specific objectives or means. Such limitations may exclude objectives or means that the lawyer regards as repugnant or imprudent.

5. An agreement concerning the scope of representation must accord with the Rules of Professional Conduct and other law. Thus, the client may not be asked to agree to representation so limited in scope as to violate Rule 1.1, or to surrender the right to terminate the lawyer's services or the right to settle litigation that the lawyer might wish to continue. . . .

Rule 1.4 Communication

(a) A lawyer shall keep a client reasonably informed about the status of a matter and promptly comply with reasonable requests for information.

(b) A lawyer shall explain a matter to the extent reasonably necessary to permit the client to make informed decisions regarding the representation.

Comment:

1. The client should have sufficient information to participate intelligently in decisions concerning the objectives of the representation and the means by which they are to be pursued, to the extent the client is willing and able to do so. For example, a lawyer negotiating on behalf of a client should provide the client with facts relevant to the matter, inform the client of communications from another party and take other reasonable steps that permit the client to make a decision regarding a serious offer from another party. A lawyer who receives from opposing counsel an offer of settlement in a civil controversy or a proffered plea bargain in a criminal case should promptly inform the client of its substance unless prior discussions with the client have left it clear that the proposal will be unacceptable. See Rule 1.2(a). Even when a client delegates authority to the lawyer, the client should be kept advised of the status of the matter.

2. Adequacy of communication depends in part on the kind of advice or assistance involved. For example, in negotiations where there is time to explain a proposal the lawyer should review all important provisions with the client before proceeding to an agreement. In litigation a lawyer should explain the general strategy and prospects of success and ordinarily should consult the client on tactics that might injure or coerce others. On the other hand, a lawyer ordinarily cannot be expected to describe trial or negotiation strategy in detail. The guiding principle is that the lawyer should fulfill reasonable client expectations for information consistent with the duty to act in the client's best interests, and the client's overall requirements as to the character of representation.

3. Ordinarily, the information to be provided is that appropriate for a client who is a comprehending and responsible adult. However, fully informing the client according to this standard may be impracticable, for example, where the client is a child or suffers from mental disability. . . . When the client is an organization or group, it is often impossible or inappropriate to inform every one of its members about its legal affairs; ordinarily, the lawyer should address communications to the appropriate officials of the organization. See Rule 1.13. Where many routine matters are involved, a system of limited or occasional reporting may be arranged with the client. Practical exigency may also require a lawyer to act for a client without prior consultation.

Withholding Information

4. In some circumstances, a lawyer may be justified in delaying transmission of information when the client would be likely to react imprudently to an immediate communication. Thus, a lawyer might withhold a psychiatric diagnosis of a client when the examining psychiatrist indicates that disclosure would harm the client. A lawyer may not withhold information to serve the lawyer's own interest or convenience. Rules or court orders governing litigation may provide that information supplied to a lawyer may not be disclosed to the client. . . .

Rule 1.5 Fees

A. A lawyer's fee shall be reasonable. The factors to be considered in determining the reasonableness of a fee include the following:

1. the time and labor required, the novelty and difficulty of the questions involved, and the

skill requisite to perform the legal service properly;

2. the likelihood, if apparent to the client, that the acceptance of the particular employment will preclude other employment by the lawyer;

3. the fee customarily charged in the locality for similar legal services;

4. the amount involved and the results obtained;

5. the time limitations imposed by the client or by the circumstances;

6. the nature and length of the professional relationship with the client;

7. the experience, reputation, and ability of the lawyer or lawyers performing the services; and

8. whether the fee is fixed or contingent.

B. When the lawyer has not regularly represented the client, the basis or rate of the fee shall be communicated to the client, preferably in writing, before or within a reasonable time after commencing the representation.

C. A fee may be contingent on the outcome of the matter for which the service is rendered, except in a matter in which a contingent fee is prohibited by paragraph (d) or other law. A contingent fee agreement shall be in writing and shall state the method by which the fee is to be determined, including the percentage or percentages that shall accrue to the lawyer in the event of settlement, trial or appeal, litigation and other expenses to be deducted from the recovery, and whether such expenses are to be deducted before or after the contingent fee is calculated. Upon conclusion of a contingent fee matter, the lawyer shall provide the client with a written statement stating the outcome of the matter and, if there is a recovery, showing the remittance to the client and the method of its determination.

D. A lawyer shall not enter into an arrangement for, charge, or collect:

1. any fee in a domestic relations matter, the payment or amount of which is contingent upon the securing of a divorce or upon the amount of alimony or support, or property settlement in lieu thereof; or

2. a contingent fee for representing a defendant in a criminal case.

E. A division of fee between lawyers who are not in the same firm may be made only if:

1. the division is in proportion to the services performed by each lawyer or, by written agreement with the client, each lawyer assumes joint responsibility for the representation;

2. the client is advised of and does not object to the participation of all the lawyers involved; and

3. the total fee is reasonable. . . .

Rule 1.6 Confidentiality of Information

(a) A lawyer shall not reveal information relating to representation of a client unless the client consents after consultation, except for disclosures that are impliedly authorized in order to carry out the representation, and except as stated in paragraph (b).

(b) A lawyer may reveal such information to the extent the lawyer reasonably believes necessary:

(1) to prevent the client from committing a criminal act that the lawyer believes is likely to result in imminent death or substantial bodily harm; or

(2) to establish a claim or defense on behalf of the lawyer in a controversy between the lawyer and the client, to establish a defense to a criminal charge or civil claim against the lawyer based upon conduct in which the client was involved, or to respond to allegations in any proceeding concerning the lawyer's representation of the client.

Comment:

1. The lawyer is part of a judicial system charged with upholding the law. One of the lawyer's functions is to advise clients

so that they avoid any violation of the law in the proper exercise of their rights.

2. The observance of the ethical obligation of a lawyer to hold inviolate confidential information of the client not only facilitates the full development of facts essential to proper representation of the client but also encourages people to seek early legal assistance.

3. Almost without exception, clients come to lawyers in order to determine what their rights are and what is, in the maze of laws and regulations, deemed to be legal and correct. The common law recognizes that the client's confidences must be protected from disclosure. Based upon experience, lawyers know that almost all clients follow the advice given, and the law is upheld.

4. A fundamental principle in the client-lawyer relationship is that the lawyer maintain confidentiality of information relating to the representation. The client is thereby encouraged to communicate fully and frankly with the lawyer even as to embarrassing or legally damaging subject matter.

5. The principle of confidentiality is given effect in two related bodies of law, the attorney–client privilege (which includes the work product doctrine) in the law of evidence and the rule of confidentiality established in professional ethics. The attorney–client privilege applies in judicial and other proceedings in which a lawyer may be called as a witness or otherwise required to produce evidence concerning a client. The rule of client–lawyer confidentiality applies in situations other than those where evidence is sought from the lawyer through compulsion of law. The confidentiality rule applies not merely to matters communicated in confidence by the client but also to all information relating to the representation, whatever its source. A lawyer may not disclose such information except as authorized or required by the Rules of Professional Conduct or other law.

6. The requirement of maintaining confidentiality of information relating to representation applies to government lawyers who may disagree with the policy goals that their representation is designed to advance.

Authorized Disclosure

7. A lawyer is impliedly authorized to make disclosures about a client when appropriate in carrying out the representation, except to the extent that the client's instructions or special circumstances limit that authority. In litigation, for example, a lawyer may disclose information by admitting a fact that cannot properly be disputed, or in negotiation by making a disclosure that facilitates a satisfactory conclusion.

8. Lawyers in a firm may, in the course of the firm's practice, disclose to each other information relating to a client of the firm, unless the client has instructed that particular information be confined to specified lawyers.

Disclosure Adverse to Client

9. The confidentiality rule is subject to limited exceptions. In becoming privy to information about a client, a lawyer may foresee that the client intends serious harm to another person. However, to the extent a lawyer is required or permitted to disclose a client's purposes, the client will be inhibited from revealing facts which would enable the lawyer to counsel against a wrongful course of action. The public is better protected if full and open communication by the client is encouraged than if it is inhibited.

10. Several situations must be distinguished. First, the lawyer may not counsel or assist a client in conduct that is criminal or fraudulent. See Rule 1.2(d). Similarly, a lawyer has a duty under Rule 3.3(a)(4) not to use false evidence. This duty is essentially a special instance of the duty prescribed in Rule 1.2(d) to avoid assisting a client in criminal or fraudulent conduct.

11. Second, the lawyer may have been innocently involved in past conduct by the client that was criminal or fraudulent. In such a situation the lawyer has not violated Rule 1.2(d), because to "counsel or assist" criminal or fraudulent conduct requires knowing that the conduct is of that character.

12. Third, the lawyer may learn that a client intends prospective conduct that is criminal and likely to result in imminent death or substantial bodily harm. As stated in paragraph (b)(1), the lawyer has professional discretion to reveal information in order to prevent such consequences. The lawyer may make a disclosure in order to prevent homicide or serious bodily injury which the lawyer reasonably believes is intended by a client. It is very difficult for a lawyer to "know" when such a heinous purpose will actually be carried out, for the client may have a change of mind.

13. The lawyer's exercise of discretion requires consideration of such factors as the nature of the lawyer's relationship with the client and with those who might be injured by the client, the lawyer's own involvement in the transaction and factors that may extenuate the conduct in question. Where practical, the lawyer should seek to persuade the client to take suitable action. In any case, a disclosure adverse to the client's interest should be no greater than the lawyer reasonably believes necessary to the purpose. A lawyer's decision not to take preventive action permitted by paragraph (b)(1) does not violate this Rule.

Withdrawal

14. If the lawyer's services will be used by the client in materially furthering a course of criminal or fraudulent conduct, the lawyer must withdraw. . . .

15. After withdrawal the lawyer is required to refrain from making disclosure of the clients' confidences, except as otherwise provided in Rule 1.6.

16. Where the client is an organization, the lawyer may be in doubt whether contemplated conduct will actually be carried out by the organization. Where necessary to guide conduct in connection with this Rule, the lawyer may make inquiry within the organization as indicated in Rule 1.13(b).

Dispute Concerning Lawyer's Conduct

17. Where a legal claim or disciplinary charge alleges complicity of the lawyer in a client's conduct or other misconduct of the lawyer involving representation of the client, the lawyer may respond to the extent the lawyer reasonably believes necessary to establish a defense. The same is true with respect to a claim involving the conduct or representation of a former client. The lawyer's right to respond arises when an assertion of such complicity has been made. Paragraph (b)(2) does not require the lawyer to await the commencement of an action or proceeding that charges such complicity, so that the defense may be established by responding directly to a third party who has made such an assertion. The right to defend, of course, applies where a proceeding has been commenced. Where practicable and not prejudicial to the lawyer's ability to establish the defense, the lawyer should advise the client of the third party's assertion and request that the client respond appropriately. In any event, disclosure should be no greater than the lawyer reasonably believes is necessary to vindicate innocence, the disclosure should be made in a manner which limits access to the information to the tribunal or other persons having a need to know it, and appropriate protective orders or other arrangements should be sought by the lawyer to the fullest extent practicable.

18. If the lawyer is charged with wrongdoing in which the client's conduct is implicated, the rule of confidentiality should not prevent the lawyer from defending against the charge. Such a charge can arise in a civil, criminal or professional disciplinary proceeding, and can be based

on a wrong allegedly committed by the lawyer against the client, or on a wrong alleged by a third person; for example, a person claiming to have been defrauded by the lawyer and client acting together. A lawyer entitled to a fee is permitted by paragraph (b)(2) to prove the services rendered in an action to collect it. This aspect of the rule expresses the principle that the beneficiary of a fiduciary relationship may not exploit it to the detriment of the fiduciary. As stated above, the lawyer must make every effort practicable to avoid unnecessary disclosure of information relating to a representation, to limit disclosure to those having the need to know it, and to obtain protective orders or make other arrangements minimizing the risk of disclosure.

**Disclosures Otherwise Required
or Authorized**

19.   The attorney–client privilege is differently defined in various jurisdictions. If a lawyer is called as a witness to give testimony concerning a client, absent waiver by the client, Rule 1.6(a) requires the lawyer to invoke the privilege when it is applicable. The lawyer must comply with the final orders of a court or other tribunal of competent jurisdiction requiring the lawyer to give information about the client.

20.   The Rules of Professional Conduct in various circumstances permit or require a lawyer to disclose information relating to the representation. . . . In addition to these provisions, a lawyer may be obligated or permitted by other provisions of law to give information about a client. Whether another provision of law supersedes Rule 1.6 is a matter of interpretation beyond the scope of these Rules, but a presumption should exist against such a supersession.

Former Client

21.   The duty of confidentiality continues after the client–lawyer relationship has terminated.

Rule 1.13   Organization as Client

(a) A lawyer employed or retained by an organization represents the organization acting through its duly authorized constituents.

(b) If a lawyer for an organization knows that an officer, employee or other person associated with the organization is engaged in action, intends to act or refuses to act in a matter related to the representation that is a violation of a legal obligation to the organization, or a violation of law which reasonably might be imputed to the organization, and is likely to result in substantial injury to the organization, the lawyer shall proceed as is reasonably necessary in the best interest of the organization. In determining how to proceed, the lawyer shall give due consideration to the seriousness of the violation and its consequences, the scope and nature of the lawyer's representation, the responsibility in the organization and the apparent motivation of the person involved, the policies of the organization concerning such matters and any other relevant considerations. Any measures taken shall be designed to minimize disruption of the organization and the risk of revealing information relating to the representation to persons outside the organization. Such measures may include among others:

(1) asking reconsideration of the matter;
(2) advising that a separate legal opinion on the matter be sought for presentation to appropriate authority in the organization; and
(3) referring the matter to higher authority in the organization, including, if warranted by the seriousness of the matter, referral to the highest authority that can act in behalf of the organization as determined by applicable law.

(c) If, despite the lawyer's efforts in accordance with paragraph (b), the highest authority that can act on behalf of the organization insists upon action, or a refusal to act, that is clearly a violation of law and is likely to result in substantial injury to the organization, the lawyer may resign. . . .

(d) In dealing with an organization's directors, officers, employees, members, shareholders or other constituents, a lawyer shall explain the identity of the client when it is apparent that the organization's interests are adverse to those of the constituents with whom the lawyer is dealing.

(e) A lawyer representing an organization may also represent any of its directors, officers, employees, members, shareholders or other constituents, subject to [other provisions on conflicts of interest].

Comment:

The Entity as the Client

1. An organizational client is a legal entity, but it cannot act except through its officers, directors, employees, shareholders and other constituents.

2. Officers, directors, employees and shareholders are the constituents of the corporate organizational client. The duties defined in this Comment apply equally to unincorporated associations. "Other constituents" as used in this Comment means the positions equivalent to officers, directors, employees and shareholders held by persons acting for organizational clients that are not corporations.

3. When one of the constituents of an organizational client communicates with the organization's lawyer in that person's organizational capacity, the communication is protected by Rule 1.6. Thus, by way of example, if an organizational client requests its lawyer to investigate allegations of wrongdoing, interviews made in the course of that investigation between the lawyer and the client's employees or other constituents are covered by Rule 1.6. This does not mean, however, that constituents of an organizational client are the clients of the lawyer. The lawyer may not disclose to such constituents information relating to the representation except for disclosures explicitly or impliedly authorized by the organizational client in order to carry out the representation or as otherwise permitted by Rule 1.6.

4. When constituents of the organization make decisions for it, the decisions ordinarily must be accepted by the lawyer even if their utility or prudence is doubtful. Decisions concerning policy and operations, including ones entailing serious risk, are not as such in the lawyer's province. However, different considerations arise when the lawyer knows that the organization may be substantially injured by action of [a] constituent that is in violation of law. In such a circumstance, it may be reasonably necessary for the lawyer to ask the constituent to reconsider the matter. If that fails, or if the matter is of sufficient seriousness and importance to the organization, it may be reasonably necessary for the lawyer to take steps to have the matter reviewed by a higher authority in the organization. Clear justification should exist for seeking review over the head of the constituent normally responsible for it. The stated policy of the organization may define circumstances and prescribe channels for such review, and a lawyer should encourage the formulation of such a policy. Even in the absence of organization policy, however, the lawyer may have an obligation to refer a matter to higher authority, depending on the seriousness of the matter and whether the constituent in question has apparent motives to act at variance with the organization's interest. Review by the chief executive officer or by the board of directors may be required when the matter is of importance commensurate with their authority. At some point it may be useful or essential to obtain an independent legal opinion.

5. In an extreme case, it may be reasonably necessary for the lawyer to refer the matter to the organization's highest authority. Ordinarily, that is the board of directors or similar governing body. How-

ever, applicable law may prescribe that under certain conditions highest authority reposes elsewhere; for example, in the independent directors of a corporation. . . .

Government Agency

7. The duty defined in this Rule applies to governmental organizations. However, when the client is a governmental organization, a different balance may be appropriate between maintaining confidentiality and assuring that the wrongful official act is prevented or rectified, for public business is involved. In addition, duties of lawyers employed by the government or lawyers in military service may be defined by statutes and regulation. Therefore, defining precisely the identity of the client and prescribing the resulting obligations of such lawyers may be more difficult in the government context. Although in some circumstances the client may be a specific agency, it is generally the government as a whole. For example, if the action or failure to act involves the head of a bureau, either the department of which the bureau is a part or the government as a whole may be the client for purpose of this Rule. Moreover, in a matter involving the conduct of government officials, a government lawyer may have authority to question such conduct more extensively than that of a lawyer for a private organization in similar circumstances. This Rule does not limit that authority. . . .

Rule 3.2 Expediting Litigation

A lawyer shall make reasonable efforts to expedite litigation consistent with the interests of the client.

Comment:

Dilatory practices bring the administration of justice into disrepute. Delay should not be indulged merely for the convenience of the advocates, or for the purpose of frustrating an opposing party's attempt to obtain rightful redress or repose. It is not a justification that similar conduct is often tolerated by the bench and bar. The question is whether a competent lawyer acting in good faith would regard the course of action as having some substantial purpose other than delay. Realizing financial or other benefit from otherwise improper delay in litigation is not a legitimate interest of the client.

Rule 3.3 Candor Toward the Tribunal

A. A lawyer shall not knowingly:

1. make a false statement of material fact or law to a tribunal;
2. fail to disclose a material fact to a tribunal when disclosure is necessary to avoid assisting a criminal or fraudulent act by the client;
3. fail to disclose to the tribunal legal authority in the controlling jurisdiction known to the lawyer to be directly adverse to the position of the client and not disclosed by opposing counsel; or
4. offer evidence that the lawyer knows to be false. If a lawyer has offered material evidence and comes to know of its falsity, the lawyer shall take reasonable remedial measures.

B. The duties stated in paragraph (a) continue to the conclusion of the proceeding, and apply even if compliance requires disclosure of information otherwise protected by rule 1.6.

C. A lawyer may refuse to offer evidence that the lawyer reasonably believes is false.

D. In an ex parte proceeding, a lawyer shall inform the tribunal of all material facts known to the lawyer which will enable the tribunal to make an informed decision, whether or not the facts are adverse.

Comment:

1. The advocate's task is to present the client's case with persuasive force. Performance of that duty while maintaining con-

fidences of the client is qualified by the advocate's duty of candor to the tribunal. However, an advocate does not vouch for the evidence submitted in a cause; the tribunal is responsible for assessing its probative value.

Representations by a Lawyer

2. An advocate is responsible for pleadings and other documents prepared for litigation, but is usually not required to have personal knowledge of matters asserted therein, for litigation documents ordinarily present assertions by the client, or by someone on the client's behalf, and not assertions by the lawyer. . . . However, an assertion purporting to be on the lawyer's own knowledge, as in an affidavit by the lawyer or in a statement in open court, may properly be made only when the lawyer knows the assertion is true or believes it to be true on the basis of a reasonably diligent inquiry. There are circumstances where failure to make a disclosure is the equivalent of an affirmative misrepresentation. . . .

Misleading Legal Argument

3. Legal argument based on a knowingly false representation of law constitutes dishonesty toward the tribunal. A lawyer is not required to make a disinterested exposition of the law, but must recognize the existence of pertinent legal authorities. Furthermore, as stated in paragraph (a)(3), an advocate has a duty to disclose directly adverse authority in the controlling jurisdiction which has not been disclosed by the opposing party. The underlying concept is that legal argument is a discussion seeking to determine the legal premises properly applicable to the case.

False Evidence

4. When evidence that a lawyer knows to be false is provided by a person who is not the client, the lawyer must refuse to offer it regardless of the client's wishes.

5. When false evidence is offered by the client, however, a conflict may arise between the lawyer's duty to keep the client's revelations confidential and the duty of candor to the court. Upon ascertaining that material evidence is false, the lawyer should seek to persuade the client that the evidence should not be offered or, if it has been offered, that its false character should immediately be disclosed. If the persuasion is ineffective, the lawyer must take reasonable remedial measures.

6. Except in the defense of a criminal accused, the rule generally recognized is that, if necessary to rectify the situation, an advocate must disclose the existence of the client's deception to the court or to the other party. Such a disclosure can result in grave consequences to the client, including not only a sense of betrayal but also loss of the case and perhaps a prosecution for perjury. But the alternative is that the lawyer cooperate in deceiving the court, thereby subverting the truth-finding process which the adversary system is designed to implement. See Rule 1.2(d). Furthermore, unless it is clearly understood that the lawyer will act upon the duty to disclose the existence of false evidence, the client can simply reject the lawyer's advice to reveal the false evidence and insist that the lawyer keep silent. Thus the client could in effect coerce the lawyer into being a party to fraud on the court.

Perjury by a Criminal Defendant

7. Whether an advocate for a criminally accused has the same duty of disclosure has been intensely debated. While it is agreed that the lawyer should seek to persuade the client to refrain from perjurious testimony, there has been dispute concerning the lawyer's duty when that persuasion fails. If the confrontation with the client occurs before trial, the lawyer ordinarily can withdraw. Withdrawal before trial may not be possible, however, either because trial is imminent, or because the confrontation with the client does not

take place until the trial itself, or because no other counsel is available.

8. The most difficult situation, therefore, arises in a criminal case where the accused insists on testifying when the lawyer knows that the testimony is perjurious. The lawyer's effort to rectify the situation can increase the likelihood of the client's being convicted as well as opening the possibility of a prosecution for perjury. On the other hand, if the lawyer does not exercise control over the proof, the lawyer participates, although in a merely passive way, in deception of the court.

9. Three resolutions of this dilemma have been proposed. One is to permit the accused to testify by a narrative without guidance through the lawyer's questioning. This compromises both contending principles; it exempts the lawyer from the duty to disclose false evidence but subjects the client to an implicit disclosure of information imparted to counsel. Another suggested resolution, of relatively recent origin, is that the advocate be entirely excused from the duty to reveal perjury if the perjury is that of the client. This is a coherent solution but makes the advocate a knowing instrument of perjury.

10. The other resolution of the dilemma is that the lawyer must reveal the client's perjury if necessary to rectify the situation. A criminal accused has a right to the assistance of an advocate, a right to testify and a right of confidential communication with counsel. However, an accused should not have a right to assistance of counsel in committing perjury. Furthermore, an advocate has an obligation, not only in professional ethics but under the law as well, to avoid implication in the commission of perjury or other falsification of evidence. See Rule 1.2(d).

Remedial Measures

11. If perjured testimony or false evidence has been offered, the advocate's proper course ordinarily is to remonstrate with the client confidentially. If that fails,

the advocate should seek to withdraw if that will remedy the situation. If withdrawal will not remedy the situation or is impossible, the advocate should make disclosure to the court. It is for the court then to determine what should be done—making a statement about the matter to the trier of fact, ordering a mistrial or perhaps nothing. If the false testimony was that of the client, the client may controvert the lawyer's version of their communication when the lawyer discloses the situation to the court. If there is an issue whether the client has committed perjury, the lawyer cannot represent the client in resolution of the issue and a mistrial may be unavoidable. An unscrupulous client might in this way attempt to produce a series of mistrials and thus escape prosecution. However, a second such encounter could be construed as a deliberate abuse of the right to counsel and as such a waiver of the right to further representation.

Constitutional Requirements

12. The general rule—that an advocate must disclose the existence of perjury with respect to a material fact, even that of a client—applies to defense counsel in criminal cases, as well as in other instances. However, the definition of the lawyer's ethical duty in such a situation may be qualified by constitutional provisions for due process and the right to counsel in criminal cases. In some jurisdictions these provisions have been construed to require that counsel present an accused as a witness if the accused wishes to testify, even if counsel knows the testimony will be false. The obligation of the advocate under these Rules is subordinate to such a constitutional requirement. . . .

Public Service

Rule 6.1 Pro Bono Publico Service

A lawyer should render public interest legal service. A lawyer may discharge this responsibility by providing professional services at no fee or a reduced fee to persons of limited means or to public service or charitable groups or organizations, by service in activities for improving the law, the legal system or the legal profession, and by financial support for organizations that provide legal services to persons of limited means.

Comment:

1. The ABA House of Delegates has formally acknowledged "the basic responsibility of each lawyer engaged in the practice of law to provide public interest legal services" without fee, or at a substantially reduced fee, in one or more of the following areas: poverty law, civil rights law, public rights law, charitable organization representation and the administration of justice. This Rule expresses that policy but is not intended to be enforced through disciplinary process.

2. The rights and responsibilities of individuals and organizations in the United States are increasingly defined in legal terms. As a consequence, legal assistance in coping with the web of statutes, rules and regulations is imperative for persons of modest and limited means, as well as for the relatively well-to-do.

3. The basic responsibility for providing legal services for those unable to pay ultimately rests upon the individual lawyer, and personal involvement in the problems of the disadvantaged can be one of the most rewarding experiences in the life of a lawyer. Every lawyer, regardless of professional prominence or professional workload, should find time to participate in or otherwise support the provision of legal services to the disadvantaged. The provision of free legal services to those unable to pay reasonable fees continues to be an obligation of each lawyer as well as the profession generally, but the efforts of individual lawyers are often not enough to meet the need. Thus, it has been necessary for the profession and government to institute additional programs to provide legal services. Accordingly, legal aid offices, lawyer referral services and other related programs have been developed, and others will be developed by the profession and government. Every lawyer should support all proper efforts to meet this need for legal services.

PRINCIPLES OF MEDICAL ETHICS

American Medical Association

Preamble

The medical profession has long subscribed to a body of ethical statements developed primarily for the benefit of the patient. As a member of this profession, a physician must recognize responsibility not only to the patients, but also to society, to other health professionals, and to self. The following Principles adopted by the American Medical Association are not laws, but standards of conduct which define the essentials of honorable behavior for the physician.

I. A physician shall be dedicated to providing competent medical service with compassion and respect for human dignity.

II. A physician shall deal honestly with patients and colleagues, and strive to expose those physicians deficient in character or competence, or who engage in fraud or deception.

III. A physician shall respect the law and also recognize a responsibility to seek changes in those requirements which are contrary to the best interests of the patient.

IV. A physician shall respect the rights of patients, of colleagues, and of other health professionals, and shall safeguard patient confidences within the constraints of the law.

V. A physician shall continue to study, apply and advance scientific knowledge, make relevant information available to patients, colleagues, and the public, obtain consultation, and use the talents of other health professionals when indicated.

VI. A physician shall, in the provision of appropriate patient care, except in emergencies, be free to choose whom to serve, with whom to associate, and the environment in which to provide medical services.

VII. A physician shall recognize a responsibility to participate in activities contributing to an improved community.

PRINCIPLES OF MEDICAL ETHICS WITH ANNOTATIONS ESPECIALLY APPLICABLE TO PSYCHIATRY

American Psychiatric Association

Foreword

All physicians should practice in accordance with the medical code of ethics set forth in the Principles of Medical Ethics of the American Medical Association. . . .

However, these general guidelines have sometimes been difficult to interpret for psychiatry, so further annotations to the basic principles are offered in this document. While psychiatrists have the same goals as all physicians, there are special ethical problems in psychiatric practice that differ in coloring and degree from ethical problems in other branches of medical practice, even though the basic principles are the same. The annotations are not designed as absolutes and will be revised from time to time so as to be applicable to current practices and problems.

Section 1

*A physician shall be dedicated to providing competent medical service with compassion and respect for human dignity.**

* Statements in italics are taken directly from the American Medical Association's Principles of Medical Ethics.

1. The patient may place his/her trust in his/her psychiatrist knowing that the psychiatrist's ethics and professional responsibilities preclude him/her gratifying his/her own needs by exploiting the patient. This becomes particularly important because of the essentially private, highly personal, and sometimes intensely emotional nature of the relationship established with the psychiatrist.

2. A psychiatrist should not be a party to any type of policy that excludes, segregates, or demeans the dignity of any patient because of ethnic origin, race, sex, creed, age, socioeconomic status, or sexual orientation.

3. In accord with the requirements of law and accepted medical practice, it is ethical for a physician to submit his/her work to peer review and to the ultimate authority of the medical staff executive body and the hospital administration and its governing body. In case of dispute, the ethical psychiatrist has the following steps available:

a. Seek appeal from the medical staff decision

From American Psychiatric Association, *Principles of Medical Ethics with Annotations Especially Applicable to Psychiatry* (1985). Reprinted by permission.

to a joint conference committee, including members of the medical staff executive committee and the executive committee of the governing board. At this appeal, the ethical psychiatrist could request that outside opinions be considered.

b. Appeal to the governing body itself.

c. Appeal to state agencies regulating licensure of hospitals if, in the particular state, they concern themselves with matters of professional competency and quality of care.

d. Attempt to educate colleagues through development of research projects and data and presentations at professional meetings and in professional journals.

e. Seek redress in local courts, perhaps through an enjoining injunction against the governing body.

f. Public education as carried out by an ethical psychiatrist would not utilize appeals based solely upon emotion, but would be presented in a professional way and without any potential exploitation of patients through testimonials.

4. A psychiatrist should not be a participant in a legally authorized execution.

Section 2

A physician shall deal honestly with patients and colleagues, and strive to expose those physicians deficient in character or competence, or who engage in fraud or deception.

1. The requirement that the physician conduct himself with propriety in his/her profession and in all the actions of his/her life is especially important in the case of the psychiatrist because the patient tends to model his/her behavior after that of his/her therapist by identification. Further, the necessary intensity of the therapeutic relationship may tend to activate sexual and other needs and fantasies on the part of both patient and therapist, while weakening the objectivity necessary for control. Sexual activity with a patient is unethical.

2. The psychiatrist should diligently guard against exploiting information furnished by the patient and should not use the unique position of power afforded him/ her by the psychotherapeutic situation to influence the patient in any way not directly relevant to the treatment goals.

3. A psychiatrist who regularly practices outside his/her area of professional competence should be considered unethical. Determination of professional competence should be made by peer review boards or other appropriate bodies.

4. Special consideration should be given to those psychiatrists who, because of mental illness, jeopardize the welfare of their patients and their own reputations and practices. It is ethical, even encouraged, for another psychiatrist to intercede in such situations.

5. Psychiatric services, like all medical services, are dispensed in the context of a contractual arrangement between the patient and the treating physician. The provisions of the contractual arrangement, which are binding on the physician as well as on the patient, should be explicitly established.

6. It is ethical for the psychiatrist to make a charge for a missed appointment when this falls within the terms of the specific contractual agreement with the patient. Charging for a missed appointment or for one not cancelled 24 hours in advance need not, in itself, be considered unethical if a patient is fully advised that the physician will make such a charge. The practice, however, should be resorted to infrequently and always with the utmost consideration for the patient and his/her circumstances.

7. An arrangement in which a psychiatrist provides supervision or administration to other physicians or nonmedical persons for a percentage of their fees or gross income is not acceptable; this would constitute fee-splitting. In a team of practitioners, or a multidisciplinary team, it is ethical for the psychiatrist to receive income for administration, research, education, or consultation. This should be based upon a mutually agreed upon and set fee or salary, open to renegotiation when a change in the time demand occurs. . . .

8. When a member has been found to have behaved unethically by the American Psychiatric Association or one of its constituent district branches, there should not be automatic reporting to the local authorities responsible for medical licensure, but the decision to report should be decided upon the merits of the case.

Section 3

A physician shall respect the law and also recognize a responsibility to seek changes in those requirements which are contrary to the best interests of the patient.

1. It would seem self-evident that a psychiatrist who is a law-breaker might be ethically unsuited to practice his/her profession. When such illegal activities bear directly upon his/her practice, this would obviously be the case. However, in other instances, illegal activities such as those concerning the right to protest social injustices might not bear on either the image of the psychiatrist or the ability of the specific psychiatrist to treat his/her patient ethically and well. While no committee or board could offer prior assurance that any illegal activity would not be considered unethical, it is conceivable that an individual could violate a law without being guilty of professionally unethical behavior. Physicians lose no right of citizenship on entry into the profession of medicine.

2. Where not specifically prohibited by local laws governing medical practice, the practice of acupuncture by a psychiatrist is not unethical per se. The psychiatrist should have professional competence in the use of acupuncture. Or, if he/she is supervising the use of acupuncture by nonmedical individuals, he/she should provide proper medical supervision. . . .

Section 4

A physician shall respect the rights of patients, of colleagues, and of other health professionals, and shall safeguard patient confidences within the constraints of the law.

1. Psychiatric records, including even the identification of a person as a patient, must be protected with extreme care. Confidentiality is essential to psychiatric treatment. This is based in part on the special nature of psychiatric therapy as well as on the traditional ethical relationship between physician and patient. Growing concern regarding the civil rights of patients and the possible adverse effects of computerization, duplication equipment, and data banks makes the dissemination of confidential information an increasing hazard. Because of the sensitive and private nature of the information with which the psychiatrist deals, he/she must be circumspect in the information that he/she chooses to disclose to others about a patient. The welfare of the patient must be a continuing consideration.

2. A psychiatrist may release confidential information only with the authorization of the patient or under proper legal compulsion. The continuing duty of the psychiatrist to protect the patient includes fully apprising him/her of the connotations of waiving the privilege of privacy. This may become an issue when the patient is being investigated by a government agency, is applying for a position, or is involved in legal action. The same principles apply to the release of information concerning treatment to medical departments of government agencies, business organizations, labor unions, and insurance companies. Information gained in confidence about patients seen in student health services should not be released without the student's explicit permission.

3. Clinical and other materials used in teaching and writing must be adequately disguised in order to preserve the anonymity of the individuals involved.

4. The ethical responsibility of maintaining confidentiality holds equally for the consultations in which the patient may not have been present and in which the consultee was not a physician. In such instances, the physician consultant should alert the consultee to his/her duty of confidentiality.

5. Ethically the psychiatrist may disclose only that information which is relevant to a given situation. He/she should avoid offering speculation as fact. Sensitive information such as an individual's sexual orientation or fantasy material is usually unnecessary.

6. Psychiatrists are often asked to examine individuals for security purposes, to determine suitability for various jobs, and to determine legal competence. The psychiatrist must fully describe the nature and purpose and lack of confidentiality of the examination to the examinee at the beginning of the examination.

7. Careful judgment must be exercised by the psychiatrist in order to include, when appropriate, the parents or guardian in the treatment of a minor. At the same time the psychiatrist must assure the minor proper confidentiality.

8. Psychiatrists at times may find it necessary, in order to protect the patient or the community from imminent danger, to reveal confidential information disclosed by the patient.

9. When the psychiatrist is ordered by the court to reveal the confidences entrusted to him/her by patients he/she may comply or he/she may ethically hold the right to dissent within the framework of the law. When the psychiatrist is in doubt, the right of the patient to confidentiality and, by extension, to unimpaired treatment, should be given priority. The psychiatrist should reserve the right to raise the question of adequate need for disclosure. In the event that the necessity for legal disclosure is demonstrated by the court, the psychiatrist may request the right to disclosure of only that information which is relevant to the legal question at hand.

10. With regard for the person's dignity and privacy and with truly informed consent, it is ethical to present a patient to a scientific gathering, if the confidentiality of the presentation is understood and accepted by the audience.

11. It is ethical to present a patient or former patient to a public gathering or to the news media only if the patient is fully informed of enduring loss of confidentiality, is competent, and consents in writing without coercion.

12. When involved in funded research, the ethical psychiatrist will advise human subjects of the funding source, retain his/her freedom to reveal data and results, and follow all appropriate and current guidelines relative to human subject protection.

13. Ethical considerations in medical practice preclude the psychiatric evaluation of any adult charged with criminal acts prior to access to, or availability of, legal counsel. The only exception is the rendering of care to the person for the sole purpose of medical treatment. . . .

Section 7

A physician shall recognize a responsibility to participate in activities contributing to an improved community. . . .

3. On occasion psychiatrists are asked for an opinion about an individual who is in the light of public attention, or who has disclosed information about himself/herself through public media. It is unethical for a psychiatrist to offer a professional opinion unless he/she has conducted an examination and has been granted proper authorization for such a statement.

4. The psychiatrist may permit his/her certification to be used for the involuntary treatment of any person only following his/her personal examination of that person. To do so, he/she must find that the person, because of mental illness, cannot form a judgment as to what is in his/her own best interests and that, without such treatment, substantial impairment is likely to occur to the person or others.

CODE FOR NURSES WITH INTERPRETIVE STATEMENTS

American Nurses' Association

Preamble

A code of ethics makes explicit the primary goals and values of the profession. When individuals become nurses, they make a moral commitment to uphold the values and special moral obligations expressed in their code. The Code for Nurses is based on a belief about the nature of individuals, nursing, health, and society. Nursing encompasses the protection, promotion, and restoration of health; the prevention of illness; and the alleviation of suffering in the care of clients, including individuals, families, groups, and communities. In the context of these functions, nursing is defined as the diagnosis and treatment of human responses to actual or potential health problems.

Since clients themselves are the primary decision makers in matters concerning their own health, treatment, and well-being, the goal of nursing actions is to support and enhance the client's responsibility and self-determination to the greatest extent possible. In this context, health is not necessarily an end in itself, but rather a means to a life that is meaningful from the client's perspective.

When making clinical judgments, nurses base their decisions on consideration of consequences and of universal moral principles, both of which prescribe and justify nursing actions. The most fundamental of these principles is respect for persons. Other principles stemming from this basic principle are autonomy (self-determination), beneficence (doing good), nonmaleficence (avoiding harm), veracity (truth-telling), confidentiality (respecting privileged information), fidelity (keeping promises), and justice (treating people fairly).

In brief, then, the statements of the code and their interpretation provide guidance for conduct and relationships in carrying out nursing responsibilities consistent with the ethical obligations of the profession and with high quality in nursing care. . . .

Code for Nurses with Interpretive Statements

1. The nurse provides services with respect for human dignity and the uniqueness of the client, unrestricted by considerations of social or economic status, personal attributes, or the nature of health problems.

1.1 Respect for Human Dignity

The fundamental principle of nursing practice is respect for the inherent dignity and worth of every client. Nurses are morally obligated to respect human existence and the individuality of all persons who are the recipients of nursing actions. Nurses therefore must take all reasonable means to protect and preserve human life when there is hope of recovery or reasonable hope of benefit from life-prolonging treatment.

Truth telling and the process of reaching informed choice underlie the exercise of self-determination, which is basic to respect for persons. Clients should be as fully involved as possible in the planning and implementation of their own health care. Clients have the moral right to determine what will be done with their own person; to be given accurate information, and all the information necessary for making informed judgments; to be assisted with weighing the benefits and burdens of options in their treatment; to accept, refuse, or terminate treatment without coercion;

and to be given necessary emotional support. Each nurse has an obligation to be knowledgeable about the moral and legal rights of all clients and to protect and support those rights. In situations in which the client lacks the capacity to make a decision, a surrogate decision maker should be designated.

Individuals are interdependent members of the community. Taking into account both individual rights and the interdependence of persons in decision making, the nurse recognizes those situations in which individual rights to autonomy in health care may temporarily be overridden to preserve the life of the human community; for example, when a disaster demands triage or when an individual presents a direct danger to others. The many variables involved make it imperative that each case be considered with full awareness of the need to preserve the rights and responsibilities of clients and the demands of justice. The suspension of individual rights must always be considered a deviation to be tolerated as briefly as possible. . . .

1.3 The Nature of Health Problems

The nurse's respect for the worth and dignity of the individual human being applies, irrespective of the nature of the health problem. It is reflected in care given the person who is disabled as well as one without disability, the person with long-term illness as well as one with acute illness, the recovering patient as well as one in the last phase of life. This respect extends to all who require the services of the nurse for the promotion of health, the prevention of illness, the restoration of health, the alleviation of suffering, and the provision of supportive care of the dying. The nurse does not act deliberately to terminate the life of any person.

The nurse's concern for human dignity and for the provision of high quality nursing care is not limited by personal attitudes or beliefs. If ethically opposed to interventions in a particular case because of the procedures to be used, the nurse is justified in refusing to participate. Such refusal should be made known in advance and in time for other appropriate arrangements to be made for the client's nursing care. If the nurse becomes involved in such a case and the client's life is in jeopardy, the nurse is obliged to provide for the client's safety, to avoid abandonment, and to withdraw only when assured that alternative sources of nursing care are available to the client. . . .

2. The nurse safeguards the client's right to privacy by judiciously protecting information of a confidential nature. . . .

3. The nurse acts to safeguard the client and the public when health care and safety are affected by incompetent, unethical, or illegal practice by any person. . . .

3.2 Acting on Questionable Practice

When the nurse is aware of inappropriate or questionable practice in the provision of health care, concern should be expressed to the person carrying out the questionable practice and attention called to the possible detrimental effect upon the client's welfare. When factors in the health care delivery system threaten the welfare of the client, similar action should be directed to the responsible administrative person. If indicated, the practice should then be reported to the appropriate authority within the institution, agency, or larger system.

There should be an established process for the reporting and handling of incompetent, unethical, or illegal practice within the employment setting so that such reporting can go through official channels without causing fear of reprisal. The nurse should be knowledgeable about the process and be prepared to use it if necessary. When questions are raised about the practices of individual practitioners or of health care systems, written documentation of the observed practices or behaviors must be available to the appropriate authorities.

State nurses' associations should be prepared to provide assistance and support in the development and evaluation of such processes and in reporting procedures. . . .

4. The nurse assumes responsibility and accountability for individual nursing judgments and actions. . . .

4.3 Accountability for Nursing Judgment and Action

Accountability refers to being answerable to someone for something one has done. It means providing an explanation or rationale to oneself, to clients, to peers, to the nursing profession, and to society. In order to be accountable, nurses act under a code of ethical conduct that is grounded in the moral principles of fidelity and respect for the dignity, worth, and self-determination of clients.

The nursing profession continues to develop ways to clarify nursing's accountability to society. The contract between the profession and society is made explicit through such mechanisms as (a) the Code for Nurses, (b) the standards of nursing practice, (c) the development of nursing theory derived from nursing research in order to guide nursing actions, (d) educational requirements for practice, (e) certification, and (f) mechanisms for evaluating the effectiveness of the nurse's performance of nursing responsibilities.

Nurses are accountable for judgments made and actions taken in the course of nursing practice. Neither physicians' orders nor the employing agency's policies relieve the nurse of accountability for actions taken and judgments made.

5. The nurse maintains competence in nursing. . . .

6. The nurse exercises informed judgment and uses individual competency and qualifications as criteria in seeking consultation, accepting responsibilities, and delegating nursing activities. . . .

7. The nurse participates in activities that contribute to the ongoing development of the profession's body of knowledge. . . .

8. The nurse participates in the profession's efforts to implement and improve standards of nursing. . . .

9. The nurse participates in the profession's efforts to establish and maintain conditions of employment conducive to high quality nursing care. . . .

9.1 Responsibility for Conditions of Employment

The nurse must be concerned with conditions of employment that (a) enable the nurse to practice in accordance with the standards of nursing practice and (b) provide a care environment that meets the standards of nursing service. The provision of high quality nursing care is the responsibility of both the individual nurse and the nursing profession. Professional autonomy and self-regulation in the control of conditions of practice are necessary for implementing nursing standards.

10. The nurse participates in the profession's effort to protect the public from misinformation and misrepresentation and to maintain the integrity of nursing. . . .

11. The nurse collaborates with members of the health professions and other citizens in promoting community and national efforts to meet the health needs of the public.

CODE OF ETHICS

American Association of Pastoral Counselors

Principle I   General

Pastoral counselors are committed to a belief in God and in the dignity and worth of each individual. They accept and maintain in their own personal lives the highest ethical standards but do not judge others by these standards.

The maintenance of high standards of professional competence is a responsibility shared by all pastoral counselors in the interests of the public, the religious community and of the profession. The pastoral counselor works toward the improvement and refinement of counseling through the establishment of ethical standards in pastoral counseling generally and especially at all pastoral counseling centers.

Pastoral counselors are accountable for their total ministry whatever its setting. This accountability is expressed in relationship to clients, colleagues and faith community, and in the acceptance of, and practice based upon, this Code of Ethics of the Association.

In the practice of the profession, pastoral counselors show sensible regard for moral, social and religious standards, realizing that any violation on their part may be damaging to their clients, students, colleagues and their profession.

Principle II   Professional Practices

In all professional matters pastoral counselors maintain practices that protect the public and advance the profession.

A. Pastoral counselors accurately represent their professional qualifications and their affiliation with any institution, organization or individual. Pastoral counselors are responsible for correcting any misrepresentation of their professional qualifications or affiliations.

B. Pastoral counselors use their knowledge or professional association for the benefit of the people they serve and not to secure unfair personal advantage, consistent with the standards and purposes of the Association.

C. Members of the Association clearly represent their level of membership and limit their practice at their respective level.

D. Announcements of pastoral counseling services are dignified, accurate and objective, descriptive but devoid of all claims or evaluation.

E. Brochures that promote the services of a pastoral counseling center describe them with accuracy and dignity. They may be sent to professional persons, religious institutions and other agencies, but to prospective individual clients only in response to inquiries.

F. Financial arrangements are always discussed at the start and handled in a business-like manner. Pastoral counselors stand ready to render service to individuals and communities in crisis, without regard to financial remuneration, when necessary.

G. Pastoral counselors neither receive nor pay a commission for referral of a client.

H. Records on clients are stored assuring security and confidentiality.

I. Pastoral counselors avoid disparagement of a colleague or other professional person to a client.

Principle III   Client Relationship and Confidentiality

Pastoral counselors respect the integrity and protect the welfare of persons or groups with whom they are working and have an obligation to safeguard information about them that has been obtained in the course of the counseling process.

A. It is the duty of pastoral counselors, during the counseling process, to maintain the re-

From American Association of Pastoral Counselors, *Code of Ethics* (1988). Reprinted by permission.

lationship with the client on a professional basis.

B. Pastoral counselors do not make unrealistic promises regarding the counseling process or its outcome.

C. Pastoral counselors recognize that the religious convictions of a client have powerful emotional and volitional significance and therefore are approached with care and sensitivity. They recognize that their influence may be considerable, and therefore, avoid any possible imposition of their own theology on clients.

D. Pastoral counselors do not engage in sexual misconduct with their clients.

E. Pastoral counselors recognize the trust placed in and unique power of the therapeutic relationship and the inherent danger of exploitation in any dual relationship with current or former clients (e.g., sexual or business relationships), and avoid exploitive dual relationships with current or former clients which compromise the integrity of therapy and/or use the relationship for the therapist's own gain.

F. Except by written permission, all communications from clients are treated with professional confidence. When clients are referred to in a publication, their identity is thoroughly disguised and the report shall so state.

G. Ethical concern for the integrity and welfare of the person or group applies to supervisory and training relationships. These relationships are maintained on a professional and confidential basis. Personal therapy will not be provided by one's current supervisor or administrator.

Principle IV   Faith Group Relationship

Pastoral counselors maintain vital association with the faith group in which they have ecclesiastical standing. They work for the improvement and growth of pastoral counseling throughout the religious community. They communicate to their own faith group and the broader religious community the implications for the life of their community of their experience in pastoral counseling. When members of this Asso-

ciation are removed from the ecclesiastical roster of their sponsoring faith group, they are to report it to the Committee of Professional Concerns for review of their membership.

Principle V   Interprofessional Relationships

Pastoral counselors relate to and cooperate with other professional persons in their community.

A. Pastoral counselors maintain interprofessional relationships, recognizing the importance of developing such relationships for the purposes of clinical consultations and referrals.

B. Pastoral counselors are sensitive to the total health needs of the clients they serve. To this end, they have access to appropriate health care professionals.

C. The affiliation of members with professional and interprofessional groups and organizations in the community is encouraged.

D. Pastoral counselors who offer specialized counseling services to persons currently receiving counseling or therapy from another professional person do so only with prior knowledge by the professional involved. Soliciting such clients is unethical practice.

Principle VI   Professional Development

Pastoral counselors continue postgraduate education and professional growth in many ways, including active participation in the meetings and affairs of the Association. Whenever appropriate, they join with other pastoral counselors and with representatives of other helping professions to promote mutual professional growth.

Principle VII   Publications and Communications

Pastoral counselors distinguish and differentiate their private opinions from those of their denomination or profession in publicity, public pronouncement or publications.

A. Pastoral counselors communicate the relationship of religion and health and the nature of the healing ministry.
B. Modesty, scientific caution and due regard for the limits of present knowledge characterize all statements and publications of pastoral counselors who supply information to the public, either directly or indirectly. Exaggeration, sensationalism, superficiality and other kinds of misrepresentation are unethical.
C. Pastoral counselors do not make it appear directly or indirectly, that they speak for the Association or represent its official position, except as authorized by the Board of Governors.

Principle VIII   Unethical Conduct

When pastoral counselors are accepted for membership in the Association, they bind themselves to accept the judgment of other members as to standards of professional ethics, subject to the safeguards provided as follows. Acceptance of membership involves explicit agreement to abide by the acts of discipline herein set forth.

Members of this Association are committed to maintain high standards of ethical practice. To this end members consult with their colleagues on the Regional Ethics Committee whenever ethical questions arise, the answers to which do not appear to be clear to them. Members who appear to violate the foregoing Code of Ethics should be cautioned through friendly remonstrance. That failing, formal complaint may be made in accordance with the following procedures. . . .

Principle IX   AAPC Ethics Committee Standards and Principles on Advertising

General: Any advertising by or for a pastoral counselor, pastoral counseling center and pastoral counseling organization (hereinafter to be referred to as pastoral counselor), including announcements, public statements and promotional activities, is undertaken with the purpose of helping the public make informed judgments and choices. Pastoral counselors *represent accurately and objectively their professional qualifications, affiliations, and functions,* as well as those of the institutions or organizations with which they or the statements may be associated. Public statements which provide theological or psychological information, professional opinions or information about availability of clinical services or products, are based on professionally acceptable findings and techniques with the full recognition of the limits and uncertainties of any such evidence.

A. Pastoral counselors may use the following information to describe the provider and services provided: name, highest relevant academic degree earned from an accredited institution; date, type and level of certification or licensure; AAPC membership level clearly stated; address and telephone number; office hours; a brief history of services offered, e.g., individual, couple and group counseling; fee information; foreign languages spoken; and policy regarding third party payments. Additional relevant information may be provided if it is legitimate, reasonable, free of deception, dignified and not otherwise prohibited by these principles. Pastoral counselors may not use the initials "AAPC" after their name in the manner of an academic degree.
B. Pastoral counselors do not advertise or announce themselves or their services in any way that falsely implies sponsorship or certification by an organization. Public statements by pastoral counselors do not contain any of the following:
   1. A false, fraudulent, misleading, deceptive or unfair statement.
   2. A misrepresentation of fact or a statement likely to mislead or deceive because in context it makes only a parital disclosure of relevant facts.
   3. A testimonial from a client regarding the quality of a pastoral counselor's services or products.
   4. A statement intended or likely to create false or unjustified expectations of favorable results.
   5. A statement implying unusual, unique, or one-of-a-kind abilities.
   6. A statement intended or likely to appeal

to a client's fears, anxieties, or emotions, especially if concerning the possible results of failure to obtain the offered services.

7. A statement concerning the comparative desirability of offered services.
8. A statement of direct solicitation of individual clients.

C. Pastoral counselors do not compensate in any way a representative of the press, radio, television or other communication medium for the purpose of professional publicity and news items. A paid advertisement must be identified as such, unless it is contextually apparent that it is a paid advertisement. Pastoral counselors are responsible for the content of such advertisement; hence, and for example, any communication to the public by use of radio or television is to be prerecorded, approved by the pastoral counselor and a recording of the actual transmission be retained in the possession of the pastoral counselor.

D. Advertisements or announcements, whether by pastoral counselors or AAPC accredited organization, of workshops, clinics, seminars, growth groups or similar services or endeavors, are to give a clear statement of purpose and a clear description of the experiences to be provided. The education, training and experience of the provider(s) involved are to be appropriately specified.

E. Pastoral counselors present themselves and their services fairly and accurately, avoiding misrepresentation through sensationalism, exaggeration or superficiality. For example, a pastoral counselor does not in any way imply, whether through individual services or those of an organization, that these services contain or will confer upon the recipient the blessings, well being or acceptance by a supreme being or any related derivative. Pastoral counselors are guided by the obligation to aid the public in developing informed judgments, opinions and choices.

F. Advertisements or announcements soliciting research participants, in which clinical or other professional services are offered as an inducement, make clear the nature of the services as well as the cost and other obligation or risks to be accepted by participants in the research.

Note: The Association Ethics Committee acknowledges the use, with permission, of "Ethical Principles of Psychologists," American Psychological Association, in developing these standards and principles. . . .

Article X   Guidelines for Sale of a Pastoral Counseling Practice

While the AAPC does not encourage the sale of a pastoral counseling practice, it is recognized that from time to time such a transaction may take place. In that instance the privacy and well being of the client will be of primary concern. . . .

THE COMMITTEE ON PROFESSIONAL STANDARDS AND RESPONSIBILITIES

American Political Science Association

RULES OF CONDUCT

A. Teacher–Student Relations

Rule 1. A faculty member must not expropriate the academic work of his students. As a dissertation adviser, he is not entitled to claim joint authorship with a student of a thesis or dissertation. The teacher cannot represent himself as the author of independent student research; and research assistance, paid or unpaid, requires full acknowledgment.

Rule 2. The academic political scientist must be very careful not to impose his partisan views—conventional or other-

From American Political Science Association, The Committee on Professional Standards and Responsibilities, *Rules of Conduct* (1968). Reprinted by permission.

wise—upon his students or colleagues. . . .

C. Political Activity of Academic Political Scientists

Rule 6. The college or university teacher is a citizen, and like other citizens, he should be free to engage in political activities insofar as he can do so consistently with his obligations as a teacher and scholar. Effective service as a faculty member is often compatible with certain types of political activity, for example, holding a part-time office in a political party or serving as a citizen of a governmental advisory board. Where a professor engages in full-time political activity, such as service in a state legislature, he should, as a rule, seek a leave of absence from his institution. Since political activity by academic political scientists is both legitimate and socially important, universities and colleges should have institutional arrangements to permit such activity, including reduction in the faculty member's work-load or a leave of absence subject to equitable adjustment of compensation when necessary.

Rule 7. A faculty member who seeks a leave to engage in political activity should recognize that he has a primary obligation to his institution and to his growth as a teacher and scholar. He should consider the problems that a leave of absence may create for his administration, colleagues and students, and he should not abuse the privilege by asking for leaves too frequently, or too late, or for too extended a period of time. A leave of absence incident to political activity should not affect unfavorably the tenure status of the faculty member.

Rule 8. Special problems arise if departments or schools endorse or sponsor political activities or public policies in the name of the entire faculty of the department or school. One of the purposes of tenure—to shelter unpopular or unorthodox teaching—is in some degree vitiated if the majority of a departmental faculty

endorses or sponsors a particular political position in the name of the faculty of the department. The simple way out of this dilemma is to adhere strictly to the rule that those faculty members who wish to endorse or sponsor a political position or activity do so in their own names without trying to bind their colleagues holding differing views. Departments as such should not endorse political positions.

D. Freedom and Integrity of Research by Academic Political Scientists

Principles for Funding Agencies

Rule 9. Financial sponsors of research have the responsibility for avoiding actions that would call into question the integrity of American academic institutions as centers of independent teaching and research. They should not sponsor research as a cover for intelligence activities.

Rule 10. Openness concerning material support of research is a basic principle of scholarship. In making grants for research, government and non-government sponsors should openly acknowledge research support and require that the grantee indicate in any published research financed by their grants the relevant sources of financial support. Where anonymity is requested by a non-governmental grantor and does not endanger the integrity of research, the character of the sponsorship rather than the identity of the grantor should be noted.

Rule 11. Political science research supported by government grants should be unclassified.

Rule 12. After a research grant has been made, the grantor shall not impose any restriction on or require any clearance of research methods, procedures, or content.

Rule 13. The grantor assumes no responsibility for the findings and conclusions of the researcher and imposes no restrictions on and carries no responsibility for publication.

Principles for Universities

Rule 14. A university or college should not administer research funds derived from contracts or grants whose purpose and the character of whose sponsorship cannot be publicly disclosed.

Rule 15. A university or college that administers research funds provided through contracts and grants from public and/or private sources must act to assure that research funds are used prudently and honorably.

Rule 16. In administering research funds entrusted directly to its care, a university or college should do its best to ensure that no restrictions are placed on the availability of evidence to scholars or on their freedom to draw their own conclusions from the evidence and to share their findings with others.

Principles for Individual Researchers

Rule 17. In applying for research funds, the individual researcher should:

a. clearly state the reasons he is applying for support and not resort to stratagems of ambiguity to make his research more acceptable to a funding agency;

b. indicate clearly the actual amount of time he personally plans to spend on the research;

c. indicate other sources of support of his research, if any; and

d. refuse to accept terms and conditions that he believes will undermine his freedom and integrity as a scholar. . . .

CODE OF ETHICS AND IMPLEMENTATION GUIDELINES

American Society for Public Administration

1. Demonstrate the highest standards of personal integrity, truthfulness, honesty and fortitude in all our public activities in order to inspire public confidence and trust in public institutions.

Perceptions of others are critical to the reputation of an individual or a public agency. Nothing is more important to public administrators than the public's opinion about their honesty, truthfulness, and personal integrity. It overshadows competence as the premier value sought by citizens in their public officials and employees. Any individual or collective compromise with respect to these character traits can damage the ability of an agency to perform its tasks or accomplish its mission. The reputation of the administrator may be tarnished. Effectiveness may be impaired. A career or careers may be destroyed. The best insurance against loss of public confidence is adherence to the highest standards of honesty, truthfulness and fortitude.

Public administrators are obliged to develop civic virtues because of the public responsibilities they have sought and obtained. Respect for the truth, for fairly dealing with others, for sensitivity to rights and responsibilities of citizens, and for the public good must be generated and carefully nurtured and matured.

If you are responsible for the performance of others, share with them the reasons for the importance of integrity. Hold them to high ethical standards and teach them the moral as well as the financial responsibility for public funds under their care.

If you are responsible only for your own performance, do not compromise your honesty and integrity for advancement, honors, or personal gain. Be discreet, respectful of proper authority and your appointed or elected superiors, sensitive to the expectations and the values of the public you serve. Practice the golden rule: doing to and for others what you would have done to and for you in similar circumstances. Be modest about your talents, letting your work speak for you. Be generous in your praise of the good work of your fellow workers. Guard the public purse as if it were your own.

Whether you are an official or an employee, by your own example give testimony to your regard for the rights of others. Acknowledge their legitimate responsibilities, and don't trespass upon them. Concede gracefully, quickly, and publicly when you have erred. Be fair and sensitive to those who have not fared well in their dealings with your agency and its applications of the law, regulations, or administrative procedures.

2. Serve in such a way that we do not realize undue personal gain from the performance of our official duties.

The only gains you should seek from public employment are salaries, fringe benefits, respect, and recognition for your work. Your personal gains may also include the pleasure of doing a good job, helping the public, and achieving your career goals. No elected or appointed public servant should borrow or accept gifts from staff of any corporation which buys services from, or sells to, or is regulated by, his or her governmental agency. If your work brings you in frequent contact with contractors supplying the government, be sure you pay for your own expenses. Public property, funds and power should never be directed toward personal or political gain. Make it clear by your own actions that you will not tolerate any use of public funds to benefit yourself, your family, or your friends.

3. Avoid any interest or activity which is in conflict with the conduct of our official duties.

Public employees should not undertake any task which is in conflict or could be viewed as in conflict with job responsibilities.

This general statement addresses a fundamental principle that public employees are trustees for all the people. This means that the people have a right to expect public employees to act as surrogates for the entire people with fairness toward all the people and not a few or a limited group.

Actions or inactions which conflict with, injure, or destroy this foundation of trust between the people and their surrogates must be avoided.

Ironically, experience indicates that conflict of interest and corruption often arise not from an external affront, but as a result of interaction between persons who know each other very well. To strengthen resistance to conflict of interest, public employees should avoid frequent social contact with persons who come under their regulation or persons who wish to sell products or services to their agency or institution.

Agencies with inspectional or investigative responsibilities have a special obligation to reduce vulnerability to conflict of interest. Periodic staff rotation may be helpful to these agencies.

Individuals holding a position recognized by law or regulation as an unclassified or political appointment (e.g. Cabinet level and Governor's appointment positions) have a special obligation to behave in ways which do not suggest that official acts are driven primarily or only by partisan political concerns.

Public employees should remember that despite whatever preventive steps they might take, situations which hold the possibility for conflict of interest will always emerge. Consequently, the awareness of the potentiality of conflict of interest is important. Public employees, particularly professors in Public Administration, have a serious obligation to periodically stimulate discussion on conflicts of interest within organizations, schools, and professional associations.

4. Support, implement, and promote merit employment and programs of affirmative action to assure equal employment opportunity by our recruitment, selection, and advancement of qualified persons from all elements of society.

Oppose any discrimination because of race, color, religion, sex, national origin, political affiliation, physical handicaps, age, or marital status, in all aspects of personnel policy. Likewise, a person's lifestyle should not be the occasion for discrimination if it bears no reasonable relation to his or her ability to perform required tasks.

Review employment and personnel operations and statistics to identify the impact of organizational practices on "protected groups." Performance standards should apply equally to all workers. In the event of cutbacks of staff, managers should employ fair criteria for selection of employees for separation, and humane strategies for administering the program.

Any kind of sexual, racial, or religious harassment should not be allowed. Appropriate channels should be provided for harassed persons to state their problems to objective officials. In the event of a proven offense, appropriate action should be taken.

5. Eliminate all forms of illegal discrimination, fraud, and mismanagement of public funds, and support colleagues if they are in difficulty because of responsible efforts to correct such discrimination, fraud, mismanagement or abuse.

If you are a supervisor, you should not only be alert that no illegal action issues from or is sponsored by your immediate office, you should inform your subordinates at regular intervals that you will tolerate no illegalities in their offices and discuss the reasons for the position with them. Public employees who have good reason to suspect illegal action in any public agency should seek assistance in how to channel information regarding the matter to appropriate authorities.

All public servants should support authorized investigative agencies, the General Accounting Office in the federal government, auditors in the state or large local governments, C.P.A. firms or federal or state auditors in many other cases. We should support the concept of independent auditors reporting to committees independent of management. Good fiscal and management controls and inspections are important protections for supervisors, staff, and the public interest.

In both government and business, inadequate equipment, software, procedures, supervision, and poor security controls make possible both intentional and unintentional misconduct. Managers have an ethical obligation to seek adequate equipment, software, procedures and controls to reduce the agency's vulnerability to misconduct. When an agency dispenses exemptions from regulations, or abatement of taxes or fees, managers should assure periodic investigatory checks.

The "whistle blower" who appears to his/her immediate superiors to be disloyal, may actually be loyal to the higher interests of the public. If so, the whistle blower deserves support. Local, state, and federal governments should establish effective dissent channels to which whistle blowers may report their concerns without fear of identification.

Supervisors should inform their staff that constructive criticism may be brought to them without reprisal, or may be carried to an ombudsman or other designated official. As a last resort, public employees have a right to make public their criticism but it is the personal and professional responsibility of the critic to advance only well founded criticism.

6. Serve the public with respect, concern, courtesy, and responsiveness, recognizing that service to the public is beyond service to oneself.

Be sure your answers to questions on public policy are complete, understandabie and true. Try to develop in your staff a goal of courteous conduct with citizens. Devise a simple system to ensure that your staff gives helpful and pleasant service to the public. Wherever possible, show citizens how to avoid mistakes in their relations with government.

Each citizen's questions should be answered as thoughtfully and as fully as possible. If you or your staff do not know the answer to a question, an effort should be made to get an answer or to help the citizen make direct contact with the appropriate office.

Part of servicing the public responsively is to encourage citizen cooperation and to involve civic groups. Administrators have an ethical responsibility to bring citizens into work with the government as far as practical, both to secure citizen support of government, and for the economies or increased effectiveness which will result. Respect the right of the public (through the media) to know what is going on in your agency even though you know queries may be raised for partisan or other non-public purposes.

7. Strive for personal professional excellence and encourage the professional development of our associates and those seeking to enter the field of public administration.

Staff members, throughout their careers, should be encouraged to participate in professional activities and associations such as ASPA. They should also be reminded of the importance of doing a good job and their responsibility to improve the public service.

Administrators should make time to meet with students periodically and to provide a bridge between classroom studies and the realities of public jobs. Administrators should also lend their support to well planned internship programs.

8. Approach our organization and operational duties with a positive attitude and constructively support open communication, creativity, dedication and compassion.

Americans expect government to be compassionate, well organized, and operating within the law. Public employees should understand the purpose of their agency and the role they play in achieving that purpose. Dedication and creativity of staff members will flow from a sense of purpose.

ASPA members should strive to create a work environment which supports positive and constructive attitudes among workers at all levels. This open environment should permit employees to comment on work activities without fear of reprisal. In addition, managers can strengthen this open environment by establishing procedures ensuring thoughtful and objective review of employee concerns.

9. Respect and protect the privileged information to which we have access in the course of official duties.

Much information in public offices is privileged for reasons of national security, or because of laws or ordinances. If you talk with colleagues about privileged matters, be sure they need the information and you enjoin them to secrecy. If the work is important enough to be classified, learn and follow the rules set by the security agency. Special care must be taken to secure access to confidential information stored on computers. Sometimes information needs to be withheld from the individual citizen or general public to prevent disturbances of the peace. It should be withheld only if there is a possibility of dangerous or illegal or unprofessional consequences of releasing information.

Where other governmental agencies have a legitimate public service need for information possessed by an agency, do all you can to cooperate, within the limits of statute law, administrative regulations, and promises made to those who furnish the information.

10. Exercise whatever discretionary authority we have under law to promote the public interest.

If your work involves discretionary decisions you should first secure policy guidelines from your supervisor. You should then make sure that all staff who "need to know" are informed of these policies and have an opportunity to discuss the means of putting them into effect.

There are occasions when a law is unenforceable or has become obsolete; in such cases you should recommend to your superior or to the legislative body that the law be modernized. If an obsolete law remains in effect, the manager or highest official should determine if the law is or is not to be enforced, after consultation with the agency's legal advisor.

There are occasions where a lower level employee must be given considerable discretion. Try to see that such employees are adequately trained for their difficult tasks.

Tell yourself and your staff quite frequently that every decision creates a precedent, so the first decisions on a point should be ethically sound; this is the best protection for staff as well as for the public.

11. Accept as a personal duty the responsibility to keep up to date on emerging issues and to administer the public's business with professional competence, fairness, impartiality, efficiency and effectiveness.

Administrators should attend professional meetings, read books and periodicals related to their field, and talk with specialists. The goal is to keep informed about the present and future issues and problems in their professional field and organization in order to take advantage of opportunities and avoid problems.

Serious mistakes in public administration have been made by people who did their jobs conscientiously but failed to look ahead for emerging problems and issues. A long list of washed out dams, fatal mine accidents, fires in poorly inspected buildings, inadequate computer systems, or economic disasters are results of not looking ahead. ASPA members should be catalysts to stimulate discussion and reflection about improving efficiency and effectiveness of public services.

12. Respect, support, study, and when necessary, work to improve federal and state constitutions and other laws which define the relationships among public agencies, employees, clients and all citizens.

Familiarize yourself with principles of American constitutional government. As a citizen work for legislation which is in the public interest.

Teach constitutional principles of equality and fairness.

Strive for clear division of functions between different levels of government, between different bureaus or departments, and between government and its citizens. Cooperate as fully as possible with all agencies of government, especially those with overlapping responsibilities. Do not let parochial agency or institutional loyalty drown out considerations of wider public policy.

ETHICAL PRINCIPLES OF PSYCHOLOGISTS

American Psychological Association

Preamble

Psychologists respect the dignity and worth of the individual and strive for the preservation and protection of fundamental human rights. They are committed to increasing knowledge of human behavior and of people's understanding of themselves and others and to the utilization of such knowledge for the promotion of human welfare. While pursuing these objectives, they make every effort to protect the welfare of those who seek their services and of the research participants that may be the object of study. They use their skills only for purposes consistent with these values and do not knowingly permit their misuse by others. While demanding for themselves freedom of inquiry and communication, psychologists accept the responsibility this freedom requires: competence, objectivity in the application of skills, and concern for the best interests of clients, colleagues, students, research participants, and society. In the pursuit of these ideals, psychologists subscribe to principles in the following areas: 1. Responsibility, 2. Competence, 3. Moral and Legal Standards, 4. Public Statements, 5. Confidentiality, 6. Welfare of the Consumer, 7. Professional Relationships, 8. Assessment Techniques, 9. Research With Human Participants, and 10. Care and Use of Animals.

Acceptance of membership in the American Psychological Association commits the member to adherence to these principles.

Psychologists cooperate with duly constituted committees of the American Psychological Association, in particular, the Committee on Scientific and Professional Ethics and Conduct, by responding to inquiries promptly and completely. Members also respond promptly and completely to inquiries from duly constituted state association ethics committees and professional standards review committees.

Principle 1: Responsibility

In providing services, psychologists maintain the highest standards of their profession. They accept responsibility for the consequences of their acts and make every effort to ensure that their services are used appropriately.

a. As scientists, psychologists accept responsibility for the selection of their research topics and the methods used in investigation, analysis, and reporting. They plan their research in ways to minimize the possibility that their findings will be misleading. They provide thorough discussion of the limitations of their data, especially where their work touches on social policy or might be construed to the detriment of persons in specific age, sex, ethnic, socioeconomic, or other social groups. In publishing reports of their work, they never suppress disconfirming data, and they acknowledge the existence of alternative hypotheses and explanations of their findings. Psychologists take credit only for work they have actually done.

b. Psychologists clarify in advance with all appropriate persons and agencies the expectations for sharing and utilizing research data. They avoid relationships that may limit their objectivity or create a conflict of interest. Interference with the milieu in which data are collected is kept to a minimum.

c. Psychologists have the responsibility to attempt to prevent distortion, misuse, or suppression of psychological findings by the institution or agency of which they are employees.

d. As members of governmental or other organizational bodies, psychologists remain accountable as individuals to the highest standards of their profession.

e. As teachers, psychologists recognize their primary obligation to help others acquire knowledge and skill. They maintain high standards of scholarship by presenting psychological information objectively, fully, and accurately.

f. As practitioners, psychologists know that they bear a heavy social responsibility because their recommendations and professional actions may alter the lives of others. They are alert to personal, social, organizational, financial, or political situations and pressures that might lead to misuse of their influence.

Principle 2: Competence

The maintenance of high standards of competence is a responsibility shared by all psychologists in the interest of the public and the profession as a whole. Psychologists recognize the boundaries of their competence and the limitations of their techniques. They only provide services and only use techniques for which they are qualified by training and experience. In those areas in which recognized standards do not yet exist, psychologists take whatever precautions are necessary to protect the welfare of their clients. They maintain knowledge of current scientific and professional information related to the services they render. . . .

Principle 3: Moral and Legal Standards

Psychologists' moral and ethical standards of behavior are a personal matter to the same degree as they are for any other citizen, except as these may compromise the fulfillment of their professional responsibilities or reduce the public trust in psychology and psychologists. Regarding their own behavior, psychologists are sensitive to prevailing community standards and to the possible impact that conformity to or deviation from these standards may have upon the quality of their performance as psychologists. Psychologists are also aware of the possible impact of their public behavior upon the ability of colleagues to perform their professional duties.

a. As teachers, psychologists are aware of the fact that their personal values may affect the selection and presentation of instructional materials. When dealing with topics that may give offense, they recognize and respect the diverse attitudes that students may have toward such materials.

b. As employees or employers, psychologists do not engage in or condone practices that are inhumane or that result in illegal or unjustifiable actions. Such practices include, but are not limited to, those based on considerations of race, handicap, age, gender, sexual preference, religion, or national origin in hiring, promotion, or training.

c. In their professional roles, psychologists avoid any action that will violate or diminish the legal and civil rights of clients or of others who may be affected by their actions.

d. As practitioners and researchers, psychologists act in accord with Association standards and guidelines related to practice and to the conduct of research with human beings and animals. In the ordinary course of events, psychologists adhere to relevant governmental laws and institutional regulations. When federal, state, provincial, organizational, or institutional laws, regulations, or practices are in conflict with Association standards and guidelines, psychologists make known their commitment to Association standards and guidelines and, wherever possible, work toward a resolution of the conflict. Both practitioners and researchers are concerned with the development of such legal and quasi-legal regulations as best serve the public interest, and they work toward changing existing regulations that are not beneficial to the public interest.

Principle 4: Public Statements

Public statements, announcements of services, advertising, and promotional activities of psychologists serve the purpose of helping the public make informed judgments and choices. Psychologists represent accurately and objectively their professional qualifications, affiliations, and functions, as well as those of the institutions or organizations with which they or the statements may be associated. In public statements providing psychological information or professional opinions or providing information about the availability of psychological products, publications, and services, psychologists base their statements on scientifically acceptable psychological findings and techniques with full recognition of the limits and uncertainties of such evidence.
. . .

Principle 5: Confidentiality

Psychologists have a primary obligation to respect the confidentiality of information obtained from persons in the course of their work as psychologists. They reveal such information to others only with the consent of the person or the person's legal representative, except in those unusual circumstances in which not to do so would result in clear danger to the person or to others. Where appropriate, psychologists inform their clients of the legal limits of confidentiality.

a. Information obtained in clinical or consulting relationships, or evaluative data concerning children, students, employees, and others, is discussed only for professional purposes and only with persons clearly concerned with the case. Written and oral reports present only data germane to the purposes of the evaluation, and every effort is made to avoid undue invasion of privacy.

b. Psychologists who present personal information obtained during the course of professional work in writings, lectures, or other public forums either obtain adequate prior consent to do so or adequately disguise all identifying information.

c. Psychologists make provisions for maintaining confidentiality in the storage and disposal of records.

d. When working with minors or other persons who are unable to give voluntary, informed consent, psychologists take special care to protect these persons' best interests.

Principle 6: Welfare of the Consumer

Psychologists respect the integrity and protect the welfare of the people and groups with whom they work. When conflicts of interest arise between clients and psychologists' employing institutions, psychologists clarify the nature and direction of their loyalties and responsibilities and keep all parties informed of their commitments. Psychologists fully inform consumers as to the purpose and nature of an evaluative, treatment, educational, or training procedure, and they freely acknowledge that clients, students, or participants in research have freedom of choice with regard to participation. . . .

Principle 7: Professional Relationships

Psychologists act with due regard for the needs, special competencies, and obligations of their colleagues in psychology and other professions. They respect the prerogatives and obligations of the institutions or organizations with which these other colleagues are associated. . . . .

Principle 8: Assessment Techniques

In the development, publication, and utilization of psychological assessment techniques, psychologists make every effort to promote the welfare and best interests of the client. They guard against the misuse of assessment results. They respect the client's right to know the results, the interpretations made, and the bases for their conclusions and recommendations. Psychologists make every effort to maintain the security of tests and other assessment techniques within limits of legal mandates. They strive to ensure the appropriate use of assessment techniques by others. . . .

Principle 9: Research with Human Participants

The decision to undertake research rests upon a considered judgment by the individual psychologist about how best to contribute to psychological science and human welfare. Having made the decision to conduct research, the psychologist considers alternative directions in which research energies and resources might be invested. On the basis of this consideration, the psychologist carries out the investigation with respect and concern for the dignity and welfare of the people who participate and with cognizance of federal and state regulations and professional standards governing the conduct of research with human participants.

a. In planning a study, the investigator has the responsibility to make a careful evaluation of its ethical acceptability. To the extent that the weighing of scientific and human values suggests a compromise of any principle, the investigator incurs a correspondingly serious obligation to seek ethical advice and to observe stringent safeguards to protect the rights of human participants.

b. Considering whether a participant in a planned study will be a "subject at risk" or a "subject at minimal risk," according to recognized standards, is of primary ethical concern to the investigator.

c. The investigator always retains the responsibility for ensuring ethical practice in research. The investigator is also responsible for the ethical treatment of research participants by collaborators, assistants, students, and employees, all of whom, however, incur similar obligations.

d. Except in minimal-risk research, the investigator establishes a clear and fair agreement with research participants, prior to their participation, that clarifies the obligations and responsibilities of each. The investigator has the obligation to honor all promises and commitments included in that agreement. The investigator informs the participants of all aspects of the research that might reasonably be expected to influence willingness to participate and explains all other aspects of the research about which the participants inquire. Failure to make full disclosure prior to obtaining informed consent requires additional safeguards to protect the welfare and dignity of the research participants. Research with children or with participants who have impairments that would limit understanding and/or communication requires special safeguarding procedures.

e. Methodological requirements of a study may make the use of concealment or deception necessary. Before conducting such a study, the investigator has a special responsibility to (i) determine whether the use of such techniques is justified by the study's prospective scientific, educational, or applied value; (ii) determine whether alternative procedures are available that do not use concealment or deception; and (iii) ensure that the participants are provided with sufficient explanation as soon as possible.

f. The investigator respects the individual's freedom to decline to participate in or to withdraw from the research at any time. The obligation to protect this freedom requires careful thought and consideration when the investigator is in a position of authority or influence over the participant. Such positions of authority include, but are not limited to, situations in which research participation is required as part of employment or in which the participant is a student, client, or employee of the investigator.

g. The investigator protects the participant from physical and mental discomfort, harm, and danger that may arise from research procedures. If risks of such consequences exist, the investigator informs the participant of that fact. Research procedures likely to cause serious or lasting harm to a participant are not used unless the failure to use these procedures might expose the participant to risk of greater harm, or unless the research has great potential benefit and fully informed and voluntary consent is obtained from each participant. The participant should be informed of procedures for contacting the investigator within a reasonable time period following participation should stress, potential harm, or related questions or concerns arise.

h. After the data are collected, the investigator provides the participant with information about the nature of the study and attempts to remove any misconceptions that may have arisen. Where scientific or humane values justify delaying or withholding this information, the investigator incurs a special responsibility to monitor the research and to ensure that there are no damaging consequences for the participant.

i. Where research procedures result in undesirable consequences for the individual participant, the investigator has the responsibility to detect and remove or correct these consequences, including long-term effects.

j. Information obtained about a research participant during the course of an investigation is confidential unless otherwise agreed upon in advance. When the possibility exists that others may obtain access to such information, this possibility, together with the plans for protecting confidentiality, is explained to the participant as part of the procedure for obtaining informed consent.

Principle 10: Care and Use of Animals

An investigator of animal behavior strives to advance understanding of basic behavioral principles and / or to contribute to the improvement of human health and welfare. In seeking these ends, the investigator ensures the welfare of animals and treats them humanely. Laws and regulations notwithstanding, an animal's immediate protection depends upon the scientist's own conscience.

a. The acquisition, care, use, and disposal of all animals are in compliance with current federal, state or provincial, and local laws and regulations.

b. A psychologist trained in research methods and experienced in the care of laboratory animals closely supervises all procedures involving animals and is responsible for ensuring appropriate consideration of their comfort, health, and humane treatment.

c. Psychologists ensure that all individuals using animals under their supervision have received explicit instruction in experimental methods and in the care, maintenance, and handling of the species being used. Responsibilities and activities of individuals participating in a research project are consistent with their respective competencies.

d. Psychologists make every effort to minimize discomfort, illness, and pain of animals. A procedure subjecting animals to pain, stress, or privation is used only when an alternative procedure is unavailable and the goal is justified by its prospective scientific, educational, or applied value. Surgical procedures are performed under appropriate anesthesia; techniques to avoid infection and minimize pain are followed during and after surgery.

e. When it is appropriate that the animal's life be terminated, it is done rapidly and painlessly.

CODE OF ETHICS

National Association of Social Workers

Preamble

This code is intended to serve as a guide to the everyday conduct of members of the social work profession and as a basis for the adjudication of issues in ethics when the conduct of social workers is alleged to deviate from the standards expressed or implied in this code. It represents standards of ethical behavior for social workers in professional relationships with those served, with colleagues, with employers, with other individuals and professions, and with the community and society as a whole. It also embodies standards of ethical behavior governing individual conduct to the extent that such conduct is associated with an individual's status and identity as a social worker.

This code is based on the fundamental values of the social work profession that include the worth, dignity, and uniqueness of all persons as well as their rights and opportunities. It is also based on the nature of social work, which fosters conditions that promote these values.

In subscribing to and abiding by this code, the social worker is expected to view ethical responsibility in as inclusive a context as each situation demands and within which ethical judgment is required. The social worker is expected to take into consideration all the principles in this code that have a bearing upon any situation in which ethical judgment is to be exercised and professional intervention or conduct is planned. The course of action that the social worker chooses is expected to be consistent with the spirit as well as the letter of this code.

In itself, this code does not represent a set of rules that will prescribe all the behaviors of social workers in all the complexities of professional life. Rather, it offers general principles to guide conduct, and the judicious appraisal of conduct, in situations that have ethical implications. It provides the basis for making judgments about ethical actions before and after they occur. Frequently, the particular situation determines the ethical principles that apply and the manner of their application. In such cases, not only the particular ethical principles are taken into immediate consideration, but also the entire code and its spirit. Specific applications of ethical principles must be judged within the context in which they are being considered. Ethical behavior in a given situation must satisfy not only the judgment of the individual social worker, but also the judgment of an unbiased jury of professional peers.

This code should not be used as an instrument to deprive any social worker of the opportunity or freedom to practice with complete professional integrity; nor should any disciplinary action be taken on the basis of this code without maximum provision for safeguarding the rights of the social worker affected.

The ethical behavior of social workers results not from edict, but from a personal commitment of the individual. This code is offered to affirm the will and zeal of all social workers to be ethical and to act ethically in all that they do as social workers. . . .

II. The Social Worker's Ethical Responsibility to Clients
   F. Primacy of Clients' Interests—The social worker's primary responsibility is to clients.
     1. The social worker should serve clients with devotion, loyalty, determination, and the maximum ap-

plication of professional skill and competence.

2. The social worker should not exploit relationships with clients for personal advantage, or solicit the clients of one's agency for private practice.

3. The social worker should not practice, condone, facilitate or collaborate with any form of discrimination on the basis of race, color, sex, sexual orientation, age, religion, national origin, marital status, political belief, mental or physical handicap, or any other preference or personal characteristic, condition or status.

4. The social worker should avoid relationships or commitments that conflict with the interests of clients.

5. The social worker should under no circumstances engage in sexual activities with clients.

6. The social worker should provide clients with accurate and complete information regarding the extent and nature of the services available to them.

7. The social worker should apprise clients of their risks, rights, opportunities, and obligations associated with social service to them.

8. The social worker should seek advice and counsel of colleagues and supervisors whenever such consultation is in the best interest of clients.

9. The social worker should terminate service to clients, and professional relationships with them, when such service and relationships are no longer required or no longer serve the clients' needs or interests.

10. The social worker should withdraw services precipitously only under unusual circumstances, giving careful consideration to all factors in the situation and taking care to minimize possible adverse effects.

11. The social worker who anticipates the termination or interruption of service to clients should notify clients promptly and seek the transfer, referral, or continuation of service in relation to the clients' needs and preferences.

G. Rights and Prerogatives of Clients— The social worker should make every effort to foster maximum self-determination on the part of clients.

1. When the social worker must act on behalf of a client who has been adjudged legally incompetent, the social worker should safeguard the interests and rights of that client.

2. When another individual has been legally authorized to act in behalf of a client, the social worker should deal with that person always with the client's best interest in mind.

3. The social worker should not engage in any action that violates or diminishes the civil or legal rights of clients.

H. Confidentiality and Privacy—The social worker should respect the privacy of clients and hold in confidence all information obtained in the course of professional service.

1. The social worker should share with others confidences revealed by clients, without their consent, only for compelling professional reasons.

2. The social worker should inform clients fully about the limits of confidentiality in a given situation, the purposes for which information is obtained, and how it may be used.

3. The social worker should afford clients reasonable access to any official social work records concerning them.

4. When providing clients with access to records, the social worker should take due care to protect the confidences of others contained in those records.

5. The social worker should obtain informed consent of clients before taping, recording, or permitting third party observation of their activities.

I. Fees—When setting fees, the social

worker should ensure that they are fair, reasonable, considerate, and commensurate with the service performed and with due regard for the client's ability to pay.

    1. The social worker should not divide a fee or accept or give anything of value for receiving or making a referral. . . .

Summary of Major Principles

I. The Social Worker's Conduct and Comportment as a Social Worker
    A. Propriety. The social worker should maintain high standards of personal conduct in the capacity or identity as social worker.
    B. Competence and Professional Development. The social worker should strive to become and remain proficient in professional practice and the performance of professional functions.
    C. Service. The social worker should regard as primary the service obligation of the social work profession.
    D. Integrity. The social worker should act in accordance with the highest standards of professional integrity.
    E. Scholarship and Research. The social worker engaged in study and research should be guided by the conventions of scholarly inquiry.

II. The Social Worker's Ethical Responsibility to Clients
    F. Primacy of Clients' Interests. The social worker's primary responsibility is to clients.
    G. Rights and Prerogatives of Clients. The social worker should make every effort to foster maximum self-determination on the part of clients.
    H. Confidentiality and Privacy. The social worker should respect the privacy of clients and hold in confidence all in-

formation obtained in the course of professional service.
    I. Fees. When setting fees, the social worker should ensure that they are fair, reasonable, considerate, and commensurate with the service performed and with due regard for the clients' ability to pay.

III. The Social Worker's Ethical Responsibility to Colleagues
    J. Respect, Fairness, and Courtesy. The social worker should treat colleagues with respect, courtesy, fairness, and good faith.
    K. Dealing with Colleagues' Clients. The social worker has the responsibility to relate to the clients of colleagues with full professional consideration.

IV. The Social Worker's Ethical Responsibility to Employers and Employing Organizations
    L. Commitments to Employing Organizations. The social worker should adhere to commitments made to the employing organizations.

V. The Social Worker's Ethical Responsibility to the Social Work Profession
    M. Maintaining the Integrity of the Profession. The social worker should uphold and advance the values, ethics, knowledge, and mission of the profession.
    N. Community Service. The social worker should assist the profession in making social services available to the general public.
    O. Development of Knowledge. The social worker should take responsibility for identifying, developing, and fully utilizing knowledge for professional practice.

VI. The Social Worker's Ethical Responsibility to Society
    P. Promoting the General Welfare. The social worker should promote the general welfare of society.

STATEMENT ON PROFESSIONAL ETHICS

American Association of University Professors

The Statement

I. Professors, guided by a deep conviction of the worth and dignity of the advancement of knowledge, recognize the special responsibilities placed upon them. Their primary responsibility to their subject is to seek and to state the truth as they see it. To this end professors devote their energies to developing and improving their scholarly competence. They accept the obligation to exercise critical self-discipline and judgment in using, extending, and transmitting knowledge. They practice intellectual honesty. Although professors may follow subsidiary interests, these interests must never seriously hamper or compromise their freedom of inquiry.

II. As teachers, professors encourage the free pursuit of learning in their students. They hold before them the best scholarly and ethical standards of their discipline. Professors demonstrate respect for students as individuals and adhere to their proper roles as intellectual guides and counselors. Professors make every reasonable effort to foster honest academic conduct and to assure that their evaluations of students reflect each student's true merit. They respect the confidential nature of the relationship between professor and student. They avoid any exploitation, harassment, or discriminatory treatment of students. They acknowledge significant academic or scholarly assistance from them. They protect their academic freedom.

III. As colleagues, professors have obligations that derive from common membership in the community of scholars. Professors do not discriminate against or harass colleagues. They respect and defend the free inquiry of associates. In the exchange of criticism and ideas professors show due respect for the opinions of others. Professors acknowledge academic debt and strive to be objective in their professional judgment of colleagues. Professors accept their share of faculty responsibilities for the governance of their institution.

IV. As members of an academic institution, professors seek above all to be effective teachers and scholars. Although professors observe the stated regulations of the institution, provided the regulations do not contravene academic freedom, they maintain their right to criticize and seek revision. Professors give due regard to their paramount responsibilities within their institution in determining the amount and character of work done outside it. When considering the interruption or termination of their service, professors recognize the effect of their decision upon the program of the institution and give due notice of their intentions.

V. As members of their community, professors have the rights and obligations of other citizens. Professors measure the urgency of these obligations in the light of their responsibilities to their subject, to their students, to their profession, and to their institution. When they speak or act as private persons they avoid creating the impression of speaking or acting for their college or university. As citizens engaged in a profession that depends upon freedom for its health and integrity, professors have a particular obligation to promote conditions of free inquiry and to further public understanding of academic freedom.

From American Association of University Professors, *Statement on Professional Ethics* (1966). Reprinted by permission.

CODE OF ETHICS OF THE EDUCATION PROFESSION

National Education Association

Preamble

The educator, believing in the worth and dignity of each human being, recognizes the supreme importance of the pursuit of truth, devotion to excellence, and the nurture of democratic principles. Essential to these goals is the protection of freedom to learn and to teach and the guarantee of equal educational opportunity for all. The educator accepts the responsibility to adhere to the highest ethical standards.

The educator recognizes the magnitude of the responsibility inherent in the teaching process. The desire for the respect and confidence of one's colleagues, of students, of parents, and of the members of the community provides the incentive to attain and maintain the highest possible degree of ethical conduct. The Code of Ethics of the Education Profession indicates the aspiration of all educators and provides standards by which to judge conduct.

The remedies specified by the NEA and/ or its affiliates for the violation of any provision of this Code shall be exclusive and no such provision shall be enforceable in any form other than one specifically designated by the NEA or its affiliates.

Principle I—Commitment to the Student

The educator strives to help each student realize his or her potential as a worthy and effective member of society. The educator therefore works to stimulate the spirit of inquiry, the acquisition of knowledge and understanding, and the thoughtful formulation of worthy goals.

In fulfillment of the obligation to the student, the educator

1. Shall not unreasonably restrain the student from independent action in the pursuit of learning.
2. Shall not unreasonably deny the student access to varying points of view.
3. Shall not deliberately suppress or distort subject matter relevant to the student's progress.
4. Shall make reasonable effort to protect the student from conditions harmful to learning or to health and safety.
5. Shall not intentionally expose the student to embarrassment or disparagement.
6. Shall not on the basis of race, color, creed, sex, national origin, marital status, political or religious beliefs, family, social or cultural background, or sexual orientation, unfairly:
   a. Exclude any student from participation in any program;
   b. Deny benefits to any student;
   c. Grant any advantage to any student.
7. Shall not use professional relationships with students for private advantage.
8. Shall not disclose information about students obtained in the course of professional service, unless disclosure serves a compelling professional purpose or is required by law.

Principle II—Commitment to the Profession

The education profession is vested by the public with a trust and responsibility requiring the highest ideals of professional service.

In the belief that the quality of the services of the education profession directly influences the nation and its citizens, the educator shall exert every effort to raise professional standards, to promote a climate that encourages the exercise of professional judgment, to achieve conditions which attract persons worthy of the trust to careers in education, and to assist in preventing the practice of the profession by unqualified persons.

In fulfillment of the obligation to the profession, the educator

1. Shall not in an application for a professional position deliberately make a false statement or fail to disclose a material fact related to competency and qualifications.
2. Shall not misrepresent his/her professional qualifications.
3. Shall not assist entry into the profession of a person known to be unqualified in respect to character, education, or other relevant attribute.
4. Shall not knowingly make a false statement concerning the qualifications of a candidate for a professional position.
5. Shall not assist a noneducator in the unauthorized practice of teaching.
6. Shall not disclose information about colleagues obtained in the course of professional service unless disclosure serves a compelling professional purpose or is required by law.
7. Shall not knowingly make false or malicious statements about a colleague.
8. Shall not accept any gratuity, gift, or favor that might impair or appear to influence professional decisions or actions.